THE NEW
GAMES
TREASURY

THE NEW
GAMES
TREASURY

More Than 500 Indoor and Outdoor Favorites
with Strategies, Rules and Traditions

By Merilyn Simonds Mohr

Illustrations by Roberta Cooke

HOUGHTON MIFFLIN COMPANY
BOSTON • NEW YORK
1997

For information about permission to reproduce selections from this book, write to Permissions,
Houghton Mifflin Company, 215 Park Avenue South, New York, New York 10003.

Library of Congress Cataloging-in-Publication Data

Mohr, Merilyn Simonds
    The new games treasury: more than 500 indoor and outdoor favorites with
    strategies, rules and traditions/by Merilyn Simonds Mohr;
    illustrations by Roberta Cooke; photography by Stephen Mark Needham.
      p.   cm.
    Enl. ed. of: The games treasury. c1993
    Includes bibliographical references (p.) and index.
    ISBN 1-57630-058-7 (pbk.)
    1. Games. I. Mohr, Merilyn Simonds. Games treasury. II. Title.
    GV1201.M67 1997
    790.1—dc21   97-23216

Printed in the United States of America
WCT 10 9 8 7 6 5 4 3 2 1

Designed by Hans Teensma/Impress, Inc. and Potter Publishing Studio
Production Editors: Susan Dickinson and Jessica Sherman
Cover and inside photographs by Stephen Mark Needham

For Claire, who likes to play

Contents

Trademark Acknowledgments

Aggravation is a registered trademark of Lakeside Games.

Balderdash is a registered trademark of Gameworks Creations.

Carroms is a registered trademark of Merdel Game Manufacturing.

Ludo is a registered trademark of Dikin.

MasterMind is a registered trademark of Pressman.

Monopoly and Sorry are registered trademarks of Parker Brothers.

Mr. Potato Head is a registered trademark of Playskool.

Othello, Cootie, Parcheesi, Scrabble, Battleship, Chutes and Ladders, Taboo, Scattergories, Password, Trouble and Yahtzee are registered trademarks of Milton Bradley.

Pick-Up-Sticks is a registered trademark of Rose Art Industries.

Pictionary is a registered trademark of Western Publishing.

Shakespeare is a registered trademark of Avalon Hill Game Company.

Slang Teasers is a registered trademark of the Aardvark Game Corporation.

Steeplechase is a registered trademark of Bendelle.

Trivial Pursuit is a registered trademark of Horn Abbot.

Wizard is a registered trademark of K. Fisher Enterprises Ltd.

Acknowledgments

THANK YOU TO THE FRIENDS who shared their games-playing past and happily played these games with me: Rose Richardson and Zalman Yanovsky; Andrew McLachlan and Lori Richards; the Herbert-Judd family; Carolyn Smart and Kenneth de Kok; the Green-Martin family; Zoe and Al Grady; Richard Peterson; Matt Cohen; Sonny and Gillian Sadinsky; Carole Blier-Carruthers; Morgan and Claire Grady-Smith; my parents, Alice and Robert Simonds; my sisters, Joey Nicolson, Donna Hallman and Virginia Simonds; and my sons, Karl and Erik. Special thanks to the regulars, Brenda Spires and Corey Holmes, and to my partner at the games table and everywhere else, Wayne Grady.

Without libraries and archives, collections such as this could not be compiled. My heartfelt appreciation to the national games associations for their assistance, to the Museum and Archive of Games, University of Waterloo, and to the Kingston Public Library, particularly to the young woman who understood that "rules are made to be broken." And my appreciation to Donald Hall for graciously allowing me to reprint an excerpt (page 175) from his book *Fathers Playing Catch with Sons,* published by North Point Press, 1985.

I am grateful to my editor, Sandy Taylor, for initiating this project and for guiding me through it; to the illustrator, Roberta Cooke, for drawings that not only clarify but enhance the text; to my copy editor, Susan Dickinson, for her enthusiasm and an attention to detail that continues to astound me; to the designers, Hans Teensma and Jeff Potter, for making visual sense of a gargantuan manuscript; to the managing editor, Alice Lawrence, for her energy and patience; and to the editor at Chapters Publishing, Barry Estabrook, who continues to make the writing game a pleasure.

House Rules:
A User's Guide

THE OLDEST BOOK OF GAMES in existence, *Libro de Juegos*, was compiled more than 700 years ago. Only 98 pages long, it is handwritten on parchment and bound in sheepskin, the script illustrated with 150 colored drawings, including a portrait of the man who commissioned the book, King Alfonso X—Alfonso the Learned— of Castile and León, Spain. Alfonso's book of games is divided into four sections: **Chess**, dicing games, **Backgammon** and miscellaneous board games such as **Alquerque**. In his preface, Alfonso explains that he intended the book for "those who like to enjoy themselves in private to avoid the annoyance and unpleasantness of public places, or those who have fallen into another's power, either in prison or slavery or as seafarers, and in general all those who are looking for a pleasant pastime which will bring them comfort and dispel their boredom."

Every book of games written since 1282 has had a somewhat similar aim, though the task has become increasingly daunting with each decade. When Alfonso set out to record the games of Spain, Chess had been in the country less than 300 years, **Checkers** for less than 200. Playing cards had not yet been invented, and copyright game boards were 500 years away. The world was still a very large place; games such as **Go, Caroms,** Spelicans and Shuttlecock (the predecessors of **Pick-Up-Sticks** and **Badminton**) were as yet confined to the Orient. Since Alfonso's reign, travel and invention have added thousands of games to our repertoire; at the same time, surprisingly few have been put permanently on the shelf.

From among the wealth of family games that exist today, I have selected those which North Americans most like to play, blending the familiar—

Snakes and Ladders, Ping-pong, Cribbage, Charades, Horseshoes and Tag—with exotic games such as **Mah Jongg** and fascinating, ancient games like **Fanorona** that are still great fun to play. You will find each game discussed under its original name, since herein often lies a clue to the game's early history. Parcheesi, for instance, is discussed here as **Pachisi**, the archaic Indian name of the game and the Hindi word for 25, the highest-scoring roll, which was originally thrown not with dice but with an earlier gambling device: cowrie shells. The oldest games, of course, have many aliases. Every country, every region, every family seems to have pet names for games; for instance, even the fairly modern card game **Oh Hell** is also played as Bugger Bridge, Bugger Your Neighbor, Up and Down the River, Blackout and Wizard. With each game, I have included as many names as I could discover; there are undoubtedly others.

Games books traditionally arrange games by theme: battle games, race games, active games, quiet games. But I have taken my cue from Alfonso and arranged the more than 300 games in this book by what the game is played *with* rather than *how* it is played. I have never heard someone say, "I feel like playing a race game." It's always, "Let's play cards!" or "What board games do you have?" The book, therefore, has five parts: board games; games with playing pieces, such as dice and dominoes; card games; mind games that demand nothing more than a keen wit; and active outdoor games. Within each part, similar games are grouped together in individual chapters. For instance, board games are segregated into those played spontaneously on homemade boards (**Tit-Tat-Toe** and **Nine Men's Morris**); games played on checkerboards (Chess and **Reversi**); and games played on commercially produced boards (**Scrabble** and **Monopoly**).

Within each chapter, the games proceed from simple to sophisticated. For instance, Chapter 8, which is devoted to card games for two players, moves from **Memory** through **Go Fish** and **Spit** to **Canasta**, Cribbage and **Pinochle.** If you come across a game that is too difficult, try one earlier in the same chapter; expert players may want to start closer to the end. Many of the games will serve simply to renew your grasp of long-forgotten rules, but they can all be learned from scratch by following the directions. If you want to delve further into the intricacies of a game, contact the games organizations listed in Sources. Many games have players' associations that sponsor tournaments, publish newsletters and maintain Halls of Fame. Even **Tiddlywinks** has a "Closet of Fame."

The short background pieces that begin each game expose the links between different kinds of play. **Crokinole**, for instance, has elements of both **Marbles** and Caroms; Mah Jongg is a lot like **Gin Rummy**, and **Anagrams** was undoubtedly a predecessor of Scrabble. If a game has its own entry elsewhere in the book, it is printed in boldface type the first time it is mentioned within a section. You will find it listed in the Games Index in the order in which it appears in the book; or turn to the General Index, where the games are listed alphabetically.

Each chapter has an introduction, which provides some historical and social context for the genre and also explains the rules, rituals and language specific to that class of games. For instance, the introduction to the group card games in Chapter 9 describes how to choose partners for a game like **Bridge** or **Euchre**, the basics of tricks and trump and the meaning of words such as revoke, side suit and void. This saves repeating the information within each trick-taking game and also avoids a cumbersome omnibus Glossary. To help you locate definitions in a hurry, the terms are printed in italics. You'll also notice that to avoid the repetition of "he or she" and "him or her," each player is assumed to be of one gender or another. It is my hope that by the end of the book, an equal number of women, men, boys and girls will have played these games.

One ritual is common to all games, and thus most appropriately mentioned here: how to decide who goes first, which player or team is It. A few games come with built-in rules for the order of play. **Croquet**, for instance, has the order painted on the stake: the person with the blue ball goes first, followed by red, black, then yellow. In Dominoes games such as **Matador**, the person with the highest doublet starts.

In Go, Black always goes first, but how do you decide who gets the black playing pieces? In two-person games, the easiest way is to flip a coin, a practice that, according to legend, was initiated by Julius Caesar. Coin money had been around for almost a thousand years, but it was Caesar who insisted that his portrait be minted on one side. In a coin flip, the person who got Caesar's head was the winner. Even serious matters such as divorce, the division of an estate or the guilt of an accused party were decided by tossing a coin. If it landed portrait side up, it meant that the Emperor, in absentia, agreed with the person who called "Heads."

To decide who goes first in games such as Chess, Checkers, Reversi or Go, one player takes a white playing piece in one hand and a black piece in the other. She puts her hands behind her back and switches the two pieces back and forth. Then she extends her closed fists to the other player, who has to guess which hand holds the black piece. If he is right, he plays black. If he is wrong, he plays white. If the game doesn't have playing pieces, put a coin in one hand and leave the other empty. If the person correctly identifies the hand with the coin, he begins.

In outdoor games, particularly games with equipment, teams decide which goes first by having one person from each team grab a stick or a bat. They take turns wrapping their fists around the stick, one above the other. The person who makes the last full fist in contact with the stick starts the game. Or a member from each team can play a round of **Scissors, Paper, Stone,** an ancient way of deciding who goes first.

To start a group game, the easiest way to determine the order of play is to roll a single die. The person with the highest number goes first, and so on, down to the person who threw the lowest number: he goes last. If there are more than six players, use two dice. If the game is a board or table game, play-ers should readjust their seating according to the roll of the die so that the play moves clockwise around the table.

If the group is simply choosing It, the "ritual of the match" is a good way to start. Have the same number of matches (or toothpicks) as there are play-ers, but break one off. Hold them in your hand so that they all look the same height, and have every player draw one. The person who gets the short stick is It. A variation on this is to dump a pile of matches or toothpicks on the table. Everyone picks up a match or toothpick in turn and continues to do so until there are no more left. The person who picks up the last one is It.

Kids often start their group games by counting out "Eeny, meeny, miny, mo" or "One potato, two potato, three potato, four." Everyone extends a fist (or both), and one person—the Potato Masher—pounds each of the proffered fists in turn. "Seven potato more," and the fist named "more" is out of the game, until there is only one fist left, the fist belonging to It.

These choosing rituals put the start of each game firmly in the hands of Lady Luck. The game itself is always a mix of skill and luck, the outcome sometimes determined more by the player's contribution, as in **Darts**, and sometimes, like **Poker**, left almost completely to chance. Games of chance often involve betting; playing for a stake adds strategy and tension to what otherwise may be a very simple game. Ironically, when money rests on the outcome, some players are less inclined to leave the course of the game to fate.

The first book of indoor games written in English was published in 1674. The author, Charles Cotton, had initially published the opening chapter as a pamphlet called *The Nicker Nicked: Or the Cheate of Gaming discovered.* "Gaming is an enchanting witchery, gotten betwixt Idleness and Avarice," writes Cotton, "an itching Disease, that makes some scratch the head, whilst others, as if they were bitten by a Tarantula, are laughing themselves to death." Games have always suffered from their association with gaming: loaded dice, marked cards, a domino tile hidden up the sleeve, a smoky back room, drink at hand, women of the night waiting for the round to end. Movies keep our minds well stocked with clichés, but that shouldn't drive games out of our homes. Quite the contrary: a family game of **Lotto**, **Barbudi** or Pinochle is more likely to produce good sports than cheaters and gamblers.

The real father of English games books, of course, is not Cotton but Edmond Hoyle. A barrister who made his living as a **Whist** tutor among "persons of quality," Hoyle sold his students a little booklet for a guinea apiece that promised to improve their game. Pirated copies of the pamphlet soon spread about London, and in 1742, Hoyle tried to recapture his own market by publishing *A Short Treatise on the Game of Whist, containing the laws of the game; and also some Rules whereby a Beginner may, with due attention to them, attain to the Playing it well.* He followed shortly with similar treatises on Backgammon, **Piquet**, Chess, Quadrille and Brag. In 1750, the treatises were combined in a compendium edition. The name Hoyle became synonymous with such compendiums, even though they had other authors and contained games Hoyle had never played.

Since Hoyle's death in 1769, his name has been attached to hundreds of books, a marketing effort to imply that *these* are the authoritative, definitive rules of the game. Ironically, it was never Hoyle's intention to teach the British public how to play games; he assumed they knew the method of play in a general way. He was interested, rather, in helping them improve their game by presenting its laws and setting out some rules "whereby a Beginner may . . . attain to the Playing it well."

My own contribution to the genre that Hoyle and Alfonso spawned is also not intended as a hard-and-fast guide to the only way to play the game, whatever it may be. Instead, this book introduces familiar and exotic games, tells a bit about the provenance and peculiarities of each and describes the basic rules of play and some interesting variations. In a tradition as old as games themselves, players, I hope, will tinker with the game, add a few house rules of their own, maybe give it another name and, in so doing, push ahead the natural evolution of the way we play.

Lewis Carroll understood the topsy-turvy world of games better than most. Both *Alice in Wonderland* and *Through the Looking Glass* can be read as renegade Hoyles, where every law of games is turned on its head and where invention is the most basic rule of all.

"That's not a regular rule: you invented it just now."

"It's the oldest rule in the book," said the King.

1

TOKEN GESTURES

Board Games

*In play there are two pleasures
for your choosing—
The one is winning, and
the other losing.*
—Lord Byron
Don Juan

1

The Paper Chase:
Games on Homemade Boards

TIT-TAT-TOE, FOR MANY OF US, is our first introduction to board games. And a simple one it is: two horizontal lines drawn across two verticals, the spaces filled alternately with X's and O's. Yet as far as archeologists can tell, it has been played by humans as long as they have been able to take stick in hand and scratch a line in the dirt. A diagram for **Tit-Tat-Toe** was among seven found incised in the roofing slabs of an ancient Egyptian temple at Kurna, built at Thebes in the 14th century B.C. The game boards had obviously been cut into the stones before they were trimmed to form tiles, which leads archeologists to speculate that they are relics of some game-playing stonemasons who relaxed, perhaps, with a few rounds of Tit-Tat-Toe during lunch.

The game didn't die with the pharaohs, of course. Ovid refers to it in his *Ars amatoria*, and boards have been found cut into the floors of Roman ruins in Britain and into the cloister seats of medieval cathedrals in Canterbury, Salisbury and Westminster Abbey. Tit-Tat-Toe and its offshoot, Nine Holes, were not child's play then; they were frowned upon as a dangerous holdover from pagan rites. Periodically, they were even banned. Records from an ecclesiastical court on the Isle of Man show that in 1699, two people were punished for "making nine holes with their knives after evening prayer."

Called the Square of Saturn in medieval Europe and the Square of Brahma in the East, the crossed-line grid on which we play Tit-Tat-Toe has been a sacred, prophetic device much longer than it has been a children's game. It is the pattern at the center of Tibetan spiritual diagrams, the design on top of Scottish ceremonial oatcakes and the framework for the Beltane fires, built in the center square for the Druids' spring celebrations and lit on the eve of May Day. An old Norse saga advises those needing guidance from the gods to sit on a freshly flayed ox hide marked with nine squares within a square to summon the spirits.

Similarly, the traditional game of **Nine Men's Morris** is played on the Morris Square, which was also found cut into the roof slabs at Kurna, into the steps of a shrine at Mihintale, Ceylon, built in the first century A.D., and into the deck of a 10th-century Viking ship. Remains of Morris games were found at the first city of Troy and in a Bronze Age burial site in Ireland. So many people in such far-flung places over such a broad sweep of time have played these games that the boards can be seen as cultural archetypes as much as playthings.

Both Tit-Tat-Toe and Nine Men's Morris are alignment games: the goal is to arrange three playing pieces in a row, which either wins the game or scores points. Alignment games and connect-the-dot territory games like **Boxes** usually start with an empty board. In a sense, these are explorer games—players strike off into virgin territory and, one way or another, exert control over the empty space. The next challenge, of course, is to exert control over an occupied space, to start with all your pieces and your opponent's pieces on the board and to make the territory yours by outwitting or capturing the opposition. Equal opponents do battle, but when the competition is unequal, imperialist war games become hunt games, pitting one or two predators against many prey. Compared with Tit-Tat-Toe, hunt games are Johnny-come-latelies. The Halatafl, or Fox Game (an early form of **Fox and Geese**), is mentioned in the *Grettis Saga*, thought to have been written by a priest living in northern Iceland around 1300 A.D. The earliest English reference is a century and a half later, when the accounts of Edward IV record the purchase of

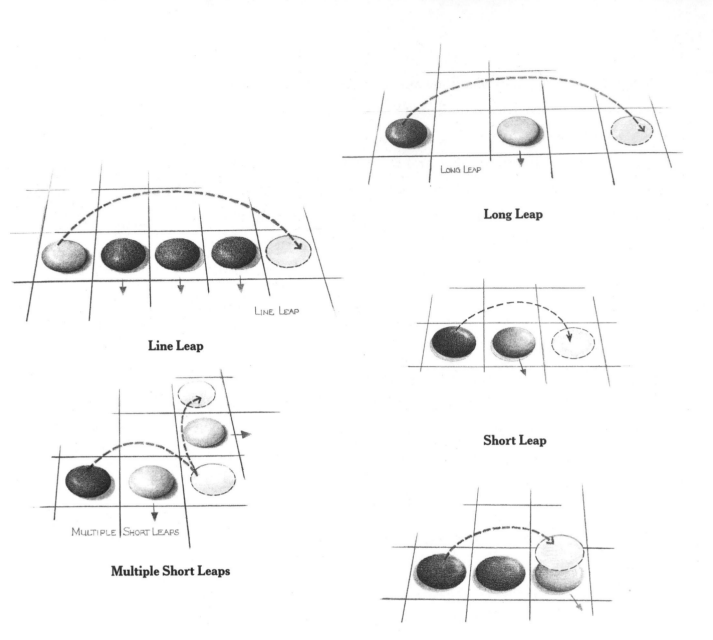

Long Leap

Line Leap

Multiple Short Leaps

Short Leap

Replacement Capture

2 foxes and 26 hounds made of silver as part of a set of Marelles, a general name for board games at the time.

All of these games—whether based on the principle of alignment, enclosure, capture or the hunt—are played on grids. Most are made up of intersecting horizontal and vertical lines; some, like the **Alquerque** boards, include diagonals. The pieces are played either in the *spaces* created by the intersecting lines, much as in **Checkers,** or on the *points*, the intersections themselves: a piece glides along a line to the next vacant adjacent point. A piece can generally move only one space or one point at a time, but it can usually move in all directions—horizontally, vertically and diagonally. Some games restrict pieces to orthogonal (horizontal and vertical) moves.

Battle games tend to be the most complex. After thousands of years of play, antagonists have devised several ways of taking prisoners and thus removing their opponents from the board. The most common is the *short leap*: a piece can jump over an opponent's piece or pieces provided the next adjacent space or point is vacant, as in Checkers. The piece that is jumped is removed from the board (indicated in the accompanying illustrations by an arrow). A *long leap*—where a piece moves along several vacant points or spaces to make a jump, landing on a vacant space beyond the captive—is less common. In a *line leap*, a whole row of opponents is captured by jumping over them to a vacant spot beyond.

To make a *replacement capture*, the aggressor lands on the same square as the captive and removes the captive from the board, as in **Chess**. **Seega** uses the *interception capture*, also known as *manacling*: a piece is captured when it is trapped between two of the opponent's pieces. Usually, the aggressor has to close the manacle (place the third piece in the row). If the victim unwittingly wanders between two opponents, it is not taken captive. The approach and withdrawal captures that distinguish **Fanorona** can remove a whole row of opponents from the board in a single move. To *capture by approach*, a piece moves to a point next in line to a row of opponents. To *capture by withdrawal*, a piece that is already at the end of a row of opponents retreats one space from the row. In both cases, the approach and withdrawal are in the same line of movement as the row of captives. The rules of most of these games specify that a piece must make a capture if possible, even if it means putting the capturing piece in jeopardy. A piece that fails to make a possible capture is *huffed*: it must be removed from the board, or in the case of hunt games, when the predator is huffed, he must return one of the captured prey to the board.

The more complex of these games call for large numbers of playing pieces (**Go-Bang** needs up to a hundred). The playing pieces can be anything at all, as long as each player's is a distinctive color or shape. Coins (pennies and dimes), beans (navy and pinto), pieces from Checkers, **Backgammon** or **Crokinole** games, bottle caps or pasta pieces (farfalle and rotini)—the choice is limited only by what is at hand. If you are playing these games in sand or on wood, you can gouge holes at the points or in the spaces and use marbles. In medieval versions of Tit-Tat-Toe and Nine Men's Morris, the pieces were sticks that players fitted into predrilled holes.

What makes hand-drawn board games so appealing is their immediacy. Because they can be played with found materials—a stick, some pebbles and a flat stretch of sand—they can be played anywhere, anytime, by anyone. The only inviolable rules are: the board must be level so that the pieces don't roll off, and it must be large enough to accommodate whatever pieces you play with. It doesn't matter whether the lines are perfectly straight or the squares exactly even. You can draw the board on a piece of paper with a pencil, scratch it in the earth or chisel it into stone; 4,000 years from now, an archeologist may dust it off and wonder just exactly how such an exotic game might be played.

MANACLE CAPTURE

Capture by Manacling

CAPTURE BY WITHDRAWAL

Capture by Withdrawal

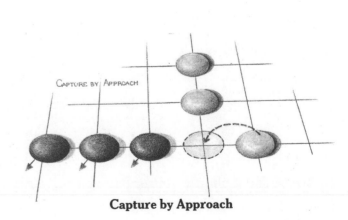

CAPTURE BY APPROACH

Capture by Approach

Boxes

- ◆ OTHER NAMES: Making Squares and Pipopipette
- ◆ NUMBER: two or more players
- ◆ EQUIPMENT: a drawn board and a pencil or crayon for each player
- ◆ DESCRIPTION: a territory game that is fun for fairly young children; easily grasped yet absorbing to play
- ◆ DURATION: depending on the size of the point-grid, a game can take from a few minutes to an hour

Triangles

IN *The History of Board Games*, Robert McConville calls this the French Polytechnic School's Game, though he does not explain why. It may come from France, but the game is a fixture in schoolyards the world over; it is the kind of pastime that is handed on from generation to generation of children. Like certain jokes, the game resurfaces regularly, each new generation claiming the invention as its own. Boxes is child's play at the beginning, but as most of the lines become joined, you will have to choose between foiling your opponent and finishing off a few squares for yourself.

The Board: Draw a grid of dots, 10 across and 10 down, 100 dots in all. (Drawing alternately one row across, then one row down helps keep the spacing even.) You can also play this game on graph paper. Draw a dot at the intersections of 10 consecutive lines, horizontally and vertically, then enclose the dots in a solid border.

The Playing Pieces: Each player needs a pencil. (They do not have to be different colors.)

The Object of the Game: To claim the most squares.

The Play: Players decide who goes first, then take turns drawing a line to connect any two dots horizontally or vertically. No diagonal lines are allowed. Each time a player connects the dots that close the fourth side of a square, she puts her initial inside, as illustrated, and takes another turn. When no more lines can be drawn, the game is over. Players count the number of squares containing their initials; the one with the most squares wins.

Variations: Boxes becomes **Triangles** if you play the game on a triangular grid. Draw a triangle with 10 dots to each side. Start with a bottom row of 10, nine in the next, up to a single dot at the top. Two players take turns connecting the dots either horizontally or diagonally. (There are no vertical lines.) The player who closes the third side of a triangle puts his initials inside; the person with the most triangles at the end wins. Award bonus points to players who make a large triangle out of small ones, all containing their initials.

For **The Snake**, players draw the

same 10-by-10-dot grid as for Boxes. The first player begins anywhere, connecting two dots horizontally or vertically, but not diagonally. The second player then connects either end of the existing line to a new dot. Players take turns connecting either end of the line with a new dot, creating a snake that

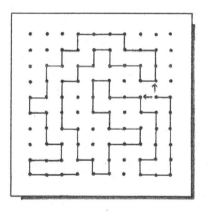

The Snake

wriggles across the grid. The line must be continuous; there can be no branches, crossings or doubling back on a line already made. The object is to avoid connecting either end of the snake to itself. Whoever makes the snake bite itself loses the game. In the game illustrated, the next person to play loses the game, since she cannot extend either end of the snake without connecting it to itself.

Two-Color Snakes is played on a two-color grid. Draw a horizontal row of five black dots, then above it, draw a row of six red dots, and so on, until you have six rows of black dots and

Boxes

Two-Color Snakes

five rows of red (30 of each color, in alternating rows).

One player uses a red pen to connect the red dots; the other player connects the black dots with a black pen. (Substitute any two crayons, as long as each is a different color.) The red player tries to make a continuous line horizontally across the board right to left or left to right; at the same time, the black player tries to draw a path vertically across the board, joining the top with the bottom in a single line. Players take turns connecting any pair of adjacent dots, horizontally or vertically (not diagonally). Lines may branch, but they may not cross. The

first player to make a continuous snake from one side of the board to the other wins. In the game illustrated, Red has succeeded in snaking across the board horizontally and has blocked Black from making a continuous vertical line. ❧

Sprouts

- NUMBER: **two or more players**
- EQUIPMENT: **pencils for each player and a large piece of paper**
- DESCRIPTION: **a territory game; the bigger the paper, the more the fun**
- TIP: **easy enough for the youngest players, but challenging for adults too**

L IKE THE FOOD for which it is named, this is a Sixties game, invented by John H. Conway and M.S. Paterson. The rules are simple, but the configurations, endless, and the strategy required is considerable. The game is confined only by the playing surface, so for a short game, play within a box drawn on a piece of paper; for a longer game with many players, use a sheet of newsprint.

The Board: At random, draw a smattering of dots (a dozen or more) on an unlined piece of paper. Draw a box around the dots to set the limits of the game, or let the edges of the paper be the boundaries.

The Playing Pieces: A pencil or pen for each player.

The Object of the Game: To be the last person to draw a line.

The Play: Players decide who goes first, then take turns drawing a line to connect two dots. The lines do not have to be the shortest distance between two points. They can take any direction, be any shape. Every time a player connects two dots, she makes her own dot at the halfway point of the line she just drew. (In the illustrated game, the solid dots were drawn on the page to begin the game; the open circles indicate the halfway points of the lines the players drew.) This dot is now part of the board, and any player can connect it to another dot. There are two caveats: a line can never cross another line, and no more than three lines can emanate from each dot. The person who draws the last line wins. ❧

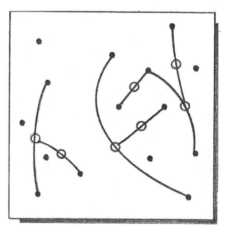

Sprouts

Tit-Tat-Toe

- ◆ OTHER NAMES: X's and O's, Noughts and Crosses and Tick-Tack-Toe
- ◆ NUMBER: two players
- ◆ EQUIPMENT: a drawn board and pencils or five playing pieces each for both players
- ◆ DESCRIPTION: an alignment game that takes mere moments; rounds of several games are usually played at once
- ◆ COMPLEXITY: for very young players

ALTHOUGH MOST Americans learn the game as Tick-Tack-Toe, the original name makes good sense: "tit" is a 16th-century word meaning a little slap; "tit for tat" is a retaliatory blow; and the toe is the third piece that secures the other two in a winning combination.

Tit-Tat-Toe is simple to play and pleasing in a way that may have less to do with the rules than with the board on which it is played. Before it became a children's game, this nine-square grid was known as the Magic Square: the numbers from 1 to 9 can be arranged so that the sum whether added across, down or on the diagonal is exactly the same. For instance, if the top row, left to right, is 8, 1, 6, the second row is 3, 5, 7 and the third row is 4, 9, 2, each line adds up to 15. Secret societies in the Middle Ages referred to the Magic Square as the Cabala of the Nine Chambers. Filled with numbers, the Magic Square concealed numerological truths about the natural world; filled with letters or symbols, it conveyed occult messages that could be read every which way. Although the square has since been stripped of its magic, it may be a lingering fascination with this ancient mystical form that keeps us coming back again and again with our X's and O's.

The Board: Draw two vertical lines, then divide them into thirds with two horizontal lines, creating a grid with nine equal squares big enough to accommodate the playing pieces. Enclose the grid in a box (this is especially important with more complex variations).

The Playing Pieces: Each player has five pieces of a different color than the opponent's. Or use pencils; one player marks X, and the other O.

The Object of the Game: To get three pieces in a row, horizontally, vertically or diagonally.

The Play: Players decide who goes first, then take turns placing a piece or marking one of the nine squares. Each player tries to get three pieces in a row, meanwhile preventing his opponent from doing the same. The first person to place three pieces in a row calls out, "Tit-Tat-Toe, three in a row!" and wins. If neither makes a row, the game is a draw—the game goes to Old Nick, Old Tom or, as we used to say, the Cat.

The loser of one game starts the next. (There is a distinct advantage in playing the first piece.) Players usually play a match: three out of five or five out of seven games.

Strategy: You can win if you place your pieces on three corners or on the center and two corners, with empty spaces between. Once you have this setup, your opponent can stop you from making a row in one direction, but on your next turn, you can make a row in the other. The game can be a

Three-Dimensional Tit-Tat-Toe

draw every time if a corner lead is countered with a center play or a center lead is countered with a corner play.

Variations: In **Two-Part Tit-Tat-Toe**, instead of five playing pieces, each person has three. (Drawing X's and O's does not work with this version.) The game begins in the usual way, with players taking turns putting their pieces on the traditional nine-square board, trying for three in a row. When all the pieces are on the board, players take turns moving them one square at a time, horizontally, vertically and diagonally, into an adjacent empty space. The game ends when one player gets three in a row or when play is stalemated. For a really reck-

less game, allow players to jump over an opponent's piece to get to an empty space on the other side, as in **Checkers**. However, no captures are allowed.

For **Three-Dimensional Tit-Tat-Toe**, draw three Magic Squares in a row, one above the other. A player can make a row of three horizontally, vertically or diagonally on any one of the three grids; she can also make a row vertically or diagonally through all three grids. For instance, if a player has playing pieces on the upper right-hand corner of the top grid, the center of the middle grid and the lower left-hand corner of the bottom grid as illustrated, she makes a winning row of three.

Expanded Tit-Tat-Toe exponentially increases the possibilities. Instead of a Magic Square, draw a grid with three verticals and three horizontals, creating 16 spaces instead of 9. Each player has eight playing pieces. The aim is to place as many pieces in a row as possible. Rows can be horizontal, vertical or diagonal, and a piece may be part of more than one row. Keep score during play: three in a row scores 1 point, four in a row scores 3 points. The person with the highest score at the end of the game wins. You can also draw a grid with 25 squares (four verticals and four horizontals) and play as above, scoring 5 points for five in a row.　～

Picaria

- ◆ NUMBER: **two players**
- ◆ EQUIPMENT: **a drawn board and three playing pieces for each player**
- ◆ DESCRIPTION: **a fast and easy alignment game, more challenging than Tit-Tat-Toe**

NORTHERN EUROPEANS and Americans play three-in-a-row games on a grid, but African and Oriental families play them on a star and call the games Achi and Yih, respectively. Instead of setting pieces within the squares, players put them on the intersections of the lines, called *points*. Spanish settlers introduced Achi to the natives of the southwestern United States; the Keres Indians of New Mexico added four short diagonals, creating the more demanding and exciting game of Picaria. Each player has only three pieces to play on the 13 points, but once the pieces are on the board, they can be moved from point to point until someone gets three in a row. A player has to decide whether to try to make a row of three or to play defensively, manipulating her pieces to block her opponent's attempts. The game becomes a duel—and the Cat rarely wins.

The Board: Draw a box, then divide it in half with a vertical line and into quarters with a horizontal line, as illustrated. Connect the corners with diagonals, to make the Achi star. (All the lines meet in the center.) Now join the tips of the horizontal and vertical lines with short diagonals. Emphasize

Achi

Picaria

with dots the 13 points where the lines of the Picaria board intersect.

The Playing Pieces: Three distinctive pieces for each player—stones, beans or checkers. X's and O's cannot be used, since the pieces are moved on the board.

The Object of the Game: To get three in a row in any direction.

The Play: Players decide who goes first. The first player puts a stone on any point on the board, except the center point. Players then take turns placing their pieces on any point. (The center is off limits only for the first play.) When all six pieces are on the board, players take turns moving the individual pieces, one at a time, along a line to the nearest vacant point. A piece can move in any direction; no jumping or captures are allowed. The first player to get three in a row wins.

Strategy: Don't worry about making a row in the first stage of the game. Place your pieces where they will have the most freedom of movement. A piece on the center point can move in eight directions; pieces on the midpoints of the outside square can move in five directions; pieces on the four points nearest the center can move in four directions; from the corner points, pieces can move in only three directions. ∾

Picaria

Go-Bang

- OTHER NAMES: **Go-Moku and Five Stones; the game has been marketed as Pegety, Ren-ju, Spoil Five and Pegtive**
- NUMBER: **two players**
- EQUIPMENT: **a drawn board and pencils or a large number of playing pieces (at least 40 each)**
- DESCRIPTION: **a challenging alignment game**

GO-BANG IS AN offshoot of the ancient Oriental board game I-Go, more commonly known to North Americans as **Go** (described in Chapter 3). The original Go is a complex surround-and-capture game, a sort of convoluted **Checkers**, that can go on for hours or even days. Go-Bang, on the other hand, is a fairly simple alignment game that has more in common with **Tit-Tat-Toe**.

Go-Bang can be played on a traditional Go board, a grid of 19 vertical and 19 horizontal lines, on a checkerboard or on a hand-drawn grid of any size. The playing pieces are called *stones*, and in fact, pebbles work admirably, especially if you play the game on a grid drawn in the sand. As in **Picaria**, the pieces in Go-Bang are placed not within the squares but on the *points*, the intersections of the lines. The bigger the board, the more playing pieces you need—and the longer the game.

The Board: Draw a beginners' grid with nine vertical lines and nine horizontal lines, and enclose it in a box. The board is empty when the game begins.

The Playing Pieces: Each player has a pile of distinctive pieces, the number determined by the size of the grid. A nine-by-nine grid has 81 points, so each player needs at least 40 pieces. Because pieces are not moved on the board, players can draw X's and O's instead.

The Object of the Game: To place five stones in a row, vertically, horizontally or diagonally.

The Play: Players decide who goes first. The first player takes the darker stones and puts one on any point. Players then take turns placing their stones on the board, trying to get exactly five in a row or to block their opponent from doing the same. Stones are never moved from point to point.

The first player to get five stones in a row wins; more than five in a row does not count.

Strategy: As soon as a player lines up four stones with a vacant point at each end—an *open four*—she automatically wins; her opponent can place a stone to block one end, but he cannot block both ends in one turn.

A player is also in a position to win as soon as he has three stones in a row with vacant points on both ends; he need only lay down another stone to be one inevitable step from victory. Consequently, when a player gets three in a row, even if there are gaps of one or two points between the stones, he says "Three" so that the other player knows enough to block the play. This may seem like giving yourself away, but as Edward Lasker, Go player since 1907, explains in his classic manual, *Go and Go-Moku*, "There is no fun in winning a game owing to a blunder of the adversary. . . . The idea is to win the game in spite of the opponent's seeing every threat."

To win Go-Bang, you have to play on more than one front, building two or more rows at the same time. Very early in most games, you will be able to play a stone that forms two rows of three at the same time, both of which can lead to open fours and victory. Because this is such an easy triumph, the Chinese play by the *rule of three and three*: a player cannot form two rows of three with a single play if both can be developed into an open four. This rule *can* be broken if making two rows of three is the only way to block an opponent from making a row of five. Beginners can ignore the rule of three and three—the game is quite absorbing without it—but for experienced players, it heightens the challenge.

In general, try to break up any attempts by an opponent to mass his stones; he can easily build out in several directions from a clump of stones. On the other hand, try to mass your own stones. Avoid getting into the position of playing an entirely defensive game, blocking your adversary at every turn, rather than building your own rows. For example, in the game illustrated, the player with the kidney beans successfully massed her stones. Her opponent can block the diagonal four in a row, but on the next turn, she will complete a horizontal open four on the fourth line from the top—and assure her victory.

Variation: An unnamed game on a similar principle can be played on a grid of seven dots across and six dots down (42 dots). One player is O and marks her dot by drawing a circle around it; the other is X and marks his dot by drawing an X through it. Players decide who goes first and take turns marking dots, trying to get four in a row, horizontally, vertically or diagonally. The first player must begin by marking a dot on the bottom row. The other player then marks a dot directly above the previous dot or anywhere in the row beside it. Play continues this way, each player allowed to mark only above or in the row beside the previous mark.　　　　⌇

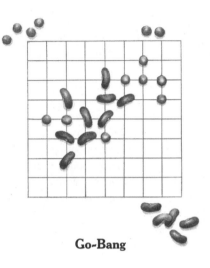

Go-Bang

Nine Men's Morris

- ◆ OTHER NAMES: **Merels, Marelles and The Mill Game**
- ◆ NUMBER: **two players**
- ◆ EQUIPMENT: **a drawn board and distinctively colored playing pieces for each player**
- ◆ DESCRIPTION: **an alignment game that introduces the concept of capture; a combination of Tit-Tat-Toe and Checkers, played on points, rather than within the squares**
- ◆ DURATION: **several minutes per game; longer for some variations**

L IKE THE MAGIC SQUARE of Tit-Tat-Toe, the board on which Nine Men's Morris is played reflects an ancient perception of the structure of the world. Called the Triple Enclosure or Morris Square, it consists of a box within a box (sometimes within another box), all joined by lines radiating from the innermost square. To the ancient Celts, the Morris Square was sacred: at the center lay the holy Mill or Cauldron, a symbol of regeneration; and emanating out from it, the four cardinal directions, the four elements and the four winds.

In *A Midsummer Night's Dream*, Shakespeare alludes to the practice of cutting life-sized Morris Squares in the grass at the end of a plowed field.

Remains of boards dating from the Bronze Age have been found, but the game was especially popular in medieval England. By the late 16th century, it was called Merels, which refers to both the game and the counters, the name deriving from an Old English word "mere," which means to mark out boundaries. Where the name Nine Men's Morris comes from is less clear. The Shorter Oxford English Dictionary suggests that "morris" is a corruption of "merels," but morris is also a Welsh word meaning dance, and the Morris (or Morrice) Dance has some interesting parallels with both the game and the mystical square on which it is played. Once commonly part of resurrection rituals in England, Europe and Asia, the Morris Dance is still performed each spring as part of the May Day celebrations in some New England communities. In Europe, dancers originally dressed

Five Men's Morris

Nine Men's Morris

Eleven Men's Morris

up as animal-men and carried deer antlers, some black and some white. Often, they blackened their faces as part of the disguise, which gives credence to the theory that the name of the dance stems from *morisco*, meaning Moorish. All of which adds considerable interest to a rather simple game in which two sets of playing pieces, usually black and white, seem to dance around the center.

The Board: On a piece of paper, draw three squares, one inside the other, decreasing in size. Adjust the size of the board to fit the pieces. If playing with pennies and nickels, the outside square, the largest, should have seven-inch sides, just about filling a standard sheet of paper. Inside the first, draw a second square, leaving a border of an inch and a half between the two. Inside the second, draw a third square with sides not less than four inches. Connect the midpoints of each side of the squares. Emphasize each intersection and each corner with a dot.

The Playing Pieces: Each player has nine playing pieces, or *merels*. The two sets of pieces should be different colors or, if coins are used, different denominations.

The Object of the Game: To get three playing pieces in a row, horizontally, vertically or diagonally; to immobilize your opponent or to reduce him to two pieces.

The Play: Players decide who goes first, then take turns putting their playing pieces, one at a time, on an intersection, or *point*, trying to get three in a row—a *mill*. When a player makes a mill, he is allowed to remove one of his opponent's pieces that is not part of a mill. And the game carries on.

After all the pieces are on the board, players continue to try to make mills by moving their pieces. A player can move a merel in any direction, along a line to the next adjacent vacant point. A merel can move only one point on each turn; no leapfrogging is allowed. Every time a player makes a mill, he takes an opponent's merel off the board. (A piece from an opponent's mill can be removed only as a last resort.)

The game ends when one player has only two pieces left or when no one can make another move. In the latter case, the player with the most merels on the board wins.

Strategy: Early in the game, place your pieces strategically, rather than trying to make mills. Freedom of movement is vital. From the midpoints of the middle square, a piece can move in four directions. The midpoints of the inside and outside squares allow three-way movement, but a merel can move in only two directions from a corner. Avoid crowding your pieces on any one square; distribute them evenly around the board so that you can block your opponent as well as make mills.

A player can move a piece out of a mill and, on the next move, slide it back into place, scoring a new mill and removing another of the opponent's merels from the board. When your opponent moves a merel out of a mill, try to block it with one of your own. If you can't, make a mill of your own as quickly as possible, and try the same tactic. The other player will be forced to choose between an offensive play (blocking your newly opened row) and a defensive one (making his own mill).

The strategic pièce de résistance is the *double mill* (also called the crisscross, the seesaw or the running jenny), composed of five pieces in two rows so that moving a piece out of one mill immediately creates another at the new point. For example, in the game illustrated on the following page, Black is certain to win, since she can move a piece from one mill to the other, as indicated by the arrows. Each time she makes another mill, she removes one of her opponent's pieces, quickly ending the game. There is no defense once a player has a double mill. The best you can do is foil the move when you see it coming and try to set one up yourself.

Variations: According to one 19th-century games manual, in the "truly rustic mode of playing the game," a player who is reduced to three playing pieces may "hop" from one spot to another on the board, instead of following the lines to an adjacent vacant point.

In **Five Men's Morris**, or Smaller Merels, there are only two concentric squares. Two players have five merels each. Otherwise, it is played exactly as Nine Men's Morris.

Twelve Men's Morris is a slower, more complicated game played on a board drawn with three concentric squares, with the diagonals as well as the midpoints of each side connected. Extremely popular in 14th-century Italy, this was the game English settlers brought to North America. Two players have 12 merels each, which they play exactly as in Nine Men's Morris except that pieces can also move along the diagonals. This is a frustrating game for players of equal skill and foresight; because there are 24 intersections and 24 game pieces, the result is often a draw. The board is used to better effect in **Eleven Men's**

Morris, in which each player has 11 pieces. In both games, the degree of movement depends on how quickly players make mills, removing pieces from the board so that other pieces can slide into new alignments. ❧

A Strategy Guaranteed to Win

Alquerque

- ◆ NUMBER: **two players**
- ◆ EQUIPMENT: **a drawn board and 24 playing pieces, 12 each of two contrasting colors**
- ◆ DESCRIPTION: **an ancient capture game, easy to learn but a strategic challenge**

ALQUERQUE WAS introduced to Europe when the Moors brought it to Spain under the name *el-qirkat*. When Alfonso the Learned added Alquerque to his *Libro de Juegos* (Book of Games), it was already 3,000 years old. Like the Magic Square and the Morris Square, the Alquerque game board is incised into the roof tiles of the ancient temple at Kurna.

The basic design unit for the game is the Achi star (see **Picaria**). Four Achi stars, drawn two on two, make the Alquerque board, which is not a battleground so much as a throw mat for a free-for-all hand-to-hand tussle. Alquerque moves are like **Checkers**— all the pieces advance one space at a time and make captures by short leaps—but the tactics are more like

Chess. The pieces, which in the *Libro de Juegos* illustrations look like pawns, can move in eight directions; at the beginning of the game, only one point is empty. The advantage, according to Alfonso, lies with the player who makes the second move. Between two players of equal skill, he predicts, the game will nearly always be a draw. As he aptly describes it, Alquerque is a game "played with the mind."

The Board: Draw a large square, and divide it in half with a vertical line and in quarters with a horizontal line. Divide each of the four squares in half vertically and in quarters horizontally, then connect the corners with diagonals. Draw a dot to emphasize the point at each intersection. The result is a 25-point grid.

The Playing Pieces: Each player has a set of 12 distinctively colored pieces, which are placed on the first two rows of points and the two right-hand points of the third row. The center point, as illustrated, is vacant.

The Object of the Game: To capture or immobilize all the opponent's pieces.

The Play: Players decide who goes first, then take turns moving their pieces along any line to an adjacent

Alquerque

**Quadruple Alquerque (above);
Zamma (right)**

unoccupied point. Moves can be made horizontally, vertically or diagonally, backward or forward, but from only one point to another in a turn. If the closest point is occupied by an opposing piece but the point beyond is vacant, a piece can jump, capturing the opponent with a *short leap* (page 22). Players must jump when the opportunity presents itself. Otherwise, the piece that could have made the capture is *huffed*—it is removed from the board. A piece can make several jumps at a time, zigzagging across the board, taking a handful of prisoners in a single turn.

The first player to capture all the opponent's pieces wins. If neither player can capture all the other's pieces, the game is declared a draw.

Variations: In **Quadruple Alquerque**, the board is quadrupled to a grid of 16 Achi squares (four on four, as illustrated). Complicated to draw, the game is equally complicated to play because of the increased possibilities for movement and capture. Each player has 40 pieces, which fill the first four rows of points and the four right-hand points of the fifth row. Only the center point is vacant. The rules are exactly the same as for Alquerque.

Another variation is **Zamma**, which uses the Quadruple Alquerque board but removes the second, fourth, sixth and eighth connecting lines on both the vertical and the horizontal, as illustrated. This vastly reduces the movement, making for a more chal-

lenging game. Played in the Sahara with camel pellets as pieces, the game dates from the time of the pharaohs. The rules are the same as for Alquerque but for one added fillip: when a piece gets to the back row of the opponent's side, it becomes a Mullah (an Islamic religious leader), much like a King in Checkers. The Mullah is not restricted to moving one space at a time; it can zoom across several unoccupied points, traveling in any one direction during a turn and capturing a distant opponent with a *long leap* (page 22).

In another twist, **Mogul Putt'han** adds a triangle to two opposite sides of the Alquerque board, making it look a little like a wrapped candy. Each player has 16 pieces set on the first four rows of the board, leaving the entire center row vacant, as illustrated. A Ceylonese variation, **Peralikatuma**, adds a triangle to each of the four sides of the Alquerque square. Each player has 23 pieces arranged on two triangles and on the first two rows of the square; three points at the center remain vacant, as illustrated. The rules for both games are identical to Alquerque; only the configuration of the board has changed.   ✍

Mogul Putt'han

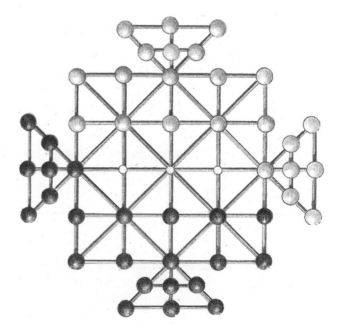

Peralikatuma

Fanorona

- ◆ OTHER NAMES: marketed as Fandango and Albuquerque
- ◆ NUMBER: two players
- ◆ EQUIPMENT: a drawn board and 44 pieces (22 of each color)
- ◆ DESCRIPTION: an elaborate capture game based on Alquerque

IN 17TH-CENTURY Madagascar, players devised a new game by setting two basic **Alquerque** boards side by side and increasing the number of playing pieces to 22 each. Not only is the board more elaborate, but the game involves the unusual capture by withdrawal and capture by approach. In Madagascar, the game was traditionally used for divination as well as for entertainment, ultimately with disastrous results. In 1895, the French invaded the island, and the ruling monarch, Queen Ranavalona III, based her military tactics on the outcome of an official game of Fanorona. The French won, and the Queen was exiled to Algeria.

The Board: Draw a rectangular grid using five vertical and three horizontal lines, creating eight equal squares (two rows of four). Divide each square into quarters, and connect the corners with diagonals. Some players also connect the midpoints of each side with diagonals. Emphasize the intersections with dots.

Fanorona

Capture by Approach

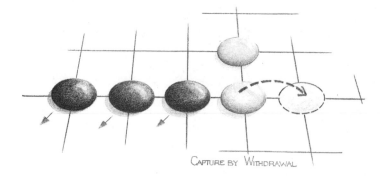

Capture by Withdrawal

The Playing Pieces: Each player has 22 pieces (White or Black) set on the first two rows and on alternate points in the third row, starting from the right and skipping the middle point, which remains vacant.

The Object of the Game: To capture all the opponent's pieces.

The Play: Fanorona is really a set of two games that are always played together, one after the other.

In the first game, White begins and moves a piece along any line to an adjacent vacant point. Players take turns, each moving a piece. If a piece moves toward a row of opposing pieces, in line with them, and lands on the next adjacent point, the row of pieces is *captured by approach*. If a piece moves away from a row of opposing pieces to a point that is still in line with the row but one space removed, they are *captured by withdrawal*. All captured pieces are removed from the board, as indicated in the illustrations by arrows.

In each player's first move, only one row of pieces can be captured. After that, a piece which makes a capture may take another turn, provided that by moving the same piece in another direction, another row is captured. If there are two possible captures with one move, the player takes only one. He is not required to take the longest row; it may be of more strategic advantage to remove the shorter one from the board.

This game ends when one player captures all the pieces of the other.

For the second game, the board is set up the same way as for the first. The loser starts, and players take turns making their moves, but during the opening phase of the second game—called the *vela stage*—the winner of the last game cannot make any captures until she has sacrificed 17 pieces to the loser. These captures must be made one piece at a time, not in rows. When the 17 pieces are captured, the vela stage is over, and play resumes as in the first game. The second game ends when one player captures all the other's pieces.

A match usually consists of two sets, or four games, the first and second always played alternately. ∽

Seega

- ◆ NUMBER: **two players**
- ◆ EQUIPMENT: **a drawn board and 24 playing pieces (12 each of two colors)**
- ◆ DESCRIPTION: **a two-part capture game**

A VERY OLD Egyptian game that has since spread to North and West Africa, Seega is played on a square grid with the pieces inside the spaces, rather than on the points of the intersecting lines. It is different from most battle games in that instead of facing each other like armies, the pieces are scattered around the board like guerrilla fighters, placed in strategic starting positions by the players.

The Board: Make a 25-square grid by drawing six evenly spaced vertical lines and, across them, six equally spaced horizontal lines. On the center square, draw a design. The board is empty when the game begins.

The Playing Pieces: Each player has a set of 12 distinctive pieces.

The Object of the Game: To capture all the opponent's pieces.

The Play: Players decide who begins, then they take turns placing their playing pieces on the board, two pieces in the first turn, one in each turn after that. Players may put their pieces on any vacant square except the center square, which must remain empty until all pieces are on the board.

The player who puts the last piece on the board begins the second part of the game—moving from space to space in an effort to capture the opponent's pieces. A piece can move horizontally or vertically, but not diagonally. It can also move onto the center square, where it is immune from attack.

A player captures a piece by *manacling* it between two of her own pieces. For example, in the game illustrated, when the black piece in the lower left corner moves up one square, the white will be manacled between two blacks: captured and removed from the board. Captures can occur only on horizontal and vertical lines, not diagonally. A piece that moves voluntarily between two opponent's pieces is not captured; the opponent must make the capture by moving the third piece of the row—the manacle—into position. The piece that completes the capture can be moved again if it can make a second capture.

A player must capture whenever possible. If a player moves a piece into a position that completes two captures at once, he must choose which prisoner to take; he cannot have both. Since a capture consists of three pieces in a row, corners are safe havens.

Seega includes three rules designed to ensure fair play. If one player's pieces are blocked and cannot move, the other player must take an extra turn and make an opening for his opponent so that the game can continue. No player can keep moving back and forth between two spaces. If he moves back and forth more than three times, he has to take a different move or lose the piece to the opposition. If a player is surrounded by the other player's pieces and refuses to come

Seega

out, she forfeits the game.

If a player captures all the other's pieces, it is a *major win*. If the game comes to a stalemate (no one can move, but there are still pieces on the board), the player with the most pieces on the board can claim a *minor win*. If players have an equal number of pieces, the game is a draw.

Strategy: Draw games, unfortunately, are common. If your opponent is unobservant, it is not difficult to position some of your pieces to create a barrier that protects the rest from an encircling attack. Break up any attempt by your opponent to do this, and for a better game, avoid it yourself. Control as many of the corners as possible, since you cannot be surrounded there.

Variation: The same board is used for **High Jump**, but instead of players positioning their own pieces during the game, the pieces are laid out before the game begins, players setting their pieces on the first two rows and on the two right-hand spaces of the third row. The center square remains vacant. Instead of capturing an opponent's piece by manacling, captures are made by short leaps, as in **Checkers**. Otherwise, the game is the same: The center square is safe, pieces can move only orthogonally (horizontally or vertically, not diagonally), and captures must be made whenever possible. ∽

Four Field Kono

- ◆ NUMBER: **two players**
- ◆ EQUIPMENT: **a drawn board and 16 playing pieces of two contrasting colors**
- ◆ DESCRIPTION: **a Korean capture game played on the points; more difficult than it seems**

WHAT DISTINGUISHES Kono is its form of capture. Instead of leaping over an opponent, as in **Checkers**, or trapping it in a manacle, as in **Seega**, a piece is taken by jumping over a comrade and landing on top of the captive—the *replacement capture* typical of **Chess**.

The Board: Draw a grid with four vertical lines and four horizontal lines, creating 16 intersections, or points.

The Playing Pieces: Each player has eight playing pieces of a contrasting color, set on the first two rows of points, as illustrated. There are no vacant points.

The Object of the Game: To capture all the opponent's pieces.

The Play: Players decide who goes first. The first player begins by making a capture, jumping over one of his own pieces and landing on the same square as an opponent, removing her piece from the board. Players take turns making captures and, when a capture is not possible, moving along the lines to an adjacent vacant point. (Moves are orthogonal, never diagonal.) The game is over when one player captures all the opponent's pieces or when the other person cannot move. If the game is stalemated, the person with the most captives wins.

Variation: Five Field Kono is played with a grid of five vertical and five horizontal lines, but the setup, motive and moves are entirely different. Each player has seven pieces laid out along the edges of the grid. The object is to move all your pieces from your side of the board to the points where your opponent's pieces started the game, much as in **Chinese Checkers**. Players take turns, moving one playing piece at a time diagonally across one square to the nearest point. Pieces can move either forward or backward, but no jumping is allowed, and there are no captures. This isn't as simple as it looks; there are surprise endings almost every time. ∽

Four Field Kono

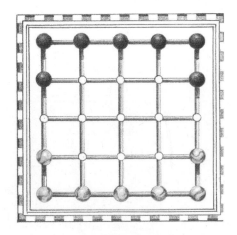

Five Field Kono

Cows and Leopards

- ◆ NUMBER: two players or by yourself, if you are honest
- ◆ EQUIPMENT: a drawn board, 24 pieces of one color (the cows) and two of another (the leopards)
- ◆ DESCRIPTION: a hunt game played on a modified Alquerque board

BATTLE GAMES start with both players' pieces on the board and limited room to maneuver; usually, there are only a few empty spaces (sometimes just one). Hunt games are also battles of a sort, but they often begin with a clear board. How a player positions her pieces and at what point the hunted increase their ranks add another dimension of strategic skill to the play. The real difference, however, lies in the proportion of playing pieces. Equal forces do battle, but in a hunt game, the hunted always outnumber the hunters, sometimes by as much as 12 to 1.

Like battle games, hunt games are universal. Cows and Leopards, for instance, originated in southern Asia, while Fox and Geese is a northern Europe variation, and Coyote and Chickens is North American. Although it is not always the hunter who has the advantage in these games,

players should take turns playing the predator and the prey.

The Board: Draw a basic **Alquerque** board with triangles off opposing sides, as in **Mogul Putt'han.** The board is empty when the game begins.

The Playing Pieces: One player has 24 "cows" of one color; the other has two "leopards" of a sharply contrasting color.

The Object of the Game: To capture or trap the opponent's pieces.

The Play: The player with the leopards begins by placing one leopard on the center point. Then the other player places a cow on any point. The players continue taking turns. The leopard at the center can move to any adjacent vacant point; the second leopard can be placed on the board at

any time during the game. The cows cannot move until the whole herd is on the board. Then the cows can move to any adjacent vacant point.

Throughout the game, a leopard can "kill" a cow by jumping over it if the next adjacent point is vacant, as in **Checkers.** The cows cannot jump; instead, they try to trap each leopard so that it cannot move. The game is over when a leopard kills eight cows or when both leopards are immobilized.

Coyote and Chickens

In the game illustrated below, the leopards are still mobile, but none of the cows are vulnerable to capture.

Variations: A similar hunt game popular in Mexico is **Coyote and Chickens.** It is played on the standard Alquerque board, with one coyote and 12 chickens (pieces of a different color). Place the coyote on the center point. Line up the chickens, five in each of the top two rows and one each on the outer points of the third row, on either side of the coyote, as illustrated. The chickens and the coyote can move in any direction, along any line, to any adjacent vacant point. The coyote can capture a chicken by jumping over it when the point immediately beyond is vacant; he can capture several at a time if the points are clear for the jumps. The chickens, for their part, try to corner the coyote so that he cannot move.

Fox and Geese continues the theme, although it is played on the **Solitaire** board and diagonal moves are not allowed. There are 13 geese, lined up on the first three rows of the cross, as illustrated. The lone fox, which starts on the center point, is free to move in any direction to any adjacent vacant point. The geese can move forward,

Cows and Leopards

Fox and Geese

left or right, but not backward. The fox tries to capture a goose by jumping over it to the next adjacent vacant point. If the fox misses a chance to jump a goose, he is *huffed* and must return one of the captured geese to the top of the board. The geese try to corner the fox so that he cannot move. As in the other hunt games, the predator wins if he can capture enough of his prey so that they are unable to surround him. All things being equal, the advantage lies with the geese. The fox's chances are better if the game is played on the expanded **French Solitaire** board with 15 geese instead of 13. Fox and Geese was also popular among the Cree and Chippewa of North America, who played it as Musinaykahwhanmetowaywin on a Solitaire grid with diagonals. The fox was a king, known as Musinay-Kah-Whan, and the geese were pawns; diagonal moves were allowed. ∾

Solitaire

- ◆ OTHER NAMES: **Pegboard and Patience**
- ◆ NUMBER: **a solo capture game**
- ◆ EQUIPMENT: **a drawn board and 32 playing pieces**
- ◆ DESCRIPTION: **simple, engrossing time-passer, like a nonverbal crossword puzzle**

ACCORDING TO popular mythology, this game was invented by a French count who, during his solitary confinement in the Bastille, worked out its properties and played it relentlessly to pass the time during the French Revolution. But the game is certainly much older than that. The Shorter Oxford English Dictionary dates the game from 1746, yet the German philosopher Leibnitz, who died in 1716, extolled its virtues. Solitaire was so popular during the 19th century that boards were often made of exotic inlaid wood, holes drilled for intricately carved pegs or shallow depressions made to hold hand-blown marbles.

The game works just as well on a humbler board made of paper. The principle is to start the game with one empty spot and to end with only one playing piece on the board. There are dozens of ways to remove all but one of the pieces, but it is another thing altogether to play the French way—removing all but one piece and leaving it in exactly the spot that was vacant at the beginning of the game. Much of Solitaire's delight lies in the hypnotic pattern of the leaps, which almost soothes the disappointment of ending up, yet again, with four pieces scattered impossibly around the board.

Add corner dots for French Solitaire

Solitaire

The Board: Draw a series of dots in the shape of a cross: three vertical rows of seven dots each and three horizontal rows of seven dots each, crossing through the middle. (The black dots are used in French Solitaire.)

The Playing Pieces: Use dried beans, pebbles or pennies, whatever fits on the grid. You'll need 32.

The Object of the Game: To remove all the playing pieces but one.

The Play: Begin the game with a playing piece on every dot except the one at the center. Move by jumping over a piece to a vacant dot on the other side; remove the jumped piece. Jumps can be made horizontally or vertically, but not diagonally.

Continue until only one piece is left on the board or until no further jumps can be made.

Variations: The original, or **French Solitaire**, board makes for a much more difficult game. Add four extra dots, one in each of the crooks of the cross, as illustrated. Put a playing piece on every dot. Start the game by removing one playing piece, and try to end the game with only one piece remaining, positioned on the dot where you removed the first piece. The French also play progressive games of Solitaire, which require numbering the dots left to right in each row, starting at #1 on the upper left and ending with #37 on the bottom right. In **Table de la Corsaire**, a player starts by removing #3 and tries to end with a piece on #35. In **Le Triolet**, a player removes #19 first and tries to end

Triangle Solitaire

with a piece on #32.

Every greasy spoon in cottage country, it seems, has a version of **Triangle Solitaire**, often made of wood with golf tees as playing pieces. Like Solitaire, it is more of a puzzle than a game, since once you figure out how to do it, the game has nothing new to offer. Instead of a cross, draw the dots in the shape of a triangle, with five dots across the bottom, then four, three, two and one.

Put playing pieces on all dots except the center. The object is to remove all the counters except one by jumping—one is left on the dot that was vacant at the start. For both Triangle and standard "cross" Solitaire, use this simple scoring system: four pegs left, there's not much hope; three pegs, you're normal; two pegs, you're pretty smart; one peg, you're a genius.　～

Salvo

- ◆ OTHER NAMES: **Swiss Navy; marketed as Battleship by Milton Bradley**
- ◆ NUMBER: **two players**
- ◆ EQUIPMENT: **four drawn grids or sheets of graph paper; a pencil for each player**
- ◆ DESCRIPTION: **a popular capture game that often lasts at least an hour**
- ◆ COMPLEXITY: **a strategic game that incorporates equal measures of luck and skill**

A LTHOUGH WAR is the theme, Salvo—or Battleship, as it is more commonly known—is not a game of aggression so much as a test of tactical skill. Each player draws two boards, one for himself and one to represent the other player's territory. Every time he fires salvos into her area, she tells him whether any of her ships are hit, and by a process of deduction, he figures out where to place his shots to sink her fleet. An absorbing game, heavily reliant on logic, it also has a lighter side, as evidenced by one of its other aliases: Swiss Navy.

The Board: Each player draws two grids, 10 squares by 10 squares, as illustrated on the following page. One grid represents the position of his home fleet; the other grid is home to his opponent's fleet. (To avoid confusion, name the grids: His and Mine.) Mark the squares alphabetically across the top, left to right (A to J). Mark the squares numerically down the left side, top to bottom (1 to 10). Any individ-

ual box can now be identified by its coordinates; for example, A6, E9, J3.

The Playing Pieces: Each player has a fleet of ships consisting of a battleship (B), five squares long; a cruiser (C), three squares long; and two destroyers (D), two squares long. Before play begins, each player marks his four ships on his own grid, positioning the ship either horizontally or vertically (not diagonally), circling the appropriate number of squares. At least one square should be left between ships; they must not touch each other, even at the corners.

The Object of the Game: To sink the opponent's four ships.

The Play: Players sit opposite each other with a tall book between them so that they cannot see each other's grids. Players can also sit across the room, across town or across the country and communicate by telephone, by mail or even by computer.

Players decide who goes first, then take turns firing a salvo of seven shots from their fleet. (In theory, three shots are from the battleship, two from the cruiser and one each from the destroyers.) The player firing the salvo calls out the coordinates of the seven squares under bombardment. At the same time, he marks them in the appropriate squares on his opponent's grid so that he will know where he has already fired. The seven squares of the first salvo are identified with the number 1, the seven squares of the second with 2, and so on.

The opponent marks the shots on her own grid, then declares what damage was done. She does not identify the coordinates of the squares; she only names the type of ship hit and the number of hits it received. For instance, "Three hits; one on a battleship, two on a cruiser."

When all squares of a ship are hit, it is sunk. The player identifies the coordinates of the downed ship. Her ability to fire shots is now reduced: a sunk battleship removes three shots from each salvo, a sunk cruiser removes two, and a sunk destroyer removes one. For instance, the player whose grids are illustrated has sunk his opponent's cruiser in the lower right, but she has already sunk both his destroyer and his cruiser, reducing his fourth salvo to only four shots.

The game ends when the loser's last ship sinks.

Strategy: Concentrate your shots in one area at a time so that you will do the most damage and can figure out as quickly as possible where your opponent's ships are. The three common strategies are to probe the four corners first, to probe the center first or to zigzag down the ABC column, then down the DEF column, and so on. Whatever your strategy, vary it from game to game so that your opponent won't start counteracting by placing his ships outside your usual plan of attack.

If you have an idea where a destroyer is, sink it quickly and reduce the number of shots in each of your opponent's salvos. Since there are only two squares in a destroyer, it is relatively easy to sink after an initial hit; a

battleship, however, may be headed in any of four directions and may take several salvos to sink.

Variation: Other than varying the number and type of ships and allowing diagonal positions, this game has no real variations, probably because each replay offers challenge enough with a whole new range of strategic possibilities.

The commercial game of **Battleship**, marketed by Milton Bradley, is only slightly different from the paper-and-pencil version. Each player has five ships: a carrier (5 spaces), a battleship (4 spaces), a cruiser (3 spaces), a

submarine (3 spaces) and a destroyer (2 spaces). The grids are made of perforated plastic inset into the tray (home fleet) and lid (enemy fleet) of a box. The play itself is simplified. Players take turns firing one shot at a time, calling out the coordinates. The opponent answers "Hit," "Miss" or "Sunk." Instead of marking the coordinates with a pen, players stick plastic pegs into the squares, red to indicate a hit and white for a miss. Players using a paper board can also change the number or type of boats in a fleet, and they can respond to individual shots. This makes the game much easier. ◡

Turn #1 — one hit on Destroyer
   #2 — two hits on Cruiser
   #3 — Destroyer and Cruiser sunk
   #4 — no hits

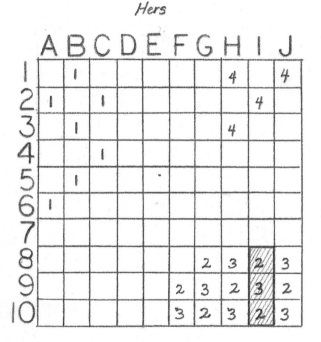

Turn #1 — no hits
   #2 — two hits on Cruiser
   #3 — Cruiser sunk
   #4 — one hit on Battleship

Salvo

2

Of Castles and Kings: Games on Checkerboards

THERE IS AN APOCRYPHAL story of a game of **Chess** played by Henry I of England, the youngest son of William the Conqueror, and Louis VI of France, also known as Louis le Gros. It was around the turn of the first millennium. Henry was beating Louis badly; there was money riding on the results. Louis called Henry something unrepeatable and threw the chessboard in his face. Henry grabbed the board and hit Louis over the head, splitting his scalp. Courtiers stopped the brawl, but apparently, the episode triggered a chain of events that ended in a dozen years of war.

Chess was intended not to stimulate battle but to simulate it. Even though it borrows from the configurations of conflict, the game was devised as a pacific test of intellectual acumen and courage. Yet from the beginning, Chess has been given larger purpose: in India, as a training ground for military strategists; in Venezuela, as a means of raising the IQ of youth; and in tournaments such as the 1972 "Match of the Century" between American Bobby Fischer and Russian Boris Spassky, as a test of national character.

It developed from the game Chaturanga, once thought to be Chinese but now believed to be Indian in origin, already in play before Alexander the Great invaded that country in 326 B.C. According to a recurring Eastern legend, Chaturanga was invented by a man called Sissa, a Brahman at the court of King Balhait of India. Tired of fatalistic dicing games such as Ashtapada—an Indian race game played with dice, somewhat like **Pachisi**—the King ordered his wise man to come up with a pastime that depended on a player's judgment and skill, rather than the will of the gods. Sissa took an Ashtapada board, an eight-by-eight grid of 64 squares, and checkered it with alternating colors. On it, he placed pieces representing the four branches of the Indian Army—the elephants, the cavalry, the chariots and the infantry—as well as the King and his chief counselor. Sissa adapted the rules from the battlefield, where strategy and skill are a matter of life and death. The King was delighted. The game was everything he had hoped it would be: Lady Luck was reduced to a bit player; when he won, it was primarily by his own wits and daring. The King ordered Chaturanga to be played in every temple as training in the art of war.

When the King asked Sissa to name his reward, the Brahman demurred, but when pressed, he asked the King to give him grains of corn on the checkerboard: one on the first square, two on the second, four on the third, and so on; each of the 64 squares doubling the amount of corn on the square before. The King thought the request reasonable until the servants started hauling in the gunnysacks. By the 64th square, he would have to give Sissa 18,446,744,073,709,551,615 bits of corn—the equivalent of 2,305 mountains, or enough to cover the entire surface of the Earth with nine inches of grain. Whether or not this accurately describes the origins of Chess, the story clearly demonstrates the myriad combinations possible on a 64-square grid, the basis of both Chess and **Checkers** and a handful of less rigorously intellectual games.

Chaturanga spread eastward along the caravan routes from India to China and, on the way, was transformed into Siang K'i, or Chinese Chess, which is played on the points, rather than the squares, with character-inscribed disks lined up on either side of a bar, representing the Huang Ho, the great Yellow River of China. According to an 11th-century tale, the Chinese Emperor met travelers playing Chaturanga, and when he discovered that commoners were moving an effigy of a king across a game board, he summarily cut off their heads and ordered that the highest rank be reduced to general and that the realistically sculptured gaming pieces be replaced with disks. Chinese Chess traveled through Korea to Japan, where it evolved into Shogi, or the Generals' Game.

From India, Chess also traveled west to Persia. The Arabs conquered Persia in the seventh century and carried the game, now known as Shatranj, throughout the Islamic world to the edge of Europe. The Moors brought it to Spain in the eighth century, and traders took it to Russia and north to Scandinavia in the ninth century; so by 1000 A.D., when Henry and Louis battled wits, it was well known on that continent. The first part of Alfonso the Learned's *Libro de Juegos* (Book of Games) is devoted entirely to Chess, although in 1282, it was not quite the same as the game we play today. Not until the 15th century did Chess begin to resemble the modern game, with a Queen as the King's counselor and Rooks, Knights, Bishops and pawns instead of elephants, cavalry, chariots and infantry.

Checkers originated in the south of France around 1100, combining elements of **Alquerque, Backgammon** and Shatranj. Originally called Fierges, the game was played on the same 64-square checkerboard and used only one kind of playing piece—the *fers*, derived from the Persian word for counselor (*farzin*) and the name of the Queen piece in medieval Chess.

At this stage in the evolution of Chess, the Queen (or Counselor) could move only one square diagonally, in any direction. Fierges adopted the move and kept it, even after the Chess Queen became more mobile and powerful. Capture in Checkers was by short leaps, as in Alquerque, rather than by replacement, as in Chess. At first, a player could decline to take prisoners, but around the middle of the 16th century, compulsory capture was introduced, the new variation called Jeu Forcé to distinguish it from the less aggressive Jeu Plaisant.

The game wasn't referred to as Checkers until it moved to North America, where, in the early 19th century, Checkers was used to describe a polite and scientific game of Draughts, its British name. In most European countries, the name of the game still refers to the matriarchal playing piece: Jeu de dames in France, Dama in Italy, Damenspiel in Germany. Only in

Canada and the United States do we refer to it by the name of the board.

The alternating colors of the checkerboard are critical to Checkers, since the playing pieces are restricted to diagonal movement on the dark squares alone. But both Checkers and Chess use the same board of 64 squares, 32 light and 32 dark (referred to as white and black, respectively, regardless of their actual colors). In both games, the board is traditionally placed so that the bottom right-hand corner square is white. (The exceptions are **Spanish Checkers** and **Italian Checkers**, in which the board is turned so that the white square is on the left.) And in both games, opponents' pieces face each other in classic battle formation.

Indeed, both Checkers and Chess seem more like intellectual contests than games. They require deep concentration, which accounts for much of their appeal; the trivialities of the day mercifully dissipate as you contemplate the next move. Many people enjoy these games, but few become masters at either Checkers or Chess, particularly the latter. Dutch psychologist Adriaan de Groot tried to discern the nature of a Chess master's genius but found few differences between those who excel at the game and the rest of us, who merely get by. Surprisingly, when making their moves, masters consider fewer choices than do novices: Instead of working through each move and its consequences, they appear to have a distinctive spatial ability that allows them to recognize patterns and emerging configurations many moves in advance.

There is no doubt that good Chess and Checkers players have unique cerebral capabilities. As early as the seventh century, Chess masters began turning their backs on the board, playing entirely from their minds. Blindfold games have since become part of the tradition, a checkerboard parlor trick taken to bizarre extremes in an attempt to prove intellectual prowess. Newell W. Banks, an American master of both Checkers and Chess in the 1920s, once played 25 Chess games and 81 Checkers games, all at the same time, six of them while blindfolded. He lost only one game; he won 22 of the Chess games and 65 of the Checkers and stalemated the rest. At the age of 60, he played six simultaneous games of Checkers blindfolded for 45 consecutive days, four hours a day. At the end of the marathon, he had won 1,131 games, drawn 54 and lost only two—without ever laying eyes on a checkerboard.

Checkers

- OTHER NAMES: **Draughts in Britain**
- NUMBER: **two players**
- EQUIPMENT: **a 64-square checkerboard and 24 pieces, 12 of each color**
- DESCRIPTION: **fewer options than Chess, but intellectually stimulating nevertheless**
- TIP: **anyone over the age of 7 or so can play**

UNLIKE CHESS, there is no single internationally recognized form of Checkers. There is standard Checkers and at least a dozen variants, with nationalist names such as Polish Checkers, Russian Checkers and Canadian Checkers. Most English-speaking countries play the game the same way, including the critical Jeu Forcé rule of compulsory capture and the consequent rule of *huffing*, removing a piece that fails to make a capture.

The first Checkers laws were formulated in 1852 by world champion Andrew Anderson and have changed little in the intervening century and a half. In card games, a card laid is a card played, and in Checkers, the same rule applies: the checker touched is the one you move. Your hand can hover, but once it alights, you have made your choice. If that piece is not playable, you forfeit your turn. In competitive play, you forfeit the game. Furthermore, anything that might annoy or distract the players is strictly forbidden—making signs or sounds, pointing, even, at one time, smoking by the spectators. In case anyone is inclined not to take the game seriously, *Foster's Encyclopedia of Games*, published in 1897, includes a rule with ominous *Merchant of Venice* overtones: "A player committing a breach of any of these laws must submit to the penalty, which his opponent is equally bound to exact." Some of these tournament laws seem a little draconian for house rules, but one worth deploying at home is the five-minute rule. If a play has not been made at the end of five minutes, you can call, "Time," and your opponent must play within the next minute or forfeit the game—or at least the turn.

Among the variations of the standard game are Spanish Checkers, which reorients the board and gives the King more mobility, and Spanish Pool (known as German Checkers in Europe), in which pieces can move backward to capture. Russian, Italian and Turkish Checkers all use the standard 64-square checkerboard, but Polish Checkers is played on a 100-square board. Also called Continental or International Checkers, the game developed in the cafés of Paris in the 18th century, supposedly the inspiration of an émigré Polish count (hence the name). Today, it has its own international organization attempting to promote it as the true test of Checkers skill. This claim is challenged by those who play Canadian Checkers—the Grand jeu de dames—on a 144-square board.

Checkers has at times been deprecated as women's Chess, implying that the more complicated war game should be left to finely honed (male) minds, but in fact, Checkers players are no slouches. The best of them plan 15 to 20 moves ahead. In 1949, the American Checker Federation was established to promote the game as "a dignified, intellectual pastime," rather than an entertainment of women, old men and children. With a membership of over 1,000, it maintains an International Hall of Fame and sponsors an annual United States open tournament followed by a world-title match. As of January 1, 1993, two new world-champion categories have been added to the roster: Man Versus Machine, and Machine Versus Machine, giving computers a chance to vie for Checkers' top honors.

The American Checker Federation also publishes a newsletter, and players anxious to get beyond the basic play-as-you-please game to more interesting strategies would do well to play out the matches printed in the newsletter. This requires temporarily numbering your board: writing on the playing squares with a soft pencil or using numbered stickers. If you are

Checkers Notation

playing on the dark squares, numbering starts in the top left, as illustrated on the facing page. Most books follow the confusing practice of reversing the color of the squares so that the pieces show up better. In these illustrations, however, the board is only lightly shaded, so the pieces can be shown in their actual positions.

The Board: A checkerboard with eight squares on each side, a total of 64 squares in alternating colors. Pieces move only on the 32 dark squares. Place the board so that each player has the *single corner* (4 or 29) on the left and the *double corner* (5, 1 or 28, 32) on the right.

The Playing Pieces: Each player has 12 wooden disks, about an inch in diameter and three-eighths of an inch thick. One set is dark, referred to as *Black*; the other is light, referred to as *White*. Most sets come with three extra disks of each color. The Black disks are lined up on the dark squares of the first three rows of one side (squares 1 through 12). The White disks are lined up on the dark squares of the first three rows of the other side (squares 21 through 32). The two rows between opponents (squares 13 through 20) are vacant.

The Object of the Game: To capture all the opponent's pieces or to block them so that they cannot move without being captured; to get a piece to the opposite side of the board, where it is crowned a King.

The Play: Players decide which person plays Black. Black always goes first, then players take turns moving one piece to an adjacent vacant square. A piece can move only one square at a time and only diagonally forward; it cannot move backward or horizontally left or right. If the next square is occupied by an opponent, a piece can jump over it, making a *short leap* to the vacant square immediately beyond. (Players may not jump over their own pieces.) The jumped piece is captured and removed from the board. A piece can make several short leaps in a single

move, capturing two or more of the opponent's pieces as it zigzags across the board, always moving forward.

Players must jump whenever possible. If more than one jump can be made in one turn, the player can choose which to take, but if it is a multiple jump, he must take it all. According to convention, a player makes the entire multiple jump, then removes the captured pieces.

If a player doesn't make a capture when such a move is possible, the *huffing* rule (sometimes called huff or blow) allows the opponent to remove from the board the piece that should have made the jump. Or he can force the other player to retract her last move and make the capture instead.

Multiple Leaps to King's Row

American laws abolished huffing some time ago; now a player must insist on the capture. Although you won't see it in competition, huffing still makes a good house rule.

If a piece gets to the farthest row of the other side—the *King's row*—it becomes a *King*, crowned with a piece captured by the other player. A King can move both backward and forward and can jump in any direction. It is mortal, however, and can be captured. If a piece lands on the King's row in the middle of a possible multiple capture, it must stop to be crowned, as illustrated above, leaving the White piece on the left undisturbed.

A player wins when he captures all his opponent's pieces or when the other player cannot make another move. The game is a draw if neither player can move or has a hope of winning. After the first game, players switch colors and play another. A match consists of an even number of games, so each player has equal opportunity to make the best of the first-move advantage.

Strategy: As a rule of thumb, the faster you take your opponent's pieces without losing any of your own, the sooner you will win. That is not, of course, as easy as it sounds. In general, keep your own checkers moving toward the center of the board, where they have the most mobility. Moving toward the outer edges soon cuts your options in half. As well as positioning yourself, however, you must block your opponent's advance and lure him into traps. Most important, you need to defend your King's row. Holding back all your first-row pieces is too restrictive, but try to keep the pieces on 1 and 3 (or 30 and 32) as long as possible. This *bridge* effectively blocks the advance of a lone opponent.

Opening moves are critical for breaking up the opposition and pushing your own pieces toward becoming Kings. Of the 49 possible first-move combinations, **11-15** followed by **23-**

19 has become such a standard that it is called the Orthodox opening. (Note: Boldface numbers designate Black.) In 1872, two Checkers masters played 72 games, and in 55 of them, this was the opening gambit. Experienced players still use it most often.

Out of the 49 possible *openings*, only two guarantee a lost game: answering either 9-14 or 10-14 with 21-17. Almost all the others have acquired nicknames. For instance, the favored opening move of beginners is the Single Corner (**11-15**, 22-18), while experienced players still use the Orthodox and the Dyke (**11-15**, 22-17); **9-14** with any reply except 21-17 is called the Double Corner; **10-14** with any reply except 21-17 is the Denny; **11-16**, 24-19 is Paisley; **9-13** with any answer is Edinburgh; **10-15** with any answer is Kelso; **11-15**, 23-18 is the Cross; **11-16** answered with anything but 23-18 or 24-19 is the Bristol and answered with 23-18 is the Bristol Cross.

All of these are two-move openings, some of which are designed to forestall captures and some of which invite jumps and counterjumps very early in the game. For beginners, it often helps to have fewer pieces on the board, so an early exchange of captures is not necessarily a bad idea, provided they are not haphazard and they leave your remaining pieces where you want them. (Try playing out this example: **11-15**, 23-19, **9-14**, 27-23, **8-11**, 22-18, **15-22**, 25-9, **5-14**.) On the other hand, more experienced players prefer a complicated game with more possi-

ble moves; they usually avoid an early exchange. This example plays through 14 moves without a single capture: **11-15**, 22-17, **8-11**, 17-13, **4-8**, 23-19, **15-18**, 24-20, **11-15**, 28-24, **8-11**, 26-23, **9-14**, 31-26.

These opening formations also have nicknames. For instance, the first four moves of the example above are called the Defiance; **11-15**, 22-17, **9-13**, 17-14 is the Boston opening; **11-15**, 22-17, **8-11**, 17-13, **15-18** is the Maid of the Mill; **11-15**, 23-18, **8-11**, 18-14 is the Waterloo; and **11-15**, 23-19, **9-13** is the Will-o'-the-Wisp.

After the opening, players work through the *middle game*, which is mostly concerned with trying to make a breakthrough of your own while preventing one by your opponent. Experience is the best teacher. You have to learn to see the traps (your own and your opponent's) materializing on the board several moves in advance. Plan ahead, and force your opponent to make a jump that lands her in line for a double jump of your own. In the game illustrated, White sacrifices one piece (*) so that Black will jump it and land within range for a White triple jump. (An exchange in which you capture more pieces than your opponent is known as a *shot*.) During the middle game, maintain at least as many pieces as your opponent. If you fall even one checker behind, you may find yourself at an insurmountable disadvantage.

One middle-game ploy is to force a wedge of pieces down the center of the board, crowding the opposition to

the edges. It isn't always true that the player who controls the center controls the game, but controlling squares 14 and 19 is critical. At the same time, Black should not let his pieces get stuck on 21 or 28, and White should be equally cautious about 12 and 5. If possible, attack your opponent's double corner; a well-filled double corner can be more defensive than a bridge.

The *end game* usually involves only a few checkers. Even if you are down to one piece each, which seems like dead-even odds, you can still win. According to some experts, what it comes down to is: Who has *the move*? Count the squares between your last piece and your opponent's. If the number is even, you have the move— the last and crucial move. Approach your opponent to block his progress. If he approaches, you will jump him, and if he backs himself into a corner, you will get him in the end. If an odd number of squares lie between your last piece and his, he can do the same to you. Your only hope is to race to a double corner (1 and 5 or 28 and 32), where you can move back and forth indefinitely, forcing the game to a draw.

If the end game involves several checkers, there is a trick to figure out whether you have the move, which can also help you decide which moves to make to turn the end game around. Think of the four dark squares in the King's row of your opponent as the tops of columns, and count the number of checkers (yours and his) that are in these columns. If the total is odd, you have the move; if it is even or zero, he does. If the total is even and you then capture a piece from one of these columns—called the *key files*— the total becomes odd, and you have the advantage. When you have the advantage, play to keep it. Capture pieces not in the key files, or match each of your opponent's captures. Anyone can develop good Checkers sense without calculating who has the move, but it may be a strategy worth adding to your repertoire.

End games often develop into standard configurations, and once you know the keys to unlock them, it

A One-for-Three Sacrifice

makes for a more interesting game. For instance, if the game comes down to two Kings against one and the lone King has taken refuge in the 5 square of the 1-5 double corner, two Kings (on 14 and 10) can flush him out thus: **10-6**, 5-1, **14-10**, 1-5, **6-1**, 5-9, **1-5**, 9-13, **10-15**, 13-17, **15-18**, 17-13, **18-22**.

The configuration to be most wary of is the *fork*: you have only two ways to move, and either way, you will be jumped. There are two kinds of forks. In the *manacle fork*, on the lower left of the board illustrated above, two Black pieces are in line, separated by a vacant square. If White moves between, Black can move one piece out of the way, but the other one will certainly be captured. In the *V-fork*, on the upper right of the board, two White pieces are lined up in front of the Black, so when the Black moves forward, it will fall into the clutches of one White or the other. This is generally a ploy of the middle game, and if you have enough pieces on the board, you can move another, distracting the opposition into dismantling the trap.

Traps to Guard Against

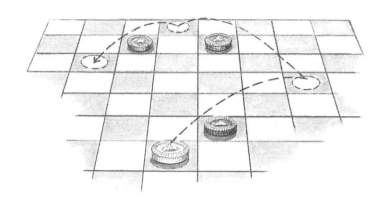

Long Leaps in Polish Checkers

Variations: In Italian Checkers, the board is placed so that the double corner is on the left, instead of the right. The game is played as above, except the King is impervious to capture by ordinary checkers: Kings can fall only to Kings. When faced with two possible moves, a player must choose the larger number of captures, or if the number of captures is equal, he must

take the more powerful piece (for instance, a King instead of a checker).

Spanish Checkers is played like Italian Checkers, except the King can move any distance along a diagonal and can land beyond the captured piece any distance, taking *long leaps* if the path is clear.

Polish, Continental or **International Checkers** is played on a larger board (10 squares by 10—100 squares in all), with 20 pieces per player set on the first four rows. Although pieces can only move forward, they can capture by making short leaps backward. A King can take long leaps, traveling any distance along empty squares to make a capture, landing on a vacant square on the other side of the captive. Provided the squares are empty, a King can land several spaces behind the captured piece and can even turn the corner to make another capture, as illustrated.

If a piece lands on King's row during a capture and can jump forward to make another capture, it must do so.

Because it has left the row, it is not made King. It must come back in a later turn to be crowned. (In standard Checkers, once a piece touches King's row, it has to stay to be crowned.)

Canadian Checkers is the biggest game of all, played on a 12-by-12-square board, with 24 pieces each. Devised by the French settlers of Quebec, who called it the Grand jeu de dames, it follows the same rules as Polish Checkers, but on a larger scale.

Spanish Pool, German Checkers or **Damenspiel** is also played by the rules for Polish Checkers, but the pieces are arranged in the standard way on a 64-square board. Instead of being made Kings, pieces that land on the opponent's back row are made Queens or Dames.

Russian Checkers or **Shashki** is the same as Damenspiel, except capturing is not compulsory and the moment a piece hits the King's row, it is crowned, even if it immediately springs out to make a capture.

Turkish Checkers is played on a

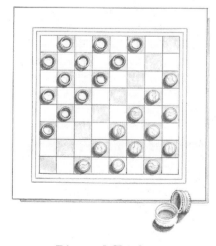

Diagonal Checkers

standard 64-square board, but each player has 16 playing pieces, arranged on the second and third rows, leaving the King's row empty. Pieces do not move diagonally; they move forward or sideways. Captures are by the usual short leaps. A piece that reaches the King's row is crowned and can move forward, backward or sideways any number of squares, so long as they are vacant. Captures are compulsory, and a player must take the largest multiple capture possible. Pieces are removed as they are jumped, instead of at the end of a multiple capture, as in standard Checkers. A player wins by capturing or immobilizing all his opponent's pieces or by reducing his opponent to a single piece against his own King.

Diagonal Checkers is an extremely simple variation on standard Checkers. Arrange the playing pieces as il-

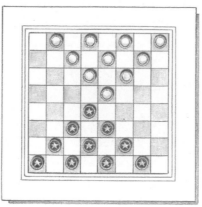

Pyramid Checkers

lustrated on the previous page so that they fan out from the double corner on the right, two in the first row, four in the next, six in the last. (There is one empty row between the Black and White.) Play is exactly the same,

though the orientation makes for an interesting game.

Pyramid Checkers is a Jeu Plaisant, a territory game without captives, which resembles **Halma** and its offspring, **Chinese Checkers**. On a standard 64-square board, each player arranges 10 pieces in a pyramid as illustrated, four in the first row, three in the next, two in the next, one in the last. No row is entirely without checkers at the beginning of the game. Pieces move diagonally, one square at a time, as in Checkers, but there is no capture. The object is to move all your pieces into your opponent's pyramid. You can jump over her pieces but not your own. ∾

Giveaway Checkers

- ◆ OTHER NAMES: **The Losing Game**
- ◆ NUMBER: **two players**
- ◆ EQUIPMENT: **a 64-square checkerboard and 24 disks**
- ◆ DESCRIPTION: **the opposite of Checkers; a fun antidote to the traditional game, especially if one person has won several in a row**

GIVEAWAY CHECKERS stands the rules of the conventional game on their head. Instead of trying to capture your opponent's pieces and end up with the most pieces on the board, you give your pieces away at every turn. Although the following describes a giveaway game of standard Checkers, any of the variations—Turkish, Canadian, International—can be played in reverse.

The Board: A standard 64-square checkerboard.

The Playing Pieces: Each player has 12 pieces lined up on the first three rows of the dark squares of the board, as in standard **Checkers**.

The Object of the Game: To get rid of all your own pieces.

The Play: Black begins. The rules for moves and jumps are identical to standard Checkers. Pieces move forward, on the diagonal only; players are compelled to jump if possible, but there is no *huffing* (removing a piece that fails to make a capture). If a capture is overlooked, the player has to take back the move and make the capture. Pieces that get to the King's row are crowned, whether they like it or not. The first person to lose all her pieces wins.

Strategy: Kings can be the key to the game; at all costs, avoid being crowned. Move your pieces to squares

from which they cannot be forced to jump to King's row. Stick to every other row, starting with the row closest to you, and don't be in a rush to capture your opponent's pieces.

On the other hand, if you can force an opponent's piece to be crowned, you can throw yourself in front of the King from four different directions and soon wipe out your own pieces, winning the game. The following opening move forces a King on the other player at a very early stage of the game (Note: Boldface numbers designate Black): **10-15**, 23-19, **7-10**, 22-17, **3-7**, 26-22, **12-16**, 19-12-3. If White had led 22-18 instead of 23-19, she would not now be stuck with a powerful monarch.

Later in the game, be careful not to force a draw by allowing one of your pieces to be blocked behind an opponent. During the end game, you do not want to have *the move*, so use the same strategies as in Checkers, but to an opposite end: give away your advantage as often as you can. ∾

Box the Fox

- ◆ NUMBER: **two players**
- ◆ EQUIPMENT: **a 64-square checkerboard, four playing pieces of one color and one of another color**
- ◆ DESCRIPTION: **a variation on the hunt game Fox and Geese, played on the dark squares of the board, like Checkers**
- ◆ TIP: **a good game for kids tired of Checkers and not yet ready for Chess**

ALTHOUGH SEVERAL hunt games are played on the Achi grid, Box the Fox is a rare example of a battle between unequal adversaries played on a checkerboard. The variations probably have more to do with cultural adaptations than with real changes in the rules of the game.

The Board: A standard checkerboard.

The Playing Pieces: Four light pieces (the geese) and one dark piece (the fox). Line up the geese on the dark squares along one side of the board, and place the fox on any one of the four dark squares on the opposite side.

The Object of the Game: The fox tries to get to the opposite side of the board; the geese attempt to immobilize the fox.

The Play: Players take turns playing the fox and the geese. (The fox has the advantage.) The player with the geese starts, then players take turns moving a piece. The geese can move forward one square at a time, diagonally right or left, as in **Checkers**; the fox can move diagonally in any direction, like the King in Checkers. There is no capture. If the fox succeeds in getting to the other side, he wins; if the geese succeed in confining the fox to a square from which he cannot escape, they win.

Strategy: Moving the geese forward in a line leaves few openings for the fox to slip through. If the geese are kept in line, they will almost surely win. To counteract the advantage of well-organized geese, you may allow the fox to start anywhere on the board. The best spot to start is on the next to last row, between the two geese that are farthest from a corner.

Variations: A similar game is listed as **Devil and the Tailors** in the 1897 *Foster's Encyclopedia of Games*. Four white pieces are placed on the dark squares of the last row of the board. These are the tailors. The devil is placed on the top left-hand dark square. The tailors can move forward only, one square at a time, diagonally. The devil can move both backward and forward, one square at a time, like a King. There is no jumping or capturing; the tailors simply try to pin the devil down so that he cannot move. If the devil can reach the free zone behind the tailors, he wins.

Wolf and Goats increases the odds and the risk. Twelve white goats are positioned on the board just as the White pieces would be laid out for Checkers. One lone wolf starts at either the right- or left-hand dark square of the first row on the opposite side of the board. The goats can move forward diagonally, one square at a time; the wolf can move in any direction diagonally, but also only one square at a time. The object is for the goats to immobilize the wolf or for the wolf to reach the other side of the board. The wolf can either capture his prey or jump over them. ∾

Reversi

- ◆ OTHER NAMES: **commercially marketed as Othello**
- ◆ NUMBER: **two players**
- ◆ EQUIPMENT: **a standard checkerboard and 64 reversible playing pieces**
- ◆ DESCRIPTION: **an imperialist game; the more territory you claim, the better**
- ◆ COMPLEXITY: **a complex game; too subtle for young children**

REVERSI WAS invented by an Englishman named Waterman in 1888. It enjoyed a brief flare of popularity, then faded into obscurity until it was resurrected in the 1970s as Othello. Many people unknowingly have the equipment for Reversi: the pieces in **Checkers** games are often stamped with distinctive designs on each side, usually stars and crowns, and there are far more pieces than necessary for a game of Checkers. But no special equipment is needed to play Reversi; a checkerboard and 64 pennies will suffice, since the coins reverse to show either heads or tails.

Although it uses the same playing surface, Reversi is nothing like Checkers. The game starts with an empty board, and once a piece is laid down, it is never moved. There are several conditions for adding a piece to the board, and if they can't be met, the player must pass. Each player uses a different side of the playing disks, either stars or

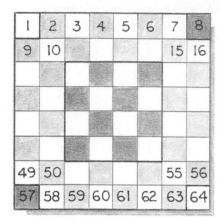

1	2	3	4	5	6	7	8
9	10					15	16
49	50					55	56
57	58	59	60	61	62	63	64

Reversi

Before

After

Capture by Manacling

crowns on checkers, heads or tails on coins. For instance, when the player who has stars lays down a piece, she traps her opponent and claims his territory by flipping over the captive crowns to become stars. Sometimes one square is captured, sometimes as many as seven in a row, making Reversi a game of rapid rallies and swiftly changing fortunes.

The Board: A 64-square checkerboard, all the squares used in play. To follow the moves discussed below, number the board 1 to 64, from the top left, row by row, to the bottom right, as illustrated above. Play begins with an empty board.

The Playing Pieces: Each player has 32 reversible pieces. If using checkers, one player is crowns, the other stars; if using coins, one player is heads, the other tails.

The Object of the Game: To claim more squares with your playing pieces than the other player.

The Play: Players decide who goes first, then take turns laying playing pieces on the board. The four center squares must be filled first.

After four pieces have been played, the game changes. A player may lay a piece on a vacant square only if it is adjacent to an opponent's piece *and* in line with one of her own, vertically, horizontally or diagonally. The opponent's piece or pieces thus manacled are turned over and become hers.

Once a piece is played, it never moves off the square, but it may be flipped several times, claimed first by one player, then the other, then the first player again. If playing a piece closes the manacle on two lines of opposing pieces, both lines are flipped. For example, in the game illustrated, the crown piece is played on the lower left square, indicated by the arrow. This closes two manacles: one vertical and one diagonal. The stars thus manacled are flipped to become crowns as illustrated in the bottom drawing.

If a player cannot play a piece adjacent to an opponent's piece and in line

with his own, he must pass. He continues to pass his turn until he can play. However, each player has only 32 turns.

The game ends when the board is filled or when neither player can make another move. Players count up their pieces on the board. Whoever has the most pieces wins.

Strategy: In the opening moves, arrange your two center pieces in a row horizontally or vertically. A diagonal is considered a weak opening. Try to place your pieces in the 16 center squares first, since these are pivotal to creating long lines. This also forces your opponent to the edge squares, which offer fewer options. The exceptions are the four corner squares (1, 8, 57, 64), which are also prime territory; a piece placed here can never be manacled and reversed. (On the illustrated board, the best squares are the high-contrast part of the board.) The worst squares are the corners on the outside of the 16-square center territory (10, 15, 50, 55). Avoid them as long as possible. Putting a piece here or in the squares on either side of an outside corner square allows your opponent to play in the corner, a situation to be avoided at all costs. It is better to forgo capturing five pieces and instead take only one if, in the process, you can claim the corner.

Position is often more important than the number of pieces you have on the board, especially early in the game. Control your moves so that you end up in the corners. In the final stages, your pieces must be set so that you can reverse long lines of your opponent's pieces. In this game, fortunes often reverse in the closing minutes of play.

Variations: For a shorter game, use only part of the board—a six-by-six-square grid. Each player has 18 playing pieces.

Except for the opening setup, **Othello** is identical to Reversi. Instead of being free to fill the center four squares any way they want, players must start with crisscrossed diagonals. Play continues as for Reversi. ∾

Halma

- ◆ NUMBER: two or four players, each playing solo
- ◆ EQUIPMENT: four checkerboards or a 16-by-16-square grid; 19 distinctively colored playing pieces each for two players, 13 each for four players
- ◆ DESCRIPTION: played almost exactly like Chinese Checkers, but without special equipment
- ◆ COMPLEXITY: ranks with Checkers and Chess as a game of skill and strategy

HALMA TAKES ITS name from the Greek word for "jump." Although much like **Chinese Checkers**, the game is played with pawnlike pieces on standard checkerboards, instead of with marbles on an indented hexagonal board. The pieces can move in eight directions—backward, forward, to each side and on all four diagonals—a feature that makes Halma an improvement over Chinese Checkers.

The Board: A grid of 256 small squares, 16 to each side. Push four checkerboards together to form a square, or adapt a single checkerboard by drawing light pencil lines through each square, horizontally and vertically, dividing it in four. (The alternating colors are meaningless in Halma.) For two players, outline the 19 squares

of the opposing *yards* or *camps* with a heavy line or tape (13 squares in each of the four corners if four are playing).

The Playing Pieces: In a two-person game, both players have 19 pieces each; Black for one player, White for the other. In four-person play, each has 13 pieces (four colors, such as Black, White, Red and Green). The game begins with the pieces in their corner yards, opposite each other in the two-person game.

The Object of the Game: To move all pieces to the opponent's yard.

The Play: Players decide who goes first, then take turns moving one piece at a time. Pieces can move one space at a time in any direction: for-

Halma

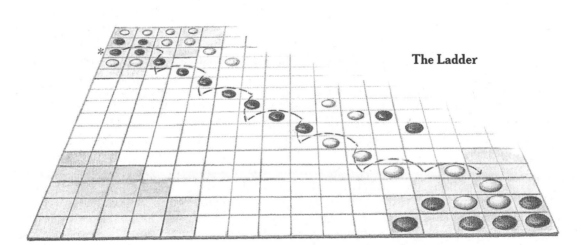

The Ladder

ward, backward, right, left, on any diagonal, like a King in **Chess**. Pieces can move only to unoccupied spaces, but they can jump over another piece (their own or an opponent's) to get to a vacant space beyond. The jumped pieces are not captured; they stay where they are. Multiple jumps are allowed and can be made in any direction, zigzagging around the board.

Whether there are two or four players, each person tries to get to the other side as quickly as possible. There is no team play, although players may agree to gang up on one particularly speedy opponent to give the rest time to catch up. The first person to take over the opposing yard wins.

Strategy: As you move your pieces out of your yard, try to form a long line, or *ladder,* that pieces can jump along, moving from the back of the yard to the head of the line in a single move. For example, in the game illustrated on the previous page, the black piece marked by an asterisk can jump a 12-piece ladder to advance from one corner to the other in a single move.

In general, move pieces out of the yard as soon as possible so that none are stranded. If you move the forward pieces into final position before removing all from the yard, you may never get them out. On the other hand, try to trap early arrivals in your own yard so that they cannot penetrate deep into your yard until your own pieces are well on their way.

When arriving at your destination, keep moving the forward pieces to make room for later arrivals.

As in **Reversi**, fortunes rise and fall during the game, and the winner is often decided in the last few moves. Close games are the rule, rather than the exception.

Variations: You can play partners, with Red and Green teaming up against White and Black. Each player helps build ladders for his partner and tries to block the progress of the other two players. A win can be declared as soon as one partner gets to the other side, or players can agree that both members of a team have to get to their yards in order to win. In this case, as soon as one player gets all her pieces home, she can use her turns to move her partner's pieces home.

A reasonable facsimile of the game can be played on a standard checkerboard with 64 squares, using only 9 or 10 playing pieces each. Arrange the pieces in the corner nine squares, and play exactly as above. The game is faster, but just as much fun and easier than finding four checkerboards to fit together. ∾

Chess

- ◆ NUMBER: **two players**
- ◆ EQUIPMENT: **a 64-square checkerboard and 16 Chess pieces each**
- ◆ DESCRIPTION: **a picturesque, dramatic war game; not necessarily ponderous and never boring**
- ◆ COMPLEXITY: **like Mah Jongg and Bridge, easy to learn but challenging to master**
- ◆ DURATION: **allow at least an hour; games can continue over several days**

ACCORDING TO Chess Master Frank J. Marshall: "You can learn the moves in 15 minutes. In another 15 minutes, you can get the idea of the game, and you can play within the hour." Marshall is an unabashed enthusiast. "As an aid to ease of mind, Chess is invaluable, since it takes the mind off the many little things in daily life that frequently disturb and irritate. Chess teaches patience, clear thinking and courage in contest. It also promotes good sportsmanship. No one who has learned the game ever regretted it, for its delights and rewards are endless."

But Chess has also had its detractors. The Koran specifically denounces its graven images. In 1291, the Archbishop of Canterbury threatened British clergy with a bread-and-water diet if they did not give up the game. More recently, J.H. Blackburne, a British Chess Champion who played every master of note between 1862 and 1914, called Chess "a kind of mental alcohol . . . unless a man has supreme self-control, it is better that he should not learn to play Chess. I have never allowed my children to learn it, for I have seen too much of its evil results."

Chess is played on a checkerboard, but all the squares are used; only the Bishops are confined to a single color. Each player has 16 pieces—eight figures and eight pawns (not traditionally referred to as pieces). All of them capture in the same way, not by short leaps, as in **Checkers**, but by replacement (page 22), landing on a space already occupied by an opponent and removing the captive from the board.

Once you are familiar with the pieces and the particular moves they make, the rules of play are quite simple. Basically, players take turns moving their pieces until one King is *checkmated*—unable to move without being captured or to bring troops to the rescue. The permutations on that theme, however, have filled volumes. To introduce some of the common moves and the kind of thinking that Chess demands, a sample game is played out below, adapted from *Chess in an Hour* by Frank J. Marshall, American Chess Champion from 1909 to 1936 (published by the Leisure League of America, 1936). Set up the pieces and pawns, and work through the game, taking time to understand each move.

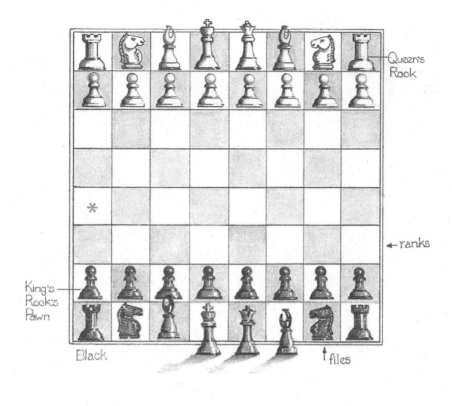

King's
Rook's
Pawn

Queen's
Rook

← ranks

Black

↑ files

Chess

If this whets your appetite, proceed to a detailed Chess manual. There are hundreds to choose from; someone once calculated that on average, on a worldwide basis, one book on some aspect of this game is published every day.

As with most old games, there are certain conventions of etiquette that Chess players observe. A move is considered to be over when you take your hand off the piece; if it is a capture, the move is over when the captured piece is off the board and your hand is removed from the capturing piece. If you are promoting a pawn, the move is over when the trade is complete and you have taken your hand off the new piece. If you touch one of your own pieces, you must play it. If you touch several, your opponent has the right to decide which one you move. If, in making a capture, you touch several of your opponent's pieces, he decides which one is actually captured.

These are tournament laws and can be waived at home, of course. If players are allowed to rethink a move, the game is often better for everybody. On the other hand, a player who constantly changes his mind or makes thoughtless moves, knowing that he can retract them, is not much fun. Decide your own house rules on this point, but make sure they are understood before the game begins. If you apply the touch-and-move rule, then you can seek a temporary injunction by declaring, "*J'adoube*" ("I adjust"), which allows you to fix a piece that has been knocked over or is edging out of its square.

Chess is a game of strategy. Given the opportunity, some players contemplate a move for hours. (The longest master game, played in 1907 between Oldrich Duras and Heinrich Wolf, lasted 22½ hours.) If you decide to impose a time rule at home, five minutes per play is reasonable. No one wants to be hounded into a precipitous move, but on the other hand, few

things are more frustrating than twiddling your thumbs for an hour while your opponent dithers.

The Board: A 64-square standard checkerboard set between players so that a White square is on the bottom right. (Regardless of the actual colors of the checkerboard, they are referred to as White and Black.) All 64 squares are in play. When the board is in position, the vertical rows are called *files*, and the horizontal rows are called *ranks*.

The Playing Pieces: Each player has eight figure pieces and eight pawns. The pieces are arranged on the first row of the board in order: Rook (or Castle), Knight, Bishop, Queen, King, Bishop, Knight, Rook. The Queen always stands on her own color (White Queen on a White square), and the King always stands on a square of the opposite color. When opponents' pieces are lined up, they face each other: Knight against Knight, Queen against Queen, and so on, as illustrated.

In the second rank are the eight pawns, lined up one in front of each piece, foot soldiers to protect the more powerful combatants in the first rank. If you draw a line between your King and Queen, you divide your troops in half. The pieces between the Queen and the edge of the board are called the Queen's Bishop, the Queen's Knight and the Queen's Rook. The pawns are designated the same way: the Queen's pawn (in front of her), the Queen's Bishop's pawn, the Queen's Knight's pawn and the Queen's Rook's pawn. The same applies to the pieces on the King's side.

Notation: In order to discuss a Chess game (or to play by mail), a system of notation has been developed naming each of the 64 squares according to the piece that controls it at the beginning of the game. The square occupied by the King's Rook is the King's Rook's square, or first square (KR1), the next square in the file is the King's Rook's second square (KR2), then the King's Rook's third

(KR3), and so on, to KR8. Each player names the board from his or her own perspective. For instance, on the chessboard illustrated on the previous page, Black's KR4 (indicated by the asterisk) is also White's KR5.

Capture is indicated by an "x"; for example, P x P means pawn captures pawn. A move is indicated by a dash: P-K5 means pawn has moved to the King's fifth square. The first letter is the piece being moved; the letter and number indicate the space the piece is moving to. When a move is described, the board is always identified from the point of view of the player making the move.

There is also an algebraic system of notation that starts at the bottom left-hand corner; it numbers the ranks (1 to 8) up the left side of the board and letters the files (A to H) across the bottom. We have used the more traditional notation that refers to the pieces, rather than the grid.

The Movement of the Pieces: The *King* can move only one square at a time, though he is free to travel in any direction, horizontally, vertically or diagonally. He can capture an undefended piece, but he himself can never be captured, nor can he move into a position where he could be captured.

If a King is in a position where he can be captured on the next move, he is in *check*. The word derives from *shāh*, the Persian word for king. A player who threatens a King must declare, "Check!" so that the other player is aware of the danger and can prepare a defense. On the next move, the King must capture his attacker, move out of the way or bring in one of his troops to ward off the attack. A King may not stay in check for even one move. If a King cannot move out of the way, bring in help or capture his attacker without putting himself in check, he is in *checkmate* (from the Persian *shāh-māt*, meaning the shah is helpless), and the game is over.

The *Queen* is the most powerful piece on the board. She can move in a straight line in all directions along any number of vacant squares.

The *Rook* (or *Castle*) is the next most powerful piece. It can move in a straight line along any number of vacant squares horizontally or vertically, but not diagonally.

The Rooks are also used in a unique move called *castling*, which a player can make only once in a game, if at all. If neither the King nor the Rook has yet been moved, the King is not in check and the squares between the two pieces are vacant, the King can move two squares toward the Rook, and the Rook can jump over the King to the square on the other side. This is the only time a King can move two squares at once and the only time the Rook is allowed to move past an obstacle in its path. Castling with the King's Rook (written 0-0) lands the King on the King's Knight's square and the Rook on the King's Bishop's square. Castling with the Queen's Rook (written 0-0-0, since the Rook moves three squares instead of two) leaves the King a little farther from the corner; he ends up on the Queen's Bishop's square, and the Rook ends up on the Queen's square. The illustration shows the position of the Black King and King's Rook and the White King and Queen's Rook, before castling (on left) and after (on right).

The *Bishop* can move diagonally forward or backward in a straight line across any number of vacant spaces. It cannot move horizontally or vertically. Each player has a Bishop on a White square and a Bishop on Black; in making diagonal moves, each Bishop is confined to his own color.

The *Knight* moves in small L-shaped jumps. He cannot move diagonally, only horizontally or vertically, taking either two steps horizontally and one vertically or two vertically and one horizontally. When a Knight leaves a square, he always lands on a square of the opposite color. The Knight is the only piece that can jump over other pieces, which means he can get out from behind the pawns at the beginning of the game, while the Bishops, Rooks and the King and Queen must wait for the pawns to move. The Knight does not capture the pieces he jumps over; he takes prisoners the same as any other piece, by removing an opponent from the square he lands on.

Before   After

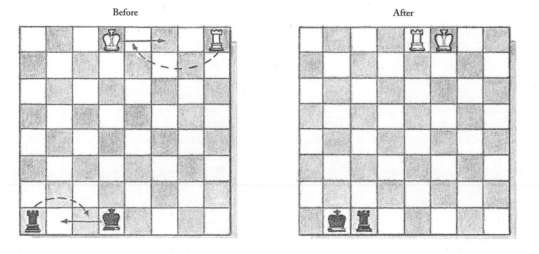

Castling With the King's Rook (lower left on each board) and the Queen's Rook (upper right)

The *pawn* is the most limited piece in Chess. It can move forward only, never backward. On the first move, a pawn can advance either one or two squares. After that, it can move only one square at a time. Although it advances straight ahead, it moves one square diagonally forward to make a capture. When a pawn reaches the opponent's first rank, it is *promoted*—replaced with another piece. This is much like crowning a King in Checkers, except King is the only promotion not allowed in Chess. The pawn can become anything else; you can even have three Queens on the board at once, if you can manage to move that many pawns to the other side of the board. Players usually promote a pawn to a Queen, which is why the practice is often called "Queening a pawn." The exchange must be done immediately.

The Object of the Game:
To immobilize or capture the other King.

The Play: Players decide who will be White. White always begins, then players take turns, moving one piece in each turn. The opening move is almost always a pawn, often the King's pawn, advanced two squares to clear a path for both the King's Bishop and the Queen. In the following sample game, detailed to give you a feeling for the basic Chess moves, White opens exactly that way (P-K4). Set up your pieces, and play along.

Black counters with the same move (P-K4), opening the board for the Black Queen and the Black King's Bishop, while at the same time blocking the White King's pawn from going farther.

The Black King's pawn is unprotected, so White moves her King's Knight to the King's Bishop's third square (Kt-KB3). Her King's Knight is in position to take the Black King's pawn on her next move.

Anxious to protect his King's pawn, Black moves his Queen's Knight to the Queen's Bishop's third square (Kt-QB3). Now, if the White Knight takes the Black King's pawn, she will

be captured in the next move by the Black Knight.

White is not willing to sacrifice a Knight in order to take a pawn, even a King's pawn, so instead of making the capture, she brings more pieces into play. The Queen is too powerful to bring into battle this early in the game, so the King's Bishop is the piece to move. White aggressively moves the Bishop to the Queen's Knight's fifth square (B-QKt5), putting the Black Knight under direct attack. As in Checkers, many Chess maneuvers have nicknames; this one is the Ruy Lopez opening (illustrated on the next page), named for the Spanish bishop who played the first international Chess tournament in 1575.

Black responds with a move named for Paul Morphy, a renowned 19th-century American master. Black moves his Queen's Rook's pawn forward one square (P-QR3), thus challenging the White Bishop, who, if she takes either the Queen's Rook's pawn

Queen

Rook

Bishop

Pawn Advance

Knight

Pawn Capture

The Moves of Individual Pieces

or the Black Knight, will be captured by the Queen's Knight's pawn. A Bishop for a Knight is not a good exchange early in the game, so White withdraws her Bishop to the Queen's Rook's fourth square (B-QR4), out of danger from the Black pawn but still in line to capture the Black Knight.

Black, seeing that White has backed off and knowing that his Queen's Knight is well protected by pawns, goes on the attack, moving his King's Knight to the King's Bishop's third square (Kt-KB3). He is now in position to capture the White King's pawn on the next move.

White sees that her King's pawn is unprotected and under attack. She decides to risk losing it in order to move her King to a safer part of the board and her Rook into the center of the action. White castles, moving her King's Rook to King's Bishop's square and her King to King's Knight's square (0-0).

Black could now take the White King's pawn, but instead, he decides to protect his own King by preparing the board for castling. He moves his King's Bishop to the square in front of the King (B-K2).

White looks at the board and asks herself, as each player should after every move, "What is under attack?" Her King's pawn is still vulnerable, so she moves to protect it. She has several choices: she can move her Queen's Knight to the Bishop's third square, her Queen's pawn forward one square, her Queen to the King's second square or her King's Rook to the King's square. She chooses the latter (R-K1).

When Black surveys the board, he sees that his Queen's Knight is still under attack, and since the middle game is well under way, he can expect White soon to make the capture. After all, Bishops and Knights are of almost equal value, so the exchange is a trade-off. He goes on the offensive, moving his Queen's Knight's pawn two squares forward (P-QKt4), in line to capture the White Bishop.

White has to move her Bishop or lose it, so she moves it back to Queen's Knight's third square (B-QKt3).

With White on the defensive, Black takes the opportunity to castle the

The Ruy Lopez Opening

King's Rook, leaving the Black King on the King's Knight's square and the Rook on the King's Bishop's square (0-0).

White has only one pawn moved forward, and all her Queen's pieces are blocked. To open up her options, she moves her Queen's Bishop's pawn one square. She is also preparing for her next series of moves. She intends to move her Queen's pawn forward two spaces. If the Black King's pawn takes it, then her King's Knight will take the Black King's pawn, the Black Queen's Knight will take her Knight, and her Queen will take the Black Knight. So far, so good. But then the Black Queen's Bishop would move forward two spaces to attack the White Queen. She would move back, giving the Bishop's pawn time to move forward another space and attack the Bishop, which Black has now successfully trapped. By moving her own Queen's Bishop's pawn forward (P-QB3) at this stage of the game, White is providing a future escape route for her King's Bishop.

Black, feeling pushed, decides to move his Queen's pawn forward. Although he could move one square, he decides to move two (P-Q4), which may mean a sacrifice; but on the other

hand, if White decides not to attack, it leaves the pawn in a strong position.

White attacks. Her King's pawn captures the Black Queen's pawn (P x P).

Then the Black King's Knight takes the White King's pawn (Kt x P).

So White takes the Black King's pawn with her King's Knight (Kt x P).

The Black Queen's Knight captures the White King's Knight (Kt x Kt).

Then the White Rook moves forward to the King's fifth square and takes the Black Knight (R x Kt).

At the end of the skirmish, Black has captured a pawn and a Knight and White has captured a Knight and two pawns, putting her ahead.

Black's Knight is now under attack by both the White Rook and the King's Bishop. If the King's Bishop moves in to take the Knight, the Bishop will be in a position to threaten both Black's Rook and his King. The Knight is guarded by the Black Queen, but he adds a second protection, moving the Queen's Bishop's pawn one square forward (P-QB3).

White is ahead but notices that her Queen's pieces are still relatively blocked. She releases two for action by moving the Queen's pawn forward two squares (P-Q4).

Black, feeling threatened by the Rook, tries to force it back by moving his King's Bishop to the Queen's third square (B-Q3).

The ploy works. White moves the Rook back to the first row (R-K1).

In doing so, White loses the tempo of her game. Black is on the offensive and attacks again, moving his Queen diagonally across to the edge of the board, landing on his King's Rook's fifth square (Q-KR5).

The action has now shifted from the center to the King's side of White's board. Her King's Rook's pawn is under attack from both the Black Queen on KR5 and the Black King's Bishop on Q3; the pawn has nothing to defend it but the King himself. If White allows the pawn to be taken by the Black Queen, the King will have to move (if the King takes the Queen, he will move into position to be captured by the Bishop, which is not allowed). If White moves her King's Rook's pawn forward one square, it will be taken by the Black Queen's Bishop and lead to inevitable

checkmate. Instead, she moves the King's Knight's pawn forward a square (P-KKt3), boldly threatening the Black Queen yet protected by both the King's Rook's pawn and the King's Bishop's pawn.

The Black Queen moves forward another square (Q-R6).

White goes on the offensive, moving her King's Bishop to capture Black's remaining Knight (B x Kt).

Black captures White's Bishop with his Queen's Bishop's pawn (P x B).

White moves her Queen to the King's Bishop's third square (Q-KB3), putting her in line to capture the Black Queen's pawn.

Black has more pieces in play than White, so he decides to sacrifice the pawn. He moves his Queen's Bishop to the King's Bishop's fourth square (B-KB4).

White decides to take the offered King's pawn (Q x P), at the same time putting the Black Queen's Bishop under attack.

Black responds by moving his Queen's Rook to the King's square (QR-K1), thus putting the White

King's Rook under direct attack and threatening checkmate in one move. The Black Queen's Rook is protected by his King's Rook.

White moves her own Rook forward and takes the Black Queen's Rook (R x R). Then the Black King's Rook moves one square sideways and takes the White Rook (R x R).

White's strategy is questionable. Her Rook, among several other undeveloped pieces, is trapped in the corner; Black's Rook is still in a position to move to K8 and checkmate White's King. To protect her King, White moves her Queen's Bishop to the Queen's second square (B-Q2); now if the Rook moves to K8, the Bishop will capture him. She could have made the same move before the exchange and saved her Rook; that blunder may cost her the game.

Black moves his Queen's Bishop to the King's fifth square (B-K5), directly diagonal to and threatening White's Queen. The Black Queen's Bishop is protected by his Rook. If the Black Queen's Bishop is allowed to stay where it is, the Black Queen can proceed to KKt7 on the next move and checkmate White's King.

White's Queen has no choice. She captures the offered Queen's Bishop (Q x B).

The Black Rook takes the White Queen (R x Q).

White tries to free up her Queen's Rook by moving her Queen's Knight to the Rook's third square (Kt-R3).

Black moves his Rook over to the King's Rook's fifth square (R-KR5).

The White King's Knight's pawn takes Black's Rook (P x R).

The Black Bishop moves deep into White territory, capturing the King's Rook's pawn (B x P) and putting the White King in check.

White moves her King one space to the right to the Rook's square (K-R1).

The Black Bishop moves out of the way (B-KKt6), so the Black Queen puts the King in check.

White moves her King back to the King's Knight's square, desperately trying to get out of the trap (K-KKt1).

The Black Queen moves forward

END GAME

White

Checkmate

another square (Q-KR7), keeping the King in check.

The White King slides over another square to the King's Bishop's square (K-KB1), but the Queen is on his tail.

As illustrated on the previous page, the Black Queen moves two squares sideways and captures the King's Bishop's pawn (Q x P), declaring checkmate. The White King has four possible moves; each means certain capture by the Black Queen. The White King is immobilized, and Black wins.

Not all Chess games are won or lost; they can also end in a draw. There are four ways to declare a draw game. If the player who has the advantage (the best pieces still on the board) does not succeed in declaring checkmate within 50 moves, the game is a draw, providing the other player requests checkmate and there have been no captures and no pawns moved.

If a person makes the same move three times in a game, that person can claim a draw before the other player makes another move.

If one player gives continual check to the other player's King (*perpetual check*), the game is a draw.

And the game is also a draw if a King is the only piece that can be moved and if, although it is not in check, it cannot be moved without going to a square guarded by an opponent.

The game described above did not include one specialized form of capture called *en passant*, or *taking in passing*. This happens when a pawn reaches the fifth square before the opposing pawns on either side have moved. Legally, a pawn can move two squares on the first move, which would bring the opposing pawn beside the oncoming pawn and out of reach of capture. This seems to give the slow starter the advantage, so in this case, the oncoming pawn can capture it as if it had moved only to the third square instead of the fourth. As an example, the Black King's pawn advances to K5. The White Queen's pawn moves to Q4. The King's pawn can capture the Queen's pawn: White's pawn is re-

moved from the board, and Black's pawn ends up on Q3, just as if the Queen's pawn had moved only one square. An en passant capture must be made at the next possible move. If you wait past the next turn, it is too late.

Strategy: Chess is played on several levels at once, which is what makes the game so complex and challenging.

In general, at the beginning of the game *develop* your pieces toward the 16 squares at the middle of the board, especially the four at dead center. If you dominate this area, you command the board, since you can move in all directions quickly. This is why the King's pawn and the Queen's pawn are usually moved first. They then control the central squares and, at the same time, release other pieces into battle. In moving your pawns forward, keep them close together, connected in a line so that the opposition cannot

The Fork

break through. Two pawns in the same file, on the other hand, leave a hole in your defense.

Queens, Rooks and Bishops can travel great distances in one move, as long as their paths are clear; keep them back until they are needed. (Watch for long open diagonals and files along which the opposing Rooks, Bishops and Queen might attack.) The Knights, on the other hand, fight at close range. These pieces are most effective if moved forward to your opponent's third or fourth rank, where the Knight will be a constant threat to the pieces on the first rank. Above all,

in developing your pieces at the beginning of the game, maintain as much mobility for all of them as possible.

At any given point in the play, each piece is working toward a capture, while at the same time protecting one of its cohorts from capture. You must therefore simultaneously play a defensive and an offensive game. After each of your opponent's moves, ask yourself, "What piece is vulnerable now?" And, at the same time, "Where can I move to threaten my opponent, weaken his defenses and get to his King?" Always keep an eye out for the weak spots in the opponent's game, and build up your attack to take advantage of them.

When a piece comes under attack, you have two choices: You can move out of the way, or you can bring in some defense so that if your opponent takes your piece, he will certainly lose his own. If a player captures your piece, then loses his own, this is an *exchange*. If, in the exchange, your opponent has to give up a valuable piece such as a Bishop in order to take a pawn, he will not likely make the *sacrifice* unless in so doing he clears a path to a more powerful piece. In trying to decide the relative merits of certain captures and sacrifices at the beginning of the game, consider the Queen worth 10 pawns, the Rook 5 and the Bishop and Knight 3 each. Bishops and Knights are not exactly equal, of course. On the board, two Bishops are a little stronger than a Knight and a Bishop, and two Bishops are certainly superior to two Knights.

Never get into an exchange in which your opponent's pieces end up deep in your territory, even if you capture more. In general, don't exchange Bishops for Knights early in the game. Beware of sacrifices on the part of your opponent; they are inevitably Greek gifts and should be looked carefully in the mouth. A *gambit* in Chess is a way of opening the game in which a pawn or a piece is sacrificed in order to put another piece in an advantageous position.

Don't wait to go on the attack. The faster you can move against the opposition, the better your advantage.

Never attack with just one piece. Have a concerted plan involving several pieces, moved in turn for a combined attack. Only in war movies do solo attacks amount to very much. And, finally, castle early so that you bring your Rook toward the center of the board and tuck away your King near a corner for safety.

Like Checkers, Chess is divided into the opening, the middle game and the end game. In general, do not move a piece twice during the *opening*. Bring the Knights out before the Bishops, and bring out both Knights before playing the Queen's Bishop. It always helps to develop both sides evenly, rather than opening only one side of your board (as White did in the sample game), and don't advance any of your troops past the halfway mark at this point in the game. Never allow your opponent to *open a file* on your King (have a column clear from the opponent's side of the board to your King).

There are dozens of famous traditional openings and their responses. Here are a few samples, many named for the master players or tournaments they have become associated with (Note: Black moves are indicated in boldface):

Giuoco Piano: P-K4, **P-K4**; Kt-KB3, **Kt-QB3**; B-B4, **B-B4**.

Ruy Lopez (most common): P-K4, **P-K4**; Kt-KB3, **Kt-QB3**; B-QKt5.

Petroff Defense: P-K4, **P-K4**; Kt-KB3, **Kt-KB3**.

Scotch Game: P-K4, **P-K4**; Kt-KB3, **Kt-QB3**; P-Q4, **P x P**; Kt x P, **Kt-KB3**.

Danish Gambit: P-K4, **P-K4**; P-Q4, **P x P**; P-QB3, **P x P**; KB-B4, **P x P**; QB x P, **P-Q4**.

Queen's Gambit: P-Q4, **P-Q4**; P-QB4, **P x P**.

English Opening: P-QB4, **P-K4**.

Zukertort's Opening: Kt-KB3, **P-Q4**; P-Q4, **P-K3**.

The *middle game* is difficult to discuss because so many moves and configurations are possible, but there are some standard forms of attack that you should learn to recognize and use. A one-on-one attack is not difficult to defend, but if you attack two pieces

at once, your opponent will not likely be able to protect both. One form of double attack is the *fork*, a simultaneous attack on two or more pieces. For instance, in the example illustrated on the facing page, if the Black Queen moves to KB7, both the White King and the Rook are threatened. White must move her King out of danger, leaving her Rook to be captured by the Queen. Forks usually result in the loss of one piece; when you are caught in one, make sure your opponent captures the least valuable booty.

Another form of double attack is the *skewer*, in which a second piece is attacked indirectly through another. For example, if the Black Queen is on K3 and the Black Rook is on the Queen's Bishop's square, as illustrated, they are on a diagonal of White squares. If the White Bishop then moves to King's Knight's fourth square, it is on the same diagonal. The Black Queen can move out of the way, but when she does, the White Bishop will capture the Black Rook.

Related to the skewer is the *pin*. In the example above, if the Queen and the Rook were reversed (Q on QB1 and R on K3), the Rook would be pinned. It would have to stay and be sacrificed so that the more powerful Queen could be moved out of the way. A pinned piece, as the name suggests, has lost its mobility and is no longer an effective guard. Kings and pawns can neither skewer nor pin, since their range of movement is too short; the Knight is also not effectively used this way because it doesn't travel in a straight line.

A more subtle ploy than the fork, pin or skewer is the *discovered check*, wherein a piece is moved out of the way, revealing a piece that directly attacks the King. The piece moved aside can also safely make a capture, because your opponent's next move must be to get the King to safety. The unmasking piece may also be positioned to deliver a check, severely limiting the King's mobility.

There are as many *end games* as there are openings. Generally, the end game begins when only a few pieces and pawns remain; some say it starts

when both Queens are off the board. At this point in play, pawns become increasingly valuable. If you can promote one to a Queen, you will stand a good chance of winning. For the end game, the King can stop skulking in a corner and can move toward the center without fear of being trapped. If the key in the opening is the development of your pieces and the key in the middle game is coordinated attack, then the key to a successful end game is accuracy. Think through each move thoroughly; the fate of your King depends on it. ❧

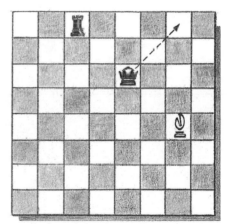

The Skewer

3

By the Board:
Games With Special Pieces

THE INVENTION OF **Monopoly** is usually credited to Charles B. Darrow, an unemployed heating engineer in Germantown, Pennsylvania, but the game was, in fact, the brainchild of an entrepreneurial woman named Lizzie Magie. And it was not originally a fantasy game designed to relieve the economic realities of the Depression; it was a game with a political point.

In 1904, Magie patented The Landlord's Game, which is instantly recognizable to Monopoly buffs: the 40 spaces that ring the board include 4 railroads, 2 utilities and 22 rental properties, as well as Jail, Go to Jail, Luxury Tax and Parking. Only Go is absent; Magie called the first space Mother Earth, which offers a clue to her motives. She conceived the game not for fun and profit but to promote an economic theory popular at the turn of the century. According to Henry George, a prominent American economist of the time, economic progress produces a scarcity of land, with the result that idle landowners reap undeserved dividends at the expense of the productive sectors of society. Magie's game was designed to prove George's point.

Although Parker Brothers had bought another Magie game, Mock Trial, it rejected The Landlord's Game as too political. Nevertheless, a few copies of the game circulated, eventually ending up at the economics departments of several major eastern universities. At the economists' suggestion, Magie named the rental properties, added property improvements and increased rents dramatically if a player held a monopoly in certain real estate. In the 1920s, the latter rule spawned a new name—Monopoly—and a shift away from Magie's single-tax concerns toward classic speculative capitalism.

During that era, a game in which players made a fortune should have been a hit, but no one took up Magie's invention. An Indiana company, however, produced a game called Finance, invented by a young man who had played The Landlord's Game in college. Finance was much like Magie's game, except the unowned properties were auctioned. A woman named Ruth Hoskins fiddled with Finance, naming the squares for well-known streets and districts in America's holiday capital, Atlantic City. Darrow heard of Hoskins' homemade game through a friend. He refined the board a little further and reorganized the rules, copyrighting them in 1933.

Darrow offered his "new" game to Parker Brothers, but it rejected the game as it had The Landlord's Game a decade before, not for political reasons this time but because the game was too lengthy and complex. So Darrow produced it himself and sold a large order to F.A.O. Schwarz, where George Parker's daughter heard about it. At her suggestion, Parker Brothers approached Darrow, bought the game and, to be on the safe side, acquired the rights to Finance and The Landlord's Game as well. Within two months, Parker Brothers was producing 20,000 sets a week. Suddenly, *The Shadow* and *Fibber McGee and Molly* had competition. In the first year of Parker Brothers' sales, in the middle of the Depression, over one million people bought the Monopoly game. Darrow became a millionaire, and Parker Brothers was rescued from the brink of financial disaster.

When Parker Brothers initially rejected Monopoly, it returned the game to Darrow with a list of 52 fundamental errors in his invention. Games manufacturers then, as now, had very definite ideas about what constituted a good family board game. It should take 45 minutes or less to play and have a specific, easily understood goal—the first person to reach it won the game. Yet many of the world's most popular board games and the board games that have survived the longest—**Go** and **Backgammon** have been favorites for more than 2,000 years—fail to conform. In fact, what the biggest board-game fads seem to have in common is an utter disregard for those very precepts.

Take **Scrabble,** for instance. Charles Lutwidge Dodgson (better known as Lewis Carroll) came up with the concept as early as 1880. "The idea occurred to me," he wrote to a friend, "that a game might be made of letters to be moved about on a Chess-board till they form words." But it wasn't actually invented until 1931. Alfred M. Butts, an unemployed New York architect who had a mania for anagrams and crossword puzzles, amused himself during the early years of the Depression by trying to turn the popular puzzles into a board game. He called it Lexiko and made up a few sets for friends. They were enthusiastic, so he sent it off to Parker Brothers, Milton Bradley and smaller games manufacturers. Their response was unanimous. "The game came back with nothing," recalls Butts. "No suggestions for improvement . . . nothing." Not even a list of fundamental errors. Butts refined his invention, renamed it Criss-crosswords and tried the games producers again. "Too high-brow," they replied. "Too complicated."

In 1948, a longtime friend, James Brunot, offered to manufacture Butts' game. He renamed it Scrabble, which the Shorter Oxford English Dictionary defines as "to struggle or strive" and "to make meaningless marks." The name perfectly describes the game—a long, drawn-out spelling bee in which your choice of words is determined by a grab bag of letters. No wonder the games manufacturers scoffed. Brunot began producing Scrabble on a small scale, about 16 sets a day, from a little red schoolhouse in Newtown, Connecticut. Sales were slow, and after a few years, he was about to drop out of the venture when, one week in July 1952, orders jumped from 200 to 2,500. A Macy's executive had played Scrabble on his summer vacation and ordered the game for his store; other department stores quickly followed suit. In 1954, production skyrocketed to 4.5 million. Once the game was a success, Selchow & Righter bought the rights, later selling them to Milton Bradley. Now, after 40 years, 100 million Scrabble games have been sold worldwide, making Scrabble the second best-selling board game in North America, after Monopoly.

Manufacturers' criteria notwithstanding, Scrabble and Monopoly are proof that the most popular board games are not mindlessly simple. They are often as complex and engaging as **Chess** or **Fanorona**. What distinguishes the games in this chapter, however, is the boards on which they are played—not checkerboards or boards you can make yourself but unique, intricate boards produced by commercial manufacturers for our playtime pleasure.

Among the first of these special board games was the Royal Game of Goose, invented in Medici's Florence in the late 16th century. A spiral track of 63 squares begins with a jester figure and ends with an elaborate portal that must be reached by an exact count on the dice. On squares marked with geese, the spots on the dice are doubled, and on other squares illustrated with a pond, a prison, an inn and a bridge, the player is penalized. For instance, at the bridge, he pays a toll of one counter; at the inn, he pays a counter for his food and lodging and loses a turn while he rests; at the well, he loses two turns while he waits for another player to come by to get him out; if he lands in prison, he pays a counter and cools his heels until someone lets him out by throwing the same number that got him in—penalties not unlike the Luxury Tax, Street Repair levy and Go to Jail square that lie in the path of the Monopoly player.

Between the Royal Game of Goose and this year's craze lie thousands and thousands of board games, most of which never got off their inventors' drawing boards, a handful of which were produced and one or two of which succeeded and survived. Most are simple race games in which tokens move from start to finish, the outcome so clearly dependent on the luck of the die that the game seldom holds players' interest for long. Variations on a theme abound. Aggravation, for instance, is **Pachisi** expanded so that six can play. Sorry is Pachisi played with a deck of cards instead of dice. Trouble is Pachisi for young children, in which a single die is noisily "tossed" by pressing the plastic dome that encases it.

This chapter describes the most basic and the most enduring of the distinctive board games. Although more complex than a deck of cards—and a lot more expensive   they all come down to the same delicate balance of skill and luck that makes any game both challenging and fun. The best linguist can lose a game of Scrabble, and in Monopoly, a player with luck on her side can bankrupt a seasoned speculator. And in games, as in life, that's what keeps most of us playing along.

Steeplechase

- ◆ OTHER NAMES: **dozens of commercial variations on the theme**
- ◆ NUMBER: **unlimited players; best with three or four**
- ◆ EQUIPMENT: **a board, two dice, a dice cup and tokens**
- ◆ DESCRIPTION: **a simple race game; all luck, no strategy**
- ◆ COMPLEXITY: **excellent first board game for young children who can count to 12**

ORIGINALLY, A steeplechase was a cross-country horse race, so named because the church steeple, the loftiest local construction, was a goal that the jockeys could always keep in view. When the steeple was no longer visible amidst the rising architecture, the race was moved to a track. Neat white rails replaced farmers' fences, and meandering streams became water jumps.

In 1895, steeplechasing was so popular that a board game was devised in its honor, complete with die-cast metal ponds, fences and leaping steeds. The legs on the miniature lead horses were widely splayed so that they rocked on the board, and the jockeys wore the colors of famous British stables.

Steeplechasing remains a major event in England. Although steeplechasing is eclipsed by thoroughbred racing in the United States, the Maryland Hunt Cup is still run every year on the last Saturday of April, one week before the Kentucky Derby, the horses and jockeys competing over a four-mile course of undulating pasture dotted with 20 post-and-rail fences.

The Board: A curlicue of 87 numbered spaces. Obstacles are set or painted on spaces 9, 32 and 52. Spaces 16, 35, 56 and 69 are marked in red. Each red space occurs immediately before a curve, which is divided into a long outside track and a shorter inside track with only half as many spaces.

The Playing Pieces: Two dice, a dice cup and a token, representing a horse and rider, for each player.

The Object of the Game: To be the first to cross the finish line.

The Play: Players each roll one die. The person who rolls the highest number goes first, then the dice cup passes clockwise around the table.

Players place their tokens at the starting post below space #1. They take turns throwing the dice, moving their horses forward the number of squares indicated. When a token lands on spaces 9, 32 or 52, the horse has stumbled and has to stay there until all the other horses have passed. (If the horse is already last in the race, it simply misses a turn.)

If a token lands on a red space—16, 35, 56, 69—it can move to the inside track; otherwise, horses must take the outside track around the curves. In the example illustrated, Black has just rolled 4 and will move his piece from #12 to #16. On his next roll, he can take the inside track on the curve.

The first horse to pass #87 wins. Just as a horse continues to run beyond the finish line, players do not have to land on the last square by an exact count.

Variation: Give each player 10 counters (poker chips, beans, gumdrops). Before each game, players put an agreed-upon stake in the center of the board—one or two counters. The first horse across the finish line wins the "pool." ❧

Steeplechase

Snakes and Ladders

- ◆ OTHER NAMES: **many commercial variations, including Milton Bradley's Chutes and Ladders**
- ◆ NUMBER: **any number of players; more than four makes a slow game**
- ◆ EQUIPMENT: **a board, a die and one token for each player**
- ◆ DESCRIPTION: **a race game with a twist, but still a game entirely of luck; kids meet their elders on equal terms**
- ◆ COMPLEXITY: **fun for anyone who can count to six**

Like **Pachisi** and **Chess**, Snakes and Ladders had its original home in India, where a similar game, Moksha-Patamu (Heaven and Hell), was used by Hindus for the religious instruction of young children. The Indian game illustrates, in 100 squares, the notion that *pap* (good) and *punya* (bad) coexist in the world; the virtuous can climb upward to Nirvana, but wickedness leads irrevocably to reincarnation as a lower, slipperier life form. In the original game, each ladder rose from a square of virtue: #12 was Faith, #51 was Reliability, #57 was Generosity, #76 was Knowledge, and #78 was Asceticism. Similarly, a player's downfall began in the jaws of a snake poised in the squares of Disobedience (#41), Vanity (#44), Vulgarity (#49), Theft (#52), Lying (#58), Drunkenness (#62), Debt (#69), Rage (#84), Greed (#92) and Pride (#95). The two high-risk evils that would take a player back to the very beginning of life's labors were Murder (#73) and Lust (#99).

Such blatant moral messages made the board eminently appealing to Victorians. Published in 1892 in Britain as Snakes and Ladders, the first English boards preserved the Hindu theme, although the virtues and vices were redistributed on the board and adapted to Western sensibilities—Penitence, Thrift and Industry led to Grace, Fulfillment and Success, while the consequences of Indolence, Indulgence and Disobedience were Poverty, Illness and Disgrace. Interestingly, while vices outnumbered virtues in the Indian game, most early Snakes and Ladders variations balance the two, and more recent versions give the players more ladders to climb than snakes to slither down. Today's games are stripped of moral overtones; in some versions, even the snakes have been replaced by "chutes."

The Board: A 10-by-10 grid in which the squares are numbered consecutively from 1 to 100. Within the grid, ladders and snakes of different lengths connect various squares.

Snakes and Ladders

The Playing Pieces: One token for each player and one die.

The Object of the Game: To move the token from square #1 to square #100.

The Play: Players roll the die. The person who rolls the highest number goes first. She throws the die and moves the number of spaces indicated. The die passes to the left, and players take turns advancing their tokens, following the numbers on the board consecutively. If a player lands on a square at the bottom of a ladder, he moves up the rungs to the square at the top of the ladder. If a player lands on a square at the top of a snake, he must slide down the beast to the square at the end of the snake. (In Hindu mythology, descent is always from head to tail, though North American games often reverse the reptiles.)

Square #100, the last square, must be entered by an exact count. If a player rolls a higher number, she passes the die to the next player and tries again on the following turn.

The first player to reach #100 wins. The other players continue until everyone has reached #100.

Variation: For a more competitive game, each player must throw a 6 to begin. A player who rolls a 6 throws again and advances on the board according to the second number thrown. During the game, when a player throws a 6, she takes another turn. (If she throws a second 6, she advances six spaces but does not take a third turn.) If a player lands on a square occupied by another token, the new arrival "bumps" the established token back to square #1. At the end of the game, instead of passing his turn when he throws a number that overshoots #100, a player moves his token to #100 then backtracks the remaining count. For instance, a player who is on #97 needs a 3 to go out. Instead, he throws a 5. He counts five spaces— 98, 99, 100, 99, 98—and lands on #98. If, in the next turn, he throws a 6, he will end up on square #96 (99, 100, 99, 98, 97, 96). As above, the first player to reach #100 by an exact count wins. ◌

Pachisi

- ◆ OTHER NAMES: **sold commercially as Parcheesi, Patchesi, Ludo and Homeward Bound**
- ◆ NUMBER: **two, three or four players; more can play as teams**
- ◆ EQUIPMENT: **a board, two dice and 16 playing pieces (four each of four colors)**
- ◆ DESCRIPTION: **a strategic race game; the model for most modern race games**
- ◆ COMPLEXITY: **children who can count can play; in its sophisticated form, it involves enough tactics to keep even Chess lovers engaged**
- ◆ DURATION: **a game lasts an hour or so; if you keep score, it can go on all night**

A MONG THE Moguls of 16th-century India, Pachisi was played on a grand scale. Akbar the Great had a life-sized marble Pachisi board inlaid in his palace garden; the playing pieces were young women, variously described by games historians as beauties who vied for the honor, members of the royal harem or slave girls. But Pachisi—named for the Hindi word for 25, *pacīs*, the highest-scoring throw of the game—predates Akbar by many centuries and is still played today under the commercial names of Parcheesi and Ludo, a slightly modified version. Ludo was introduced to Britain in 1896, 22 years after Selchow & Righter had trademarked Parcheesi. Neither became a fad, but Parcheesi has sold steadily for more than a century, making it the third all-time best-selling board game in North America, after **Monopoly** and **Scrabble.**

Scrabble and Monopoly are 20th-century American inventions, but Pachisi is played today almost exactly as it was 500 years ago on the other side of the world. Players move their pieces, one by one, out of the Start Square, around the board's outside track and up the center path; the first player to get all four pieces into the center wins. What has changed since Akbar's day is the equipment. Instead of cowrie shells, dice determine the moves; the *char-koni*, or throne, at the center has been democratized into Home; and the playing pieces no longer run down the track. Nevertheless, Parcheesi and Ludo boards have retained some of the game's exotic origins. In the first Selchow & Righter version, Home looks like an elaborate Asian stamp, and the Start Squares, tucked in the arms of the cross where the Mogul's gardens once grew, are decorated with intricate Indian motifs.

Akbar determined his moves by a throw of six cowrie shells, which served as Indian currency at the time. He directed his playing piece according to how many shells landed with their open sides up. If two, three, four or five shells fell open, the piece moved that many squares. If only one shell lay open, the piece moved 10 squares; if all six shells landed open side up, the piece moved 25 squares— *pachisi.* You can imitate the original game by substituting six coins for the dice, counting the number of "heads" just as Akbar counted his open-sided shells.

The Board: A cross-shaped arrangement of spaces, each arm being three squares wide and eight squares long. The arms converge at a large central square called Home. The middle row of squares leading to the center is the Home Path, usually colored red. The two outer rows form the track around which the playing pieces move in a counterclockwise direction, as indicated in the illustration. Twelve squares in this outer track—three on each arm of the cross—are specially marked Safety Points, representing castles where pieces are safe from attack and capture. The Safety Point to the left of the Start Square is the gate through which each playing piece begins its journey around the board.

The Playing Pieces: There are 16 playing pieces, four each of four different colors, and two dice.

The Object of the Game: To move all four pieces around the board's outside track and up the Home Path to Home; the first player to get all four pieces Home wins.

The Play: To decide who goes first, players take turns throwing one die. The person with the lowest number begins, then play continues clockwise around the board.

The first player rolls the dice. If she throws a 5, she moves a piece out of the Start Square and onto the Safety Point to the left. According to the original rules, a player must roll an actual 5, but house rules often allow a total count of 5 as well (for instance, 2-3 or 4-1). If a player throws double 5s, she can move two playing pieces onto the track, or she can move one piece out, then advance it, counterclockwise, five spaces. If the first player does not roll a 5, she passes the dice to the left. Players take turns rolling the dice, using the count to move pieces out of their Start Squares, then counterclockwise around the outside track.

Safety Point

Start Square

Home Path

Pachisi

At every turn, players decide which of their four playing pieces to move and how to count the dice. The dice can be added together to move one piece forward or counted individually to advance two pieces. For instance, a player who throws a 3 and a 4 can move one piece seven spaces, or he can split the roll, advancing one piece three spaces and another piece four spaces. A player can also use the count from one die and simply ignore the other. Every time a player throws a 5, she can move another piece out of the Start Square.

When a player throws doubles, he takes an extra turn. If all his playing pieces are out of the Start Square and on the track, he counts both the top and bottom spots on double dice. For example, double 5s are counted as 5-5-2-2. (Don't bother with a calculator: the top and bottom spots on a die always add up to 7, so a double roll inevitably totals 14.) He can move one piece 14 spaces, play the four numbers separately or use them in combination. For instance, a player who throws double 5s (5-5-2-2) can move one piece five spaces, another seven spaces

Red sends Yellow back to its Start Square.

and another two spaces. The entire count must be used, however. If not, the player forfeits the roll.

There is a penalty in Pachisi for too much luck. If a player throws three sets of doubles in a row, he may not move any piece forward on the third throw, and the piece closest to Home has to go back to the player's Start Square. Remember: If you throw doubles once you have a playing piece back in the Start Square, you count only the top spots on the dice.

If a playing piece lands on a space occupied by an opponent, the opponent is captured. For instance, in the game illustrated, Red rolls 3 and moves to the same square as Yellow; Red *captures* the yellow piece, sending it back to its Start Square. (Captures are not compulsory.) The capture earns the red player a 20-space bonus that he can use to move any red piece forward. A bonus cannot be split between two playing pieces. The bonus must be used by one piece, or it is forfeited. (In the example illustrated, the lead Red is only 11 spaces from Home, and the other two Reds are trapped behind a Yellow blockade, so the bonus is forfeited.)

Multiple captures are particularly rewarding. For instance, the red player may roll 3-6, thereby capturing a blue piece three spaces ahead and a yellow piece six spaces ahead, sending them both back to their Start Squares, clearing the path and earning two 20-space bonuses in the process. The whole roll is nullified, however, if all the red playing pieces are less than 20 spaces from Home. Remember: Use each 20-space bonus in its entirety, or forfeit it.

On a Safety Point, a playing piece cannot be captured. If a Safety Point is already occupied, a piece of the same color can join it, but an opponent cannot land there. There is one exception. A piece moving out of the Start Square has the right-of-way. If the Safety Point to the left of the Start Square is occupied by an opponent, the emerging piece sends the occupying piece back to its own Start Square and earns the usual 20 spaces for a capture.

Two playing pieces of the same color occupying a single space constitute a *blockade*. The two pieces are safe from capture, and no other piece, not even one the same color as the blockade, can pass. If all his pieces are trapped behind a blockade, a player cannot move in that turn. A blockade mounted on the Safety Point to the left of the Start Square traps an opponent's pieces inside. A blockade is a temporary device; the two pieces cannot be moved together even when doubles are thrown. A piece can be moved out of a blockade, however, and another moved into it on the same roll, re-creating a blockade in exactly the same place.

When a piece has made an almost complete circuit of the board, it moves up its Home Path. If the other pieces need help, a player can choose not to take the piece Home but to move it around the board again, capturing and blockading along the way. A playing piece on the Home Path cannot be captured. Some players also impose a no-passing house rule: a playing piece cannot pass another on the Home Path unless it gets Home on that move. Pieces can enter Home only on an exact count (either die or the sum of the two). Every time a player gets a piece Home, she earns a 10-space bonus. She can use the bonus to advance another piece, but it cannot be split. If no piece can be moved 10 spaces, the player forfeits the bonus.

The Score: In traditional Pachisi, there is no score; the first player to get all four pieces Home wins. Instead of earning bonus spaces for captures and arriving Home, however, you can earn bonus *points*: a capture scores 20 points; Home scores 10 points. The game ends when one player gets all his playing pieces Home, but the player with the most points wins. This transforms the game from a race to a chase, where captures are more important than heading Home and several circuits around the board are not unusual.

Strategy: Use the two rear pieces as a blockade to stall the players behind you while your other two pieces advance in front. You have to know when to switch strategies, however. As long as you maintain the blockade, you are playing with only half your pieces. A good time to break a block-ade is when you get a roll that moves a piece to a Safety Point. When rolling the dice, the magic numbers are 5, 7 and 12, the number of spaces between Safety Points.

Variations: In Two-Person Pachisi, each player controls two sets of playing pieces, located in Start Squares opposite each other. Play continues until one player gets one set of pieces Home. A good strategy in Two-Person Pachisi is to play one set of pieces offensively and the other defensively, a kind of kamikaze Pachisi that sacrifices one set in long, bitter blockades so that the other can race Home.

Partnership Pachisi is played with four people, but it is like the two-person version in that the two players opposite each other work together to capture opponents and build blockades. This works especially well if you keep score instead of giving bonus moves. The winner is the team with the most points after one set of playing pieces gets Home.

Beginners' Pachisi emphasizes the element of luck and requires less strategic thinking from players. Play with only one die; for a faster game, use two dice, but always count the two together. Allow players to move a playing piece out of the Start Square on the first throw, regardless of the number rolled. For those with short attention spans or low frustration levels, this gets the game going sooner. The remaining three pieces still need a 5 to get onto the track. Depending on the age and skill of the players, allow captures, but not blockades.

Double Pachisi is a two-person or two-team game played with a doubling cube, used exactly as in **Backgammon**.

Ludo is a simplified form of Pachisi. The track is a little smaller—each arm is three squares wide and six long—and there are no Safety Points where pieces are immune from attack and capture. Although Ludo is played with only one die, the rules of play are exactly the same as those of Pachisi.

Backgammon

- ◆ OTHER NAMES: **played as Trictrac by the French**
- ◆ NUMBER: **two players**
- ◆ EQUIPMENT: **a board, four dice, a doubling cube, 15 white pieces and 15 black**
- ◆ DESCRIPTION: **a complicated race game; easy to learn but can involve great strategy**
- ◆ DURATION: **individual games last only 20 minutes; a match may take several hours**

SOME CREDIT Ardashir, a third-century Sassanian ruler of Persia, as the inventor of Backgammon; others point to an Indian named Qaflän. One theory supposes it evolved from **Pachisi**; another, from the Egyptian race game Senat. Whatever its genesis, the recorded history of the game begins early in the first century A.D., when Claudius, Emperor of Rome, played a game called Tabula (in English, Tables), using a board recognizable as the one we play on today: a rectangle lined on two sides with long, narrow triangles, like the mirrored image of a mountain range. Two players race their pieces around the oval track created by the points, hopping from peak to peak just as they do from space to space in other race games.

Tables was played under various names during the Middle Ages, the game of choice until **Chess** swept Europe. In the early 17th century, it was revised and again became popular as Gammon in Scotland, Trictrac in France, Puff in Germany and Tablas Reales (Royal Tables) in Spain. By 1743, when Edmond Hoyle produced the first treatise on the game, the English were calling it Backgammon, a name that derives either from the Welsh words *back* and *gammon*, meaning little battle, or from the Saxon words *bac* and *gamen*, meaning back game, one of three traditional strategies of play.

Some of the terminology of the game, however, is a holdover from earlier times. The board is divided into an *inner table* and an *outer table*, as in the game of Tables. In setting up the playing pieces, the inner table was traditionally the side of the board closest to the light, "whether it be a window or the gas," writes R.F. Foster in his 1897 *Foster's Encyclopedia of Games*. With contemporary lighting, players have free choice. In the following de-

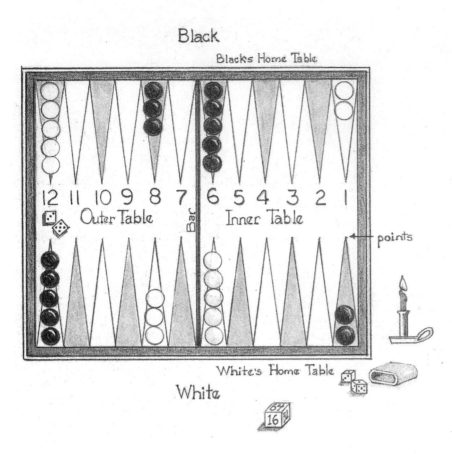

Black

Black's Home Table

12 11 10 9 8 7   6 5 4 3 2 1

Outer Table   Bar   Inner Table

points

White's Home Table

White

Backgammon

scription, the inner table is on White's right (and Black's left). Each player refers to his own side of the inner table as his *home table*.

The 20th century added the *doubling cube* to Backgammon. Invented by an anonymous American in the 1920s, this significantly ups the ante of the game. Usually, a match consists of several Backgammon games played at once. The winner of each game earns a point, and the first to get 10 points wins. The doubling cube changes winners' scores dramatically; games are played to 20 or 50 points or more. The cube looks like a die but is imprinted with the numbers 2, 4, 8, 16, 32 and 64. (Make your own by printing new numbers on a regular die.) At the beginning of the game, the cube is placed on the table with 64 faceup, indicating that no one owns it. At any time (but probably when his game is going particularly well), a player can pick up the cube, turn it so that 2 is faceup and offer it to the other player. If she accepts the cube, the game is now worth 2 points to the winner. If she rejects the cube, she forfeits the game, but the stakes remain

at the original level: her opponent earns 1 point.

If a player accepts the cube, it is hers, and she has the right at some juncture (presumably when her own fortunes have improved) to turn the number to 4 and offer it back to her opponent. If he accepts, the game is worth 4 points; if he declines, he forfeits the game, and she earns 2 points for a win. The stakes can be doubled any number of times until the last play of the game. All of this can be done verbally, of course, without an actual cube; either way, doubling forces players to play strategically a game that, in the end, is not as simple as it looks.

If you don't refine the skills for Backgammon, you can always resort to magic. According to an ancient Icelandic formula, "If thou wishest to win at Backgammon, take a raven's heart, dry it in a spot on which the sun does not shine, crush it, then rub it on the dice."

The Board: The board is rectangular, with a row of 12 triangles, or *points*, projecting from opposite sides toward the center. (The color of the triangles is irrelevant.) A vertical *bar* down the center divides the board into the *inner table* and the *outer table*. So that moves can be described, the points are numbered from 1 to 12, moving from the far edge of the inner table toward the far edge of the outer table. Points 1 to 6 are on the inner table; 7 to 12 are on the outer. In general, a player moves the pieces one at a time along the points in a loop that extends from his opponent's 1-point to his own 1-point. The opponents travel in opposite directions, Black moving clockwise and White moving counterclockwise. (Some sources number the points in the direction of White's travel, 1 to 24.)

The Playing Pieces: Each player has two dice and 15 pieces of contrasting color, sometimes called stones. Each player puts five pieces on his own 6-point; three pieces on his 8-point; two pieces on his opponent's 1-point; and five pieces on his opponent's 12-point, as illustrated above.

The Object of the Game:
To be the first to move all your pieces around the points to your home table and bear them off.

The Play: The players, designated as White and Black, sit with the board between them. For this game, the inner table is on White's right.

Each player has his own dice and throws into the table on his right. If the dice come to rest on top of a playing piece or each other or the edge of the board, they are *cocked* and must be rolled again. If the dice bounce onto the other table or outside the board, they are also rolled again. Each die advances a piece the number of spots shown on the face. A player can move two pieces, one for each die, or a single piece twice, once for each die.

Pieces can only move forward; they can never step back. Players must move if possible, even if it means landing in an undesirable spot, and they must use the full count of each die or forfeit it. A player can elect to use the count from only one die, but if he has a choice between one die and the other, he must take the higher number if possible. If a player throws doubles, the spots are doubled again. For instance, a throw of 5-5 counts 5-5-5-5 and constitutes four separate moves.

To start the game, each player throws one die. The person with the highest number chooses whether to be Black or White, then takes the numbers from the two dice as his opening moves. After the first turn, each player throws both of his own dice; play alternates back and forth between the players.

The playing pieces move along the points according to the count on the dice, then come to rest at the base of the triangle. A player can have as many pieces as she wants on any one point, but having only one or two pieces on a point has certain consequences. As soon as a player has two pieces on a point, she has *made the point*; it is *closed*, or *blocked*, as long as the two pieces stay there. An opponent's piece can jump over a closed point, but it cannot land there. He must move a different piece or, failing that, not move at all. If a player blocks six points in a row, trapping one or more of his opponent's pieces behind the blockade, the player has made a *prime*.

A single piece occupying a point is called a *blot*. An opponent can land on the point and *hit* the blot, sending it to the bar at the center of the board. From the bar, the piece can reenter the game only by moving to a point on the opponent's home table; the numbers of the two reentry points are dictated by the next roll of the dice. For

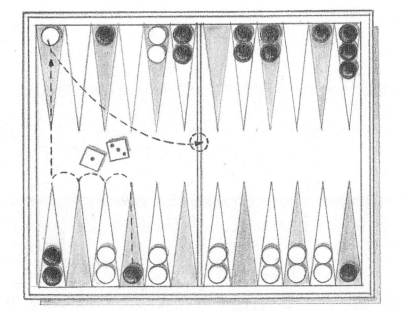

Black hits White's blot.

example, in the game illustrated on the previous page, White has a blot on Black's 12-point; Black rolls 4 and jumps over White's 10-point, which is closed, landing on White's blot and sending her piece to the bar. On her next turn, White throws 4-5; her piece can go to Black's 4-point or 5-point. Both are closed, however, so White cannot move. On her next turn, she throws 3-6. Black's 3-point is open, so she moves the piece off the bar and onto the 3-point. She can now use the count from the other die. Anxious to get off Black's home table, she moves the same piece forward six points. If all six points on Black's home table had been closed, it would be a *shut-out*. White would not throw the dice but would simply pass until a point opened on Black's home table.

When a player has all 15 pieces on her home table, distributed between her own 1-point and 6-point, she can start removing them from the board, a process called *bearing off*. Every time she throws the dice, she can remove pieces from the two points designated by the numbers on the dice. For instance, if she throws 1-2, she bears off a piece from the 1-point and a piece from the 2-point. She may choose instead to move within her home table, advancing a piece from the 6-point to the 4-point and another from the 3-point to the 2-point. If she does not have a piece on the point specified by the die but has one on a higher-numbered point, she moves that piece forward. If all the points above the number rolled are vacant, a player can bear off from her highest occupied point. For instance, if she rolls 5-6 and has a piece on the 4-point and another on the 2-point, she can bear off both.

The first player to bear off all his playing pieces wins.

The Score: A win scores 1 game point. If a player bears off all his pieces before the other player removes any of hers, he has a *gammon*, which doubles what the game is worth (either 2 points or twice the number shown on the doubling cube). If the other player still has one playing piece on the winner's home table, it is a *backgammon*

and scores triple—3 points or three times the number on the doubling cube. A match is usually played to 10 points, although players may agree to a different target score, especially if playing with a doubling cube.

Scores can also be settled on the basis of how many of the opponent's pieces remain on the board after the winner bears off her 15 pieces: 1 point for each piece on the loser's home table, 2 points for each piece on his outer table, 3 points for each piece on the winner's outer table and 4 points for each piece on the winner's home table.

Strategy: There are three basic approaches to Backgammon: the running game, the block game and the backward or back game. Choosing between them is based on a simple principle: When you're ahead, advance as fast as you can; when you're behind, trail as long as you can.

In the *running game*, you try to outrace your opponent, getting your pieces home and off the board before he does. The running game, which relies heavily on the luck of the dice, is a good opening strategy if you get several high throws at the start. Keep a low profile, protecting your pieces by moving them to points you hold, and when reduced to two on a point, move them together when you roll doubles.

In the *block game*, try to block your opponent at every turn, closing points whenever possible, spreading your pieces out in groups of two over the board, the ultimate goal being a prime, which is impossible to break through. This is a defensive game that gradually switches to a racing game to bring your pieces home.

The *back game* is a spoiler's game. Instead of racing ahead, you try to keep your pieces on your opponent's home table, especially on the 1-point and the 2-point. You even try to get hit so that you can reenter in your opponent's home area and close as many points as possible, thus making it impossible for your opponent to bear off.

Given Backgammon's long history, it is not surprising that certain opening moves have been developed, as in

Chess. Dating from Edmond Hoyle's time, the following are the standard openings used with each of the combinations possible on your first roll of the dice. (B-1 indicates Black's 1-point, and so on. White is assumed to make the first move, but if you switch the point designations, the same holds true for Black.)

6-6: Two from B-1 to B-7; two from B-12 to W-7
6-5: One from B-1 to B-12
6-4: One from B-1 to B-11
6-3: One from B-1 to B-10
6-2: One from B-12 to W-5
6-1: B-12 to W-7; W-8 to W-7
5-5: Two from B-12 to W-3
5-4: One from B-1 to B-10
5-3: W-8 to W-3; W-6 to W-3
5-2: B-12 to W-8; B-12 to W-11
5-1: B-12 to W-8; B-1 to B-2
4-4: Two from B-1 to B-5; two from B-12 to W-9
4-3: B-12 to W-9; B-12 to W-10
4-2: W-8 to W-4; W-6 to W-4
4-1: B-12 to W-9; B-1 to B-2
3-3: Two from B-12 to W-7 or two from W-8 to W-2
3-2: B-12 to W-8 or B-12 to W-10; B-12 to W-11
3-1: W-8 to W-5; W-6 to W-5
2-2: Two from W-6 to W-4; two from B-1 to B-3
2-1: B-12 to W-11; B-1 to B-2
1-1: Two from W-8 to W-7; two from W-6 to W-5

According to Hoyle, a player should close her own 5-point as soon as possible, then close her 7-point (also called the *bar-point*). Next in priority is her 4-point. Hoyle also recommends closing the opponent's 5-point and 7-point as a defensive ploy. In general, with each throw of the dice, try to move your pieces so that you close as many points (especially consecutive points) as possible, take possession of your own 5-point or your opponent's, close your own bar-point or close points on your home table.

As soon as possible, move the pieces that are on the opponent's 1-point so that they won't be blocked. Advance them to the 5-point or the 7-point, where they can help prevent the other player from entering his home table.

Don't crowd pieces on a point, piling up seven or eight. This limits your moves and keeps your pieces out of play. Use them instead to close points against the opposition or to move into your home table.

Never hit a blot in your home table unless you are absolutely sure you can close that point as soon as the hit is made. (Or make a double hit, which gives you enough time to cover the blot.) Your opponent has to reenter the board on your home points, and if you have a blot there, you are vulnerable. If you get hit, you will pay the maximum price, traveling all the way back to the beginning of the race.

As in Chess, don't expose a blot unless your opponent takes an even greater risk by making the hit, and guard against decoy blots set out by your opponent. If you must leave a blot, try to isolate it. If a blot is eight points away from the nearest opponent, he will have to use both dice to get to you. (Seven is the most probable throw with two dice.) Leaving a blot one space in front of an opponent is also a good tactic. In general, getting hit early in the game is less devastating than ending up on the bar when you are almost ready to bear off.

During the end game, always bear off if you can, rather than move your pieces forward within the home table. If neither die will bear off a piece, instead of advancing two pieces a little, combine the count and bear off one piece.

The doubling cube carries strategic consequences of its own. As well as calculating your odds of winning, you have to estimate the value of owning the cube. In general, don't double too early, and have the courage to refuse the cube and cut your losses. If your opponent offers it to you early in the game and you have about a 25 percent chance of winning, it is probably wise to take the cube, rather than forfeit the game. Fortunes can shift, you have lots of time to catch up, and if you are neck and neck, you can offer the cube back to your opponent near the end of the game, forcing him to choose between a low-score forfeit and winning the game. If you think you have more than a 50 percent chance of winning, then by all means offer the cube to your opponent. It puts the cube in your opponent's hands, which is risky, but it also earns you more points if you win.

Chinese Checkers

- ◆ NUMBER: two, three, four or six players (never five)
- ◆ EQUIPMENT: a board and a set of 10 colored marbles for each player
- ◆ DESCRIPTION: a simple territory game; no captures, but some strategy
- ◆ COMPLEXITY: requires no counting or spelling; even young children can play
- ◆ DURATION: a 15-minute diversion at most

Chinese Checkers

A SIMPLIFIED VERSION of **Halma**, Chinese Checkers was patented in the United States around 1880 by J. Pressman & Co., New York, as Hop Ching Checkers. Instead of a checkerboard, the game is played on a six-pointed star laced with a grid; where lines intersect, the points are indented to hold the colored marbles. Because a piece can move in only six directions instead of eight, as in Halma, Chinese Checkers is not as challenging, but the unusual board and smooth, round pieces make the game a pleasure to play.

The Board: A six-pointed star, each point colored to hold 10 matching playing pieces. Pieces are played on the intersections of the lines.

The Playing Pieces: Ten marbles per person, each set a different color, usually red, yellow, blue, green, white and black. (Games played on bigger stars allot 15 or 21 pieces each.) Players set the pieces in the matching point of the star. Even numbers of players choose colors that are across the board from each other. When three play, the occupied points of the star alternate with the vacant points.

The Object of the Game: To move all 10 pieces into the point of the star directly opposite. (With three people, each player moves her pieces to the point on the right, as illustrated on the previous page.)

The Play: Players decide who goes first, then take turns. The turns pass clockwise around the board, each player moving one piece in a turn. A piece can be moved in any direction, forward or backward, along any line, to the next adjacent vacant point. If the adjacent point is occupied (by one of the player's own pieces or by an opponent's) and the point beyond it is vacant, a piece may jump, as in **Checkers**. (There are no captures in this game.) If the marbles are positioned appropriately, a piece can make multiple leaps in one turn. A piece cannot, however, move one point and then jump.

The first player to get all 10 marbles to the point directly across the board wins. The others keep playing until all the players occupy their new territory.

Strategy: Establish *ladders* from your side of the board to the target territory so that marbles can make extended multiple jumps, moving as far as possible in a single turn. (See page 53.) Similarly, block any ladders your opponent tries to build.

Variations: New tactical possibilities are opened up by allowing long leaps. A piece can jump any other piece that is in line with it, provided the jumper can land an equal distance on the other side, with nothing but the jumped piece in between. Multiple long jumps are also allowed.

For an interesting tournament, line up **Chess**, Checkers and Chinese Checkers boards side by side (the latter set up for two players). Players make a move on each board in turn, playing the three games simultaneously. The similarities and differences between the three will flex your mind to the limit. ❧

Go

- ◆ OTHER NAMES: **known in Chinese as Wei-ch'i and in Japanese as I-Go**
- ◆ NUMBER: **two players**
- ◆ EQUIPMENT: **a board, 180 white pieces and 181 black pieces**
- ◆ DESCRIPTION: **the ultimate territory game; deceptively straightforward**
- ◆ DURATION: **a game with beginners takes one to three hours; with professionals, up to three days**

Go

ALTHOUGH IT IS most commonly known by its Japanese name, Go originated in China. The first books dedicated to the subject were published during the T'ang Dynasty (618-907 A.D.), but it is mentioned in writings as early as 625 B.C., and many believe it has been played since 2000 B.C. It spread to Korea, where it is played as Pa-tok, then on to Japan, where it was enthusiastically adopted in the sixth century A.D. Initially a court game, by the 13th century, it was a favorite of samurai warriors, carried with them to the battlefield. In the 16th century, learning Go was compulsory at Japanese military academies, and although that practice faded with the fall of the shogun, millions of Japanese still play regularly. According to *Cassell's Book of Sports and Pastimes*, published in 1881, I-Go was introduced to modern civilization by a Mr. Cremer, Jr., who declared the game "intellectually as exhilarating as **Chess** and, in its method, very superior to Draughts."

The Go board, like many of the paper boards in Chapter 1, is a basic grid of 19 horizontal and 19 vertical lines. The pieces, or *stones*, are played on the 361 *points* where the lines intersect. Although now made of glass or plastic, the stones were originally rounds of dense white shell and black slate. The boards were about a foot and a half square, raised on short feet to a comfortable level for the players sitting cross-legged on the floor. The underside of the thick board was hollowed out, so as each stone was played, it produced a resounding click.

The basic principle of Go is easy to grasp: Players take turns placing stones on the points of the grid. Pieces are never moved from point to point, but when a string of stones encloses an opponent's stones, the territory is captured and the captive stones are removed from the board. The object of the game is not the prisoners so much as the surrounded territory. At the end of the game, the player with the most captive points on the board wins.

As simple as it seems, Go has been compared to playing five simultaneous games of Chess, one on each corner and one in the middle of the board—a challenge for any intellectual athlete. Beginners should start by learning the subtle principles of play on a 9-by-9-line grid, advancing to a 13-by-13-line grid before finally tackling a full-fledged game of Go. The rules don't change, only the size of the playing field.

The Board: A 19-by-19-line grid. Pieces are played on the points where lines intersect. Nine points on the board are emphasized with "stars," as illustrated. The board is vacant at the beginning of the first game. In later games, the loser may start with two or more pieces on the stars, as a handicap.

The Playing Pieces: 180 white stones and 181 black stones.

The Object of the Game: To capture the most territory.

The Play: Players decide who takes the black stones and who takes the white. Black always plays first.

To begin, Black places a stone on any point (including the points around the outside edge of the grid). Players take turns, each person placing one stone on the board during a turn. Unless they are captured, the stones stay where they are placed; they never move from point to point. At any time, a player can choose to *pass*, forfeiting his turn.

In placing the stones, a player tries to surround the opponent's pieces and thus capture the points or territory they occupy. A piece placed on a vacant board has four *liberties*—four lines connecting it to other points. A

When White plays a stone on Black's last liberty (left), Black is captured (right).

piece is captured when it loses all its liberties, when every theoretical escape path is blocked. For example, in the following illustrations, an asterisk indicates Black's one remaining liberty, or escape route. If White plays a piece on this vacant point, Black is completely surrounded, without a liberty, and is captured. In the illustration above, one Black piece is captured; in the illustration on page 78 (bottom), seven Blacks are captured. A piece or pieces completely trapped within an opponent's chain of stones are considered *dead* and are removed from the board. (Pieces that are secure from capture are *alive*.) The captured pieces now belong to the captor, as does the vacant territory within the chain—for the moment.

Territory on the edge of the board cannot be completely enclosed. It is considered captured when surrounded on three sides (the border completes the chain).

A player can choose not to play the final piece to close a surrounding

chain, allowing the threatened pieces to keep their last liberty. They are considered *prisoners* and, unless the other player alters the situation, are counted as captured stones at the end of the game.

If a chain of stones surrounds a group of pieces but within the surrounded pieces there is at least one vacant point—called an *eye*—the territory is not considered captured. According to the *suicide rule*, a player cannot place a stone in her own eye; this would put the entire group of stones at risk of being captured should the opponent be able to surround it. For example, in the illustration on page 78 (top), Black still has one liberty—an eye. He may not put a stone here, since all his pieces would then be at risk; in the next turn, White would simply lay a stone as indicated by the dashed circle, completing the chain and capturing all six Blacks. Similarly, it would be suicide for a player to place a stone in an opponent's eye; her piece would immediately be captured. A

A Black "Eye"

Black has one liberty.

player may put a piece in *atari*—put it at risk by playing it on a vacant point surrounded by her own or her opponent's pieces—only when, by doing so, she makes a capture.

Obeying this rule could lead to an unending round of capture and recapture, known as *ko*, the Japanese word for eternity. For example, in the illustration on the facing page (left), Black may play a piece on the asterisk, even though it is atari, because in doing so, the White piece on the left is captured. But White cannot replace that piece and capture the Black, since this violates the rule of ko. To avoid this, a player, after being captured, must first add a stone elsewhere on the board before returning his opponent's attack at the same site. If there are three ko's on the board simultaneously, the game is a draw.

Whenever a stone or cluster of stones is captured and removed from the board, either player can place stones on the points of the vacated territory, provided he or she does not commit atari.

If opposing stones are so interlocked that neither player can try to surround the other without endangering himself, the situation is declared a stalemate, or *seki*. That part of the board remains untouched until the end of play, and the enclosed area is not claimed by either player.

When the players place all their stones, when both players pass in succession or when neither player can seal off any more territory or make more captures, the game ends. (This is probably the only game that, according to the rules, can end by mutual consent, instead of conquest.)

In typical Oriental style, customs and courtesies, rather than outright rules, dominate the final stages of the game. Isolated vacant points—the neutral no-man's-land between claimed territories—are filled in by either player, not necessarily in turn. Prisoners—pieces which are not fully surrounded but which could have been captured by playing one more stone—are considered dead (or *virtually dead*) and are removed from the board and counted as captives. Captured territo-

ries are rearranged into convenient rectangles so that the vacant points can be easily counted. Finally, players use their captives to fill in the vacant points claimed by the other.

The Score: Players add up the vacant points within their territories. The player with the highest total wins.

For the next game, players switch colors, since Black always has the advantage of playing first. If one player wins three games in a row, he gives the other a handicap of two pieces. The nine "stars," or emphasized points, on the board indicate where the handicap pieces are placed.

Strategy: The object of the game is to build chains, both to surround your opponent's stones and to avoid being surrounded yourself. (A chain is not just a string; it is also a cluster.) Avoid chains that are too small and compact, but conversely, don't make a chain so large and spread out that your opponent can attack from within.

Building a secure chain, or *live chain*, depends on eyes. The game can be summed up as a struggle to make eyes within your own chain and to prevent your opponent from making eyes within his. A cluster of stones with two eyes is virtually immune from attack. Beware, however, of false eyes: If the cluster of stones is strung out, an opponent may be able to place a piece on a vacant point between them and enclose part of the group. For example, in the game illustrated on the facing page (bottom), the dashed circles represent all the points where White could play a piece and thus capture one or more Blacks. There was a false eye in the cluster on the lower right, but the cluster in the upper right is protected by two good eyes.

In the opening, control the corners first, then the sides of the grid, leaving the center for last. For maximum flexibility, start your plays on the third and fourth lines from the borders. In building your chains, try to think multidirectionally. Make your stones do double or triple work. Disconnected stones are vulnerable, while stones just a point or two apart can easily be linked, preventing enclosure. Remember: A chain is not necessarily made stronger simply by adding more stones. Make sure that the stones you add increase your options by giving the chain more liberties. Increased liberties mean fewer opportunities for your opponent to enclose your pieces.

Although captives are not the primary goal—claiming territory is—the stones you take are useful at the end of the game. In a sense, a capture scores twice: it gives you a vacant territory point, and it also earns you a piece with which to wipe out one of your opponent's vacant points at the end of the game.

Go is extraordinarily complex. There are, for instance, 21,000 variations in corner openings alone. These elementary rules and tactics will enable you to get started. To continue, refer to the book *Go and Go-Moku* (see Sources).

The Rule of Atari

The Rule of Ko

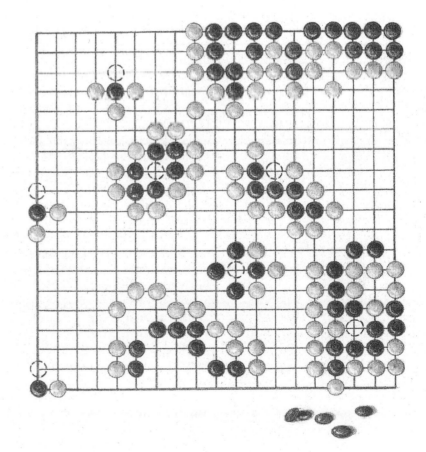

White can complete a chain in seven places, but a stone in the bottom right gains the most territory.

Monopoly

◆ NUMBER: **three to seven players; four or five is best**
◆ EQUIPMENT: **a special board, two dice, 7 tokens, 32 houses, 12 hotels, 28 title deed cards, a set of 16 cards each for Chance and Community Chest and play money in denominations of $1, $5, $10, $20, $50, $100, $500**
◆ DESCRIPTION: **a territory game; equal parts skill and chance**
◆ DURATION: **played by the rules, it usually takes two hours to finish**

MONOPOLY PROVES the point that game fads owe as much to timing as to inventive, entertaining boards. Monopoly had been around, under various aliases, since 1904, yet it didn't really catch on until 1935, when a population laid low by the Depression was primed for a cheap trip into the fantasy world of high finance, personified by the waggish Uncle Pennybags, the Jiggs look-alike who scampers through Chance and Community Chest.

Parker Brothers subtitled Monopoly "a trading game," which is akin to calling the New York Stock Exchange a trading post. Make no mistake about it: Monopoly is cutthroat capitalism at its best—or worst. The aim of the game is to bankrupt everybody at the table, and in the attempt, even the mildest-mannered players become Simon Legrees. The ruthless and the greedy triumph; wimps are left in the dust. Few games provoke such acrimony, but at the same time, few games keep players at the board for so long.

Parker Brothers, concerned about the indefinite playing time, stipulated when it bought the rights to Monopoly that it be allowed to produce a shortened variation. The first game sets came with "Rules for Short Games of Monopoly" printed on a separate sheet. However, even the original rules, if adhered to rigorously, produce a game that usually ends within two hours.

One of the reasons Monopoly often goes on longer is that players introduce house rules which give them more cash, extending the game by forestalling bankruptcy. For instance, according to the rules, fines and taxes are paid to the Bank; the money is *not* tucked under Free Parking as a bonus for anyone who lands there. Free Parking is just that—a place to rest from the rigors of real estate wheeling and dealing. A player who lands directly on Go does *not* collect $400; the salary for passing Go is $200, regardless. Other common house rules not in the actual game include denying a jailed player the right to collect rent, buy or sell property or erect buildings (in fact, even jailed citizens retain their trading rights); sending a token that lands on an occupied square back to Go (any number of tokens can legally occupy a square); and including immunity in property deals. For instance, a player might trade Park Place for St. Charles Place plus the right to land on both Park Place and Boardwalk without ever paying rent. (In the American and Canadian version, properties are named after well-known streets and districts in Atlantic City, New Jersey. In other countries, the properties may bear local designations.)

Each twist in the rules creates a slightly different variation in a game that has been evolving for the better part of a century. For the record, the following rules are adapted from Parker Brothers' first edition. Do with them what you will.

The Board: An outside track of 40 squares includes 22 properties, 4 railroads, 2 utilities, a Luxury Tax square, an Income Tax square, 3 Chance squares and 3 Community Chest squares; corner squares are marked Go, In Jail, Free Parking and Go to Jail. Before play begins, shuffle the Community Chest and Chance cards and set them facedown in the designated areas at the center.

The Playing Pieces: Each player selects a token and puts it on Go. One of the players agrees to act as the *Banker*, who oversees the distribution of money (salaries, bonuses, windfalls and prizes), title deeds and buildings. The Banker should be familiar with the rules of the game, good at math and not easily ruffled. If no one volunteers, players roll one die; the person with the highest number is Banker. (The Banker keeps her own assets separate from the Bank's.) Before the game begins, the Banker gives each player $1,500 in the following denominations: one $500, seven $100, two $50, five $20, seven $10, five $5 and five $1. (Later versions specify two each of $500, $100 and $50, six $20 and five each of $10, $5 and $1.) The rest of the money stays in the Bank, along with the title deed cards and the houses and hotels. The Bank may sell all its buildings and properties, but it never runs out of cash. When there is no more money in the till, the Banker mints more, creating homemade dollars.

The Object of the Game: Through buying, selling and renting properties, to become the wealthiest player, reducing all others to bankruptcy.

The Play: Each player throws the dice; the player with the highest total begins. The first player throws the dice and moves around the board, in the direction of the arrow, the number of spaces indicated by the total of the two dice. Play moves clockwise around the table, each player rolling the dice, advancing the token the indicated number of spaces, then playing out whatever options he has according to the space he lands on. (Any number of tokens can occupy a square.) In the course of the game, players circle the board several times; each time they land on or pass Go, they collect $200.

If a player lands on an *unowned property*, he can buy it from the Bank. (Once a player owns a property, he collects rent from every player who lands on it.) If he decides to buy, the player pays the Banker the price listed at the bottom of the property square. The Banker gives him the title deed card, which he places faceup in front of him.

If the player decides not to buy the property, the Banker puts it up for sale by *auction*. Bidding starts at any price, and anyone may bid, even the player who just turned down the option to buy. The property goes to the highest bidder, who pays the Banker and receives the title deed card, which she lays faceup in front of her.

The railroads and utilities are properties just like Vermont Avenue or St. James Place. If a player who lands there declines to buy, they are auctioned to the highest bidder.

If a player lands on Chance or Community Chest, she draws a card from the appropriate stockpile, follows the instructions and returns the card facedown to the bottom of the deck. The exception is the Get Out of Jail Free card, which a player can keep to use later or sell to another player. After the card is used, it is put on the bottom of the pack.

The Luxury Tax square exacts a flat fee of $75. If a player lands on the Income Tax square, he pays the Bank either a flat rate of $200 or 10 percent of his total worth (cash on hand plus the printed price of properties and the cost price of buildings), but he has to decide which option to take before he adds up his assets.

A player who throws *doubles* gets another turn. If a player throws three sets of doubles in a row, however, he goes to *Jail* (without passing Go). A player can land in Jail by throwing triple doubles, by landing on the Go to Jail corner or by drawing a Go to Jail card. If she owns a Get Out of Jail Free card or can buy one from another player at a mutually agreed price, she moves immediately to the Just Visiting part of the square and continues on her way at her next turn. She can also pay $50 and move into the visiting area. If she has neither a card nor the cash, she stays in Jail and rolls the dice when it is her turn. If she throws doubles on any of her next three turns, she gets out of Jail and advances that number of squares. If, after three throws, a player has not thrown doubles, she must pay the $50 fine, then advances the number of spaces shown on the dice. A jailed player retains all her privileges, however: she can collect rent and buy, sell, trade, improve or mortgage properties.

Every time a player lands on an *owned property* (either by a roll of the dice or as a result of a move dictated by a Chance or Community Chest card), the owner collects rent according to the rates on the title deed card. Rent increases with every property improvement. If the property is mortgaged, the landlord collects no rent. However, if a player owns all the properties of that color, he can charge double rent on any unimproved, unmortgaged properties in the group, even if the other properties in the group are mortgaged or have buildings on them. Landlords must be on their toes; if they don't ask for the rent before the next player rolls, they forfeit the fee.

Free Parking

Once a player owns all the properties of one color, she can improve their rental values by erecting houses and then hotels on each site. The price of buildings is listed on the title deed card. A player does not have to wait her turn to buy a house. Any time the dice are changing hands and she has both the money and the title deeds to all the properties of a group, she can buy buildings. Properties have to be improved evenly; if one property has a house, the next house she buys must go on another property in the group. She cannot build three houses on Vermont Avenue, for instance, and leave Connecticut and Oriental Avenues vacant. After a player has four houses, she can buy a hotel for the cost of the houses plus a cash fee (the amount is on the title deed card), but there must be four houses on each of the properties in the group before one gets a hotel. There is a limit of one hotel to a site.

If the Bank runs out of houses to sell, a player has to wait until someone else sells houses back to the Bank before she can buy. Even a very rich player who can afford to skip the housing stage and buy a hotel directly must have the houses available in the Bank when he purchases the hotel. If there are only a few houses or hotels left and more than one player wants

them, the Banker sells them by auction to the highest bidder. Bidding starts at the lowest purchase price listed on the title deed of each property the bidders intend to improve. Under no circumstances can a player move a house or hotel from one property to another or sell a house or hotel to another player.

There are several ways a player can raise cash. He can sell houses and hotels back to the Bank, which pays half price for them. Just as they were added evenly, buildings must be removed at an equal rate from all the properties in a group. For instance, a player cannot sell one hotel and leave that property vacant while there are hotels on the other two. Instead, he can raise money by converting each of the three hotels to four or fewer houses. If all the hotels are resold at once and not converted to houses, the Bank buys each for half the price of five houses on that property.

Properties without houses or hotels can be *mortgaged*. The Bank pays the mortgage value listed on the title deed card, which is then turned facedown in front of the player. (The player still owns the property; he does not relinquish the title deed card to the Bank.) Before a property is mortgaged, all the houses and hotels on that color group must be sold back to the Bank. No

rents can be collected on mortgaged property, and no buildings can be erected on it. A player cannot add houses to the other unmortgaged properties in the color group, but he can still collect rent on them and can charge the double rate for having the entire color group in his possession. To bring a mortgaged property back into play, the owner must pay the Bank the mortgage fee plus 10 percent interest. (He also must pay full price for any houses he rebuilds on the site.) A player can give a mortgaged property to the Bank as payment for a debt, in which case it is worth the amount of the mortgage minus 10 percent interest. The Bank immediately puts the property up for auction at its original board price.

A player can also raise money by selling undeveloped properties, railroads and utilities to other players for a mutually agreed price. No property can be sold, however, if houses or hotels are standing on any of the properties in that color group. A player must strip the entire color group of its assets before selling any single property in the set.

A player can also sell a mortgaged property privately. The new owner can pay back the mortgage plus interest to the Bank immediately. He can choose not to pay back the mortgage right away, but he still has to pay 10 percent interest on receiving the property, and when he does repay the mortgage, he pays an additional 10 percent. A debtor can offer to give his landlord a piece of mortgaged property in exchange for rent, but it is up to the landlord to decide how much the property is worth.

If a player owes more rent than he is able to pay in cash, he can pay the landlord in undeveloped property at the printed board price. (All buildings must be stripped from the color group first.) Or he can ask the Bank to auction his properties and try to pay his rent with the proceeds.

If, after selling off his houses and hotels and mortgaging properties, a player still cannot pay the rent, he must declare bankruptcy and turn over his mortgaged properties to the landlord. If a player declares bankruptcy because he cannot pay his taxes or the penalties imposed by a Chance or Community Chest card, the Bank takes over his assets and sells them off by auction. (The Get Out of Jail Free card has no monetary value and is simply returned to the deck.) Either way, the bankrupt player leaves the game.

When everyone else is bankrupt, the remaining, very rich player wins.

Strategy: The temptation in Monopoly is to race around the board buying up every available property, but some districts are more desirable—and some monopolies more valuable—than others. When you land on a property, consider carefully whether you want to buy it, weighing the amount of money you have to invest against the likely return on investment from the property.

The orange and red groups balance relatively low purchase price with relatively high rents, so they are prime real estate. Boardwalk is also valuable, since players are sent there by Chance as well as by a throw of the dice. Don't neglect the railroads. They are good investments early in the game, though their value later pales as the hotels claim the big rents. The same is true for the utilities. Collect them early, but eventually mortgage them or trade them for profitable properties. In deciding what to collect, keep in mind the calculations of mathematician Irvin Hentzel, who has determined that players most frequently land on Go, Reading Railroad, Pennsylvania Railroad, St. James Place, Tennessee Avenue, New York Avenue, Free Parking, Illinois Avenue, B&O Railroad and Water Works.

After a few circuits, all players will likely have some properties, but no one will have a complete color group. Now is the time for wheeling and dealing amongst yourselves. There are few rules governing private enterprise between players. Undeveloped properties can be bought, sold and traded for whatever price you can get. You may trade one valuable property for two of lesser value or for cash or for a combination of the two. (Houses and hotels

cannot be traded.) The negotiations can take place anytime, but the actual transaction can occur only during your turn or the other party's turn or when the dice are being passed. A good house rule is to allow property trades only during the turn of one of the traders. And don't be shy about intervening in other players' deals, conning them into making a trade that will benefit you later. If you secretly covet a property that someone is about to trade, use every ounce of schmooze to convince him that it is the worst deal he has ever made in his life.

Collect a color group, and improve the properties as soon as you can, developing one color group at a time. This is especially true if you decide to collect the cheaper properties. You have to collect maximum rents before your opponents develop their ritzier places, which, even with a single house, can bankrupt you if you haven't made some profits first. Get three houses on each property of a set, then move on to improving your next color group. This virtually guarantees an instant income, since players can rarely get past a whole group with one throw. There are not enough houses and hotels to raise the rents on every property to their maximum, so make improvements early. Remember: Seven comes up more often than any other number, so if an opponent is heading for your property and you want to buy some houses, develop the one seven spaces away.

Play defensively. If your properties are studded with houses and there are no more in the Bank, it is a good idea to keep them, rather than convert them to hotels. This prevents your opponents from adding houses to their properties. It may also prevent them from easily converting buildings into cash. If your opponents have only hotels and there are no more houses in the Bank, they cannot trade in a single hotel. Properties must be devalued equally, so in order to raise a few dollars, a player has to strip an entire color group of its buildings.

Bidding for properties can sometimes absorb a large part of the game, and here, psychology comes into play.

Uncle Pennybags From the Chance and Community Chest Cards

Don't let your opponents know how much you want the property, and try to convince the others that the site is worthless. Keep your bids low, or don't even enter the fray until near the end. If no one bids, make a ridiculously low offer. The Bank has to sell to the highest bidder, even if that bid is only a dollar. If you pay less than the mortgage value, the property is a bargain. In trades with other players, get the best deal you can; unlike the Bank, the other players are under no obligation to give up the property you want.

Avoiding Jail is obvious advice, but if you land there early in the game, it is usually worth paying the fine so that you can keep moving and buying. If it takes you three turns to get out, the prime properties may be gone. On the other hand, late in the game, you can comfortably stay in Jail, collecting rents without ever having to pay any yourself.

At the beginning of play, you can buy with abandon, knowing that you will not be paying much rent as you travel around the board. But as the game progresses, be careful not to overextend your finances, investing in so many property improvements that you are hard-pressed to pay rents and fines. Keep a close eye on other players' properties, and keep enough dollars in your cash reserves to cover any throw of the dice. Always have a rough idea of your total assets; if you land on the Income Tax square, you need to know whether the $200 levy is preferable to the 10 percent tax.

It is acceptable to use all your powers of persuasion to squirm out of a bankruptcy, promising to clean the bathroom as well as turning over Park Place and Boardwalk. The landlord decides what she will accept. Players should remember, however, that bankruptcy is the goal. Being ruthless may be the only way to end the game. And if the Bank is your creditor, it is game over for you. As in real life, the Banker does not make deals.

There are a few points in the original game that are unclear. If a roll of the dice lands you on a utility, you pay 4 or 10 times the number shown on the dice. You do not roll again to cal-

culate your rent. If a Chance card sends you to the utility, however, you throw the dice to calculate the rent. If a player owns both utilities and one is mortgaged, you still pay 10 times the amount on the dice when you land on the unmortgaged one.

If a Chance card instructs you to move to the nearest railroad, you must move forward to that railroad (unless the card specifically states backward). You can collect a salary every time you pass Go when following the directions of a Chance or Community Chest card. If a Chance card directs you to advance to a property and allows you to buy it if unowned, you can decide not to make the purchase. In that case, the Bank immediately puts the property up for auction, and it is sold to the highest bidder.

The Community Chest card that assesses for street repairs applies only to your own houses and hotels. Likewise, the Chance card assessing property repairs is payable on the improvements that exist on your own properties at the time you draw the card. Even if you have to sell buildings to raise the cash to pay the levy, the amount is still based on what you owned at the beginning of the turn.

Variations: There are two approved ways to shorten the game. In **Time-Limit Monopoly**, the players agree beforehand when the game will end, usually after an hour. The Banker shuffles the title deed cards and deals two properties to each player, including himself. Players immediately pay the Bank the printed board price for the cards they are dealt. The game proceeds as before, but when the time is up, the Banker calls, "Game over." The player who is in the middle of a turn completes her moves, but otherwise, no further trading transpires. Each player adds up his or her assets, including cash, the printed price of properties, utilities and railroads (mortgaged properties are worth half the board price), houses at cost value and hotels at the cost of five houses. The richest player wins.

In the **Second Bankruptcy** variation, the game ends as soon as two

players have declared bankruptcy. When the Banker is assured that the second player cannot meet his obligations, he declares, "Game over." The second bankruptcy turns over to his creditor everything he has, then the remaining players add up their assets, and the richest player wins.

Staggered Starts compensates for the advantage the first player usually enjoys, getting first option on the properties around the board. Instead of everyone starting from Go, the first player starts at Go, the second at Just Visiting, the third at Free Parking and the fourth at Go to Jail (this person does not, of course, land behind bars).

In **Auction Monopoly**, no player automatically has the right to buy a property. When someone lands on a square, all players bid for the title deed. The person on the property starts with a bid at least equal to the mortgage value; bidding moves clockwise around the table, with players either passing or raising by at least $10. Passing on one round does not eliminate a player from the auction; she may bid again when it is her turn. After a round in which everyone passes, the property goes to the highest bidder. Players must be able to pay the amount they bid, either in dollars or cash plus mortgaged property. ✺

Save these until you need them.

Scrabble

- **NUMBER:** two, three or four players, playing alone; more can play as teams
- **EQUIPMENT:** a Scrabble board, 100 tiles, a tile holder for each player, paper and pencil for scoring and a dictionary
- **DESCRIPTION:** a simple spelling game or a competitive test of vocabulary skill
- **COMPLEXITY:** anyone who can spell can play, from about age 8 up; most fun between well-matched opponents
- **DURATION:** tournament games are limited to an hour; at home, they usually last the evening

ONE OF THE time-honored ploys of Scrabble is to try to pass off made-up words as the real thing. When a player begins her turn with a slow, drawn-out question—something like, "Suppose one exporting company ships more boxes of books than a competitor, you could say that company outships the other, right?"—you know there is a concocted word sitting on her tray. She may be persuasive, but in this game, the ultimate arbiter is the dictionary.

Scrabble turned the dictionary into a best-seller; at the height of the Scrabble fad in the mid-1950s, bookstores couldn't keep them in stock. According to the rules, if a word is in the dictionary, it is fair play. The question is, Which dictionary? Zax, an obsolete tool for trimming roofing slates (but still an extremely useful word), is not in Funk & Wagnalls, but it does appear in Random House. Alfred M. Butts, who invented the game, used Webster's when he played; at our house, the Shorter Oxford English Dictionary settles disputes; Funk & Wagnalls Standard College Dictionary was originally used for Scrabble tournaments; and the bible among serious Scrabblers today is the Merriam-Webster's Official Scrabble Players Dictionary.

Although it is tempting to browse, the dictionary is on the table solely to arbitrate official challenges. There is no harm in discussing potential words, but once a word is laid on the board, it can be challenged as long as the next player has not yet laid a tile. (If the next player has already taken her turn, the questionable word can still be challenged later in the game if it is modified.) If the challenged word isn't in the dictionary, the player retracts it and loses her turn. In tournaments, a challenger who is proved wrong loses his next turn, and if more than two are playing, all the players who join in a wrongful challenge lose their turns. House rules don't usually penalize a doubting Thomas, although competitive linguists may agree to dock a challenger's score by the number of points the disputed word is worth.

There are only a handful of forbidden words in Scrabble. Players may not make proper names or any words that normally start with a capital letter, such as the names of cities, months or days of the week. Abbreviations and words spelled with apostrophes or hyphens are not permitted, but archaic, colloquial and slang words are, as long as they are in the dictionary. Even letters of the alphabet qualify, including odd spellings like aitch (H) and doubleyou (W). Foreign words are not acceptable, however, unless, like pâté or chic, they have been adopted by the English language.

Although it is fun to play multilingual Scrabble, it is difficult to play with a standard English set. Each language has its own peculiarities in the number of each letter represented in the tiles. The French version of Scrabble, for instance, has 15 Es, and the Dutch game has 10 Ns and two Js.

You will soon be frustrated by the lack of Qs if you play French Scrabble with an English game.

In tournaments, players are allowed up to three minutes per turn. This doesn't seem like much when you are trying to figure out a word, but it is an eternity when you are waiting to lay down your bingo. To avoid disputes, decide how long each turn should be before the game begins. Use an egg timer to keep everybody honest.

Some final advice: Before buying a Scrabble game at a yard sale, count the tiles. There should be 100, but if the game was owned by a family with a dog, there may be some missing. The tiles for early Scrabble games were made in Germany by a company that produced perfectly uniform, beautifully glazed wooden squares. The chemical in the finish, however, was as irresistible to dogs as catnip is to cats. The manufacturer was deluged by letters from Scrabble players seeking replacements for the tiles their dogs had consumed. So be forewarned: If you have an old Scrabble game, do not leave it out on the dining room table overnight. We did, and the next morning, the tiles had gone the way of good kibble.

The Board: The board is a grid, 15 squares on each side, 225 squares in all. At the center is a pink square marked with a star. This is where the game begins. Fanning out from the star are 61 "premium" squares: 24 light blue Double Letter Score squares; 12 dark blue Triple Letter Score squares; 16 pink Double Word Score squares; and 8 red Triple Word Score squares around the outer rim of the board.

The Playing Pieces: A wooden rack for each player and a stockpile of 100 tiles.

There are 42 vowels and 56 consonants as well as two blanks, which are wild and can be used as any letter you want. Once a blank is played as a certain letter, it remains that letter throughout the game. Every tile is imprinted with a letter and a subscript number indicating the number of

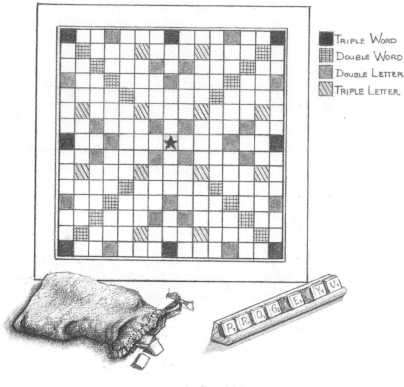

Scrabble

points it scores. (Blanks score no points.)

9-A_1	1-J_8	4-S_1
2-B_3	1-K_5	6-T_1
2-C_3	4-L_1	4-U_1
4-D_2	2-M_3	2-V_4
12-E_1	6-N_1	2-W_4
2-F_4	8-O_1	1-X_8
3-G_2	2-P_3	2-Y_4
2-H_4	1-Q_{10}	1-Z_{10}
9-I_1	6-R_1	

The Object of the Game:
To form interlocking words, as in a crossword puzzle; to place words on the board so that they score the highest possible points.

The Play: Place the board between the players and within reach, and spread out the tiles facedown. For tournaments, the tiles are kept in a deep cloth bag; at home, we use the gold-embroidered indigo bag with drawstrings that Crown Royal whiskey comes in. Whatever the system, the letter must be hidden until the tile is drawn.

Players each turn up one tile. The person who draws the letter closest to A begins. (Blanks supersede A.) The drawn tiles are returned to the tile *pool* and reshuffled. The first player then draws seven tiles and sets them on his rack. Moving clockwise, the rest of the players do the same.

The first player forms a word of two or more letters and places it on the board, horizontally or vertically, so that one letter covers the center star. (Diagonal words are not allowed.) The numbers on the tiles are added up, then doubled (the pink star has the same effect as a Double Word Score). The first player notes his score, then draws from the pool the same number of tiles that he laid on the board. (Players always have seven tiles in their racks.)

The person to the left of the first player then takes a turn, laying one or more letters on the board to lengthen the existing word, to form a new word using one letter of the existing word, or both. For instance, the first player sets down STOCK. The second player has the letters O, Q, R, S, I, N, G. She can add ING to the existing word to make STOCKING. Or the S, I, N, G can be played vertically, incorporating the T to create a new word, STING. Or S, I, N, G can be played

vertically at the end of the existing word to create two new words: STOCKS horizontally and SING vertically. To score, the player adds up the points of the letters in any new words created, including letters that were already on the board. For instance, STOCKING would count 15; STING would count 6; SING, although a smaller word, would count 17 (5 for SING and 12 for STOCKS, a new word). The S counts twice, once as part of the word STOCKS and again in SING.

In forming new words, all the letters that touch must make sense when read horizontally and vertically.

Words can be lengthened by adding prefixes or suffixes but not by adding syllables in the center. For instance, STOCK can be lengthened by adding GUN to the beginning or by adding PILE to the end.

Instead of taking a turn, a player may return some or all of her tiles to the pool, shuffle them in, then draw enough to restore her rack to seven. In making an exchange, a player forfeits the right to lay down a word in that turn. A player can also pass without exchanging any tiles, a useful ploy when she has a good word but no place on the board to play it. But you cannot wait forever to lay down that special word; three passes in a row forfeit the game. (A player can pass only if there are still tiles in the bag.)

Play continues clockwise around the table until all the tiles are drawn. Players then make words in turn without drawing replacements. If a player cannot make a word with the tiles he has, he passes, but he is not out of the game. When it is his turn again, he plays if he can. The first player to use up all her tiles ends the game. More often, the game ends when everyone has a tile or two left, but no one can make any more words.

The Score: One player is usually designated scorekeeper. Players add up their tiles after each turn and announce the total to the scorekeeper, who keeps a running tally for each player.

The score for each turn is the total

face value of all the letters in all the words created or modified in that play plus the bonus points earned for using premium squares. A letter on a Double Letter Score counts twice its face value; on a Triple Letter Score, three times its face value. If a word covers a Double Word or Triple Word Score, the value of the letters is added up, then multiplied by two or three, respectively. If the word includes both a letter score and a word score, count the letter score first, then the word score. For instance, if you spelled QUIET vertically, starting on a Double Letter Score and ending on a Double Word Score, you would add up the value of the letters first, scoring 20 points instead of 10 for the Q on the Double Letter Score. The total word count is 24 (10 x 2+1+1+1+1), which would then be multiplied by two, since the T is on a Double Word Score, making a total score of 48. Blanks themselves score nothing, but if a blank lands on a Double Word or Triple Word Score, the total value of the word is still multiplied. (Remember: As a starting bonus, the word score of the first player is automatically doubled.)

A premium square counts only for the player who first lays a tile on it. If another player later makes a word using a letter that is on a premium square, it simply counts as the face value of the tile. However, if a player puts a letter on a premium square that figures in two words, the premium square counts twice. For instance, if the S that starts the word SING and ends the word STOCKS was put on a Double Word Score, the score of both words would be doubled.

A seven-letter word that uses all the player's tiles in one turn is called a *bingo* and scores a bonus of 50 points —an improvement added by James Brunot when he began to market the first Scrabble game.

At the end of the game, the total of each player's unplayed tiles is deducted from his score. The person with the highest final score wins. In two-person Scrabble, the combined scores for beginners will likely be in the 300 to 400 range. If you and your opponent hit

600, you are average; 700 to 800 puts you in the professional league; if your games regularly total over 800, you and your Scrabble buddy should sign up for the next tournament.

The world record for a single Scrabble game is 725 points, scored by an Australian during competition. The highest total at an official American game is 719, scored in 1982 by Chris Reslock, an Ohio taxi driver. Even expert players usually tally much lower scores. The 10 best players at the 1992 National Scrabble Open averaged 405 points per game. For an average player, breaking 300 is cause for a hearty pat on the back.

Strategy: To decide how many of each letter to include in the game, Scrabble's creator, Alfred M. Butts, laboriously counted the proportion of letters in daily newspapers. His analysis, however rudimentary, has proved sound: the letter distribution has not been altered since the game's invention. It is the source of much of the game's frustration and also the secret of success. Experts earn their scores not with large vocabularies but by being adept at anagrams, rearranging scrambled letters to form many different words.

Professional Scrabblers also memorize lists of specific, vital words. There are 94 acceptable two-letter words, among them the usual AH, OX, PI, EF and YE and the not-so-usual AA, KA, MU and UT. There are no two-letter words containing C, Q, V or Z; on the other hand, X combines with all five vowels to make five two-letter words: AX, EX, OX, XI, XU. Of the vowels, A combines with 19 letters to make two-letter words, more than any other vowel.

The written form of most letters of the alphabet is a three-letter word (GEE, KAY, VEE, WYE), though most house rules also accept two-letter alphabet plurals such as PS and QS. It is a good idea to memorize some unusual three-letter words too, since your opponent may leave a combination like AX exposed below a Triple Letter Score, unaware that ZAX is a word. So is GOA, KAB, MAE,

TEG, DOR, HOY and YOW. Knowing unusual words that include the high-scoring letters Q, J and Z can win you the game. For instance, ZYGOSIS, CACHEXY, PYREXIC and SJAMBOK. And while the Shorter Oxford English Dictionary does not list a single word that uses Q without its usual partner U, nine are admissible in tournament play: FAQIR, QAID, QANAT, QAT, QINDAR, QINFARKA, QINTAR, QOPH, TRANQ. Finally, keep prefixes (INTER-, RE-, MIS-, UN-) and suffixes (-MENT, -LY, -ABLE, -NESS, -ER) in mind. If you don't draw the high-scoring tiles yourself, "topping" and "tailing" existing words will allow you to benefit from your opponent's good fortune.

Experts normally earn about a quarter of their points from bingos. Even average players often get one bingo per game. You can increase your bingo options by remembering that the six most common letters in the Scrabble game spell SATIRE. There are 69 words that can be formed by adding an extra letter to satire, among them TIRADES, GAITERS, AIRIEST, TRAIPSE and RATITES. You can make 45 seven-letter words from the base of RETINA (including PERTAIN, NITRATE and TAURINE) and 44 bingos from the basic nonword SANTER (SALTERN, TREPANS and WANTERS). By building on an existing word, you can sometimes stretch a seven-letter word between two Triple Word Scores for the maximum scoring opportunity.

The obvious strategy is to get the maximum number of points for each word you lay on the board. Do not play your letters hastily. Calculate the score for each possible play; sometimes a strategically placed two-letter word will earn more points than a five-letter one. And it is not always the unusual words that are the big winners. The highest word score in sanctioned North American play is 302 points, scored by Ron Mason of Toronto, Ontario, for the well-placed word REEQUIPS. Jack Eichenbaum of Flushing, New York, once earned 293 points for the word ANTIQUES. As

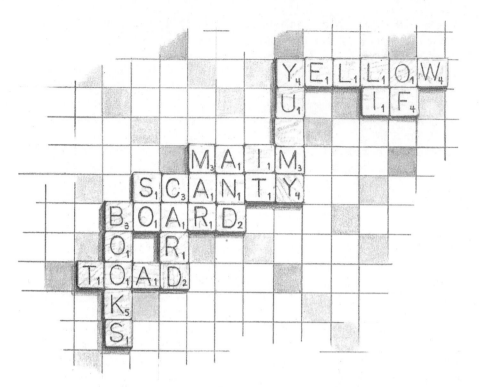

Competitive Scrabble

veterans know, blanks are priceless, and the high-scoring consonants may not be worth the reduced number of words they appear in. If you save blanks and low-scoring consonants (R, S, T, N) and get rid of duplicate vowels, you will likely have a bingo within a few turns.

As a rule, Scrabble players fall into two camps. There are those who play cutthroat Scrabble, giving their opponents few openings for play, even to the point of using premium squares for low-scoring words simply to foil the other person's chances for a high score. And there are those who play what can most appropriately be called cooperative Scrabble, keeping the board open and playing for personal-best scores and the satisfaction of being able to use every single tile. Both the game's inventor, Alfred M. Butts, and the man who made Scrabble a success, James Brunot, belong in this camp. Players should discuss their Scrabble strategy before the first tile is drawn. If one player is playing competitively and the other cooperatively, the game will be a disappointment and a frustration for both.

In cooperative Scrabble, players frequently help each other find words on the rack or a place to lay down a

bingo. Brunot admits that he and his wife often exposed Triple Word Scores for each other. Competitive Scrabble involves a different approach: You must not only be aware of your own score but also assess what opportunities each new word offers your opponent.

The player who starts has an advantage in that his first word is automatically doubled, but how that first word is placed can quickly pass the advantage to the opponent. In opening, avoid positioning your first word directly over the central star; instead, offset it to make use of a Double Letter Score. For instance, the word GROAN is worth 6 points (2+1+1+1+1). If centered on the star, it is simply doubled for 12 points, but if it is offset to the left, the G lands on the Double Letter Score, for a total of 16 points (2 x 2+1+1+1+1 = 8, doubled). At all costs, avoid offsetting a word that can be lengthened with a prefix or a suffix until the opening word reaches the Triple Word Score. For instance, if you start GROAN on the star, it scores 14 (2+1+1+1+1 x 2 = 7, doubled), but the next player can add ERS and score 27 (2+1+1+1+1+1+1+1 = 9, tripled) or add ING and score 30 (2+1+1+1+1+1+1+2 = 10, tripled). It is better to start with a short word and keep the Triple Word Scores out of your opponent's reach.

An opening word with a lot of vowels is easiest to build on; conversely, lots of consonants may make life difficult for your opponent. If your first draw gives you a rack of vowels and not much else, consider waiving the right to make a word and, instead, exchanging some of your letters. This is always an option but is particularly useful at the beginning if the best you can do is a score under 10.

There are a few general rules for competitive Scrabble. Never open up a Triple Word Score for your opponent. Try to keep your high-scoring letters away from Double Word Scores; make sure only you take advantage of the few valuable letters in the bag. Use the past tenses of verbs where possible, and make nouns that cannot be pluralized with a simple S. Avoid using words that take prefixes. To thwart bingos, make short words that block your opponent's access to seven empty spaces in a row. Always try to make double words, adding a letter such as S or Y to the end of a word, scoring both horizontally and vertically. But don't leave openings for your opponent to do the same.

In a cooperative game, the tiles are usually splayed expansively across the board, with lots of space between; players extend long words in exposed locations to give themselves and their opponent new letters to build on. Conversely, in competitive Scrabble, the board is as tight-fisted as Scrooge. Players tend to make short words, laid parallel to existing words so that three or four words are formed in a single turn. For example, MAIM can be spelled across the top of the last four letters of SCANTY, producing the vertical words MA, AN, IT and MY. If the final M lands on a Double Word Score, MAIM scores 38. Playing a tight game will leave almost half the board bare, but it requires fluency in arcane two- and three-letter words and an ability to see the potential for stretching words like EASY into QUEASY or AIL into FRAILTY.

Learning to balance the rack will benefit both competitive and cooperative Scrabble players. A balanced rack has a roughly equal number of vowels and consonants. Human nature being what it is, players often accumulate the high-value consonants, saving them for some unimaginable whammy of a word, then find themselves without the simple vowels to finish the game. Even if you have to play relatively low-scoring words, try to keep the distribution of vowels and consonants even. If you draw three vowels at once, exchange them. (Some house rules allow players who draw three or more of the same letter to throw any duplicates back in the pool and draw again.) Although two Ls or two Ts are usable, duplicates are generally to be avoided. If you draw a third, you will be hard-pressed to make a word. So if you have a duplicate, play it. Don't be fooled into thinking that all seven-letter words hold pairs. The exception to

this rule, of course, is S and the blank. You can never have too many of either. Because there are more vowels than any other letters, it is worth your while to memorize a few words that are heavy with them; for instance, ADIEU, IOTA, HOODOO and QUEUE.

Remember which tiles have already been played. There is no sense waiting for a Q to mate with your U when the only one in the game is on the board and out of reach. The letter distribution is printed at the side of every board; consult it regularly. In your rack, don't isolate your high-value letters. Keep the letters mixed and evenly spaced. When trying to make words, shift the letters around; new combinations may leap out at you.

are almost impossible. Short words are the order of the day, but judiciously placing an A next to an X can earn a lot of points, perhaps the winning points. Since there are few, if any, draws to look forward to, you have to play what you have, rather than hoping for better combinations. If you are behind, it may not pay to go out. Instead, try to keep the game limping along so that you can get as much mileage as possible from your remaining letters. This is especially true if the high scorers are already on the board and if your chances of earning points from your opponent's rack are limited.

Variations: With the blessing of both Butts and Brunot, several Scrabble variations have evolved, though

Anagram Scrabble, before (left) and after

In competitive Scrabble, the end game is the most exciting. House rules often stipulate that the person who goes out first earns double the point total of the letters left in his opponent's rack. In this kind of game, you try to keep the point count in your rack low, while at the same time trying to score as many final points as you can. In any kind of end game, bingos

few players tire of the original game. In one variation, players must open with a word of five letters or more. If the player who earns the right to go first cannot open with a long word, he passes, and his opponent, or the player on his left, may open with a five-letter word. If no one can open with a five-letter word, the first player attempts a four-letter word, and so on. A long opening word lets the board "breathe" and provides more opportunities for play early in the game.

Ecology Scrabble is so named because the blank is constantly recycled throughout the game, which makes for a higher-scoring and much less frustrating game. When a blank is played on the board, it stays there until a player, on her turn, exchanges the designated letter for the blank, which she can then use as any letter she pleases. The exchange does not constitute a move—she can still make a word elsewhere on the board—and she does not have to use the blank in that turn. The only caveat is that a player may not exchange a letter for a blank during a turn in which she passes. Late in the game, the blank can be "frozen" by playing it as a letter for which all the tiles are already exposed. For instance, a player lays down a blank as the U in the word QUICK. All four Us are already on the board, so your opponent can never retrieve the blank—of course, neither can you.

Double-Bag Scrabble attempts to compensate for the plethora of vowels

Butts put in the game. Before play begins, separate the vowels and consonants into two piles or put them in different bags. At the beginning of the game, you can draw your seven tiles from both bags in whatever proportion you like (four consonants and three vowels is usual). During the game, you can restock your rack from either bag or both, but you have to draw *all* your replacement tiles before looking at any of them. It may not improve the scores, but it certainly reduces the frustration.

Solitaire or **Stopwatch Scrabble** pits a lone player against the clock, instead of a human opponent. A player has 15 minutes to make all his moves, plus 3 minutes' grace for keeping score. Since an average two-person game consists of 15 to 18 moves per player, this is about a minute a move. Use a stopwatch, set up two racks, and play both, timing the plays of each. You can use any amount of time for each turn, but you are penalized 10 points for every minute you go over the total game limit. You can stretch the time limit as much as you like. For average players,

a 30-minute game is reasonable.

In **Anagram Scrabble**, players can rearrange the letters of a word already on the board into a new word, provided that they add one letter to the board and that all the connecting words still make sense. The player gets full credit for the new word but not for any premium squares it covers and not for any connected words that remain the same. Interconnecting words that are changed to new words by the rearrangement also score. For instance, GAMES is spelled horizontally on the board with RAM rising vertically from the M and GENUS descending from the G. Another player may add an I and rearrange the letters of GAMES to form IMAGES; in the process, RAM becomes RAG and GENUS becomes MENUS. The entire configuration still makes sense, and the player scores for three new words.

In **Bonus-Point Scrabble**, players agree on a category, such as colors, animals or foods, before play begins. Every time a player makes a word in that category, he scores a 25-point bonus. ∾

4

Sowing Seeds:
Mancala Games

Proposing to play **Mancala** is something like suggesting a game of cards. Like cards, Mancala can be played dozens of ways: the name refers to a genre of games, rather than one specific pastime. Although rarely seen on this continent except at Third World bazaars and exotic import stores, Mancala boards are as prevalent in Africa as Bicycle cards. Just as **Go Fish** and **Snap** are among the first real games a child here learns to play, African children grow up with Mancala and play it all their lives. If cards are the North American favorite and **Pachisi** is the national pastime of India, then Mancala is Africa's game.

The word comes from the Arabic *manqala*, which comes from the verb *naqala*, which means "to move." And indeed, movement is the crux of this game. Mancala boards are carved with a series of shallow cups called *holes*: players take turns moving or *sowing* small objects—referred to generically as *seeds*—from hole to hole, with the intent of winning the game by capturing the most seeds. (Most boards have a reservoir or *storehouse hole* at each end where players keep their captured seeds.) This is a resolutely two-person pastime, although like dominoes and **Checkers**, Mancala games tend to draw a crowd of interested onlookers.

The very earliest boards come from northeast Africa. Boards have been found carved into the stone of the pyramid of Cheops and in the temples at

Luxor and Karnak, establishing Mancala as one of the oldest games in the world. Mancala is still played in Egypt and over the millennia it has spread throughout Africa and into Asia, the Caribbean and South America.

The people of each region tend to put their own distinctive stamp on the game—lengthening and widening the board, varying the distribution of seeds at the start of play, adjusting the rules of capture—so much so that anthropologists have used Mancala to help determine the ancestral origins of slaves brought to the New World. African-Caribbeans, for instance, can sometimes trace their tribal origins by the form of Mancala they play. According to the noted games historian R.C. Bell, four variants of **Wari** are played by blacks of Guiana and the Caribbean which perfectly match the distinct games played in Dahomey, Togoland and Nigeria.

Among African-Americans, however, the seed game provides no such clues to their homeland: slaveowners in the United States apparently were rigorous in prohibiting traditional pastimes, concerned that their slaves would be reminded of home, so Mancala gained no foothold here.

When Europeans began to travel widely in the 19th century, they discovered Mancala and brought it north to Europe where, unfortunately, it has remained little more than a curiosity. Mancala, the Egyptian game, and Wari, the oldest and most basic form of the game, may sound vaguely familiar, but there are hundreds, perhaps thousands, of variations. The names alone are compelling— **Songo, Qelat, Nambayi, Bao**. Many of them derive from the playing pieces. **Okwe**, played by the Ibo tribe of Nigeria, is a Mancala game named for the tree that bears the fruit that provides the seeds for play; Songo is the Cameroonian word for pebbles; **Andot**, played in the Sudan, takes its name from dried manure pellets, which, in a desert climate, serve admirably as "seeds."

Mancala, like **Tit-Tat-Toe** and **Nine Men's Morris**, is a testament to human ingenuity and propensity for play. The "board" can be as simple as holes scooped in the sand between two players; the pieces can be pebbles, sticks or seeds. North American players will likely have to make their own, since the few commercial boards, such as Oh-War-Ree and Kalah, are not widely distributed. Yet even with common, unsophisticated materials, the variables of holes and seeds produce a game that can be simple enough for toddlers, yet as subtle, complex and intriguing as **Backgammon** or **Chess**.

Although Mancala can be played with buttons in an egg carton or pebbles in holes dug in sand, some African boards, particularly those of the Swahili and Baganda tribes, are beautifully finished. My own is hand-carved and hand-painted in intricate designs of deep red, yellow, blue and green. Like the more familiar checkerboard, Mancala boards vary from small, folding portable models to oversize boards chiseled in limestone, permanent fixtures in public places or at crossroads in the desert.

However, if many of the boards seem crudely worked, it is not because the carvers lacked skill. Rather, in some areas tradition dictates that the boards be roughly hewn from a single log and polished not by the carver but by the fingers of many players caressing the holes through many games.

Most Mancala boards are flat, although they may also be curved: many of the oldest surviving examples in museums and in old illustrations show a pronounced bananalike curve. This seems to indicate nothing more than personal preference, although superstition has it that if a man who always played on a curved board dies, other villagers are well advised to restrict themselves to flat boards for a time, to reduce the chance of his ghost joining the game.

Given Mancala's age, it is not surprising that many such superstitions have grown up around it. Traditionally, only elderly widowers were allowed to make Mancala boards. And, as with many Native North American and Mexican pastimes, the game was not only played for amusement but was also part of religious events. Mourners would play Mancala to amuse the spirit of the dead awaiting burial, though only during the daylight hours. According to beliefs still held in parts of the Caribbean and Africa, when night falls, ghosts join the players and claim the spirits of the living as prizes in the game. In fact, some refuse to play at night under any circumstances, lest they lose their souls.

Wari, the first game in this chapter, is the simplest and probably the oldest Mancala game. Most of the principles of play are evident in it; all the games that follow can be seen as variations and refinements on this basic theme. Wari is a *single-lap* game, as are Songo, **Bechi** and **The Cow Game**. Single-lap is the standard term, but single pickup would be more appropriate: in this type of Mancala game, each player scoops the seeds from one hole and, moving in one direction, distributes them—*sows* them—one per hole around the board, making a capture if there are a certain number of seeds in the last hole. Then the turn is over. In other words, in single-lap games, a turn consists of one pickup from a hole and one lap of the board, regardless of whether or not the seeds stretch all the way around. In fact, if there are many seeds in one hole, a lap may also consist of several go-rounds of the board.

The five games beginning with **Ayoayo** and ending with **The Game of Daughters** are *multiple-lap* games. A player scoops up the seeds from one hole, sows them one at a time in a given direction and, depending where the last seed falls, he may be allowed to pick up that holeful of seeds and continue around the board again. In multiple-lap games, a player may, in the course of one turn, pick up seeds from several holes and make several rounds of the board.

Some of the games on the following pages are played on boards as small as two rows of four holes each; others are played on boards as large as four rows of eight holes each. Each game offers a new twist: a different arrangement of seeds, a change of direction in sowing, a slightly different method of capture, new rules for claiming ownership of certain holes. Thirteen games with 19 variations are included, yet this is only a fraction of the Mancala games played in Africa.

For an exhaustive list, complete with rules for more than 100 games, refer to Larry Russ's *Mancala Games*. (See Sources, page 402.) A mathematics professor and Dean for Undergraduate Academics at Stevens Institute of Technology, Russ became interested in Mancala in the 1960s. "Because many of these games, whose origins extend back thousands of years, were gradually being lost in the face of increasing urbanization, racial violence and open warfare, I began writing my book to assure that a knowledge of this important cultural element does not vanish," he wrote to me recently. "I also wanted to make these games more widely known so that Americans of African descent would have the opportunity to play the games of their ancestors." Besides, he adds, "these games are among the most interesting, challenging and enjoyable games to be found anywhere in the world."

Indeed. One of the reasons for Mancala's enduring fascination is that these games do not come with lengthy codes or hard-and-fast rules. Over its long history every variation of seeds and holes has undoubtedly been tried. Thus, Mancala is perfect for families who like to create their own house rules. Nothing is sacrosanct: feel free to play games designed for four-hole boards on a five-, six- or seven-holer, or create new rules as you go along.

But first, play a few Wari games to become accustomed to the basic principles and terminology. Part of the charm of such ancient, regionally specific games lies in preserving their language, so although you may be handling ball bearings and dropping them into cardboard egg cartons, you will be "sowing seeds," just as the denizens of the desert did six thousand years ago.

Wari

- OTHER NAMES: Woro, Awèlé, Kboo, Kpo, Poo, Aware, Ayoayo, Ayo, Kale and Aghi
- NUMBER: two players
- EQUIPMENT: **a Mancala board with two rows of six holes and storehouse holes at each end; 48 playing pieces**
- DESCRIPTION: **a speedy game of capture, easy to learn even for children**
- COMPLEXITY: **a very basic, single-lap Mancala game**
- DURATION: **10 minutes, tops**

WARI offers a good introduction to Mancala games because it is relatively simple and yet teaches the concepts necessary to move on to more complex games and strategies. Although it is played on a board with two rows of six holes, many of the variations use almost identical rules with boards of different sizes: two rows of four, five or seven holes.

Many consider the two-row Mancala games like Wari among the very oldest in the family. This venerable game is still played among several African tribes and is widespread in Senegal, Gambia, Guinea, Sierra Leone, Liberia, Ghana, Togo, Nigeria, Cameroon and Gabon. In the Western Hemisphere, it has been noted in Suriname, Guyana, Grenada, Barbados, St. Lucia, Martinique and Dominica.

Those just learning the rules will likely play slowly, but between skilled players, even children, Wari proceeds with lightning speed, players scooping up the seeds and dropping them into the holes with swift clickety-clicks.

The Board: The Wari board has two rows of six holes each. There is a reservoir at each end that is not involved in play but acts as a storehouse for captured seeds. The board is placed between the two players. Each player controls the row closest to him and the storehouse on the right.

The Playing Pieces: The game requires 48 small pieces, such as nuts, dried beans or shells. Four seeds are deposited in each hole at the beginning of play.

The Object of the Game: To capture the most seeds by the time all the holes are empty.

The Play: Players decide who goes first by flipping a coin or by playing **Mora** (page 333). The first player scoops all four seeds from one of her own holes (it doesn't matter which) and "sows" the seeds one at a time into the next four holes, moving counterclockwise. No seeds are dropped into the storehouse hole.

The two players take turns scooping the seeds from one of their own holes and sowing the seeds one at a time in the holes immediately to the right. If the last seed is dropped into an opponent's hole that contains only one or two seeds (no more), the player captures those seeds. Counting the last seed sowed, the hole contains two or three seeds, so the move is called a "capture by twos and threes." The cap-

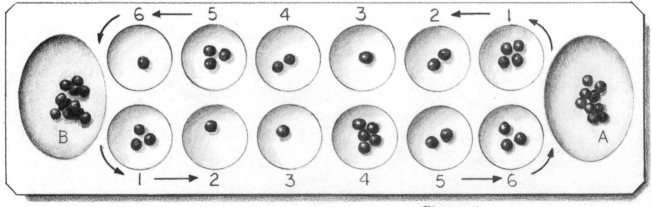

Wari

tured seeds are added to the player's storehouse. In the illustrated game on page 96, if player A takes the five seeds from her 4th hole and drops them one by one, the last seed will fall into player B's 3rd hole. Since player B's hole contains only one seed, player A can make a capture by twos: she removes the captured seed and her own seed to her storehouse.

Remember, a player can only make a capture on his opponent's side of the board, and only if he is sowing his last seed in a hole that already holds either one seed or two. If there are three or more seeds, no capture is made: the player simply adds his seed to the hole and his turn is over.

When a player makes a capture, he may also capture the seeds in the preceding holes provided the holes are on the opponent's side of the board and provided they contained only one or two seeds *before* the player added the new round. For instance, in the game illustrated, player A could also capture the seeds in B's 2nd hole since it contained two seeds before A sowed her round. B's two seeds, plus the one A just added, would be removed to A's storehouse. At the end of the turn, player A will have five more seeds in her store, her 4th hole will be empty and so will her opponent's 2nd and

3rd holes.

A player is not required to make a move that results in a capture, but if he does make such a move, he must take the captured seeds and put them in his storehouse.

The number of seeds in each hole will vary dramatically as the seeds are sowed again and again. Enough seeds may accumulate in one hole that they can go around the board more than once. In this case, the player skips over the original hole in the second go-round. As a general rule, the hole from which a player takes seeds at the beginning of his turn remains empty at the end of his turn.

At any time, a player may count the seeds in his own holes or in his opponent's. This is especially necessary if the distribution becomes very uneven and a hole is filled to capacity.

As the game draws to an end, many holes will be empty. A player may not leave his opponent's holes empty, however, if it is possible to move seeds into them.

According to some Wari manuals, a player may never capture all the seeds on his opponent's side in a single turn, leaving her opponent with nothing to play. However, other players allow this move, which effectively ends the game. According to Larry Russ, au-

thor of *Mancala Games*, this move is called, appropriately, "cutting off the head."

The game ends when a player cannot make a move because all the holes on his side of the board are empty. The opponent's seeds must be arranged in such a way that he cannot possibly pass any seeds to his opponent's side of the board, as is the case in the Wari game illustrated below. The seeds remaining on A's side of the board belong to A and are added to A's store.

It is also possible for the last seeds to continue to circulate with no captures possible by either player. In this case, the players may agree to end the game and each take half the remaining seeds, regardless of which side of the board the seeds are on. Alternatively, the players may leave the circulating seeds on the board and disregard them in the final tally. Or they may agree that each player add the seeds from his own side of the board to his store.

A game may also be declared finished when one player has 25 seeds in her storehouse, that is, one more than half the seeds in play. A tie game occurs when both players capture 24 seeds or when both players have an equal number of seeds in their storehouses and the remaining seeds are

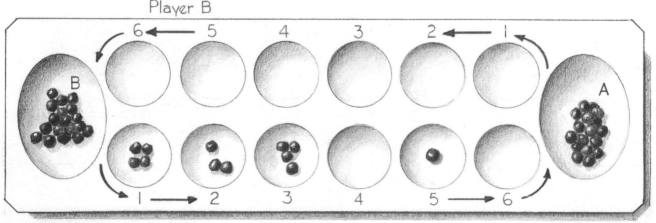

Wari

circulating with no possibility of capture by either player.

Each player adds up the number of seeds in his store: the player with the most seeds wins.

Strategy: A good Wari player pays attention to exactly how many seeds are in each hole on the board, how far they will stretch during sowing and which holes are vulnerable as a result. Consider that each seed represents an intervening hole. For instance, if a hole contains five seeds, the last one will be sowed in the 5th hole to the right. If that hole contains one or two seeds, they are vulnerable to capture.

Always work defensively to keep the seeds on your side of the board distributed so you have at least three in each hole. Analyze likely moves by your opponent and protect vulnerable holes before she can get to them. For instance, in the illustration on page 96, player B has four holes that are potentially vulnerable (i.e., contain one or two seeds): his 2nd, 3rd, 4th and 6th holes. However, only the 3rd hole is vulnerable in this turn because it is the only one player A can reach with her seeds. (Note that she can reach it from either her 4th or her 6th hole.) Player B can protect himself by scooping his 3rd hole, leaving it empty, and sowing the seed in the 4th hole so it has three pieces; a capture can no longer be made from either hole.

Instead of acting defensively, player B could go on the offensive and scoop his 5th hole containing three pieces, which he would sow in his 6th hole and player A's 1st and 2nd holes. Since A's 2nd hole only has one seed, B would make a capture, adding two seeds—the one from the 2nd hole and his own—to his store. Only experience will teach whether it is best to sacrifice a seed in order to capture one. In this case, the odds are even, although one of the moves might make more sense in terms of long-range strategy.

As a general rule, try to distribute seeds in such a way that you are in a position to threaten several of your opponent's holes at once. He can only move to protect one or two of them,

which may still leave you with a capture. By the same token, limit the number of holes you leave vulnerable at any one time. The two strategies for protecting a vulnerable hole are to empty it or, if there are already two seeds in it, to add a third.

Avoid situations in which you have seeds in several holes all bearing on one vulnerable hole. For instance, in the first illustration, both the 4th and 6th holes of player A bear on B's 3rd hole. Such an unfortunate distribution of seeds severely limits a player's options in a game where you want as many plays as possible to choose from.

In general, if you have a heavily loaded hole, wait until you have maximum capture potential before sowing from it. By adding another seed or two to the loaded hole, you may be able to play to your opponent's 6th hole at a time when several previous holes are also vulnerable. The best strategy for "cutting off the head" is to accumulate enough pieces in one hole that you can round the board once and make it to the far end (hole number 6) on the opponent's side. If the opponent is already reduced to a few seeds, a player may be able to capture them all in this one move.

Toward the end of the game, try to keep as many seeds as possible on your own side and distribute them lightly among several holes so you have maximum mobility. Move seeds onto your opponent's side only if it is essential to do so. The final moves should be designed to get your remaining seeds in positions similar to the illustration on page 97, where they cannot possibly be sowed onto your opponent's side of the board.

Variations: In a variation played by the Mende people of Sierra Leone, each player on the opening move may sow the seeds one at a time or he may choose to sow two seeds into the 1st hole, then one into each of the next two holes, or he may sow three seeds, then one. In all subsequent turns, the seeds are sowed one per hole, as in standard Wari. A variation from the island of St. Lucia allows players in their first turn to drop all four seeds

into the next hole.

In a variation from West Africa, a player must always leave an opponent with at least one seed on his side of the board. In other words, "cutting off the head" is not allowed. The player may choose to make a move that would remove all the opponent's seeds, but he may capture nothing. The penalty for capturing all the opponent's seeds is stiff: the offending player loses all of his remaining seeds. The rule is waived at the end of the game when there are three or fewer seeds circulating on the board. If it is a player's turn to move and there are no seeds on his side of the board but there are three or fewer on the opponent's side, the two players split the remaining seeds, with the odd one going to the player in possession of the seeds when the turn began.

In **Oware**, a version played in Ghana, captures are allowed from holes containing three seeds, as well as from holes with two seeds or one. Otherwise, the rules are the same as for Wari.

Another variation, also from the west coast of Africa, is **Érhérhé**, a cutthroat Wari that continues through several rounds. The rules of play are the same except that captures are made when a hole contains either one or three seeds, but not two.

After the first game, the player who captured the most seeds fills each hole on his side of the board with four seeds and puts the remainder in his store. The loser from the first game fills as many holes as possible with four seeds and puts the leftovers (three or less) in his store. Each of the loser's holes will either contain four seeds or be empty, in which case it is called a "burned hole." It seems only fair that the loser should go first in this second game.

At the end of the second round, the winner again fills all his holes and puts the excess in his store; the loser fills whatever holes he can and play begins. Rounds continue until one player does not have enough seeds to fill even one hole, whereupon he is declared the absolute loser of the game.

Songo (the Cameroonian word for

pebbles) is much like basic Wari, except that a Songo board has two rows of seven holes and play begins with five seeds in each hole. Sowing is clockwise. If the final seed falls into a hole that contains one or three seeds, they are all captured.

Vai Lung Thlan is not an African game, but is a single-lap Mancala played by the Lushei Kuki people in the eastern region of India, bordering Pakistan. The rules, however, are similar to Wari. The board has two rows of six holes each, with five seeds in each hole to begin the game. A player can pick up seeds from any hole on his side of the board and sow them, one per hole, in a clockwise direction. If the last seed is sowed in an occupied hole, the turn is over. However, if the last seed is sowed in an empty hole, the player captures that final seed and puts it in his storehouse. If any holes that precede the capture hole in sequence contain a single seed, it is also captured. The game continues until all seeds are captured and, since seeds are captured one at a time, the game is much slower than Wari. ❧

The Cow Game

- ◆ OTHER NAMES: **Um El Bagara and Mangala**
- ◆ NUMBER: **two players**
- ◆ EQUIPMENT: **a Mancala board with two rows of five holes and storehouse holes at each end; 50 playing pieces**
- ◆ DESCRIPTION: **a single-lap Mancala game with two-directional movement**
- ◆ COMPLEXITY: **a simple game, easy enough for children**
- ◆ DURATION: **15 minutes or so**

THE COW GAME is played in northern Sudan where the Nile cuts through the Nubian Desert. Not surprisingly, the game is typically played with holes hollowed out of the sand, rather than a board.

Although the rules of play and capture are similar to **Wari**, the sowing of seeds in The Cow Game is either clockwise or counterclockwise, depending on which hole the seeds are taken from. This changes the game considerably, though the tactics are essentially the same as for Wari.

The Board: This board has two rows of five holes each, with a storehouse hole at either end. The board is placed (or carved in the sand) between two players. Each player controls the row closest to him and the storehouse on the right.

The Playing Pieces: The game requires 50 seeds, five in each hole at the beginning of play.

The Object of the Game: To capture the most seeds.

The Play: The direction in which the seeds are sowed depends on the hole they are taken from. Sowing from the two holes on the left is clockwise; sowing from the two holes on the right is counterclockwise; sowing from the middle hole can be in either direction.

Players decide who goes first. The first player scoops all five seeds from one of his own holes and sows them, one per hole, in the appropriate direction. After the last seed is sowed, the turn ends. The players alternate sowing seeds from one of their holes.

If the last seed is dropped into an opponent's hole that contains one or three seeds, these seeds are captured (capture by twos and fours). At the same time, the player may capture the seeds from any holes preceding the capture hole that contain two or four seeds as a result of the sowing in this turn.

No move can be made from a hole containing a single seed. If a player cannot make a move, he passes and the opponent makes her move.

The Cow Game

The game ends when neither player can make a move. Players capture any seeds remaining on their side of the board and add them to their storehouse. They tally the total number of captured seeds: the player with the most seeds wins.

Variation: A children's variation, called **The Little Goat Game**, or **Um El Tuweisat**, is played on a small board with two rows of three holes, each containing three seeds at the start of the game. The rules are the same as above, except that captures are only by twos: the single seed that is in the hole and the seed that is sowed. ∽

Bechi

- ◆ NUMBER: two players
- ◆ EQUIPMENT: a Mancala board with two rows of four holes and storehouse holes at each end; 48 playing pieces
- ◆ DESCRIPTION: a single-lap Mancala game with two-directional movement and captures from any hole; successive rounds of play
- ◆ COMPLEXITY: increased options for capture require keen observation, memory and strategy
- ◆ DURATION: at least half an hour

THIS TWO-DIRECTIONAL variation on single-lap Mancala is played by the Kunama people in Eritrea, on the southwestern shore of the Red Sea. Refinements on the basic **Wari** game make Bechi a much more subtle and complex pastime. Players are no longer limited to making captures from their opponent's row: a player can capture seeds on either side of the board, but only from holes that have been previously used to begin a move, and only holes that, including the seed sowed in that turn, contain an even number of seeds. These rules give players more options, but the increased variables also make strategic demands. Like **Érhérhe**, the game continues through several rounds until one player has too few seeds to fill even one hole.

The Board: A Bechi board has two rows of four holes each, with a storehouse hole at either end. Each player controls the row closest to him and the storehouse on the right. A player begins his moves from his own side of the board, but can make a capture from either his own row or his opponent's.

The Playing Pieces: The game requires 48 seeds, six in each hole at the beginning of play.

The Object of the Game: To capture the most seeds.

The Play: Sowing is clockwise from the two holes on the left and counterclockwise from the two holes on the right.

Players decide who goes first. The first player scoops all the seeds *except one* from any hole on his side of the board and sows them, one per hole, in the appropriate direction. After the last seed is sowed, the turn ends. The players take turns scooping all but one seed from a hole and sowing the seeds clockwise or counterclockwise, depending on the hole they were taken from.

Captures can be made from either the opponent's row or the player's own row of holes. However, seeds can only be captured from a hole that has already been used to begin a move.

If the last seed is sowed in a hole containing an odd number of seeds (the sowed seed makes the number even), the player captures them all and puts them in his storehouse. If holes in sequence *following* the capture hole also contain an even number of seeds, these are captured in the same turn. (Note that this is different from the usual practice of making captures from holes that *precede* the capture hole in sequence.)

If a player cannot make a move, he passes and continues to do so until he can move.

The game ends when neither player can make a move. Each captures the seeds remaining on his own side of the board and tallies them with the captured seeds in his storehouse. The player with the most seeds wins.

Bechi does not end after one round. The winner of the first round puts six seeds in each of her holes and the remainder in her storehouse. The loser puts six seeds in as many holes as possible, choosing which holes he wants to fill. Any remaining seeds are added to his store. (Holes must be filled with exactly six seeds: five or fewer are put in the store.) Holes that are empty at the beginning of the round are out of play for the remainder of the round.

Players alternate taking the first turn. Rounds continue until one player cannot fill even one hole to begin a new round.

Strategy: Players familiar with Wari will have to adjust their thinking somewhat for Bechi. Since one seed is always left behind in the hole and since the direction of movement varies, calculating which holes are vulnerable is more complicated. In the illustration on page 101, player A cannot pick up from her 2nd hole because it contains only one seed. She would not pick up from her 1st hole because the two seeds (leaving one behind) would end in her opponent's 3rd hole, which would result in an uneven total of seeds and therefore no capture.

Player A can, however, pick up two seeds from her 3rd hole, sowing the last seed to her opponent's 1st hole, which contains a single seed. Adding the sowed seed makes an even number of seeds, so these are captured. Player A would make the same capture if she scooped her 4th hole, leaving one behind and moving one forward to her opponent's 1st hole and making the capture.

Player B, on the other hand, has very limited options. His 2nd hole is empty and his 1st hole only has one seed, so no move can be made from either. If he starts from his 3rd hole, he can pick up one seed and move it to his 4th hole, which would create an uneven number and therefore no capture. He may decide to do this, to build up the 4th hole with the hope of capturing it before his opponent does. Or he may decide to scoop the five seeds from his 4th hole, and sow them across his opponent's holes, ending at

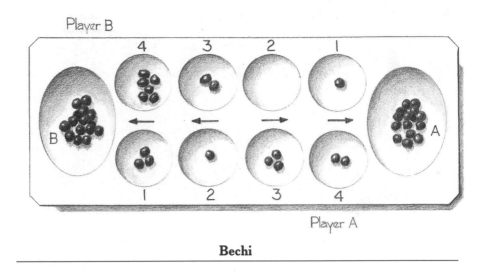

Bechi

his own 1st hole, making a capture. The disadvantage to this move is that it would leave him with three empty holes and only one potential move in his next turn.

Since captures can be made from any hole, players have twice as many options to consider, both defensively

and offensively. The risk in letting a hole build up, hoping to capture it yourself, is that your opponent may strike it rich if he gets there first. The safer course—though one with a lower payoff—is to keep seeds distributed fairly evenly among the holes. ∾

Qelat

- ◆ NUMBER: **two players**
- ◆ EQUIPMENT: **a Mancala board with two rows of six holes; 48 playing pieces**
- ◆ DESCRIPTION: **a single-lap Mancala game with two-directional movement and created storehouses**
- ◆ COMPLEXITY: **strategically sophisticated**
- ◆ DURATION: **15 to 20 minutes**

LIKE BECHI, Qelat is a two-directional game, but it is played on a 12-hole board and has no designated storehouse holes. As the game proceeds, each player creates up to six storehouse holes on the board. When a hole becomes a storehouse, it is no longer in play; the game narrows from 12 holes to four during play, with obvious strategic consequences.

The Board: A Qelat board has two rows of six holes. Each player controls the row closest to him. There are no storehouse holes. Instead, storehouses called *waldas* are created as the game proceeds. Each player

may designate his own extreme right and left holes, as well as the two outside holes on each end of his opponent's row, as waldas. As illustrated on the next page, player A has six potential waldas: her own 1st and 6th holes and her opponent's 1st, 2nd, 5th and 6th holes. Player B also has six potential waldas. If, in the course of the game, all of these become waldas, only the 3rd and 4th holes on either side will remain open for play.

The Playing Pieces: The game requires 48 seeds, four in each hole at the beginning of play.

The Object of the Game: To capture the most seeds.

The Play: Sowing is clockwise from the three holes on the left and counterclockwise from the three holes on the right.

Players decide who goes first. The first player scoops all the seeds in one of his own holes and sows them, one per hole, in the appropriate direction. After the last seed is sowed, the turn ends. Players take turns scooping the contents of a hole and sowing them.

If the last seed is sowed in a hole that contains three seeds (the sowed seed makes four) and if that hole is a potential walda for the player, that hole is converted to a walda.

Once a hole is declared a walda, it belongs to the player who designated it. It cannot be used to start a move—once sowed there, seeds are never picked up—and seeds are not sowed in it during play. A walda is effectively out of play as a hole; it is used only as a storehouse for other captured seeds.

Players continue to create waldas by making "fours" in one of the four

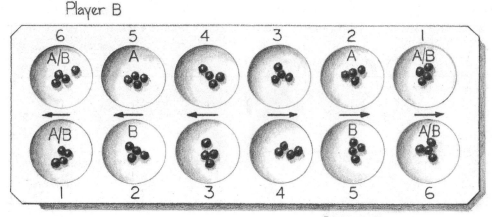

Player B

Qelat

outside holes. If captures by four are made in any of the middle holes (the 3rd or 4th holes in either row), the seeds are removed and put into one of the player's waldas. Such captures cannot occur until a player has created at least one walda.

If a player cannot move, he passes until he is able to move. When neither player can move—when all the seeds are in the waldas—the game is over. Players tally the total number of seeds in their waldas. The player with the most seeds wins.

Strategy: Determining which holes are vulnerable is a little more challenging in Qelat simply because not all the holes in the board are in play. To figure out where the final seed will end up, a player has to take into account that certain holes are closed. Players must be doubly diligent, therefore, to avoid making mistakes and leaving their seeds at risk.

The complication of the waldas is balanced somewhat by the fact that captures are only made by fours. There are fewer captures in this game, as a result, and much of the strategy hinges

on thinking several moves ahead and trying to get into a position where there are three seeds in a hole that is vulnerable from your side of the board.

It is a good idea to create waldas as soon as possible, especially in the outside holes, since these can be claimed by either player. There is no competition for the 2nd and 5th holes; close these holes on your opponent's side as soon as possible. Similarly, try to keep any number of seeds but three in the 2nd and 5th holes on your side, thus preventing your opponent from converting them to waldas.   ∾

Ayoayo

- ◆ OTHER NAMES: **Yovodji (in Benin), Tamtam apachi (in Ghana) and Warri (in Barbados)**
- ◆ NUMBER: **two players**
- ◆ EQUIPMENT: **a Mancala board with two rows of six holes and storehouse holes at each end; 48 playing pieces**
- ◆ DESCRIPTION: **a simple multiple-lap Mancala game**
- ◆ COMPLEXITY: **the most basic of the multiple-lap games**
- ◆ DURATION: **about 20 minutes**

THE PRECEDING GAMES were all single-lap Mancalas—that is, a player picked up the seeds from one hole and sowed them one per hole until the final seed was sowed, signaling the end of the turn. Ayoayo and the subsequent games in this chapter are multiple-lap, or

multiple-pickup, games. A player scoops the seeds from one hole, sows them one at a time and, if the last seed falls in a hole that already contains seeds, these are scooped up and the sowing continues, so that in the course of one turn a player might make several rounds of the board.

Ayoayo is played by the Yoruba in Nigeria. Ayo means "game" and is a generic Yoruban name for several different forms of Mancala.

The Board: The Ayoayo board has two rows of six holes with a storehouse hole at either end. Each player controls the row closest to him and the storehouse hole on the right.

The Playing Pieces: The game requires 48 seeds, four in each hole at the beginning of play.

The Object of the Game: To capture the most seeds.

The Play: Players decide who goes first. The first player scoops the seeds from a hole on his side of the board and sows them, one per hole, counterclockwise. If his last seed falls in a hole which is occupied (this is inevitable on the first turn), he scoops up the seeds in this hole (including the seed he just sowed) and sows them, one per hole, to the right. The player continues moving around the board, scooping up seeds if his last seed falls in an occupied hole and continuing until his last seed falls in an empty hole.

If the empty hole is on his opponent's side, the turn is over.

If the empty hole is on his own side and the opponent's hole immediately opposite is empty, the turn is over.

If the empty hole is on his own side and the opponent's hole opposite is occupied, the player captures the opponent's seeds and puts them in his storehouse, ending his turn.

Players take turns sowing seeds counterclockwise in multiple laps and capturing seeds from the opponent's hole opposite whenever the last seed falls in an empty hole on his own side.

For instance, in the game illustrated on page 104, player A picks up the six seeds from her 5th hole and sows them to the right. The last seed falls in her opponent's 5th hole, which already contains three seeds. She picks these up (four seeds in all, including the last seed sowed) and continues sowing, dropping her last seed in her own 3rd hole, which is empty. Her opponent's 4th hole opposite contains five seeds, which A captures, transferring them to her storehouse. This is a sore disappointment to player B, who was hoping, on his next turn, to pick up the seeds from his own 3rd hole, sowing them so the last seed would fall in his own 6th hole, which contained a single seed. He would then sow these two, ending in A's 2nd hole, where he would pick up four seeds (three plus the last seed sowed), which would run to A's 6th hole. The two seeds from that pickup would land B in his own empty 2nd hole, making it possible for him to capture the seven seeds in A's 5th.

If a player starts his turn from a hole that contains 12 seeds or more (enough to go all the way around the board), he skips over that hole when sowing past it.

If there are no seeds on the opponent's side of the board, a player must, if possible, move seeds into the opponent's holes. If the player cannot do so, the game is over and the player captures all the seeds on his own side, adding them to his store.

If there are no seeds at all on a player's side, he cannot move. The game is over. The opponent collects all remaining seeds on her side of the board and adds them to her storehouse.

Players count the number of seeds in their storehouse holes. The player who captures the most seeds wins.

Strategy: Multiple-pickup games constitute a second, more complex level of Mancala, akin to moving from **Whist** to basic **Bridge**. Many of the principles are similar, but because a player can make several pickups in a turn, he must carefully assess all the possible ways of getting from his original pickup hole to an empty hole on his own side of the board that is opposite a hole filled with seeds.

In general, players should keep their own holes empty and their opponents' holes filled, because captures can only be made by landing in an empty hole on your own side of the board. Players who can think several moves ahead are at an advantage, as they can fill holes gradually through several turns, building up resources to be captured later in the game. Of course, an opponent can foil the best laid plans by starting his turn from a carefully seeded hole, which is why players are advised to work on building up several holes at once.

Variations: The Masai of Kenya and Tanzania play a similar multiple-lap game on boards that range from 6 to 10 holes per side. **Endodoi** is almost identical to Ayoayo, with three exceptions. When a player drops his last seed in an empty hole and makes a capture from the opponent's hole, he also picks up the last seed from his own side of the board and adds it to his store. As a result, at the end of each capture two opposing holes are empty. If a player scoops a hole with

more than 12 seeds, he does *not* skip that hole when sowing around the board. And, if the opponent's holes are all empty, a player is not obliged to move seeds into them.

Tegre comes from southern Ethiopia and is very similar to Ayoayo, but with an interesting variation added to the rule of capture. When a player's last seed is sowed in his own empty hole, he captures any seeds in the opponent's hole opposite, then uses the single seed from his empty hole to continue the game, moving it into the next hole, picking up whatever seeds are there and continuing to sow. Each game consists of several rounds. The winner of one round fills his holes with four seeds each and puts the rest in his storehouse. The loser fills as many holes as he can with four seeds and puts the remaining few in his store. The winner plays first in the next round. Rounds are played until one player is reduced to 12 or fewer seeds. The other person wins the game.

Bao is played in East Africa on a board with two rows of eight holes each, and only two seeds in each hole at the beginning of the game. Although the equipment is different, the rules of play are almost exactly like Ayoayo. Play proceeds with multiple pickups and the sowing of seeds in a counterclockwise direction until a seed lands in an empty hole. If the hole is a player's own, he captures any seeds in the opponent's hole opposite. What is different here is that a player cannot start his turn with a pickup from a hole that contains only one seed, unless all the seeds on his side are singletons. (*Bao* means "board" and is a generic name for several Mancala games; a completely different game by the same name appears on page 107.)

People in western Kenya play another variation called **Ndoto**, also on a board with eight holes per side and two seeds in each hole. In this version, a player can start his turn by picking up from a hole with one seed only if the next hole is empty. Walter Dreidger, of the University of Nairobi, noted that in some cases Ndoto begins with both players making their first

Ayoayo

move simultaneously, scooping up the seeds from the holes on their far right; the first player to finish sowing makes the next move and players take turns thereafter. (Captures are not allowed on the first move.)

Dabuda is played by the Afar people of Djibouti, a tiny nation at the narrows between the Gulf of Aden and the Red Sea. This variation uses an even bigger board—two rows of 10 holes each—although it can also be played (and often is, particularly by children) on a board with six holes. The game begins with four seeds in each hole. Sowing is counterclockwise. The rules of capture are the standard rules of Ayoayo, except that, as in Endodoi, when a player captures the seeds from his opponent's hole, he also captures the single seed in his own hole opposite. Dabuda includes one unique rule precipitated, presumably, by the length of the board. A player must start his turn from a hole that contains sufficient seeds that the last one will be sowed either on his opponent's side of the board or in one of his own empty holes. ∽

Gamacha

- ◆ OTHER NAMES: Yada (in Ethiopia)
- ◆ NUMBER: two players
- ◆ EQUIPMENT: a Mancala board with two rows of 12 holes; 44 playing pieces
- ◆ DESCRIPTION: a multiple-lap game with an unusual opening setup and first move
- ◆ COMPLEXITY: moderately complex
- ◆ DURATION: a half hour per game

SEVERAL VARIABLES can be manipulated to add interest to the basic Mancala game: the length of the board, the configuration of the holes, the distribution of seeds at the beginning of a game, the rules for picking up and sowing the seeds and the method of capture. Each refinement, however inconsequential it might seem, can change the manner of play dramatically.

If there is one common feature of Mancala games, it is that almost all begin on a level playing field: an equal number of seeds occupies each hole on the board. Gamacha, however, varies this usually standard practice by filling only alternate holes. As a result, one player has six filled holes on his side of the board, while the other has only five holes filled. In most Mancala games, the goal is to capture the most seeds; in Gamacha, the goal is to empty the opponent's holes of seeds. This complicates the game considerably.

The Board: The Gamacha board has two rows of 12 holes each. There are no storehouse holes. Each player controls the row closest to him.

The Playing Pieces: The 44 seeds are distributed as illustrated, with no seeds in the 12th holes, four in the 11th, and the rest of the holes alternating zero and four until the 1st hole, which is empty on one side of the board. One player will have five occupied holes; the other will have six.

The Object of the Game: To remove all the seeds from the opponent's holes.

The Play: Several games are usually played in series. In the first game, players flip a coin, or play **Mora** (page 333) or another Mancala game to see who goes first. The loser takes the side of the board with only five occupied holes and goes first.

In the first move, the player picks up the seeds from the 7th hole and puts them in the opponent's 6th hole.

The other player then begins by taking the seeds from any hole on his side of the board, so long as when the seeds are sowed, the last seed ends up on the opponent's side or is sowed to an empty hole on the player's own side. Sowing proceeds counterclockwise.

The illustration on page 105 shows the distribution of seeds at the beginning of a game. Player B can sow seeds from his 6th hole (the last seed will fall in his own empty 10th hole) or he can sow from his 9th and 11th holes (the last seed will end up in A's 1st and 3rd holes respectively).

Players take turns picking up seeds from holes on their own side of the board and sowing them so that either

Player B

Player A

the last seed ends up on the opponent's side or in an empty hole on their own side.

If the last seed falls into an empty hole on the opponent's side, the turn is over.

If the last seed falls into an empty hole and the opponent's hole opposite is empty, the turn is over.

If the last seed falls into an empty hole on the player's own side, and the opponent's hole opposite is occupied, the player captures his opponent's seeds. (The last seed sowed remains in the hole on his own side of the board.)

The game is over when a player has no seeds on his side and therefore cannot move. The other player wins, regardless of how many seeds each has captured during play.

The winner of one game takes the side with only five filled holes and begins the next game.

Variations: Several games use elongated boards with a variable arrangement of seeds. **Sadeqa**, from southern Ethiopia, starts with four seeds in the 10th holes and alternates four and zero all the way to the 1st hole, except that the 4th hole on one side contains only one seed. The player *without* the single seed makes the first move. The game is played exactly as above except that the winner takes the side with the single seed and the other player makes the first move.

A game that goes by the same name is played in western Ethiopia with a slightly different seed distribution: the four and zero alternation carries through the entire board, even the 4th

hole. The player who makes the first move removes either one, two or three seeds from one of his holes and places them all in the hole immediately to the left, capturing any seeds in the opponent's hole opposite. For instance, in the game illustrated, if player A began by moving one seed from her 6th hole to her 5th, she would capture all four seeds from her opponent's 6th hole. Except for this unusual beginning, the rules for Gamacha apply.

Tapata or **Tagega**, a variation from southern Ethiopia, also varies the opening configuration of seeds. Played on a board with two rows of 12 holes each, three seeds are put in holes 11, and 12; 10 is empty; three seeds each are put in 9 and 8; and so on, two holes seeded and one empty, down

to the 1st hole, which is empty. Movement during play is counterclockwise. On her first turn, a player may only take seeds from the right half of her side of the board (holes 7 through 12). The player may choose any one of these holes, but if the last seed is sowed in a hole on her own side of the board, she skips over the rest of her own holes and drops the seed into the 1st hole on the opponent's side. For instance, in the game illustrated, if A picked up the seeds from her 8th hole, the last seed would normally fall in her 11th hole, so she skips over her own 11th and 12th holes and drops the seed into B's 1st hole. After this first move, play proceeds as for Gamacha.

Sadeqa

Player B

Player A

Tapata

Player B

Player A

Giuthi

- ◆ NUMBER: **two players**
- ◆ EQUIPMENT: **can be played on Mancala boards of various sizes: 2x5 through 2x10; most commonly 2x6 and 2x8; with storehouse holes at each end; number of seeds varies, though six per hole is usual**
- ◆ DESCRIPTION: **a multiple-lap game with sowing in alternate directions**
- ◆ COMPLEXITY: **more complex rules of capture; reverse directions adds challenge to planning moves ahead**
- ◆ DURATION: **15 minutes or so per round; an hour or more per game**

IN THE 1930s, the renowned anthropologist L.S.B. Leakey found a mandible of one of the earliest Homo sapiens on the shores of Lake Victoria, also noted games played by contemporary East Africans. In his 1937 book, *White African,* he describes the game Giuthi, played by the Kikuyu. The same game is also played by the neighboring Embu tribe. In fact, games by the same rules are played throughout the region on boards of various sizes, with two rows of holes varying in number from five to 10. The number of seeds per hole also varies, from four to nine. Such widespread variation usually indicates an old game and also attests to its broad entertainment value.

The significant variation that leads to Giuthi's inclusion here is the direction of movement. Earlier games have included clockwise and counterclockwise sowing, sometimes within a single game, with movement clockwise from the holes on the right and counterclockwise from the holes on the left. Giuthi takes the notion one step further and includes movement both left and right during a single turn. On his first pickup, a player decides whether to move right or left, and he switches direction at every pickup thereafter during that turn. Not only does the direction reverse repeatedly during a round, but the length of the board changes in the course of a game. After each round, the board is short-ened or lengthened, depending on how many seeds the loser captured during the previous round. At some points, there are six holes per side in play, and at others only two.

The Board: A two-row board with five to 10 holes per row and a storehouse hole at either end. Boards with six or eight holes per row are most common. Each player controls the row closest to him and the storehouse on the right.

The Playing Pieces: The game can begin with four to nine seeds per hole, although six seeds per hole is usual.

The Object of the Game: In each round, to capture the most seeds; eventually, to reduce the opponent to four or fewer seeds.

The Play: Players decide who goes first. The first player scoops the seeds from any of his own holes that contains two or more and sows the seeds in either direction, as desired. If the last seed is sowed in an occupied hole, he picks up the contents (including the seed just sowed) and distributes them, one per hole, in the *opposite* direction. If the last seed from this lap falls in an occupied hole, he picks up the seeds and sows, switching direction once again. Each time seeds are scooped from a hole, the direction re-verses, until the last seed falls into an empty hole.

If the empty hole is on the opponent's side of the board, the turn is over.

If the last seed falls into an empty hole on the player's side of the board and the hole opposite is empty, the turn is over.

If the opponent's hole opposite contains seeds and, during this turn, the player has dropped a seed into that hole, then the player captures all the seeds in the opponent's hole as well as the last one sowed in his own hole. Captured seeds are collected in the storehouse hole on the player's right.

If, however, the last seed falls into an empty hole on the player's side and the player has not added a seed to the opponent's hole opposite during the turn, no capture is made. In explaining this rule, the Kikuyu cite the proverb, "You can't steal the other man's cattle without crossing into his territory."

For example, in the game illustrated opposite, player B might pick up the seeds in his 5th hole and sow them counterclockwise, ending in player A's 3rd hole. He picks up those seeds (four in all, including the one he sowed) and reverses direction, sowing clockwise and ending in his own 5th hole, which is now empty. During the turn, he sowed A's 2nd hole (once each way, so that now it contains seven seeds). He therefore makes the capture, adding seven seeds to his storehouse.

In the same illustration, if A picks up the seeds from her 6th hole and moves counterclockwise, the last seed will end in B's 2nd hole. A will pick up these seeds, switch direction and sow clockwise ending in her own 4th hole, which is empty. However, she cannot capture the seeds in B's 3rd hole opposite because she has not sowed seeds to that hole during her turn.

After a capture, if the next hole in sequence on the player's side of the board is empty, he may also capture any seeds in the opponent's hole opposite. This is the case for all empty holes in a row on the player's side. The only thing that stops the multiple captures is an occupied hole on the player's side or an empty hole on the opponent's side. In the game illustrated and described above, B's last seed fell in his own 5th hole and he made a capture. His next hole, the 6th, is also empty, so he could capture seeds from A's 1st hole. Unfortunately, that hole is empty, so B's turn ends.

A turn cannot begin from a hole containing only one seed. If a player cannot make a move, the turn passes to his opponent until the player can make a move.

Players alternate turns until neither one can make a move. Each player then adds whatever seeds remain on his side of the board to his storehouse. The player with the most seeds wins.

To start the next round, the loser arranges his seeds as he wishes in the holes on his side of the board. He can put any number in any hole so long as there is at least one per hole. The opponent (the winner of the previous round) then distributes her seeds in exactly the same way and puts the remainder in his storehouse. The opponent's seeds are a mirror image of the player's, that is, holes 1 and 6 contain the same number of seeds.

If the loser of the previous round

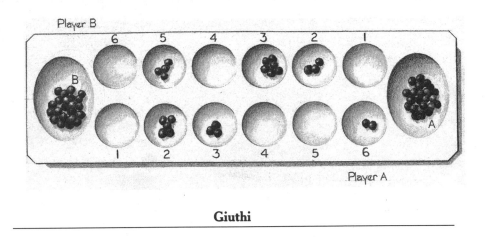

Giuthi

has less than half his original number of seeds, he may "shorten" the board for the next round: players use only four holes per side instead of six. If he has less than a quarter of his original seeds, he may shorten the board to three holes per side. If he has less than an eighth, he may shorten the board to two holes per side. If the loser regains seeds in succeeding rounds, the board must be restored to the appropriate size, based on the number of seeds in his possession at the beginning of the new round.

The winner of one round starts the next, and play continues according to

the same rules. Several rounds will likely be played before one of the players is reduced to four or fewer seeds.

Variation: Some play that the loser of one round need not use all his seeds in setting up the following round: he may use as many as he wishes and leave the rest in his storehouse. Another rule, which evens the odds and lengthens the game, states that if the loser has less than half the original number of seeds, the opponent has to put twice as many seeds in each of her holes as the loser put in his. 〜

Bao

- ◆ NUMBER: **two players**
- ◆ EQUIPMENT: **a Mancala board with two rows of seven holes and storehouse holes at each end; 56 playing pieces**
- ◆ DESCRIPTION: **a multiple-lap game in which players claim holes, thus protecting seeds from capture**
- ◆ COMPLEXITY: **moderately complex; strategy hinges on which holes to close and when**
- ◆ DURATION: **a game consists of several rounds and can last more than an hour**

BAO is a generic name applied to many Mancala games played in the region of east central Africa around Tanzania. The rules below were culled from an early-20th-century missionary manuscript in the

archives of the National Museum of Tanzania at Dar es Salaam. It was played by the Bondei people who lived near the Tanzanian coast.

An interesting feature of this form of Bao is the opening move: the first

player may rearrange the seeds any way he wishes, so long as both rows of holes are identical. However, what gives Bao its strategic edge is the making of a "child." Players not only capture seeds, but can gain ownership of holes during play. Such a hole is called a *child*, which is then partially closed; it can collect seeds but they are protected from capture.

The Board: The game is played on a Mancala board with two rows of seven holes each and a storehouse hole at either end. Each player controls the row closest to him and the storehouse on the right.

The Playing Pieces: The game requires 56 seeds, four in each hole at the beginning of play.

Player B

Player A

Bao

The Object of the Game:

To capture the most seeds in each round; to eventually reduce the opponent to four seeds or fewer.

The Play: Players decide who goes first. The first player may rearrange the seeds as he wishes, provided both sides of the board are identical at the start of the game, i.e., holes 1 and 7, 2 and 6, 3 and 5 contain the same number of seeds. If he rearranges the board, the other player goes first. If he leaves the board with four seeds per hole, he goes first, although he cannot make a capture or claim a child until his opponent has done so.

Bao is a multiple-lap game in which seeds are sowed counterclockwise. The person who moves first picks up seeds from any hole on his side of the board and sows them one per hole.

If the last seed falls into an empty hole on the opponent's side of the board, the turn is over.

If the last seed falls into an empty hole on the player's side and there is at least one seed in the opponent's hole opposite, the contents of both holes are captured and transferred to the storehouse. If the next hole on the player's side is also empty and there are seeds in the opponent's hole opposite, these are captured too. Captures continue so long as there is an uninterrupted sequence of empty holes on the player's side and filled holes opposite. An occupied hole on the player's

side or an empty hole on the opponent's side ends the string of captures.

If the last seed drops in an occupied hole on either side of the board (unless it is an opponent's hole containing three seeds), the player picks up the seeds, including the last one sowed, and continues another lap.

If the last seed falls into an opponent's hole that contains three seeds (the last seed makes four), the hole becomes a child, which means it henceforth belongs to that player. If any seed dropped by either player lands in a child, the move is immediately over. Seeds cannot be removed from a child and a child can never be captured.

If an opponent's 1st hole contains three seeds, a player may not make a child by taking a single seed from his 7th hole and dropping it in his opponent's 1st hole. In this case, the player must pick up all four seeds and continue his laps. For instance, in the game illustrated above, if A picks up the single seed in her 7th hole and drops it in B's 1st hole, she must pick up those seeds and continue with another sowing. However, if she picks up the four seeds from her 4th hole instead, and sows them to the right, the last seed will fall into B's 1st hole, which will then become A's child.

The second lap cannot begin on the player's side unless he has already moved through the opponent's holes. In other words, since B has two seeds in his 2nd hole and four in his 4th, he

may not pick up the seeds in the 2nd, sow the last in the 4th and start the second lap here. Instead, he must simply pick up the seeds in the 4th hole, and sow to the opponent' side ending in A's empty 1st hole.

When one player cannot make a move, the round is over. Players collect their captures, the contents of their child holes and any seeds that remain on their side of the board. Players tally their seeds: the player with the most seeds wins.

For the second round, the loser refills his holes, putting four seeds in each, starting from the left. Any remaining seeds (fewer than four) are put in the next hole. The winning player from the previous round copies this arrangement exactly and puts any leftover seeds in his storehouse. Empty holes are considered closed to play during that round. If a player is reduced to 12 seeds or fewer, so that he can only fill three holes or fewer, neither player is allowed to make a child.

The winner of one round goes first in the next. The rules of play are the same except that rearranging the seeds before the first move is not allowed, and the first player is allowed to capture and to make a child before his opponent. Closed holes are skipped over during sowing.

Rounds continue until one player has four seeds or fewer. ～

The Game of Daughters

- OTHER NAMES: Um El Banat (in Sudan), Mazageb (in Ethiopia) and Weg (in southern Ethiopia)
- NUMBER: two players
- EQUIPMENT: a Mancala board with two rows of six holes each and storehouse holes at each end; 48 playing pieces; six markers for each player
- DESCRIPTION: a multiple-lap game in which players own daughters (holes on the opponent's side of the board) and capture seeds from the opponent's daughters
- COMPLEXITY: moderately difficult with potential for both defensive and offensive play
- DURATION: each game consists of several rounds of 15 minutes or so

THE GAME OF DAUGHTERS is similar to **Bao**. The "child" has taken on the female gender but it functions similarly: it is a hole that can collect seeds but is the property of one player, even though it is on the opponent's side of the board. According to Larry Russ, this is an Arab game played by the Kababish in northern Sudan. The board is usually dug out of sand, making it one of the world's most portable pastimes.

The Board: The Game of Daughters is played on a board with two rows of six holes each and a storehouse hole at either end. Each player controls the holes closest to him and the storehouse on the right.

The Playing Pieces: The game requires 48 seeds, four in each hole at the beginning of play. Each player must have six markers—chips of two distinct colors, leaves of two shapes or six leaves and six twigs—with which he can indicate that an opponent's hole belongs to him.

The Object of the Game: To capture the greatest number of seeds.

The Play: Players decide who goes first. The first player scoops the seeds in any hole on his side of the board and sows them, one per hole,

counterclockwise.

If the last seed falls in his own occupied hole or an opponent's hole that contains any number of seeds except three, he picks them up and starts another lap, sowing one per hole. Laps continue until the last seed is sowed into an empty hole or an opponent's hole that contains three seeds.

If the last seed falls in an empty hole on either side of the board, the turn is over.

If the last seed falls in an opponent's hole that contains three seeds (four including the last seed sowed), this hole becomes a *daughter* and is marked by

the player with a leaf or colored chip to indicate that the hole belongs to him. After a player makes a daughter, his turn is over.

Players take turns making moves. Seeds are sowed in the daughters in the course of play, but a move cannot begin from a daughter hole.

If a player drops his last seed into his own daughter, his move is over. No capture is made and no seeds are removed from the daughter.

If a player drops his last seed into an opponent's daughter (which will be on the player's own side of the board, of course), the dropped seed and one other are removed from the daughter and put in the player's storehouse. (If the daughter is empty, the lone seed goes to the store.) The player then continues his turn, picking up the seeds from any hole on his side that is not a designated daughter.

In the game illustrated below, player A cannot move from her 3rd or 6th holes because these are her opponent's daughter holes. If she starts from her 5th hole, the last seed will end up in B's 2nd hole, which is A's own daughter. Her turn will be over and she'll make no capture, so this is not a good option. If she picks up the five seeds in her 4th hole, the last seed will fall in B's 3rd hole, which contains three seeds. The dropped seed

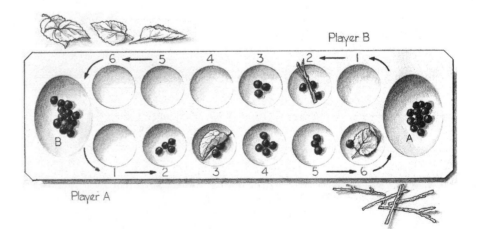

The Game of Daughters

makes four, so this hole becomes another daughter for A. Another option is for A to pick up the four seeds in her 2nd hole. The last seed will fall in her own 6th hole, which is one of B's daughters, so A can capture a seed from the hole and add it, together with her own last seed, to her store-house.

If a player cannot move, he passes until he can take a turn. When neither player can move—when all the seeds are in daughter holes or in the store-house—the round is over. Each player removes the seeds from his own daughters and adds them to his store. The player with the most seeds wins.

This game is usually played in rounds. To begin the second round, the player with the most seeds fills as many holes as she can, first on her side of the board, then on her opponent's side, starting with his 1st hole. If the winner has three seeds left, she takes one from her opponent to make up the fourth for one more hole. If she has one or two seeds left over, she gives these to her opponent to make four for his last hole. The holes a player fills at the beginning belong to her during play, so that as rounds continue, one player might start with nine holes and the other player with three.

Players take turns going first in each subsequent round. The game continues until one player is reduced to fewer than four seeds, not enough to fill one hole for another round. ∾

Deka

- ◆ NUMBER: two players
- ◆ EQUIPMENT: a squarish Mancala board with 12 holes arranged around one large elongated central hole; 24 playing pieces; six markers for each player
- ◆ DESCRIPTION: a multiple-lap game in which holes are closed by "threes"
- ◆ COMPLEXITY: a relatively simple circular game
- ◆ DURATION: a half hour or so; the game isn't over until most of the seeds are in the center hole

DEKA is one of several games that are played on what looks like a circular board. Instead of holes arranged in rows, they are arranged in the round, often with a central reservoir where pieces are deposited during play and where they can be stored when not in play.

Although the arrangement of holes is novel, play often proceeds as in the two-row multiple-lap Mancala games: movement is counterclockwise, and if there are seeds in the hole where the last seed drops, the player picks them up and continues his turn with another lap.

Deka, according to Larry Russ in *Mancala Games*, is played by the Uombe people in the lower regions of the Republic of Congo, formerly Zaire.

The Board: A Mancala board with 12 holes: each player controls the five holes immediately in front of him and the one in the middle on the right. As shown in the illustration,

player A controls holes 1 to 6; player B, holes 7 to 12.

The Playing Pieces: The game requires 24 seeds, two per hole at the beginning of play. Each player should have six distinctive markers to indicate holes he has closed.

The Object of the Game: To empty all the seeds from the opponent's holes.

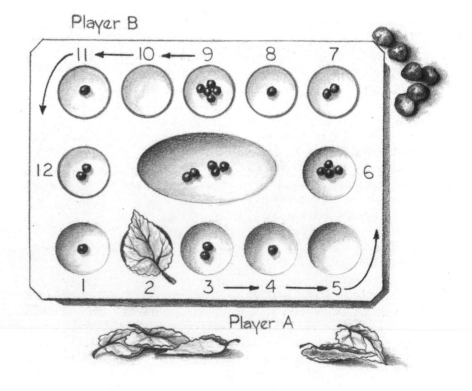

Deka

The Play: Players decide who goes first. The first player scoops the seeds from any hole on his side and sows them, one per hole, counter-clockwise.

If the last seed falls in an empty hole, the turn is over.

If the last seed falls in an occupied hole (other than an opponent's hole containing two seeds), the player picks up these seeds, including the last seed sowed, and continues with another lap.

If the last seed falls into an opponent's hole that contains two seeds (three including the last seed sowed), the hole is deemed *closed*. The player removes the three seeds and puts a marker in the hole. Then he continues with his turn, sowing the seeds in the usual way, except that when he comes to a closed hole on his own side of the board, he skips over it. When he comes to a closed hole on his opponent's side, he skips over it, adding a seed to the large hole at the center of the board instead, then continues on his way. If the last seed is dropped in the center hole, the turn is over.

A player may close more than one hole in a turn, but no one may close the two end holes, 6 and 12.

When a player has no seeds on his side of the board, he cannot move. The game is over, and he has lost.

Variations: Another tribe in the same region, the Nyanga, play by the same rules on a 14-hole board, six per side with two end holes.

In **Imbelece**, the end holes can be closed. This variation is also played on a 14-hole board.

Nambayi is played on an 18-hole board, but the two end holes are not used in play. The game begins with three seeds instead of two in each hole, and the holes are closed by making "fours"—a final seed added to a hole that already contains three. ☙

Abalala'e

- ◆ NUMBER: two players
- ◆ EQUIPMENT: a Mancala board with three rows of six holes each; 54 playing pieces
- ◆ DESCRIPTION: a multiple-lap game in which players capture seeds, much as in Ayoayo
- ◆ COMPLEXITY: a fairly simple three-row Mancala
- ◆ DURATION: a half hour or so

According to Larry Russ, archeological evidence suggests that three-row Mancala games are variations on established two-row games and, therefore, are a more recent refinement. Indeed, for those who like to play **Ayoayo** or any of the simple two-row, multiple-lap capture games, this form of Mancala will be a snap. The extra row complicates the movement and raises the stakes for captures, which makes for more intriguing play.

The Board: Abalala'e is played on a Mancala board with three rows of six holes each, with a storehouse hole on either side. Each player controls the row closest to him and the three right-hand holes of the middle row as well as the storehouse on the right.

Sowing starts at the far left (the player's 1st hole), moves counterclockwise along the player's holes to the center of the middle row, jumps up to the far right of the opponent's side of the board and proceeds along the opponent's holes to the center of the middle row, then begins again on the far left on the player's row. In other words, in the illustrated game on page 112, sowing moves from the player's holes 1 through 9 in order, then to the opponent's holes, 1 through 9, and back to the player's 1st hole.

The Playing Pieces: The game requires 54 seeds, three in each hole at the beginning of play.

The Object of the Game: To empty the opponent's holes of all seeds; to capture the most seeds.

The Play: The game begins with both players simultaneously scooping the seeds from their 1st holes and sowing them, one per hole, counter-clockwise. When the last seed falls in a hole that contains seeds, the player scoops them up and continues in laps around the board until the last seed of a lap falls in an empty hole. The first player to finish this move makes the next move. Thereafter, players take turns.

A player starts his move by scooping all the seeds from one of his own holes and sowing them in laps until the last seed is sowed in an empty hole.

If the empty hole belongs to the opponent, the turn is over.

If the empty hole belongs to the player, and the opponent's holes vertically above it are also empty, the player's turn is over.

If a player's last seed falls in his own empty hole and one or two of the opponent's holes directly above contain seeds, the player captures those seeds and puts them in his storehouse. He then continues his turn by moving the single seed (his last seed sowed) to the next hole, and proceeding in laps if possible, or making a capture if appropriate.

Play continues until one player cannot move because there are no seeds in her holes. The other player then captures all the seeds that remain on the board. The players add up their captured seeds; the person with the most seeds wins.

This game can also be played in

rounds. The loser of the first round fills as many holes as he can on his side of the board (in order, holes 1 to 9), leaving the last hole with only one or two seeds, if necessary. The winner fills the rest of the holes, putting any leftover seeds in his storehouse. The holes a player fills belong to him for that round.

In the second and subsequent rounds, the opening move is not simultaneous. Instead, the winner of one round makes the first move in the next. Rounds continue until one player loses all his seeds. ∼

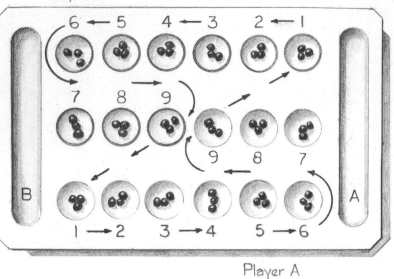

Abalala'e

Gabata

- ◆ NUMBER: **two players**
- ◆ EQUIPMENT: **a Mancala board with three rows of six holes each; 54 playing pieces; nine distinctive markers for each player**
- ◆ DESCRIPTION: **a multiple-lap game in which players capture seeds and take possession of holes**
- ◆ COMPLEXITY: **the extra row of holes complicates the movement, but otherwise almost identical to The Game of Daughters**
- ◆ DURATION: **a half hour for a round; a couple of hours for a full game**

GABATA comes from northern Ethiopia and nearby Sudan. Although it is played on a three-row board, it is almost identical to **The Game of Daughters**, which is played on two rows. The captured holes here are called *wegues* and the movement is tricky to get used to, but otherwise the rules of play will be familiar from earlier games in which holes are claimed by one player or the other.

The Board: Gabata is played on a board with three rows of six holes each and a storehouse hole at either end. As in Abalala'e, each player controls the row closest to him, the three right-hand holes of the middle row

and the storehouse on the right.

Sowing is also the same as in Abalala'e. A player starts at the far left (i.e., from his own 1st hole), moves counterclockwise along his own holes to the center of the middle row, jumps up to the far right of the opponent's 1st hole and proceeds left along his opponent's holes into the middle row, then begins again on the far left of his own row. (See illustration above.)

The Playing Pieces: The game requires 54 seeds, three in each hole at the beginning of play. Each player must have at least nine markers—two different sets of buttons, coins or chips in two shapes or colors—to designate his claimed holes.

The Object of the Game: To collect the most seeds; eventually, to reduce the opponent to fewer than three seeds.

The Play: Players decide who goes first. The first player scoops the seeds from any one of his holes and sows them, one per hole, in the appropriate direction.

If the last seed falls in an empty hole anywhere on the board, the turn is over.

If the last seed falls in a hole containing seeds (unless it is an opponent's hole with three seeds), the player picks up the seeds, including the one just sowed, and continues on another lap.

If the last seed is sowed in an opponent's hole containing three seeds (the one just sowed makes four), the hole becomes the player's *wegue* and is marked to indicate which player claims it. No captures are made and the turn is over.

If the last seed falls into a player's own wegue, his turn is over.

If the last seed falls into an opponent's wegue, this seed and another are taken from the hole and put in the player's storehouse. (If the wegue is empty, only the final seed is added to the store.) The player continues his turn by picking up the seeds from any of his holes not designated as a wegue.

No player can start by picking up the seeds from a wegue, either at the beginning of a turn or midway through a turn when starting a new lap.

A player cannot make a wegue during the opening move of a game.

If a player cannot move, she passes and waits until she can make a move. Play continues until neither player can move. When this happens, all the seeds are in wegues. Players take the seeds from their own wegues and add them to their storehouses. The player

with the most seeds wins.

The game is usually continued in rounds. The winner of the first round fills his own holes and as many of his opponent's holes as he can, starting on the opponent's far left (his 1st hole). If he has two seeds left over, the loser contributes one to complete it, but the hole belongs to the winner. If the winner has one seed left over from filling the holes, he gives it to the loser. The loser fills the rest of the holes. Whatever holes a player fills at the beginning of the round belong to him for the remainder of the round.

Each round is played by the same rules. Players take turns going first. When one player does not have enough seeds to fill even one hole, the other player is declared the winner.

Variation: Some players include the rule that a move cannot be started from the extreme left-hand hole (i.e., a player's 1st hole) unless it contains more than three seeds or unless this is the only hole that contains any seeds at all. This rule makes it easier to capture the 1st hole and convert it to a wegue. ∽

Njombwa

- ◆ OTHER NAMES: Mofuba (in Transvaal)
- ◆ NUMBER: two players
- ◆ EQUIPMENT: a Mancala board with four rows of eight holes each; 58 playing pieces
- ◆ DESCRIPTION: a multiple lap game in which players circle their own rows only, but capture seeds from opponent's rows
- ◆ COMPLEXITY: simpler in movement than three-row Mancala, but more complex capture strategies
- ◆ DURATION: an hour or more

THE BOARDS for four-row Mancala games are imposing: some have as many as 100 holes, gouged out of a large slab of wood or constructed with interlocking twigs. In some ways, however, four-row Mancala is a little easier to grasp than three-row, at least when it comes to the sowing movement. In these games, each player controls the two rows closest to him: his outer row and his inner row. He sows only in his own two rows, although he captures seeds from his opponent's adjacent rows. Captured seeds are removed from the board and kept in a storehouse or simply by the player's side.

The Board: Njombwa is played on a board with four rows of eight holes each. A player controls the two rows closest to him. Each player sows

counterclockwise around his own two rows, as illustrated.

The Playing Pieces: The game requires 58 seeds, distributed as illustrated, with two seeds in each hole of the outer rows and two seeds in each of the inner rows except for holes 15 and 16. Hole 15 has one seed and the last hole in each player's inner row is empty. (See page 114.)

The Object of the Game: To capture all of the opponent's seeds.

The Play: Players decide who goes first. The first player scoops the seeds from any one of his holes that contains two or more. He sows the seeds, one per hole, counterclockwise. If the last seed falls in a hole that contains seeds, he picks them up (includ-

ing the last one sowed) and moves in laps counterclockwise around his two rows.

If the last seed falls in an empty hole in the player's outer row, his turn is over.

If the last seed falls in an empty hole in the player's inner row, and the hole in the opponent's inner row directly opposite is also empty, the player's turn is over.

If the last seed falls in an empty hole in the player's inner row, and the hole in the opponent's inner row directly opposite is occupied, the player captures any seeds in the holes of both the opponent's inner and outer rows. The captured seeds are removed from the board and the player's turn is over.

Players take turns. They can start moves from a hole containing a single seed only if no other hole on their side of the board contains more than one seed. If a move begins with a single seed, it can only be moved if the next hole is empty.

The player who captures all his opponent's seeds wins.

Variations: In the Republic of Congo, a variation called **Dwong** is played that is identical to Njombwa, except that the holes in the outer rows contain four seeds each at the beginning of the game.

Another variation, **Baruma**, begins the game with two seeds in each hole of the outer rows; all the inner holes are empty except for each player's 9th hole, which contains three seeds. The rules of play are the same except that captures are only made from the opponent's inner row. Seeds in the outer row cannot be captured.

A variation called **Maruba** has been noted among the Bapedi of South Africa. The opening arrangement of seeds is the same as Njombwa, as are the rules of play, except that every time a player makes a capture from the inner row, he may take the seeds from one other hole belonging to his opponent. ∾

Player B

Player A

Njombwa

Nsumbi

- ◆ NUMBER: two players
- ◆ EQUIPMENT: a Mancala board with four rows of eight holes each; 64 playing pieces
- ◆ DESCRIPTION: a multiple-lap game in which captured seeds are sowed back onto the board
- ◆ COMPLEXITY: the most complex of the Mancala games
- ◆ DURATION: an hour or more

NSUMBI, played in the south of the Republic of Congo and northern Zambia, is typical of the four-row Mancala games that include a rule that elevates the strategic potential to that of **Backgammon** or **Chess**. Instead of captured seeds being removed from the board (as is almost always the case), the seeds are resowed on the player's rows; there is no storehouse and all the pieces remain in play throughout the game. According to noted games collector R.C. Bell, the most complex four-row Mancalas come from eastern and southern Africa.

The Board: Nsumbi is played on a board with four rows of eight holes each. Each player controls the two rows closest to him. Seeds are sowed counterclockwise around a player's two rows only, as in Njombwa.

The Playing Pieces: The game requires 64 seeds, two per hole at the start of play.

The Object of the Game: To reduce the opponent to one seed or none per hole.

The Play: Players decide who goes first. The first player scoops the seeds from any one of his own holes and sows them, one per hole, counterclockwise.

If the last seed falls in a hole with seeds, he picks these up (including the last seed sowed) and continues making laps around his outer and inner rows, until the last seed falls in an empty hole. The other player then takes his first move, proceeding in laps as above. No captures can be made during the first move of each player.

In subsequent turns, a player may not begin from a hole containing only one seed. He sows seeds, one per hole, counterclockwise in multiple laps.

If the last seed falls in an empty hole, his turn is over.

If the last seed falls into an occupied hole on his outer row, his turn continues.

If the last seed falls into an occupied hole on the player's inner row and the two holes in the opponent's rows opposite both contain seeds, the opponent's seeds are captured. The player continues his move by sowing these captured seeds in the holes on his own side of the board, beginning with the hole to the right of the one that began the last lap. (If you can't remember which hole that is, it will probably be the first empty hole clockwise from the hole where the final seed was dropped.) Laps continue until the last seed falls into an empty hole.

Only one capture can be made per turn.

Play continues until one player has only empty holes or single seeds, in which case she cannot move, since a turn cannot begin from a hole containing one seed. The other player is the winner.

Variation: In Ethiopia, a game called **Bare** is played on a four-row board with 12 holes per row and two seeds in each hole at the beginning of the game. Rules of play are identical except for the opening move, which is simultaneous, as in Abalala'e. Both players start at the same time, and whoever finishes the initial move first takes the next turn. No captures are allowed in the opening move.

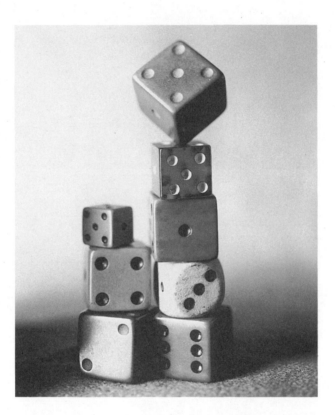

2

BULL'S-EYES AND BONES

Games With Playing Pieces

We figured the odds as best we could,
and then we rolled the dice.
—President Jimmy Carter
The New York Times, July 10, 1976

5

Shake, Rattle and Roll: Dice Games

According to Sophocles, the Greeks invented dice during the siege of Troy, but archeologists know better. Four-thousand-year-old dice, almost identical to the spotted cubes we play with today, have been found in Egyptian tombs; dice have turned up in Chinese excavations dated to 600 B.C.; in fact, every major culture around the world seems to have independently developed some form of dice early in its history. Long before there were written records, knucklebones—the cube-shaped astragalus bone in a sheep or a dog where the ankle joint connects to the leg—were being tossed from woven baskets, the results determining how inheritances were divided and which candidate would rule. At the time, a roll of the dice was not viewed as a random event but, rather, as a mouthpiece for the gods. There was no such thing as chance, only divine will.

The god of wisdom, prophecy and the dead is said to have invented dice; the outcome of each roll is controlled by Fortuna, more popularly known as Lady Luck. Dice were so popular in Europe during the Middle Ages that French academies taught dicing games and dice makers formed their own guild. Christians, however, called them "devil's bones," after their pagan origin. Successive generations of moralists have tried to ban them, but dice remain with us still, one of the world's most enduring, most portable and least expensive games.

What is it about dice that makes them such a persistent part of human history? The gambling instinct, some might say, or put another way, our craving to glimpse the future, to pit our intelligence and intuition against the forces of fate. Ironically, dice had a bipartisan birth in both church and casino: in religious ceremonies, the die was cast to divine the will of the gods; in the agora, the die was cast for fun and profit. The spotted cubes have long since become part of the language, a metaphor for risk and moxie. Julius Caesar was the first of a long line of politicians to invoke it. "*Iacta alea est*," he said as he crossed the Rubicon in defiance of Rome. "The die is cast."

Caesar's dice were probably ivory or bone, but today's dice are usually little plastic cubes, often white, sometimes red or transparent, stamped with dots—officially called spots in North America, pips in England—on each of their six sides. The numbering system was settled on early; even the Greeks labeled the faces 1 to 6 and positioned the numbers so that opposing faces always add up to seven: 1 and 6, 2 and 5, 3 and 4. In North America, the spots have their own pet names. Two 1s or a 2 is called snake eyes; 3 is cross-eyes or cock-eyes; 4 is little Joe; 5 is Phoebe; 6 is my sister; 8 is Ada; 9 is my Carolina; 10 is big Dick; and 12 (6-6) is boxcars.

Before polymers, dice were made of wood, stone, metal, glass, even amber and gemstones—anything that could be whittled into a cube and painted or scratched with spots. Some cultures used two-sided dice, instead of cubes, for games of chance. In India, dice were cowrie shells, which were counted according to whether they landed facedown or open side up. Cowries were the currency of the day, and in fact, pennies can be used exactly the same way. If you throw six pennies and four fall heads up, it is the same as throwing a die that lands with four spots facing up. North American natives also used two-sided dice—buffalo bones, peach pits, walnut shells, woodchuck teeth or pottery pieces with painted markings to distinguish the two sides. Pyramidal dice, pentahedral (five-sided) and octahedral (eight-sided) dice have been around almost as long as there have been people to toss them. Today, they are used mostly in role-playing games such as Dungeons and Dragons.

If you play dice games at a casino, you'll throw *perfect dice*, which says nothing about your skill but much about the way they are made. Perfect dice are as close as technology can bring them to being true cubes, exactly as long as they are high and wide, within fractions of a millimeter. The spots are drilled out and filled with paint, equal in weight to the material that was removed. The dice are then polished until the sides of the cubes are perfectly flush and the edges sharp; all this to ensure that each die has an absolutely equal chance of falling on any one of its six faces. *Drugstore* or *candy-store dice* are not perfect cubes, but they are close enough for those of us who are playing for fun rather than the family fortune. Almost all drugstore dice have recessed spots, and many have rounded corners, though the squared-off kind are better for kids and slippery tables—they don't roll away as easily.

Standard dice are just over half an inch square, with spots about one-eighth inch in diameter, but there are also *peewee dice* that are one-quarter inch square and *oversize dice* up to an inch across. *Chinese dice* are quite small, usually black. Although the spots are arranged conventionally, the one spot is much larger and deeper than the others and the four spots are painted red. Many Western games also use special dice. The six faces of *poker dice* are stamped with playing-card denominations: 9♠ or ♣, 10♦, Jack, Queen and King of no particular suit and A♠ or ♣. With five of these dice, players can put together "hands" for a game of **Poker Dice**. There are also *crown and anchor dice*, with a crown, an anchor and the four playing-card suits stamped on their six sides. Most unusual, perhaps, are the four- or six-sided cylindrical dice with little handles on top and a pointed nipple on the bottom so that they can be spun like tops. These spinning dice are called *teetotums* by the British in India and *dreidels* by Jewish families around the world, and their sides are usually stamped with directions for the gambling game Put and Take or with numbers or Hebraic letters for the Hanukkah game of **Dreidels**. Finally, there are dice imprinted with letters on each side, rather than numbers, so that when a dozen or more are tossed, the players spell as many words as they can within a minute, as in the commercial game Boggle.

Whatever is incised on the sides, dice can and will be tampered with; cheaters prefer to know in advance how the die will fall. The unprincipled player might shave off a corner, *load* a die by weighting one side with heavy metal paint in the spots or *mark* the faces with duplicate 3-4-5 so that certain combinations can never come up; for instance, the losing totals of 2, 3 and 12 in **Craps**. This is not a modern vice. The first written reference to dice, the Sanskrit epic *Mahabharata,* mentions loaded dice.

Dice are most common, perhaps, as the means of determining moves in board games, but games can also be played solely with dice. Most are games of chance, games traditionally associated with the road to ruin. When Rabelais' heroes Pantagruel and Gargantua disembark on Sharper's Island, Pantagruel remarks that the island, formed of two huge cubic blocks of white bone, had occasioned "a greater loss of life and property than Scylla and Charybdis."

But there is skill in dicing games, and it rests in understanding the mathematical probabilities of throwing any specific combination of numbers. With six numbers on a die, there is one chance in six that a specific side will fall faceup. In other words, the odds are five to one against you that a certain number will appear. With two dice, there are 36 possible combinations of numbers. You can never throw a 1, and there is only one chance in 36 that you will throw a score of two (1-1). There are six combinations, however, that add up to seven (4-3, 3-4, 5-2, 2-5, 1-6, 6-1). When you throw three dice, there are 216 possible combinations; 1,296 with four dice, and so on, multiplying by six for every extra die added to the cup.

To calculate the odds of a certain number or total showing up, figure out the number of throws that will produce a desired combination and subtract it from the total possible combinations. For instance, out of 1,296 possible combinations with four dice, there are only four ways to produce a total of five (2-1-1-1, 1-2-1-1, 1-1-2-1, 1-1-1-2), so the odds against throwing a five with four dice are 1,292 to 4, or 323 to 1. Using the example above, two dice produce 36 combinations. There are six ways to throw a seven, so the odds against throwing a seven are 30 to 6, or 5 to 1.

Although dice can be shaken and tossed from the hand, a variety of receptacles have been invented for the express purpose of shaking dice to make sure that the little cubes spin at random before they fall. Ancient Greeks fashioned conical beakers, American aboriginals wove special baskets, and the Romans used metal cups, quite like the leather or plastic dice cups we have today. In games using a dice cup, the dice are vigorously shaken, then *thrown* or *rolled* onto the table. With games like Poker Dice, they are allowed to roll freely out of the cup, but in **Liar's Dice**, they are thrown *under the cup*—the cup is overturned, trapping the dice while they are still moving and exposing them only when they come to a halt.

In games like Craps, players *shoot* the dice, shaking them in the cup of their hand so that the others can hear the cubes move freely—the click-click-click is proof that the shooter isn't holding the dice in a winning pattern, waiting to drop them onto the table. Convention requires that the shooter, to prove his innocence further, must roll the dice onto the playing surface away from himself. To guarantee a random throw, some players set up a *backstop*—a cereal box or a tall book—to bounce the dice against.

The top side of a die—the side pointing skyward—is the one that counts. Whether thrown from the hand or a dice cup, dice count only if they lie flat on the playing surface. If one or more dice are *cocked*—tilting at an angle—all the dice have to be rethrown. At any time, a player can snatch the rolling dice and say, "No dice!" The shooter must then rethrow. No one can do this if any one die in that roll has already stopped.

Players usually decide who starts a game by throwing one die. The person who rolls the highest number is the *first shooter*, the second highest shoots second, and so on. In the case of a tie, the two players roll again. Players can rearrange their seating so that the cup is always passed to the left. The person who loses one game usually gets the chance to start the next.

Dice are not as popular as they once were. A recent cruise through local department stores failed to turn up a single set, and even specialty games stores had only a few cubes, shoved to the back of a shelf behind Nintendos. Yet dice will undoubtedly outlive video games and whatever electronic pastimes follow. Dice games are compelling and unique: the feel of dice rattling in your hand, the spill and click of cubes on the table, random numbers determining fortunes, a new chance with every throw. Children love them, partly because they are faster and more active than most card or board games and partly because, being dependent more on luck than on skill, they give kids equal odds against adults. Even young children can play, since most of the games are based on simple matching. Whatever math is needed can usually be accomplished on fingers and toes.

Bugs

- OTHER NAMES: **Beetle and Cootie**
- NUMBER: **suitable for the youngest players; two to six people, though a small group is best**
- EQUIPMENT: **one die; paper and a pencil or crayon for each player**
- DESCRIPTION: **the fun of Hangman, without the spelling; kids don't have to be able to add to play**

A DICING VARIATION of Mr. Potato Head, Cootie was introduced by Schaper Toys in 1948, that company's first foray into the world of games. Players threw a die and, according to the number thrown, assembled a big plastic flea from the parts in the box. The manufacturers promised "an exciting, educational game for all ages," though it is hard to figure out exactly what lessons were to be learned. An equally entertaining game can be played with pencil and paper. Encourage the players to stray as far from conventional insect anatomy as they like.

The Object of the Game:
To be the first to draw a bug.

The Play: Give each player a sheet of paper and a pencil, or set out a common tub of crayons. Players determine who goes first, then each in turn rolls the die and draws the body part that corresponds to the number thrown. For instance, if a player rolls 2, she can draw the head; if she rolls 3, as illustrated, she can draw one leg. She cannot start her bug, however, until she throws a 1 for the body; and she can't add the eyes and the antennae until she throws 2 and draws a head. Each bug has a body, a head, two eyes, two antennae, six legs and a tail. The first player to finish the bug wins.

The Score:

1 = Body	4 = One Eye
2 = Head	5 = One Antenna
3 = One Leg	6 = Tail

Variation: For a faster game (with more players), use two dice. After a game or two, kids will undoubtedly develop more complicated creatures to draw. ∽

Bugs

Dreidels

- NUMBER: **two or more players**
- EQUIPMENT: **a dreidel and counters (a bag of pennies or candies)**
- DESCRIPTION: **a traditional game of pure chance; especially fun for young children**

A GAME THAT originated in medieval Germany, Dreidels is now a traditional part of the Jewish celebration of Hanukkah, the Festival of Lights. It is played with a teetotum, a spinning die with four sides inscribed with the letters N, G, H and S, the first letters of the words *Nes Gadol Hayah Sham*, which translates, "A great miracle happened here." The miracle occurred in 165 B.C., when the Maccabees recaptured the Temple of Jerusalem from the Syrians.

They had only enough oil in their lamp for one day, but somehow, it kept burning for eight days until reinforcements arrived. Hanukkah—and the game of Dreidels—celebrates the Maccabees' victory.

The game was adapted from a German betting game and is still usually played for candies or a more valuable pot. Woody Allen, for one, admits to having earned pin money in public school hustling Dreidels. If you can't find a dreidel (check the

local synagogue), you can easily make one by drilling a hole through a small cube of wood and inserting a dowel so that it extends a half-inch on the bottom. Sharpen this short end to a point, and paint the Hebrew letters on the sides.

The Object of the Game:
To win the counters.

The Play: Each player has an equal number of counters (pennies, beans, candies). Before each game, the players ante two counters to the center of the table—the kitty, or pot. Players decide the order of play, then the first player spins the dreidel. If it stops with the N facing up, as illustrated on the following page, he does nothing. If G is facing up, he takes all the counters. If H faces up, he takes half the counters; and if the letter S faces up, he has to put a counter in the center. Then he passes the dreidel to the next player. Before the next player spins, players ante. If there is nothing in the center, everyone antes two counters; if half the kitty remains in the center, each player antes one counter. Otherwise, they ante nothing. The next player spins, and play continues around the table until one person has won all the counters. ❧

Dreidels

Going to Boston

- ◆ OTHER NAMES: **Yankee Grab**
- ◆ NUMBER: **any number of players; most fun with four or more**
- ◆ EQUIPMENT: **three dice, a dice cup and counters (at least 10 per player)**
- ◆ DESCRIPTION: **a fast, easy time-passer; kids can play as soon as they can count**

Young children like this game, but the staying power of the rest of the family may be limited unless a kitty, or pot, is added to each round.

The Object of the Game:
To get the highest score (and win the kitty) on each round.

The Play: Players throw one die; the person with the highest score shoots first. The first shooter throws the dice from the dice cup and sets aside the highest number. If the highest number is a pair, he keeps only one and returns the other to the dice cup. He throws the two dice and again sets aside the highest, then throws the last die. Each player must take three turns. The total of the three dice is the player's score. Each of the other players takes a turn. The person with the highest score in the round wins.

The game is more fun if each player starts with 10 counters. Before the round begins, everyone antes one counter—a coin, a matchstick or a candy—into the kitty at the center. The player with the highest score in the round wins the kitty. (In the case of a tie, players split the kitty or leave the counters in for the next turn.)

Variation: For kids with advanced math, instead of adding all three dice together, add the first two and multiply by the third. The scores are higher, and with a lot of people playing, there is less chance of a tie. ❧

Dice Golf

- ◆ NUMBER: **any number of players**
- ◆ EQUIPMENT: **three dice, a dice cup, paper and pencil**
- ◆ COMPLEXITY: **requires no math, only the ability to recognize doubles**

Although golf as we know it originated in Scotland sometime before 1457, the Romans played a similar game called Paganica, hitting a feather-stuffed ball across the fields with a club. This dicing version is of indeterminate age, but it can be played without leaving the house.

The Object of the Game:
To throw doubles and to have the fewest throws in 18 turns.

The Play: Players roll one die, then shoot in order, the highest number going first. (Rearrange seating according to order, if you like.) The first shooter throws the dice. If all the numbers on the dice are different, this counts as a *stroke*, and he throws again, counting as a stroke each throw in which all the dice are different. When he finally throws a double, he makes the hole. He records the number of strokes it took (including the last throw with the double), then passes the dice cup to the next player. Each player throws the three dice until he or she gets a double and makes the hole. For instance, if the next player throws

	Kelly	Laura	Grace
1	2	1	1
2	1	5	4
3	1	10	5
4	1	1	2
5	1	1	3
6	3	1	3
7	4	1	1
8	4	1	4
9	2	4	3
10	2	3	2
11	1	5	1
12	2	2	1
13	2	1	1
14	1	1	1
15	2	5	2
16	1	2	2
17	1	1	4
18	1	5	2
	32	50	40

3-1-6, 2-3-5, 4-4-1, she scores three strokes for that hole. Each round is one hole of golf. The game ends after 18 holes.

The Score: Write 1 to 18 in a column, and record the number of strokes (throws) each player takes for each hole, as illustrated. At the end, add up the strokes to get the final score for each player. The lowest total wins. ∾

Dice Golf

Ohio

- ◆ OTHER NAMES: **Martinetti and Centennial**
- ◆ NUMBER: **any number of players except one (a boring solo game)**
- ◆ EQUIPMENT: **three dice, a dice cup, a chalkboard or paper and pencil and markers**

IN ITS MOST GENERIC form, this is probably the precursor to all track-style board games. The players draw a grid on a chalkboard or paper, with the numbers 1 to 12 marked in order in the squares as illustrated. Each player has one marker. It doesn't matter what the markers are as long as they are distinguishable from one another. You can use a penny, a nickel, a dime and a quarter for four players; dinky cars or troll dolls, if the squares are big enough.

The Object of the Game: To be the first to move your marker from 1 to 12 and back again.

The Play: Players roll one die; the person with the highest score shoots first. The first shooter throws the dice. If he gets a 1, he moves his marker to the first square; if he doesn't, he passes the dice cup. Each player in turn must move his marker from square to square, in sequence (1-2-3-4-5, and so on), but the dice can be added together to produce the correct number. For instance, if a player throws 1-2-2 on his first throw, he can move all the way to the fifth square: 1, 2, 2+1, 2+2, 2+2+1. If he is on the tenth square and throws 5-6-1, he can move to 11 (5+6), then to 12 (5+6+1). If a player overlooks a total he could use and passes the dice cup, another player can claim it. Each move earns a player an extra throw; when he throws numbers he can't use, the turn passes to the next player. The first player whose marker travels from 1 to 12 and back to 1 wins. ∾

Ohio

Sevens

- ◆ NUMBER: **any number of players; five is fun**
- ◆ EQUIPMENT: **six dice and a dice cup**
- ◆ COMPLEXITY: **some strategy is involved, especially by the first shooter**

SEVEN HAS LONG been held a number of mystical power. The Babylonians believed in seven sacred planets, the Jews decreed that the Earth was created in seven days, and the Christians abide by seven virtues and seven deadly sins. There are seven days in the week and seven stages in a person's life, and when you are in seventh heaven, according to the Muhammadans, you will have 70,000 heads, each with 70,000 faces, each with 70,000 mouths, each with 70,000 tongues. Sevens come up a lot in this game too, but they are bad luck, not good.

The Object of the Game: To score the highest total of the dice that remain after eliminating those which add up to seven.

The Play: The players throw the dice, then shoot in order, highest first. (Rearrange the seating so that the dice cup can pass to the left.) Each player in turn rolls the dice and eliminates combinations that add up to seven. These dice do not count. The object is to get the highest possible score with the remaining dice. The first shooter is allowed three throws, but he can take only one or two if he chooses. The other players may take the same number of throws as the first shooter or fewer. The player with the highest score in each round wins.

For instance, the first shooter throws 4-3-1-1-1-3. She eliminates the 4 and the 3, because they add up to seven. She could keep the remaining 1-1-1-3 as her score (6) and pass the dice to the next shooter, but instead, she throws the four dice again, hoping for something better. On her second throw, she gets 5-2-6-6. She eliminates the 5 and the 2. She can take the remaining dice as her score (12), or she can throw again. Since 12 is the highest score possible with two dice, she ends her turn and passes the cup. The rest of the players have two throws in which to beat her score of 12. If players ante before each round, the one with the highest score takes the kitty, or pot. ∽

Drop Dead

- ◆ NUMBER: **any number of players**
- ◆ EQUIPMENT: **five dice and a dice cup**
- ◆ DESCRIPTION: **similar to Yacht, but not as complex**

FIVE IS ANOTHER ancient mystical number, composed of 2 and 3, the first even and odd numbers. Two symbolizes diversity and has a long history of bad luck; three is a compound of unity (1) and diversity and represents the guiding principles of creation. In this game, the power and adversity of 5 and 2 render each roll that contains those numbers scoreless.

The Object of the Game: To add up the totals of dice thrown; to avoid throwing 2 and 5.

The Play: Players roll one die; low shooter goes first. Each player in turn rolls all five dice and adds up the numbers. If the roll includes a 2 or a 5, there is no score, and each 2 or 5 is eliminated, becoming a dead die. The remaining dice are rolled again. The player keeps throwing until all five dice are dead, keeping a running tally of his score on throws that did not contain the deadly 2 or 5. When all five dice are dead, the turn passes to the player on the left.

For instance, the first roll yields 1-3-4-5-6. There is no score, the 5 is eliminated, and the other four dice are rolled again. The second roll yields 1-3-3-6. This scores 13, and all four dice go back in the dice cup. The third roll yields 2-4-5-5. No score, and only one dice can be rolled. It comes up 2—a dead die. The final score is 13, and the dice cup passes to the next shooter. The person with the highest score after one round wins. For added interest, players can ante to a pot in the middle of the table before a round begins; the winner of each round takes the pot. ∽

Straight Shooter

- OTHER NAMES: Sequences
- NUMBER: any number of players, but a good solo game too
- EQUIPMENT: six dice and a dice cup
- DESCRIPTION: a simple time-passer that is lots of fun
- DURATION: the score roller-coasters so that a game for two can last half an hour

THIS IS A SIMPLIFIED version of the next game, Farkle, and is a good way to introduce kids to the concept of scoring for certain prescribed combinations, which is also the principle of Yacht and Generala.

The Object of the Game:

To roll sequences of 1-2 or more; the first to reach 100 points wins.

The Play: Players roll one die; the person with the highest score shoots first. Each player throws the dice and scores for the sequences that appear. For instance, a roll of 5-6-1-2-3 scores 10 points. If a player rolls 1-1-1, her score is cancelled; she starts again at zero. Continue around the table, each player throwing once in turn, until one player reaches the target score.

The Score: The sequences are scored as indicated. The first player to reach 100 wins.

Scoring System: Straight Shooter	
1-2	5 points
1-2-3	10 points
1-2-3-4	15 points
1-2-3-4-5	20 points
1-2-3-4-5-6	25 points
1-1-1	score cancelled

Farkle

- OTHER NAMES: 10,000
- NUMBER: good played alone or with two or three; four or more is a slow game
- EQUIPMENT: six dice, a dice cup and a scorepad
- DESCRIPTION: a big-stakes game that calls for a steady heart and a lucky hand
- COMPLEXITY: good for kids, though the scoring is a little complex
- DURATION: with three players, a game takes half an hour

THIS HIGH-ROLLING numbers game can keep even adults absorbed for an evening. Scoring combinations are set aside, and the rest of the dice are rethrown in the hopes of getting a higher score. Only 1s, 5s, three of a kind and a run of 1-2-3-4-5-6 score. It isn't unusual to score over 2,000 points in one turn, but in this game, you have to quit while you are ahead. If you throw a Farkle—a throw with no scoring dice—you lose all the points you have accumulated in that turn. The name of the game is a euphemism for the expletive that such bad luck can elicit.

The Object of the Game:

To keep rolling 1s, 5s, triples or runs; to be the first to score 10,000.

The Play: Players roll one die to establish the order of play. (Rearrange seating so that dice cup can pass to the left.) In turn, each player rolls all six dice. If there are no 1s, 5s or triples or there is no run, the dice cup passes to the next player. Any 1s, 5s or triples are set aside, and the rest of the dice are rolled again. If a player throws a run or if all six dice have been set aside as counters, she puts them back in the dice cup and rolls again, continuing the tally.

The player keeps a running total of her score. As long as she throws a counter—1, 5, three of a kind or a run—she keeps rolling. At any time, she can decide to stop and claim her points, but as soon as she rolls a Farkle (a scoreless throw), her turn ends.

For example, if the first roll is 5-1-4-3-6-6, the 5 and the 1 are set aside and score 150. The other four dice are rolled: 3-3-3-2. The 3s are set aside and added to the score (150+300 = 450). The 2 is rolled and comes up a 5 (450+50 = 500). All six dice have scored, so they are rolled again: 5-4-6-2-2-2. The 2s and the 5 are set aside. If she stopped now, her score would be 750 (500+200+50), but instead, she rolls the remaining two dice. They come up 3-4—a Farkle. The player's turn is over, the score for the turn is zero, and the dice cup passes to the next player.

Each player must score 500 points in one turn to open. Until then, none of his points score. Once a player opens, he can record the points earned in each turn provided he quits before he throws a Farkle. Players keep a running tally of their points, playing to 5,000 or 10,000 (which gives the

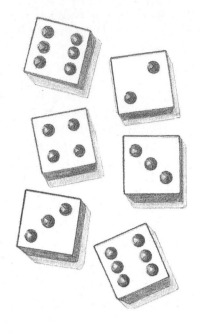

Farkle

game its alternate name).

If a player with accumulated points throws a Farkle, the next player can pick up the scoreless dice, roll them and, if she gets 1, 5, a triple or a run, score all of the previous player's points. (Both players must already be open.) For instance, the first player had a running total of 750, threw the two dice, got 3-4 and Farkled. The dice cup passes to the second player, who decides to throw the two dice. He rolls 5-3, scoring 800 (750+50). He then rolls the 3 again, continuing where the first player left off. If the first player has an extremely high score, this is well worth the risk.

The Score: A die showing 1 is worth 100, 5 is worth 50 and three of a kind are worth 100 multiplied by the numerical value (indicated by # in the boxed scoring system). For instance, three 6s are worth 600, and

Scoring System: Farkle
1 = 100 points
5 = 50 points
#- # - # = # x 100 points
1-1-1 = 1,000 points
1-2-3-4-5-6 = 1,000 points
3 Farkles = −1,000 points

three 2s are worth 200. The exception is three 1s, which score 1,000 points. A run of 1-2-3-4-5-6 also scores 1,000. (Incomplete runs do not score.) If a player throws a completely scoreless first roll in three successive turns, he loses 1,000 points. ∾

Help Your Neighbor

- ◆ NUMBER: **two to six players; best with six**
- ◆ EQUIPMENT: **three dice, a dice cup and at least 10 counters per player**
- ◆ DESCRIPTION: **an extremely old dicing game in which you are the agent of your neighbor's fate**
- ◆ COMPLEXITY: **no strategy, all luck; fast-moving (fortunes won and lost in an hour)**

WE HAVE A two-gallon jar full of pennies that stands in the corner of the dining room, always ready for the moment when a wave of generosity prompts a round or two of Help Your Neighbor.

The Object of the Game: To be first to get rid of your counters.

The Play: Each player takes a number from one to six, representing the faces of a die; the first shooter is 1, the next shooter is 2, and so on. (Assign the numbers at random, or throw one die: the highest throw is 1, the second highest is 2, and so on.) If there are five players, the 6 is dead and is ignored when it comes up in a throw. With four players, both the 5 and 6 are dead. With three players, each takes two numbers; for instance, 1-2, 3-4, 5-6. With two players, each takes three numbers: 1-2-3 and 4-5-6. Players have 10 counters each.

In turn, each player throws the dice. If a player's number comes up, she must put a counter in the pot, one counter for each number. For instance, if the first shooter rolls 4-3-3, the number-four player puts in one counter and the number-three player puts in two. Pass the dice cup clockwise around the table, each player taking a turn rolling the dice. The first player to run out of counters wins and takes the pot. The next round begins with the second shooter. ∾

Aces in the Pot

- NUMBER: two or more players; best with at least four or five
- EQUIPMENT: two dice, a dice cup and counters; on each die, 1 is an Ace
- DESCRIPTION: fortunes rise and fall fast; the winner is uncertain until the very last moment

IN MANY DICING games, the 1 is referred to as an Ace, which may indicate that these particular entertainments evolved from playing cards.

The Object of the Game:
To avoid throwing 1 or 6; to be the last person at the table with a counter.

The Play: Before the round begins, give each player two counters. The players each throw one die; the highest number begins. The first player starts, then each player takes a turn, throwing both dice. If a player rolls one Ace (1), he puts one counter in the pot, or kitty, at the center of the table; if he throws 1-1, both counters go in the pot (Aces in the Pot). If he throws a 6, he gives a counter to the player on his left; if he throws 6-6 he gives both counters to the player on his left (Sixes to the Side). Any other throws are safe. Pass the dice cup to the left, players throwing once in each turn and giving counters to the pot or to the player on their left as indicated by the numbers on the dice. Only players who have counters may throw the dice; if they have no counters left, they say, "Pass."

When the dice come to the last player to hold a counter, she must take three throws of the dice. If she avoids throwing a 6 in those three throws, she wins the pot. If she throws a 6, she passes her last counter—and the dice cup—to the player on her left, who must also take three throws. The first player to toss the dice three times without throwing a 6 wins the pot. Before the next round begins, give two counters to each player; the person to the left of the first shooter starts. ❧

Yacht

- OTHER NAMES: Cheerio, Yot and, in its commercial incarnation, Yahtzee
- NUMBER: any number of players; in solo Yacht, go for your personal best
- EQUIPMENT: five dice, a dice cup and a pencil and paper for scoring
- COMPLEXITY: involves strategy; children must be able to add to keep score
- DURATION: a game for three kids takes about 20 minutes, but they'll want to keep playing for hours

YAHTZEE WAS introduced in the early 1950s, another product from Edwin S. Lowe, the man who brought Bingo to Americans. Lowe bought the rights to the dicing game from a Canadian couple that had approached him to package a few samples of the game as gifts for their friends. They had invented it, they said, to play on their yacht, and they called it, not surprisingly, The Yacht Game. Lowe liked the game, changed the name and marketed it as Yahtzee, still available on games-store shelves.

Yahtzee, or Yacht, bears a very close resemblance to Puerto Rico's most popular dice game, Generala. In changing the name from battles to boats, the symbolism of the scoring system has been lost. A Yacht is five of a kind; in the Puerto Rican version, this is a General, complete with five stars. Generala is a more sophisticated adult game—in Puerto Rico, Generala is played in bars for drinks and cash—while Yacht is easily grasped by the 8-to-10 age group. Start younger players off by playing without the poker hands, simply trying to roll as many 1s as possible in the first turn, 2s in the second, and so on, up to 6s. With both Yacht and Generala, keep the scorepad obvious so that players can remember the combinations they have yet to score.

The Object of the Game:
To throw a maximum score in each category.

The Play: Roll the dice to determine the order of play. The lowest total rolls first, then the dice cup is passed clockwise around the table. In each turn, players have three rolls of the dice. On the first throw, the player shakes the dice and tosses them onto the table. He sets aside any 1s and returns the other dice to the dice cup. If he got his maximum score on the first throw, his turn ends. Otherwise, he throws a second time. He sets aside any additional 1s and throws a third and final time. After the third throw, he notes his score in the 1 column, and the dice cup passes to the left.

Every player tries for 1s, then 2s, moving in order from the top of the scorepad to the bottom. (If a player trying for 3s rolls five 6s, they don't score.) A Little Straight is 1-2-3-4-5; a Big Straight is 2-3-4-5-6. A Full House is three dice of one number, two of another, as in 3-3-3-2-2. Four of a Kind is exactly that. Choice Hand is the best score you can throw in your three rolls. A Yacht is five of a kind. When players have scored for each of the 12 categories in turn, they add up their scores. The player with the highest total wins.

The Score: Before the game begins, rule off the score sheet as illustrated, or buy a Yahtzee scorepad at a games store. Players try for the highest score in each category, shown in brackets.

After three throws, each player adds together the numbers on the dice that fulfill the category. For instance, if you are trying for 5s and after the third throw you have 5, 5, 5, 2, 6, add together the three 5s for a score of 15. The Little Straight scores 15, and the Big Straight scores 20. With a Full House, add up the numbers. For instance, 3-3-3-2-2 scores 13. In Four of a Kind, score both the four identical numbers and the odd number. For instance, 4-4-4-4-6 scores 22. With the Choice Hand, add all five dice together, whatever they are. Yacht always scores 50 points, regardless of the number on the dice. With Little and Big Straights, Full House, Four of a Kind and Yacht, a player scores only if she rolls exactly what is called for. An incomplete Full House or part of a Straight scores zero. The highest score possible in a game of Yacht is 278.

Variations: Once you become familiar with the categories, add strategy to the game by filling them in according to your choice, rather than in order from 1 to Yacht. Each player decides after her first throw what she will try for. She may change her mind during the three throws, but at the end of her turn, she must assign the score for that turn to one of the categories on the scorepad. Once a score is entered, it cannot be changed or moved. For instance, on the first throw, she rolls 2-2-3-4-5 and decides to go for a Big Straight. She rethrows the 2 and gets a 3, rethrows again and gets a 4. She did not score the Big Straight; the best she can do is enter 8 in the 4 cate-

gory for the two 4s. A player can also opt to score zero in a category. For instance, if a player's final throw is 1-3-4-5-6 and only Little Straight, 5s and 6s remain to be filled, she can choose to score zero for Little Straight, rather than use up the 5 or 6, which are relatively easy to fill with higher scores. In general, scores tend to be higher when players choose the categories, instead of filling them consecutively. The maximum total possible, however, is lower: 277 instead of 278, since the

Yacht Score Sheet

highest score for a Full House would be 29 (six 6s would count as a Yacht).

The main difference between Yacht, its variations and **Yahtzee** is in the method of scoring. In the latter, Full House, Little Straight and Big Straight score 25, 30 and 40 points, respectively (regardless of the numbers in the Full House). There is a 35-point bonus if the scores for categories 1 through 6 add up to 63 points or more.

Generala ups the ante by scoring categories differently if you fill them in one throw, rather than two or three. Five of a kind in one throw is a Big General and wins the game automatically. Five of a kind made on the second or third throw is a Small General and earns 60 points. Four of a Kind on the first throw is worth 45 points; on the second or third throw, 40 points.

A Full House on the first throw is 35 points, regardless of the numbers in the Full House; on the second or third throw, it is always 30 points. Any straight (1-2-3-4-5 or 2-3-4-5-6) on the first throw is 25 points; on the second or third throw, it is 20 points. In this category only, 1 is wild and can become either a 2 or a 6 to make a straight. For the rest of the categories, the point numbers (1 to 6) are scored as their total spot value, as in Yacht. There are only 10 categories, instead of 12; the Straight counts as one instead of two, and there is no Choice Hand. If Generala is played for money—a penny a point to a dollar a point—the value of each point is decided beforehand; the person with the highest total wins the difference between his score and each loser's score.

Crag uses three dice, and each player takes two throws per turn. Another category is added: Crag is scored when a pair and a number add up to 13; for instance, 4-4-5 or 5-5-3. A Crag counts 50. Any group of three different numbers that add up to 13 counts 26. Also, because there are three dice, Four of a Kind is replaced by Three of a Kind, which counts 25, and there are four straights: High Straight (4-5-6), Low Straight (1-2-3), Even Straight (2-4-6) and Odd Straight (1-3-5), each counting 20.

Double Cameroon Score Sheet

Double Cameroon uses 10 dice and is scored almost exactly like Yacht, with a couple of differences as indicated on the score sheet illustrated. Each player in turn throws the dice no more than three times. At the end of the third throw, the player divides the 10 dice into two groups of five and assigns them to two different categories. After five turns, all the categories are filled. The player with the highest score wins. The maximum possible is 214; and 170 is considered good. Because there are more options, there are more chances for strategy. As a rule, use early throws to try for specific combinations, writing off your failures as 1s, 2s, 3s, and so on. ❧

Craps

- ◆ OTHER NAMES: **African Golf, Rolling the Bones and African or Galloping Dominoes**
- ◆ NUMBER: **any number from two to more than a dozen players; best with a large group; players can join in and drop out at any stage in the game**
- ◆ EQUIPMENT: **two dice, counters and, if desired, a backstop**
- ◆ DESCRIPTION: **fast and fun, with or without the stakes**

CRAPS IS AN OFFSHOOT of the British game Hazard, but it took a circuitous route through France and the American South to reach the form in which it is played today. Some speculate that the name derives directly from the French settlers in New Orleans, who were called Johnny Crapaud (from the French for toad, referring to their taste for amphibians). Their favorite dicing game supposedly evolved from Crapaud to Craps. But the name more likely comes from crabs, the 16th-century British term for what we call snake eyes today—two dice that come up 1-1, a losing throw in Hazard, which the French played as Krabs.

In *Scarne on Dice*, games writer John Scarne speculates that blacks took up the game from the French in New Orleans in the early 1800s, simplifying and streamlining the rules into the American game of Craps. This spread up the Mississippi and through the rest of the country, arriving at gambling houses early in this century. So what is now considered a casino banking game began as a private game among friends, a pastime played with dice, cheaper and easier to carry than cards, a game that could be played on the run, snatching a few minutes from the daily grind. Craps is still a good family game, albeit an extended family, since the more players the merrier. Unlike casino Craps, the stakes at home can be counted in pennies or jelly beans.

Much of the allure of Craps lies in its language. All through the game, players talk to the dice, cajoling them, sweet-talking them into giving up their best numbers, kissing them, cursing them, nursing them. There is a lot of chatter in a Craps game, as in

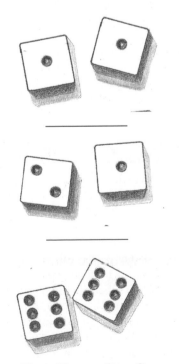

Three Ways to Crap Out

Poker, and nothing is written down. *Mouth bets* are binding. Once a player has made a bet, he has to go through with it, unless he calls it off by saying, "No bet" before the dice are rolled. But the other bettor has to hear him for the bet to be off.

A critical term in the game—to *fade*—gives credence to the French line of evolution. In French casino gambling games, a betting round ends when the banker says, "*Les jeux sont faites.*" ("All bets are laid.") Friends simply say, "*Faites!*" (pronounced fate), which sounds distinctly like fade. When the shooter's bet is faded —covered by other bettors—the Craps game begins.

In the movies, soldiers and street urchins shoot Craps anywhere they can find a patch of flat dirt to crouch around. In gambling houses, shooters circle round a table stenciled with a layout where bets are placed. At home, play it on the living room floor or around the kitchen table, anywhere you can shoot the two dice out of your hand and give them a little room to rock and roll. If you want, set up a large book or a cereal box as a *backstop* for the dice to bounce against.

There are no official rules for Craps, as there are for **Bridge** and **Euchre**, although there are as many variations on the theme as for any card game. According to generally accepted play, no one can touch the dice after they have come to a standstill until all bettors have seen them. If either die is cocked or rolls outside the designated center (the *boneyard*), the roll is void. Traditionally, the person who just lost the dice gets first chance to fade the next shooter's bet.

The Object of the Game:
To avoid crapping out.

The Play: Players agree on maximum bets before play begins. The first shooter decides what to bet on his roll and throws that number of counters into the boneyard, saying, for instance, "I'll shoot five. Who'll fade me?" This means he bets five counters that he'll win and asks who will bet against him or, in other words, cover his bet. Any player can say, "I'll take it" and fade (cover) the entire bet, putting down five counters. A player need not fade all of the bet, however. One player might say, "I'll take two"; and another, "I'll take three." The players who fade the bet must add their counters to the shooter's before he rolls. They are betting *wrong* (against the roll), and the shooter is betting *right*. (The shooter can withdraw, or *drag down,* any part of his bet that isn't faded.) When the shooter's bet is faded, the shooter shakes the dice and rolls them into the boneyard.

If the dice add up to 7 or 11 on the first roll, it is a *natural,* or a *nick,* and the shooter wins. He takes the counters that are in the center, or the pot, makes a new bet and shoots again.

If the dice add up to 2, 3 or 12, it is a *crap.* The shooter has *crapped,* and he loses the counters in the pot. He keeps the dice, however, makes a new bet and shoots again.

If the total is any other number—4, 5, 6, 8, 9, 10—that number becomes the shooter's *point.* He keeps rolling the dice until he rolls the same number again (*makes his point*) and wins. If he throws a 7 before he makes his point, he loses (*craps out,* or *sevens out*), and the dice pass to the next player. When a shooter loses, the bettors each take double the amount they put in the pot (their original bet and the shooter's stake).

When the shooter either wins a natural or makes his point, he wins all the counters in the pot (his own plus the faders' bets). He keeps the dice and may bet on a new round as he pleases. If he *shoots the works,* or *lets it ride,* he bets everything he won in the last round—his own stake and his winnings. The standard is for a player on a winning streak to let it ride three times, then drag down to the original bet. A shooter may also choose to end his winning streak at any time, passing the dice even though he has the right to throw again. A shooter loses the dice only if he fails to make his point or if he decides to stop betting.

As well as the opening stakes and fading, there are always *side bets* amongst other players around the table and between the shooter and other players as to whether or not the shooter will win. After rolling a point, the shooter might make a *come bet* in addition to his original stake, wagering that he'll make the point in the next series of rolls. A come bet is calculated as if there had been no previous rolls.

For instance, if a player rolls a point of 8, makes a come bet, then rolls an 11, this is a meaningless roll as far as the center bet is concerned—it can be lost only with a 7 or won with an 8—but the throw wins the come bet, since 11 is a natural.

Strategy: Two dice can come up 36 different ways. The most common combination is 7, because there are six ways that two dice can add up to that total: 1-6, 6-1, 2-5, 5-2, 3-4 and 4-3. This works to your advantage in the first throw but works against you when you are shooting to make your point. The most uncommon combinations are 2 and 12, because there is only one way to make either total: 1-1 and 6-6 (snake eyes and boxcars). Similarly, there are five ways to make 6 or 8, four ways to make 5 or 9, three ways to make 4 or 10 and two ways to make 3 or 11.

Commit this to memory before you bet any money in Craps—even pennies. Before you shoot the dice, you have almost even odds; the chances are 251 to 244 that the shooter will lose. But once you throw a point, the odds are definitely against you. If the point is 4 or 10, the odds are 2 to 1 against making it; if the point is 5 or 9, the odds are 3 to 2 against making it; if the point is 6 or 8, the odds are 6 to 5 against making it. ∾

Barbudi

- ◆ OTHER NAMES: **Barbooth and Even-Up Craps**
- ◆ NUMBER: **any number of players, two at a time**
- ◆ EQUIPMENT: **two peewee dice and two dice cups**

A BORDER-TOWN GAME, Barbudi is played mostly in cities such as Detroit, Chicago, Buffalo and Niagara Falls that snuggle up to Canada, where the game is traditionally a favorite among dicers, particularly of Middle Eastern descent. It has some betting features in common with **Craps,** but the winning combinations are unique, and the game is for two, although other players can watch and take part in the betting action on the side. Barbudi is best played on a long table with the two opponents at either end, each holding a dice cup and taking turns shooting the dice down the length of the table toward the other until one wins.

The Object of the Game: To throw a winning combination.

The Play: Players roll one die; the player throwing the highest number is the first shooter. The other player is the fader. The fader bets that the shooter won't win and places his bet (up to the limit established before the game) in the pot. The shooter then covers all or part of the bet; spectators may cover whatever is left. Either the shooter or the fader may also decide not to bet and pass the dice to the next two players. Others can make side bets on whether the shooter or the fader will win.

The shooter throws the two dice. If he rolls 3-3, 5-5, 6-6 or 6-5, he wins and takes the pot. If he throws 1-1, 2-2, 4-4 or 1-2, he loses. Any other throws don't count. If the shooter loses with 1-2, he keeps the dice. If the shooter loses with a pair, the dice pass to the fader, who throws. If the fader wins, he takes the pot; if he throws a losing or meaningless combination, the dice pass back to the shooter. The two continue to alternate until someone throws a winning combination.

The Score: Barbudi is an all-or-nothing proposition. All throws are meaningless except the following:

If the shooter or the fader throws 3-3, 5-5 or 6-6, he wins and keeps the dice.

If the shooter or the fader throws 6-5, he wins, but in both cases, the shooter gets the dice.

If the fader throws 1-1, 2-2 or 4-4, he loses, and the shooter gets the dice.

If the shooter throws 1-2, he loses, but he keeps the dice and continues to roll as long as he wins.

If the shooter throws 1-1, 2-2 or 4-4, he loses, and the fader becomes the shooter. If two are playing, they simply switch roles; if there are more people who want to play, the fader becomes the shooter, and the next person in line to play becomes the fader. ❧

Poker Dice

- ◆ NUMBER: any number of players, but five is best
- ◆ EQUIPMENT: a dice cup, five poker dice and counters

POKER DICE IS especially popular in Central America, where leather dice cups are sold with a secret compartment in the bottom, to store the specially marked dice.

The Object of the Game:
To get the best possible poker hand in three throws of the dice.

The Play:
Each player in turn rolls the five dice and picks out all, none or some of the dice to keep toward a poker hand. The rest of the dice are rolled again. After the second roll, the player may stand pat or roll all or some of the remaining dice one last time. Following the third roll, the player declares her final hand, returns the dice to the dice cup and passes it to the next player.

When everyone has rolled a poker hand, the best hand wins. (As the round progresses, players have to remember only the best hand.) In case of a tie, the players throw a play-off round. If playing for counters, each person antes one or more counters before the round, and the best hand wins the pot.

The Score:
The rank of poker "hands" in dice is the same as that in the card game of **Poker** except for five of a kind. With Poker Dice, flushes and straights count, as indicated by the scoring system, and within each category, the highest number wins. The best poker hand wins each round, and each round is a *leg*. If there are two players, the winner of two out of three legs wins the game and takes the accumulated pot. With more players, everyone plays two legs, and the winner of the first leg plays a deciding game with the winner of the second leg.

Variations:
Poker Dice played with standard dice is sometimes called **Indian Dice**. The 1 is ranked high like an Ace, so the numbers rank high to low, 1-6-5-4-3-2. In this version, flushes and straights don't count. Rank the hands from lowest to highest, as in Poker Dice.

With Indian Dice, you can play **Deuces Wild**, in which the 2 can count as any number, or **Aces Wild**, in which the 1 counts as any number. Players can also agree that before a roll, each shooter can declare the number which is wild for that round.

In another variation much like **Sevens**, the first player is allowed three throws, but if he stops after the first or second throw, the other players in the round must do the same, taking only as many throws as the first shooter. ❧

Two Pairs in Poker Dice

Liar's Dice

- NUMBER: **a rare game of dice for two; more can play, but the game is boring with more than four**
- EQUIPMENT: **a dice cup, five dice—either poker dice or regular dice (1 or Ace high)—and 10 counters per player**
- DESCRIPTION: **a combination of Poker Dice and I Doubt It**
- COMPLEXITY: **best for adults and kids 8 to 12 who love the subterfuge and whose hands are big enough to hide the dice; only fun if played fast and loose**

As IN MOST CARD and dice games, variations on this game abound, but a favorite way to play is to incorporate the principles of **I Doubt It** with a standard game of **Poker Dice.** Some gambling clubs have specially built screens that separate opponents in Liar's Dice so that players cannot see each other's dice over the partition. At home, two players can set a large hardcover book between them, or groups can play simply by throwing under the dice cup. Half the fun, after all, is trying to keep your hand secreted from peering eyes.

The Object of the Game: To be the last player with a counter; to avoid a penalty by successfully lying about your poker hand; to catch other players' lies.

The Play: Each player starts with 10 counters. Players throw the dice, and the one with the highest poker hand shoots first. Players each ante one or more counters into the pot. The first shooter tosses the five dice, letting them come to rest under the dice cup. Carefully, without allowing anyone to see, he peeks at the dice and selects the ones he wants to keep. He hides these under his hand, throws the rest and continues for three throws of the dice, always sheltering the dice from view as he selects his final hand. After three throws, he declares his hand, but as in I Doubt It, he is not required to tell the truth. He can understate or exaggerate the value of his hand; either way, it is a lie. (Players must declare in full, saying, "Four Aces" or "Full House, three fours and two kings.")

The other player (or the player on the shooter's left) can accept the call or lift the dice cup to expose the dice. If the shooter was bluffing, the shooter puts a counter in the pot. If the shooter was telling the truth, the other player pays a counter to the pot. If the next player in turn decides to accept the shooter's call and not expose the dice, then the dice pass to her, and she has three throws to improve on his hand—or, more correctly, to bluff the player on *her* left into believing that she has bettered it. Play continues around the table until only one person has a counter left. That person—the best liar—wins the pot.

Dudo

- OTHER NAMES: **commercially marketed as Perudo**
- NUMBER: **two or more players; five or six is best**
- EQUIPMENT: **a set of five dice and a dice cup for each player and a reserve cup for discarded dice**
- DESCRIPTION: **a lighthearted bluffing game like Liar's Dice**
- DURATION: **like Go, it takes only moments to learn but is complex enough to hold players' interest for hours**

ACCORDING TO LEGEND, King Atahualpa of the Incas taught this game to the Spanish conquistador Pizarro more than 400 years ago, but it wasn't until recently that it attracted widespread European attention. In 1990, Cosmo Fry (of Fry's Cocoa fame) began to market the game in England as Perudo. Fry calls it the "Liar's Dice of the Andes," and one enthusiastic player exclaimed, "It's the second most addictive thing ever to come out of South America." The game, which comes with leather dice cups and a woven Peruvian dice sack, is extraordinarily expensive, but it is just as much fun played with a few 99-cent sets of dice and some unbreakable, opaque kitchenware.

Essentially a guessing game, Dudo requires each player to estimate how many of a certain number on the dice are hidden under the other players' dice cups. For instance, with six players, there are a total of 30 dice in play, so the chances are that when everyone rolls, there are five 6s, five 4s, and so on. In reality, of course, there could be thirty 6s. This is complicated by the fact that 1 is referred to as Ace, and Aces are wild; they can be any number at all. A game of luck and moxie, the only skill comes in trying to read the faces of the other players and to figure out exactly when to call their bluff.

The Object of the Game: To estimate correctly the total number of dice on the table that show any given number; to be the last player with dice in your dice cup.

The Play: Players roll one die to

determine the order of play; the person with the highest number declares first.

All the players simultaneously shake their dice, then upend their dice cups on the table. Each person peeks at his or her own dice, being careful not to let anyone else see what was thrown. The first player makes his call, declaring how many dice on the table show a particular number; for instance, the player with the hand illustrated below might declare seven 2s, even though he has only one. The player to his left can declare a higher amount of the same number (for instance, nine 2s), or he can declare the same or a higher amount of a larger number (for instance, seven 3s). The first player may not call Aces. Subsequent players are allowed to call Aces, but because there are no wild numbers to consider (1s themselves are wild), the guess is reduced by half. For instance, after a player declares seven 2s, the next player might declare four Aces. The person following then has the option of declaring five Aces or nine of any other number (double the number of Aces plus one).

Whenever a player believes that the previous call is impossible or unlikely, she can challenge it by saying "Dudo!" ("I doubt it!" in Spanish). As soon as a challenge is made, all the players expose their dice. All the dice that show either the last declared number or an Ace are counted. For instance, if the challenged player declared nine 5s, then all the 5s and all the 1s are counted. If there are nine or more, the player's call was correct. The challenger loses a die, putting it in the reserve dice cup. If the count reveals less than nine, the challenger is proved right and the challenged player loses a die. The challenge ends the round.

The player who lost a die begins the next round. In each round, one player loses a die, so the odds of a certain number showing up gradually decrease. Play continues until one player is reduced to one die. This person is *palafico*, and he automatically starts the next round. (Each player is palafico only once—in the round immediately after he loses his fourth die.) In a palafico round, 1s are not wild, and the palafico can begin with a call of Aces if he wants. Whatever the opening call, the other players must call a higher quantity of the same number; the number doesn't change during the round. For instance, if the palafico declares four 2s, the next player must declare five or more 2s; the player after that calls six or more 2s, and so on, until someone challenges a call. (When the game is reduced to two players, the palafico rules are waived.)

A player who loses her fifth die leaves the game. The person on her left starts the next round. The last player still in the game wins. ❧

Dudo

6

The Boneyard: Dominoes Games

WHEN THE HEROES OF Rabelais' *Gargantua and Pantagruel* disembarked on Sharper's Island, they found it inhabited by the 21 Devils of Chance—one for each of the distinct couplings that would eventually appear if two dice were rolled again and again. Fusing together the top faces of these dice after each roll produces dominoes. A standard set of 28, the basis of most games, includes tiles that represent the 21 pairings of two dice plus the seven unions of a blank—with a die and with itself.

Given the long history of dice, it seems odd, then, that dominoes took so long to appear. They showed up in Italy in the early part of the 18th century, 200 years after Rabelais wrote his fable, and spread from there throughout Europe, arriving in England with prisoners returned from the Seven Years' War, only a decade before American independence. Dominoes dating back to 1120 A.D. have been found in China, but even this is relatively recent, considering that dicing games can be traced into prehistory. Traders and travelers such as Marco Polo likely brought dominoes from the Far East to Europe, and immigrants carried them across the Atlantic to North America. The other

Chinese tile game, **Mah Jongg**, came to this continent from the opposite direction, traveling across the Pacific from Shanghai to San Francisco early in this century.

Originally carved from ivory and ebony, dominoes today are primarily made of wood, though the game is gradually succumbing to the plastic revolution. Most are imported from China: pressed hardwood tiles generally a quarter-inch thick, three-quarters of an inch wide and an inch and a half long. One side of the rectangle is uniformly black, embossed with a fanciful design (lying facedown on a table, they look like angular Oreo cookies). The flip side is divided into two equal squares, each square impressed with the face of a die, white spots against a black background. The white-on-black probably named the game: in French, *domino* is a priest's winter hood, black on the outside, white on the inside.

Technically, Dominoes is the name of the game; the pieces are sometimes called tiles or stones, but usually bones. Each half-tile is called an *end*. An end with no number is a *blank*, and a tile with the same number on both ends is a *doublet*. The highest-ranking tile in a standard set of 28 is the six doublet, giving the set itself the name *double sixes*. You can also buy *double nines*, a set of 55 dominoes that goes to nine, and even *double twelves*. (Inuit, who play their own form of Dominoes, use a set with 148 pieces.) Some games, especially those played with more than four players, call for the larger sets, but for most family play, the standard double sixes will suffice.

The Chinese call dominoes "dotted cards," and both the terminology and individual games reflect a curious combination of the genres. The bones are *shuffled* before each game—turned facedown and slid amongst each other to mix up the numbers. (On large bones, a small metal stud is embedded midway between the ends so that when they are shuffled, they spin easily without marring the faces.) All players have the right to shuffle, one at a time, before the game begins. Players then *draw* their bones at random and set them on edge in front of them so that no one can see their *hands*, just as in cards. (Experts hold as many bones as possible in the palm of one hand, which works for five or six but is uncomfortable for all but Paul Bunyan in games where players have up to a dozen at a time.) The bones that remain facedown after the draw are the *boneyard*. When a player has no appropriate bones in his

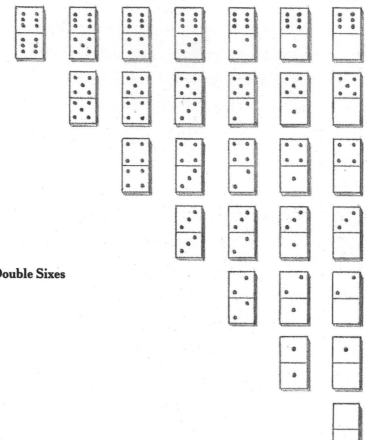

A Set of Double Sixes

hand, he must *dig in the boneyard*, which is the same as drawing from the stockpile in cards, though the expression sounds a little more macabre than "Go fish!"

All 28 bones makes up a *deck*, and as in cards, the deck is arranged by *suits*. There are seven suits, as illustrated: 1s, 2s, 3s, 4s, 5s, 6s and the blank suit. Each end of a bone belongs to a suit, which means that every bone belongs to two suits. For instance, the 2-6 bone is the sixth one in the 2 suit and also the second one in the 6 suit. The exceptions, of course, are the doublets, which belong to only one suit. When comparing two bones, the one with the most spots (both ends added together) is the *heavier* bone; the other is the *lighter*. When you draw your bones at the beginning of a game of Dominoes, arrange them in suits, running from heavier on the left to lighter on the right.

(Switch this order from time to time so that your opponents cannot tell where your strong suits lie.)

With 28 bones, there are 1,184,040 possible hands. You will rarely, if ever, draw two hands the same. Each new hand must be played for itself. At first, Dominoes is a game of pure luck; you are at the mercy of the bones you draw. But as the game unfolds and more bones are exposed, it shifts to a game of calculation and strategy, in which you plan moves that foil your opponent and advance your own cause based on which bones you figure the other player holds in her hand. It takes a few rounds to get used to seeing the bones in suits and keeping track of which bones in the 6 suit haven't been played and which in the 5 suit your opponent might hold. The two most complete books on Dominoes are written by a mathematician and a banker, which suggests the kind of logic these games hone.

After the bones are shuffled, the first one exposed in play is called the *set*. The player who lays the first bone on the table is called the player *on set*. There are two ways to determine who is on set. All the players draw one bone from the boneyard; the heaviest or lightest bone sets in the first hand, as the players decide. If you are playing partners, those who draw the two heaviest bones play together. If the total is a tie, for instance, 6-4 and 5-5, the bone with the heavier end (6-4) is considered higher. Blanks count zero. The other way to decide who goes first is to call out doublets, starting with the highest: "Does anyone have double sixes? Double fives?" The person with the heaviest doublet starts the game. (The double blank is the lowest-ranking bone.) If none of the players has a doublet, they take turns digging in the boneyard until one draws a doublet and starts the game.

The principle of Dominoes is simple. After the set, the second player matches one end of a bone in her hand with one end of the set on the table. Depending on the game, players match suits, playing a 6 from the hand against a 6 on the table, or they make matches that add up to a given number, playing a 2 against a 5 or a 3 against a 4 to add up to seven. Play moves clockwise around the table, or if two people are playing, they take turns, each player matching a bone to one of the two exposed, or *open*, ends of the *layout*—the growing chain of bones on the table.

Traditionally, doublets are laid *à cheval*, or crosswise, to the layout. This does not create two open ends on that side instead of one; it simply makes the doublets easier to spot. When a bone is placed on the other side of the doublet, it is laid perpendicular to the doublet, in line with the rest of the chain. If, as the layout grows, players run out of room for a straight length of chain, they can place a bone at right angles (not crosswise), so the chain turns a corner. This still leaves only two open ends against which to match your bones.

Beyond this, there are very few rules. In general, if a player has a playable bone, he must lay it on the table. If he doesn't have one in hand, he draws from the boneyard. In most games, he keeps drawing until he gets a playable bone; in some games, there is a limit to the number of bones each player can draw in a turn. The boneyard is not usually emptied completely. With two players, the boneyard is closed when there are two bones left; with three players or more, it is closed when only one remains. This ensures that a player cannot figure out exactly what the others hold. When the boneyard is closed, a player who cannot play from her hand, says, "Go," and the others continue taking their turns. She is not out of the game, however. When it is her turn again, she may be able to make use of the bones still in her hand.

Dominoes games are of two basic types. *Block games* are a race, the object being to rid your hand of bones before your opponent does. You give her as few opportunities to set and make her draw as often as possible while, at the same time, playing your hand so that you can always make a match and rarely need to draw. A favorite block tactic, and one that usually ends the game, is to make both open ends the same suit—a suit in which all the bones are either in the layout or in your hand. In *point games*, the matches you make during the game not only use up bones but score points too, so the strategy shifts from running an all-out race to doing some skillful footwork before the finish line.

The first player who succeeds in playing, or *posing*, all her bones declares, "*Domino!*" which signals the end of the game. In the late 1800s, the game was so popular that the cry "Domino!" became slang for "Finished!" and could be heard in classrooms across the country. After one declares Domino, the other players add up the spots on the bones still in their hands. The total either counts against each player or goes to the winner as her score. Games are usually played to a specified number of points.

If the game is *blocked*—no one can make another move—the hand ends and the game is *closed*, even though everyone still has bones. Since all players have bones in their hands, the winner is the one with the lowest total of spots—the *lightest hand*. In the event of a tie, the bones are shuffled, and the players each draw a tile: the lightest wins. In either case, the winner scores the difference between the total of his spots and the total of his opponent(s).

One final caution: Although the game uses only 28 little bones, it can take up a lot of space. The living room rug is not ideal; the bones in your hand will tip over. A card table will do, but a large kitchen table or an expanse of bare, smooth floor is best. When the game is over, stack the bones on end like miniature high rises and rediscover the domino effect.

Block and Draw Dominoes

- ◆ NUMBER: **two to five players**
- ◆ EQUIPMENT: **one set of double sixes (28 bones)**
- ◆ DESCRIPTION: **the original and the simplest game of Dominoes**
- ◆ TIP: **the best way to learn the fundamentals of play**

THIS IS THE basic game of Dominoes, played by matching the bones according to suits. If the pastime is unfamiliar, play a few rounds before moving on to more complicated games. Block and Draw will initiate you to the calculations and strategies unique to Dominoes. Be forewarned: The simplicity is entirely superficial.

The Object of the Game: To match ends according to suits; to be the first to call "Domino!"

The Play: Shuffle the bones. With two players, each draws seven bones. If more than two are playing, subtract the number of players from 8 to determine the number of bones each player draws. For instance, five players would each draw three bones.

The player with the highest doublet sets, laying the doublet faceup on the table. The second player lays a bone perpendicular to the doublet, matching the doublet's suit. For instance, in the example illustrated below, 4-4 was set, then 4-3 was played against it. The next player had two choices: he could match the 3 of the new bone or the 4 on the other side of the doublet. Since he had no 3s, he played the 5-4. Play moves clockwise around the table (or back and forth between two opponents), each player in turn matching one of the two open ends of the layout.

If a player does not have a bone that matches either end of the layout, she can draw from the boneyard until she gets a match. With two players, two bones must be left in the boneyard; with more, one remains in the boneyard. If a player does not have a match and no more bones can be dug from the boneyard, he says, "Go," and the other players continue to take turns as long as they can.

The first player to get rid of all his bones calls "Domino!" and wins the hand. Otherwise, the game ends when no one can make another move. After scoring, turn the bones facedown, shuffle, and draw a new hand. The loser goes first, setting her highest bone. There are usually several hands in a game.

The Score: When a player calls "Domino!" the others add up the spots on the bones still in their hands (blanks score zero). The total is the winner's score. If the game is closed (no one can move), the players each add up the spots on the bones left in their hands. The lightest hand wins. The winner earns the difference be-

tween her score and the scores of the other players. For instance, if three players are left with bones totaling 12, 15 and 20, respectively, the person with 12 wins, and her score is 3 (15-12) plus 8 (20-12), for a total of 11. The first player to reach 50 or 100 wins the game.

Strategy: Keep in hand the bones that give you the most options. If you have four or more bones with ends in one suit, try to make both open ends of the chain in that suit—your opponents are unlikely to have any. By forcing them to dig in the boneyard, you will increase their hands. With luck, the boneyard will be closed by the time you have to draw, and you can simply pass, hoping that your opponents' next plays will give you a chance to match your remaining bones. Early in the game, you can dig in the boneyard to supplement your hand, but later in the game, do your best to unload your heaviest bones so that you will have few points to give to the winner.

Block and Draw can also be played offensively. If you have a run in one suit, try to block the game early by playing that suit on both ends of the layout. Your opponents will have to dig the boneyard empty, and when the game is closed, you will reap a high score from what they have drawn.

Variations: For very young children, simplify the game even further by eliminating the draw and playing only **Block Dominoes**. Divide the bones evenly between opponents, two players taking 13 each, three players 9

Block and Draw Dominoes

Cross Dominoes

Double Cross Dominoes

each, and four players 6 each. Always leave one or two bones out of play. Take turns laying down bones until one player calls "Domino!" or no one can make another move. This is a game of pure luck, since fate decides whether the bones to unblock the game are in the boneyard—or in the other players' hands.

Cross Dominoes increases the number of open ends from two to four. The first player sets her highest doublet. In the next four turns, players match bones to the middle of both sides as well as both ends of the doublet, creating a cross. For instance, in the game illustrated above, a 5-5 was set; the next players laid down 5-3, 5-6, 5-2 and 5-1 in turn, creating four open ends with 3, 6, 2 and 1 available for matches. No other bones can be played until the doublet has been completed with the four bones that create the cross. Cross Dominoes is a faster game with more options; it also takes up less space.

Double Cross Dominoes is played exactly like Cross Dominoes with the added rule that a doublet must be played crosswise on one arm of the cross before play can proceed on any

of the four open ends. For example, in the game illustrated at lower left, the 2-2 was set and matched with 2-1, 2-3, 2-6 and 2-4. Players had to draw until someone could play a doublet on one arm of the cross. Once the 3-3 was laid down, all four ends were open for play.

Maltese Cross Dominoes is the most trying of these variations, one that can empty the boneyard in a flurry of digging early in the game. The opening doublet is set and four bones matched to it to create a cross. Doublets must then be played crosswise on each arm of the cross before play can proceed. For instance, in the illustration below, before the 1-6 could be laid down, doublets had to be played on all arms of the cross. Continue as for Block and Draw.

Sebastopol is Maltese Cross Dominoes played with four people and without a draw. After the shuffle, each player takes seven bones, leaving none in the boneyard. The player with the 6-6 sets. Play moves clockwise around the table, creating a Maltese cross, as above, then players match on the four open ends. If a player has no match, he says "Go," and the

Maltese Cross Dominoes

Double Nine Cross Dominoes

shuffled, then four players draw 13 each, five draw 11 each, six draw 9 each, seven draw 7, eight or nine draw 6, and ten players draw 5 each. The player who has the double nine sets; if no one has 9-9, the bones are reshuffled and redrawn. After the 9-9 is set, players lay matching bones on both ends and each side to make a cross, then diagonally in the four angles between the arms to make an eight-pointed star, as illustrated below. Matches can be made on other arms before the star is complete. Play continues clockwise around the table, matching on eight open ends, until a player calls "Domino!" or the game is closed. ∾

turn passes to the next player.

Double Nine Cross Dominoes is a good family game for four or more. Use a set of double nines (55 bones). Up to three players draw seven bones each to start; four or more players draw five bones each. The person with the highest doublet sets, then bones are matched to the two ends and the two sides, as in Cross Dominoes. (All but two bones can be drawn from the boneyard.) Play proceeds with matches on all four open ends, and every time a doublet is played, two more ends are opened for matches. For example, in the game illustrated above, 3-3 was set, and play proceeded on the two sides and the two ends of the doublet. After the 7-7 was played, 7-4 was laid on its other side. The ends of the 7-7 are now open, so the next player can lay down 7-0.

Finally, **Cyprus** is also played with a set of double nines. The bones are

Cyprus

Blind Hughie

- ◆ OTHER NAMES: **Blind Dominoes and Billiton**
- ◆ NUMBER: **two to five players**
- ◆ EQUIPMENT: **one set of double sixes (28 bones)**
- ◆ COMPLEXITY: **all luck, absolutely no strategy; kids love it**

THE NAMES Blind Hughie and Blind Dominoes have an obvious genesis: a player doesn't see her hand until she plays it. But Billiton is a little more exotic and mysterious. The anglicized spelling of Belitung, a major tin-producing island off the former Dutch colony of Sumatra, Billiton may be an imperialist pastime or an Oriental import.

The Object of the Game:

To match ends according to suits; to be the first to call "Domino!"

The Play: Shuffle the bones facedown. Draw to determine who sets; the heaviest bone plays first.

Reshuffle, and deal the bones equally to all players: 14 each to two players, 9 each to three players (one left over), 7 each to four players and 5 each to five players (three left over).

Players do not look at their bones but arrange them facedown in a vertical row, long sides flush. With two or four players, the heaviest bone from the draw sets. If there are leftovers after the deal, one is set, and the person who drew the heaviest bone plays first.

The first player turns over the top

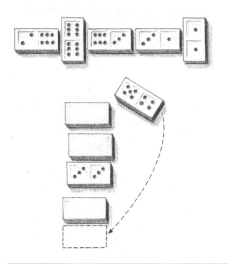

bone in his row. If it matches the set, he plays it and turns over the next bone in his row, playing it if he can.

When he flips over a bone that does not match, he puts it facedown at the bottom of the row. (Unplayable doublets are moved to the bottom of the row but left faceup.)

Play moves clockwise around the

Blind Hughie

table. The first player to get rid of all her bones calls "Domino!" and wins the accumulated spot total of the other players. If the layout is blocked, the player with the lightest hand wins, scoring the difference between her hand and the hand of each of the other players. ❧

Bergen

- ◆ NUMBER: two to four players, each playing alone
- ◆ EQUIPMENT: one set of double sixes (28 bones)
- ◆ DESCRIPTION: like a Block and Draw game with points; some elementary strategy involved

ALTHOUGH *bergen* is German for mountains, old games books refer to this as "the Bergen game." This may indicate that the game comes from Bergen, Norway, or from Bergen op Zoom, a coastal town in the Netherlands, which suggests a Dutch origin for both Bergen and the preceding game of Billiton (**Blind Hughie**). As in all **Block and Draw** games, the ends are matched according to suit, but in this case, a player scores points if he also manages to leave both open ends in the same suit—a *double-header*. If one open end is the same suit as a doublet on the other, he scores for a *triple-header*.

The Object of the Game: To match ends according to suits; to win points by making both ends the same suit; to be the first to call "Domino!"

The Play: Shuffle the bones, and draw six each. The player holding the lowest doublet sets and scores for the first double-header, since both open ends are the same suit. Play continues, matching a bone in hand with one of the open ends according to suit. Play-

ers who do not have a playable bone draw one, but only one, from the boneyard. Two bones always remain facedown in the boneyard. Players score every time they lay down a bone that makes a double-header or a triple-header. For instance, in the game illustrated below, Timothy scored a double-header for starting with 1-1. Bill laid down 1-3, then Timothy played 1-4, both scoring no points. When Bill laid down 3-4, he scored for a double-header (4s on each

end). Next, Timothy will play 4-4 and score for a triple-header—a doublet and an open end all of the same suit. Play continues until one person calls "Domino!" or the game is closed. Several hands are played to reach the target score.

The Score: Players score 2 points for a doublet, 2 points for a double-header and 3 points for a triple-header. Domino scores 1 point. If the game finishes without a Domino, the player without any doublets earns the game point. If all players have doublets, the one with the lightest doublet scores. If no one has a doublet, the lightest hand scores the game point. The first player to reach 15 wins. ❧

Bergen

Matador

- ◆ OTHER NAMES: **Russian Dominoes and All Sevens**
- ◆ NUMBER: **two to four players**
- ◆ EQUIPMENT: **one set of double sixes (28 bones)**
- ◆ DESCRIPTION: **essentially Block and Draw Dominoes, but players must be able to add to seven**

RUSSIAN DOMINOES has one rule that varies significantly from conventional play: a person can draw from the boneyard even when he has a playable bone in hand. This small element of choice shifts the weight of the game from luck to strategy and makes Matador as engaging as **Euchre** or **Cribbage**. Instead of matching ends according to suits (6 to 6, 3 to 3), players in this game match ends that add up to seven (3 to 4, 6 to 1 or 5 to 2, as illustrated at the bottom of the page). The game takes its name from four special bones called *matadors*: bones that add up to seven by themselves (3-4, 5-2, 6-1) and the double blank. A matador acts as a wild card or a trump. It can be played at any time and is the only bone that can unblock an end which has been closed with a blank.

The Object of the Game:
To match ends that add up to seven; to be the first to call "Domino!"

The Play:
Shuffle the bones. Two players draw seven bones each; three or four players draw five each. The player with the highest doublet sets, and others follow in turn clockwise around the table. In this game, doublets are played end to end, in line with the others, rather than crosswise. Players may lay down a bone only if the matching ends add up to seven. For instance, a 6 against a 1, a 4 against a 3 and a 5 against a 2. Only a matador can be played against a blank. Matadors can be played anytime, regardless of which suits are the open ends. Like the doublets, matadors are laid down in line with the layout; the player decides which end to leave open. Players can dig in the boneyard even if they have playable bones. A player without a playable bone must draw until he gets one or until the boneyard is empty of all but two bones. The game ends when one player empties her hand and calls "Domino!" or when no one can play another bone.

The Score: Making sevens is the matching requirement; it does not earn points. Matador is scored like conventional **Block and Draw Dominoes**: the player who calls "Domino!" wins the spot total of the bones that are left in opponents' hands. If the game is blocked, the player with the lightest hand wins,

Russian Cross Dominoes

Matador

scoring the difference between the spot total of her hand and that of each of her opponents. The first player to reach 50 or 100 wins.

Variations: Players can agree to lay doublets in line with the layout but to lay matadors crosswise against a blank. In this case, only a blank can be played against a matador.

Russian Cross is played like Matador, except bones are played against the two ends and the two sides of the set bone to create a cross, as in **Cross Dominoes**. Play then proceeds with players making matches on four open ends, instead of two. For example, in the game illustrated on the previous page, 4-4 was set, and 3-2, 3-5, 3-6 and 3-1 were played against it before any of the arms were extended. The blank doublet cannot be set to start the game, since this would use up all four matadors in the first few plays.

Russian Double Cross adds the rule that a doublet must be played against one arm of the cross before any of the other arms are open for matches, just as in **Double Cross Dominoes**. Remember to play all doublets in line with the layout, rather than crosswise as in Block and Draw.

In **Triangle Cross**, the person with the blank doublet begins. Matadors must be played on three faces of the doublet before play can proceed. Once the three matadors are played, both ends and both sides are open for play.

Double-Nine Matador uses the 55 bones of a set of double nines, so this is a game that more than four can play. Six or fewer players draw seven bones each; more than six draw five. The game is exactly like Matador with one crucial difference: instead of seven, the magic number is 10. There are six matadors (5-5, 6-4, 7-3, 8-2, 9-1 and the double blank), and matching ends must add up to 10. This game is usually played to 200 points. ∽

All Fives

- ◆ OTHER NAMES: **Muggins**
- ◆ NUMBER: **two, three or four players**
- ◆ EQUIPMENT: **one set of double sixes (28 bones)**
- ◆ DESCRIPTION: **a point game that requires simple math; some strategy**

THIS GAME represents a fundamental shift from previous games. In **Matador** and the basic **Block and Draw** games, players are only concerned with the ends of the bones which touch—they have to be the same suit, or they have to add up to a certain number. In All Fives, bones are matched according to suit, but in playing each new bone, you score points if the two open ends add up to a multiple of five.

The Object of the Game: To match ends according to suit; to make the open ends add up to a multiple of five; to get rid of your bones first.

The Play: Shuffle the bones. Each player draws seven bones if two are playing, five if three or four are playing. The highest doublet sets, then play moves clockwise around the table. Each person plays a bone, matching ends of the same suit but trying, whenever possible, to make the open ends of the layout add up to 5, 10, 15 or 20. Doublets are laid crosswise and count their full value. For instance, in the game illustrated below, Alice begins (A1) by laying down 5-5 and scoring, because the bone adds up to 10. Bob (B1) plays 5-0 and also scores for making 10. Alice plays 5-4, Bob plays 0-2, then Alice plays 4-4, again making 10 (4+4+2). Bob plays 4-3 and scores 5 (3+2), Alice places 2-6, then Bob lays down 6-6 and scores 15 (3+6+6).

The blank doublet scores zero but can be laid down to take advantage of a previous score. For instance, if one end is 5-5, a double or single blank laid on the other open end scores 10. If a player makes a multiple of five without noticing it, any player can call "Muggins!" as soon as the next play is made and score the unobservant player's points. When a player cannot follow suit, he draws from the bone-

| B4 | A4 | B2 | B1 | A1 | A2 | A3 | B3 |
| 15 pts. | | | 10 pts. | 10 pts. | | 10 pts. | 5 pts. |

All Fives

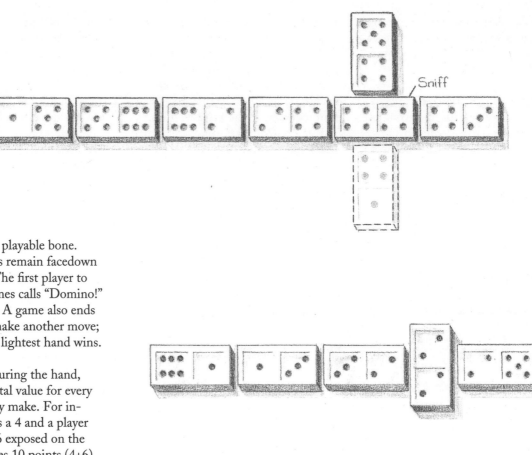

Sniff

yard until he gets a playable bone. (The last two bones remain facedown in the boneyard.) The first player to get rid of all his bones calls "Domino!" and the hand ends. A game also ends when no one can make another move; the player with the lightest hand wins.

The Score: During the hand, players score the total value for every multiple of five they make. For instance, if one end is a 4 and a player lays a bone with a 6 exposed on the other end, she scores 10 points (4+6). If 5-5 is the first set, the player scores 10. The highest possible score in one turn is 20 points: 4-4 on one end and 6-6 on the other.

At the end of the hand, players who still have bones add up the spots and round the total to the nearest multiple of five (1 and 2 are rounded downward; 3 or more are rounded upward). The player who calls "Domino!" wins the rounded-off points of her opponents. For instance, the winner gets 10 points from a player with a spot total of 12 and also 10 points from one with a spot total of 8. The player with the lightest hand wins a blocked game and scores her adversaries' totals minus her own, rounded to a multiple of five. The player who reaches 100 first wins.

Strategy: In this game, the ability to score usually leapfrogs around the table. When one player scores, the total of the open ends is divisible by five; the next player is unlikely to be able to lay down a bone that will also make the open ends divisible by five. The 6-1, 5-5 and 5-0 are valuable bones, because they can turn an opponent's

scoring opportunity into a scorer for you too. For instance, if the last person scored and one open end is 4, the other open end is either a 1 or a 6; the 6-1 will score, whichever way it is played. Your opponent is now in the unenviable position of having to break up the even fives.

Timing is important. Save these valuable bones until the point in the game when you can most benefit from the switch in tempo. Drawing from the boneyard can also be useful. If you have more bones than your opponent, try to maneuver the last plays so that you can make several in a row while she passes. If you have a good hand, do not try to go out quickly but, rather, try to prolong the game so that you can score as often as possible before it is over. If your hand is not good, you might play defensively, trying to block the game early before your opponent has a chance to score.

Variations: Two simple varia-

tions—**All Threes** and **Threes and Fives**—are both played exactly as All Fives, except in the first case, the object is to make the open ends add up to multiples of three, and in the second, to make the open ends add up to multiples of either three or five.

A more challenging variation is **Sniff**. Sniff is shuffled, dealt and played exactly like All Fives, except for one important difference. Before the game begins, players draw from the boneyard; the player with the heaviest bone sets first, and he may set any bone he likes. The first doublet, regardless of when it is set, is called the *sniff*. For instance, in the game illustrated above (top), the 6-5 was set, followed by 6-2, 5-1, 2-4 and then the sniff, 4-4. It may be placed end to end in line with the layout, in which case only its open end counts. Here, the player placed it end to end so that she could score 5 (4+1). Alternatively, the sniff may be placed crosswise, in which case the total value counts. In the next game illustrated on the previous page (bottom), a player laid the first doublet (2-2) crosswise so that he could score 10 (6+2+2). Once a sniff is played crosswise, the two new ends continue to count toward the multiples of five in each subsequent play. When the next player lays down 2-5 against the side of the doublet, she scores 15 (6+2+2+5). If she had laid 2-5 against one end of the sniff, she would not score (6+5+2 = 13).

Whether the sniff is laid crosswise or in line, it can be built on with other bones, creating a four-armed layout and four open ends that count toward multiples of five. For instance, in the top illustration, after the sniff (4-4) is laid, the next player lays the 4-5 against the side of the doublet and scores 10 (1+5+4). The next player lays 4-3 against the open end of the sniff and scores nothing, but the following player lays down the 4-1 on the other side of the sniff and scores 10 (1+5+3+1) Only the first doublet is a sniff; other doublets may be laid either in line or crosswise to the chain, as benefits the player, but no more ends are opened for play.

In Sniff, players don't have to play when they have a playable bone. They may dig in the boneyard, or when the boneyard is closed, they may pass, even though they have bones to play. (Players may agree to limit draws from the boneyard to one per turn.) The hand ends when one player calls "Domino!" or when none of the players are able, or willing, to play. In this case, the lightest hand wins and scores the total of the others' points, without subtracting his own. As in All Fives, players earn points for each multiple of five they make. Final scores at the end of each hand are rounded to the nearest five, and games usually go to 200 points. ∾

Five-Up

- ♦ NUMBER: two, three or four players; best as a four-handed partnership game
- ♦ EQUIPMENT: one set of double sixes (28 bones)
- ♦ DESCRIPTION: like Bridge, easy to learn but difficult to master
- ♦ COMPLEXITY: requires addition, subtraction, division and a calculating mind
- ♦ TIP: takes All Fives a step beyond Sniff

THE SUBJECT OF an entire book by an Italian-American banker, Dominic Armanino, Five-Up is Dominoes for thinkers. It developed in the San Francisco area in the early part of this century and, 50 years later, was such a preferred noonhour pastime that the city's largest club built an entire separate floor to accommodate its Dominoes devotees. Fortunes wax and wane throughout the game, and as Armanino says, "The luck and skill factors are happily so proportioned that defeat can always be attributed to luck, and victory to skill." Games for two or three are described under Variations; the directions below are for four people playing as partners.

The Object of the Game:
To match ends according to suit; to make open ends add up to a multiple of five; to be the first to go out.

The Play:
Shuffle the bones, and draw for partners, the two heaviest bones playing together. The player with the heaviest bone sets for the first hand; the set rotates clockwise for the rest of the hands in the game.

Reshuffle. Starting with the player on set and moving clockwise around the table, each player draws five bones. The first player may set any bone he chooses. Players take turns laying down bones, matching the ends according to suits and, as often as possible, making the open ends add up to five. Up to this point, Five-Up is like **All Fives.**

Doublets are always laid crosswise, and when another bone is laid against it on the other side, the doublet becomes a *spinner*. The two ends of the spinner are now open for play, although each is included in the count only after a bone has been played on it. For instance, in the game illustrated on the following page, 3-1 is on the table. The next player lays the 1-1 crosswise against the 1, scoring 5 (3+1+1). His opponent lays 1-2 on the other side of the doublet and scores 5 (3+2). He does not include the open ends of the doublet in the count, but the doublet has now become a spinner. The 1-5 is played on one open end of the spinner, scoring 10 (3+5+2). The fourth player lays 2-3 on the open 2; this adds up to 11 (3+5+3) and does not score. When 1-4 is laid on the last open end of the spinner, the player will score 15 (3+5+3+4). All four ends of the chain are open, and from this point on, at least four numbers must be included in every count. Each doublet played on the layout can become a spinner, opening more and more ends to the count.

If a player has no playable bones, she draws from the boneyard until she gets a bone she can play. One bone must be left in the boneyard facedown; after the boneyard is closed, players who cannot play pass.

The hand is over when one player calls "Domino!" or when play is blocked and no one can move.

The Score: Each multiple of five counts 1: 10 counts 2, 15 counts 3, 20 counts 4, and so on. When a hand is over, the player who declares "Domino!" wins 1 point for her team for every five spots left in the opponents' hands. (Round up or down to the nearest five.) If the game is blocked, the team with the lightest combined hands wins and earns 1 point for every five spots left in the losers' hands. Several hands are played until one team reaches 61. It is easiest to keep score on a cribbage board, recording points as they are totaled for each hand.

Strategy: The basic strategy is the same as for all Dominoes games: try to play bones which will force your opponents to draw from the boneyard, and try to go out first so that your opponents are left with a handful of bones. Along the way, try to score as often as possible and prevent your opponents from doing the same. When playing partners, if you cannot score, try to play to your partner's hand so that she can score.

Given the increased number of ends to play off, Five-Up calls for great attention. It is easy to overlook a count, and if your opponents notice, they declare "Muggins!" and score your points.

Hold onto the *kickers*, the bones Armanino calls the *sweethearts*, which automatically score after an opponent scores—the blanks, 5-5 and 6-1—as well as the singles that play off their own doublets to score (1-2, 2-4, 3-1, 4-3, 5-0 and 6-2). About half your hand will be kickers; play them to best advantage.

Doublets are a mixed blessing. They increase the number of playing ends, they give you more options if you are strong in that suit, but because both numbers are the same, there are only half as many places where a doublet can be played. Hold onto doublets to make them most useful, but watch what is played so that you aren't left holding an unplayable doublet after all bones of that suit are on the table. When you are on set, play a doublet if you have bones of a matching suit in your hand. There are four playable faces on every doublet—two sides and two ends—so the play is guaranteed to come back to you. Where possible, use the doublet to establish your strong suit, and play off it as long as you can. A doublet with no matching number in your hand is called a *lighthouse*.

Always try to think ahead and fig-

Five-Up

ure out which plays can be made on the bone you lay. Try to avoid playing to the kickers, which will turn the tempo of the game against your team. If your opponent can follow your play with a scoring play, the odds, according to Armanino, are 10 to 3 that he will earn the same score or more. Check the layout to see whether the bone that would score highest on your play has already been played; this makes your play safe. For example, suppose the open ends of the layout are 4, 3 and 5 with an unplayed open end of a 1-1 spinner. You hold a 5-5, 3-3 and 3-1. If you play the 3-3 for a score of 3 (3+3+4+5 = 15), your opponent could play the 3-6 and score 3 also (6+5+4 = 15). If you play your 3-1 on the 1-1, however, you would still score 3 (3+5+4+3 = 15), but the only possible scoring play after that is the 3-3 played in line—and that doublet is in your hand. Not only is the play safe, but if everyone else passes, you may be able to score two more times by playing the 3-3 in line, then the 5-5 in line. The doublet 5 is your kicker; play it last.

At all times, keep track of the total count of the open ends. This lets you

know which of your bones can score and helps you catch your opponents' missed scores, which you can then claim for yourself. Perhaps most important, it keeps the steady slap-click of the game going.

Because there are so many open ends, adding up the count can be a complicated business. Make a clockwise circuit around the layout adding up the spots on the open ends. Then add or subtract to find the nearest multiple of five. For instance, if the count adds up to 17, you need to subtract 2 to make 15 or add 3 to make 20. You can do this by changing the 6 to a 4 (playing 6-4) or changing the 1 to a 4 (playing 1-4). If you have more than one option—for instance, changing a 6 to a 4 or a 3 to a 1—think ahead and determine which is the best defensive play.

Variations: In Five-Up for two, players also draw five bones to begin. The boneyard is closed when only two remain facedown. The game is usually played to 21.

In **Seven-Toed Pete**, four players draw to determine who sets, then reshuffle the bones and draw seven each, instead of five, to begin the hand. Each person plays alone. The set must be a doublet or a scoring bone (2-3, 1-4, 5-0, 5-5, 6-4). If the first player cannot set, she passes, and the turn moves clockwise around the table until a player can set. Each time a player lays down a doublet or scores a point, he plays again. This creates a game with a different tempo and strategy, since players aim for sequences that can be laid down one after the other. When playing his last bone, a player must score if possible. If he plays a doublet or scores, the game does not end; the other players continue to lay down what they can, in turn, until play is blocked, then the lightest hand (or the team with the lightest combined hand) wins. If the player with one bone left cannot score, the round is closed, and the hands are tallied as in Five-Up. ❧

Mah Jongg

- NUMBER: four players (no partners); less pleasing variations for two or three
- EQUIPMENT: 136 Mah Jongg tiles (plus eight optional tiles), two dice, four wind disks and counters
- DESCRIPTION: like Rummy, but prettier—gin with tonic, a twist of lime and a hand-painted silk umbrella
- COMPLEXITY: a complex, fascinating and formal game that takes an hour to learn, a lifetime to master
- DURATION: in China, a hand takes five minutes (Slap! Click! Pung! Chow! Mah Jongg!); beginners should count on about an hour per hand, an evening for a round

MAH JONGG looks daunting. Few games have so many and such unfamiliar pieces. They look like the bones used in **Dominoes**, painted with Oriental characters and symbols that make the game at once enticing and intimidating. It is a bit of a shock, then, to discover that Mah Jongg (emphasis on the Mah with a soft French-sounding J in the Jongg) is a simple game much like **Pinochle** or **Gin Rummy**, in which players draw and discard, trying to reshape their hands into scoring combinations. The ritual of laying out the tableau and making the opening moves accounts for much of the game's charm.

Mah Jongg has been played in China for centuries. Typically, the rules varied from region to region and were rarely written down. Sometimes called the Game of Four Winds, it became popular in teahouses during the nationalistic fervor of the Boxer Rebellion and, by the early years of this century, was considered China's national pastime. Shortly after World War I, Joseph P. Babcock, an American representative of the Standard Oil Company in Shanghai, played a few rounds and enjoyed it so much that he simplified and codified the rules and published them as Mah Jongg, taking the name from the Chinese word for the mythical "bird of 100 intelligences," pictured on one of the tiles. He imported the exotic game to the United States and started one of the biggest fads in this continent's history. His little red book *Mah Jongg: The Fascinating Chinese Game* went through nine printings between 1920 and 1923. In 1922, he exported 131,400 Mah Jongg sets from Shanghai to the United States; the next year, 1.5 million. The game outsold radios. At its height, 15 million Americans were playing Mah Jongg, sitting in silk kimonos, sipping green tea from lacquered cups and listening to Eddie Cantor sing *Since Ma Is Playing Mah Jongg*.

Babcock's games were exquisite: hand-carved ivory or bone tiles painted with herons, bamboo stalks and delicate red-and-black Chinese characters. Each set arrived with four extra blank tiles and the promise that should you lose one, the company would happily carve you another if only you would tell them the design and include 20 cents return postage from Shanghai. The counters were slivers of dyed ivory, and the dice imperfect hand-fashioned cubes. The sets were housed in wooden boxes with dovetailed corners, the front hinged to reveal the full stack of 144 tiles, with a tray on top for the counters, dice and wind disks.

Mah Jongg's popularity was brief. By 1924, the game was in steep decline, its devotees quickly won over to the new fad of crossword puzzles. According to *Panati's Parade of Fads, Follies, and Manias*, Mah Jongg has survived mostly among middle-aged Jewish women, becoming to the Synagogue what Bingo is to the Catholic Church. Although sets of these exquisite tiles are increasingly hard to find, they can usually be ferreted out in the Chinatown districts of big cities or in curio shops in vacation areas like the Adirondacks or Cape Cod, where at one time, every summer house was equipped with the game. (Old bone or ivory tiles will likely be dirty or discolored. Do not wash with water. Rub with a dry cloth or one very slightly moistened with alcohol. It is important, of course, to keep the backs clean so that players can't tell which tiles you have in your hand.)

Mah Jongg sets today are made of plastic, and their designs are more likely stamped than carved, but the pieces remain the same. Because the language and the designs are foreign, take some time to become comfortable with them before you start to play.

There are three *suits* in Mah Jongg: Characters, Bamboos and Dots, top to bottom as illustrated. Each suit runs from 1 to 9. The tiles of the Dots suit (also called Circles or Balls) look like the bones in a traditional Dominoes set but are painted with concentric colored circles instead of spots; there is also a numeral on each tile. The Character tiles (sometimes called Cracks or *Won*) are painted with Chinese symbols and a numeral from 1 to 9. The first tile of the Bamboo suit (sometimes called Sticks or Bams) is decorated with the bird of 100 intelligences; tiles 2 to 9 are painted with numerals and the appropriate pieces of bamboo. Individual tiles are referred to as 1 Bamboo, 5 Dots, 8 Characters, and so on. The 1 and 9 of each suit are called the *head tiles* and are worth more; tiles 2 to 8 are the *middle tiles*.

There are four tiles of each number in a suit: 36 Dots, 36 Characters and 36 Bamboos, a total of 108 suit tiles.

The four *Winds* and the three *Dragons* are called the *honor tiles*. The Winds are inscribed with a Chinese character and a letter designating N (North), S (South), E (East) and W (West). The Dragon tiles are im-

Characters, Bamboos and Dots

printed with a vermilion swordlike character for the Red Dragon and a jade character that looks like Napoleon's hat for the Green Dragon; the White Dragon is an utterly blank tile. There are four each of the four Winds (16) and four each of the three Dragons (12), making 28 honor tiles.

Mah Jongg sometimes comes with eight optional tiles: four *Seasons* and four *Flowers* (or sometimes eight of one type). These decorative, scenic tiles function as wild cards in the game and are usually inscribed with a numeral (1 to 4) as well as a Chinese character and a scene. Babcock included them in his game but did not recommend playing with them; they are described under Variations.

A complete Mah Jongg set, for those who glean theirs from an antique shop or an auction, consists of 108 suit tiles, 28 honor tiles and 8 optional tiles. The backs of all tiles are completely blank. As well, there are two dice, four *wind disks*, marked N, S, E, W, which determine the seating arrangement, and *counters*, or *bones*, that are used to score the game. The counters vary according to the set but are usually dyed ivory bars and disks that represent different points, like poker chips. There should be four kinds of counters, worth 500, 100, 10 and 2 points, respectively. Babcock's counters were marked with spots like dice (5, 1, 10 and 2), but other sets may simply contain chips of four different colors. Use the most numerous color for the lowest denomination. Omit the 2 counter if necessary, and round off scores to multiples of 10.

Winds, Dragons and Seasons

Opening the Wall in Mah Jongg

The Object of the Game:
To collect high-scoring sets; the first to hold a complete hand—four sets and a pair—declares "Mah Jongg!"

The Sets: The tiles individually have no value; they score only in combinations or sets. There are three kinds of sets. *Chow* is a sequence, or run, of three tiles of the same suit; for instance, 4-5-6 Bamboos or 7-8-9 Characters. (A chow cannot have more than three tiles in sequence.) *Pung* is three of a kind; for instance, three 5-Dots or three Green Dragons or three North Winds. *Kong* is four of a kind, as in four 9-Bamboos or four West Winds.

The object of the game is to collect four sets and a pair. This is called a *woo*, or a *complete hand*. A player with a complete hand declares "Mah Jongg!" and scores for going out, much as in Gin Rummy.

Any set will help a player make a complete hand and go out, but after the hand is over, the sets can also contribute to the score. Chows are worth nothing at all. Pungs made up of middle tiles score only half as much as three of a kind with head tiles. So in deciding which sets to collect, keep a close eye on the scoring system below.

If you are just learning the game, practice sorting the tiles into different kinds of sets until you have the words chow (a sequence), pung (three of a kind) and kong (four of a kind) firmly in mind. It will also improve your game if you have a sense of their ultimate worth in scored points.

The Seating: A formal rigmarole determines who sits where around the table. You can skip it and use Babcock's simplified method, but the ritual is quite fun and puts players in the proper frame of mind for the game.

Traditionally, before play begins, the four wind disks are placed upside down in a row in the center of the table. One of the players throws the two dice. Starting with himself and moving clockwise around the players at the table, he counts the number shown on the dice. The seat where the count stops is temporarily designated the East seat. The player in the East seat throws the dice and counts clockwise, starting with herself, the number of places shown on the dice. The player designated by the second count picks up a wind disk from one end of the row; the player to her right picks up the next disk, and so on, around the table. The player who picked up the East Wind moves to the seat that was temporarily designated East. The others sit according to the directions of the winds: West across the table from East, South on the right of East and North on the left. (In Mah Jongg, the winds are opposite from the Western tradition, with east and west reversed from what we consider their rightful positions.)

Babcock's simplified routine is to throw the dice. The highest score is the East Wind, to his right is the South Wind, and so on. However it is decided, the East Wind plays first.

The Play: Before play begins, give each player counters worth 2,000 points: two 500-point bones, nine 100-point bones, eight 10-point bones and ten 2-point bones. Turn the 136 Mah Jongg tiles facedown in the center of the table, and thoroughly shuffle them like the bones in Dominoes. Each player chooses 34 tiles at random and, without looking at them, stacks the tiles in front of him, facedown, in a *wall* 17 tiles long and 2 tiles high. The four walls are shoved together, as illustrated, to form a hollow square in the middle of the table—a Chinese walled city.

The game begins by *opening the wall*. To decide who gets the honor of opening the wall, the East Wind throws the dice and, starting with himself and moving clockwise around the table, counts the number shown on the dice. The player designated by the end of the count throws the dice again. She adds the total of her throw to the total of the first throw; then, starting at the right-hand corner of her wall and moving to the left, she counts the number of tiles indicated by the two throws.

For instance, if the first throw was 2-3 (5) and the second was 6-3 (9), the total is 14 (5+9). The player starts at the corner, counts 14 from right to left and removes the fourteenth pair of tiles from the wall. These are the *loose tiles*. She sets the loose tiles on top of the wall to the right of the opening, as illustrated. This marks the end of the wall. The *draw* begins from the left side of the opening. (If the total is more than 17, the player rounds the corner and opens the wall in front of the player on her left.)

Set aside the dice. They won't be used again until the next hand.

The players now draw tiles from the wall for their hands. The player who is the East Wind begins, taking the two pairs of tiles to the left of the opening. Moving counterclockwise around the table, each player does the same, drawing four tiles at a time from the left side of the opening, until everyone has 12 tiles (three draws of four tiles each). The players then draw one more tile so that each hand contains 13 tiles. Finally, East draws one last tile. At the end of the draw, North, West and South have 13 tiles each and East has 14; the city wall is almost half gone. Players stand their tiles outside the wall, facing them so that no one else can see their hands. Players arrange their tiles in numerical sequence within suits.

During the course of the game, players try to collect a complete hand by drawing new tiles from the wall and discarding unusable ones in the center. East begins by discarding one of her tiles faceup in the middle of the hollow square. Play moves counterclockwise to South. South may either take the discard or draw from the wall. After he does one or the other, he discards a tile from his hand. (Players

may discard any tile, even the one just drawn from the wall.) Play continues counterclockwise, each player drawing from the wall or picking up the last discard, then discarding back to the center. As a courtesy, each player names the tile discarded, saying, "1 Bamboo" or "5 Dots." Don't overlap the discards. Everyone should be able to see clearly what has been discarded during the hand.

When it is his turn, a player may pick up the discard *only* if he can use it to make a pung (three of a kind) or a chow (a sequence). If he decides he can use the discard, he picks it up, adds it to two other tiles from his hand, then lays the set faceup in front of him (outside the wall, not within the hollow square). He now has an *exposed hand* as well as a *concealed hand*. Note in the scoring system that sets in the concealed hand are worth more than sets in the exposed hand. After laying down the pung or the chow, the player discards so that the number of tiles in his exposed and his concealed hand still adds up to 13.

All the discards except the last one are *dead*. They provide useful information but are never picked up. Only the last discard can be picked up, and when a player does so, the tile always becomes part of the exposed hand. The concealed hand contains only tiles drawn from the wall.

When it is your turn, you can either chow (make a sequence) or pung (make three of a kind) from the previous player's discard. However, you can also pung out of turn. Whenever a tile is discarded that completes three of a

kind in your hand, you do not have to wait for your turn. You simply call "Pung!" take the discard and lay it faceup with two others of the same denomination on the table in front of you. Then you discard, and play carries on, the player to your right taking the next turn. (When someone pungs out of turn, one or two people may lose their rightful turn to draw.)

If it is your turn and you pick up the discard, intending to chow, and another player calls "Pung!" the punger gets the tile, even if he declares his intention after you picked up the tile. If you have already exposed your own tiles for the chow, however, the discard is yours.

The rules for declaring kong are a little different. A complete hand (winning hand) is always four sets and a pair. At the beginning of the game, each player has 13 tiles, so if the last tile that the player draws is not discarded, he can make four chows or pungs and a pair (4 x 3 = 12+2 = 14). A kong, however, is four of a kind, so a winning hand of four sets and a pair must contain extra tiles if it contains a kong. (If one of the sets is a kong, the hand has 15 tiles; if two are kongs, the hand has 16, and so on.) To keep the correct number of tiles in hand, a player who makes a kong draws an extra tile from the loose tiles at the end of the wall.

For instance, if a player has three of a kind in his hand, he can pick up a discard of the same denomination and lay a kong faceup on the table. He draws the first loose tile at the end of the wall, the one farthest from the

Wind Disks and Counters

opening, then discards a tile.

If a player has three of a kind in her concealed hand and draws a matching fourth from the wall, she can declare a kong and lay it on the table, turning the last tile facedown to indicate that the fourth was not a discard. This is scored as a concealed kong. As before, she draws a loose tile, then discards.

If a player draws a tile from the wall that matches an exposed pung (three of a kind) on the table, he can add the single tile to the pung, expanding it to a kong. He draws the first loose tile from the wall and discards. (A player may not, however, pick up a discard to make an exposed pung into a kong.)

A player with a kong in hand need not lay it down immediately. She may save it hoping to use one of the four in a run, making two sets instead of one. Likewise, if she draws a fourth, she doesn't have to lay it down on the exposed pung immediately. A player can declare a kong during any turn, but only after drawing from the wall, not after picking up a discard. On any one turn, a player can declare more than one kong, but he may not declare a kong after declaring a chow or a pung.

After laying down a kong, a player always draws a loose tile and discards. After two kongs, therefore, the first two loose tiles will be gone. To maintain the supply of loose tiles, the last pair of tiles at the end of the wall is lifted to the top of the wall, to the right of the opening. When these two are taken, another pair is lifted onto the wall, and so on.

When a player completes four sets and a pair, either by drawing the final necessary tile from the wall or by punging or chowing a discard from the table, he calls "Mah Jongg!" and lays his concealed hand faceup on the table beside his exposed hand.

A player who is one tile short of declaring Mah Jongg is said to have a *waiting hand*, or *set hand*. If the tile she needs is discarded, she may pick up the discard and declare "Mah Jongg!" even if she is out of turn and intends to use the discard in a chow or a pair. If more than one player want the discard, the one who declares Mah Jongg gets it. If more than one player with a set hand wants the discard, it goes to the player closest in order of play to the person who discarded it.

A player does not discard after declaring Mah Jongg. Note that a player can never declare Mah Jongg by completing a kong, because this is always followed by drawing a loose tile to make up the correct number of tiles in the hand. He may, however, complete his hand with the loose tile he draws —and win a special bonus.

One final point: If a player declares a kong by adding a fourth tile to an exposed pung (three of a kind), another player with a set hand may steal that fourth tile to complete his hand and declare Mah Jongg. Babcock calls this, predictably, *stealing the fourth to win*. This move also scores bonus points.

It sometimes happens that no one

Scoring System: Mah Jongg

Exposed Combinations (completed from discards)	Points
Three of a Kind (middle tiles 2-8)	2
Three of a Kind (head tiles 1 and 9)	4
Three of a Kind any Winds	4
Three of a Kind any Dragons	4
Four of a Kind (middle tiles)	8
Four of a Kind (head tiles)	16
Four of a Kind any Winds	16
Four of a Kind any Dragons	16
Pair of any Dragons or player's own Wind	2

Concealed Combinations (completed by drawing from the wall)	
Three of a Kind (middle tiles 2-8)	4
Three of a Kind (head tiles 1 and 9)	8
Three of a Kind any Winds	8
Three of a Kind any Dragons	8
Four of a Kind (middle tiles)	16
Four of a Kind (head tiles)	32
Four of a Kind any Winds	32
Four of a Kind any Dragons	32
Pair of any Dragons or player's own Wind	2

Bonus Scores (for the winning hand only)	
Mah Jongg (for winning the hand)	20
Drawing winning tile (rather than discard)	2
Drawing winning loose tile	10 *
No score other than Mah Jongg	10
No chow, concealed or exposed	10
Stealing fourth to win	10
Mah Jongg on the last tile drawn	10

*score this or the previous bonus, not both

Double Honor Scores (applies to all hands; calculated last)
Three or four of your own Wind, concealed or exposed: Double total score
Three or four Dragons, concealed or exposed: Double total score
Hand all one suit except for Dragons and Winds: Double total score
Hand all one suit: Double total score three times
Hand entirely honor tiles (Winds and Dragons, no suits): Double total score three times

---

declares Mah Jongg. When the wall is reduced to the *dead portion*—the last 14 tiles (seven pairs including the loose tiles)—the game is declared a *draw*. No scores count. The tiles are turned facedown and shuffled, and a new hand is begun. The same player continues as the East Wind.

If a player wins at the last moment by drawing the final tile from the *live portion* of the wall, she wins a special bonus. The move, in Chinese, is called *plucking the shadow of the moon from the bottom of the sea.*

The Score: The player who declares Mah Jongg has a complete hand of four sets and a pair to score. If the final tile drawn by the winning hand is a discard, the set it is added to scores as an exposed combination; if the final tile is drawn from the wall, that set scores as a concealed combination.

Once Mah Jongg is declared, the other players can regroup the tiles in their concealed hands to create the best possible scoring combinations. Chows have no value in either the exposed or the concealed hand except to complete the woo, so tiles from chows should be rearranged into pungs and pairs where possible. Tiles in the exposed part of the hand must stay where they are. Players lay down the tiles from their concealed hands, placing one tile crosswise across the other two in a concealed pung. This differentiates it from an exposed pung, which is worth less.

Players each count their own hands according to the scoring system illustrated on the previous page, adding up the points and the bonuses, then doubling if they deserve it. When each score is calculated, players settle accounts using the counters they received at the beginning of the game.

First, all the players give the winner counters equal in value to her score. For instance, if South declares Mah Jongg and scores 42, then the others each give her counters worth 42.

For the player who is the East Wind, the stakes are always doubled. If East wins, each player pays her twice the amount of her score. If East loses, she pays the winner double.

A Complete Hand, Including Two Chows in the Exposed Hand (left) and a Chow, a Pung and a Pair in the Concealed Hand (right)

After the winner is paid off, the losers settle scores between themselves. Each player gives counters to anyone who has a higher score; the amount of the payment is the difference between their scores. For instance, if East scores 24, West scores 18 and North scores 12, then West pays East 6, and North pays East 12 and West 6. (Rounded off to multiples of 10, the scores would be: South 40, East 20, West 20, North 10. Five or more is rounded up; four or less is rounded down.) North and West would pay South 40; East would pay South 80; West would pay East 0; and North would pay both East and West 10. Don't forget: East pays double the difference between her score and the other losers.

The average score of a winning hand is about 40 points; players will likely never see the highest score possible: 63,488. The doubling and tripling bonuses, however, can shoot scores into five digits, so most players establish a limit of 300 or 500 points per hand before play begins.

Each game is over when a player declares Mah Jongg or when players declare a *draw game*. The East wind disk (and therefore all the wind disks) pass to the right, the tiles are turned facedown and shuffled, and a new

game begins. In Mah Jongg, players usually play a *round* of several games until each player has a turn as East Wind. This may be more than four hands, since when East declares Mah Jongg, he continues as East; only when East loses do the wind disks move. The winner of each round is the person with the highest value of counters. Before each new round, players again draw for seats.

Strategy: The formalities of building and opening the wall and even of establishing the players as the four Winds seem complicated at first but are actually quite simple in play. The reverse is true of the game. While it seems very simple the first time through, it is in fact wonderfully complex, a game of skill to challenge the most inveterate game players.

Keep track of the number of tiles in your hand, recounting often to make sure you have 13 tiles plus one additional tile for each kong. This is especially true after part of your hand is exposed. If you end up with more or fewer tiles, yours is a *dead hand*: you cannot complete a Mah Jongg, and you automatically score zero, which raises your payouts to the winner and other losers to the maximum.

Arrange your tiles with the Dragons, your own Winds and completed and hoped-for combinations on one end and potential discard tiles on the other. Don't leave any spaces between the tiles; this might tip off other players as to the makeup of your hand.

Assess your hand for both its scoring possibilities and your ability to complete a Mah Jongg. Try to make a plan of action at the beginning, but be prepared to shift quickly depending on the discards and draws that come your way. Watch for combinations that can be completed in as many ways as possible: a chow that is open at both ends (4-5 or 7-8, rather than 8-9) or a sequence of two that contains a pair (it can be completed as a pung or a chow). If you have a choice, complete the most difficult set. For instance, if you hold the 5, 6, 8 and 9 Bamboos and the 7 Bamboos is discarded by the player before you, pick up the 7 for a 7-8-9 Bamboos chow. Another 7 or a 4 will complete the 5-6.

Discard your least desirable tiles: single Winds other than your own, single suits and 9s of a suit, since they are hardest to meld into a run. You can safely discard opponents' Winds early in the game when they are unlikely to have a pair in hand that allows them to pung. Some players always keep their own Wind, even singles, and single Dragons in hopes of getting two more so that they can double their score. At some point, you have to decide how close the others are to declaring Mah Jongg and divest yourself of hopeless tiles—usually the single Dragon or single Wind.

Never pick up a discard unless the chow or pung it makes improves your hand substantially. The exposed hand is worth less, and it hints at how close you are to completing a Mah Jongg.

Keep your eye on the discard pile, calculating which tiles are dead and which may still appear during discards and draws. Sometimes, you can lure the player on your left into discarding exactly what you want. For instance, if you have the 5, 6, 8 and 9 Bamboos, you can discard the 9 in one turn and the 8 in the next; your opponent might then feel safe enough to discard the 7 or even the 4.

Limit Hands: Mah Jongg

Hand From Heaven: When East picks up a complete Mah Jongg in his 14 tiles at the beginning of the game, he scores the limit (300).

Hand From Earth: If any player other than East picks up a set hand of 13 tiles and can pung East's first discard for Mah Jongg, he scores half the limit (150).

Lucky Thirteen: If any player picks up a set hand and cannot complete it with the first discard, he can declare his set hand before he makes his first draw. Provided he never discards any of the original 13 tiles, he may score one-third the limit (100) when he finally draws or pungs the necessary tile to complete the woo.

Snake: 1 to 9 of a suit plus one each of the Winds with any tile paired. All tiles but the last must be drawn from the wall. This scores the limit (300).

Thirteen Hidden Orphans: Thirteen single tiles concealed in the hand—one each of the four Winds, the three Dragons and one head of each suit—all drawn from the wall (since the entire hand is concealed). Drawing one matching tile completes the hand, and it scores the limit (300). If that one essential tile is never drawn, the hand scores nothing.

Seven Twins: Any seven pairs, making 14 tiles in all. The fourteenth can be drawn or punged, and the completed hand scores half the limit (150).

Three Great Scholars: A pung or kong of each of the Dragons (Red, White and Green), plus any chow or pung and a pair. Scores the limit (300).

The strategy of most beginners is to collect the sets first and to wait for one last draw or discard to produce the final pair. Yet this is the most difficult hand to complete. Instead, keep a pair in hand from the earliest possible moment. Sacrifice a pung if you have to in order to preserve your pair. The easiest set to go out on is a middle chow, since any one of eight tiles can complete the chow—and the Mah Jongg.

If your hand is close to completion early in the game, you may want to hold on for a few more rounds, hoping the draw from the wall will improve your score. As with most strategy games, however, it is a matter of timing that can be learned only with practice. In general, the East Wind, who plays for double stakes, should go out as soon as possible.

Most beginners play offensively,

trying to build a high-scoring complete hand as fast as possible, but much of Mah Jongg's skill comes in defensive play. Since a player will lose 12 hands out of 16, on average, she should try to cut her losses to a minimum, as well as maximize her score when she wins. If the original draw gives you six or more single tiles that are not part of any set, chances are you won't make Mah Jongg. If luck is with you, it will become evident in the first few draws. Otherwise, play defensively; ignore chows and go for the high-scoring pungs. Lay down as little as possible in the exposed hand, punging from your draws, rather than discards. Draw from the wall whenever possible. If you know you cannot win the hand, play so that the person with the fewest counters (lowest overall score in the round) wins.

Be alert to discard patterns among your opponents. Pay particular attention to the discards of the person on your right, since it is your discards he is waiting for. Be careful not to help him win. If it is the player on the right who is losing the round to this point, do what you can to help him win and thus deprive the overall winner from increasing her lead. Watch for indications that one player is trying for a one-suit hand. Under most circumstances, players discard uniformly from all suits.

In general, discard what others have already discarded and avoid breaking new ground by discarding something completely new. When the live portion of the wall is nearly gone and a draw game is a distinct possibility, players with low scores should do their best to make sure that a draw game is declared and that the player with a high-scoring hand does not get a chance to count it. Be conservative with discards, even if it means sacrificing from sets in order to discard a tile that you know the high scorer cannot use. On the other hand, at the same point in the game, the player with a high-scoring hand should try to let one of the others win if possible, since he will at least score.

And good luck—this one is worth the effort.

Variations: Players can agree to score for any or all of the special *limit hands* listed on the previous page, or they can invent their own. A limit hand is some special grouping of tiles that scores the maximum for a player who both collects the group and declares Mah Jongg. Limit hands seem to be an American innovation. According to some critics, the emphasis on these specific combinations, which made the game so complex, caused Mah Jongg to fall from favor. The best game, in fact, is the simplest, with the focus on strategic play, rather than on collecting specific high-scoring hands.

Later versions of Mah Jongg include Four Seasons tiles, sometimes called Flowers, Flower Gardens or Goofs. The game contains two series of four each, making eight Season tiles altogether. (The two series are usually different colors, and each series is numbered 1 to 4.) Each player has his or her own Season: East being Season 1; South, Season 2; West, Season 3; and North, Season 4. A Season cannot be discarded and therefore can be drawn only from the wall. It is declared immediately by placing it faceup in the exposed hand. The player then draws a loose tile from the dead portion of the wall. If players draw a Season at the beginning of the game, they can declare it in turn, before East's first discard. Each player then draws a loose tile to replace the Season. Each Season scores 4 points. If a player holds one of his own Seasons, he adds the value of the Season to his score, then doubles his total score. If he holds both of his own Seasons, he doubles his total score twice. If a player holds all four Seasons (1 to 4) of one color, she doubles her total score three times. All players can take advantage of the Seasons.

Although Mah Jongg is best played with four people, the *Seattle Daily Times* declared in the 1920s that **Two-Handed Mah Jongg** was, "with the exception of **Cribbage** and **Piquet**, the first satisfactory husband-and-wife game that has come along." In Mah Jongg for two, the entire set of tiles is used, each player drawing 68 tiles and building both the wall in front of him or her as well as the wall to the right. The two players alternate as East and West. In the preliminaries, East rolls the dice for himself and South; West rolls for herself and North. During play, East can double his score if he holds three or four East Winds or South Winds; West can double her score if she holds three or four West Winds or North Winds. Play continues as for four people. It is much easier to win a complete hand, so players usually agree that they cannot declare Mah Jongg unless they hold a complete hand with two or more doubling combinations. Keep the limit for the hand at 300 points.

In **Three-Handed Mah Jongg**, the four West Winds are removed, leaving 132 tiles. Each player draws 44 tiles, building a wall of pairs 22 tiles long, which, when shoved together, creates a triangular walled city. In determining seats, there is no West. Otherwise, play is exactly the same. Scores tend to be a little lower than in the four-handed version; the limit hands are therefore often raised to 600 points. ∽

7

Pieces of the Action: Games With Special Equipment

THE HISTORY OF GAMES is to some extent the history of fads. **Tiddlywinks** arose from obscurity at the end of the last century to become a national craze in the early teens. The opulent **Mah Jongg** took the twenties by storm, while the modest wooden **Pick-Up-Sticks** was, appropriately, a phenomenon of the Depression. Like most other fads, Pick-Up-Sticks was not an invention so much as a clone. Eugene Levay, a toy buyer for Gimbel Brothers department stores, bought the game in Hungary, where it is called Marokko. American toymaker O. Schoenut Inc. grudgingly agreed to make the sticks. The game was introduced at Easter 1936, and almost three million sets sold within the first year.

Ping-pong rode a similar, if slower, wave. It first emerged during the gaming heyday of Victorian England, one of many outdoor games miniaturized for the drawing room. Tabletop Billiards and Tabletop Croquet suffered an early demise, but Tabletop Tennis persisted under such onomatopoeic names as Wick-wack, Click-clack, Whiff-whaff, Ping-pong and Flim-flam, as well as Gossima, an early attempt to market the frivolous game with the flimsy ball under an exotic name. Its popularity was short-lived; the British

Ping-Pong Association, formed in 1902, disbanded in 1905. After World War I, however, the game was resurrected when Parker Brothers registered the trademark name "Ping-Pong" and started selling the official equipment for what quickly became America's hottest indoor sport. The game was an international fad, particularly popular in Hungary. Shortly before World War II, a young Hungarian Ping-pong star, Victor Barna, toured the United States, slamming and smashing his way into the headlines. Almost overnight, Ping-pong was transformed from a wimpy after-dinner entertainment to the indoor equivalent of Wimbledon. At the height of the Ping-pong mania in the late 1930s, an estimated 10 million Americans regularly played.

Although most of the games in this chapter enjoyed a bright moment in the gaming spotlight, they have shown remarkable staying power. After more than a hundred years, all are still widely available, and most people, at one time or another, have either played the games or seen them played. More active than most table or board games, these pastimes have players crouching on the floor flicking plastic disks into cups, shifting their butts to the edge of their chairs for a tricky **Crokinole** shot, throwing pointed projectiles at targets and slamming lightweight balls around the basement rafters.

The games themselves are all relatively simple contests of physical skill that can be played on an elementary level; in the hands of a dedicated practitioner, however, these games become exquisitely refined. With the exception of Pick-Up-Sticks, all the games in this chapter are played seriously in tournaments organized by national and worldwide associations. This comes as no surprise for **Darts**, perhaps, but few realize that since 1972, the International Federation of Tiddlywinks Associations has been organizing Tiddlywinks matches. In the United States, the North American Tiddlywinks Association maintains an archives and a "Closet of Fame," featuring the clothing and equipment of famous players. The United States Table Tennis Association, founded in 1933, still oversees 280 tournaments a year, many of them televised, with the tables wired to reproduce a resounding PING-PONG. And aficionados of the sport maintain not one but two halls of fame—in Seattle and in Colorado Springs. Every two years, the United States competes with teams from 100 countries for the Table Tennis World Cup; at last count, China had five million registered competitive players. This game has even entered the political lexicon. In 1971, an American team was invited to visit the People's Republic of China, leading to the "normalization" of relations between those two countries and coining a new phrase: "Ping-pong Diplomacy."

Players take these games seriously. There are surprisingly few variations in Ping-pong, Crokinole and such, possibly because national associations publish official rules of play that keep the games standardized. The inventive impulse has been turned instead on the equipment. Darts, for instance, were once little more than cut-off arrows tossed at an upended tree trunk or the butt of a wine barrel. In 1898, an American replaced the feathers on a dart with a patented folded-paper flight, and in 1936, a Hungarian living in Britain substituted metal for the standard wooden shaft. Today, a novice is faced with a dizzying array of darts, from brass torpedoes to tungsten bombs fitted with turkey feathers.

The fascination with playing pieces is probably what has made these games so enduring—and so marketable. During the 1920s, games manufacturers tried to include all the games with special playing pieces on one omnibus board. The 1919 Sears, Roebuck & Company catalog, for instance, advertised a 29-inch-square "moderate-priced board . . . complete with full set of equipment to play fifty-seven games," including **Chess, Checkers**, Crokinole, Tabletop Billiards, **Caroms**, Tiddlywinks, Nine-Pins, **Go-Bang, Backgammon**, Shuffleboard and dozens more. This misguided attempt to corner the market didn't last long. Manufacturers soon realized that there were huge profits to be made in selling each of the 57 games individually.

Today, basements and attics across the country are littered with the bits and pieces of these games, incomplete and instructionless. The basic rules and the language, unique to each game, can be found in the following pages; most of the equipment—Ping-pong balls, Crokinole cookies, **Jacks**—can still be bought in games or sporting-goods stores. Best of all, none of them have lost the charm and excitement that first made them fads.

Jacks

- ◆ OTHER NAMES: **Jackstones, Dibs and Fivestones**
- ◆ NUMBER: **excellent solo game or play with friends; each person plays individually**
- ◆ EQUIPMENT: **12 or more jacks and a small ball with good bounce**
- ◆ COMPLEXITY: **good eye-hand coordination is an asset; kids should be 5 or older**
- ◆ TIP: **not a good table game; best played squatting or sitting on the floor**

LIKE DICE, JACKS has its roots in Knucklebones, the classic tossing game of prehistory. Under the name of Fivestones, Aristophanes described the game more than 2,000 years ago, and still as Fivestones, it was cataloged by William Newell in his 1883 book *Games and Songs of American Children.* Today, the game is commonly called Jacks, which comes from Jackstones or Chuckstones—stones tossed in the air, sometimes together with the bouncing of a ball, the object being to catch the stones in the palm or on the back of the hand. Although stones work admirably in the following games, the little six-pronged metal jacks sold in stores are an inexpensive delight.

Playing Jacks is something that, like riding a bicycle, you never forget. This year, a close friend who just turned 40 received a set of Jacks from Santa. She spent a happy Christmas morning impressing her young children with her skill and reliving her youth, when she was a Jacks champion of local renown.

Equipment: A set of 12 or more six-pronged metal jacks and a small bouncing ball, about an inch in diameter. Oversize foam-rubber jacks are appropriate for young children; they require only a fraction of the dexterity demanded by the original jacks. If you can't buy the real thing, play the game with dice, **Go** pebbles or small, smooth stones. One set of jacks can be shared by all players.

The Object of the Game: To pick up jacks in the time it takes to bounce a ball.

The Play: Jacks is really a series of challenges. When you perfect one challenge, move on to the next; when you flub it, start over. If several people are playing, when one person misses, she passes the jacks to the next player, who then attempts to complete all or part of the sequence.

Spread the jacks on the floor. Throw the ball in the air, pick up a single jack with your throwing hand, then catch the ball after it bounces once. Transfer the jack to your other hand, throw the ball up again, and pick up another jack in the time it takes the ball to bounce once. Continue until you have picked up all the jacks, one at a time. (This is called Ones, or Onesies.) The trick is to throw the ball high so that you have enough time to pick up the jack and also to throw the ball straight so that it bounces directly back to you to catch. The jacks should be spread out; some players disallow the turn if you touch or move other jacks during the pickup.

After you have completed ones, try picking up the jacks by twos, then by threes, and so on, until you can scoop up all the jacks in the time it takes the ball to bounce once. If this is too difficult, try a double bounce, picking up the jacks—one at a time, then two at a time, then three—in the time it takes the ball to bounce twice.

Variations: In Sequences, pick up one jack on the first throw, two on the second, three on the third, and so on, until all the jacks are in your hand. Then try doing this without transferring the jacks to your other hand between tosses of the ball: toss the ball, then collect and hold the jacks and catch the ball, all with the same hand.

Next, with all the jacks in your

Eggs in a Basket

Toad in the Hole

For **Toad in the Hole** (also called Peas in a Pod and The Cave), lay your nonthrowing hand on the floor with the thumb flat and the fingers curled around to create a burrow, as illustrated. Scatter the jacks near the mouth of the burrow. Throw the ball in the air, pick up a jack with your throwing hand, toss it into the "hole" of your other hand, and catch the ball after one bounce. Toss the toads in the hole one at a time, then two at a time, until you pitch them in all at once. Then try throwing them into the hole in sequence.

For **Horses in the Stall**, lay your nonthrowing hand palm down, thumb and fingers spread and resting on their fingertips to create four "stalls." Throw the jacks between your fingers, one jack to a stall, while the ball is in the air. After all the "horses" are in their stalls, take them out, one at a time, catching the ball after a single bounce.

To play **Jumping the Ditch**, line up four jacks in a row. Toss the ball, then pick up the first and third jack without disturbing the others, and catch the ball after its first bounce. Toss the ball again, and pick up the second and fourth. Once you perfect this, line up six jacks, and pick up the first, third and fifth on the first toss. Add more challenge by increasing the number of jacks and arranging them in a circle or a square (take only the corners first, then the walls). Use your imagination to set up more and more complex challenges. ∽

hand, toss the ball, and spread the jacks on the floor, catching the ball after the first bounce. Toss the ball again, and pick up all the jacks, catching the ball after its first bounce.

Eggs in a Basket demands more speed. Scatter the jacks on the floor. Hold your nonthrowing hand on the floor, palm up and fingers cupped like a basket, as illustrated on the previous page. Toss the ball, pick up a jack, put it in your basket hand, then catch the ball after its first bounce. Pick up the jacks, and put them in the basket one at a time, then by twos, threes, and so on, and finally in sequence.

Crack the Eggs adds another step. Pick up a jack, tap it against the floor, and transfer it to your basket hand before catching the ball.

Pick-Up-Sticks

- ◆ OTHER NAMES: **Jackstraws and Jerkstraws**
- ◆ NUMBER: **two to four players; more can play, but it is a long wait between turns**
- ◆ EQUIPMENT: **one set of 41 pick-up-sticks, various colors**
- ◆ COMPLEXITY: **a humbling game for adults; a test for steady-handedness**
- ◆ TIP: **best played on the floor; carpets make the game easier, but a slick-surfaced table or floor is more challenging**

Pｉｃ-Up-Sticks is this century's version of Jerkstraws or Juggling-Sticks, which in turn evolved from an ancient Chinese game called Spillikins or Spelicans. Where Pick-Up-Sticks are identical, elongated, plastic toothpicks, Spillikins was played with 30 intricately carved six-inch slivers of ivory, each topped with a unique figure or symbol. Both Spillikins and Jerkstraws included a hooked stick, much like a crochet hook, with which players retrieved individual sticks from the pile. The ivory sticks were ranked according to the intricacy of their carvings: the most difficult to remove—the saw—scored 50 points.

By comparison, the lightweight plastic Pick-Up-Sticks sold today seem pale imitations indeed. Wooden sticks are difficult to find, but you can make your own by cutting the finest dowels into seven-inch sticks and sharpening both ends in a pencil sharpener or hand-sanding them to smooth points. A coat of varnish or a rubbing of wax will make the sticks slick enough for an interesting game. The name, by the way, comes from the children's counting rhyme, "One, two, buckle my shoe; Three, four, shut the door; Five, six, pick up sticks."

Equipment: A set of 41 multi-colored sticks. If some have gone missing over the years, the game can also be played with fewer.

The Object of the Game: To retrieve as many sticks as possible, removing each individually without disturbing any others.

The Play: Throw a die to determine the order of play. The player who goes last grasps the sticks in one hand and sets her fist on the floor, the sticks pointing straight up like a bouquet. She lets go and pulls away her hand in one swift motion. (This produces a tight fan of sticks. Let young players hold the bundle of sticks a few inches above the floor; when they let go, the sticks disperse farther, making them a little easier to pick up.)

Starting with the player who rolled the highest number on the die, players try to pick up the sticks, one by one, using only their fingers and neither touching nor disturbing any sticks other than the one they are trying to lift. You can pluck a stick from the pile between pinched fingers or lever it away from the others by pressing on one pointed end, as illustrated, raising the other end so that you can grasp it with your free hand. The other players watch carefully, calling out when a stick so much as shivers.

When a player successfully removes one stick, he gets another chance and continues to remove sticks, one by one, until he drops a stick or jiggles another close by. He then leaves the stick where it fell or rolled, and the turn passes to the player on the left. The game ends when the last stick is picked up.

In some games, one of the sticks is black. The person who retrieves the black stick can use it as a wand to lift or lever another stick off the pile and into a position where it can be more easily picked up. The same rule applies, however: no other sticks can be moved in the process.

The Score: Players count the number of sticks they have at the end of the game. The person with the most sticks wins. You can also give the colors different values; for instance, green may be worth 3 points, red 5, blue 10 and black 20. This adds an element of strategy and risk to the game, since it is to a player's advantage to pick up the most valuable sticks first.

Pick-Up-Sticks

Tiddlywinks

◆ NUMBER: **any number of players; usually two to six; four is best**
◆ EQUIPMENT: **a shooter and several winks for each player and a shallow cup**
◆ DESCRIPTION: **a tongue-poking-from-the-side-of-the-mouth game of skill**
◆ TIP: **best played on the floor**

RECENTLY, A Tiddlywinks game turned up at a local antique store: $35 for an incomplete set of winks and shooters, with a whiskey shot glass substituted for the little cup. As overpriced and deficient as it was, the game was a temptation: they just don't make Tiddlywinks like they used to. The disks in the old games are made of bone or, later, of a celluloid plastic that feels slick in the fingers and comes in intense opaque colors. Today's games, for the most part, are cheap imitations, but despite inferior materials, the game is still fun and demands a surprising measure of skill. Don't relegate this game to the children's toy box. Victorian Tiddlywinks illustrations show adults, not kids, squidging the winks; at the height of the Tiddlywinks craze, there were intercollegiate championships, and in the late 1930s, it was the favorite pastime of the surrealists who congregated in Mexico.

Where the name comes from is a mystery. A "tiddlywink" in British dialect is an unlicensed public house, but it is also a little chunk of floating ice. The game likely began as a barroom pastime, with patrons flicking coins into a shot glass, using free drinks as stakes. Whatever its origins, it has evolved into a game of skill not unlike **Crokinole** and **Marbles**. At home, the game is best played on a table with a thick fabric tablecloth or on a rug-covered floor, both of which combine firm support with a nonslip surface, so the winks jump high into the air but stay where they land. In French, the game is called Jeu de Puce—the Flea Game—and this is exactly what the winks resemble: high-hopping fleas.

Equipment: Each player has a *shooter*—a colored disk about an inch in diameter, which the British call a *squidger*—and several *winks* (sometimes prosaically called counters) of the same color, but about half the size of the shooter. (There were usually six winks in older games; three in contemporary sets.) The shooters and winks are rigid but slightly pliable, so when the shooter is pressed firmly against the edge of a wink, the wink skips forward. If you can't find an actual Tiddlywinks game, small, slick poker chips, markers from old board games, heavy cardboard disks or flat buttons will work. You can also play with coins: quarters as shooters and dimes as winks.

The target for the winks is the *cup*, a glass or plastic dish about 1½ inches in diameter and an inch or more high. (These dimensions are variable: a peanut-butter-jar lid will do.) Some games come with a fold-out cloth or a plastic sheet marked like a target with a series of concentric circles or squares. The cup fits in the center, marked 25, and the rings that extend out from the cup are marked 20, 15, 10 and 5.

The Object of the Game: To land all your winks in the cup.

The Play: To determine the order of play, players line up their winks in a row at the start line. The distance can vary with the age and skill of the players but should never be less than a foot. Each player in turn takes her shooter between her thumb and first two fingers, then presses the edge of the shooter against the edge of a wink and bears down sharply so that the wink flies upward and forward toward the cup. This is called *squidging the wink*. The player who lands a wink closest to the cup starts. If two players tie, they squidge again.

The first player squidges a wink; if he *pots the wink* (lands it in the cup), he gets another turn. If he doesn't, the turn passes to the left. At each turn, a player can squidge a new wink from the start line or squidge one of the winks from where it landed in a pre-

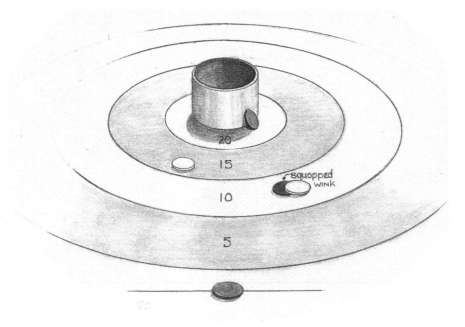

Tiddlywinks

vious turn, trying to move it closer to the cup. (A good strategy is to make many small jumps toward the cup, instead of trying to make it in one flying leap.) Winks must be played from where they land. If a wink goes completely off the table or out-of-bounds (off the target cloth), put it back at the starting position. A wink must lie flat to be squidged. If a wink is tilted against the cup, the player has to knock it away by hitting it with another wink and, on a subsequent turn, try to pot it. If a player's last wink is propped this way, the player has to wait until an opponent knocks it free.

If one wink lands on top of another, the bottom wink is said to be *squopped*. (Much of the strategy of the game is a matter of deciding whether to squoop another's wink or to try to pot one of your own.) A player cannot squidge a squopped wink. She has to wait until the top wink is played. For instance, in the example illustrated, Black has to squidge the wink on the start line because one wink is leaning against the cup and the other is squopped on

the 10-ring. If a squopped wink is a player's last, she passes her turn until her wink is free. The game ends when one player pots all his or her winks.

The Score: At the end of the game, players add up their scores according to where their winks landed on the target. A wink on a dividing line is pushed into the lower scoring area. Score each round individually—the highest score wins—or play a game to 500 points.

Variations: This is an excellent two-person game. With more players, either each person can play for himself or herself or players can play as partners; for instance, Red and Yellow against Blue and Green. Even without partners, the game can become strategic, as two players gang up on a high-scoring third to squoop her winks so that she can't move.

Castle adds an element of risk to Tiddlywinks. Draw concentric circles on a large piece of paper: 2 inches in diameter, 5 inches in diameter and 10

inches in diameter. Place the cup (the castle) in the center. Players start from the outside line and try to reach the castle. The space between the two-inch and five-inch line is the moat. Any winks that land here drown and must be removed permanently from play. The first player to get a wink in the castle wins.

Some early Tiddlywinks games came with miniature inch-high bowling pins that were set up to be knocked down by the leaping winks. For an easier simulation of a large-scale sport, place 18 cutoff paper cups on the living room floor for a game of **Tiddlywinks Golf.** Each player snaps a single wink from hole to hole, keeping a tally of the number of strokes needed to get the wink in each hole.

For a fairly raucous game with three or four kids, run a **Tiddlywinks Race.** Mark a starting line and a finish line about six or eight feet apart. The route will be circuitous, but the usual rule applies: the first to cross the finish line wins. ❧

Crokinole

- ◆ NUMBER: two players or four, playing as partners
- ◆ EQUIPMENT: a Crokinole board and six "cookies" per player (usually red or black)
- ◆ DESCRIPTION: one of the most active, entertaining and sociable sit-down games
- ◆ COMPLEXITY: all ages can play together; kids often whup adults
- ◆ TIP: the basics can be learned in minutes; technique improves with practice

CROKINOLE IS A bit like **Marbles,** brought indoors and made adult and respectable with its own polished wooden board and flattened round playing pieces, instead of skittering glass balls. The origins of the game are obscure. The first American board dates from 1880, but the game was played in Canada several decades before that, initially among the Mennonites of south-central Ontario. In play, Crokinole has ele-

ments in common with the British game of Squails, in which wooden disks were shoved by hand toward the center of a round table, and with **Caroms,** an Indian game in which players flick wooden rings across a fenced wooden board so that they rebound off the sides and into netted corner pockets. But whereas Squails was a pub pastime and Caroms was played for money, Crokinole was a game of impeccable moral character,

associated with neither gambling nor drink. Canada's largest department store, Eaton's, marketed it in the latter part of the last century as a game "with no objectionable features whatever"—hardly a rousing endorsement, but a recommendation sure to win favor among moralistic Victorians.

Despite its British, Indian and Mennonite origins, Crokinole derives its name from *croquignole*, French for a small, hard biscuit, which each of the chunky wooden playing disks, or *cookies*, resembles. *Croquignole* is also the word for the distinctive flick of the finger with which the cookies are shot as a player tries to displace one of his opponent's disks or sink a 20.

Crokinole boards can still be bought, though many are now made from pressed hardboard, a poor imitation of the original mahogany or maple. If you find a good old board at an auction or a garage sale, wash it down with a wood cleaner and wax it well. Make sure the shooting surface

Crokinole

is smooth and level, without cracks, splits or heaves. If necessary, replace the rubber sheathing on the posts; this deadens the force of the cookies caroming off metal. You may be able to buy replacement cookies at a games store; if not, wooden checkers will do, although a smooth surface on the disk is preferable. You can also make your own cookies by slicing maple dowels and sanding the pieces.

Crokinole is a simple game with few rules. Shoot for a 20 whenever you can; if there are opponents on the board, get them out of the way first; ditch the opponent's cookies, and in the end, leave as many of your own cookies in the high-scoring ring as possible. None of these moves tax the brain severely. Above all, Crokinole is a social sport. Kibitzing among the players is not only allowed but essential. Partners regularly advise each other on shots and angles, agreeing between them who will pick off which cookie and how. With practice, members of the family will all become crack shots. One household brings out the board every night after supper; the loser does the dishes, a house rule that has improved their game immensely.

Equipment: The Crokinole board looks like a horizontal wooden target, octagonal in shape, usually 30 inches across. Its playing surface is marked off in three concentric circles, with a shallow depression in the mid-

dle, as illustrated above, Crokinole's answer to the bull's-eye. Around the outside is a narrow *ditch*, or gutter, bounded by a low fence. The concentric circles increase in value toward the center. Next to the ditch is a 5-point ring, then a 10-point ring, a 15-point ring and a 20-point hole in the middle, just slightly larger than a cookie. (Each ring is 3½ inches wide; the hole is 1⅜ inches.) The 5-point ring is divided by thin lines into four quadrants, one each for four players. Eight short posts surround the 15-point ring, a stockade that makes the high-scoring center particularly hard to hit.

Each player needs six Crokinole cookies, 1¼ inches in diameter and ⅜ inch thick, with smoothly rounded edges. One player has red or natural disks, the other black. The board usually comes with a set of 12 natural and 12 dark-stained cookies, enough for four players.

The Object of the Game: To land your cookies in the hole or as close as possible; to accumulate the highest score in each round.

The Play: Players sit opposite each other with the board centered so that each player is in front of a quadrant. If four are playing, partners sit opposite each other. Each player has six cookies; one player or team has black, and the other has natural (or red). Players each shoot a cookie to-

ward the center. If someone lands a 20, remove the cookie; otherwise, leave the cookies on the board until all players have a turn. The person who lands a 20 or who lands closest to the 20 goes first; play continues clockwise around the board.

The first shooter sets her cookie on the outside rim of the 5-point ring, anywhere between the quadrant lines. As long as the tiniest sliver of cookie kisses the ring line or the quadrant line, the shot is legal. The board is clear, so she shoots for a 20. If she is successful, she lifts out the cookie and sets it aside, off the board. If she misses, the cookie stays where it stops. Either way, the turn passes clockwise to the next player. Each person gets one shot at a time. Players take turns shooting until all the cookies have been played.

If a player misfires—hits too weakly or accidentally hits his cookie—he can retrieve it as long as it doesn't reach the 10-point ring. When the board is clear and a player is shooting for a 20, the cookie must come to rest in the 15-point ring; if not, it is removed to the ditch. This prevents players from positioning their cookies in defensive spots behind the posts for a guaranteed 10 points.

As long as there is an opponent's cookie on the board, a player must aim for it. If she misses, her cookie goes in the ditch. A combination shot—hitting one of your own cookies so that it hits an opponent's cookie—is allowed, but if neither cookie hits the opponent, both go in the ditch.

Generally, if a cookie touches the outside rim of the 5-point ring after it is shot, it is considered out of play. You may decide, however, to leave those cookies on the board and eliminate only cookies that are actually in the ditch. If a cookie goes into the ditch, then caroms back onto the board, it must be returned to the ditch. If it hit any cookies when it jumped out of the ditch, they stay where they come to rest. Don't put them back where they were.

A cookie that hangs over the edge of the 20-hole or is cocked inside the hole is not considered a 20 until it lies flat. Players may not jostle the board when a cookie is cocked. If a future shot by any player knocks the cookie flat, it scores 20 for its owner. Some house rules allow players to turn the board to make a shot, but this may knock over a cocked cookie. Instead, a player should get up from the chair to line up a shot on the farthest reaches of the quadrant. Some persnickety players allow only leaning: the board must not be moved, chairs cannot be tipped, and one cheek must be firmly in contact with the seat at all times.

The person with the last cookie has the *hammer*, the most advantageous shot of the round. When the hammer is shot, the round is over. Players (or teams) add up their scores, record the final results and start a new round, the player to the left of the first shooter in the last round starts the next.

The Score: Cookies score according to the ring they are in at the end of the game. Any cookies that touch a line are moved into the lower-scoring ring. For instance, if a cookie is on the boundary between 5 and 10, it scores 5. Then players cancel out the black and white cookies on the board. For instance, if there is both a white and a black cookie in the 5-point ring, they cancel each other and go in the ditch. Likewise, three whites in the 10-point ring cancel out two blacks in the 15-point ring. They all go in the ditch, leaving only one black cookie in the middle ring for a score of Black 10. White has a 20, however, so the final score is White 10.

Players can also add up their own cookies and then subtract the loser's score from the winner's to determine the number of points the winner earns. Either way, only the winner scores in each round; the loser gets zero. The score after each round is tallied, and the first player or team to reach 100 points wins.

For a longer game, add or subtract the winner's score from the running total at the end of each round. For instance, after the first round, Joan has 45 points and Ted has 20, so Joan scores 25 (45-20). In the next round, Joan earns 10 and Ted earns 25, so

Ted scores 15 for the round (25-10). Ted's score for that round is subtracted from Joan's running score, so the final tally after round two is 10 points for Joan. Continue until one player or team reaches 100 points (the other will have zero).

With differential scoring, games between equals go on and on. A Canadian player with the St. Jacobs (Ontario) Crokinole Club remembers one game in his father's store that was played three hours a night for five consecutive nights; it was finally settled by declaring a time limit. The score, after 15 hours of play, was 20-0.

Technique: Most of the skill of Crokinole rests in the flick of the finger. There is no officially sanctioned form, but the best players seem to rest their thumb on the surface of the board, tucking the forefinger (or middle finger) against the ball of the thumb, as if making the OK sign. You can lay your forefinger horizontally against the surface or shoot with your forefinger perpendicular to the surface, as illustrated below, whichever gives you the best aim. Keep the cookie snug up against the forefinger; flicking

the finger forward propels the cookie in the same direction. Many beginners come away with bruised fingernails from holding their fingers too far away from the cookie and batting it, instead of pushing it forward. The flick is gentler than you'd expect. To get the feel of it, practice sinking some 20s before you play a game.

A good Crokinole player sinks a 20 every time the board is clear. This takes accuracy and control. You need a harder flick to send your opponent's cookie flying into the ditch and an understanding of angles and rebound if you want to sink a 20 after knocking your opponent off the board. (Veteran billiard and Marbles players have an advantage here.) Knocking off two opponents while sinking a 20 is not unusual; knocking five opponents into the ditch, then sinking a 20 with the same cookie is the stuff of legends.

Variation: Very skilled players can try **Ricochet Crokinole**. Players have to hit a post before hitting an opponent's cookie or sinking a 20. This is closer to Caroms and requires considerable technique.   ∾

Crokinole Shooting Technique

Caroms

- ◆ OTHER NAMES: **known under various spellings, including Carums, Carroms, Carooms and Kairams**
- ◆ NUMBER: **two players or four, playing as partners**
- ◆ EQUIPMENT: **a Caroms board; nine white disks, nine black disks, one red queen and a striker for each player**
- ◆ DESCRIPTION: **a game of angles and accuracy, like a combination of Marbles and Tabletop Billiards**

Originally from India, Burma and Yemen, Caroms became well known in North America as one of dozens of games offered on the omnibus game boards of the turn of the century. Manufactured for years as a separate board game by an American company called Carrom Industries, it is among the most ubiquitous and least-understood boards in the recreation rooms of America.

The board is a rectangle of wood, usually plywood, about two feet square and framed to keep the disks within its borders. The corners are cut out and fitted with string pockets, much like a billiard table. (The entrance to the pocket is one and a half times the diameter of the striker.) The board is divided into four triangles by diagonals, the foul lines that define one person's area of play. At the center of the board is a series of three concentric circles: the outside one 7 inches in diameter, the middle one 6 inches in diameter and the center one 1¼ inches in diameter, exactly the size of a disk. The circles are set within two concentric squares: one 15 inches on each side and the other 18 inches on each side. The outer one is the baseline, and the space between the two squares is the shooting rectangle, where the striker is placed to take a shot at the disks in the circle.

The disks may be solid wooden pieces like **Crokinole** cookies or wooden rings, just over an inch in di-ameter. Each player has nine disks of a distinct color and a striker, 1⅓ inches across, often made of bone or ivory. There is also a red queen, which is placed in the center circle on the board. At the beginning of a game, the white disks are arranged in a Y extending from the queen, as illustrated in the detail. Three black disks are nestled in the crook of each arm of the Y, and within the three black disks, a single white disk is placed.

The Object of the Game: To knock your own disks into the pockets; to knock the queen into a pocket; to leave as many of your opponents on the board as possible.

The Play: Players decide who gets the black pieces; black goes first. The first player puts the striker in the shooting rectangle on his quarter of the board. He flicks it toward the cluster of disks, aiming to knock one of his own into a pocket. (The motion is a finger flick, as in Crokinole.) The striker must go over the front line of the rectangle. A player's fingers can extend over the foul lines that define his quarter, and his fingers and hand may extend over the base line, but no

Caroms

other parts of his body can touch anywhere else on the board.

If one of the player's disks goes into a pocket, he gets another turn. He returns his striker to the shooting rectangle and shoots again. The striker does not have to hit the disk directly into a pocket. It can hit a disk that bumps a second one into the pocket or ricochet off the walls of the board. Every time one of his disks goes into a pocket, the player gets another turn. If a player pockets an opponent's disk, however, his turn ends. The disk stays in the pocket, and the other player now has a chance to shoot. Each player continues to shoot only as long as one of his or her own disks lands in a pocket.

If a player pockets his own striker, his turn is over and he has to pay a penalty. His opponent takes one of the player's disks out of a pocket and puts it anywhere in the center. If a player pockets his striker and a disk at the same time, the opponent takes the pocketed disk plus a penalty disk and puts them both in the center.

If a disk skips off the board, the turn is over, and the disk is put back at the center of the board. If the striker skips and lands on a disk, the striker is simply removed. If a disk was pocketed as a result of the turn, the player gets another shot. Likewise, if a disk lands on a striker, the striker is removed and the disk left in place. If his own disk was pocketed during that turn, the player shoots again.

Anytime after a player has pocketed one of her own disks, she can try to pocket the queen. After hitting the queen into a pocket, a player must pocket another disk; otherwise, the queen is returned to the center together with all the player's disks that were pocketed in that turn.

The round, or *board*, is over when one player pockets all her disks—whether the queen is pocketed or not.

Several boards are usually played in each game.

The Score: The player who pockets all her disks scores 1 point for each of her opponent's disks still on the board and 5 points if she has pocketed the queen. (The queen scores only if pocketed by the winner of that round.) If the winning player already has 24 points or more, the queen's value drops to 1 point. The first player to score 29 wins the game. Three games are usually played at a sitting.

Variation: Instead of pocketing the red queen at any time during the game, players save it for last. Players cannot pocket it until all the rest of their disks are in the pockets.

Darts

- ◆ NUMBER: **two-person Darts is best; stage a round robin of playoffs if more want to play**
- ◆ EQUIPMENT: **a dartboard, three darts per person and a chalkboard (or paper) for keeping score**
- ◆ COMPLEXITY: **best played with people of equal skill; technique improves rapidly with practice**
- ◆ DURATION: **a basic game takes only 10 minutes or so, but several hours can happily be passed with popcorn, conversation and Darts**

ALTHOUGH DARTS, in the sense of Cupid's cutoff arrows, have existed for centuries (the first reference in English is 1314), the game of Darts is a relatively recent phenomenon. A miniature archery board was sold as part of the game Dartelle in the 1880s, but the numbered pie-like dartboard used today only appeared in 1896, invented by a Lancashire carpenter named Brian Gamlin. The game was hugely popular in pubs and took on the legitimacy of indoor sport when the London tabloid *News of the World* sponsored the first major competition in 1927. Since then, competitive Darts, and the family dartboard, has spread around the world. Britain, of course, is still the home of Darts—a 1980 survey showed that 10 percent of Brits play regularly—but Darts has also found a home in America's recreation rooms.

Darts is played on a standard international board, known colloquially as the *clock*, the *treble* or the *No. 1*. The best boards are made of tightly packed hemp or sisal bristles—about 16 million of them that knit back together after a dart is pulled out. Cheaper boards made of wound paper soon become riddled with holes and aren't worth the investment.

Choosing the actual darts is not so simple. A dart has four parts—needle, body, shaft and flight—each of which comes in a variety of materials and designs. Originally made of wood, the body material of choice for experts nowadays is tungsten, a high-density metal that makes for sleek yet solid darts. Most dart bodies, however, are brass and come in several shapes, as illustrated on the following page: the straight barrel has its weight evenly distributed along the length; the center-weight barrel is built like a middle-aged banker; the torpedo barrel is widest and heaviest where the shaft meets the tip. Regardless of shape, most are ridged for a better grip.

A metal needle point is fixed into one end of the body, and a shaft, usually plastic, is screwed into the other end to hold the flight. Both the shaft and the point can be replaced as they become damaged or dull. (Profession-

Straight, Center-Weight and Torpedo Barrels (left to right)

als always carry special dart sharpeners to keep the point honed.) The flight gives the dart stability as it flies and is usually made of plastic. The best and most expensive flights are made from the leading wing feathers of a turkey; the second best are paper flights, which a player folds and slots into the end of a shaft before a game. But for starters, plastic will suffice. All flights must be replaced regularly.

Darts are a personal investment: test the weights and sizes for what feels comfortable. Throw a few at a dartboard (games shops usually have practice boards set up). The maximum length and weight of darts is 12 inches and 1.75 ounces, but what you buy will likely be the length of a pencil and weigh between half an ounce and an ounce. Shop for thinness, precision and balance. As with most things in life, you get what you pay for.

Perfect equipment does not ensure a perfect game, of course. Practice the techniques described below until your stance, grip and concentration are second nature; professionals throw darts several hours a day. If you think that's a lot of Darts, consider this: in 1976, four men at the Rose and Crown Pub in Santa Ana, California, played non-stop Darts, in shifts, for 725 hours 6 minutes—more than 30 days of round-the-clock Darts.

Equipment: A standard dartboard is 18 inches in diameter, with a 2-inch band around the outer edge for the numbers and an inner scoring circle about 13 inches wide. The board is divided into a 20-piece pie, with the numbers 1 to 20 cleverly arranged so that each high number is sandwiched between two lower ones; the highest scores are earned at maximum risk. A narrow ring around the outside of the wedges—the crust around the pie—is the *doubles* ring; a dart that lands inside this ring scores double. About halfway through the pie is the *trebles* ring; a dart that lands in this band scores triple. At the center of the board is the bull's-eye; the very center scores 50, and the narrow ring around the center scores 25. Traditionally, the board is black, with the scoring wedges colored alternately black and yellow or black and white. The doubles and trebles rings are often green and red; the outside of the bull's-eye is usually yellow, with red at the center. A web of thin metal wires (the *spider*) divides the board into scoring *beds*, so a dart can never land squarely on a boundary. The upper section of the board is called *upstairs*, and the lower section *downstairs*; the left half is the *married man's side* (the right side is unnamed).

Hang the dartboard where it is convenient and will get lots of use—a kitchen wall is perfect. There should be about 10 feet of open space in front of the wall. According to the rules established in 1976 by the World Darts Federation, the minimum throwing distance is 7 feet 9¼ inches, but there are a lot of regional variations. Anything from six to nine feet is acceptable, and eight feet is probably most common. At floor level, measure out from the wall eight feet, and with electrician's tape or a grease pencil, draw the toe line on the floor. Professionals call this the *oche* (pronounced like hockey without the h). Hang the board so that the center of the inner bull's-eye is 5 feet 8 inches from the floor, with the 20 segment at the top and the 3 at the bottom. If the players are amateurs, mount a square of cork on the wall behind the board, large enough to catch any wild throws. For a professional touch, light the board from above and in front so that the darts cast no shadows. Keep your darts—three for each player—and a chalkboard for scoring nearby.

The Object of the Game: To throw three darts so that they strike the target in a particular scoring order; to be the first to go out and to win the highest score.

The Play: The order of play is decided either by a toss of a coin or by *bulling-off*: each player throws a dart, and the person who lands it closest to the bull's-eye goes first. If your opponent begins, take heart in an old Darts proverb: win the toss, lose the game.

For all the games below, the basic rules apply. Players take turns throwing, each player throws three darts at a turn, and a player who oversteps the oche with any part of the foot does not score the points earned by that throw. Darts that land in the wall around the board, stick into the flight of another dart, bounce off the metal rings or fall out of the board before the player can retrieve them do not score; the player may not throw again. However, a player who drops a dart before or during a throw can rethrow.

Players alternate turns until one has completed the sequence—throwing 1 to 20 in numerical order or in order around the board—or has reduced his score to zero.

Players usually play a number of *legs*; for instance, two out of three or three out of five games. It is customary for the winner of one leg to *stay on* and play the next person who chalks her initials on the board, a signal that she wants to challenge the winner.

The Score: Each player adds up the total of his three darts after each turn and marks it on the chalkboard. In some games, players have to *double in*—throw a double before their darts can count—or *double out*—throw a double to go out on an exact count. Players keep a running tally of their scores, subtracting or adding depending on the game. The first person to reach zero or the person with the highest score at the end of the game wins.

Technique: A few minutes of watching a British pub match or an international Darts tournament on television proves that stance and grip are a matter of individual taste. You can stand and throw any way you like, as long as you feel balanced and comfortable. Beginners might try resting the toe of their front foot against the oche, with the back foot about 12 inches behind, at a 45-degree angle. Center your weight over the front foot (leaning is allowed). As for grip, a dart is not a pencil. Hold it instead so that the point is supported. Your elbow should act as a pivot, your arm moving forward smoothly and your hand releasing the dart just before the arm is fully extended. After throwing the dart, your arm continues forward. If you don't follow through, the dart will likely take a nose dive. Most of the action is in the wrist, rather than the arm. The type of dart you use will also influence the delivery. A fast push motion works well with heavy darts, while a gentle lobbing throw is more appropriate with a lighter dart. Sight along the dart, focusing on the part of the board you want to hit.

As with most long-standing games, certain moves have accrued nicknames. The 20 is known as the *top*. Hitting 20, 1 and 5 in one turn is called *bed-and-breakfast*, or sometimes *brewer*. Landing three darts in order in the single, double and treble beds of one number is *shanghai*. All three darts in one double or treble bed is *three in a bed*. When you score a single number, instead of the attempted double, you have *cracked*. When you have

Dartboard

Doubles ring
Scoring Bed
Bull's-eye
Trebles ring

99 left in a game of 501 or 301, you are *in the wilderness*. The double-1 is the *madhouse*, or *up in Annie's room*. A score of 111 is a *Nelson* (from the saying, "One eye, one arm, one . . . .); a score of zero is *Oxo*; a score of 100 is a *ton*; and 33 is *feathers*. *Mugs away* means losers go first.

Variations: The basic tournament Darts game is **501**. It is a two-person game in which each player starts with an opening score of 501 and throws the highest scores possible to bring the total down to zero. From the first throw, the total points of each turn are added up and subtracted from 501. Players must double out. If a player scores too many points on his last throw, he *goes bust*, which means the whole turn is ignored, and he has the same score as before. For instance, if a player's remaining score is 4 and he throws a 5, he goes bust, and the turn doesn't count. Next time, if his dart lands in the doubles ring of the 2, he wins.

In 1986, professional British Darts player John Lowe completed 501 in nine darts during a televised match. He scored three triple-20s in his first turn, three triple-20s in his second turn and triple-17, triple-18 and double-18 in his third and last turn. In an interview after the game, he shrugged his shoulders and said, "A win is a win." Nevertheless, it's something to shoot for.

A variation of 501 is **301**. Each player starts with 301 points and subtracts the points scored with each dart, reducing the score to zero. The main difference is that players must double in as well as double out. No points are scored until a player lands a dart in the doubles ring. Between players of unequal experience, this can give one player a critical head start.

Designed more as practice rounds, the variations **101** and **201** can be over in as little as three or four throws. **Round the Clock**, or **Round the World**, is a simple practice game that hones accuracy. Doubles and triples

Shanghai

don't count. Each player has to throw the numbers in sequence from 1 to 20, then the outer and the inner bull's-eyes. The record time for going Round the World with doubles is 2 minutes 13 seconds—and the player pulled out his own darts!

Twice Round and Two Tops is a British variation in which players start at 1, throw to 20, start at 1 again, then throw to 19 and finish off with two double-20s (tops). In this version of the game, doubles count, both as the single number and as the double, allowing the player to skip ahead to the number following the double. For instance, a player throws 3, then double-4, which counts as the required 4 and also as 8; the player then throws for 9. Doubles thrown above 10 allow you to skip only one number. For instance, a player might throw 11, double-12, then 14, skipping 13 as a reward for the double-12. A *perfect game* is 12 throws of the darts: double-1, 3, double-4, 9, double-10, double-1, 3, double-4, 9, double-10, double-20, double-20.

Another form of Round the Clock is **Shanghai**, in which players throw

darts at each number in sequence, 1 to 20, but they throw all three darts at the number, trying to score as high a total as possible. Doubles and triples count, so the highest total for 1s is 9, the highest for 8s is 72 (3 x triple-8). If a player fails to hit the number with any of the three darts, he is out of the game. And if a player hits a single, double and triple of the appropriate number in one turn, she has gone shanghai and wins the game. If no one goes shanghai, the highest score wins.

Tac-Tics, also known as **Mickey Mouse**, uses only the numbers from 10 to 20 and the two bull's-eyes; each is in play until every player has hit it three times, at which point the number is eliminated. (Sometimes, only the numbers 15 to 20 and the bull's-eyes are used.) As the name suggests, Tac-Tics is a highly strategic game and one of the most fascinating and fun in Darts, although it is best between players of equal skill.

The object is for a player to hit a number three times. Doubles count as two hits, triples as three. When a player has three hits on a number, it belongs to him, and any further hits

on that number—by him or his opponent—score for him. (A number doesn't score until it belongs to a player.) When his opponent has hit the number three times, the number is removed from play. For example, if a player opens by throwing a triple-20, the number is "his" and scores for him until his opponent hits it three times. He has to decide whether to aim for the 20 and start building his score or to try for triples on 19 and 18 and claim those numbers for himself too. His opponent, on the other hand, has to decide whether to aim for the triple-20, 19 and 18, to close down those numbers and thus stop the other player's score-building potential, or to aim for the triple-17, 16 and 15 and claim those numbers for herself so that she can start building a score. In the scoreboard illustrated, the 20 belongs to Y, who has scored for one of his own hits and two of M's. When M hits it one more time, the 20 will be out of play, and Y will have scored 80.

Score the game by writing the numbers 10 to 20 down the center of the chalkboard, with the players' scores noted on either side. Mark an X beside a number on a player's side each time she hits the number. As soon as she has three hits, each subsequent hit scores for her until her opponent also has three hits. Then the X's and the number are rubbed off the board; the score, of course, stays. The highest score wins. ❧

Tac-Tics

Ping-pong

- **OTHER NAMES:** Table Tennis
- **NUMBER:** two or four players; solo games for the agile only
- **EQUIPMENT:** Ping-pong balls, a paddle for each player, a net, a table and a bare minimum of 12 feet of open space
- **DESCRIPTION:** can be played as a smash-bang game or a genteel pinging sport
- **COMPLEXITY:** kids must be as tall as the table to play; no upper age limit
- **DURATION:** the International Table Tennis League has a time limit of 20 minutes per game, but it rarely takes that long

According to a turn-of-the-century article in *The New York Times*, Ping-pong "started with cigar-box lids for bats, champagne corks for balls and a row of books for a net." You can try this, but the game is probably best played with the right equipment, a setup that looks a little like a tennis court for trolls. Although the table is only nine feet long, you need several feet of open space at either end for an active game—the recommended playing area is 25 by 15 feet. Official rules also require players to wear clothing of a single dark color on their upper body (pullovers, if worn, must match the shirt), so as not to distract the opponent. And one very serious manual cautions against polishing the table lest pools of reflected light put players off their game.

Home-style Ping-pong is a little more flexible. Most families put the table in the basement, where balls bounce off the heating ducts and the furnace in what poet and essayist Donald Hall calls gas-furnace pong. In *Fathers Playing Catch with Sons*, Hall describes his lifetime affiliation with Ping-pong, sometimes the formal game but now one he plays daily with his wife, "keeping five or six balls in play—not, alas, at the same time, but in sequence—so that we need seldom stop to pick up the errant ball; when we do pause, we pick up the whole bunch. We are each other's hysterical backboards, furiously serving and returning, volleying a ball that would surely overshoot the table, hitting a ball on the second bounce or the slide if we must, keeping the air loose with a white ball flying. And if a ball pops up to the ceiling, zaps between two-by-fours and drops on the table, we hit it again; if a crazy shot hits the cement-block wall and veers toward one of us, we pretend we play squash and keep it in play. And when a ball is gone to the dirt floor, one of us immediately serves another so that our play is one long rally with a few ball-searching interruptions. In the heat of the moment, when a ball drops to the floor, sometimes each of us serves a new ball at the same time—and we work double-pong for a few seconds at least." Hardly tournament play, but formidable house rules, nonetheless.

Equipment: The table is 5 feet wide, 9 feet long and 30 inches high, made of a material resilient enough to give the ball an eight- or nine-inch bounce—usually ¾-inch plywood. The tabletop is stained a dark, unreflective green and bordered with a ¾-inch white line. (At the ends of the table, this white line is called the *baseline*.) A thin white line down the center divides the table into courts for four-person play.

The table is bisected by a net strung tightly between clamps so that it is six inches high along its entire length. The balls were originally made of light rubber covered with knitted webbing, but these were replaced by celluloid balls in the late 1890s. A ball is just over an inch in diameter, hollow and feather-light, weighing only an ounce and a half. Old balls are often *wobblers*, so misshapen from Ping-pong smashes that they no longer bounce true. But a new ball can wobble too. Spin it on a flat surface to see whether it is true, and pinch both sides slightly to see whether it has equal "give" all round.

Before 1900, paddles (also called bats or rackets) were made of metal, glass, plaster or wood covered with vellum, sandpaper, cork or leather. In 1905, just before Ping-pong's first demise, the rubber-faced paddle appeared. Paddles today are either solid wood or a thin sandwich of wood covered on both sides with dark, stippled rubber. The pimpled surface controls the ball and, if hit appropriately, can give the ball considerable spin. For a while in the 1950s, there was a sponge-faced paddle, but it was banned from competition in 1959.

The Object of the Game: To return the ball over the net, keeping it in play; to be the first to score 21 points.

The Play: A toss of a coin decides who serves. The server chooses which end of the table she wants to play. Each player has five serves, regardless of who scores, then the serve passes to the other player. The serve alternates during the game, each player serving five times per turn.

The server hits the ball so that it bounces once on her side of the table, then over the net. The other player lets it bounce once, then hits the ball in return. The ball is struck back and forth over the net, always bouncing once on a side before it is hit.

When a player hits the ball before it bounces on her side, fails to return the ball over the net or returns it so that it does not bounce on the other side of the table, her opponent scores a point.

As long as the ball hits the tabletop, even if it barely skims the white line around the edge, it is in play. If it definitely hits the *side* of the tabletop, it is a dead ball and is considered a miss by the last player to strike it (and earns a

The Ping-pong Handshake Grip

point for the other). If a player drops his racket after he hits the ball, the ball is still in play (unless the dropped racket falls on the net). The butterfingered player picks up his paddle and continues if he can. He cannot, however, hit the ball with his open hand if he is unable to retrieve his paddle quickly enough.

Volleying—returning a ball that has not hit the table—is strictly illegal and scores a point for the other player. Likewise, if the server misses the ball during the serve, the other player scores. The same applies if a ball is hit twice by one player or bounces twice on one side of the table; the other player wins a point. If a player touches the table or the net with anything other than the ball while the ball is in play, the opponent scores a point. (For example, a player leaning forward to reach a net ball can't support himself with his free hand on the table.) However, if the ball touches the net or a player serves before her opponent is ready, then it is considered a *let*, and the player takes the serve again, with-

out penalty. (This holds true regardless of how the ball is hit after it dribbles over the net to the other side.)

A game is over when one player reaches the target score with a 2-point margin. After the first game, players switch ends, and the loser of the first game serves first in the second game. Players usually play the best three out of five.

The Score: Each player keeps track of the points he or she scores. (Scores are so low that mental arithmetic should suffice.) Play continues until one person scores 21. Games must be won by at least 2 points. When the score is 20-all, players take turns serving, instead of taking five serves each. The player who first earns a 2-point lead wins.

Technique: A Ping-pong paddle is held much like a tennis racket—a handshake grip—except you hold it close to the blade, your forefinger extended and resting along the back of the paddle, your thumb along the

front as illustrated at left. Shift the forefinger and thumb until the grip feels comfortable. Asian players tend to hold the handle between the thumb and forefinger, like a pen.

Beginners usually start with the simple *push* or *block* shot. Hold the paddle at right angles to the table, and hit the ball horizontally as it bounces straight up from the table. This shot keeps the ball in play but is easy to return. With two players using push shots, the ball can bounce back and forth indefinitely. If your opponent sends the ball back with a spin on it, however, it is difficult to adjust the angle of the blade quickly enough to push the ball back over the net.

Forehand or backhand *drives* are harder to return and are therefore better offensive strokes. Turn your body slightly in either direction, tilt the paddle toward the net and swing it toward the ball with an upward stroke, using your whole arm to hit the ball, brushing over it and ending the stroke with the paddle high in the air above you. This motion propels the ball forward with great speed and gives it a *topspin* (forward rotation).

Forehand and backhand *chops* are defensive shots: downward strokes of the paddle, the blade tilted away from the net to produce a *backspin* (backward rotation). Start with the paddle high above your shoulder, then chop forward and down behind the ball at a 45-degree angle. The ball usually stays low and has enough of a spin on it that your opponent sends it back into the net.

A *smash* shot is almost guaranteed to win the point. Aside from sheer speed, you can also score points by *angling* the ball past the other player or putting it out of reach, by placing either a *deep ball* that bounces just inside the baseline, a *short ball* that bounces close to the net or a *drop shot* that barely clears the net, falling too close to be returned.

Before playing a game, practice a few serves. Lay the ball in the palm of your open, outstretched hand. According to regulations, the thumb must be free, the ball neither cupped nor pinched. (If you are right-handed, the paddle is in your right hand and the ball in your left; vice versa if you are left-handed.) Throw the ball straight up, and hit it with the paddle. Don't throw the ball up too far; a few inches is enough. If you hold the ball about eight inches behind and above the baseline, its first bounce will be just shy of the middle of your court, and the ball will be steadily in play.

The open-palm serve is not always used in the recreation rooms of the nation, but it became mandatory for competitive play after the American teams developed a *knuckle-spin* serve, squirting the ball out of their free hand onto the paddle, giving it such a spin with their fingers that it could never be returned. You can serve any way you like, but outlawing the knuckle-spin seems fair. Confound your partner instead by varying the length and speed of your serve.

Variation: In Doubles Ping-pong, the narrow line that divides the table in half lengthwise—the *service line*—comes into play. A toss of the coin decides which team serves first, and the players on that team decide between them who serves first.

The server stands at the right side of the table and serves so that the ball bounces once on the right half-court,

crosses the net diagonally and bounces on the other team's right half-court. Play can continue in order, with the ball bouncing from the server's right half-court to the opposition's right to the server's left to the opposition's left—A to C to B to D, as illustrated —so each player has a turn to hit the ball.

In home games, however, after the initial serve and return, the ball can be hit anywhere as long as the players take turns returning it. Some players even waive this rule, playing a free-for-all game in which either partner can hit the ball, calling it first to avoid collisions. Formal order of play is a good idea for beginners or for players of unequal skill; everyone gets some practice controlling the ball.

After the first server takes five turns, the serve passes to the other team and the players on the first team switch courts. For instance, the game begins with A serving to C. After five serves, the serve passes to C. A and B switch places, so C is serving to B. After C's five serves, the serve goes to B. C and D switch places, so B is serving to D. Finally, D serves, and A and B switch places, so D is serving to A.

Scoring for doubles is the same as for singles; game is 21 points. ❧

Service in Doubles Ping-pong

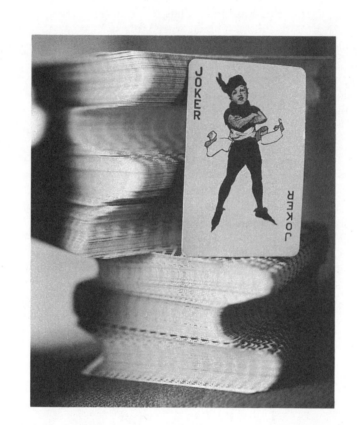

3

TRICKS
OF THE TRADE

Card Games

Behold four Kings in majesty revered,
With hoary whiskers and a forky beard
And four fair Queens, whose hand sustain a flower,
Four Knaves in garbs succinct, a trusty band,
Caps on their heads and halberts in their hand;
And parti-coloured troops, a shining train,
Draw forth to combat on the velvet plain.
—Alexander Pope
The Rape of the Lock

8

Beating the Devil:
Card Games for One

GAMES FOR ONE PLAYER are childish and simple," wrote Captain
Crawley in *The Card Players Manual* (1876). "When a man is
reduced to such a pass as playing cards by himself, he had better give up." Despite Crawley's advice, the popularity of solitary
card games has never waned; attitudes, however, have changed. "Patience,"
writes David Parlett in his 1979 classic, *The Penguin Book of Card Games*, "is
the mental equivalent of jogging. Its purpose is to tone the brain up and get
rid of unsociable mental flabbiness."

North Americans, more attuned perhaps to isolation than virtue, generally call one-person card games Solitaire, but Patience is the original name.
First described in a 1783 German manual as Patiencespiel, the game appeared
just 20 years after card layouts began to be used for cartomancy—fortune-
telling—which lends credence to the theory that Patience was, initially, a
lighthearted attempt to forecast the future. Supposedly a favorite with young
ladies, the game predicted nuptial destiny: if a player completed a sequence on
the Ace of Hearts, she would find love; on Diamonds, she would be courted;
Clubs foretold marriage; and Spades, a future of "single blessedness."

By the 19th century, hundreds of different Patience games were being played in Russia, Denmark, Iceland and England. During the 1890s, British games inventor Mary Whitmore-Jones compiled a seven-volume collection of Patience games. (She also invented a portable Patience board to expand the laps of card-playing long-distance travelers.)

The game that most of us know as Patience, or Solitaire, is really **Klondike**, a North American contribution to the genre and one of a large group of Solitaire games based on the principle of building sequences on certain foundation cards—in this case, Aces. Most other Solitaires are based on the principle of elimination: instead of arranging orderly piles, the object is to eliminate all the cards on the table by discarding those which match or which add up to certain numbers. Elimination games used to be much more popular. In *Foster's Encyclopedia of Games* (1897), five of the six Solitaires were elimination games. In the current *Hoyle's Modern Encyclopedia of Card Games*, 40 out of the 45 Solitaires are based on building sequences.

Whatever the Solitaire game, a win depends on two things: how much choice is allowed in the plays and how much information is revealed by the cards. The oldest forms of Solitaire—and most elimination-type games—offer hardly any choice at all: you deal the cards and play them as they lay. Some attention is required, but the outcome depends more on chance than on skill. This kind of Solitaire is a good way to introduce children to playing cards by themselves. Anyone who can recognize numbers and do simple math can play, and whether brilliant Uncle Harry or 4-year-old Sarah deals the cards, the result is usually the same. The thrill lies in making the game "come out," and the attempt can keep anyone engrossed for hours.

If there is little choice in the plays, it hardly matters how many cards you can see, but where there is choice, the amount of information revealed is crucial. If some cards remain hidden, the game is one of judgment and intuition. If, on the other hand, all cards are exposed for play, the game is one of pure analysis. It is like a puzzle—a problem presented for solution—yet it is still a game, because a new problem arises with every deal.

Although players have their preferences, the perfect Solitaire game demands enough strategy to keep you engaged yet includes enough twists—of logic or fate—to make you wonder whether, this time, you'll win.

Given the infinite ways these conditions can be met, it is no wonder that so many variations of Solitaire exist or that players become so hooked. Lewis Sutter, a self-professed New York Solitaire addict, estimated that he played 150,000 games in the first 10 years of his retirement, keeping a record of every win and loss. The results fill 10 huge ledgers. Sutter is not alone. The game may be solitary, but when you play, you join company with thousands around the world who are initiated to Solitaire's particular equipment, language and even rituals.

Although you can play with regular decks of cards, half-sized Solitaire cards bring sprawling games such as **Black Hole** back to manageable size. This also explains why Solitaire is so popular with young children: the small cards fit easily in little hands and can even be shuffled by a child.

Solitaire has its own lexicon, common to all manuals and serious aficionados. The *tableau* is the basic layout, the way the cards are dealt before the game begins. There is aesthetic as well as intellectual pleasure in the game, since the arrangement of cards is often as intricate and as delightful as the play itself. In the tableau, cards may be dealt horizontally in *rows* or vertically in *columns*. If the cards are dealt in *piles* or *overlapped*, only the final one is available for play. If cards are dealt *singly* in rows or columns, each one can be played. Sometimes a *reserve* of a specified number of cards is dealt.

Games such as Klondike, which are won by building up sequences, have *foundation cards* in the tableau, often Aces. Sometimes the foundation cards are removed from the deck before the deal and placed at the top of the playing area. The foundations may also appear during play.

The *stockpile*, or *stock*, is the cache of cards that remains after the tableau is dealt. These are usually held facedown and turned up one at a time or in little fans of three to bring more cards into play.

The *discard pile* is home for unplayable cards. Also called the waste pile, deadwood and talon, the stack of discards is sometimes turned over and reused as a stockpile a second or third time.

Sequences are series of cards in numerical order from low to high (an *ascending sequence*) or from high to low (a *descending sequence*). In Solitaire, Aces are almost always low, so a *complete ascending sequence* is A-2-3-4-5-6-7-8-9-10-J-Q-K. A *complete descending sequence* is K-Q-J-10-9-8-7-6-5-4-

3-2-A. A *continuous sequence* just keeps going: 4-3-2-A-K-Q-J. A *reversing sequence* can switch from ascending to descending, and vice versa, at any time: 9-8-7-6-5-6-7.

Depending on the rules of the game, sequences may be all of one suit; they may be of one color (for instance, Hearts and Diamonds together); they may alternate red and black suits; or they may be randomly colored, the sequences built only according to the denomination of the cards, 1-2-3-4-5 regardless of suit. Even within one game, the rules for building sequences on the tableau are usually different—and generally more liberal—than the rules for building sequences on the foundation cards. Sometimes sequences on the tableau can be moved as a unit—*en bloc*—which is a great advantage in winning the game.

Despite the richness of the language and the layout, Solitaire was initially not considered a true card *game* at all, because there was no opponent. Anyone who plays Solitaire knows, of course, that there is competition: you play against yourself, against the deck and against the forces of fate that arrange the cards each time you shuffle and deal. When you play alone, you play to beat the devil.

Those who take a dim view of Solitaire assume that solo cardplayers make certain they win every time. But devotees forswear such hollow victories. The real virtue of Solitaire is not patience but impunity: to play fair, even when there are no witnesses.

Of course, that's not to say that Solitaire has no room for creativity. With no one to object, you can fiddle with the rules as much as you like, which may explain the plethora of variations and the confusion of names among Solitaire games. "It is competently estimated," states *The Modern Hoyle*, "that there are 1,000 varieties of Solitaire, 999 of which are called **Idiot's Delight**."

Idiot's Delight

- ◆ EQUIPMENT: **one deck of 52, Ace high**
- ◆ DESCRIPTION: **a fast, easy time-passer; takes relatively little space**
- ◆ COMPLEXITY: **starter Solitaire; all luck, no strategy**

ANYONE WHO CAN count and recognize suits can play this game, yet despite its mindlessness, or perhaps because of it, it is a pleasant way to pass a half-hour. This game is at least as entertaining as most television sitcoms—hence, its name.

The Tableau: Shuffle the cards, and deal four cards faceup in a row.

The Object of the Game: Through a process of elimination, to end up with only four cards in the tableau.

The Play: If the opening tableau holds two cards from the same suit, discard the one with the lower number. If there is a pair, discard both. For instance, if the first deal yields 9♣, 9♥, 2♣ and 8♣, discard both 9s and the 2, since it is the lower of the two remaining Clubs. (If you lay down three of a kind, discard two.) Deal another four cards, filling the open spaces and covering any cards that remain from the previous deal. Don't make a move until all four are dealt, then remove pairs and the lower of two same-suit cards. This exposes cards underneath. Continue to remove pairs and low cards until you can no longer make a move. Deal another four cards, playing until the stockpile is gone. Since there is only one deal, Idiot's Delight rarely comes out, but it is fun to try.

Variation: In Aces Up, Aces are not removed during play. You win when all cards but the Aces are eliminated from the tableau—an almost unprecedented feat, but don't let that stop you from trying.

Monte Carlo

- ◆ EQUIPMENT: **one deck of 52, Ace low**
- ◆ DESCRIPTION: **a good basic matching game for anyone who can recognize pairs**
- ◆ COMPLEXITY: **fast and won about half the time**

ONLY THE VALUES of the cards count in this game. Players don't have to recognize suits; they need only spot pairs, which makes it an excellent introductory Solitaire for children.

The Tableau: Shuffle the deck, and deal 20 cards faceup in four rows of five cards each. Do not overlap the cards. The rest of the deck is the stockpile, which remains facedown.

The Object of the Game: To reduce the stockpile to zero.

The Play: Find pairs adjacent to each other—horizontally, vertically or diagonally—and discard them. You may remove only two cards at a time, even if, for example, there are three Aces in a row.

Fill the empty spaces with the cards that are directly below, sliding them up to fill the vacancies. Look again for pairs. When you can't eliminate any more cards, deal from the stockpile to bring the tableau back to 20.

For example, in the game illustrated, two 8s that touched diagonally have been removed from the tableau.

Cards are slid into the vacancies from the rows below, then vacancies in the bottom row are filled by dealing from the stockpile. When 10♠ is moved up, the pair of 10s can be discarded.

Repeat the play, discarding pairs, sliding cards into the empty spaces and refilling the tableau from the stockpile.

The game is over when you can't make any more moves; if the stockpile is gone, you win.

Variations: There are hundreds of similar matching games whose goal is to eliminate the stockpile or the entire tableau. **Sirap,** from Robert Harbin's *Family Card Games,* takes less space than Monte Carlo. Deal three rows of three cards each, faceup (nine cards in all). Discard *all* pairs; the touching rule does not apply.

Fill empty spaces from the stockpile. Whether the stockpile can be

Monte Carlo

Stockpile   Discard Pile

eliminated is entirely a matter of luck, but the game is more engaging because it is less likely to come out.

Adding up the values of the cards brings a measure of mathematical skill and strategy to matching games. Instead of removing two cards at a time, three, four or more may be taken away, provided they add up to the magic number. The tableau for **Take Eleven** is exactly as in Sirap, but instead of discarding pairs, remove cards that add up to 11: for instance, 9 and 2 or 5, 3, 2 and Ace. Ace counts 1; other cards count according to their denominations. Face cards have no value. Treat them as spaces: when a face card appears, deal another card on top. Remove both when you make 11.

Take Fourteen brings the face cards into play: Jacks count 11, Queens 12 and Kings 13. Deal 10 cards faceup in two rows of five cards each. Discard combinations that add up to 14. Deal cards from the stockpile to fill the spaces. Both games are won by emptying the stockpile.

Pyramid is easily won but has the added interest of a complicated tableau. Deal one card faceup in the top row, two in the next, then three, and so on, to the bottom row of seven cards. From this pyramid, remove cards that add up to 13, counting face cards as above. (Kings, which are worth 13, are removed by themselves.) In this game, the top card on the discard pile can also be used in play.

For **Take Ten**, deal 13 cards faceup in three rows: a row of five, then three, then five. Discard any *two* cards that add up to 10; you may not take more than two at a time. The exception is that the 10, Jack, Queen and King of each suit *must* be removed as a group. Deal cards from the stockpile to replace discards. You win by clearing the entire tableau, which is not a difficult task.   ∾

Clock Solitaire

- ◆ EQUIPMENT: **one deck of 52, Ace low**
- ◆ DESCRIPTION: **a very simple matching game**
- ◆ COMPLEXITY: **depends entirely on luck**
- ◆ TIP: **good for children who are just beginning to tell time**

COMPARED WITH the slap-dash pace of **Idiot's Delight**, a single game of Clock Solitaire can absorb a child for 15 minutes or more. One of a subspecies of Solitaire that relies on a pretty tableau, this game involves no strategy, so put away the left side of your brain and enjoy.

The Tableau: Shuffle the cards, and deal 12 facedown in a circle to represent the numbers on a clock face. Put a card facedown in the middle. Repeat three more times, creating 13 piles of four cards each. The entire deck is used up in the deal; there is no stockpile and no discard pile.

The Object of the Game: To complete the clock face with a set of four of a kind, faceup, each at its correct number (Kings in the center).

The Play: To begin, turn over the top card of the center pile. Put this card faceup in its correct position on the clock face: Jack at 11 o'clock, Queen at 12 o'clock, Ace at 1 o'clock, 2 at 2 o'clock, 6 at 6 o'clock, and so on. Every time you place a card on the clock face, remove a card from the bottom of that pile. Play this card in the appropriate place on the clock face, and remove a card from underneath that pile. When you draw a King, put it in the center, remove a card from under the center pile, and begin the play again.

For example, in the game illustrated, K♦ was just turned up from the bottom of the 9 pile. It will be played faceup in the center, and another card will be drawn from the bottom of the center pile.

The game ends when all four Kings are exposed. With luck, the clock will also be complete, all cards faceup and in the correct positions. ❧

Clock Solitaire

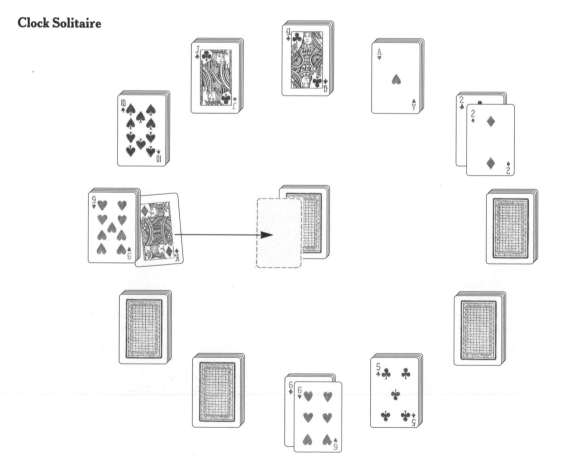

Trusty Twelves

- EQUIPMENT: **one deck of 52, Ace low**
- DESCRIPTION: **a good game to introduce the concept of sequences**
- COMPLEXITY: **fast and relatively easy; requires some judgment and skill**

THIS SIMPLE GAME, and the dozens like it, eliminates cards from the tableau not by matching or counting but by means of sequences, the basic premise of more sophisticated Solitaires.

The Tableau: Shuffle the deck, and deal three rows, each containing four cards faceup (12 cards in all). The rest of the pack is the stockpile; turn it facedown.

The Object of the Game: To eliminate the stockpile by building partial descending sequences of mixed suits.

The Play: Check the opening tableau for cards that form part of a sequence from King high to Ace low. Suits do not matter. For instance, if the tableau contains 9♠, 10♣ and 8♥, move 9♠ onto 10♣ and 8♥ onto 9♠. (Don't overlap the cards; it takes up too much space.) Only single cards may be moved, so start sequences on the highest card possible. As soon as there is an empty space, fill it from the stockpile. The new card may offer a better option than what is in the tableau. When the moves stop, so does the game.

Variation: The tableau in **Knotty Nines** contains only nine cards, dealt faceup in three rows of three. The rules are exactly the same as Trusty Twelves, but as the name implies, it is much more difficult to win. ∾

Kitty in the Corner

- EQUIPMENT: **one deck of 52, Ace low**
- DESCRIPTION: **involves sequences, not suits, and a little skill**

OFTEN CALLED Puss in the Corner, this simple Solitaire is especially good for kids, since, with a bit of strategy, it comes out almost every time.

The Tableau: Remove the four Aces from the deck, and place them faceup in a square. Shuffle the deck, then hold it facedown as the stockpile.

The Object of the Game: To build complete ascending sequences on each Ace. The suits can be mixed, but sequences must be all black or all red.

The Play: Deal cards one at a time from the stockpile. A red 2 can be played on A♦ or A♥; a black 2, on A♠ or ♣. Any other card is discarded, faceup, to a *kitty*, or discard pile. You are allowed to make four kitties, one at each corner of the Ace square. The top card in each kitty can be played at any time.

Continue to deal through the stockpile, building sequences on the Ace foundation piles. When the stockpile is finished, pick up a discard pile, turn it facedown, and play the cards one by one. Deal through each discard pile only once. When you are finished, with a little luck, you will be left with four complete sequences in the center and no kitties in the corner.

The secret to winning this game is clever discard. Make one discard pile for 2-3-4, another for 5-6-7, a third for 8-9-10, reserving the fourth for the royal family, J-Q-K. When the stockpile is finished, deal through the discard pile with the lowest numbers first. For a more challenging game that won't always come out, build on the Aces by suit, instead of color. ∾

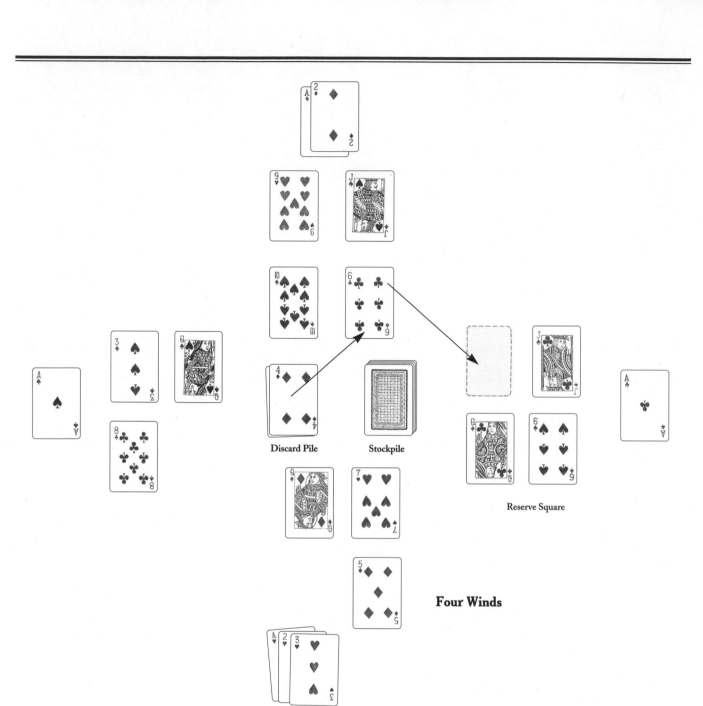

Discard Pile   Stockpile

Reserve Square

Four Winds

Four Winds

- ◆ EQUIPMENT: **one deck of 52, Ace low**
- ◆ DESCRIPTION: **involves sequences *and* suits**
- ◆ COMPLEXITY: **fairly long game; complex to play but not difficult to win**
- ◆ TIP: **needs a large playing surface, about three feet square**

THE TABLEAU for this game looks like a cross, with an Ace at each tip and four "reserve" cards forming each arm. This is a two-part game, in that a card from the stockpile can be played directly on an Ace, or it can be placed in the reserve for that Ace until it is needed.

The Tableau: Remove the four Aces from the deck, and position them well apart, like the points of a compass. Shuffle the cards, and deal four faceup to the inside of each Ace. These are the reserve squares. Leave space at the center for the stockpile (facedown) and the discard pile.

The Object of the Game: To build up the Aces by suits in complete ascending sequences.

The Play: Start the sequences by moving any appropriate cards from the tableau to the appropriate Aces: for instance, 2♥ and 3♥ onto A♥. (Stack the cards on the Aces; don't overlap them.) This creates spaces in the reserve squares that can be filled either from other squares or from the stockpile, but only with cards that are the same suit as the Ace governing that square. Once a card is moved to a reserve square, it cannot be moved again, except to the Ace.

After making moves from the tableau, turn over the first card in the stockpile, placing it faceup in the discard pile. You may play the card on an Ace, put it in a reserve square or leave it in the discard pile. Continue to deal through the stockpile, one card at a time, playing cards from the stockpile and the discard piles onto the Ace

sequences and the vacancies in the reserve squares whenever possible. When the stockpile is gone, turn over the discard pile, and deal through it, one card at a time. Only two deals are allowed (one through the stockpile and one through the discard pile).

Don't be in a hurry to fill the spaces in the reserve squares. Every open space increases your options and improves your chances of success. Open spaces allow you to move cards from one reserve square to another, creating a new space to hold a card in reserve until you need it to build a sequence. For example, in the game illustrated, 4♦ is dealt. Only the Ace and the 2 are on the Diamond foundation pile, so 4♦ can't be used now, but you don't

want to bury it in the discard pile. There is a space in the Club reserve and 6♣ in the Diamond reserve. Move 6♣ to its own reserve, and put 4♦ in the space created. The game can almost always be won if you are careful to move only low cards into the reserve squares on the first deal, allowing the high cards to languish in the discard pile until the second deal.

Variation: To make the game a little harder, leave the Aces in the deck. Lay out the tableau as described, but without the compass points. The Aces are set out as they come up in the deal, with the player choosing which reserve square gets which Ace. Play exactly like Four Winds. ∾

Klondike

- ◆ EQUIPMENT: **one deck of 52, Ace low**
- ◆ DESCRIPTION: **a long-standing favorite, usually played simply as Solitaire**
- ◆ COMPLEXITY: **a fast game of chance, rarely won**

Canada's contribution to Solitaire, Klondike became popular during the 1896 Yukon gold rush for which it was named. Described in one memoir as a "vicious gambling Patience," Klondike was undoubtedly responsible for a few fortunes changing hands. The so-called sourdoughs put up $50 for a pack of cards and, at the end of the game, got $5 back for each card played on an Ace. Since five or six cards is average, a player stood to lose $20 a game.

The Tableau: Shuffle the deck, and starting at the left, deal a row of seven cards facedown. Deal a second row on top of the first, starting with the second card from the left. Deal a third row, starting on the third card, and so on, until there are seven piles of cards, with one card in the first pile and seven in the last. Turn the top card of each pile faceup. The remaining 24 cards are the stockpile, turned facedown.

The Object of the Game: To build complete ascending same-suit sequences on the Aces, which appear during play and are moved above the tableau to become foundations.

The Play: On the tableau, move cards from one pile to another, building descending sequences of alternating colors. When a card is moved, turn the one underneath faceup, and continue play. As Aces appear, place them above the tableau, and build ascending sequences on them, 2 to King, following suit. (Once a card is played on an Ace, it cannot be brought back to the tableau.) When a pile in the tableau is eliminated altogether, the space can be filled only by a King.

In the game illustrated on the following page, 9♦ was moved onto 10♣ and 3♠ onto 4♥. Such sequences can no longer be played as single cards; they *must* be moved as a unit. For example, 3♠-4♥ can be moved to 5♣,

but when 3♥ is dealt from the stockpile and played on the foundation cards above, 3♠ cannot be relocated to 4♦ in order to free up 4♥ for the ascending Heart sequence. (Many players waive this rule.)

After laying out the tableau, play as many cards as possible. Then turn the top card of the stockpile faceup. Play it on an Ace or on the tableau; if it can't be used, discard it faceup. (The top card of the discard pile is always available for play.) Continue to deal through the stockpile, one by one.

In Klondike, a player may go through the stockpile only once, one card at a time. Occasionally, this is enough to build complete sequences on the Ace foundation cards, but more often, you will be stumped while most cards lay trapped in the tableau or on the discard pile.

Some house rules allow a player to turn over the discard pile and deal through the pack a second time. Another variation allows a player to deal cards from the stockpile in fans of three, making three passes through the stockpile. This not only prolongs the game but, according to *The Modern Hoyle*, markedly improves the odds: you are likely to get 10 to 12 cards on the Aces and win one out of every five or six games.

Variations: Klondike can also be played with two players and two decks of cards. Each player lays out his or her own tableau, facing each other. The game is played exactly as above except that the foundation Aces are held in common: all eight are available to both players, which substantially increases the chances of winning.

Can-Can takes twice as much room as Klondike, at least three feet of playing surface. Shuffle a 52-card deck, and deal a row of 13 cards facedown. Turn the first and the last faceup. Deal a row of 11 cards on top of the facedown cards. Again, turn the first and last faceup. Continue until there are 13 piles of cards, the first and last each containing one card and the middle pile containing seven. All the top

cards are faceup. Lay the three remaining cards faceup in front of you, as illustrated opposite.

The game is played exactly like Klondike, except there is no stockpile. All moves are made within the tableau and to the Aces. It seems as if this layout exposes more cards for play, but while there are 16 faceup in Can-Can, there are 7 in Klondike's tableau, and another 24 appear during the first pass through the stockpile. Because there are more cards laid out before you, the game requires more attention. The element of luck, however, remains unchanged.

Gold Rush starts with the standard Klondike tableau. Deal cards one at a time from the stockpile. As soon as one of the cards can be played, you have made a "strike," and the discard pile is your "claim." Start a new discard pile with the next card from the stockpile. When you deal a card that can be played, this discard pile becomes a second claim. Continue playing, creating a new claim after each card that is played. At any time, you can play the top card of each claim, substantially increasing your chances of winning the game.

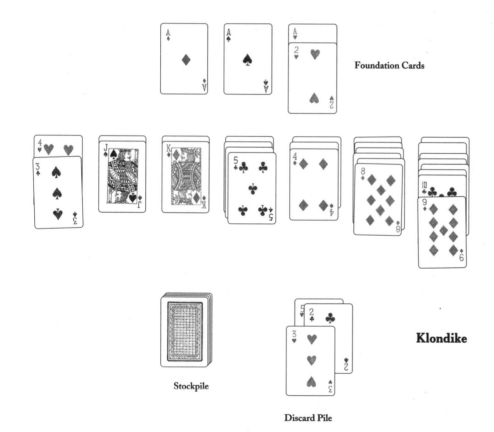

Foundation Cards

Klondike

Stockpile

Discard Pile

Can-Can

Yukon combines Klondike with some elements of **King Albert**. Deal the cards in a standard Klondike tableau. There are 24 cards left. Deal these four at a time, faceup, on the first six piles, overlapping the cards slightly so that you can see all the numbers. This uses the entire deck; there is no stockpile. Play the game exactly like Klondike, moving only the card at the end of each column. Because four other cards are visible under the one that is playable, you can plan your moves ahead.

If you get stumped, switch to **White Pass**, a variation that gets players past obstructions. Square up any column, and flip it over so that the faceup cards are facedown, and vice versa. This opens a whole new series of plays. Continue until you reach another block, then use White Pass to keep going.

Finally, there is **Whistler**, played exactly like Klondike, but instead of building descending sequences in the tableau with alternating red and black cards, sequences are built according to the denomination of the card, regardless of suit. Sequences on the foundation Aces are built up in the usual way. Whistler is a much easier and much faster game and is virtually a guaranteed win.
ᓚᘏᗢ

Yukon

Fascination

- ◆ OTHER NAMES: **based on the old-time Storehouse, sometimes known as Demon, modified for gambling as Canfield**
- ◆ EQUIPMENT: **one deck of 52, Ace low**
- ◆ DESCRIPTION: **a better lap-top game than Klondike; takes up less space**
- ◆ COMPLEXITY: **more complicated than Klondike; less chance of winning**

P LAYED WITH a smaller tableau than **Klondike** and with the added element of the reserve pile, Fascination increases the role of luck. Not surprisingly, it was adopted in the 1890s by gamblers, notably one Richard A. Canfield, who operated a casino in Saratoga Springs, New York. He gambled with Fascination—which he renamed after himself—much as the sourdoughs did with Klondike, selling a player a deck for a buck a card and paying him back $5 for every card moved to the foundation piles, with a $500 jackpot if the player won the game. Canfield became popular at the same time as Klondike, and the two games have become confused in some manuals. Despite their common past, however, they are quite different in play.

The Tableau: Shuffle the deck, and deal 13 cards facedown in a pile. This is the reserve. Place it to your left, and turn the pile faceup. Beside it, deal a row of four cards faceup. Then deal a single card faceup, above the row. This is the foundation card. The remainder of the deck is the stockpile.

The Object of the Game: To build complete ascending sequences on the foundation cards, following suit.

The Play: As the other three suits of the foundation card show up during play, place them alongside the first. Instead of running from Ace to King, sequences start with whatever foundation card is dealt. For instance, if 6◆ is

the foundation card, the other foundations are 6♠, 6♥ and 6♣, and the sequence will be 6-7-8-9-10-J-Q-K-A-1-2-3-4-5.

On the five faceup cards in the tableau (including the reserve pile), build descending sequences, alternating red and black. Instead of stopping at Ace, sequences in this game are continuous. For instance, 3♥-2♠-A◆-K♣-Q◆. As in Klondike, sequences must be moved as a unit. When a space opens up in the tableau, it can only be filled by the card or the sequence on the reserve. In the example illustrated, when

J♠ is moved to Q◆, the 9♣-8♥-7♣ sequence will be moved from the reserve to fill the vacancy. When the reserve is empty, the spaces in the tableau can be filled from the stockpile.

You don't have to fill spaces right away. Wait until a good card appears.

Deal cards from the stockpile in fans of three. If the top card is played on the tableau or the foundations, the card below can be played; if the top card cannot be played, the two below are trapped.

When the stockpile is done, turn over the discard pile, and deal the cards by threes again, going through the

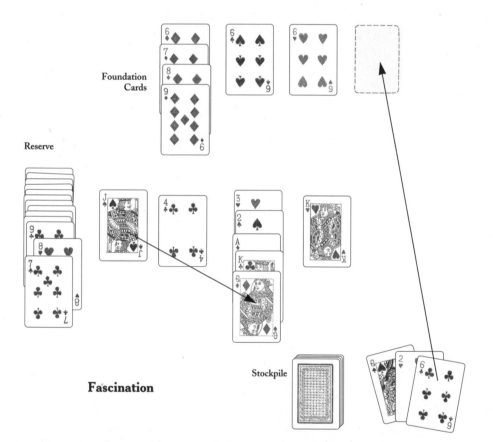

Foundation Cards

Reserve

Stockpile

Fascination

pack as often as you want until you are stumped or the game is won.

Variations: With **Canfield**, gamblers had a choice of turning up the cards in the stockpile one at a time or three at a time. If you played them one at a time, you were allowed to go through the stockpile once. With triplets, you dealt the stockpile three times. Like most gambling games, it seems to offer a choice, but either way, the results are usually the same.

Demon is an additional rule more than a variation. Play Fascination until you are down to six cards in the stockpile, then deal through them one by one, instead of by threes. In **Grand Demon**, a player is allowed to bring back one card from the foundation to the tableau if it will help with a sequence. Both variations give the player a little more choice, expanding the game's options and thereby increasing its interest.

A very old, simplified form of Fascination is called **Help Your Neighbor**. The four Aces are foundation cards, and there is no reserve.

Four cards are dealt faceup in a row, and the cards of the stockpile are turned up, one by one. Play is the same as Fascination, except spaces can be filled from the stockpile, the discard pile or other columns in the tableau. A good introduction to Fascination, it soon pales, because without the handicap of the reserve, you can always beat the devil if you go through the stockpile often enough.

Storehouse is also a simplified forerunner to Fascination. Deal 13 cards faceup in a pile as a "storehouse" and, beside it, a row of four cards faceup. Instead of a random foundation card, place the four 2s above the row as they come up in play; build on them by suit

in ascending order from 3 to Ace. Play proceeds as for Fascination, except you deal cards from the stockpile one at a time. Turn over the discard pile, and go through it two more times, three deals in all.

Pounce is Fascination for groups; as many as 12 can play. Each player has his or her own deck of cards and plays a personal game of Fascination, except the foundation cards are held in common in the center. Whoever gets there first makes the play. The player who empties his or her reserve first yells "Pounce!" and wins the game, regardless of how many cards are built on the foundations. Caution: This game is pandemonium. ༄

Trefoil

- OTHER NAMES: Clover
- EQUIPMENT: one deck of 52, Ace low
- DESCRIPTION: a game of same-suit sequences, both on the tableau and on the foundation Aces
- TIP: needs a large playing surface

DRAWING ITS NAME, not so much from the plant—a three-leaved, yellow-flowered weed—as from a figurative reference to the Trinity, this old game has an attractive layout exposing all cards.

The Tableau: Place the four Aces across the top as foundation cards. Shuffle the deck, then hold it faceup, and deal all the remaining cards in fans of three, scattering them randomly under the foundations, as illustrated on the following page.

The Object of the Game: To build up the Aces in complete ascending sequences according to suits.

The Play: Move the top card from each trefoil either to a foundation Ace to build an ascending same-suit sequence or to another trefoil to build a descending same-suit sequence. For instance, in the game illustrated on the following page, 9♦

in the top-right trefoil can be moved either to 8♦ on the foundation or to 10♦ on the trefoil directly below. Move only one card at a time. (To make the devil a little more beatable, some players allow themselves to move sequences.) Spaces opened in the tableau remain unfilled.

When you can't make any more moves, gather up the trefoils, shuffle the cards, and deal them in new trefoils. There may be a one- or two-card trefoil at the end. Continue play until you are stumped, then reshuffle, and lay out the tableau a final time. On the last deal, if a King blocks a lower card of the same suit, you can switch the two. Even with this advantage, however, Trefoil is difficult to win.

Variations: Trefoil played with two decks is called **House in the Woods**. The eight Aces are laid out as foundations. The remaining cards are shuffled and dealt in trefoils—32 of them. Play exactly like Trefoil. The

game takes longer but has a better chance of coming out.

House on the Hill also uses two decks, but the foundations are four Aces and four Kings. Build ascending sequences on the Aces and descending sequences on the Kings. On the trefoils in the tableau, sequences can go either way—up or down the hill.

The person for whom **La Belle Lucie** was named must have been a paragon of patience, because the game is even harder to win than Trefoil. Shuffle a single deck, and deal it all in trefoils—17, with a one-leaf trefoil left over at the end. Instead of placing the Ace foundation cards above the trefoils at the beginning of the game, move them into position as they become available. Play exactly like Trefoil. Players are granted one advantage: after the third deal, a player can pull a card—called the *merci*—from within any trefoil and play it on any sequence. This game is also known as Midnight Oil; prepare to burn it if you want to win.

Shamrocks calls for a little more strategy. As in La Belle Lucie, the entire deck is dealt in threes, with a single-leaf shamrock left over. Aces are released during play to become foundations. This game, however, ignores suits on the tableau. Move cards to create mixed-suit sequences, *either* ascending or descending. Lest this sim-

Trefoil

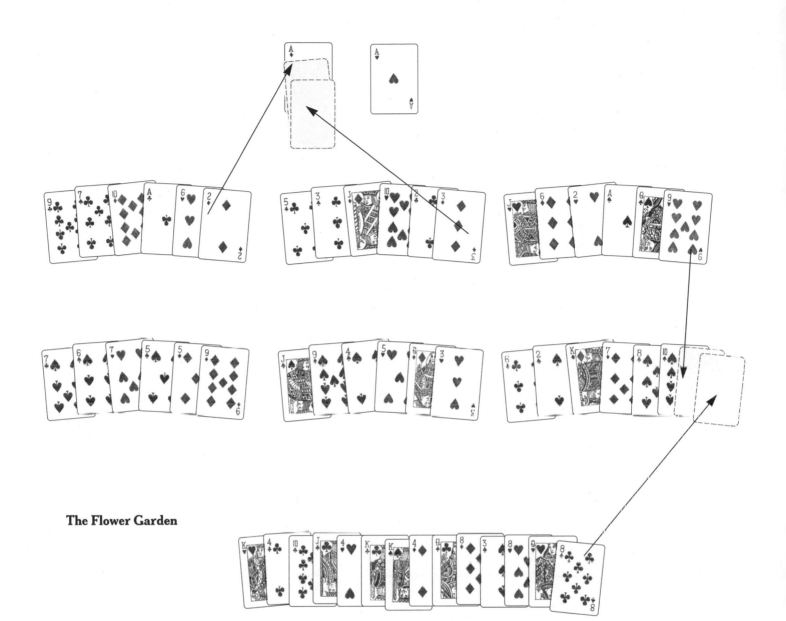

The Flower Garden

plify the game too much, another rule is added: shamrocks may contain no more than three cards. Therefore, unless an Ace is dealt as the top card of one of the shamrocks in the tableau, the game is lost before it is begun. As in Trefoil, if a King covers another card of the same suit, you may switch the two. Mobility is the key, so keep one-leaf shamrocks as long as possible. Only one deal is allowed.

The Flower Garden, popular in France as Le Parterre, puts a few more cards, quite literally, in the player's hands. Shuffle a 52-card deck, and deal six "gardens" of six cards each, overlapping them so that all the denominations show. Fan the 16 remaining cards in your hand like a bouquet. As Aces become available during

play, use them as foundations to build ascending sequences according to suit. Play any card from your bouquet to the end card of each garden bed to create descending sequences in alternating red and black.

For instance, in the game illustrated above, 9♥ is moved from the top-right bed to 10♠ in the bed below, then 8♣ is added to the sequence from the bouquet. In **Klondike**, sequences are vertical, but in The Flower Garden, they are built sideways from the end of each garden bed. Move cards one by one, not in sequences. When a whole bed is gone, start a new one with a King, your only opportunity to release cards covered by the monarch. There are no second chances; the tableau is dealt only once.

Contemporary games inventor and historian David Parlett adds his own variation on this theme. **Black Hole** begins with a black Ace in the center of the tableau; the rest of the deck is dealt in threes around it. The top card of each trefoil is playable. Move cards from the tableau to the Ace, creating random ascending and descending sequences, regardless of suit, until all cards are in the "black hole." As Parlett points out, this is a game of perfect information. By looking at the tableau and forecasting the moves, you can calculate whether you win or lose without moving a single card. As a Patience game, this qualifies as a marathon more than a jog. ❧

St. Helena

- ◆ OTHER NAMES: **Big Forty and Forty Thieves**
- ◆ EQUIPMENT: **two decks of 52, Ace low**
- ◆ COMPLEXITY: **cumbersome for young children; requires strategy**

ONLY ONE OF many games with names that refer to the Little Emperor, St. Helena begs the question of whether Napoleon actually whiled away his exile with a double deck of cards. The truth is, enough journals exist from both Elba and St. Helena to give the lie to the myth. Napoleon played **Piquet** and **Whist**, but researchers have found no evidence that he had any use for Patience.

The Tableau: Shuffle two 52-card decks together. Deal a row of 10 cards faceup. Deal three more rows on top of the first, overlapping each row: 10 columns with four cards in each, all 40 "thieves" visible. The remainder of the pack is the stockpile.

The Object of the Game:
To build up the Aces in complete ascending sequences according to suits.

The Play: In the course of play, as Aces appear, set them above the columns as foundations. The last card in each of the 10 columns can be moved to another column to create same-suit sequences in descending order; for instance, 5♦ can be moved to

6♦. Only single cards can be moved, not sequences. When a space opens in the tableau, you may fill it with a card from the tableau or the stockpile.

With the stockpile facedown, turn over the cards one by one, and play them on the tableau or the foundations. (Only one deal through the stockpile is allowed.) If a card cannot be played, discard it. String out the discard pile, overlapping cards so that you can see them all. Only the top card can be played at any given time, but with luck, you will be able to work back through the discards to get to the one you need.

For instance, in the example illustrated, J♣ is turned up next in the stockpile. It is played on Q♣, then 10♣ is added from the discard pile. This releases 3♥, which is played to the foundation, as is 4♥ from the sixth column, which uncovers 9♣ for the sequence in the first column, releasing

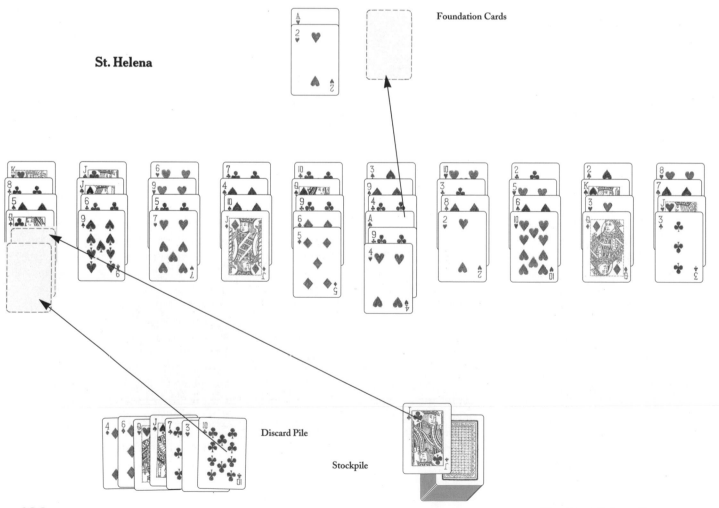

St. Helena

Foundation Cards

Discard Pile

Stockpile

196

A♠ for the foundation.

The key to this game is strategy. Open spaces as soon as you can, keep track of duplicates, don't cover cards you may need in the near future, order your plays carefully, and don't make a play just because it is possible.

Variations: An earlier, easier version, **Lucas** also uses two decks but needs an even larger playing surface. Remove the eight Aces from the decks, and place them above as foundations. Shuffle the two decks together, and deal 13 cards faceup in a row. Deal two more rows, creating 13 columns, three cards in each. The remaining cards form the stockpile. Play exactly like St. Helena.

Famous Fifty is named after a group of baseball fans who traveled to the World Series every year by Pullman. The tableau contains 10 columns of five cards each, which, although it follows the rules of St. Helena, makes this two-deck game easier to win.

Maria Louisa, which is also played with two decks, has a tableau of nine columns with four cards in each. As the Aces appear during play, they are placed as foundation cards and are built up in same-suit ascending sequences. On the tableau, descending sequences are created in alternating red and black, as in **Klondike.** This game is a little easier still, because the alternating colors give you twice as many options.

Bisley uses a single deck. Shuffle the cards, and deal 13 faceup in a row, then continue with three more rows until the deck is used up. (Four rows altogether.) As you turn up Aces in the deal, set them above the tableau as foundations. As a result, the fourth row will have only nine cards. There is no stockpile; all the cards are exposed. Build same-suit ascending sequences on the Aces. On the tableau, build ascending or descending same-suit sequences. As Kings become available, place them below the tableau, and build descending same-suit sequences there. Spaces opened in the tableau remain empty. As with all the Lucas-style games, if you move sequences *en bloc,* you can win every time, but the rule is, move only one card at a time.

Beleaguered Castle

- ♦ EQUIPMENT: **one deck of 52, Ace low**
- ♦ DESCRIPTION: **a game of calculation with all cards exposed**
- ♦ TIP: **needs a large playing surface**

Like **St. Helena,** Beleaguered Castle is essentially a game of judgment. A player's success depends on whether she can play her moves so as to release the necessary cards to continue building sequences on the Aces in the middle of the tableau.

The Tableau: Lay the four Aces in a column. Shuffle the cards, and deal a column of four cards, faceup, to the right of the Aces, then a column of four cards to the left. Continue dealing until the deck is used up, alternating right, then left, overlapping the cards in each row slightly so that all the cards show. In the end, four rows of six cards each fan out from the Aces. There is no stockpile.

The Object of the Game: To build complete ascending sequences on the Aces according to suits.

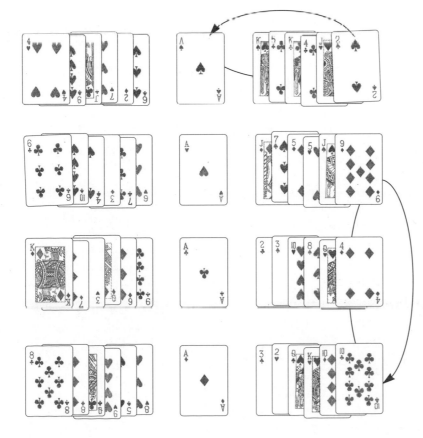

Beleaguered Castle

The Play: Play only the outside card in each row, moving it to an Ace to build an ascending same-suit sequence or to another row to build horizontal descending sequences of mixed suits. For instance, in the game illustrated on the previous page, 2♠ can be moved to A♠, and 9♦ can be moved to 10♣, then 8♣ can be placed on the 9. Move cards one at a time, never *en*

bloc. When a space opens, fill it with any card. As in most games of this type, clever manipulation of the open spaces leads to success.

Variations: In **Citadel**, a space is left in the middle, and the entire deck is dealt as described above. When an Ace appears during the deal, place it in the middle, and as cards appear that

can be played in sequence on the Aces, do so. This gives you a head start in beating the devil.

Streets and Alleys also buries the Aces in the shuffled deck, but during the deal, they are dealt into the rows with the other cards, rather than being removed to the center. Releasing the Aces makes this game difficult to win. ∽

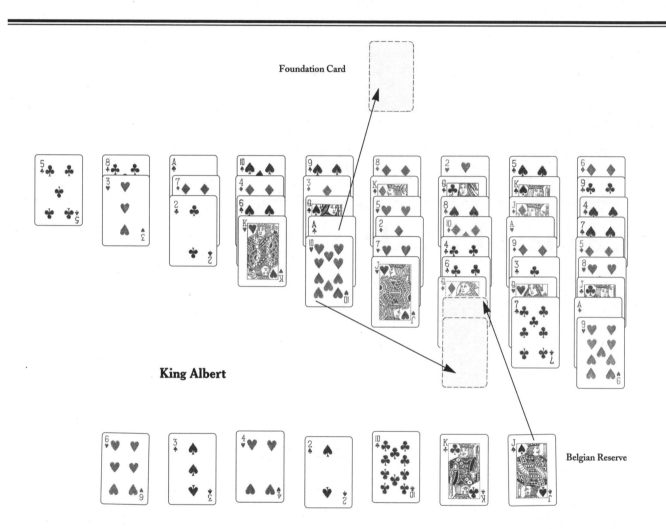

Foundation Card

King Albert

Belgian Reserve

King Albert

- ◆ EQUIPMENT: **one deck of 52, Ace low**
- ◆ DESCRIPTION: **a game of strategy more than luck**
- ◆ TIP: **if you can win at Chess, you'll beat the devil at this**

ALTHOUGH A DEVOTEE of Patience, Queen Victoria's husband Albert did not lend his name to this game. According to Walter Gibson in *How to Play Winning Solitaire*, it was named after King Albert I of Belgium, a World War I hero. One of the most challenging Solitaires, it is a devilishly hard game to win, but it no doubt helped to pass the time in the trenches of France.

The Tableau: Shuffle the deck, and deal nine cards faceup in a row. Start the second row with the second card on the left, and deal eight; in the next row, deal seven, and so on, until the last row has only one card. Overlap the cards as you deal so that you can see them all, creating columns, rather than piles. Lay the remaining seven cards below the columns, faceup. This is the Belgian Reserve.

There is no stockpile and no discard pile.

The Object of the Game:
To build complete ascending sequences on foundation Aces according to suits.

The Play: The seven cards in the reserve and the card at the end of each column can be moved to build descending sequences of alternating red and black suits. As Aces appear, move them above the columns as foundations for ascending sequences of the same suit. For instance, in the game illustrated, J♠ is played from the reserve to Q♦, which allows 10♥ to be added to the sequence, releasing A♣, on which 2♣ can then be played. Cards must be moved one at a time, never *en bloc*. This requires great forethought.

Spaces in the tableau can be filled with any card, but don't be in a hurry. Spaces offer mobility, the only way to release buried cards. If you move a King into a space (the rule in **Klondike**), you will lose the use of that space for the rest of the game. It is also a good strategy to build up the foundation Aces evenly and to avoid long sequences in the tableau, since they have to be dismantled one card at a time.

When the game is stalled, some players allow themselves to move a card from the foundation back to the tableau, but not to the reserve. Sometimes this is enough to get the moves going again. Because it involves so much strategy, this is one Solitaire that you will get better at with practice. ∾

Spider

- ◆ EQUIPMENT: **two decks of 52, Ace low**
- ◆ DESCRIPTION: **for experienced cardplayers; the most challenging, absorbing Solitaire of all**
- ◆ DURATION: **each game can take up to half an hour**
- ◆ TIP: **needs a large playing surface**

A LTHOUGH THE ORIGIN of its name is unknown, Spider has been around for most of this century and remains one of the best, combining an equal measure of luck and skill. In one of W. Somerset Maugham's short stories, a character complains that he can never get Spider to come out, but according to *The Modern Hoyle*, skillful players can, in fact, beat the devil one time in three. This, apparently, was Franklin D. Roosevelt's favorite Patience game, perhaps the inspiration for the New Deal.

The Tableau: Shuffle two decks of cards together. Deal 10 facedown in a row. Repeat three more times, creating 10 piles of four cards each. Deal an extra card facedown on each of the first four piles (this will make the deck come out even), then deal a card faceup on top of each of the 10 piles. The remaining 50 cards form the stockpile.

The Object of the Game:
To build eight same-suit descending sequences from King to Ace within the tableau.

The Play: There are no distinct foundation cards in this game. You

Spider

Stockpile

build descending same-suit sequences on the faceup cards in the tableau; when one is complete, King to Ace, it is removed from the tableau. Only same-suit sequences count, but to manipulate the cards, mixed-suit sequences are allowed, with one caveat: same-suit sequences can be moved as a unit; otherwise, cards must be moved singly. For example, in the game illustrated on the previous page, 3♥-2♠ in the ninth column cannot be moved to 4♥ to make room for 3-2♠ on 4♠.

When a faceup card is moved from a pile, turn over the card below. It is important to get all the cards into play as soon as possible. Open spaces can be filled with any card or same-suit sequence. To get Kings out of the way, you must move them to a space, but if you move them too early, you will lose the added mobility that a space offers.

When you can no longer make any moves, deal another row of cards from the stockpile onto the end of each col-umn. This produces new moves and, at the same time, blocks some of your hard-earned sequences. (Any open spaces must be filled from other columns before you deal another round from the stockpile.) Continue playing until you are stumped again, then deal another row.

When the stockpile is gone and all moves are blocked, the game is over. ❧

9

Double or Nothing: Card Games for Two

COMPARED WITH **Tit-Tat-Toe** and **Mah Jongg**, playing cards are a relatively recent gaming phenomenon. There is nothing resembling cards in the Egyptian hieroglyphs; they don't appear on ancient Greek amphoras; none are etched in Roman ruins; even Chaucer doesn't mention them, although his pilgrims indulge heartily in dice. The first literary reference, in fact, is in the early 14th century, a mere 600 years ago, making playing cards a more recent invention than **Backgammon**, **Checkers** or **Chess**.

Exactly where cards came from has kept games historians busy for generations. "When the origin of a thing is remote or mysterious, it has been the custom to attribute it to the Devil or to Asia," writes W. Gurney Benham in *Playing Cards: The History and Secrets of the Pack*. Indeed, some suggest that cards came from the Orient, where playing tablets and disks were used long before. Some have even tried to make a connection between the four suits of playing cards and the four ranks of early Chess. The timing suggests that the Crusaders may have brought cards from the Holy Land, though this theory is entirely unsubstantiated; and neither did the Gypsies bring them, for cards entered Europe before the Gypsies arrived. The best early references give credence to the theory that the Moors brought them from Africa or that the Saracens introduced them from Arabia.

"It is no good groping for the inventor," writes Benham. "We may as well give up this conundrum, as we must give up others of the same sort. Who knows the original inventor of cricket, of football, of golf or of draughts and dominoes? Of these, its greatest men, the world knows nothing."

What can be established with certainty is that the first playing cards were made in Italy at least as early as 1325. The original deck had four suits and 10 numerals, like today, but four, not three, picture cards—King, Queen, Knave and Valet or Page. The suits are similar to contemporary Tarot cards, and they still appear on Mexican playing cards: full-color Cups, Swords, Coins and Batons, or Clubs. The Germans changed the suits to Hearts, Acorns, Bells and Leaves, but it was the French who brought order to the pack, kicking the Valet out of the royal family, reducing the deck to 52, splitting it into black and red and settling on the easily identifiable symbols of Spades, Hearts, Diamonds and Clubs. Diamonds, like coins, is for wealth, and Hearts is for love. The French substituted the trefoil for the club, and the British kept both the three-leaved plant and the name. Spades, however, has nothing to do with digging. It comes from the Spanish-Italian *espadas* and an Old English word "spado," which, until the 18th century, was used for sword. The British adopted the French pike head for the symbol on the black card and called it a Spade. Incidentally, the expression "to call a spade a spade" is almost as old as playing cards themselves, but it refers to revealing your weapon, not your hand.

The cardboard court is not a collection of no-name kings and queens, as you might suppose. Each is a portrait, the name of the sitter often written on early cards. It is an unusual gathering. The King of Hearts is Charlemagne, his Queen is Judith from the Bible (sometimes Helen of Troy), and the Knave is a French marquis, a member of Joan of Arc's Council of War who nicknamed himself La Hire. The King of Spades is David, the Queen is the Greek goddess Pallas, and the Knave is the mythical French hero Renaud, a Christian Achilles. The King of Diamonds is Julius Caesar, his Queen is

Rachel, and the Knave is Hector de Maris, half-brother to Lancelot of Round Table fame. The King of Clubs is Alexander the Great, the Queen is Hecuba, and the Knave is Lancelot himself. Real and mythological, drawn from the ancient and medieval spiritual and political worlds, the characters are all dressed as if in attendance at Henry VIII's court.

Numerous powers have tried to unseat this eclectic royal band. In 1526, Henry VIII himself ordered all cards confiscated and burned (along with dice, bowls and the board game of Tables) so that the working man would have more time to learn archery. Christmas was the only time that a working-class Brit could legally play cards. A more serious challenge to the cardboard court came with the French Revolution. The tax on playing cards was lifted, and card playing became a fad, but the Kings and Queens in the deck were politically incorrect. "All emblems which denote royalty, scourge of the human race, are proscribed," proclaimed a 1793 edict from the Council of the Commune at Thiers. "Packs of cards consist partly of cards known under the names of Kings, 'Dames,' Valets. The former show fleurs-de-lis, scepters, crowns. The republican should reject such emblems. They must be removed from those who do not blush to encounter them." The royal face cards were banned; the Kings were redrawn as Sages and Geniuses; the Queens, as Virtues and Seasons; the Jacks, as Heroes and Workers. In one republican pack, the Kings were deposed by Molière, Voltaire, La Fontaine and Jean Jacques Rousseau. In another, the surrogate Queens carried slogans: Joan of Arc (the Queen of Hearts), for example, bore the banner *"Rien ne m'arrête"* (Nothing stops me). After deposing their own monarchs, Russian Communists tried to follow the French lead with playing cards, but both countries' attempts were failures. Napoleon restored the royal face cards, and Russia dropped its campaign in 1928.

Religious antagonism toward playing cards has been more enduring and a little surprising, given the identity of some of the royal family members. In 1423, a Franciscan friar, Saint Bernard of Siena, preached a sermon at Bologna denouncing cards as the invention of the devil, a line that preachers have repeated, on and off, ever since. Particularly vigorous in their disapproval were the Puritans, who forbade any contact with what they termed "the devil's picture book." In 1656, a Plymouth Colony law fixed the penalty for card playing at 40 shillings for adults; children and servants "to bee corrected att the discretion of theire parents or masters and for the second offence to bee publickly whipt." The French replaced the royal visages with paintings of seasons, and even the face of Victor Hugo; while in New England, special decks were designed in which all the cards bore numerals: no portraits, no frivolous decoration at all. The games of Rook and Flinch, still played by those intent on keeping graven images out of their grasp, were invented specifically for these faceless cards.

Yet the old royal families have hung on. The cards North Americans buy today are based on a series produced in England in 1750 by a manufacturer named Bamford. He copied the designs from a set of cards found in the binding of an old register in Rouen, dated at 1567. Compared with the cards hand-painted 425 years ago, the details in a brand-new pack of cards are remarkably unchanged, right down to the pattern of the Queen of Clubs' robes and the Jack of Hearts' mustache and curly hair.

In the early 1800s, the royal family was cut in half to make "two-headed" cards that can be read in the hand no matter which way they are picked up. Until the end of the 19th century, the flip sides of playing cards were traditionally blank, a protection against those who would mark the cards. As a result, playing cards were often pressed into service when paper was scarce. The earliest playing cards manufactured in the United States are preserved not because of an interest in games but because their back sides were used as invitations for social events and as admissions for lectures. In Canada, when the French provinces ran out of paper money in 1685, the Seigneur cut playing cards into quarters and paid his soldiers with the signed pieces.

Many of the card games in this chapter have a history as long as cards themselves. Some will be familiar, like **Go Fish**, even though it is 400 years old. Others, such as **Piquet** and **Klobiosh**, are less well known today, but their very survival attests to how challenging and entertaining they are. Some of the rituals may seem quaint and the language a little foreign, but such games forge a curious and honorable link with a long line of cardplayers in the past.

All card games except Solitaire begin with the ritual of deciding the deal. After the cards are shuffled, the players *cut the deck*: one person lifts up part of the deck, the other player lifts up another part; then they compare the cards on the undersides of the lifted parts. Depending on the game, the person with the high or the low card deals first. If the two cards are the same value, the players either cut again or rank the suits: Spades high, then Hearts, Diamonds and Clubs, in descending order.

The dealer is the *younger hand*, and the nondealer is the *elder hand*, always given the honor of playing first. After the cut to see who deals, the dealer shuffles the cards again and deals, giving a card to the elder hand first, then dealing alternately to the two players, one or more cards at a time, as specified in the game.

Most two-person games are based on matching cards, as in **Memory**, or on the principle of draw and discard, as in **Gin Rummy**, players picking up cards from a common stockpile in an attempt to collect particular *sets* (two, three or four of a kind) or *sequences* (a run of consecutive numbers, usually of the same suit).

Like most group games, however, complex card games for two involve *tricks*. The elder hand goes first. She takes a card from her hand and lays it faceup in the middle of the table; the dealer does the same, playing a card of the same suit if possible. These two cards are the trick. The person who played the higher card wins the trick. He collects the two cards and places them facedown in front of him. These cards are out of play and cannot be looked at for the rest of the hand. The player who wins the trick plays the first card for the next trick.

Trump, from the French *triomphe*, is a key part of most trick-taking games. Before the hand is played out in tricks, one suit is named trump; the cards in that suit outrank any card of any other suit. Within the trump suit, the usual ranking applies, with Ace high and 2 low. If only one trump is on the table, it automatically wins the trick; if more than one is played, the higher trump card takes the trick. In two-person games, the trump suit is usually decided by chance, by turning up the top card on the stockpile; in group games, players often bid for the right to make trump.

In most cases, trump can be played only if the trump suit is led or if a player has a *void* (no cards at all) in the suit led—players must always follow suit. In some games, players are obliged to trump if they can't follow suit;

sometimes a player with a void in the suit led has the option of either playing trump or throwing off a card from a *side suit* (one of the other two suits).

The best two-person games have two stages or more, which makes them complicated to learn but more challenging to play. In **Cribbage**, Piquet and Klobiosh, players first assess their cards and score them for *melds* before they play out the hand. Meld comes from the German word *melden*, "to announce," and means that players collect and lay down certain scoring combinations of cards—the *sets* of seven of a kind in **Canasta**, the critical *point totals* of 15 in Cribbage, same-suit *sequences* in Gin Rummy or Queen-King *marriages* in **Pinochle**. Much of the strategy in two-person games comes from assessing a hand for melds, bidding on melds or melding (exposing the combinations) at a judicious time.

Given the nature of the court cards, some of these melds make for interesting marriages. Take Pinochle, for instance. The *coup d'état* of the game is to mate Hector, one of the noblest knights of the Round Table, with Pallas, the Greek goddess of war and wisdom who sprang fully armed from the head of Zeus. A feat worth celebrating, indeed.

Memory

- OTHER NAMES: **Concentration and Pelmanism**
- NUMBER: **best for two players, but can be played with more**
- EQUIPMENT: **one deck of 52**
- DESCRIPTION: **a simple matching game for young children**
- TIP: **needs a very large playing surface**

AN EXCELLENT TONER for short-term memory, this game is fun for two but easily accommodates 10 or more players. No math or strategy is required, just good recall and the ability to recognize cards. The British call it Pelmanism, after the memory-training system taught at the turn-of-the-century Pelman Institute.

The Deal: Cut the deck; high card deals. The dealer shuffles the deck and lays all the cards facedown on the playing surface, with none overlapping.

The Object of the Game: To accumulate cards by matching pairs.

The Play: The elder hand (non-dealer) goes first, turning any two cards faceup. If the cards match—for instance, K♦ and K♠ or 4♣ and 4♠—the player removes the two cards and turns them facedown beside her. Then she takes another turn, flipping over two more cards. If they do not match, she turns them facedown in exactly the same spot. The other player then turns two cards faceup. Players try to remember where the cards are so that they can make matches in a later turn. Peeking is strictly forbidden, as is marking the cards with little bends, tears and scratches. After all the cards have been matched, the player with the most pairs wins.

Beggar My Neighbor

- NUMBER: **a good game for two players; can be played with more**
- EQUIPMENT: **one deck of 52, Ace high**
- DESCRIPTION: **fast-paced, elementary trick-taking game**
- TIP: **excellent for beginning cardplayers**

A SLIGHTLY MORE sophisticated version of Snap and War, the excitement of this game lies in waiting for the luck of the draw to decide the winner.

The Deal: Cut the deck; high card deals. The dealer shuffles and deals the cards one by one to each player until the deck is gone. (Or divide the deck roughly in half.) Players hold their cards in a pile facedown.

The Object of the Game: To win all the cards, reducing the other player's hand to zero.

The Play: The elder hand (non-dealer) goes first, placing his top card faceup on the table. The other player turns over her top card and plays it on the first. If it is a number card, the players continue turning over their top cards one at a time, placing them on the common discard pile.

As soon as one player lays down a face card, the other has to pay: one card for a Jack, two for a Queen, three for a King, four for an Ace. The pay cards are dealt from the player's stockpile and laid out in a separate pay pile. If they are all number cards, then the player who laid down the face card takes the pay cards and adds them facedown to the bottom of her stockpile. If, however, a face card or an Ace is played as a pay card, the debt is cancelled, and the other player has to pay.

For instance, in the game illustrated, the dealer laid down a Queen. The elder hand paid out two cards; the second was a King. The dealer then had to pay three cards. He dealt 2-8-5 from his stockpile. There are no face cards, so the elder hand picks up both pay-card piles and adds them facedown to her stockpile. Play continues until one player has "beggared" his neighbor, taking all the cards and leaving the other with none.

Variations: With up to six players, use a single deck of cards; for more, use two decks. Distribute the cards clockwise around the table until the entire deck is dealt. Starting with the player on the dealer's left, players turn the top card of their stockpiles faceup one at a time, playing onto a discard pile in the middle. When one person turns up a face card or an Ace, the next player in turn has to pay. If a Jack, Queen, King or Ace is among the pay cards, the next player in turn has to pay, and so on. When the pay cards are all number values, the player who laid the last face card on the discard pile collects all the pay cards. As players run out of cards, they drop out of the game, until only one person is left—the winner.

Everlasting, sometimes called Battle or War, is another matching game that kids happily play for hours. Divide a deck of 52 in half, or deal it equally between two players; each starts with a stockpile of 26. The players then turn their top cards faceup at the same time, laying them side by side in the middle of the table. The higher value takes the trick (ignore suits), and the winner adds the two cards facedown to the bottom of her stockpile. When both players turn up cards of the same value, it is war. Each plays three more cards faceup. The person whose third card is higher wins all eight cards. Play continues until one player holds all the cards.

Snap is Everlasting at breakneck speed. This raucous game is hard on a deck of cards but great fun, when it doesn't end in tears. Divide the deck in half, or deal the whole deck facedown to the two players. Each simultaneously turns over the top card, flipping it faceup in the direction of the opponent so that no one has an advantage. If the cards do not match, the players flip over another, at exactly the same time. (Each has his own discard pile.) The split second that the players turn up a pair, they yell "Snap!" The first to yell takes both discard piles and adds them to her stockpile. The game ends when one player has "snapped" all the other's cards.

Slapjack is similar to Snap, except players have a common discard pile and take turns flipping cards until one exposes a Jack. The first player to slap her hand on the Jack takes it—and all the cards under it. If two people slap the Jack at the same time, the hand directly on the card wins. Even if one player loses all his cards, play

continues, since he can renew his stockpile by slapping the next Jack.

Gops adds strategy to these fatalistic match-ups. Its name is an acronym of Game Of Pure Strategy, which is an exaggeration: there is some skill involved, but the game does not rank with **Chess**. Divide the deck into suits, giving one suit to each player. A third suit, shuffled well, is placed facedown between them. The fourth is out of play. For instance, one player takes Hearts, the other takes Diamonds, with Spades in the middle. (Clubs are out of play.) Turn the top Spade faceup. Players decide what to bid for the card, and each lays a card of that value facedown on the table. (Ace counts 1, King 13, Queen 12, Jack 11, and the others according to their numbers.) Both players turn up their bidding cards at the same time. The higher card takes the Spade. The bidding cards are discarded, another Spade is turned faceup, and a new bid is made, until all Spades are captured. When two bids are the same, the Spade is set aside and won with the next bid. The player with the most Spades (or the highest value of Spades) wins.

Elder Hand

Pay Cards

Discard Pile

Pay Cards

Dealer

Beggar My Neighbor

Spit

- ◆ NUMBER: **a game for just two players**
- ◆ EQUIPMENT: **a deck of 52, Ace low**
- ◆ DESCRIPTION: **a fast-paced, two-person race that combines Klondike and Snap**
- ◆ COMPLEXITY: **all luck and timing, little skill; young kids love it, so do teens**
- ◆ TIP: **an aggressive card game, best played on the floor**

SPIT BELONGS TO the huge genre of matching games within the Stops family of cards. Players each try to get rid of their cards by building sequences on common discard piles. The sequences are eventually "stopped" because certain cards are out of play, which triggers a new round of "One, Two, Three, Spit."

The Deal: Cut the deck; high card deals. The dealer shuffles the cards and deals the entire deck alternately to the two players. Each person then lays out a row of five cards facedown, as illustrated on the next page. On top of these five, each player lays a row of four cards facedown, starting with the second card on the left; then

a third row, starting with the third card from the left, a fourth row and a fifth row, which is just one card laid on the pile at the far right. Turn the top card of each pile faceup. This uses 15 cards. The remaining 11 cards are the player's stockpile. Both players put their stockpiles facedown between them. The top card of each stockpile is turned over and set next to the stockpile, creating two discard piles in the center.

The Object of the Game: To be the first to get rid of all your cards by building reversing sequences of mixed suits.

The Play: Both players say in unison "One, Two, Three, Spit." On this signal, players move cards from the layout in front of them to either

Elder Hand

Elder Hand's Stockpile

Discard Piles

Dealer's Stockpile

Dealer

Spit

discard pile, building up sequences regardless of color or suit and reversing the direction of sequences at random. For instance, in the game illustrated, 2♦ was played on 3♥ then A♣, 2♠ and 3♣. If the dealer plays her 4♥, the elder hand (nondealer) can play his 3♦ and 2♥. (The discards here are laid out; in play, they would be stacked.)

Players can move cards from their own layout to either discard pile; they can also move cards singly or *en bloc* within the layout, creating random reversing sequences in order to release cards that can be played to the discard piles. When neither player can make another move, they say in unison "One, Two, Three, Spit" and turn over a new card from the stockpile. Play moves quickly, because if one player gets stuck, the other soon plays a card that makes it possible to move again. Whenever both players are stuck, the play stops momentarily, they say "One, Two, Three, Spit" and turn a new card from each stockpile, in unison, to get the play going.

Play continues in this manner until the stockpiles have been used up. The split second both stockpiles are gone, each player tries to put his hand on the smaller discard pile, yelling "Spit!" The person to do so gets the small pile and turns it over as his new stockpile. The other person turns the larger discard pile over as her new stockpile. On the signal "One, Two, Three, Spit," the new round begins. This time, one person will finish the stockpile before the other and must wait until the other is done. The person who finishes first gets to choose the smallest pile, and another round begins.

Played this way, the person who gets the smallest pile in the first round almost surely wins. If players continue to vie for the smallest pile, trying to slap their hand on it and yell "Spit!" first, the loser has a fighting chance of reversing fortunes. Either way, the first person to get rid of all his cards—both in his layout and in his stockpile—wins. ❧

Go Fish

- ◆ OTHER NAMES: **Fish Pond or simply Fish**
- ◆ NUMBER: **at least two players; as many as five**
- ◆ EQUIPMENT: **one deck of 52, Ace high**
- ◆ DESCRIPTION: **a simple matching game for beginning cardplayers**

DERIVED, ACCORDING to David Parlett in *A History of Card Games*, from a 16th-century Italian gambling game called Andare à Piscere, Go Fish is one of the simplest of a long list of games based on the principle of exchanging cards with other players in order to collect matched sets.

The Deal: Cut the deck; low card deals. The dealer shuffles the deck and deals seven cards, one at a time, to each player. The remaining cards are fanned facedown between the players in a stockpile, or stream. Players arrange their cards by values—Kings together, 5s together, and so on.

The Object of the Game: To get the most sets of four of a kind.

The Play: The elder hand (non-dealer) begins, asking the other player for a card to match one that she holds in her hand. He has to give up all the cards of that denomination in his hand; if he has none, he says "Go fish!" She draws a card from anywhere in the stream. If it is the one she asked for, she takes another turn and continues asking for cards as long as she gets what she asks for, either from the other player or from the stream. (A successful fisher must show the matching card on request.) Most often, the fishing is unsuccessful, and the turn passes to the other player.

During his turn, a player who has four of a kind, or a *book*, lays the cards faceup in a pile on the table. Each time he makes a book, a player earns an extra turn. When a player successfully lays down all her cards in books,

she is not out of the game. She draws a card from the stream and asks the other player for a card to match the one she just drew. When a player has laid down all her cards and the stream is gone, the game is over. The player with the most books wins.

Variations: With two or three players, deal seven cards each; with four or five players, deal five cards each. The player to the left of the dealer begins. Players ask for cards from specific players, addressing them by name: for instance, "Jason, do you have any Queens?" The game ends with the first person to empty his or her hand after the stream is gone.

Happy Families was a popular commercial variation of Go Fish. The cards were imprinted with characters such as Mr. Dip the Dyer and Mr. Dose the Doctor. Players tried to reunite the characters into families: for instance, Mr. Dip with his wife and son and daughter. If a player didn't have the requested character card in his hand, he answered, "Not at home."

Happy Families can also be played with a regular deck and three or more players. Deal all the cards, facedown, one at a time to the players. (The deal need not come out evenly.) The point is still to collect books, but instead of asking for any and all the cards of a certain denomination, a player asks for a specific card that matches one in his hand. For instance, a player holds 10♦. Instead of asking for any 10s, he asks, "Henry, do you have 10♥?" If the answer is "No," the turn passes to the left. There is no stockpile to draw from, so players have to deduce from the answers which cards their oppo-

nents hold. As soon as a player collects a book, he shows it and wins 1 point. If a player forgets to show a book in the turn in which it was made, he forfeits the point. Play stops as soon as one player lays down all her cards in books. The person with the highest score wins.

Authors is a 19th-century commercial game played exactly like Happy Families, but with a different set of cards. Instead of members of a family, players collect all four cards that represent books by a single author. Rather than asking for 10♥, a player might ask Henry for *Little Women* by Louisa May Alcott. This is one of dozens of playing-card games devised for instructional purposes, a twist that is almost as old as playing cards themselves.

Old Maid, also called Slippery Lizzie, is a Go Fish-style game that uses a 52-card deck with one Queen removed. The object is to form pairs, rather than books of four, and to avoid being left holding the odd Queen. Deal the entire deck facedown one at a time. Players remove any pairs they were dealt, then fan the rest of the cards in their hands. The dealer offers the back of her card hand to the other player (or to the player on her left, if more than two play). He draws one card. If the draw completes a pair, he discards them and draws again. If no pair is made, he offers his hand to the dealer or the player on his left. Play continues until all the cards have been paired except the odd queen—the Old Maid. Whoever holds the Old Maid is the loser. The French and Germans play a similar scapegoat game, removing a Jack and playing it as Le Vieux Garçon and Schwarzer Peter, respectively.

In a version called **Black Maria**, the Queen of Clubs is removed from the deck. Players collect pairs of the same color, either red or black. The loser is the person left with the Queen of Spades—the Black Maria. ༄

Cassino

- **OTHER NAMES:** sometimes spelled Casino
- **NUMBER:** perfect for two; variations for three or four playing individually, or four as partners
- **EQUIPMENT:** a standard deck of 52; Ace counts as one; face cards have no numerical value; scorepad and pencil
- **DESCRIPTION:** simple but unique "fishing" game; excellent for developing card memory
- **COMPLEXITY:** suitable for children, challenging for adults; strategy varies greatly in the course of a single hand
- **DURATION:** less than an hour per game; about 10 minutes per hand

ACCORDING TO the *Oxford English Dictionary*, the game Cassino and the word casino appeared at almost exactly the same time, about 200 years ago. Today "casino" conjures images of Las Vegas, but when the word was coined in 1789, it referred to any public room used for social gatherings. The card game preserves that original meaning: it is a purely social pastime and has nothing to do with betting or playing for stakes. In fact, Cassino is so respectable that R.F. Foster's *Hoyle*, published at the peak of Victorian morality, recommends Cassino as "one of the few games of cards that are unhesitatingly admitted to the domestic circle."

The game is correctly spelled Cassino, though it often appears as Casino. Casino is the diminutive for *casa*, the Italian word for house. Cassino is also a town in Italy. Generally, the game is thought to originate in that country, but I wonder if in fact the game takes its name not from a place, but from a person, namely G.D. Cassini, the 18th-century astronomer whose name has been immortalized in the cassinoid, a curve that Cassini thought should replace the ellipse in explaining planetary movements. This is not as far-fetched as it sounds, for the cards in a game of Cassino seem to move in swiftly turning arcs, rather than the angular give-and-take of draw-and-discard games or the resolutely centrifugal movement of most trick-taking games.

Whatever the origin of the name,

Cassino is a great game for players of all ages. It is often the first sophisticated card game a child learns. As one card aficionado noted, "My dad taught me this two-player game after giving up on trying to get me to play **Cribbage**." A child who can't yet count to 15 but can manage the count to 10 will love Cassino.

Cassino has survived for 200 years, however, not because it is easy but because it is a quick-paced, challenging pastime that can be played at many levels. Although quite simple in principle, it is a subtle game of strategy in which the primary elements are constantly changing, requiring keen observation and great flexibility of mind.

Cassino is essentially a fishing game: players capture cards by matching one or more cards from their hand to one or more cards that have been

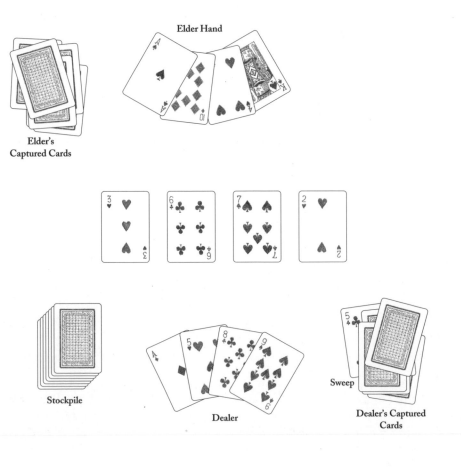

Elder Hand

Elder's Captured Cards

Stockpile

Dealer

Sweep

Dealer's Captured Cards

Cassino

laid on the table in a "pool." This type of game has far more variations in Asia than in the West, where trick-taking games take precedence. **Go Fish** and Cassino are the only two that regularly appear in English-language card-playing manuals, and the former is far more well-known than Cassino. This wasn't always the case: in 1897, Foster lists Cassino as America's national game.

The Deal: One person shuffles the cards; the other cuts. Each player draws one card from the deck; high card deals. The dealer deals two cards to his opponent, lays two cards faceup on the table, then deals two to himself. He repeats the round so that each player has four cards in hand and there are four cards faceup on the table between them. The rest of the pack lies facedown on the dealer's left.

After all four cards from the first deal are played, the dealer gives four more cards to each player, two at a time. No more cards are laid on the table. After the second set of cards is played, there is another deal and so on until the entire pack is dealt. Before dealing the final round, the dealer must announce, "Last deal!"

After the last four cards are played and the hand is scored, the opponent gathers up the cards and shuffles them well. (This is especially important in this game.) The deal alternates between the two players, regardless of who wins each hand.

The Object of the Game: To score points by collecting as many cards as possible, especially Spades, Aces and special counting cards: the Big Cassino (10♦) and the Little Cassino (2♠). Although Spades count in scoring, suits have no significance during play.

The Play: The elder hand (non-dealer) goes first. Each player at her turn must play one card from her hand. She can use a card from her hand to capture one card from the table by *pairing*; she can capture more than one by *combining* cards on the table; she can add a hand card to one

or more cards on the table, thus *building* for her next turn; or, if none of these is possible, she must lay a card faceup on the table, which is called *trailing*. The cards a player captures are collected facedown in a single pile in front of her.

Pairing is the easiest way to capture cards. A card from the hand is matched with a card of the same denomination on the table. For instance, an Ace is paired with an Ace, a 10 with a 10. This is the only way that face cards can be captured. Face cards can only be paired once, but other cards can be taken two, three or four at a time. For instance, if there are two Aces on the table, an Ace in the hand will take both in one turn. But if there are two Jacks on the table, a Jack in the hand takes only one. (Some play by the rule that a face card in the hand can take any number of the same face card from the table, but limited face-card pairing makes for a better game.)

Combining allows a player to add together the values of two or more cards on the table, and take them with a card from the hand whose value equals the combined total. For instance, in the game illustrated, a 2 and a 6 are on the table; the dealer can capture both with an 8 from her hand. However, two or more combinations can be taken with one card. If the cards on the table are combined another way (7+2 and 6+3), the dealer can capture all four cards with her 9. Removing all the cards from the table at once is called a *sweep*, which scores an extra point. Players keep track of sweeps by turning one of the captured cards faceup. In the game illustrated, the dealer already has one sweep, as indicated by the faceup 5♣.

Building allows a player to add a card from his hand to one or more cards on the table, providing the combined value equals another card in his hand. For instance, the elder hand in the game illustrated cannot match any single card or combination on the table, but he can add the Ace from his hand to the 3 on the table and announce "Building 4s," since he does have a 4 in hand. Only one card can be played at a time, so the player has

to wait until his next turn to match the 4 from his hand to his build of 4s on the table, and then he will collect all three cards. If a player builds in one turn, he cannot trail in the next: he must either collect his build, add to it or capture other cards from the table in a different play.

A player may use only one card from his hand for a build, but he may combine several cards on the table. For instance, instead of building 4s, the elder hand could combine the 6 and the 3 on the table and add the Ace from his hand, announcing "Building 10s." On his next turn, he would match the 10 from his hand to the 6-3-Ace build on the table and thus capture four cards. If there had been other matching combinations on the table, a 7 and 3, for instance, these could also be added to the build in the first turn. The elder hand would then collect six cards on his next turn: 6+3+Ace, 7+3, and 10.

Building is risky. An opponent can capture a build if she holds a card of the right value. By paying attention to which cards have already been captured, a player can judge how safe it is to build.

In subsequent turns, any player can increase a build, his own or his opponent's, by adding a card from the hand. For instance, if the elder hand had added his Ace to the 3 for a build of 4s, the dealer on her turn could have added her Ace to the same build, announcing "5s," since she has a matching 5 in hand. The elder hand has protected himself, however, by building 10s, which is as high as a build can go.

Any number of cards can be added to increase the value of the build to 10. (Face cards cannot be built.) A build can be frozen, however, by adding to it a card representing the total value. For instance, a 3 and 2 are joined to make a build of 5, that subsequently is increased with an Ace and then a 2 to make a build of 8. By adding an 8 from the table to freeze the build, a player can ensure that the build is increased no further.

Note: A build can be increased *only* by adding a card from the hand, not by adding a card from the table. A build can, however, be frozen with a card from either the table or a player's hand.

In every turn, a player *must* play one card from her hand. If she cannot use a card to capture or to build, she must trail—lay a card on the table. As a result, the number of faceup cards often increases beyond the original four.

Players take turns until the four cards of the first deal are played, then the dealer distributes another four, two at a time. Play continues until all the cards are dealt and played. Whoever makes the last capture of the hand wins all the remaining cards on the table, but this does not count as a sweep.

The Score: Each player adds up the total number of cards collected and the total number of Spades. Extra points are awarded for sweeps, Aces and the Big and Little Cassinos. The total number of points possible in each hand is 11, plus points for sweeps. Several hands are played in each game: the first player to score 21 points wins. (In cutthroat Cassino, players stop at 11, which is usually two hands.)

Penalties: If a player builds without holding a card representing the value of the build in hand, the opponent, if he discovers the error, adds a point to his own score. The build is declared invalid, the "built" cards are spread faceup on the table and play continues.

If a player trails instead of capturing cards or increasing a build from the previous turn, the opponent can force her to take the build. The trailed card

is left on the table and the offending player misses her next turn.

Strategy: The key to Cassino is keeping track of cards, especially 8s, 9s and 10s. Face cards can only be captured by pairing, so if there is one on the table and one in your hand, there are still two elsewhere, either in your opponent's hand or in the undealt deck. If you can keep track of the cards, you'll know when your 10 is the only one left to take a combination or a build.

In general, go for number of cards over all else. Make combinations with as many cards as possible. Collect cards that score whenever possible: give preference to capturing Spades, Aces and the Cassinos. In the illustrated hand on page 212, if the dealer uses her 9 to capture the two nine-combinations on the table, she captures five cards, including two Spades, thus increasing the possibility of having the most cards and most Spades, while at the same time earning a point for a sweep. Not bad for one play.

In general, avoid trailing a Spade, an Ace or a Cassino card unless you are fairly sure of collecting it in your next turn. For instance, if you are dealt the 10♦, keep it as long as you can, until two other 10s are played and you can safely pair it with the last 10 or use it to capture a build of 10. In the game illustrated, by building 10s, the elder hand hopes to keep the valuable Ace of Spades for himself while also hanging onto his Big Cassino. If he collects his build, he earns a guaranteed three points.

When trailing, it is a good policy to lay down low-value cards (except for Aces and the Little Cassino, which score). Keep high cards in hand, since they can capture combinations. Trail low-value cards that you know you can build on with other low cards in your hand to make a total which you also hold. For instance, if you hold 2, 3, 5, 6, trail the 2 in the hopes you can add the 3 in your next turn for a build of 5. When building, try to build a high value or freeze the build so your opponent cannot add to it.

Variations: Three or more can play Cassino, following the same rules as above. The game is a little slower and risks are greater since there are more unknown cards in opponents' hands and more players to steal builds. The deal passes to the left, and the first player to earn 49 points wins. If players tie for the most cards or the most Spades, neither wins the points.

Partnership or four-handed Cassino exhausts the pack in three deals. One partner collects the cards and the partners pool their scores. Except for reducing the risk of losing builds, there isn't much room for cooperative play.

In **Royal Cassino**, face cards have values: the Jack is worth 11, the Queen 12 and the King 13. Aces can be either 1 or 14 as each player decides. All cards can be built or taken in combination as well as pairs. This increases the combining and building possibilities markedly. Nothing stays on the table very long, making it difficult to plan moves ahead. Scores tend to be higher as sweeps are more common.

In **Spade Cassino**, all Spades score points: the Jack and the 2♠ (Little Cassino) score two points each and all the other Spades score one. A game is 61 points. (A Cribbage board simplifies scoring.)

In **Royal Spade Cassino**, the rules of both variations above apply: face cards have numerical values and all Spades score.

In **Draw Cassino**, instead of playing the four cards of each round before dealing the next four, as soon as a card is played one is drawn from the stockpile to replace it. The draw feature speeds up the game, especially for two players, and changes the strategy considerably, since there are no distinct rounds during which players feel safe to build as opponents are reduced to only one or two cards. Spade or Royal Cassino can also be played as draw rather than dealt games. Our own family favorite is **Royal Draw**. But be forewarned: this game takes some getting used to, since it reverses the more familiar rummy procedure of drawing first, then discarding. ༄

Conquian

- ◆ OTHER NAMES: **Coon Can, Rum Poker and Double Rum**
- ◆ NUMBER: **two players**
- ◆ EQUIPMENT: **a 40-card deck of Spanish cards or a standard deck with face cards removed; Ace is low; counters such as matches or poker chips**
- ◆ DESCRIPTION: **a simple precursor to Gin Rummy**
- ◆ COMPLEXITY: **very easy to learn; fun for all ages; high degree of luck in the draw**
- ◆ DURATION: **slower than Gin, and much harder to win**

CONQUIAN is the earliest form of true **Rummy**: it appeared in a games manual for the first time when R.F. Foster explained the rules in his 1897 *Hoyle.* Foster traces the game to the early 1860s, and it was apparently played among the Apaches in the 1890s, but beyond this, Conquian's origins are murky. At the end of the 19th century, it was hugely popular in Mexico—Foster calls it Mexico's national game—and also in the American states along Mexico's border. Because it is played with a Spanish deck, some suggest the game comes from Spain, but according to David Parlett in *A History of Card Games,* it doesn't surface in European games manuals until well into the 20th century.

Conquian appears, then, to be a Mexican invention. The name may be derived from the Mexican expression *Àcon quién?* meaning, With whom? Whatever its origins, it appears to be the true predecessor of **Gin Rummy,** and, given that "gin" sounds much like "quién," this may account for Gin's peculiar name. In 1897, Foster wrote that Conquian is "quite different from any other in its principles" and predicted it would "grow in popularity as it becomes better known." Indeed, Conquian will seem very familiar to card players who enjoy Gin, the game that has since rendered Conquian all but extinct.

Conquian is most fun played with a Spanish deck, in which the suits are Bastos (Clubs), Copas (Cups), Oros (Gold) and Espados (Swords). You

can remove the 8s, 9s and 10s from a standard deck to create a substitute Spanish deck, but it may be wiser to discard the face cards and play with Ace through 10, since those unfamiliar with Spanish cards often overlook 6-7-J and 7-J-Q sequences.

As its alternate name, Rum Poker, suggests, Conquian is largely a game of luck, one best played for counters rather than points. (A many-handed version of Conquian called Panguingue, or Pan, is a popular gambling game.) Unlike Gin Rummy, however, Conquian players can't improve their hands during the game by adding cards from the stockpile: they are dependent on the turned-up card to complete whatever partial sets and sequences were dealt. As a result, games often end in a draw and the pot builds up, adding excitement to what is otherwise a relatively static game with limited room for strategic play.

The Deal: The deck is shuffled; players cut for the deal; low card deals. Each player receives 10 cards, two at a time. The remaining 20 cards are stacked facedown as the stockpile. The loser deals the next hand. If the hand ends in a draw, the deal alternates.

Each player receives 10 counters.

The Object of the Game:
To collect and lay down sets of three or four matching cards or same-suit sequences of three or more; to go out by laying down 11 cards in sets and sequences.

The Play: Each player antes one counter to the pot before play begins.

The elder hand (nondealer) starts by turning the top card of the stockpile faceup and placing it beside the stockpile. If the card matches two in his hand to create a set or sequence (called, colloquially, a *rope*), he slides the turned-up card to his side of the table and lays down the cards from his hand to complete the set or sequence. Then he discards from his hand so that, counting the meld (the cards on the table) and the cards in his hand, he still has 10 cards.

On his first turn, a player can meld any sets or sequences he was dealt, even if he cannot use the stockpile card. In this case, there is no discard.

If he cannot use the upcard and doesn't want to meld, the elder hand passes. The dealer can then slide the upcard to her side of the table, providing she can add at least two cards from her hand for a meld. If she does so, she then discards from her hand. (On this first turn, she may also meld any sets or sequences she was dealt.)

If the dealer doesn't want the upcard either, she passes, turning it facedown. (Once a card is turned facedown it cannot be looked at again.) Having passed on the upcard, she then turns over the next card on the stockpile. If she wants it, she slides it to her side of the table, melds with cards from her hand and discards. If she doesn't want it, she passes and her opponent either takes it or turns it facedown and turns up the next card on the stockpile.

Play continues in this way. The turned-up card is never actually taken into a player's hand. Whoever turns it over has first chance to move it to his side of the table to meld with it or use it to extend one of his existing melds. If he doesn't want it, he passes. If the second player doesn't want the card either, she turns it facedown and turns the next card on the stockpile faceup.

Whenever a player uses the upcard to meld, he discards, placing a card from his hand faceup between the two players. The discard is then used exactly as if it were an upcard from the stockpile: the opponent can use it to meld or, if he doesn't want it, he turns it facedown and turns the next card on the stockpile faceup.

At any time during his turn, a player can add cards from his hand to an existing meld. He can also borrow cards from existing melds of four or more to make new melds. (The existing meld must not be depleted to fewer than three cards.) For instance, in the game illustrated, the dealer holds a 6♦ in her hand, has a 6-5-4-3♠ sequence melded, and the upcard is 6♥: she can take the 6 from the meld and the 6 from her hand and add them to the upcard to meld a set of 6s.

A player is required to take the stockpile card if it can be added to any of his existing melds. If he neglects to do so and passes on the card, his opponent can force the move by picking up the card, placing it on his opponent's set or sequence, and saying, "Discard!" A player is not required, however, to use the turned-up card to meld from his hand. Such a play cannot be forced because the opponent never knows what cards the other player holds.

A player can also force an opponent to use his discard by placing it directly on the opponent's meld (providing it matches, of course). In the game illustrated, after using the 6 in a meld, the dealer will discard her King, laying it directly on the elder hand's melded set of Kings, thus forcing him to discard from his hand. If she discarded the King instead to the center of the table, her opponent is not obliged to use the card to extend his meld. Toward the end of the game, such force-plays can effectively empty a player's hand, leav-ing him completely reliant on the luck of the stockpile to complete a meld and go out.

The game is finished when one player lays 11 cards on the table in sets and sequences. A winner may use the final card to make new melds, add to existing melds or both, but when he goes out, there is no discard.

If the last card of the stockpile is turned up and no one can go out, the game is considered a draw.

The Score: The player who goes out first takes the pot. If the hand is tied, the pot is carried forward to the next hand.

Instead of counters, the game can be played for points. The player who goes out first scores points equal to the value of the cards remaining in his opponent's hand. In draw games, the player with the fewest points scores the difference between the total value of his hand and his opponent's. If using a Spanish deck, face cards count 10.

Strategy: One of the distinguishing factors of Conquian is that players see every card turned faceup on the stockpile. No cards are drawn and added to the hand: cards are either turned down or laid on the table in sets or sequences. One hopes for a good hand in the deal above all, and after that, prays for good cards to appear early in the stockpile.

What little strategy there is hinges on the discard. It is a good tactic not to lay down more meld cards than necessary. For instance, if you hold the 2, 3, 5 of Hearts and the 4♥ is turned up, you can slide it to your side of the table and lay down the 2 and 3, but keep the 5 in hand in hopes of melding it with other cards. The more options you leave open, the greater the potential for being able to meld all 11 cards and win the game. Also, you want to keep your opponent in the dark about the sets and sequences you are collecting.

When discarding, get rid of single cards that cannot fit with others to become sets or sequences. Keep cards that maximize options. For instance, a 7♥, 7♠, 6♠ can be completed with four cards: 7♣, 7♦, 8♠, 5♠. In the game illustrated, the K♥ is a good discard because it matches nothing in the dealer's hand, while the other four cards represent two potential sets and a potential sequence. Furthermore, the King is a high-value liability for her yet a useful offensive tool: with it, she can force the elder hand to disrupt his hand.

A feature that has persisted in the more ruthless forms of Rummy is the notion of *forcing*, whereby a player must take the upcard if it fits into one of his existing melds, thus forcing him to discard. This tactic can be used effectively toward the end of a game, to keep a player with only one or no cards in hand, not enough to make a set or sequence, and therefore forcing him to wait until a card is turned up that matches a meld already on the table.

If you play for points instead of counters, the strategy changes somewhat, since you don't want to be left with high-counting cards in hand. Discard high cards whenever possible and meld all cards as soon as possible. Empty your hand if your opponent appears to be close to going out. No melding opportunities are lost, since cards can be rearranged on the table; the disadvantage is that more of your cards are exposed to your opponent so he can foil your plans by holding on to the discard you need to go out. ༄

Gin Rummy

- ◆ OTHER NAMES: **Poker Gin or simply Gin**
- ◆ NUMBER: **a classic two-person game**
- ◆ EQUIPMENT: **one deck of 52, Ace low, and a scorepad**
- ◆ DESCRIPTION: **a cutthroat strategy game with a characteristic knock, a high frustration level and complex scoring**
- ◆ DURATION: **fast-paced; only a few minutes per hand, several hands while the teakettle boils**

ACCORDING TO American card authority John Scarne, the Rummy family of card games evolved from Whiskey Poker, a swift gambling game played for drinks in 18th-century American saloons. Whiskey Poker became Rum Poker; then the unsavory last name was dropped and the first name colloquialized until Rummy was proper enough for family play. Gin Rummy is a two-handed variation, supposedly perfected by Elwood T. Baker, a **Whist** teacher at the Knickerbocker Whist Club in New York. It wasn't well known, however, until the early 1940s, when it became a Hollywood fad and spawned one of Broadway's longest-running shows, *The Gin Game*.

In the Rummy family of games, players draw cards one by one from the stockpile and discard after each draw, attempting to reorganize their hands into melds. The wild cards, penalties and melding rules vary, but the two-handed version—Gin—is a classic and, strategically, among the best.

Like all the Rummys (particularly **Canasta**), Gin Rummy is extremely frustrating. Losing is bad enough, but in Rummy games, the loser not only scores zero but does not even have the satisfaction of playing out his hand. The winner cuts her opponent off mid-meld and walks away with the prize. A run of bad luck can make you crazy. "All lunatics are bound to be Gin players," writes Damon Runyon in *The Lacework Kid*, "and in fact the chances are it is Gin Rummy that makes them lunatics."

The Deal: Cut the deck; low card deals. The winner of each hand deals the next. The dealer shuffles the deck and deals 10 cards to each player one at a time. The remaining cards are placed facedown between the players as a stockpile. The top card of the stockpile is turned faceup beside it; this is the discard pile.

The Object of the Game: To make sets and sequences, reducing the unmatched cards in the hand to as few and as low-scoring as possible. The first to reach the target score of 100 points wins.

The Play: Throughout the game, each player in turn takes either the top card of the discard pile or the top card of the stockpile, then discards, always leaving 10 cards in hand. The aim of drawing and discarding is to meld the 10 cards into *sets* of three or four of a kind or into *sequences* of three or more consecutive cards of the same suit: for instance, K-Q-J♥ or 3-2-A♣. The sets and sequences have no scoring value, but at the end of the game, players are penalized for unmatched cards.

First, the elder hand (nondealer) decides whether he wants the faceup card. If he doesn't, he says "Pass" and offers it to the dealer. If the dealer takes it, play begins, and she makes the first discard. If she doesn't want it either, then the elder hand begins, drawing the top card from the stockpile and discarding from his hand. Play continues, each player in turn drawing from either the discard pile or the stockpile, then discarding.

When a player can meld all 10 of his cards, he knocks on the table to announce the hand is finished. (A player knocks after the draw and before the discard.) He lays his discard facedown on the discard pile and lays the rest of his cards faceup on the table, arranged in melds so that the other player can see there are no unmatched cards. He declares the fact that *all* his cards are melded by saying "Gin."

A player does not have to wait until he has Gin to knock. He can also knock if, at any time, the unmatched cards in his hand add up to less than 10. The procedure is the same. Draw, then knock on the table to signal the end of the hand, discard facedown on the discard pile, lay the hand faceup on the table, with the melds together and the unmatched cards to one side, and declare the count; for instance, "Down for 6," if the unmatched cards add up to 6 points. (In both cases, a player who goes out must discard.)

Once a player knocks and lays down his hand, the other player does the same, laying her cards faceup on the table, grouping the melds. Because the player who knocks has not *gone Gin*—in other words, he still has unmatched cards—the opponent is allowed to *lay off* her unmatched cards on the other's melds. For instance, in the game illustrated, M knocked, declaring "Down for 8," and laid down a sequence and two sets of three of a kind, with 8♥ left unmatched. H can lay off her unmatched 7♣ on the sequence and her K♣ on the set of Kings. Having disposed of as many cards as possible, H lays down her unmatched cards and declares her count aloud.

If the players get down to the last two cards of the stockpile and neither has knocked, the hand must be abandoned. The last two cards remain facedown, and neither player scores.

The Score: There are two stages to scoring Gin Rummy. First, each hand is scored. The players set aside their melds—these are out of play and do not score—and add up their unmatched cards according to their numerical values; face cards count 10, Aces 1.

A player who goes Gin scores 25 points plus her opponent's total in unmatched cards.

A player who knocks without going Gin scores the total of his opponent's unmatched cards minus the total of his own unmatched cards. For instance, in the game illustrated, H has 7♦, Q♣, 5♠, 6♠ and 6♥ unmatched, for a total of 34. M has 8♥ unmatched, for a total of 8, so M scores 26 (34-8).

If, after laying off her unmatched cards on the other hand, the opponent has a lower total of unmatched cards than the player who knocked, she gets a bonus of 25 plus the difference between her count and his. For example, if H had J♣ instead of 7♣, she could play Q-J♣ on the 10-9-8♣ sequence. And if she had 4♠ instead of 6♥ to make another meld, she would only be left with 7♦ unmatched. Her total would be 7, compared with his 8, in which case H would score 26 (the 25-point bonus plus 8 minus 7). John

Scarne disapproves of the practice. He suggests only a 10-point bonus in this situation, which he calls an *underknock*.

In each hand, only one player scores. It is called the *box score*, or *line score*. As each hand is played, the scores are tallied but entered on a new line, so it is clear how many hands each player has won within the 100-point game.

The player who reaches 100 first earns a bonus of 100 points. Each player also earns a bonus of 20 points for every hand won. The box scores and bonuses for each player are tallied, and the loser's total is subtracted from the winner's to calculate the margin of victory. When playing for money, this is what determines the payoff, usually a penny a point. In the game illustrated, this hand puts M's score over 100, so he wins the game and earns the 100-point bonus. M earns an 80-point bonus for winning four hands; H won two and earns a 40-point bonus. The final score is M 292 and H 92. If they were playing for a penny a point, H owes M $2.00.

If one player wins every hand, he skunks his opponent and earns double his total points.

Strategy: Order the cards in your hand according to potential sets and sequences, grouping single unmatched cards in suits. Decide which combinations to strive for in drawing and discarding. One astute Gin player insists that the hand be picked up one card at a time after the deal so that each card is impressed upon your memory. Avoid ordering your hand high to low, and keep reordering the cards, partly to confuse your opponent and partly to keep yourself alert to each card's potential.

No one wants to be stuck with high-scoring face cards at the end, but it is also unwise to be known as a player who always collects 2s and 3s. Play the hand you are dealt, even if it is all Kings and Queens.

Holding onto consecutive cards doubles your chances of making a

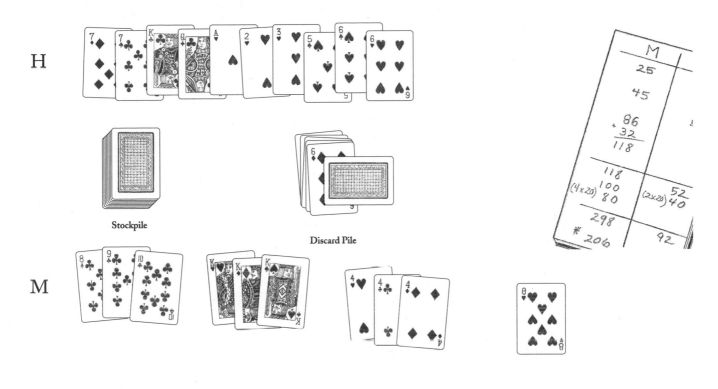

sequence. For instance, if you keep 9-8♦, there are two cards that can complete the sequence: 7♦ and 10♦. But if you keep 7♦ and 9♦, you could spend the whole game waiting for 8♦. Look for combinations that can go either way, keeping 8♣, 8♥ and 9♥ so that any one of four cards—7♥, 8♦,8♠, 10♥—completes the meld. Remember: There is nothing above the King or below the Ace, so when you start sequences with these cards, your options are cut in half.

Get to know your opponent's hand. Watch what he discards and picks up. If he discards 6♦ but picks up 6♥, he is probably collecting a sequence of Hearts. Be wary of discarding anything that will help. It is often a good idea to discard a card of the same value as one your opponent previously discarded: for instance, if he threw 6♦ last turn, you throw 6♣ this turn. Keep in mind, however, that he may hold 4-5♣ and be trying to elicit the 6♣ with his discard.

Some players pick up cards they don't really want in order to mislead their opponent, a practice known as *spitballing*. Be suspicious of an opponent who exclaims, "Great! Exactly what I need!" He is probably trying to distract you. By remembering what your opponent picks up, you can assess whether he can build on your sequences and sets. If you think he can, wait and try to go Gin so that he cannot discard on your melds.

In general, however, go out as soon as possible. You deprive yourself of the satisfaction of making Gin, but the earlier you knock, the more likely you are to earn a high score from your opponent's unmatched cards. Remember: There is only a 5-point difference between a 25-point Gin and the 20-point box-score bonus. When your hand is close to Gin, with only a few low-scoring unmatched cards, you may choose to wait a few draws, since even if your opponent beats you to the knock, your unmatched cards might allow you to underknock and win.

After a few draws, assess your opponent's chances of knocking, and if he seems close, discard the high-value cards in your hand. You can do this by picking up a 3 from the discard pile, even though you don't want it, so that you can discard a King. You may not be able to avoid losing, but you can control to some extent how much your opponent scores. (Some players *always* pick up cards under 4, unless it means discarding from a meld.)

In Gin, the most valuable card is 7. There are, according to John Scarne, 15,820,024,220 possible 10-card combinations in the game, and 7 works in more of them than any other single card, with fewer negative consequences. The King and the Ace are the least useful cards.

Variation: Some players designate the Ace worth 15 and allow it to be played either high or low. This "round the corner" variation changes the value of holding Kings and Aces for sequences. ~

Canasta

- ◆ NUMBER: **two players; variations for more**
- ◆ EQUIPMENT: **two decks of 52, Ace low, plus four Jokers**
- ◆ DESCRIPTION: **complicated and frustrating, but not difficult**
- ◆ COMPLEXITY: **easy to learn, but hard to master**
- ◆ DURATION: **set aside an evening; an average game takes an hour and a half**
- ◆ TIP: **caution—this game can be hazardous to relationships**

CANASTA is also a type of Rummy, but unlike **Gin Rummy**, the melds earn points and players pick up the whole discard pile, instead of just the top card. This lengthens the game and shifts the emphasis from going out to collecting high-scoring sets of cards.

One of the few widespread North American pastimes of South American origin, Canasta was first played in Uruguay around 1940, then spread in a myriad of variations to Argentina and throughout the rest of Latin America to the United States. In 1950, order was brought to the game by the Official Laws of Canasta, published by the Canasta Committee of New York's Regency Club and endorsed by **Bridge** guru Ely Culbertson. For a few years in the 1950s, Canasta edged out Bridge as America's favorite card game. Its allure has faded somewhat, but it still has a place in history as the last great card-game fad.

Canasta is the Spanish word for basket and refers to the main thrust of the game: to collect melds of three or more cards of the same value. There are dozens of variations, all equally fascinating and frustrating. You can collect melds for an hour, only to have your painstaking plans dashed when your opponent melds out, leaving you with a fistful of cards and unfulfilled dreams. Not necessarily vicious, Canasta nevertheless brings out the cutthroat in cardplayers. More than one couple has had to forswear the game to preserve a marriage.

The Deal: Cut for the deal; high card deals. For subsequent hands, the deal alternates between players. The dealer shuffles two full decks of cards together, Jokers included, and deals 15 cards facedown to each player one at a time. The remaining cards are turned facedown on the table as a stockpile. The top card is turned faceup beside it. This is *el pozo*, the pot, where cards are discarded faceup. If the upturned card is a red 3 or a *wild card* (a Joker or a 2), another card is turned faceup on the discard pile. Players organize their cards numerically in sets: for instance, all the 4s, then 5s, then 6s. Sequences and suits are of no consequence.

The Object of the Game:
To lay down melds of three or more of a kind, striving for canastas (seven of a kind). The first player to reach 5,000 points wins.

The Melds:
When a player has a set of three or more of a kind, he can lay the meld faceup on the table in front of him. (Except in the opening meld, one of the cards may be wild.) After a meld is laid down, a player can add cards to lengthen it to a canasta. A *natural canasta*—seven of a kind—is squared with a red card on top. A *mixed canasta*, which contains wild cards (up to three of the seven cards can be Jokers or 2s), is squared with a black card on top. An eighth card or wild cards can be added to a finished canasta, slipped under the bottom of the stack, but if a wild card is added later to a natural canasta, it becomes mixed. A black card is laid on top, and at the end of the game, the mixed canasta scores less. Jokers and 2s cannot be melded alone. Likewise, red 3s are never melded but are laid down one at a time for bonus points. Three or four black 3s can be melded, but only when a player goes out; no wild cards can be added to a meld of black 3s. Once a card is laid down in a meld, it cannot be moved or retrieved.

The Play: The elder hand (non-dealer) goes first, either drawing the top card of the stockpile or picking up the discard pile, which, at the beginning of the game, is just a single card. Throughout the game, each player in turn either draws the top card of the stockpile or picks up the entire discard pile, then discards one card. If she draws from the stockpile and discards, she is left with 15 cards in hand; if she picks up the discard pile, then discards one card, her hand will expand according to the size of the pile.

Whether the discard pile is one card or a dozen, a player cannot pick it up until he lays down an opening meld worth 50 points or more. (Wild cards cannot be used in opening melds.) He can include the top card of the discard pile in the opening meld, then pick up the rest of the pile, or he can lay down the opening meld, then pick up the entire pile.

For instance, the top card of the discard pile is 9♥, and the player has 9♦ and 9♠ in hand, as well as three Queens. Cards from 8 to King are worth 10 points each, so the player picks up 9♥ from the discard pile and lays down a set of 9s (30 points) and a set of Queens (30 points), for a total opening meld of 60 points. Having opened successfully, she picks up the rest of the discard pile, arranges her hand in sets, then discards one card.

Once a player has made an opening meld, she can, on her next turn, draw a card from the stockpile or pick up the discard pile. To pick up the pile, a player must be able to add the top card to an existing meld or lay it down in a meld, either with a natural pair or with a matching card and a wild card. (A player with only one card in his hand cannot pick up a discard pile that contains only one card.) After picking up the discard pile, a player can lay down as many melds as he wants before discarding.

When a wild card or a red 3 is turned over as the first card in the discard pile, it is placed crosswise, and another card is turned over top. The pile is considered *frozen*. To unfreeze it, a player not only needs the correct points for an opening meld but also must match the top card of the discard pile with a natural pair. For instance, if the top card is 7♦, she could unfreeze the pile if she has 7♣ and 7♥, as well as enough points to lay down an opening meld. After a frozen pile is picked up, the usual rules apply to the discard pile. A player can refreeze the discard pile at any time, however, by discarding a wild card, laying it crosswise on the other cards. (During play, red 3s are never discarded; they are laid down to score points.) To pick up the frozen pile, a player must again match the top card with a natural pair. Whoever does so, gets *all* the cards, including the valuable wild card—a *pozo premiado*, or prize pot.

If a player is dealt a red 3, he lays it faceup on the table at his first turn and draws another card from the stockpile to replace it. If he draws a red 3 from the stockpile, he lays it down immediately and draws another card.

A black 3 does not freeze the discard pile, but it does make the pile inaccessible to the next player. The discard pile can be picked up only if the top card is laid down in a meld, and black 3s can only be laid down when a player is going out, which is not going to happen immediately upon picking up the pile. So a black 3 blocks an opponent from picking up the pile in his next turn. Instead, he must draw from the stockpile. As soon as he discards, however, the pile can be picked up as usual.

A player can end the hand at any time by *melding out*—laying down all the cards in her hand, disposing of the last one either on the discard pile or in a meld. A player must have at least two canastas to meld out. When one player melds out, the other shows his hand, and both calculate their scores. Sometimes a player can conceal her cards well enough that she can lay down her opening meld and meld out in the same turn, earning 200 points

Scoring System: Canasta

Bonus Points	Points
Natural Canasta (no wild cards)	500
Mixed Canasta (up to three wild cards).	300
Melding out	100
Concealed melding out	200
Each red 3	100
All four red 3s	800

Card Values	
Joker	50
2 and Ace.	20
K, Q, J, 10, 9, 8	10
7, 6, 5, 4 and black 3	5

Opening Melds	
Minus Score	15
Score of 0 to 1,495	50
Score of 1,500 to 2,995	90
Score of 3,000 or more	120

instead of the standard melding-out bonus of 100.

If play continues down to the last card of the stockpile and the final card is a red 3, the game ends immediately. If it is anything but a red 3, the players then take turns picking up the top card from the discard pile as long as it can be used to make a new meld or to match an existing one. When no more discards can be used, the hand is over. In both cases, when the scores are tallied, neither player wins the melding-out bonus and they must subtract the cards in their hands from their totals.

When the hand is over, players record their scores. Each game requires several hands.

The Score: There are two stages to scoring Canasta. When the hand is over, players add up their bonus points first: 500 for each natural canasta, 300 for each mixed canasta, 100 for each red 3, and so on, as listed in the scoring system on the previous page. After the bonuses are counted, each player adds up the values of the cards that were laid down in the melds.

Unmatched cards in the loser's hand are added up and deducted from his score. A red 3 left in the hand counts

100 points against a player.

The final scores for the players are recorded after each hand. The first player to reach 5,000 points wins. The loser of one hand deals the first hand in the next.

As the game progresses, the total required for an opening meld increases. If a player's total score is less than 1,500 points, the opening meld is 50 points; if it is 1,500 to 2,995, the opening meld is 90; if it is 3,000 or more, the opening meld is 120. If a player's score falls below zero, the opening meld drops to 15.

For example, in the game illustrated, M has just gone out. She scores 500 for the natural canasta of Queens, 300 for the mixed canasta of 4s, 200 for the two red 3s, 100 for melding out and 350 for the card values, for a total of 1,450. H scores 100 for a red 3 and 160 for the card values, for a total of 260, minus 40 points for the unmatched cards in his hand. The final score for the hand is: M 1,450; H 220. Both are under 1,500 points, so in the next hand, each still needs only 50 points for the opening meld.

Strategy: Early in the game, keep as many wild cards and different pairs

H

Discard Pile   Stockpile

M

as possible. Lay down an opening meld as soon as you can and take the discard pile; you need the extra cards to build melds. (Melding without picking up the discard pile impoverishes the hand.)

Because each card in a meld contributes to the final score, collect high-scoring cards, discarding 5-pointers. Black 3s are the exception. Save them to use as discards to block your opponent from picking up a discard pile that contains cards you desperately want. The black 3s buy time and cost only 5 points each if left in your hand; hoard as many as you can.

Pay attention to your opponent's melds and discards. Figure out what he is collecting, and avoid discards that will help him build canastas. If you must discard what your opponent wants, do so when the pile is small. The player who picks up the big discard piles has the scoring advantage.

There is a trade-off in laying down melds. If you lay them down early, your opponent will know what you are collecting and foil your attempts at canastas. If you hoard your melds, you may be stuck with a handful of cards

when your opponent goes out. Timing is all. Hoard early in the game, making your opening meld with as few cards as possible, but when it looks as though the other player may go out, lay down as much as you can—at the very least, your high-scoring cards. Don't hold onto wild cards too long. Sometimes it is worth adding them to a natural canasta, since the added count compensates for the reduced bonus.

Don't hesitate to freeze the discard pile if your opponent has melded and you haven't. It will slow her down, but since you still have all your cards, you are more likely to have the natural pairs to unfreeze it. The danger is that once your opponent has access to the discard pile, she will take it repeatedly before you make an opening meld. In this game, the person with the most cards usually wins.

Variations: For a shorter two-person game, draw two cards at a time from the stockpile, and discard one.

Canasta for three to five players is exactly the same as the two-person game, except each person receives

13 cards.

Partnership Canasta is played with four people. Instead of 15 cards, deal 11 to each player. The two people sitting across from each other are partners. Only one member of the partnership has to make the opening meld before both players can pick up the discard pile. For convenience, the melds can be laid down in front of one player only. Partners can play to each other's melds. In this variation, only one canasta is required to go out, but before going out, a player must ask his partner, "May I go out?" If the answer is "No" or if the player then finds he cannot go out, the team is penalized 100 points. Scoring is the same. The deal passes to the left. Six-handed Canasta is exactly like four-handed, played in partners, three against three.

Wild Card Canasta, sometimes called Cuban Canasta, deals 13 cards to two players and allows wild-card melds. Games go to 7,500 points.

In **Bolivian**, **Samba** and **Brazilian Canasta**, three decks are shuffled and dealt, sequences are collected as well as cards of the same value, and scores run to 15,000 points. ∾

Cribbage

- ◆ NUMBER: **two players; variations for more**
- ◆ EQUIPMENT: **a deck of 52 and a special scoring board, with four pegs and a double track of 60 or 120 holes**
- ◆ DESCRIPTION: **a social game that does not preclude conversation**
- ◆ COMPLEXITY: **moderately challenging; requires a little strategy and attention, some judgment and luck**
- ◆ DURATION: **easily mastered in 15 minutes; a game takes about half an hour**

ONE OF the classic two-handers, Cribbage was apparently invented by the 17th-century British poet and soldier Sir John Suckling, considered by his contemporaries to be the greatest gamester of his time. Legend has it that he devised the game while at the French court on the lam after he attempted to rescue a col-

league from the Tower of London. Although the game undoubtedly has predecessors—Cribbage has elements in common with the more sophisticated **Piquet**—Suckling probably refined it, naming it after the dealer's unfair advantage, the "crib" of discards.

The game of Cribbage is based on

certain valuable combinations of cards—pairs, three or four of a kind, runs, flushes and, especially, sets that add up to 15. Players score points during play by matching their cards with those of their opponent, but they also score after the cards are played, by adding up the value of the combinations in their own hands.

Each point is scored as it is earned, during play and after. The game moves quickly, and a scorepad soon becomes a mess of scratched-out numbers. A Cribbage board is worth the investment. Usually made of wood, it is a rectangle perforated with a double row of holes, either 30 along each side, for a total of 60, or a curlicue S of 120, snaking from one end of the board to the other, with a winning hole at the end. Each player has two pegs of a distinctive color. A player counts her first score with one peg, then uses the

Cribbage

Dealer

The Crib

Cribbage Board

Starter

Elder Hand

second peg for the next score, counting forward from the first. The pegs leapfrog along the track, the lead peg indicating a player's current total and the back peg indicating the previous score, so there can be no dispute as to where she started each count. Not only is the board a neat way of keeping score, but it turns Cribbage into a race, the finish line—and the skunk line—clearly in sight.

The Deal: Cut the deck; low card deals. For subsequent hands, players take turns dealing. Several hands make a game. The loser of one game deals first in the next. The dealer shuffles the deck and deals six cards facedown to each player one at a time. The re-

maining cards are the stockpile. They are turned facedown at the end of the Cribbage board, on the dealer's left.

The Object of the Game: To form scoring combinations of cards in your hand and during play. The first player to cross the finish line, scoring 121 points, wins.

The Crib: Players assess their hands for flushes, runs, sets of matching cards and combinations that total 15. (See Scoring the Hand, facing page.) They decide which four cards to keep, then discard the other two facedown to a *crib* pile. In each hand, the crib belongs to the dealer.

The Starter: After the discard, the elder hand (nondealer) cuts the stockpile. The dealer takes the top card of the bottom portion and lays it faceup on the top of the stockpile as the *starter*. If it is a Jack, the dealer earns 2 points, traditionally announced as "Two for his heels." If he forgets to score the points before the first card is played, he forfeits them.

The Play: The elder hand begins by laying a card from his hand faceup on the table and announcing its value. (Ace counts 1, face cards count 10, and others count according to their numerical value.) The other player then lays down a card, announcing the total of the two. (Each player has his own discard pile.) Players continue to lay down cards until the total approaches 31. If a player cannot lay down a card without going over 31, she says "Go," and the other person plays as many cards as possible up to, but not over, 31. Whoever plays the last card scores 1 point for a total below 31 (Go) and 2 points for making 31 exactly. The lead then passes to the other player, and the count begins again at zero.

Play continues until all the cards in both hands have been played. Then the individual hands are scored, and the person who has the deal collects the cards, shuffles the deck and deals a new hand.

Several hands are played before someone wins the game.

Scoring in Play: Players score points during the game, as indicated by the scoring system. Laying down a card that brings the total to 15 scores 2 points; for instance, the elder hand says "Six" and lays down 6♠; the dealer lays down 9♦ and declares "Fifteen," scoring 2 points. If the elder hand then laid down 9♥, he would also score 2 points for a *pair*. Making three of a kind scores 6 points; four of a kind scores 12. Playing a third card to create a numerical sequence counts 1 point per card. The cards do not have to be in order, but they must be played one after the other. For instance, if the elder hand lays down 7♦ and the dealer follows with 9♥, the elder hand can play 8♣ and score 3 points; if the dealer then plays 6♦, she scores 4 points for making a sequence of four.

Scoring the Hand: After playing the hands, each person gathers up his discards and scores his own hand, using the turned-up starter as a fifth card to create combinations. Score 2 points for each set of cards with a combined face value of *15*: for instance, 7 and 8; 9 and 6; a 10 or any face card together with 5, 1 and 4 or 2 and 3. A *pair* also counts 2 points. *Three of a kind* counts 6 points, and *four of a kind* counts 12. A *run* of three or more cards in numerical sequence is

worth 1 point per card. Certain standard combinations such as the double run (5-6-6-7) and the triple run (5-6-6-6-7) can be scored at a glance, as indicated in the scoring system. A *flush*—four cards of the same suit—scores 4 points; if the starter is also in that suit, score 1 extra point, for a total of 5. (Flushes do not score during play.) A Jack in the same suit as the starter counts 1: "One for his nobs."

There is a ritual to announcing the score. A player holding 10♦, 10♥, J♠ and 5♠, with J♥ as the starter, would say: "Fifteen 2, fifteen 4, fifteen 6, fifteen 8 and two pairs makes 12," pegging it on the board as he calls it.

The elder hand has *first show* and scores first. Then the dealer shows his hand and scores it. Finally, the dealer turns the crib faceup and scores it too. In the crib, a flush counts only if the

starter is the same suit; there is no 4-point flush within the hand itself. Otherwise, it scores the same.

In the hand illustrated on the previous page, the dealer earns 2 points for turning up a Jack starter; 10 points for a double run of four in her hand; and in the crib, 4 points for two sets of 15 and 2 points for a pair, for a total of 18 points.

The elder hand earns 6 points for three sets of 15 and 2 points for a pair, for a total of 8 points.

If a player overlooks a chance to score, either during play or during the show, the other player calls "Muggins!" and takes the points. To be fair, this rule should be invoked only by players of equal skill.

The first player to reach 121—the game hole—*pegs out* and wins. If the other player has not yet reached the

---

Scoring System: Cribbage

In Play	Points
Total of 15	2
Pair	2
Three of a Kind	6
Four of a Kind	12
Run of three or more . . . . 1 point/card
Turned-up Jack	2
Go	1
31	2

The Hand	
Total of 15	2
Pair	2
Three of a Kind	6
Four of a Kind	12
Run of three or more . . . . 1 point/card
Four-Card Flush	4
Five-Card Flush	5
Jack same suit as starter	1
Double Run (7-6-6-5)	8
Double Run of Four (8-7-6-6-5)	10
Triple Run (7-6-6-6-5)	15
Quadruple Run (7-7-6-6-5)	16

Card Values	
Ace	1
Face Card	10
Numerals . . . . face value

Game is 121 points.

halfway mark, he is *in the lurch*, or *skunked*, and loses two games, not one. Players often play a *rubber* match: two games out of three.

Strategy: Because the crib belongs to the dealer, he can discard valuable cards—pairs, two cards in a run or a flush—knowing that they will still contribute to his score. The elder hand, however, must avoid giving away points with her discards. Since a third of the cards in a deck have a value of 10, the elder hand should never discard 5s, face cards or 10s, a pair or two cards that need only one more to complete a run; for instance, a 9 and 7 need only an 8 to score 5 points: 3 for the run and 2 for 15. Instead, she should discard widely separated cards in different suits and cards with little potential for adding up to 15. Sometimes, she has to *balk*, to ruin her own score in order to avoid giving game-winning points to the dealer in his crib.

As a player comes close to pegging out, the discard strategy changes. Early in the game, keep a high-scoring hand. Near the end, keep cards that will score during play; for instance, low cards that may win "Go" points. The starter is no longer a big factor. Instead of keeping pairs and in-hand combinations of 15, keep individual cards that allow you to make 15 no matter what your opponent leads.

Although the hands themselves are valuable, skillful play usually wins the game. Generally, it is suicide to lead a 5 or a 10-value card. Instead of avoiding combinations that might help your opponent, however, you can lead him on. For instance, you may lead a 7, knowing that if your opponent plays an 8 to score 15, you can play 9 and score 3 for a run. Leading from a pair is also good strategy: if your opponent plays a matching card, you can play another one and score 6 for three of a kind.

For the record, the highest-scoring single hand counts 29 points: a Jack and three 5s, with the starter a 5 of the same suit as the Jack (four 15s by combining the Jack with a 5; four 15s by combining the 5s; four of a kind; and his nobs). Hands valuing more than 20 are rare, 10 is considered good, and 7 is about average. No hand can possibly total 19, which explains why a player with four scoreless cards traditionally declares "Nineteen."

Variations: Five-card Cribbage predates the six-card version and is different only in that five cards are dealt and two discarded, leaving three in each hand and four in the crib. Before play begins, the elder hand pegs 3 points—"three for last"—to compensate for the extra card in the dealer's crib. Since points are harder to score, the game usually goes to 61, instead of 121. Many older Cribbage boards have a single circuit of 60 pegs, navigated once for five-card Cribbage and twice for six-card Cribbage.

Although two-handed Cribbage is better, three people can also play. Deal five cards to each player and one to the crib. The same rules apply, except players discard only one card to the crib. The player to the left of the dealer cuts for the starter and leads first in play. Triangular Cribbage boards are made to score three-handed Cribbage, either to 61 or 121, but if you can't find one, you'll have to resort to a scorepad instead. ∽

Russian Bank

- ◆ OTHER NAMES: **Rabouge or Robuse**
- ◆ NUMBER: **two players**
- ◆ EQUIPMENT: **a standard deck of 52**
- ◆ DESCRIPTION: **competitive Patience, building same-suit sequences**
- ◆ COMPLEXITY: **requires close attention more than skill; players are mostly at the mercy of the cards and their own ability to spot moves**
- ◆ DURATION: **about 15 minutes a game**

MOST PATIENCE or Solitaire games can be played by two people as a race, each playing separately but competitively to see who can get the furthest fastest. Solitaire can also be played interactively, with players building on each other's Aces, as in double **Klondike** or **Pounce**. There is a third option: players can take turns playing one game, each moving the game forward as far as possible in his turn before ceding to the other player, who also moves it forward, each trying to bring the game to completion during his turn.

Russian Bank falls in the last category. It is one of the few card games that has remained truly a folk game: it is played in myriad variations and rarely appears in two places with precisely the same rules. The name is a mystery, too, since it has little to do with either Russia or gambling (banking games are traditionally played for stakes).

Russian Bank was first played as Rabouge or Robuse in mid 19th-century Europe; by the turn of the century a double-decker version was being played in France as **Crapette** or Crippette. Just after the First World War, a simplified form became a fad in the United States under the name Russian Bank, the same one described here.

The Deal: Shuffle the cards. The two players cut the deck; high card deals. The dealer deals the entire deck, one at a time, facedown, so that each player has 26 cards. The deal alternates between hands. (Shuffle the cards very well between hands to break up sequences.)

The Object of the Game:
To be the first to get rid of all 26 cards.

The Play: The elder hand (non-dealer) begins by laying the top four cards of her hand in a row faceup on the table. This is half the *tableau*. Then she turns over the fifth card. She can play it to the tableau if it is the same suit and next in rank, either ascending or descending. For example, if she turns up 6♥ and there is a 7♥ on the table, she can play the 6 on it. If she can't play the turned-up card on the tableau, she sets it aside, faceup, to begin her discard pile or *talon*.

The dealer then takes his first turn, laying the first four cards from his hand on the table faceup, to complete the tableau (eight cards faceup in two rows between the two players). He turns over his fifth card and if it is the same suit and next in rank to any of the eight cards in the tableau or the card in his opponent's talon, he plays it. If he cannot play the card, he turns it faceup to begin his talon.

Once a card is played on the tableau, the rank sequence is established and must be followed by both players. Aces are not played separately; they are played next in sequence to 2s and Kings. For example, if the 6♥ is played on the 7♥, a descending sequence is started and must be continued, playing the 5, 4, 3, 2, A, K, Q, and so on to the 8, at which point the sequence is complete.

At any turn, a player can lay a card on his opponent's talon, following the same rules for building an ascending or descending suit.

During his turn, a player can move cards within the tableau, but only one at a time. When a space opens in the tableau, it must be filled by the player who created it. He can fill it with the

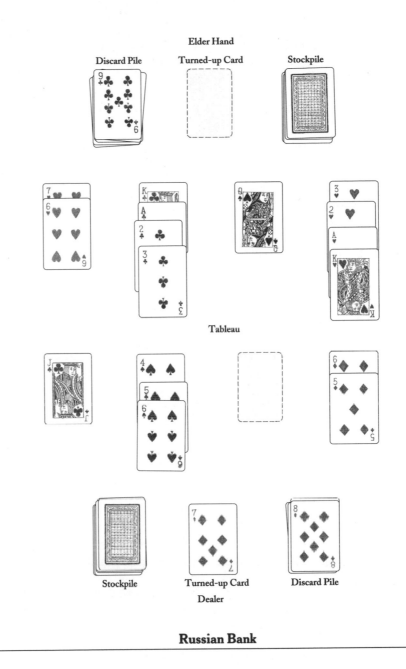

Elder Hand

Discard Pile   Turned-up Card   Stockpile

Tableau

Stockpile   Turned-up Card   Discard Pile

Dealer

Russian Bank

top card from the talon or with any *end card* (the final card in any sequence in the tableau).

Each player continues to build sequences and turn over cards from his hand as long as he can make a play. As soon as he turns over a card that he cannot play to the tableau or to his opponent's talon, he discards it in his own talon and the turn passes to his opponent.

The first player to get rid of all 26 cards wins.

Strategy: As in most forms of Solitaire, much of the outcome depends on close observation and the

luck of the cards. A player can use a space in the tableau, however, to reverse the direction of a sequence. For example, in the game illustrated, the dealer has turned up a 7♦. There is a 6-5♦ sequence on the board, which is useless to him because it is a descending sequence: the next card must be 4♦. However, there is also a space open on the tableau. He can move the 5♦ into the space, play the 6♦ on it, and add the 7♦, deftly reversing the sequence from descending to ascending and at the same time opening another space so he can continue his play. He can fill that new space with the 8♦ from his talon, then move the 8♦ to the ascending Diamond sequence and reopen the space once again.

It is a good idea to *load* cards on your opponent's talon whenever possible. This not only gives you an advantage in going out, but may open spaces in the tableau, which will allow you to manipulate the sequences so you can play more of your cards. Russian Bank becomes cutthroat in a hurry once players realize the potential of loading.

Don't forget that sequences are continuous: Kings build on Aces and vice versa. ∽

Crapette

- ◆ OTHER NAMES: **Double-deck Russian Bank and sometimes Russian Bank**
- ◆ NUMBER: **two players**
- ◆ EQUIPMENT: **two standard decks of 52, each with a different back design**
- ◆ DESCRIPTION: **three games of Patience in one; fairly leisurely as each player takes care not to miss moves or proceed out of order**
- ◆ COMPLEXITY: **requires very close attention; players usually win by spotting opponent's errors in order of moves**
- ◆ DURATION: **at least a half hour per game**

CRAPETTE, also called Double-deck Russian Bank and sometimes just **Russian Bank**, uses two decks of cards: choose decks with different patterns on the backs so you can separate them again after the game. This game requires a fairly large playing surface because there are eight cards in the tableau column as well as eight in the foundation column. It expands on the principles of Russian Bank by adding a stockpile (distinct from the hand), which complicates the rules of order considerably. One important difference in play, which takes some getting used to for devotees of Russian Bank and **Stung**, is that discards cannot be used to build foundation sequences.

Experienced Crapette players are real sticklers for rules, since winning often depends on taking advantage of an opponent's errors and oversights. For this reason, players should agree beforehand on the finer points in the order of play. Because procedural errors can cost a player her turn, some people play Crapette as a four-person game: two who actually play the cards, each with a consultant to keep an eye on moves.

The Deal: Players shuffle and cut one of the decks: low card has the choice of decks and plays first. Players then shuffle each other's decks, hand them back, and each player deals himself 12 cards facedown in a *stockpile* that is placed to his right. Above the stockpile, in a *tableau* column, each player deals four cards faceup. The remaining cards are the player's hand, which he puts facedown on his left (usually at the end of the tableau column his opponent has dealt). Players should leave considerable space between the two tableau columns because two *foundation* columns of four Aces each will be placed here as the Aces turn up during play.

The Play: The player who cut the low card goes first. Plays must be made in absolutely strict order. In general, moves are made first from the two tableau columns to the center foundation columns, then moves are made between cards in the tableau columns, then from the tableau to the opponent's stockpile and discard pile or talon. Each move will create certain consequent moves, and these must be completed before beginning the next set of moves. (See the Order of Play box on page 230.)

The first player begins by moving any Aces from the tableau into the center, creating a foundation column. He then moves cards from the tableau to the foundation cards, building same-suit sequences, low to high, on the Aces.

After making these moves, a space or spaces may be opened in the tableau. The player turns over the top card on his stockpile and uses it to fill a space. He continues to make any moves created by the new card. When that series of moves comes to an end, he turns over the next card in his stockpile and fills the next space. When all the spaces are filled, he turns over the top card of the stockpile. For the rest of the game, the top stockpile card is always visible, even though it may not be immediately in play.

When there are no more moves to the foundation cards, the player moves cards within the tableau, building alternate red and black sequences, high to low, as in **Klondike**. Each move must be followed through to completion before initiating another set of moves. Once there are sequences built on the tableau, a space may be filled with either the end card of a sequence or the top stockpile card. Filling spaces from the tableau takes precedence if, by doing so, a card is exposed that can be played to the foundation.

When the first player completes all possible moves within the tableau, he can then play the upturned card on his stockpile—first to the foundation column, and if that is not possible, to the tableau. If the upturned stockpile card is not playable, the player turns to his hand (the pile of cards on his left). He turns the top card faceup and plays it first to the foundation cards, and if that is not possible, he plays it to the tableau. If that is also impossible, the player signals that his turn is over by placing the card faceup between the stockpile and his hand, thus starting his discard pile or talon.

The opponent begins by turning the top card on her stockpile faceup. (She cannot play from the stockpile yet, but seeing this card may affect strategy.) She proceeds in the same order of play, looking first for moves the other player may have missed. She moves cards from tableau to foundation cards first, then within the tableau. Any spaces opened in the tableau are filled at the conclusion of that move with the faceup card on her stockpile or with the end card from a tableau sequence.

She is also allowed to build in *either* ascending or descending same-suit sequences on her opponent's talon and stockpile, using cards from the tableau or from her own stockpile. This is called *loading*. Sequences may be built up or down and they may reverse. Loading is permitted only after moves to the foundation cards and moves within the tableau are exhausted.

After making all possible moves on the tableau, the opponent then turns to the faceup stockpile card, playing it to the foundation column first, or the tableau or the other player's stockpile or talon. She continues to turn up new stockpile cards as long as they can be played. If she cannot use the upturned stockpile card, she leaves it faceup and moves to her hand, turning up the top card and using it first to play to the foundation and if that is not possible, then to the tableau or her opponent's talon or stockpile. She completes all the moves initiated by playing the first hand card, then turns up another. Her turn ends when she can find no more moves for the hand card: she signals that she is finished by laying the unplayable card from her hand, faceup, on her talon.

The game continues with each player taking alternate turns. Plays to the center always take priority. A card may not be kept in the tableau and built on if it can be played to a foundation card.

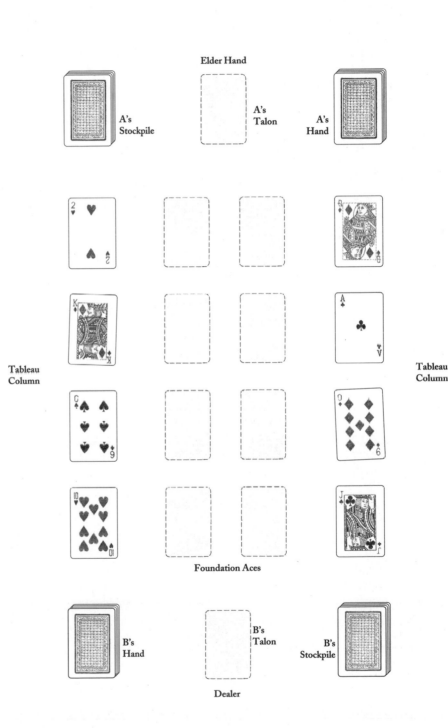

Tableau spaces are filled as they are created, at the end of the sequence of moves initiated by creating the space. The space may be filled with the end card from one of the sequences in the tableau, or from the stockpile until the stockpile is gone, then it can be filled from the hand.

Moves are allowed as long as the player observes the priorities: play to the foundation first, fill tableau vacancies, move within the tableau or to the opponent's stockpile and talon, then play from the stockpile until all moves are exhausted, then play from the hand. A turn is always over when a player holds a hand card that has nowhere to go but the talon.

The top card of the talon can be played on by the opponent, but it is never available for play. After all the cards in the hand are played, the talon is turned facedown to form a new hand so play can continue. (Do not shuffle the cards.)

If a player violates any of these priorities, the opponent may declare, "Crapette," and if he is proved correct, the offender's turn ends immediately. (In our family, we used to signal errors with a loud and rather rude but effective "Bzzzzz." However, remembering to say the word, "Crapette!" and not just, "Stop!" or "Hey!" puts a little more onus on the observer and tightens up the game.)

The first player to get rid of all her cards wins.

Score:
Crapette is not usually scored: for longer games, players usually play a rubber of three hands. However, scores can be accumulated by awarding 30 points to the player who gets rid of his cards first, plus 1 point for each card in the loser's hand and talon and 2 points for each card in the loser's stockpile. A game can be 60 or 100 points.

Variation:
Conventionally, only one card at a time is moved from the tableau, and the tableau is maintained in neat packs, rather than overlapping rows. For a speedier game, try playing with the rule that on the tableau, cards can be moved as sequences.

Strategy:
It is a good idea to load cards on your opponent's stockpile or talon whenever possible, therefore making it harder for him to be the first person to be rid of all his cards.

Look for moves on the tableau that will release cards valuable to the foundation. For instance, if there is J♥, 10♠, 9♦ and a Q♠, J♦, 10♣ on the tableau and a sequence on the Ace of Spades up to 9, move the 9♦ to the 10♣ and release the 10♠ to be played on the foundation.

The best strategy is close attention. When looking for plays, get in the habit of looking at the cards in order: center foundation cards first, then tableau, then opponent's stockpile and talon. Once this habit is established, you'll rarely risk losing your turn by making a mistake in the rule of order. ∾

Order of Play: Crapette

Moves must be made in the following order:
- from tableau to foundation
- within tableau, sequence to sequence
- from tableau sequence to space (to facilitate foundation play)
- from tableau to opponent's stockpile and talon
- from player's stockpile to foundation
- from player's stockpile to tableau space
- from player's stockpile to tableau sequence
- from player's stockpile to opponent's stockpile and talon
- from player's hand to foundation
- from player's hand to tableau
- from player's hand to opponent's stockpile and talon

Cards within the tableau are moved one at a time.
Each set of moves must be finished before beginning the next.
Spaces are filled from the tableau or the stockpile, and when the stockpile is gone, the hand. Tableau takes precedence if a foundation play is involved.
If a move from the hand creates foundation plays from both the stockpile and the tableau, the stockpile takes precedence.
Except for the beginning of the game and when a player is stopped mid-move, the top stockpile card is always faceup.
A player who notices violations may call "Crapette!" ending the opponent's turn.

Stung

- NUMBER: **best for two players; as many as eight can play**
- EQUIPMENT: **a standard deck of 52**
- DESCRIPTION: **competitive Patience, building alternating sequences as in Klondike**
- COMPLEXITY: **intermediary between Russian Bank and Crapette; good practice for the strict order vital to Crapette**
- DURATION: **about 15 minutes a game**

LIKE RUSSIAN BANK, Stung uses a single deck, but the similarity ends there. In this game, the tableau is laid out in a single column and the sequences are built horizontally. On the tableau column, descending sequences are built in alternating red and black suits. Whenever an Ace appears, it is placed in a separate column, the foundation column, where ascending sequences are built by suit. The enlarged tableau creates more opportunities for play and, as a result, the order of play becomes significant—in deed, vital—to the game.

The Deal: The cards are shuffled and players cut the deck; low card deals. The dealer distributes all the cards, one at a time, facedown, moving clockwise around the table.

The Tableau: The first few turns are taken up with creating the tableau. The elder hand (nondealer), or the player to the dealer's left, goes first, turning over his top card. If it is an Ace, he plays it to the foundation column; otherwise, he lays it on the table to begin the tableau column. Players take turns turning up the top card of their piles, playing it to the cards on the tableau, to the spaces in the tableau or to the foundation column.

The Play: As soon as there are four cards in the tableau column, play begins in earnest.

In each turn, a player turns up the top card of his stockpile and makes every legal move possible, building alternate red and black sequences, high to low, on the tableau cards; building same-suit sequences, low to high, on the foundation cards; and building either ascending or descending same-suit sequences on the opponent's discard pile or *talon*. If a turned-up card cannot be played, it is set faceup in the player's talon.

Cards may be moved, one at a time, within the tableau, from the tableau to the foundation, and from a player's talon to the tableau, to the foundation or to his opponent's talon, but moves must follow in strict order, as indicated in the Order of Play box on page 232. When a move creates a space in the tableau, it must be filled with the end card of a sequence if that will expose a card that can be moved to the foundation column. Otherwise, the space must be filled from the talon.

Every time a player turns over a card in his hand to begin his turn, he must follow the prescribed order of play. Playing the card will initiate a series of moves that must be followed through before starting a new set of moves opened up by the next play.

If a player violates the order of play, his opponent can declare "Stung!" He places the top card from his talon (or, if he has no talon, the top card from his hand) on her talon. The tableau, the foundation and other cards are restored to the positions they occupied before she made the error. The more players in the game, the more dramatic the "sting," as offenders risk having eight more cards added to their pack.

When all a player's cards are used up, he turns his talon facedown and continues. (Shuffling is not allowed.)

The game is over when one player wins by getting rid of all her cards.

Strategy: Loading, which is a key feature in other games of this nature, is not so advantageous in Stung, as the sequences on the tableau are alternate and those on the talon are same-suit. The best tactical advice is to be observant, particularly toward the end, when variables are plentiful and a mistake can cost you the game.

In the game illustrated on the following page, for instance, the dealer has just turned up 9♣. If he played it on the 10♥ on the tableau, the elder hand could immediately say "Stung!" because seven moves must precede this one. First, the dealer must make a move from the tableau to the foundation row, moving the 4♣ to the 3♣, a move his opponent missed in her last turn. Then he moves the 4♣ to where the 4♣ had been, opening a space, which he fills from the tableau. He must move the 4♦, since this releases the 5♣ to be played to the foundation. The first space is then filled from the talon, as is the second (3♠ and K♥ respectively). This frees the 9♠ which is played on the 10♥ in the tableau, which in turn frees the J♠, which can be played on the elder hand's talon. With all of this accomplished, the 9♣ no longer has a place on the tableau, so the dealer discards it to her talon and the turn passes to the elder hand. ☙

Stung

Order of Play: Stung

- from tableau to foundation
- from one tableau sequence to another
- from one tableau sequence to a space in order to facilitate a foundation play
- from your own talon to the foundation
- from your own talon to a space in the tableau
- from your own talon to a sequence in the tableau
- from your own talon to your opponent's talon

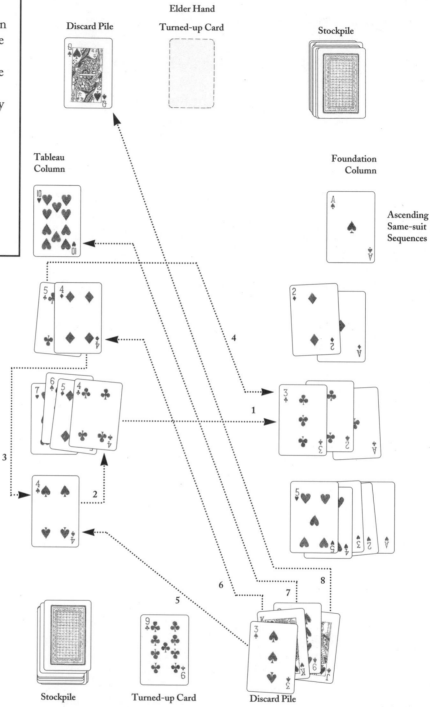

Elder Hand

Discard Pile   Turned-up Card   Stockpile

Tableau Column

Foundation Column

Ascending Same-suit Sequences

Descending Alternating Sequences

Stockpile   Turned-up Card   Discard Pile

Dealer

Spite and Malice

- ◆ NUMBER: two players
- ◆ EQUIPMENT: two standard decks of 52, plus four Jokers; suits are disregarded, only numerical values count
- ◆ DESCRIPTION: a simple but very competitive double Solitaire
- ◆ COMPLEXITY: multiple discards make this the most strategic of the Russian Bank family of games
- ◆ DURATION: in most cases, a half hour or more per hand; a rainy afternoon for an entire game

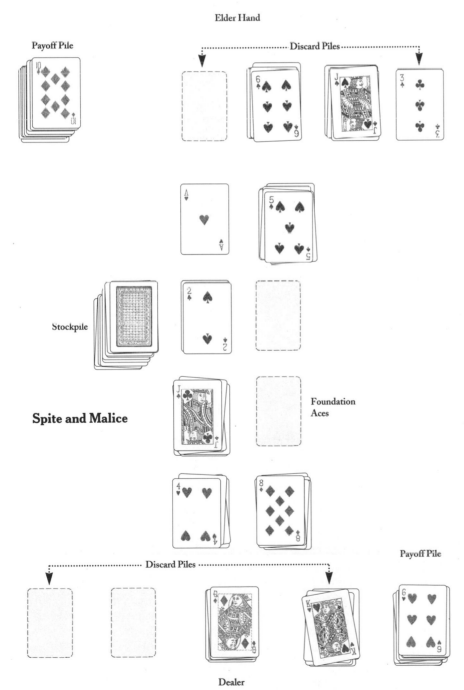

Elder Hand

Payoff Pile

Discard Piles

Stockpile

Spite and Malice

Foundation Aces

Discard Piles

Payoff Pile

Dealer

THIS AMERICAN TWIST on **Russian Bank** was a 1970s fad. The name comes from the fact that it can be a deadly offensive game in which most of the play is devoted to blocking an opponent's progress rather than advancing one's own. Forget about suits in this game: only the numerical values of the cards count. The Joker can have any value and is named by the player who plays it.

The most distinctive feature of Spite and Malice is the discard; players can have up to four discard piles, and these repositories can make all the difference in winning.

The Deal: Players divide a deck, without Jokers, into two stacks of 26 cards. Each player takes one stack—the *payoff pack*—and turns the top card faceup. High card plays first. (If there is a tie, the cards are reshuffled and new cards turned up.) The second player takes the other deck, adds the Jokers, and shuffles these 56 cards. She deals five cards facedown to her opponent, then five to herself, and sets the rest of the deck in the center of the table as a *stockpile*.

The Object of the Game: To be first to get rid of the payoff pile.

The Play: The first player checks his hand for Aces, which he lays in the center of the table to begin the foundation. Henceforth, whenever a player has an Ace or a 2 in hand or on his payoff pile, he must play it to the foundation; other cards are played at a player's discretion. Sequences are built on the foundation cards in ascending order, Ace to King, regardless of suit or color.

The first player plays as many cards from his hand and his payoff pile as possible to the foundation. After finishing his builds (if any), he takes a card from his hand and lays it faceup in front of him to begin his discard pile. Then he draws one or more cards from the stockpile until he once again has five cards in hand.

The other player then takes her turn, playing cards from her hand and her payoff pile to the foundation cards, starting new foundations with Aces whenever possible. When she has made all possible moves, she lays down a discard and replenishes her hand from the stockpile. If she can play all five cards from her hand to the foundation, she draws five more from the stockpile and continues her turn.

Play continues alternately. On the second turn, when the player discards, he must match his previous discard or build a sequence on it, either ascending or descending, regardless of suits. (For a tougher game, allow only descending sequences.) If he cannot, he discards to a new pile. At any juncture in the game, a player can have a maximum of four discard piles. In subsequent turns, a player may use cards from his discard piles, hand and payoff pile to build on the foundation cards. (Unlike previous games, a player may not build on his opponent's discard piles.)

At any time, a player may choose not to discard, in which case he ends his turn by saying, "Go." He waits until the beginning of his next turn before drawing from the stockpile to replenish his hand to the original five.

When the stockpile is reduced to 12 cards, the completed foundation piles (i.e., built from Ace to King) are gathered together, shuffled well and added to it. If the stockpile runs out before any of the foundation Aces are built to Kings, all the piles are gathered up, shuffled and returned to the stockpile.

Jokers are wild: they can have any value, except Ace. A player names the value when he plays the Joker to a foundation pile. When the pile is shuffled and returned to the stock, the Joker again becomes wild. A player can name the Joker one value when he discards it and name the same Joker a different value when he plays it to the foundation. However, if a player discards a Joker to end his turn, he doesn't have to name the value until later. For instance, a player discards a Joker and the next turn, he holds 9, 6, 5, 3, none of which match the top cards on any of the discard piles. He simply calls his unnamed Joker a 9 and discards the matching 9.

When a player can neither build nor discard, her hand is frozen and the turn goes to her opponent, sometimes through several turns until cards are played on the foundation that open up moves for the frozen player. A player can also choose to freeze her hand, refusing to build or discard if conditions aren't quite right. (Much of the strategy of the game hinges on this point.) The only requirement is that a player must always play an Ace or a 2 if she has one in her hand or on her payoff pile (provided, of course, there is a foundation Ace to play the 2 on).

If both players' hands are frozen, all the cards except those in the payoff piles are gathered up, shuffled, and five cards each are dealt to the players, the remainder going to the center as the stockpile. Play continues as if the game were just beginning.

At any time, a player can demand a count of her opponent's payoff pile, while also counting her own.

The first player to get rid of all his payoff pile cards is the winner. If no one manages this, players can agree to end the game and whoever has fewer payoff cards at that point wins.

The Score: The winner earns one point for each card still remaining in the loser's payoff pile. A game is 50 or 100, depending on how long the evening stretches.

Strategy: In general, always build from the payoff pile first, since you have to get rid of these cards to win. Then build from the hand because every play from the hand allows you to draw a fresh card with new potential from the stockpile. The least desirable is to build from the discards, although this, too, can be useful in building to a point where the hand or payoff cards come into play.

Build in descending sequences on the discard piles rather than by matching cards. Thus, when one discard can be played to a foundation pile, you will be able to transfer an entire sequence and stand a better chance of opening up a play for the top payoff card. As a rule, avoid building ascending se-

quences if you want to save yourself frustration.

Building on the foundation cards beyond 2 is entirely optional. As a rule, the more builds the better, though there are some circumstances in which it is a good idea to block builds. For instance, if your opponent's hand is frozen and you hold the card that, if played on the foundation, would open up a move from his payoff pile, it would be wise to avoid making the build and keeping his hand frozen, providing you can make other moves.

Don't be shy about keeping four discard piles going. The more the better, as each pile increases your options for play. If you have a choice between making a discard sequence and making a new pile, do the latter.

The game starts very slowly, as players wait for the Aces to come into play. At this stage, use Jokers freely to get through as many sequences as possible and release whatever Aces are in the stockpile. The game speeds up toward the end, when most of the Aces are out of the stockpile and payoff piles. As the payoff piles are reduced to a few cards, hoard your Jokers so you can use them to go out.

At the end of the game, be careful not to build foundations to a point where your opponent can play a payoff card. Stop a card short of the card she has on her payoff pile, or use your Jokers to move past it. For instance, if she has a 6 turned up on her payoff pile, and a foundation is built to 4, don't play your 5. Wait until you draw a 6 and can play both the 5 and 6, forcing her to wait for another foundation Ace to build up to 6. This may mean hoarding 5s, in which case, keep them in hand if you can, so she doesn't know where her key cards lie.

Variation: Some play with the rule that discard piles must be built only in descending sequences, which results in many more frozen hands.

The game can be played with three or four people, using six decks of cards, six Jokers and hands of 13 or 17 cards. This is chaotic, but fun. ∽

Piquet

- ◆ OTHER NAMES: Piquet au Cent, Picket, Sant, Saunt and Mountsaint
- ◆ NUMBER: strictly for two players
- ◆ EQUIPMENT: a Piquet deck of 32 (A-K-Q-J-10-9-8-7 of each suit) or a regular deck of 52 with 2s through 6s removed and a Cribbage board or pencil and scorepad
- ◆ DESCRIPTION: a fast-paced two-part game that scores for both hands and tricks
- ◆ COMPLEXITY: challenging scoring and strategy
- ◆ DURATION: a good way to pass a lunch break; one game (six hands) takes an hour

ORIGINATING IN France about 500 years ago, Piquet was a fad in the 16th century, much like **Canasta** in the 20th century. In 1534, Rabelais included it in the games Gargantua played; it was a favorite of the exiled Napoleon; and in 1892, a cardplayers' congress in Vienna voted it *the* classic card game of all time. Although manuals published after World War I tend to dismiss it as "a fossil"—probably because of its aristocratic origins and formal rules of play—Piquet has never disappeared and today remains a challenging two-person game.

Piquet is the national pastime of France; it has gained allegorical status there akin to Baseball in the United States. The name is French for "peg," indicating the importance of scoring to the game. In the 16th century, elaborate mechanical markers were devised specifically to score Piquet, but a **Cribbage** board works equally well. Piquet is more complex and sophisticated than Cribbage, however, on the level of Bezique, **Bridge** and Skat. A fair amount of information is revealed at the beginning, and after the luck of the deal, the outcome depends entirely on the players' skill.

Like Cribbage and **Klobiosh**, this elegant, courtly game is really two games within one. First, there is the exchange of cards and the declaration of melds, then the hands are played out in tricks.

The Deal: Cut the deck; high card deals. For subsequent hands, players take turns dealing. The dealer shuffles the deck and deals 12 cards, in groups of two or three, to both players. The remaining eight cards are turned facedown as the stockpile; five, reserved for the elder hand (nondealer), are laid crosswise over the remaining three, which belong to the dealer. Players sort their hands according to suits. If a hand contains no face cards, the player declares *cartes blanches* and scores 10 bonus points. (Sometimes it is advantageous to keep that information secret and forgo the bonus.)

The Object of the Game: To create scoring combinations and to take tricks. The first player to reach a score of 100 points wins.

The Exchange: Before play begins, players may exchange some of their cards to improve their hands, both for the declaration and for potential tricks (see the scoring system on the following page). The elder hand makes the exchange first, discarding at least one card and no more than five. He draws replacement cards from the stockpile reserved for him; after he has done so, he is allowed to peek at any of the five cards he has not claimed.

The dealer is not required to exchange any cards, but she has access to her own three as well as any cards the elder hand left unclaimed. If she discards, she draws her replacements first from the elder hand's unclaimed stock, then from her own. For instance, if the elder hand takes three cards, the dealer can exchange up to five. If she decides, in fact, to exchange four, she would first draw the two left by the elder hand, then take two from her own stock. Any unclaimed cards in the stock belong to the dealer, but she can look at them only after play begins and only if she turns the cards faceup so that both players can see them. Each player can always look at his own discards but not those of his opponent.

If the elder hand declares cartes blanches, the exchange is a little more complex. The elder hand draws replacement cards from the stockpile but does not look at them. After the dealer makes her exchange, the elder hand shows his cartes blanches to her, then discards and picks up his replacement cards.

The Declaration: After the exchange, players assess their hands according to the scoring system on the following page. The elder hand starts this phase of the game by declaring in turn, how many points, sequences and sets he has in his hand. After each declaration, the dealer must reply. If she holds something better, she says, "Not good," and she scores. If the dealer's hand is worse than what the elder hand declares, she says, "Good," acknowledging that the elder's hand is better, and he scores. If the dealer holds exactly what the elder hand declares, she replies, "Equal," and special provisions come into play to break the tie.

Scoring the Hand: *Point* refers to the number of cards in any one suit. For instance, if the elder hand has six Clubs, he declares, "Point of 6." If the most the dealer has in any one suit is five Diamonds, she replies, "Good," and the elder hand scores 6 points, one for each card. If both players have the same number of cards in a suit, they add up the values of the cards: Ace counts 11, face cards 10 and all the others as marked. If the totals are the same, no one scores. If one is higher, that player scores the value of the highest card in the suit.

For instance, in the hand illustrated on the facing page, the elder hand has A-10-8-7♥ and declares, "Point of 4." The dealer also has four of one suit, so she responds, "Equal." The elder hand replies, "36" (11+10+8+7). The dealer has four Spades worth 39 (10+10+10+9) and four Clubs worth 35 (11+9+8+7). She decides to declare the Spades and replies, "Not good," claiming 10 points for her highest card in that suit, the King. Her highest Club, an Ace, was worth more, but Clubs would not have won the declaration. Having declared Spades, she can only claim the highest card in that suit. If the other player asks, the winner of the point must reveal the value of the card that scored.

A *sequence* is a run of consecutive cards in any one suit. A sequence of three, a *tierce*, scores 3; a sequence of four, a *quart*, scores 4; and sequences of five to eight cards—called *quint, sixième, septième, huitième*—score 15 to 18, respectively (the number of cards plus 10). The elder hand declares his best sequence by name and highest card. For instance, in the game illustrated, the elder hand has A-K-Q♦, so he says, "Tierce to the Ace." Length always wins; the high card comes into play only if the number of cards in the sequences is the same. The best the dealer holds is a tierce to the King in Spades, so she replies, "Good." If the players tie, neither scores for any of the sequences they hold. If there is a winner, however, he scores for the declared sequence as well as for any others in the hand. (In the example, the elder hand scores only 3; he holds no other sequences.) Sequences that score must be shown on request.

A *set* is a group of three or four cards of the same value, 10 or higher. Three of a kind—a *brelan*—scores 3; four of a kind—a *quatorze*—scores 14. The elder hand declares his best set, the dealer replies, "Good" or "Not good," and the winner scores all his or her brelans and quatorzes. (A quatorze always beats three of a kind; in case of a tie, the higher value wins.) Players don't have to show their sets or indicate which suit is missing from three of a kind. In the illustrated hand, the elder hand has three 10s, so he declares, "Brelan," and the dealer replies, "Not good," scoring 14 for her quatorze of 9s.

The declarations and scoring must proceed in order: cartes blanches, point, sequence, set. If a player scores for the point, sequence and set and scores 30 points in declarations before the other player scores at all, she wins a *repique*—a bonus of 60 points. In some versions, another bonus of 50 is given to the player who holds a hand in which every card counts toward a scoring combination—*cartes rouges*.

The Play: After the declarations, the hands are played out in tricks. The elder hand leads first. There is no trump; the higher card in the suit that was led always takes the trick. The dealer must follow suit, but she does not have to play her highest card; she can choose to lose the trick. Whoever wins the trick turns it facedown in front and leads to the next. Play continues until all the cards are gone.

Scoring in Play: A player scores 1 point for every card worth 10 or more that is led. (No point for leading 7, 8 or 9.) If the player who leads wins the trick, there is no additional score. If the opponent takes the trick, however, she scores 1 point. The last trick always scores 1 point for the winner, regardless of who led. A player who wins seven or more tricks earns a bonus of 10 points; a player who wins all 12 tricks scores 40, a *capot*. If, after the first lead, the elder hand reaches 30 points before the dealer scores at all, the elder earns a *pique*—a bonus of 30 points.

After the first hand, the elder hand

gathers all the cards, shuffles and deals the next hand. Play continues, the players dealing alternately, until one player reaches 100 points. If the other player has not yet scored 50 points, he is left *in the lurch*, and the winner is considered to have won not one but two games. (Five games are usually played at a time.)

Traditionally, each player calls out her score as the declarations and tricks proceed, writing down only the final score of each hand. If this is too much mental math, keep track as you go, jotting the numbers on a scorepad or pegging on a Cribbage board with the holes beyond 100 masked over.

Strategy: Since there is no trump, voids (no cards in a suit) are unimportant. In making exchanges, however, never throw away a *stopper*—a low card you can play to save your King if your opponent leads the Ace.

Try to figure out what is in your opponent's hand; only a few cards are not in play, and most declarations must be revealed on request. A player does not have to declare the best card or combination in his hand, however: he can lie. As long as it wins, he can declare a lesser card, *sinking* his score but possibly gaining an advantage by hiding the true value of his hand.

For instance, he declares a sixième when he really holds a huitième or declares a point total of 39 instead of the true value of 51. By sacrificing declaration points, he conceals his strength so that he can take all 12 tricks and earn the 40-point capot at the end of play.

Variation: In Rubicon Piquet, instead of ending the game at 100 points, opponents play exactly six hands—a *partie*—and keep a running tally. The winner of the partie earns a 100-point bonus. If the loser's score is 100 points or more, it is deducted from the winner's. If the loser's score is less than 100, however, it is added to the winner's score. This lends piquancy to the final hand. The loser takes great risks to boost his score over 100 or, if that is impossible, avoids declarations and purposely loses tricks to keep his score—and his opponent's bonus—as low as possible. If the game is played for money, even a penny a point, the final score becomes a matter of great concern. ❧

Piquet

Elder Hand

Cribbage Board

Dealer

Elder Hand's Discards

Stockpile

Dealer's Discards

Pinochle

- NUMBER: a classic two-hander; can be played with more
- EQUIPMENT: special Pinochle deck of 48 (two each of A, 10, K, Q, J and 9 in each suit) or two decks of regular cards with 2s through 8s removed
- DESCRIPTION: a two-part game that scores for melds as well as cards won in tricks
- COMPLEXITY: complicated scoring; extremely high degree of skill and subtlety
- DURATION: a game lasts an hour, with little room for conversation; more like Chess than Checkers, more like Bridge than Euchre
- TIP: requires strict attention, a good memory, some calculation and acute judgment

PINOCHLE (pronounced PEA-knuckle) is the most illustrious contribution the United States has made to card games. It first appeared in an American Hoyle in the 1880s under the name Penuchle and, despite confusion over the spelling, has since become one of the country's favorite card games, second only to **Bridge**. Similar to the German game Sixty-Six and the French game Bezique, Pinochle is a game of marriages, with special points for matching Kings and Queens and joining the Jack of Diamonds with the Queen of Spades. The latter union is called the *pinochle*, a word that some speculate derives from binocle: on early cards, this Knave and Queen faced each other in profile; the two cards together presented one visage with two eyes. The game uses the German ranking of cards—Ace, 10, King—and the French term *dix* (pronounced deece) to designate the lowest trump card, the 9, which earns a bonus of 10 points.

In various forms, Pinochle can be played by up to eight players, but the classic two-handed Pinochle remains one of the best, not only within the Pinochle family but also in the genre of two-person games in general. No matter how expert the player, the game remains challenging, yet the basics are easily grasped. In difficulty, it is similar to **Canasta** and **Klobiosh**, less cutthroat than the former and a little more strategic than the latter.

The Deal: Cut the deck; high card deals. In subsequent hands, the deal alternates between players. The dealer shuffles and deals 12 cards facedown, by threes or fours, to each player. The next card is turned faceup as the trump, and the remaining cards (the stockpile) are turned facedown crosswise over top. If the trump card is the dix—the 9—the dealer scores 10 points. Players arrange their cards in sequence A-10-K-Q-J-9 within suits. Remember: 10 is the second highest card in all suits.

The Melds: Players assess their hands for potential scoring combinations, or *melds*, as illustrated in the scoring system on page 240. A King and Queen of the same suit is a marriage; the King and Queen of the trump suit is a royal marriage; and a run of Ace to Jack of trump is a royal sequence. The 9 of trump also scores. The Q♠ and J♦ makes a special marriage—a pinochle. Also, four-of-a-kind Aces or face cards score.

Every time a player wins a trick, she earns the privilege of laying down a meld and scores the appropriate points. (Only one meld to a turn.) A card from a previous meld can be used to make a new one: for instance, if Diamonds are trump, Q♦ from a four-Queen meld can be matched with K♦ to make a royal marriage. There are certain exceptions. Each face card can be used for only one set of four of a kind. Bigamy is not allowed: one Queen cannot make separate marriages with two Kings. For each meld, at least one card must be played from the hand. And a card cannot count in two melds created in the same turn. For instance, if K♠ and J♦ are on the table and you lay down Q♠, you can count either the Spade marriage or the pinochle, but not both. Cards in the meld are still part of a player's hand. They can be used to lead to a trick or to take one.

The Object of the Game: To build high-scoring melds and to take high-scoring cards in tricks.

The Play: The elder hand (non-dealer) leads with any card. The dealer can play any card at all: she can follow suit, play trump or discard from a side suit. The highest card takes the trick, unless it is trumped. If two cards of the same value are played, the one that was led wins the trick.

The player who wins the trick puts the cards facedown in front of him. (Tricks cannot be looked at during play.) Winning the trick earns him the right to lay down one meld, which he does if he can. Then the winner draws the top card from the stockpile, and the loser does the same. After the draw, both players have 12 cards (counting those in their hands and those exposed in melds).

After the first trick is taken but before the draw, the dealer may, if he holds the dix, put it faceup at the bottom of the stockpile and take the exposed trump in exchange. When the other dix shows up, the player declares it as soon as he wins a trick. In both cases, the player who declares a dix scores a bonus of 10 points and still has the right to meld.

The winner of the first trick leads to the next, taking the card either from his hand or from the meld. Play con-

Elder Hand

Melds

Tricks

Stockpile

Trump

Dealer

Pinochle

tinues. The winner of the trick has the right to make one meld, using some cards from an earlier meld or all new cards from the hand. For instance, in the game illustrated, Spades are trump. The elder hand took the first trick and melded J♦ and Q♠ (a pinochle) for a score of 40. He had three other Jacks, so he also took the next trick and melded J♥, J♣, J♠ with J♦ to score 40 for four of a kind. After the trick and the meld, both players draw replacement cards from the stockpile. As long as there is a stockpile, each player has 12 cards, counting the cards in the exposed melds and those in the hand. Note that in the illustrated hand, the dealer has no melds, because she has not yet taken a trick. In the next round, the elder

hand will lead A♣, hoping to win another trick and meld her K♠ to Q♠ for a royal marriage. The dealer may decide, however, to trump the trick so that she can meld her four Aces. If she can keep the lead and take more tricks, she can also meld her K-Q♣ marriage and her dix, the 9♠.

Continue taking tricks, making melds and drawing replacement cards until the stockpile is gone. The faceup trump is the last card drawn, and it goes to the player who loses the twelfth trick. This signals the beginning of the end game, a change in rules and usually a change in strategy too. The moment the stockpile is gone, both players pick up their meld cards from the table and add them to their hands. No more melds can be

made; players are now entirely concerned with taking tricks. From this point on, players must follow suit whenever possible, even when trump is led. If a player has a void (no cards) in the suit led, he must play trump if he has it. Players continue playing the cards to tricks until the hand is finished.

The Score: During the game, players keep a running score of their own melds. After the last trick, players add up the value of the cards in the tricks they took: Ace counts 11, 10 counts 10, King counts 4, Queen counts 3, Jack counts 2, and 9 counts zero. When the two players add up the values of the cards in their tricks, the combined total should be 240 points (the tally of all the counters in the Pinochle deck). The player who takes the last trick of the game scores a bonus of 10. Each player adds the total point value of his trick cards to the total from his melds. Scores of 7 or more are bumped up to the nearest 10; below 7, reduced to the nearest 10. For instance, totals of 193 and 277 would become 190 and 280, respectively. The deal then moves to the other player. Several hands are played until one player reaches 1,000. If both pass 1,000 in the same hand, the game continues to 1,250, then 1,500, and so on, until one player reaches the target first or *declares* in midplay.

The Declaration: If a player believes she has reached 1,000 points while still in the middle of a hand, she declares herself out. She must win the next trick she leads, and if she does, play stops, and the players tally their scores. If her total points are over 1,000, she wins, even if the other player's score is higher—the reward for taking a risk. If she overestimated her score and it is not over 1,000, the opponent wins, regardless of his score.

If a player who has declared fails to win the next trick, the hand is played out, and at the end, the player with the highest score wins, no matter who actually reached it first. If one player declares himself out, the other may also declare herself out if play has not yet stopped. Then the first player to lead and win a trick wins, provided that player's total is over 1,000 points.

Strategy: Pinochle requires a lot of attention, because you are playing out several, sometimes conflicting, strategies at once. You are trying to collect four-of-a-kind Aces and court cards as well as marriages; at the same time, in taking the first tricks, you want to make sure your Aces and 10s end up in your own trick pile; and you want to keep enough high cards and trump cards to be able to win tricks so that you can meld when you are ready and capture your opponent's high cards during the end game. With all this to think about, there is little time left for socializing.

Scoring System: Pinochle

Melds	Points
A-10-K-Q-J of trump (royal sequence)	150
K-Q of trump (royal marriage)	40
K-Q of any suit (marriage)	20
Q♠-J♦ (pinochle).	40
9 of trump (dix)	10
Four Aces (one of each suit)	100
Four Kings (one of each suit)	80
Four Queens (one of each suit)	60
Four Jacks (one of each suit)	40

Card Values	
Ace	11
10	10
King	4
Queen	3
Jack	2
9	0

Last Trick Bonus 10

Game is 1,000 points.

The first part of the game is more strategic than the end game. The goal is to get cards out of your hand and onto the table so that they will score twice: once in a meld and again to win tricks. Don't forget that you can play cards from the melds to the tricks, saving the cards in your hand for future melds. If you have a poor hand, play a wide-open game, paying little attention to melds and scoring as many tricks as possible.

Knowing when and how to meld is crucial. John Scarne, who bills himself as the world's foremost authority on cards, advises "sacrificing (as cheaply as possible) the first few tricks to one's opponent and then trying to win the last few tricks," when you can take better advantage of winning the right to meld.

Unless it is trump, play your longest suit every time you have the lead. (It is rarely a good idea to lead trump.) Eventually, your opponent will give up discarding 9s and Jacks (the two least valuable cards, except in trump) and will start throwing valuable face cards your way. Tens are good leads, since they are high cards, but keep the

Kings and Queens for future melds.

During the early part of the game, guard your Kings and Queens. A hand with four Kings and four Queens is called a *round house* and can score up to 240 points, counting the marriages and the four of a kinds. If the trump K-Q can make a sequence, the score is 390. Put down a royal marriage as soon as possible, in case you draw the cards to complete a royal sequence.

Try to keep track of which melds have become impossible when cards are buried in the tricks. Watch your opponent's discards to predict which melds he is collecting. By the thirteenth trick, a good Pinochle player knows exactly what is in his opponent's hand.

As the first part of the hand draws toward the end game, try to prevent your opponent from taking tricks and winning the chance to make last-minute melds. On the twelfth trick, you may have to choose between winning the trick and melding or purposefully losing so that you can pick up the exposed trump card to add to your hand. In the end game, the more Aces and trump cards you have, the better. ∼

Klobiosh

◆ OTHER NAMES: **Clabber, Clobber, Klob and Klaberjass**
◆ NUMBER: **for two players; variations for three or four**
◆ EQUIPMENT: **one deck of 32 (A-K-Q-J-10-9-8-7 of each suit) and a scorepad**
◆ DESCRIPTION: **two-part game that includes melds, tricks, trump and bidding**
◆ COMPLEXITY: **slightly more complicated than Pinochle**
◆ DURATION: **each game to 500 takes less than an hour**

ONE OF THE CLASSIC two-handers in cards is Klobiosh, or, as Damon Runyon preferred, Klob. The game is derived from Klaberjass (a klaberjass is the clover Jack, or Jack of Clubs) and is a member of a family of games in which the Jack, or *jasz* (pronounced yahss), reigns supreme. In the trump suit, the highest card is not the Ace but the Jack. In Klobiosh, the second highest trump card is the 9, known as the *menel* (pronounced muh-NELL).

Although derived from Jass, Klobiosh was apparently born in Hungary as the four-hander Kalabriás

and spread with Jewish emigration around the world. It is an odd duck of a game. It incorporates the ranking system, the card values and the King-Queen marriage of **Pinochle**, the high-trump Jack of **Euchre** and a second deal of cards reminiscent of **Poker**. The language and the ritual of deciding the maker, however, are unique.

Sometimes referred to as Jewish Euchre, Klobiosh is primarily a men's gambling game, played in smoky back rooms for high stakes. But it is also one of the most entertaining and challenging games for two—fast-paced

and unpredictable. Schmeissing is a little difficult to grasp and varies among players, so clarify the details before you begin, especially if playing for money. My Jewish friends taught me to play the game as follows, and they learned it, they assure me, at their *zeyde*'s knee.

The Deal: Cut the deck; low card deals. (For the cut, cards rank A-10-K-Q-J-9-8-7.) In subsequent hands, players alternate the deal. The dealer shuffles the deck and deals six cards to each player, three at a time. The rest of the cards are placed facedown between the players. The top card is turned faceup beside the stockpile. The players bid to become the *maker* (see below): either the suit of the turned-up card becomes trump, another suit is named or the deal is scrapped. (No-trump hands are not played in this game.)

If the turned-up card becomes trump, whoever holds the 7 of trump (the lowest card, or the *dix*) may exchange it for the turned-up card. After the trump suit is named and the dix exchanged, the dealer gives three more cards to each player from the stockpile, then turns the bottom card of the stockpile faceup. (This has no purpose other than to expose an extra card, which may be a crucial trump.)

In the trump suit, cards rank J-9-A-10-K-Q-8-7. In the other suits, cards rank A-10-K-Q-J-9-8-7. Players organize their cards by suit accordingly.

The Maker: The player who decides the trump suit is the maker, and he has to win the hand. If the maker's score at the end of the hand is lower than his opponent's, he forfeits his points to the other player. Deciding the maker, therefore, is critical.

The elder hand (nondealer) begins. If he wants the turned-up suit to be trump, he says, "I accept" or "I call it," and play begins. If his hand is not strong in the turned-up suit, he passes. The dealer may now pass or call up the turned-up suit as trump.

There is, however, a third option. A player can say "Schmeiss" (pronounced

---

Scoring System: Klobiosh

Melds in Hand   Points
    Best sequence of three of one suit 20
    Best sequence of four or more of one suit 50

Melds in Play
    Bella (K-Q trump, both played) 20

Card Values
    Ace (any suit) 11
    10 (any suit) 10
    King (any suit) 4
    Queen (any suit) 3
    Jack (all suits but trump) 2
    9-8-7 (all suits but trump) 0
    Jack of trump 20
    9 of trump 14
    8-7 of trump 0

Last Trick Bonus 10

Game is 500 points.

---

shmice), which is a succinct way of saying, "Let me in on that suit, or the round's over." If the other player says "No," the hand is thrown in. If the other player says, "Yes, you're in," the schmeisser becomes the maker, and the turned-up suit is trump.

Schmeiss is a defensive play, a blocking maneuver that brings the bidding to become maker to a premature halt. To understand it more fully, refer to Strategy (page 243).

So, in the first round, if one of the players calls up the turned-up suit, it becomes trump. If one of the players schmeisses, the other decides either to throw in the cards or to play with the turned-up suit as trump. If both players pass on the turned-up card, it is turned facedown, and the second round begins.

In the second round, the elder hand can pass, he can name one of the other three suits as trump or he can schmeiss, in which case he does not name a suit but simply asks the other player whether or not he wants to play out the hand. If the other player says "No," the hand is thrown in. If the other player agrees to play the hand, the elder hand then names the trump suit and play begins.

If the elder hand passes, then the dealer has the chance to name trump. If she also passes, then the hand is thrown in. (The dealer cannot schmeiss in the second round.)

The player who accepts or names trump is the maker.

The Melds: After the maker is decided and the extra cards are dealt, players assess their hands for sequences of three or more cards in one suit. (For this part of the game, all suits are ranked as usual: A-K-Q-J-10-9-8-7.) A three-card sequence counts 20; four or more counts 50.

The elder hand announces his best sequence, declaring, "None," "20" or "50." The dealer replies, "Good," "Not good" or "Equal," as in **Piquet**. If the sequences are equal in length, the dealer asks, "How high?" and the elder hand declares the top card. If the sequences are still equal, a sequence in the trump suit wins. If neither player

Klobiosh

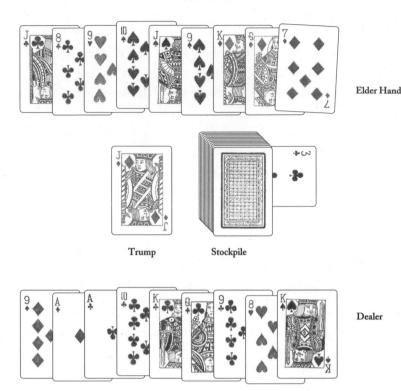

Elder Hand

Trump   Stockpile

Dealer

has a trump sequence, no one scores. The winner shows the winning sequence and scores it, as well as any other sequences in her hand.

The K-Q of the trump suit is known as *bella*. This meld is not declared at the beginning with the other sequences but, rather, during the game. When the second card of the marriage is laid on a trick, the player declares "Bella!" and scores 20 points. It doesn't matter whether the King or the Queen is played first.

In the hand illustrated, the elder hand has accepted the turned-up card, making Diamonds trump. After he exchanges 7♦ for J♦, he announces "20" for his K-Q-J♦. The dealer replies "Equal," because she has a sequence of three Clubs. "How high?" she asks. "King," replies the elder hand. The dealer's top card is an Ace, so she scores 20. The elder hand, however, can still score during the game with his K-Q♦, the bella.

The Object of the Game: To score points by taking tricks and making melds.

The Play: The elder hand leads

to the first trick, playing any card. The other player follows suit if possible; otherwise, he plays a trump if possible. A player can play a card from a side suit only if he has a void (no cards) in the suit led and no trump cards. High card wins unless trumped; a player must follow with a higher trump whenever possible. The person who wins the trick leads to the next. Play continues until all the cards are gone.

The Score: At the end of play, both players add up the value of the cards taken in tricks. In all suits except trump, Ace counts 11 points, 10 counts 10, King counts 4, Queen counts 3, Jack counts 2 and the 9, 8 and 7 count nothing. In trump, Jack counts 20, 9 counts 14, and the other cards score as for nontrump suits. The player who takes the last trick scores a bonus of 10 points.

Players add up their individual scores, including sequences, bella and cards taken in tricks. If the maker has more points, both players score what they make. If the maker has the same number of points as the opponent, the maker scores zero, and the other player scores what he earned. If the maker has fewer points than the opponent, he is *bête*: the maker scores zero, and the other player adds the maker's score to his own.

The first player to reach 500 points wins. If both players go over 500 in the same hand, the higher score wins.

Strategy: Much of the strategy in Klobiosh involves knowing when to take a risk. When you bid to become maker, you do so with only six of your nine cards in hand. Sometimes the draw brings you valuable trump cards; sometimes it gives your opponent the menel and the jasz, and you go bête, even with what looked like a promising hand at the beginning. During the game, 12 out of 32 cards are not in play, so there is a good chance that some high cards are buried.

In general, the average card count for a deal is around 100. Do not make or accept trump unless you have at least 40 points in hand, counting the value of your high trump cards and other Aces and 10s. When choosing a trump suit, holding the Jack and the 9 are more important than a long run of cards in that suit. A singleton Jack of trump (no other trump cards) plus an A-10 combination in another suit often allow the maker to score, while a hand with the K-Q-8-7 of trump but only a few other high cards rarely will. The second part of the deal generally adds about 20 points to your hand, but don't count on it during the bidding.

The melds and last-trick bonus often score the deciding points in a hand. If you can score a 50-point meld and the bella, it is unlikely that your opponent will beat that with points collected in the tricks. Therefore, holding the Q-J-10-9 of one suit and only the K-Q of trump is enough to become maker, even though your trump holdings look pretty slim.

The schmeiss is a risky maneuver that adds some of the piquancy of Poker to the game. Schmeiss is a Yiddish word meaning a sharp blow, such as comes from a whip, and it can have that effect on your opponent.

The strategy for declaring schmeiss differs slightly according to whether you are the dealer or the elder hand and whether it is the first or second round. Beginners tend to schmeiss a lot, but in general, the ploy is best reserved for special occasions.

In the first round, the elder hand schmeisses if he thinks his hand is probably good enough to win in the turned-up suit but not good enough to defeat his opponent if he passes and she accepts it. If your hand is really strong, of course, you will simply accept the turned-up suit. By schmeissing, you take the risk that the other player agrees to play, but it is worth it if you get to throw in a dubious hand or if you manage to squeak through in the turned-up suit.

For example, in the hand illustrated, the elder hand had good Diamonds and the dix to exchange for J♦. Otherwise, his hand was not strong, so he said "Schmeiss." Because the dealer had a strong hand—the Ace and menel in Diamonds as well as A♣ and 10♣—she refused to throw it in. Diamonds became trump. Neither player did well in the draw, so the maker will likely win the hand.

If the elder hand passes on the turned-up suit, the dealer should schmeiss if she has a marginally good hand and if she suspects that her opponent has a good hand in another suit, particularly one in which she is void or weak. In the first round, schmeissing is obviously of more strategic importance to the dealer, since if she passes, the turned-up suit is eliminated and the other player has free choice in naming trump.

In the second round, the strategy is a little different. Only the elder hand can schmeiss. (By the time the bidding gets to the dealer, there is nothing left to block.) The elder hand forces his opponent to make a decision to play the hand without knowing what trump suit will be called. In this position, you should schmeiss if you have a marginally good hand in one of the remaining three suits and if you suspect

that the other player will name a suit in which you are weak or void. For example, if you don't have a single red card in your hand and Diamonds were turned down, it is a safe bet that the other player will name Hearts if he gets the chance. If you have a half decent hand in either Clubs or Spades, you might have a chance of winning the hand. But if you aren't too sure, schmeiss and hope that your opponent throws in the cards.

In this game, it is not unusual to throw in several hands in a row, especially as the score approaches 500. Play the tricks thoughtfully, trying to keep your Aces and 10s in your own trick pile and holding back a trump card for that last trick. Ten points can make or break you in the final tally.

Variations: You can vary the schmeiss rule, allowing it only in the first or second round of bidding or eliminating it from the game.

Klobiosh is commonly played with four. People sitting opposite each other play as partners. If one person schmeisses, the player to his left decides whether the hand is played or thrown in. After deciding the maker, deal two (not three) cards to each player.

In three-handed Klobiosh, the players take turns bidding, melding and playing, moving clockwise around the table from the dealer. The two non-makers become partners against the maker, who must score more than the other two combined. If the maker loses, the other two divide his score.

Belotte is Klobiosh with extra scores for four of a kind: four Jacks count 200, and four 9s, Aces, 10s, Kings or Queens count 100. A five-card sequence is worth 50, a four-card scores 40, and a three-card scores 20, as in Klobiosh. A player who wins the declaration for sets or sequences can score for all the sets and sequences in hand. The schmeiss is called the *valse*, or waltz. If the maker fails to score the most points, he loses his points, but his opponent doesn't get them. ∼

10

Dealer's Choice:
Card Games for Three or More

BOTH THE MANUFACTURE and the playing of cards was at one time taken very seriously, even by the courts. In 18th-century France and England, the sale of playing cards was taxed and their manufacture, therefore, tightly controlled, much as alcohol is today. Card makers were registered, and anyone else caught making the playthings was severely punished. Just a few years before the French Revolution, a master card maker by the name of Firmin Saint-Paul went bankrupt in Paris and subsequently set up a small secret factory in a village about 30 miles away. His punishment, when he was caught, was severe: he was branded on the right shoulder with a red-hot iron, chained in the galleys for five years and banished from Paris for another nine. When he was caught selling contraband playing cards a few years after his release, he was sent to prison for life. In England, one Richard Harding was sentenced to death in 1806 for forging 2,000 Ace of Spades.

Cheating at the card table was likewise frowned upon. In October 1777, a Norwich tradesman was found guilty of cheating his mates at cards and sentenced to six months in prison, with an additional fine of £20. If the fine wasn't paid, the court ordered, he would be made "to stand on the pillory for one hour, with his ears nailed to same."

Card playing, and presumably card making, has lightened up a bit since then. While solitary and two-person games are often played to pass the time, group games are just as likely to be social occasions, and regular ones at that. **Euchre, Bridge, Whist** and **Poker** have all spawned weekly clubs where friends meet and socialize over a deck of cards, year after year. Poker nights are a traditional male purview, while the afternoon Bridge Club has been a welcome social outlet for stay-at-home women for much of this century. One group of Canadian women in Kingston, Ontario, has been meeting for a Bridge game once a week since 1945.

Before Bridge, Euchre was the national card game of American non-gamblers. Although not as popular as it was, it still holds sway in rural areas, where Euchre parties mitigate long, snowbound winters. The spirit of group play is caught in this correspondent's report on "Yewker" in *The Westminster Papers* of June 1875: "This ill-bred game ov kards is about twenty-seven years old. It was first diskovered by the deck hands on a Lake Erie steamboat, and handed down by them, tew posterity in awl its juvenile beauty. It is generally played by four persons, and owes mutch ov its absorbingness to the fackt that you kan talk, and drink, and chaw and cheat while the game is advancing."

Pulling up a few more chairs to the card table brings some new rules into play. The matter of who deals first, who plays first and who plays with whom must be settled before a group game can begin. There are standard procedures for dealing and playing most group games, and although you don't have to follow them slavishly, they manage to get the details out of the way so that players can concentrate on the strategy of the particular game.

First, the group has to decide who deals. Shuffle the deck, and fan it out on the table. Everyone takes a card, and the person who draws either the lowest or the highest card deals, as determined by the game or by the people at the table. If the game is played in partners, the draw also decides who plays together: the two highest cards are partners and get the first choice of where to sit. The person who holds the higher card of the pair is the dealer.

Anyone can ask to shuffle the deck of cards before the deal, but the dealer always shuffles them last. Before distributing the cards, the dealer hands the shuffled deck to the player on his right, who cuts the deck, lifting a section of cards off the top and setting it beside the rest. The dealer puts the bottommost part on top of the other and begins to deal.

The dealer starts by giving a card to the player on his left, then continues distributing cards to each player, moving clockwise around the table. The last card in the round goes to the dealer himself. Although some games specify dealing two or three cards at a time, most games are dealt one card at a time, facedown. Players may declare a *misdeal* if a card is accidentally turned faceup during the deal or if the dealer gives the wrong number of cards to one or more players. The dealer can correct his mistake if the others agree; otherwise, the cards are gathered, shuffled and dealt again, usually by the same dealer, unless the dealer enjoys certain advantages in the game. In that case, the deal passes to the player on his left.

Many games involve playing several hands until a target score is reached. After the first hand, the deal usually passes to the player on the first dealer's left, and so on, around the table.

In games such as Bridge and **Hearts**, the entire deck is dealt among the players. In Euchre, **Pitch** and other *short games*, only a certain number of cards are dealt. Some games begin with a short deal, then players increase their hands by drawing from the stockpile or receiving a second deal.

Group games are often just games for two played with partners, the players who sit opposite from each other forming a team and scoring points together. Games in which players play for themselves alone are called *round games*.

Tricks and *trump* are involved in all the best group games. Just as in two-person games with tricks, each player in turn plays a card faceup in the center: the group of cards is a trick. The person to the left of the dealer leads to the first trick, and everyone follows suit, if they can. The person who plays the highest card in the suit led wins the trick and, with it, the right to play the first card for the next trick. The score may be the total of the number of tricks taken, as in Whist, or the total of the values of the cards taken in the tricks. In a few games, such as Hearts, the point is to avoid taking any tricks at all, not because the tricks score against you but because a trick may contain a Heart, and Hearts carry stiff penalties.

Trump is central to the best trick-taking games. In relatively simple games, such as Whist, the suit that becomes trump is decided by chance, by turning up a card. In more complex games, however, the players bid for the right to decide which suit will be trump, since it is often the key to winning the game. When a card from the trump suit is played, it wins the trick. If two trumps are played on one trick, the higher trump takes it. In most cases, a trump can be played only if the trump suit is led or if a player has a *void* (no cards at all) in the suit led. Remember: Players always have to follow suit. In some games, players must play a trump if they can't follow suit; in others, a player with a void in the suit led can either play a trump or throw off a card from a *side suit* (one of the other two suits).

In playing out a hand in a game of cards, it is polite to wait your turn. In serious play, there are penalties for playing or bidding out of turn, but usually, it is just good manners to abide by the routine. One of the most serious offenses in trick-taking games is failing to follow suit when you have a card of that suit in your hand. This is called a *revoke*. You can correct the mistake by replacing the card you played with the proper card, provided another trick hasn't yet been played. The wrong card you played is treated as a *penalty card*: it must be laid faceup on the table, and your opponents can force you to play it at the first opportunity. The other players are also allowed to take back any cards they played after the revoke, since the changed circumstances could affect their strategy. In some games, there are more severe penalties. If the bidding player revokes in Bridge, for example, two tricks are erased from the offender's score and added to that of the other team.

Amongst friends, most irregularities can be resolved amicably. In fact, they sometimes prompt new rules, giving birth to yet another variation of a venerable old game. Only a few games, such as Whist and Bridge, have their rules codified as "Laws." These are a good way to learn the game, but remember: Games are for play, and if you can make a game more fun or more challenging by bending a rule into a new shape, do it.

I Doubt It

- OTHER NAMES: **Cheat**
- NUMBER: **best with three or four players whose hands are big enough to hold up to a third of the deck at once**
- EQUIPMENT: **one deck of 52, Ace low; with 4 to 8 players, two decks; with 8 to 12 players, three decks**
- DESCRIPTION: **matching game for beginning players and wily veterans**
- DURATION: **a good waiting-for-dinner pastime; takes about 10 minutes**

IN A WELL-THUMBED book from the local library, this was the only game that was circled. Beside it was written, in the rounded letters of a tyro critic, "Good Game." Kids love I Doubt It, because not only are they allowed to lie, they *must* lie. Watching them trying to keep a poker face is almost as much fun as playing the game.

The Deal: Cut the deck; low card deals. The dealer shuffles the deck and deals one card at a time, facedown, to each player until all cards are dealt. (Some players may have an extra card.) Players arrange their hands according to denominations—5s, 6s, 7s, and so on. Suits and sequences don't count.

The Object of the Game: To be the first to play all the cards in your hand.

The Play: The player on the dealer's left goes first. He pulls one to four cards from his hand, discards them facedown in the center of the table and announces the number of cards and their denomination: for instance, "Three Aces." Moving clockwise around the table, the next player lays her cards on the discard pile in the center and announces 2s, the next 3s, and so on, up to Kings, after which the next player begins again with Aces.

At any time, a player may cheat, playing different cards than he announces in order to get rid of the cards in his hand more quickly. For instance, "Three Aces" may actually be 4♦, 10♥ and A♣. Players may not pass, so if they do not have a card of the right denomination, they must cheat.

If someone thinks a player is cheating, he calls "I doubt it!" or "Cheat!" before the next person plays. (You may not call a player a cheat before he actually announces what he is laying down; if two players doubt at the same time, the one nearest the player's left is the accuser.) The accused shows what he played. If he cheated, he has to pick up the whole pile of discards. If he has laid down exactly what he said, the accuser must take the pile.

Play continues until one person plays her last card without being called a cheat.

Strategy: To foil other players, arrange your cards in the order they will be played. For instance, if you are the first of three players, arrange your hand A-4-7-10-K-3-6-9-Q-2-5-8-J. This will also make your deficiencies obvious.

Sometimes, it is a good idea to be a doubter early in the game in order to get the cards you'll need. In general, cheat early; honesty pays off near the end. Risk major cheats when the discard pile is small so that you won't end up with a handful of cards if you are caught. For minor cheats, practice passing off two cards aligned as one.

To win I Doubt It requires good bluffing skills: beware of giveaway body language. Ironically, the player whose face normally wears a guilty smirk often wins. ∽

Pig

- NUMBER: **up to 13 players; the more the merrier**
- EQUIPMENT: **one deck of 52**
- DESCRIPTION: **a fast-moving, aggressive exchange-and-elimination game**
- COMPLEXITY: **only matching skills required; same level as Go Fish and Snap**

MOST PEOPLE have played this game—it is a favorite at children's birthday parties—although they may know it as something other than Pig. Also called Spoons and Donkey, it is essentially a scapegoat or elimination game in which there are many winners, but only one loser.

The Deal: Cut the deck; low card deals. From the deck, remove one set of four of a kind for each player. For instance, if there are three players, take four 6s, four 10s and four Kings. (Choose any denominations you like.) Set the remaining cards aside. The dealer shuffles the sets together well and distributes all the cards, dealing them one at a time, facedown, to each player. Players arrange their hands with cards of the same denomination together.

The Object of the Game: To collect a set of four matching cards; not to be the last player to notice when the game is over.

The Play: Each player takes an unwanted card from his hand and places it facedown in front of the player to his left. Then he picks up the card the player on his right has placed in front of him. He discards another to his left, picks up one from his right, and so on. Players must always discard before picking up; they may never have more than four cards in hand at once. The exchanges need not be simultaneous: half the fun is screaming at your neighbor to hurry up.

When one player collects a set of four of a kind, she stops passing cards and puts her finger on her nose. As soon as the others see the signal, they do the same. The last to put his finger on his nose is the Pig.

Variations: Instead of a free-for-all, some players prefer to exchange cards only when a leader says "Pass," a good idea if there are children of different ages playing.

The game can also change according to the reward or penalty applied. Give five pennies to each player, then before the first round, put a penny in the center. Instead of putting his finger on his nose, the first player to collect a set drops his cards faceup and grabs the penny. The others quickly put their fingers on their noses, as above. The last to notice the game is over pays a penny to the kitty, or pot, the prize for the winner of the next hand.

Spoons is Pig played as an elimination game. Spoons are put in the center, one less than the number of players. As soon as a player collects a set of four of a kind, she grabs a spoon, then

so does everyone else. The one who doesn't get a spoon is out of the game.

Players continue to play new rounds, each time reducing the number of sets and the number of spoons by one, until only two players remain, vying for a single spoon. Whoever gets it wins. Some people put candies in the center, one less than the number of players, but this seems unnecessarily cruel.

Donkey replaces spoons with coins. The player who fails to get a coin in a round earns one letter of the word DONKEY. The same coins are reused for each round. When a person spells DONKEY (six losses), she is out of the game. Players can stop there or play until there is a winner—the only person who is not a full-fledged DONKEY. ∾

Michigan

- ◆ OTHER NAMES: **Boodle, Newmarket, Chicago and Saratoga; the basis of Rummoli**
- ◆ NUMBER: **three to eight players**
- ◆ EQUIPMENT: **two decks of 52, Ace high, and counters**
- ◆ DESCRIPTION: **a great family game that can be learned in seconds; fun for people of all ages to play together**

MICHIGAN IS a good card game on its own, for a long time the most popular of the Stops family of games (see **Crazy Eights**). It is more often played today in its board-game incarnation—Rummoli. You don't need a board, though: just use a standard deck of cards and designate certain ones as pay cards.

The Deal: Deal cards from one deck faceup around the table, one at a time. The first person to get a Jack is the dealer. From the second deck, the dealer takes out A♥, K♣, Q♦ and J♠. These are the *boodle*—the *money cards*, or the *pay cards*—which are laid out in the center of the table. Every player is given 20 counters, and before the deal,

each antes one counter on each pay card. (According to some house rules, the dealer antes two counters, one for each hand.) The dealer then shuffles the first deck and deals all the cards, one at a time, facedown, one hand to each player and two hands to himself. (The deal may not come out evenly.)

The Object of the Game: To get rid of all your cards first; to play a pay card and claim the reward.

The Play: All players assess their hands. The dealer looks at one of his. If he likes it, he keeps it and offers the other hand to the rest of the players, who bid for it. The winner pays the dealer the agreed-upon amount. If the dealer does not like his first hand, he

lays it down and picks up his second hand. The first hand is dead; no one may buy it. In the example illustrated, the dealer kept his hand because it has the A♥ pay card. The player to the left bought the extra hand and discarded his own.

The person to the left of the dealer begins play by laying down the lowest card he has in any suit, announcing it out loud: for instance, "Two of Spades." The person with the next card in sequence in that suit plays it and announces the card, "Three of Spades." Then the player with 4♠ lays it down, and so on, until the sequence stops. At that point, the person who played the last card before the stop chooses a new suit and plays her lowest card in that suit.

Whenever a player lays down a card that matches a pay card, she collects the counters on that pay card. If she neglects to do so before the next player lays down a card in sequence, she forfeits the payoff.

When the cards are all played out, the hand is over. The deal passes to the left, the cards are shuffled, everyone antes, and a new hand is dealt. Play continues until one player is

Michigan

The Boodle

Discarded Hand

Dealer

Counters

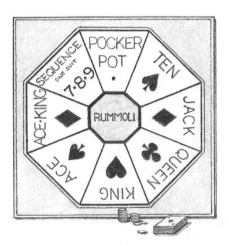

Rummoli

bankrupt or until only one person remains in the game.

Variations: Cards do not have to be taken from another deck to play **Rummoli**, since it comes with a board that is painted with the boodle: 10♠, J♦, Q♣, K♥, A♠, A-K♦ and any sequence of 7-8-9 in one suit. There is also a poker pot and a pot in the center that is won by the player who gets rid of all her cards first.

Before the deal, each player antes a counter to each pay card as well as one to the poker pot and one to the center pot. Play begins with the poker pot. Players choose their best five cards (according to the rules of Poker), and starting with the player on the dealer's left, each shows his hand. The person with the best hand (see page 286) wins the poker pot. Play then proceeds with the player on the dealer's left announc-

ing the lowest card in his hand and laying it down. The others continue in sequence. When that sequence stops, the person who played the last card must switch color of suits. For instance, if 3-4-5-6-7♦ was played and stopped there (no one declared 8♦), the person who played 7♦ then plays her lowest Spade or Club. As in Michigan, players collect the counters on the pay cards as they are called. The game ends when one person gets rid of all her cards. She collects the counters in the center pot as well as a counter from each of the other players for every card they are left holding when she goes out. The counters that are still on any pay cards remain there until a player collects them in some subsequent round: 7-8-9 and A-K are often heaped with counters when someone finally cashes in. ❧

Play-or-Pay

- OTHER NAMES: Stops, Sevens, Parliament, Card Dominoes and Fan Tan (or Fan-tan)
- NUMBER: three or more, the more the merrier, though best with five
- EQUIPMENT: a standard deck of 52, Ace low, counters such as beans, matches or poker chips
- DESCRIPTION: a simple matching game with a tense finish
- COMPLEXITY: appropriate for young children but fun for a crowd
- DURATION: 20 minutes, less with fewer players

IN MOST MANUALS, this game is called Fan Tan or Fan-tan, which is misleading because it has nothing whatsoever to do with Fan Tan, a Chinese gambling game based on guessing the number of beans in a pot. Counters, such as beans or poker chips, are used in this game, too, but they are only a convenient way of keeping score, not a betting tool.

Play-or-Pay is one of the simplest in the family of matching games known as Stops. (See also **Spit, Michigan** and **Crazy Eights**.) In these games, players try to be the first to get rid of their cards by building sequences, at the same time withholding cards in an effort to "stop" the others from playing cards to the table. Designed to be fast-paced, the game often starts slowly but builds to a hectic finale.

The Deal:
Players shuffle the cards and cut for the deal; low card deals. Working clockwise around the table, the dealer deals the entire deck, one card at a time, facedown. Depending on the number at the table, some players may have an extra card, but the disadvantage evens out over several hands. The deal moves to the left in subsequent hands.

Players arrange their hands in suits, high to low. Each player receives an equal number of counters, usually 25 or more.

The Object of the Game:
To be the first to get rid of all cards dealt.

The Play:
Before play begins, each player puts one counter in the pot. Every time a player cannot play a card, he must "pay" another counter to the pot: hence the name, Play-or-Pay.

To start the game, the player on the dealer's left lays a 7 in the center of the table. If he has more than one 7, he can choose which to play. If he has no 7, he pays a counter to the pot. Play passes to the next player, and the next, until someone has a 7 to lay down.

The next player may either lay another 7 beside the first, thus beginning the row of four foundation 7s, or she may match the suit of the first 7 and lay the 8 above it or the 6 below.

Play continues clockwise around the table, with each player laying down only one card at a turn: either a 7 or a card that builds ascending and descending same-suit sequences on the 7s. If a person cannot play, she pays a counter to the pot. Eventually, all four 7s are laid in a row and sequences are built in columns from the 7 up to the King and down to the Ace in each suit.

When a player lays down his last card, he declares, "Out!"

Penalties:
If a player passes and later is found to hold a 7, she must pay three counters to the pot and five counters each to the players who hold the 6 and 8 in that suit. If a player passes and later is found to hold a playable card other than a 7, he has to pay three counters to the pot.

The Score:
The losing players pay a counter to the pot for each card left in their hands. The winner then collects all the counters in the pot.

The cards are reshuffled and a new hand is dealt. Play continues until one player wins all the counters or until everyone decides to end the game. In this case, the player with the most counters wins.

Strategy: The basic tactic of the game is to play your cards in an order calculated to get all your cards quickly on the table and, at the same time, withhold cards that might help other players go out first.

If you hold a lot of cards in one suit, move into that suit as soon as possible. In general, play cards that will open the way to other cards you hold in that suit.

Aces and Kings, being the end cards of sequences, are useless as "stoppers." The cards closest to the Ace and King are the least valuable stoppers. Play these cards first, rather than playing a card that might open or extend new sequences. This minimizes the options open to other players.

The best stoppers are 8s, 6s and a lone 7. Hold onto these as long as possible, thus preventing other players from playing their cards and adding considerably to the pot. In the game illustrated on the following page, one of the players is holding onto the 7♠, thus preventing others from playing any Spades at all. She is also stopping the descending Heart sequence by withholding the 6♥, while she continues to lay down her Clubs.

Especially among a large group, Play-or-Pay often becomes a sophisticated bluffing game, as no one knows exactly who holds the critical stoppers.

Variations: According to Foster's 1897 *Hoyle*, a standard game begins not by laying down a 7, but by laying down any card the first player chooses. The next person must play the card next highest in value to the one laid down, building only ascending same-suit sequences. For instance, if the first player lays down 10♦, the next player must lay down J♦. If she does not have this card, she pays a counter to the pot. Players continue playing the next card in ascending sequence if they can, paying if they can't, gradually building the suit to the King, followed by the Ace, 2, 3 and so on until the suit is complete. Each suit is turned facedown when it is complete. The person who plays the card that completes one suit starts the next with any card he chooses. The first player to rid herself of all her cards wins the pot which, in this variation, is considerable.

In **Five-or-Nine**, instead of opening with a 7, the first player starts by laying down either a 5 or a 9. The card that is chosen establishes the standard and replaces the 7 in the rules above. Because there are eight possible opening cards, players' options are increased considerably. On the down side, if the first player cannot play a 5 or 9, he has to pay five counters instead of one to the pot. The same penalty applies to other players until someone lays down a 5 or a 9. In a further variation, players can agree that every suit can be opened with either a 5 or a 9, thus adding flexibility and interest to the game, though the pot at the end is liable to be smaller.

Play or Pay

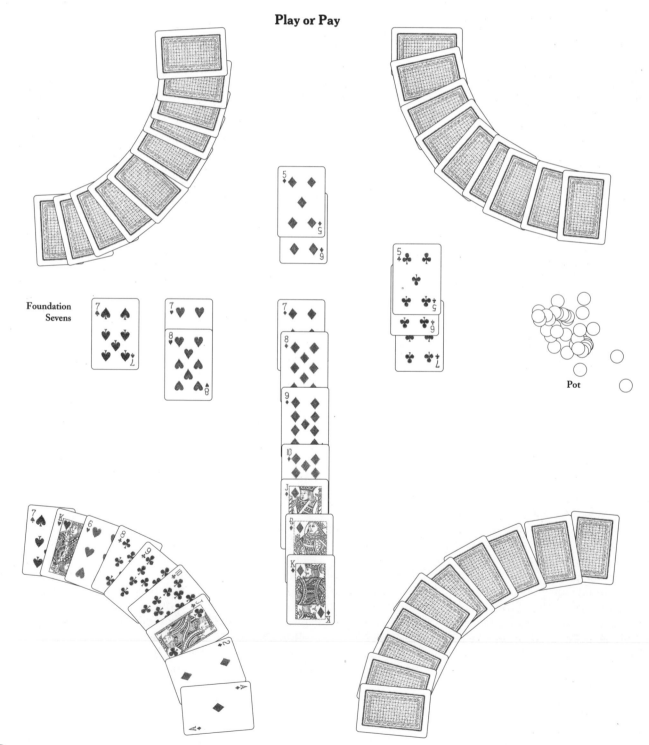

Foundation Sevens

Pot

Rummy

- OTHER NAMES: **Seven-Card Rummy**
- NUMBER: **two to six, four is best**
- EQUIPMENT: **a standard 52-card deck, Ace low, pencil and scorepad or counters for scoring**
- DESCRIPTION: **a basic draw-and-discard game**
- COMPLEXITY: **a relatively simple game, excellent for developing card sense in children; good family play**
- DURATION: **10 or 15 minutes per hand**

RUMMY is a 20th-century card game, yet despite its relative youth, its roots are already blurred. Many card historians assume it is derived from **Conquian**, popular in Mexico and bordering American states in the late 1800s. But as David Parlett points out in *A History of Card Games*, Rummy also closely resembles Chinese card games, where draw-and-discard is as common a feature as tricks are to North American and European games. **Mah Jongg**, in fact, is basically Rummy played with tiles instead of cards. Parlett cites the Chinese games of Khanhoo and Kon Khin as being remarkably like Rummy, and they may in fact be the true precedents to Conquian, which may have been imported not by Mexicans, but by Chinese immigrants to the American southwest.

Rummy's name, originally spelled Rhummy, is equally mysterious. Some suggest an origin in alcoholic drink, but Parlett makes a good case for Dutch derivation, since *roem* is the Dutch word for meld, the laying down of sets and sequences, which is central to Rummy games. There are some other interesting contenders: *rompha*, an ancient term that denotes scoring combinations, which is also the root of *triomphe* or triumph; or *ronfle* from the Celtic *rum*, meaning "a gathering together."

Whatever its origins, Rummy attracted a slow but steady following until, by mid-Depression, one survey showed that more people knew the rules to Rummy than to any other card game. And the game's popularity is not limited to North America. A poll commissioned by Waddingtons Playing Card Company in 1981 showed that Rummy was the game most commonly played in Britain, over **Whist**, **Cribbage**, **Poker** and **Bridge**.

The basic principle of the game is simple: players draw from a stockpile to improve the cards in their hands, gradually collecting sets of matching cards or cards in same-suit sequences; the first to organize all 10 cards into sets and sequences wins.

Rummy is an excellent game for families. The concepts are easily grasped yet the game is challenging enough to hold parents' interest. And children quickly develop card sense. In its early days, Rummy was played as a children's game called Nosy. The name comes from the "scoring" method. The winner would take the loser's remaining cards, compact them into a pack and thwack the loser across the tip of the nose, one thwack for each card left in his hand. A powerful incentive not to be left with too many cards, certainly!

Rummy is more than a single game, it is a family of games characterized by draw-and-discard. It begs to be embellished, and indeed, myriad variations exist. They take two basic forms: one concentrates on collecting melds in order to go out; the other concentrates on collecting melds in order to score points. Standard Rummy, Boathouse Rummy and **Gin Rummy** are of the former variety; Five Hundred Rum and **Canasta** belong to the latter school. Both forms of the game are equally entertaining and both have attracted nationwide fads: Gin Rummy during the Second World War and Canasta during the '50s.

The archetypal Rummy, however, is Seven-Card Rummy, originally played by three or four people. In the basic rules that follow, the deal has been adapted for a wider range of players.

The Deal: Shuffle the cards and cut for the deal; low card deals. Working clockwise around the table, the dealer deals one card at a time, facedown: 10 cards each in a two-person game; seven cards each to three or four players; six cards each for five or six players. The rest of the pack is laid facedown in the center of the table as a *stockpile*. The top card is turned faceup beside the stockpile to form the discard pile. This faceup card is called the *upcard*. Players arrange their hands, grouping cards into *sets* of the same value (for instance, three Queens or two 9s) and into *same-suit sequences*, such as 7-8-9♥.

After each hand, the deal passes to the left. Traditionally, seven hands make a game.

The Object of the Game: To be the first to *meld* or lay down all one's cards and go out.

The Play: The player to the dealer's left goes first. He begins his turn by taking either the upcard from the discard pile or drawing the top card from the stockpile. He ends his turn by discarding one card from his hand, setting it faceup on the discard pile. Between drawing and discarding, he can meld or lay down three or more cards in a set or a sequence.

The turn passes to the left. Each player in turn takes a card into his hand—either the upcard or the top stockpile card—and lays down whatever melds he can, then discards to signal the end of his turn.

During her turn, a player can also *lay off* or *rummy* single cards on her own or her opponents' melds. For instance, in the game illustrated, it is player B's turn. The upcard (J♥)

matched nothing in her hand, so she drew from the stockpile—the 7♦—which she can rummy on player C's melded sequence of 6-5-4♦. Player B has two potential sets and sequences in hand, so she discards her 4♥.

Play continues until one player gets rid of all her cards during her turn by laying off, melding and/or discarding. In standard Rummy, a discard is not required to go out; a player can lay down all her cards in melds and rummies and declare that she is out, without playing a discard.

If the entire stock is drawn before anyone melds out, the next player may take the upcard or, if he doesn't want it, he can turn the discard pile over to create a new stockpile. (The cards are not shuffled.) He draws the top card and play continues as before.

The Score: When one player goes out, the others add up the value of the cards they are left holding: face cards are worth 10 points, Aces are worth one, and each of the other cards count according to their pips. (Some play that court cards are worth 11, 12 and 13 for the Jack, Queen and King respectively.)

The winner earns points equal to the value of each of the other players' hands. If a player lays down his entire hand at once, melding it in one complete *spread*, he "goes rummy" and collects double points from each player.

Players keep a running tally of individual scores. Whoever has the highest score after seven hands wins the game. Instead of a scorepad and pencil, some prefer to keep score with poker chips or matchsticks so players can watch their mound of winnings grow.

Strategy: Although tactics vary with the number of players, true Rummy masters are those who can remember every card that is discarded and by whom, as well as who picked up what from the discard pile. This information gives a player a clear picture of what her opponents are collecting. Even if you don't have that kind of memory, try to take note of the discards that affect you. There is no point in collecting Queens if you hold two,

Rummy

and the other two are buried in the discard. Even if only one is buried, your chances of picking up a Queen to complete your set are reduced by half.

It is good defensive strategy to meld sets over sequences. Sets limit your opponents' ability to rummy cards on your melds, since only one card can complete a set of three Kings, whereas two cards, one at the beginning and one at the end, can complete any sequence other than A-2-3 or J-Q-K. It is better offensive play to collect sequences, however, for much the same reason: more cards are available to complete them.

In general, discard high cards whenever possible as these count more against you when a player goes out. Of course, this can become predictable. Sets of Queens or Kings are often easy to collect because players discard these high-value face cards first. The more players there are at the table, the more

likely they are to hold on to low cards rather than be caught with high-value ones in their hands.

Saving split sequences, such as 7♥ and 9♥ or 3♣ and 5♣, is tempting but not generally a good idea, since only one card can complete the run. However, a sequence-set combination such as 9♥-9♣-8♣ is highly desirable because the number of cards that can complete the set is greatly increased, in this case, 9♦, 9♠, 10♣ or 7♣. Assess every combination for the number of cards available to complete it: the lower that number, the less your chance of drawing the card you need.

It is risky to try to "go rummy" and hold all cards in hand until melding out, but the payoff is great. It has a strategic advantage, too: other players are prevented from rummying on your cards because you have no melds on the table, thus greatly reducing their potential for going out.

Two-person games tend to be more strategic, as you can affect the other person's hand by withholding certain discards you know she needs. With three or more players, you can only affect the game of the person to your left, and he has no power of retribution over you.

Variations: In **Block Rummy**, a player must have a discard to go out. Also, if the stockpile is exhausted before anyone melds out, the game is over when everyone passes the final upcard. All the players show their hands and count their points: the player with the lowest score wins, but he must deduct his score from the points he takes from each of the other players.

Knock Rummy brings some features of Gin to the multi-player game. Deal and play are as in standard Rummy, but no cards are melded to the table; all sets and sequences are collected in hand. The object is to reduce the number and value of unmatched cards in hand as quickly as possible. When a player has a very low count in unmatched cards, or none at all, he knocks on the table to signal the game is over. (He can only knock during his own turn, after drawing from the stockpile.) He then discards and all players meld whatever they can. Cards cannot be rummied on other players' melds.

The knocker earns the difference in points between his unmatched cards and the unmatched cards of the others, plus 25 points if he goes rummy, laying down *all* his cards in melds. If another player ties the knocker for lowest points left in hand, the knocker loses points equal to the value of his hand to each of the other players. If another player has fewer points than the knocker, the knocker pays him a penalty of 10 points for being undercut *and* loses his points to the other players. If more than one player undercuts the knocker, each collects 10 points from him.

No knock is allowed after the stockpile is reduced to the same number of cards as there are players. Play continues until all the stockpile cards are gone, then hands are melded and the player with the lowest count in unmatched cards wins.

In **High-Low Rummy**, Ace ranks high or low: it can begin or end a sequence as a player desires. Each Ace counts 11 points.

In **Round-the-Corner Rummy**, the Ace counts *both* high and low in melds, so players can lay down A-2-3 and Q-K-A as well 2-A-K. An Ace left in the hand counts 11 points.

Boathouse Rummy includes the round-the-corner feature of a flexible Ace that counts 11. Furthermore, to increase the risk, if a player picks the upcard instead of drawing from the stock, he is penalized: he must take an extra card, either from the stock or the next card in the discard pile, but he only discards one card. No melds are allowed during the game. To win, a player must go rummy, laying down his entire hand, which, obviously, may contain more than the number of cards dealt.

Call Rummy gives the advantage to attentive players. If someone discards a card that he could have added to a meld on the table, another player can call, "Rummy!" He lays the discard on the meld himself, then makes a discard from his own hand. Play then resumes in the usual order.

Continental Rummy was once as popular for ladies' afternoon card parties as Canasta. Players usually number five to eight. For five, use two 52-card decks plus two Jokers; for six to eight, use three packs; for nine to 12 players, use four packs. As in Boathouse Rummy, the Ace can be both high and low. Twos and Jokers are wild. Each player is dealt 15 cards, three at a time. The rest of the cards are the stockpile: the top card is turned over to start the discard pile.

In this variation, only sequences are collected; there are no sets. To go out, a player has to meld her entire hand using one of these combinations: five three-card sequences, three four-card sequences and a three-card sequence; one five-, one four- and two three-card sequences. Play continues as usual with each player drawing from the stockpile or taking the discard, then

Scoring System: Continental Rummy

Going out	1 point
Going out on first turn	7 points
Going out on first turn without drawing a card	10 points
Each 2 melded	1 point
Each Joker melded	2 points
No 2s or Jokers melded	10 points
All melded cards from one suit	15 points

discarding a card from her hand. A player cannot meld until she goes out.

The player who goes out earns from each player one point for going out, one point for each 2 and two points for each Joker she melds, 10 points if she goes out without using a Deuce or a Joker, seven points for going out on the first turn, 10 points for going out on her first turn without drawing a card and 10 points for having all 15 cards in one suit. In some cases, a player will collect for one or more of these.

Five Hundred Rum, sometimes called **Michigan Rum** or **Pinochle Rummy**, adds another scoring twist that changes the strategy considerably. All players score points for the cards melded, and subtract the point value of the cards left in their hands. There is no bonus for going out, only the advantage of having no points to subtract from the meld total. Running scores are kept through several hands and the first to reach 500 wins. Scores are much higher than in standard Rummy, of course, and players are tempted to collect higher-value sets and sequences and to delay going out so they can amass more points.

One deck is used for up to four players, two decks for five or more. Ace can be high or low. In two-hand play, each person is dealt 13 cards; with three or more players, each person receives seven. The rest become the stockpile and the upcard is turned up beside it to start the discard pile.

Play continues as usual, drawing and discarding with the object of collecting and melding sets and sequences. However, in addition to taking either the top card of the stock or the upcard on the discard pile, a player may pick up two or more cards from the top of the discard pile, or even the whole stack, so long as he melds the bottom card of what he picks up. He may meld it by rummying it on one of his previous melds or by combining it with cards in his hand to make a new set or sequence or by combining it with other cards he picked up to create a new set or sequence. This feature can add a lot of cards to a hand, which increases the risk should an opponent go out, but it also increases the potential for earning a high score.

In the game illustrated, it is player C's turn. In her previous turn she picked up 5♦ and she already had 5♣, so in this turn she will pick up the discard pile back to an earlier discard of 5♠. She will meld the three 5s, add the 10♥ to the sequence she melded in her last turn, and rummy the 3 to player D's set of 3s (though she does not actually put the 3 on the set but keeps it in front of her). The rest of the cards go into her hand, and she'll discard the King to reduce the total points she holds.

During any turn, a player can rummy cards on other players' melds, though he keeps the rummied cards on the table in front of him (as player A has done) because the rummied cards also contribute to his score. When rummying, a player must identify to which meld he is adding. This is particularly crucial with Aces, since Aces count as one point when melded in a low sequence (A-2-3) but otherwise count as 15, whether in a Q-K-A meld or left in the hand when someone goes out.

The strategy of Five Hundred is quite different from standard Rummy. Instead of trying to go out, the object is to try to get as many cards and thus as many points as possible, at least early in the game. As the risk of someone going out increases, players try to empty their hands. But early on, hold on to cards instead of melding so that you can pick up the discard pile and use it to meld. Many players discard from sets, intending to collect them later, a dangerous but lucrative practice

when it works. Players must be diligent about their own discards, taking care not to add cards to the discard pile that will complete sequences or sets when combined with other discards.

The game ends when a player gets rid of the last card in his hand; a discard is not required. If the stockpile is exhausted before anyone goes out, play continues so long as anyone can draw from the discard pile, but the game ends as soon as a player cannot or will not do so.

Vatican is a sophisticated Czechoslovakian variation for two to five players, but is best with three or four. It requires two decks complete with two Jokers, 106 cards altogether. Thirteen cards are dealt to each player with the remainder facedown in the center as a stockpile. Jokers are wild, Aces are high or low and the object is to go out first by melding all your cards. Melds are, as usual, sets or sequences of at least three, but the difference here is that melds are not the property of one player but rather are communal and can be broken up and re-formed by any player. In turn, each player may draw a card from the stockpile, make a meld or do both. There is no discard. Once a player makes a first meld, he may, at his turn, draw from the stockpile, make one or more melds from his hand or break up and re-form any melds on the table, provided that he also adds to at least one of the melds from his own hand. The melds, when rearranged, must always contain at least three cards in same-suit sequence or three cards of the same value. Jokers are wild but a Joker can only be moved from one meld to another if it is replaced by the card it represents. No card can be taken from a meld and put back into the hand. The first player to meld all his or her cards wins. ～

Five Hundred Rum

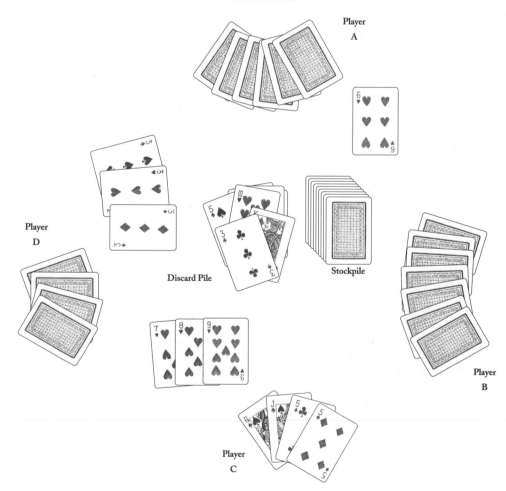

Crazy Eights

- OTHER NAMES: **Eights, Swedish Rummy and, commercially, Uno**
- NUMBER: **up to eight players, but best with two, three or four players or partners**
- EQUIPMENT: **one deck of 52; two decks for six players or more**
- DESCRIPTION: **a Stops game, like Rummoli, but without the boodle and with "wild" cards that change the course of play**
- COMPLEXITY: **excellent for kids ages 8 and up; must be able to match cards by suit and denomination**
- TIP: **great family game for mixed ages**

CRAZY EIGHTS is another off-shoot of the Stops family, in which players try to get rid of their cards but are stopped from doing so because they lack the next in a sequence. One of the earliest Stops games was Comet, all the rage in the late 1700s and named for the comet that Edmund Halley correctly predicted would return in 1759. Because Stops games are gentle, relatively unskilled family fun, they have never lost their appeal. Crazy Eights is something of a newcomer—it doesn't appear in games manuals until about 1940—but it is among the most strategic survivors of Comet and has replaced **Michigan** as America's favorite game of Stops.

The Deal: Players draw cards from the deck; the first to draw a Spade deals. The dealer shuffles the deck and deals five cards one at a time, facedown, to each player. The remaining cards are placed facedown in the center as the stockpile. The top card is turned faceup beside the stockpile. This is the starter. If the starter is an 8, the dealer buries it in the stockpile and turns over the next card as the starter. Players arrange their cards in numerical order within suits.

The Object of the Game: To get rid of all the cards in your hand.

The Play: The player on the dealer's left begins by laying a card on the starter that matches it either in suit or denomination. For instance, if the starter is 9♥, the first person can play a Heart or a 9. Moving clockwise around the table, each player lays down a card, matching the suit or the denomination of the last card played. If a player has neither in her hand, she draws from the stockpile until she can play. A player can, if he wants to, draw from the stockpile even if he has a card in his hand he can play. (If he

Scoring System: Crazy Eights

Card Values	Points
8	50
K-Q-J-10	10
9	9
7-2	face value
Ace	1

Game is 500 points.

holds only an 8, he may want to save it to use at a more strategic point in the game.)

The 8s are wild: they can be played at any time, regardless of the last discard. When a player lays down an 8, she can name a new suit. For instance, if 4♦ was the last discard, the next person can lay down 8♥ and say, "Clubs." The following player then must play either a Club or an 8.

Play continues until one player has discarded all her cards or until the stockpile is gone and no one can lay down another card.

The Score: When one player goes out, the other players add up the value of their remaining cards according to the scoring system: Ace counts 1; face cards count 10; other cards count according to their denominations, except 8s, which count 50. The totals from the other players are added together: this is the winner's score. Losers don't score. The first player to reach 500 points wins.

If the hand ends before anyone goes out, each player adds up his or her unplayed cards. The person with the lowest point total takes from each player the difference between their scores. For instance, if three players end the hand with scores of 35, 53 and 62, the person with 35 wins and earns 18 points (53-35) from one player and 27 points (62-35) from the other, for a score of 45. If there is a tie, the two winners add up the scores of the losers and divide the total in half, then each winner subtracts his own point total from his half of the losers' points to get his final score.

Variations: Crazy Eights is also a good two-person game. Deal seven cards each and play as above.

In **Rockaway**, Aces are wild, instead of 8s, and carry a penalty of 15, rather than 50.

A variation called **Switch** or **Crazy Jacks** uses two decks, with 10 or 12 cards dealt to each player. Aces are wild and change the suit for the next player. If Q♠ is discarded, the next player has to pick up five cards. A 2 forces the next player to pick up two cards. Each succeeding 2 multiplies the penalty by two. For instance, if a 2 is discarded, the next player picks up two cards and discards another 2; the next player must pick up four cards; if she also discards a 2, the following player must pick up eight cards. Playing a 4 doubles any penalty for the next player. For instance, if a 4 is discarded after Q♠, the next player must pick up 10 cards. Playing a Jack reverses the direction of play, so instead of moving clockwise around the table, play moves counterclockwise.

A very similar game is marketed

with special cards as **Uno**. The Uno deck has 108 cards in four colors instead of suits. There are five special cards: a +2 Card indicates that the next player draws two extra cards from the stockpile; a Reverse Card, with arrows, indicates that the direction of play reverses; a Skip Card forces the next player to pass; a four-colored Wild Card changes the color in play, just as an 8 does in Crazy Eights; and a +4 Wild Card changes the color and also forces the next player to pick up four cards. In Uno, players are dealt seven cards each. Play proceeds exactly as in Crazy Eights, except as a player lays down his second last card, he must declare "Uno." When scores are tallied, cards count their face value except the +2 Card, Reverse Card and Skip Card, which each count 20, and the Wild Card and +4 Wild Card, which each count 50.

Go Boom

- ◆ NUMBER: **two or more players**
- ◆ EQUIPMENT: **for up to six players, a deck of 52, Ace high; for larger groups, two decks**
- ◆ DESCRIPTION: **like Crazy Eights, but this game introduces the concept of taking tricks**
- ◆ TIP: **a good game for developing "card sense" in beginning players**

THIS SIMPLE GAME is a good first step toward more complicated card games such as **Euchre, Oh Hell** and **Bridge**. The strategy is elementary but can be applied to all trick-taking games. The name is a euphemism for "Go Bust," which is the point of the game: to reduce your holdings to nothing.

The Deal: Cut the deck; low card deals (Ace is low for the cut). The dealer shuffles the deck and deals seven cards to each player one at a time, facedown. The remaining cards are placed facedown in the center as a stockpile. Players arrange their cards by suits.

The Object of the Game: To be the first to use up all the cards in your hand by playing to tricks; tricks don't score.

The Play: The player on the dealer's left begins, playing any card she chooses. Moving clockwise around the table, each player lays down a card that matches either the suit or the denomination of the card led. For instance, if 10♣ is led, players may lay down any Club or any 10.

The highest card of the suit led wins the trick. (There is no trump.) If all the cards are the same denomination, the one played first wins. The winner of each trick plays the first card for the next round.

If a player does not have a card of the correct suit or denomination, he draws from the stockpile until he gets a card he can play. (In some versions, no more than three cards can be drawn at a time.) If the stockpile is gone, he passes.

Play continues until one player lays down her last card. The rest of the players play to the final trick, then count the cards that remain in their hands.

The Score: The tricks have no value; they are simply a way of getting rid of cards. The first player to empty her hand wins. The other players add up the value of the cards still in their hands (Ace counts 1; face cards count 10; other cards count according to their number). The winner's score is the total of what is left in everyone else's hand. For each hand, only the winner scores.

Several hands are played for each game. The first player to reach 200 points wins. (For young children, a target score of 100 points is high enough.)

Strategy: There are 13 cards of each suit and only four cards of each denomination, so when you have a choice, match suits rather than numbers. As you discard, try to keep some cards of every suit.

High cards give your opponent points in the final score, but they also allow you to take tricks, an advantage near the end of the game, because the trick-taker controls the lead and is more likely to be able to empty her hand of its last cards. At the beginning of the game, let others have the lead: discard low cards, and save your high cards for the last few tricks. When you notice that other players are down to two or three cards, discard your high counters. Save Aces until last: they are the highest cards for taking tricks but count low in scoring.

Hearts

- OTHER NAMES: **Omnibus Hearts, Black Maria and Black Lady**
- NUMBER: **an exciting "round" game for three to six players; four is best**
- EQUIPMENT: **one deck of 52, Ace high**
- DESCRIPTION: **a penalty-avoidance game like Old Maid**
- COMPLEXITY: **tricks but no trump; strategic demands are similar to Whist**

HEARTS HAS BEEN included in English-language games manuals for only slightly more than a century, yet it is one of America's most popular games, and the only one in the family of negative trick-avoidance games with an international reputation. Hearts is cutthroat in all its many forms, but standard Hearts, sometimes called Omnibus Hearts, is considered the best.

The Deal: Cut the deck; low card deals (Ace is low for the cut). With four players, the full deck is used. To make the deal come out even with three players, remove 2♣ from the deck; with five, remove both black 2s; with six, remove all four 2s. The dealer shuffles the deck, the player on his right cuts, then all the cards are dealt clockwise one at a time, facedown, to the players in turn. Players arrange their cards by suits, grouping the penalty cards—all the Hearts and Q♠—together.

The Object of the Game: To avoid winning tricks that contain any of the 13 Hearts or Q♠; the lowest score wins.

The Play: Before play begins, each player takes any three cards from her hand and passes them to the player on her left. Then she picks up the three cards passed to her. Players must pass their cards before picking up the new cards. (With five or more players, pass only two cards.)

The player to the dealer's left leads any card to the first trick. (If everyone agrees, a Heart may not be led until the third trick.) Players follow suit if possible; otherwise, they discard from another suit. The highest card of the suit led takes the trick. (There is no trump.) The winner puts the trick facedown in front of her. Play continues until the last trick is taken. At the end of the hand, players add up the penalty cards in the tricks they won.

While the object of the game in general is to avoid getting any Hearts or Q♠, a player may also try *shooting the moon*, or *going for control*—trying to take all the penalty cards. He must have a very strong hand, with several Aces, high Hearts and a way to capture or protect Q♠. The reward for taking the gamble and getting all the penalty cards is great—all the others get 26 points added to their scores.

The Score: Each heart counts 1 point against the player who holds it; Q♠ counts 13 points, a penalty that has earned this card the nickname Black Maria or Calamity Jane. However, if a player holds all the Hearts and Q♠, she deducts 26 from her score and the others add 26 to theirs. The game ends at 50 points: when one player reaches or goes over 50, the player who has the lowest score wins.

Strategy: In choosing three cards to pass, get rid of high Hearts and A-K♠, unless you have Q♠ as well. It isn't a bad idea to keep Q♠ as long as you have a couple of low Spades so that you aren't forced to take a trick with Q♠. If possible, create voids (no cards at all) in some suits so that you can discard Hearts or Q♠ when those suits are led. Shorten long suits, and get rid of Aces, since you don't want to win tricks. Because there is no trump, long suits are an advantage, especially if you are sure you can get the lead.

Although players are mostly concerned with avoiding penalty cards for themselves, Hearts is also a conspiracy game. If one player is going for control, the rest can work together to make sure he fails. Likewise, players can slow down or speed up the game by deciding who to dump penalty cards on. If your score is lowest, try to push the player with the highest score over the 50 mark. If you are vying for lowest score, dump Hearts on your nearest competitor, not on the high scorer.

Early in the game, when there are unlikely to be voids, you can risk leading a high card, but because the aim is to avoid winning tricks, low leads are generally more common throughout the game. A Spade is the usual opening lead, since it is to everyone's advantage, except the player holding Q♠, to smoke out the Black Maria early so that it won't be discarded on an unsuspecting trick later. A low Heart is also a safe lead and one that may tip you off to a player's intention to go for control. In general, play high cards early in the game, saving low cards for later when other players have voids that allow them to dump their Hearts. Late in the game, make sure you have a few low exit cards. The worst scenario is to end up with several high cards that give you the lead and, coincidentally, everyone's unwanted last-ditch Hearts. And keep a close count on the Hearts—if they have all been played, it is perfectly safe to take the last few tricks.

Variations: Instead of scoring to 50 points, play four hands, varying the exchange each time: pass to the left, pass to the right, pass across and sit tight (no cards passed). The person with the lowest score after four hands wins. Sometimes, J♦ or 10♦ is designated a bonus card, allowing the lucky holder to deduct 10 points from his score.

In **Heartsette**, the full 52-card pack is dealt, no matter how many are playing. Any cards that are left over after an equal deal are set aside facedown as the *widow*. Whoever takes the first trick adds the widow to his pile of tricks. He may look at the widow but may not show the cards to anyone else.

In **Pink Lady** or **Bloody Mary**, Q♥ also counts 13 points, which raises the total penalty count to 38: 13 each for the two Queens and 12 for the remaining Hearts. The play is the same, but the game goes to 100 points instead of 50.

In **Sweepstake Hearts**, the score is settled differently. At the end of the hand, players each put a number of counters into the center equal to the number of penalty points they scored. All those who are *clear*—have no penalty points against them—divide up the pot. If one player shoots the moon and scores all the penalty points, she gets the pot. If everyone is *painted*—has at least 1 penalty point—the pot remains untouched until the next hand.

In **Spot Hearts**, the score is tallied according to the numerical value of

the Hearts: Ace counts 14, King 13, Queen 12 and Jack 11.

In **Hearts for Two**, deal 13 cards each to two players; the remainder is the stockpile. The elder hand (nondealer) leads, and play is the same, except the winner of each trick draws the top card from the stockpile and the loser takes the next, keeping the hands to 13 cards each until the stockpile is exhausted. Players then play out the rest of their hands in tricks. Penalty cards score as in standard Hearts. ⌒

Oh Hell

- ◆ OTHER NAMES: **Bugger Bridge, Bugger Your Neighbor, Up and Down the River, Blackout and the bowdlerized Oh Well or Oh Pshaw**
- ◆ NUMBER: **three to seven players; four is best**
- ◆ EQUIPMENT: **a deck of 52, Ace high, a scorepad and pencil**
- ◆ DESCRIPTION: **a relaxing trick-taking game that allows friendly conversation without being mindless; requires skill comparable to Hearts**
- ◆ COMPLEXITY: **the scoring system is too involved for most children under the age of 12**
- ◆ DURATION: **learned in a few minutes; a game absorbs the better part of an evening**

OH HELL TAKES trick-taking games a step further, in that not only must tricks be won but the players must accurately predict how many they can take. The game's origin is unknown, although it is likely a 20th-century invention, since it was not described until the Depression.

The Deal: Cut the deck; the person who draws the lowest card shuffles and deals the first hand. In subsequent hands, the deal moves clockwise around the table.

In the first hand, each player gets one card, in the second hand two cards, and so on, until the last hand, when the entire deck is dealt. With three players, there are 15 hands, with four players 13, with five players 10,

with six players 8 and with seven players 7.

For each hand, the dealer distributes the appropriate number of cards, one at a time, facedown to the players, then turns the next card faceup. This is the trump suit. The rest of the deck is set aside facedown; it is not used again until the cards are shuffled for the next hand. In the last hand of the game, no trump card is turned up.

The Bidding: Starting with the person on the dealer's left, each player bids the number of tricks he thinks he can win. He may bid zero, but he may not pass. Each bid is noted on a special scorepad, as illustrated. After everyone has bid, the scorekeeper announces whether the hand is overbid

(more tricks bid than each person has cards), underbid or even—the same number of tricks bid as there are cards.

For a more interesting game, disallow even bids. The scorekeeper gives the status of the hand (overbid, underbid or even) when everyone but the dealer has bid, then the dealer makes the last bid: he cannot make a bid that will bring the total to the same number as there are tricks in that hand. For instance, if each player is dealt three cards, there will be three tricks in that hand. If the first player bids one and the second bids two, the hand is even. The dealer, therefore, cannot bid zero: she must bid at least one.

The Object of the Game: To win exactly the number of tricks bid; more or fewer are penalized; the highest score wins.

The Play: The player on the dealer's left leads to the first trick. Players must follow suit if they can. If not, they may trump or discard from a side suit. The highest card in the suit led wins the trick unless it is trumped, in which case the highest trump wins the trick.

The winner of each trick lays the trick facedown in front of her, setting the next one crosswise so that the tricks can easily be counted by all players. The winner of one trick leads to the next.

Play continues until all the cards are taken in tricks, then the score is recorded, the cards are gathered and shuffled well, and a new hand is dealt.

At the end of the final hand, which is played without trump, the player with the highest score wins.

The Score: Precise bidding is the key to success. Players who take exactly the number of tricks they bid score the amount of the bid plus 10. For instance, if a player bids five tricks and takes five, her score for that hand is 15 (5+10). Players who *bust*—go over or under their bids—score zero. Decide beforehand how to score a successful bid of zero: it can earn 10 points (the amount of the bid plus 10), 5 points or the total number of tricks in the hand (2 in the second hand, 3 in the third hand, and so on).

In the score sheet illustrated, the four players were overbid in the third hand. The first player bid two and took two, scoring 12 (21+12=33); the second player bid zero and took none, scoring 10 (10+10=20); the third player bid one and took one, scoring 11 (20+11=31); and the fourth player bid one and took none, scoring zero.

Strategy: The dealer always has the advantage, since he bids last. If he is unsure how many tricks he can win, it is good strategy to make the bid even, because he may then get the co-operation of other players who want to make their bids.

If the bid is even, the game is simply a matter of distributing the tricks properly amongst the players, and it is to everyone's advantage to see that this happens. If the bid is over or under, the game becomes competitive. If the hand is overbid, players are vying with each other for the tricks because there

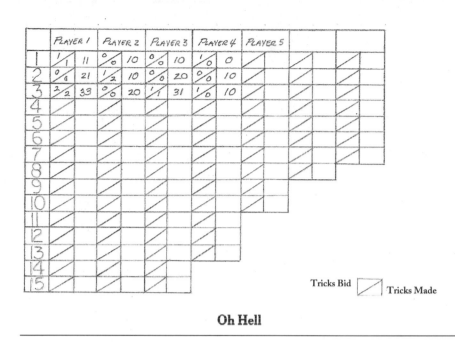

Tricks Bid [/] Tricks Made

Oh Hell

aren't enough to go around. If the hand is underbid, players are trying not to take tricks: someone will be stuck with the extras.

In general, it is easier to lose tricks than to win them, so underbidding is safer than overbidding, especially with four or more cards. It is best to hold both high and low cards in a suit; several middle cards are unlikely to win many tricks.

Variation: A commercial variation of Oh Hell called **Wizard** adds a little more strategy to the game. The Wizard deck is like a conventional 52-card deck with four Jesters and four Wizards added. (You can duplicate this by borrowing two Jokers and four Aces from another deck with the same back pattern. Mark the faces of the Aces with a W to indicate that they are Wizards.) Jesters are the lowest

cards, and Wizards are the highest, outclassing trump. The cards are dealt as for Oh Hell, but with three players, there are 20 deals, with four players 15, with five 12 and with six 10. Play is exactly the same, except a Wizard or a Jester may be played on a trick at any time. Jesters are throwaways and simply allow you to save a King or a Queen to take a later trick. Wizards take any trick. If two Wizards are played, the first one laid down takes the trick. If a Jester is led, the next card played sets the suit. If only Jesters are played in a round, the first one played takes the trick. In Wizard, players who correctly predict the number of tricks they will take score 20 points plus 10 points for each trick. A player who predicts incorrectly, loses 10 points for each trick over or under his bid.   ᕬ

Nine-Five-Two

- OTHER NAMES: similar to Sergeant-Major, Bismarck and Dutch Whist
- NUMBER: a game for three players—no more, no less
- EQUIPMENT: one deck of 52, Ace high
- DESCRIPTION: a three-part compound game; the strategy changes for each player with each hand
- DURATION: low-scoring but lots of fun; absorbs an entire rainy day, with players peaking and bottoming out several times before a winner is declared

OTHER THAN the obsolete Hombre and the convoluted Skat, there are few card games designed specifically for three players. Many, such as **Canasta** and **Cribbage**, can be adapted for three players, but this is a game that only a trio can play. It is an especially good family game, because fortunes rise and fall with skill and also with the position played: if you have to make nine tricks this turn, you can take comfort in knowing that you will only have to make five tricks in the next hand.

The Deal: Cut the deck; low card deals. The dealer shuffles and deals the cards one at a time, facedown, to each player until all the cards are distributed. During the deal, he lays aside a kitty of four cards: he may deal them one after the other or at random throughout the deal, but the last card cannot go to the kitty. Players arrange their 16 cards in sequence within suits. The dealer names trump according to the strongest suit in his hand. After he names trump, the dealer adds the kitty to his hand, then discards four unwanted cards.

The Object of the Game: To score more tricks than the required nine for the dealer, five for the second player and two for the third player; the first player to reach the target score wins.

The Play: The person on the dealer's left leads to the first trick.

Players follow suit, and if they cannot, they either trump or discard from a side suit. The winner of the trick gathers the cards and turns them facedown in front of her so that the number of tricks can easily be counted by everyone. No players may refer to trick cards after they are taken. The winner of one trick leads to the next. Play continues until all the cards have been played in tricks.

The Score: There are 16 tricks in each hand: the dealer must take nine, the second player must take five, and the third player must take two. This is called *book*. There is no score for making book. For each trick overbook, a player scores 1 point. For each trick underbook, a player loses 1 point. The game can start at 10 and go to 20, or it can start at zero and go to 10, in which case some players will have minus scores.

Players who underbook suffer a further penalty. In the next hand, before trump is declared, a player who overbooked is allowed to *hit* the player or players who underbooked: for each trick overbook, the winner gives one card to a person who underbooked. He passes her his lowest card in a suit, and in return, she gives him her highest card in that suit. For instance, in the first round, the dealer (Tracy) takes nine tricks, the second player (Jan) takes seven, and the third player (Lori) takes none. That means Jan overbooked two and Lori underbooked two. In the second round, Jan

gives Lori 3♦ and 2♥, and Lori returns her two highest cards in those suits: K♦ and A♥. The cards exchanged may be all in one suit or spread among several. If Jan gave Lori 10♠ and Lori's highest Spade was an 8, she would simply return Jan's card, which indicates she has nothing higher. If one player is hitting the other two, he would give a card or cards to each player before picking up any in return.

Before the game begins, players should decide how long they want to play: a game of 10 points often takes more than an hour.

Strategy: Although he has to make the most tricks, the dealer has the advantage in Nine-Five-Two: he makes trump, and he has the kitty, which can be his salvation if he underbooked during the last round and has lost his best cards in the exchange. The most difficult hand to play is that of the second player, since she has to take five tricks yet has no control over trump. She does, however, lead to the first trick, which gives her some power. The third player has the least control and is under the least pressure to perform. It usually isn't difficult to take two tricks out of 16.

When you hit another player in an exchange, try to reinforce your hand for trump cards. In general, offer the low card of a weak suit or one you think might be called trump. For instance, if you have a long suit of Spades, only a few low Diamonds and high cards in neither, you should hit for Diamonds, since it is more likely that the dealer has Diamonds and will make that suit trump. Hitting tells the person on the other end of the exchange where you are weak, and if it is the dealer you are hitting, she can use that against you, making your weak suit trump. When hitting the dealer, therefore, use the scatter-gun approach, hitting for high cards in several suits instead of two or more cards in one. This protects you no matter which suit is trump. ∽

Napoleon

- OTHER NAMES: Nap
- NUMBER: three to six players; four are best
- EQUIPMENT: a standard 52-card deck; Ace high; counters such as poker chips or coins
- DESCRIPTION: a Euchrelike trick-taking game with trump
- COMPLEXITY: fairly elementary, good for families; teaches simple bidding and trump
- DURATION: quick and easy: five minutes or less per hand

NAPOLEON, sometimes referred to as Nap, followed Loo as an early 20th-century British fad. It is still an excellent family game, especially good for teaching children the basics of trick-taking and trumping. Because the outcome is not particularly dependent on skill, a beginner has little to fear from an expert, who is just as easily defeated by the luck of the draw.

The name of the game and its variations suggest an origin in the trenches during the summer of 1815, when Wellington and the Prussian commander Gebhard Leberecht von Blücher defeated Napoleon near the village of Waterloo. Despite its terminology, however, the game actually appeared somewhat later, around the mid-1800s, and seems to commemorate not the vertically challenged emperor, but Napoleon III, who retired to Britain and who was, according to Edmond Taylor, author of *The Fossil Monarchies*, "the nearest thing Europe has ever produced to a Mississippi river-boat gambler."

Although the game was born in England, its imperial associations have all but died out even there. Today, it is played mostly under its drowsy nickname, Nap.

Napoleon is, appropriately, an alliance game. Instead of each person playing for himself, players join forces to defeat the highest bidder. Because alliances shift from one hand to the next, the dynamics at the card table are quite different from traditional partnership and solo games.

The game itself is elementary, although many variations have evolved to add interest. Stakes also increase enthusiasm: players buy or receive a certain number of counters, usually 50, from a designated banker before play begins. When a player's supply is exhausted, he can buy more. According to Foster's 1897 *Hoyle*, British players of the time usually played Nap for a penny a point; in North America, nickel and quarter Nap were more usual. Considering that a nickel at the turn of the century would buy two pounds of butter, and a six-room house could be rented for $6 a month, the stakes seem high indeed.

The Deal: Players shuffle the deck and cut for the deal; low card deals. (For the cut, Ace is low.) The dealer deals five cards facedown to each player, in groups of two and then three or, if desired, one at a time. The remaining cards are turned facedown: except in certain variations, these cards do not come into play. The loser of one hand deals to the next.

The Object of the Game: To be the highest bidder and thus earn the right to name trump; to win the number of tricks bid.

The Bidding: The player to the left of the dealer begins. He may pass or he may make an opening bid of two, which means he contracts to take two tricks. (Some permit an opening bid of one.) No trump suit is named. Bidding proceeds by turn clockwise around the table. Each player must either pass or make a higher bid than the last. There are no second bids. If everyone passes, the dealer is required to bid one and play the hand. A bid of five is known as *Napoleon* or *Nap*.

The highest bidder is required to take the number of tricks he bid. The other players join forces to try to defeat the high bidder.

The Play: The highest bidder leads to the first trick. The suit led becomes the trump suit. Players must follow suit if possible, but a player does not have to take a trick unless he wants to. The highest trump played wins the trick; the winner of each trick leads to the next.

In subsequent rounds, players must follow suit if possible. If they cannot follow suit, they can play trump if they wish. The highest trump played wins the trick; if no trump is played, the highest card of the suit led wins the trick.

Tricks are turned facedown and stacked so that they can be counted by all players. (A facedown trick cannot be looked at again.) One person among the opponents should gather all the tricks for the opposition.

The Score: Players can score with points, each keeping track individually. If the bidder is successful, he earns points equal to the number of tricks he bid. For instance, if he bid two, he scores two points, even if he took more than two tricks. If he fails to make his bid, he earns nothing and each of the other players scores the number of points he bid.

More usually, the game is scored with counters. If the bidder makes his bid, he collects that number of counters from each of the other players. (Again, if he bid two and took four tricks, he still only collects two counters from each player.) If he fails to make his bid, he *pays* that number of counters to each of the other players. A Nap (a bid of five) is worth 10 counters if it is accomplished, but it costs the bidder only five counters to each other player if he fails to take all five tricks.

Strategy: With four players, there are only 20 cards in play and 32 buried in the stockpile. With fewer players, the odds are even higher that a card is buried and not held by an opponent. As a result, Queens and Jacks often take tricks, and a run of three in one suit is worthy of a bid of three. With so many cards out of play, whether you make a bid is largely a matter of luck.

The established probabilities in this game are as follows. Four trump cards in hand wins three tricks. Three trump cards, Jack or higher, will win two tricks. Three lower trumps are probably good for a trick and a half. Two trump cards that include either the Ace or King are worth one trick; any other two trumps can only be counted as half a trick. In the side suits, an Ace or King is worth a trick; a Queen with a couple of lower cards can be counted as half a trick. For bids up to three, players can safely include all side-suit cards, but for bids of four or five, players should rely entirely on trump holdings and side Aces and Kings.

These probabilities hold fairly true with a large group of players, but if there are only three or four at table, lower cards will likely reap greater yields. In any case, this is a game for risk takers. Only experience will give you a true sense of when a high bid is worth the risk.

During play, the three opponents should work together against the bidder. In general, leave no trick to your partners that you can win yourself. If possible, lead singletons and create

Scoring System: Napoleon		
Player Bids:	If Successful, Scores	If Unsuccessful, Pays Penalty
Bid of 1	1	1 to each player
2	2	2
3	3	3
4	4	4
5 (Napoleon)	10	5
5 (Wellington)	20	10
5 (Blücher)	30	20

voids that you can trump into. Indicate your weak areas to your partners by discarding low cards in that suit. A high discard usually indicates strength in that suit.

Variations: Two can play by dealing an extra, dummy hand, which remains facedown while the players bid. The loser of the bidding plays both hands against the winner, taking care to play cards in proper order to the tricks.

If a bidder is very sure of his hand and is certain he can make five tricks, or Napoleon, he can double the stakes by bidding *Wellington*. Or, for the brave of heart, stakes can be tripled by declaring *Blücher*. The loser of a Wellington bid pays out 10 counters to each player; the loser of a Blücher bid pays out 20. This order of events is historically appropriate since Wellington defeated Napoleon, but only because Blücher arrived on the scene with his Prussian troops.

In **Misery Napoleon,** a bid of mis-

ery, or *misère,* is possible in which the bidder offers to play no-trump and to win no tricks at all. The "miz" bid falls between a bid of three and a bid of four. If the bidder wins he scores three.

In **Peep Napoleon,** a one-card widow is dealt facedown after all the other cards are dealt. As each player comes up to bid he may peep at the widow, but it costs a counter to do so. The highest bidder picks up the widow and discards a card from his hand before play begins.

In **Purchase Napoleon,** before making a bid, each player can discard as many cards as he wants and draw new ones from the stock of undealt cards, paying one counter per card to the pot. Only one round of exchanges is allowed. Any player winning five tricks on a Nap bid takes the whole pot, which obviously may stand and increase through several hands. Also known as **Écarté Nap,** this variation adds considerable excitement in the bidding and the play.   ∽

Hombre

- ◆ OTHER NAMES: Ombre, Renegado and Solo
- ◆ NUMBER: three players—no more, no less
- ◆ EQUIPMENT: a Spanish deck of 40 cards, or a standard 52-card deck with 8-9-10s removed; coins or chips as counters
- ◆ DESCRIPTION: introduces the concept of bidding to name trump
- ◆ COMPLEXITY: simple trick-taking game with interesting Spanish twists
- ◆ DURATION: 15 minutes per hand

THE ENDURING fascination of Hombre, or Ombre, may be surmised from a line in Alexander Pope's poem *The Rape of the Lock:* "Her joy in gilded chariots when alive, And love of *Ombre* after death survive." Indeed, Pope includes a card-by-card account of a game Belinda plays. At the time Pope wrote his poem, the game had been popular in England for about 50 years. It had been brought back by the Cavaliers around 1660, but Hombre is several centuries older than this; its origins have been traced to the 14th century. In fact, Hombre deserves a place in every card aficionado's repertoire if only because it is among the oldest of card games, as old as playing cards themselves.

Referred to as "that noble Spanish game" and "a royal game," Hombre was described in the very first games manual. Rarely played now in its original form (you'll be hard-pressed to find a mention in any modern Hoyle's), it has nevertheless been responsible for a clutch of offspring, which, although they are quite dissimilar, go under the common name of Solo. The nickname derives from the fact that, unlike games in which each player plays for himself (**Rummy** and **Hearts**) or games in which players work together as partners (**Whist** and **Bridge**), in Solo games, one player names trump and plays against the combined forces of the other two. Each player scores for himself, and from one hand to the next will likely find himself playing with and against the other individuals at the table, as they win or lose the right to name trump.

Whether one prefers the fixed alliances of games like Bridge or the more fluid and temporary treaties at play in Solo games comes down to a matter of temperament. In 1830, Charles Lamb wrote a humorous essay in which one Sarah Battle muses on the distinct properties of Whist and Quadrille, a direct descendant of Hombre: "The skirmishes of Quadrille . . . reminded her of the petty embroilments of the little Italian states, depicted by Machiavel; perpetually changing postures and connections, bitter foes today, sugared darlings tomorrow; kissing and scratching in a breath; — but the wars of Whist were comparable to the long, steady, deep-rooted, rational antipathies of the great French and English nations."

Ombre, sometimes pronounced "umber," is an Anglicization of *hombre*, the Spanish word for man, which refers to the solo player who is the focus of the game. Hombre's real heyday was at the end of the 17th century, and its popularity persisted for more than a century. Special triangular tables were even designed for the game. As late as 1884 one standard card-playing manual stated, "Of all games, undoubtedly the most interesting, diversified, and widely known is Ombre." But even then, Hombre was in decline, at least in England, where Thackeray noted, "Card-playing is greatly out of mode: very likely there are not six ladies of fashion in London who know the difference between Spadille and Manille"—terms unique to the Solo family of games.

Hombre may have the honor of being the first card game in which a player bids for the right to name the trump suit, a remarkable evolution which is the basis of some of today's most sophisticated and challenging card games, particularly Bridge. In fact, it was Whist and Bridge that eventually edged Hombre out of the games room, so much so that by 1975, another European card-playing manual dismissed Hombre as "a game for card gourmets and snobs."

Hombre is included here, at the risk of provoking accusations of elitism, because it is an entertaining and unique form of cards designed specifically for three, which increasingly is the number sitting down to the family card table. Despite its gender-specific name (or perhaps because of it), Hombre has always been a favorite of women: Catherine of Braganza, the queen of Charles II of England, loved it, as did Maria Theresa of France, though her husband, Louis XIV, declared it tedious. As one manual put it, Ombre "better suits the Genius of the Ladies, to whom Complaisance and good Manners must Prejudice the Gentlemen in its favour."

The game began as a four-hander, was adapted for three players as Renegado (or Traitor, a variation that survives today as Tresillo) and eventually migrated to other countries as a three-hander with the four-handed name. The terms are mostly corruptions of Spanish words, and the game uses the Spanish deck of 40 cards as well as the Spanish tradition of counterclockwise movement, but French terms also creep in, reminders of this game's wide travels and long heritage.

The Deal: Cards are dealt facedown, to the *right*, as is the Spanish custom: nine cards to each player. The remaining 13 cards form the stockpile, which is set facedown in the center of the table.

High to low, cards rank K-Q-J-7-6-5-4-3-2, in the black suits and A-K-Q-J-2-3-4-5-6-7 in the red suits.

Note that there are no Aces in the black suits. That's because these two Aces count among the three highest trumps, which are called *matadors*. Regardless of which suit is named trump, the three matadors in order from high to low are the Ace of Spades, called the *Spadilla*; the lowest card in the trump suit (the 2 if Clubs or Spades or the 7 of Hearts or Diamonds), called the *Manilla;* and the Ace of Clubs, called the *Basta*. If a red suit is trump, the fourth best card is the Ace of Hearts or Diamonds, called the *Punta*. The Punta, however, is not considered a matador.

Matador is the Spanish word for killer, a term as appropriate to the card table as the bullring, since these three powerful trumps can take out any trick. The actual names of the three matadors are not as easy to translate and may derive from earlier evolutions of the language. Spadilla is a mystery, unless it is Spade pronounced with a Spanish lilt. Manilla may possibly come from *manillar*, or handlebar, since it is the trump in the middle. The Basta is the third and final matador, "enough" to take the cards of the trump suit. The Punta, the highest of a red trump suit but not a matador, is the "pivotal point" between matadors and the traditional trump suit.

The Object of the Game:
To name trump, and then to win more tricks than either of the other players.

The Trump:
Each player, beginning to the right of the dealer, either passes or declares himself to be "Hombre," which means he undertakes to win an individual majority of tricks.

The Hombre announces the trump suit, then he discards as many cards as he wishes from his hand and draws the same number of replacement cards from the stockpile. This is known as the *simple game.*

The player to the right of the Hombre can override him by saying he will play "*sans prendre,*" or solo—without discarding and taking replacement cards. The original declarer can still be the Hombre if he replies that he, too, is willing to play Hombre Solo, playing his hand exactly as dealt.

If everyone passes, the player who holds the Spadilla is obliged to become Hombre and play a simple game. If no one holds the Spadilla (it may be in the stockpile) the hand is abandoned and the deal moves to the right.

The Play: After the Hombre draws from the stockpile, the other players in turn, counterclockwise, may also discard as many cards as they wish and draw the same number of replacements from the stockpile. The third player to draw may look at all the remaining stockpile cards to see what the other players missed.

The player on Hombre's right leads to the first trick and the others follow, counterclockwise around the table. All players must follow suit if possible; otherwise, they can play any card. The highest card in the suit led wins the trick unless trump is played, in which case the highest trump wins.

If trump is led, players must follow suit, although matadors are an exception to that rule. The three matadors may be held back, even if trump is led. If a matador is led, however, and a player has no other trump, he must play a matador if he has one.

Hombre wins if he takes more tricks than either opponent individually. For instance, if Hombre wins four tricks and the other players win three and two respectively, Hombre wins the hand. He is *sacardo*, which means to take out one's opponents.

If Hombre loses, he is said to be *beasted.* If he has the same number of tricks as another player, he loses by *puesta* (Spanish for stake or bet). If either opponent wins a majority of the tricks, he loses by *codilla*, a mysterious reference to the knee or elbow joint

The Score: Hombre is usually played for counters, such as poker chips or coins, which is the best method for keeping score.

Players contribute equally to the pot before a hand is dealt—usually three counters each. If Hombre is sacardo, he wins the pot. If he is beasted by puesta, he pays a double stake to the pot in the next hand. If he loses by codilla, he pays the double stake to the winner, instead of the pot, which remains intact for the next hand. In other words, if the stake is three counters each per hand, a loser by codilla pays six counters to the player with the most tricks; the pot of nine counters is carried forward, everyone antes again, and the winner of that hand collects 18 counters in all.

If Hombre takes the first five tricks in a row, he is sacardo, and the hand can end right there. He can, however, opt to continue to play, going for *vole*, a "flight" or "blowup" of all nine tricks. If he is successful and takes all nine tricks, he collects half the amount of the pot from each player.

Hombre

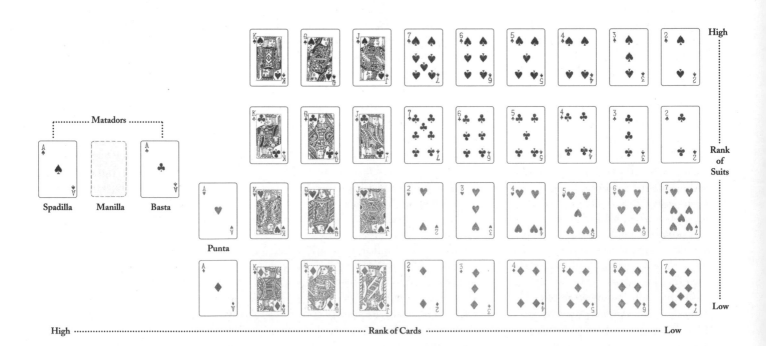

If he fails to win vole, he has to pay each player half the amount of the pot. Either way, he wins the pot, the reward for his sacardo.

If the hand is abandoned, players add another counter each and deal another hand.

Strategy: The two opponents work together to defeat the Hombre. In most cases, this means that one of the opponents will be allowed to take most of the tricks, since the Hombre can only be defeated by an individual, not by their combined tricks. ∽

Matadors (high to low)	
Spadilla	Ace of Spades
Manilla	2♣, 2♠, 7♥ or 7♦
Basta	Ace of Clubs

Non-Matadors	
Punta	A♥ or A♦

Solo

- ◆ OTHER NAMES: German Solo, Frog (a corruption of Frage), Hearts Solo, Solo Whist
- ◆ NUMBER: four players
- ◆ EQUIPMENT: a 32-card deck (a standard deck with 2-6s removed, Ace high); coins or poker chips as counters
- ◆ DESCRIPTION: a four-hander similar to Hombre; players bid in a formal ritual to name trump
- ◆ COMPLEXITY: three games within one; more intricate than Hombre; not appropriate for children
- ◆ DURATION: 20 minutes per hand

HOMBRE generated a four-handed offspring called Quadrille, which became so popular in Europe it made Hombre itself virtually extinct. Quadrille is one of the five games treated by Edmond Hoyle. A very complicated enterprise appropriate to 18th-century courts, Quadrille survives today in a simpler but no less engaging four-handed form known as Solo. Unlike most card games for four, in which two players usually work in partnership through several hands, Solo brings the fickle temporary alliances of Hombre to the four-player card table. Scores are counted individually but play is cooperative, with partners changing at every deal—the best of all possible worlds, some might say.

Solo is rarely found in North American card-playing manuals, perhaps because it isn't played much on this side of the ocean, or perhaps because there is such a plethora of variations and disparate games described under similar names that sorting them out is no mean feat. The game described below is usually, more specifically, known as German Solo. There are many others that travel under the Solo name—French Solo, Spanish Solo, Hearts Solo, English Solo or Solo Whist—each with its own refinements. The game's cosmopolitan, European nature is evident in the linguistic variety of its terms, drawn from French, German, Spanish and English. This can make Solo somewhat confusing for Hombre players, as many of the same Spanish terms are used, though they designate different cards: *Spadilla* in this game is the Queen of Clubs, the seven of the trump suit is the *Manilla* and the Queen of Spades is the *Basta*.

Because scores are calculated individually, Solo is often played for stakes instead of points. Because each hand is complete in itself, the game can end at any time, rather than waiting for some arbitrary point level to be reached.

The Deal: Players draw cards from the deck: the first Club determines who deals. The dealer deals eight cards in batches of three, two, then three, facedown to the left.

The three top-ranking trump cards (regardless of which suit is trump) are, high to low, the Queen of Clubs, the 7 of the trump suit and the Queen of Spades. These are the matadors, known respectively as the Spadilla, Manilla and Basta. All the side suits rank, high to low, Ace to 7.

The Object of the Game: To win the bid to name the trump suit and to win, alone or in partnership, five tricks (Frage or Solo) or eight tricks (Tout).

The Games: Games are played *in color*, which means that Clubs are trump, or *in suit* which means that one of the other three suits will be named trump. There are three basic games:

In the simple game, or *Frage* (from the German, meaning question or "I ask"), the successful bidder must win five tricks. After the bidding is over, he announces whether the game will be played in color or in suit (if that was not already established in the bidding). If the game is to be played in suit, he declares which suit is trump, then he asks for a strategic Ace that he lacks (or a King, if he holds all Aces). The player who holds that Ace or King does not identify himself except by playing the card to a trick at the earliest opportunity. Nevertheless, holding the asked-for card makes that player the bidder's partner for the entire hand: he is obliged to help out from the beginning, whether the bidder knows who his assistant is or not. Frage is the lowest-value game, earning four points if played in color, two points if played in suit. Both the bidder and the partner earn the points if they make five tricks, and both lose the points if they fail to make the contract.

In a *Solo* game, the successful bidder plays alone against the other three players to win five tricks. The bidder declares whether the game will be played in color or in suit and, if the latter, he names the trump suit before play begins. A successful Solo earns eight points if played in color, four points in suit.

In a *Tout* game (from the French, meaning all), the successful bidder declares his intention to play solo *and* to take every trick. The game is worth 32 points in color, 16 points in suit.

The Bidding: Players bid for the right to name trump by declaring which game they think they can win. The value of the games is as follows, low to high: Frage in suit, Frage in color, Solo in suit, Solo in color, Tout in suit, Tout in color.

The player to the dealer's left begins. He can either pass or declare, "I ask." This indicates he is prepared to play the lowest-value game: Frage in suit. The player to the bidder's left passes if he doesn't think he can win this game. If he has a good hand, one that he thinks can win the next level, he responds by questioning the first bidder as to whether he will play the game of the next highest value.

"Is it in color?" the second bidder asks. If the answer is yes, the second bidder can either pass or continue with the next question:

"Will you play solo?" he asks, which implies Solo in suit.

Each question ups the bid, since each implies a game that is worth more points. In asking each question, the second bidder is indicating that he is prepared to undertake the game in question. So when the first bidder says yes to the Solo in suit, the second bidder then asks, "Is it in color?" indicating that he also has the cards to play and win a Solo game in color. If the first bidder answers yes, he is agreeing to that game. The second bidder, if he has the cards, then asks if the first bidder will play Tout or finally, Tout in

---

---

color. If at any point the first bidder doesn't think he can win the game in question, he answers, "No."

When the first bidder removes himself from the bidding with a negative response, the bid rests with the second bidder, and it is up to the third player to question him, upping the bid further if he thinks he can make the next level of game or, otherwise, passing.

In short, asking a question implies that the questioner is willing and able to play the game he is asking about, as does a positive response to the question. A pass or a negative response indicates the bid is beyond the potential of the hand.

Bidding continues until each player has one opportunity to either bid or pass. If all four players pass without bidding, whoever holds the Spadilla must show it and play a forced or *Forcée* Frage game in suit. If a player holds both black Queens, the Spadilla and the Basta, he must either play a Solo suit game or call for an Ace. The player holding the Ace names trump other than the suit of the called Ace. *Forcée* games earn double points.

After everyone has bid or passed, the successful bidder names the game he will play, which can be of a higher value than the one agreed to in the bidding, but cannot be any lower. Then he calls color (Clubs) or suit, in which case he goes on to name the specific suit that is trump (Spades, Hearts or Diamonds).

The Play: The player to the left of the dealer leads to the first trick.

Players must follow suit if possible; otherwise they can play any card, trump or not. The trick goes to the highest trump or to the highest card in the suit led. The winner of each trick leads to the next.

The hand is abandoned as soon as the player who bid Frage or Solo takes five tricks. If he opts to continue, he *must* take all the tricks. In other words, continuing to play after he takes the fifth trick is a promise to make Tout. If he fails, he must pay the appropriate penalty.

The Score: Players tally scores individually at the end of each hand. Either the bidder and his partner win points, or, if the bidder doesn't make his bid, his opponents earn points. Players decide before the play begins what they will play to: 50 or 100 or whatever.

The game is usually played for stakes rather than scores. Winners earn counters from their opponents or pay up a certain amount per point if they fail to make their game. Debts are settled at the end of each hand.

Strategy: Much of the strategy of this game takes place during bidding rather than play. It is easy to be lured into making a higher bid than intended: beware of players who can tempt you beyond the limit of your cards. Tout hands are extraordinarily rare; Solo hands are possible, but should be bid on the basis of what is actually in hand, not relying on your as-yet-unnamed partner to supply a trick or two. For Frage, you should have three sure tricks in hand: the risk is low if you don't make it, and you can probably rely on your partner for one trick and the luck of the cards for the other. Remember that once play begins, if your partner seems to have a hand that perfectly matches yours, you can opt to go Tout halfway through the game, earning the benefit of the high stakes without taking the risk during bidding.

Variations: In traditional play, the suit made trump in the first deal remains the trump suit throughout the

---

game. This removes some of the interest from subsequent bids and leaves much of the pleasure of the game up to the luck of the deal.

Older versions also include a fourth game, the *Grossfrage*, or Big Question, which is like Frage except that the partner reveals himself as soon as the Ace is called. The partner names trump, which need not be the suit of the called Ace. If everyone passes, whoever holds the Spadilla must play the Grossfrage game. Frage and a forced Grossfrage score two points in suit, four in color; a bid Grossfrage wins four points in suit, eight in color.

Hearts Solo is a three-handed version played with a deck of 24 cards, made by removing the 8♥ and all the Diamonds but the 7 from the Solo deck. Diamonds (instead of Clubs) are always *color* but there are only three trumps in that suit: Spadilla, Manilla and Basta. The only game in the bidding is Solo. If no one makes that bid, the hand is played in color and the winner of the last trick loses the value of a Solo.   ∽

Solo

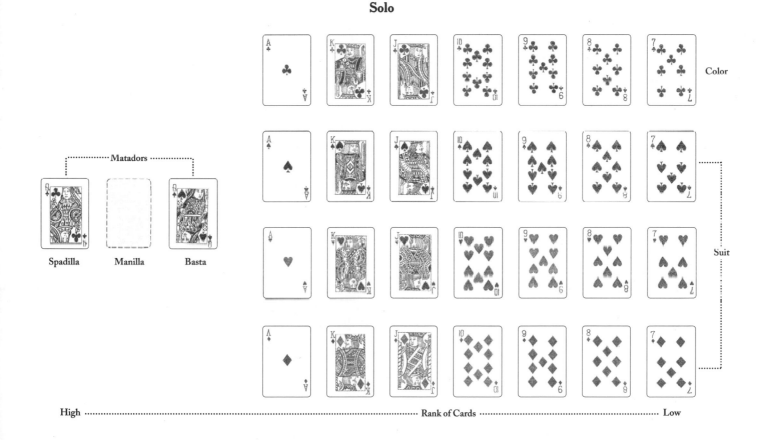

Skat

- **OTHER NAMES: American Skat**
- **NUMBER: three players only**
- **EQUIPMENT: a 32-card deck (a standard deck with 2-6 removed). Cards in the four suits rank A, 10, K, Q, 9, 8, 7; suits rank, high to low, Clubs, Spades, Hearts, Diamonds; Jacks, ranked by suit, form a fifth "grand" suit of highest trump; scorepad and pencil for scoring or poker chips as counters**
- **DESCRIPTION: a trick-taking, Jacks-high trump game like Euchre; several games within the game; certain cards are captured for points**
- **COMPLEXITY: comparable to Bridge in depth and complexity; exotic lexicon and intricate scoring procedure; hands down, the most challenging and strategically intriguing game for three**
- **DURATION: an hour or so**

FOUNDED in the early 19th century by the Brommesche Tarock Club in Altenburg, Skat is considered by many to be Germany's national card game. Altenburg to this day bills itself as "the birthplace of Skat." Aficionados play the game competitively in clubs and also as a family pastime. Indeed, it is popular throughout northern Europe. Skat emigrated to North America—the American Skat League was established in St. Louis in 1898—but the game on this side of the Atlantic differs significantly from its Teutonic forebear.

Skat evolved from two games: **Tarok,** which uses the Tarot deck, and Schapkopf, a very old Middle European game, which translates as "sheepshead." Like **Bridge,** Skat was quickly taken up by the university crowd, and during its first half-century or so was played in myriad variations. Its evolution was so swift and varied that players from different parts of the country, or even different card-playing circles within the same town, could hardly sit down for an afternoon of "Skat-bashing" (a few rounds of Skat) without spending an hour going through the rules first and agreeing on which would govern play.

When the Second Reich unified the Germans in 1871, Skat benefited from the harmonizing spirit. The First

National Skat Congress met in Altenburg in 1886 and agreed on a set of General Rules for German Skat. Nevertheless, the game continued to evolve. During the First World War, it moved from the study halls to the trenches, where it was simplified considerably. American Skat, the game described below, is further streamlined, but even it is played with local idiosyncrasies. Given Skat's resistance to codification, it may be useful, when sitting down for a game with people you've never played with before, to go through a brief checklist of the specific rules that will be followed.

The name of the game, Skat, is the German word for discard. It may also be a corruption of one of the Italian terms used in Tarok, *scart* or *scarto,* meaning what is left. Or it may come from the old Anglo-Saxon word *skatt,* meaning money, since the game is a favorite for gambling.

Skat, in fact, is not one game, but many. The three players bid on the right not only to name the trump suit (as in Bridge), but also to name the variation of Skat that will be played in that particular hand. These fall into two broad categories: if the object is to win tricks, it is called a *game;* if the object is to lose tricks, it is called a *nullo.*

Skat is an alliance game like **Hombre** and **Solo:** in each round, the

successful bidder becomes the Player and the other two join forces as the Opponent. Newcomers to this type of game are advised to play a few rounds of these simpler card games to become familiar with the notion before attempting the more complex Skat.

Indeed, Skat will seem like a catchall, with bits and pieces familiar from several other games: card values are the same as in **Pinochle,** the Jacks, or *wenzels,* are like the bowers in **Euchre,** and like **Piquet** and **Cribbage,** Skat is at least two games in one. It shares with **Klobiosh** an exotic lexicon, in this case, mainly Franco-Prussian. Don't let that put you off: once you know the lingo (much of it is immediately understandable to English-speakers) and have mastered the complex scoring system, Skat offers unprecedented three-handed card-playing mental exercise and fun. Like other French card games, it uses the 32-card deck (7 to Ace), but it is by far the best *mélange à trois.*

The Deal: Players each draw a card from the shuffled deck; low card deals. If two cards are of the same value, the rank of the suit decides the dealer. The player on the dealer's left in called the *Vorhand* (V), the next player is the *Mittelhand* (M) and the dealer is the *Hinterhand* (H).

M, to the right of the dealer, cuts the deck. The dealer gives each player in turn three cards, then lays two cards facedown on the table in front of him. This is the *skat,* in other games called the widow or the cat. The dealer then deals a round of four cards, followed by a round of three. At the end of the deal (which uses up all the cards), players each have 10 cards in hand and there are two in the skat.

Players arrange their cards by suit, ranking them high to low A, 10, K, Q, 9, 8, 7. Jacks are collected in their own "grand" suit, ordered according to suit rank: Clubs, Spades, Hearts, Diamonds.

The Object of the Game:
First, to become the Player, the person who, as the highest bidder, wins not

only the right to decide which Skat game is played, but also the chance to score. (Only one person, the Player, scores in each hand.) Once the game is named, the object is to take half the tricks, to capture enough high-value cards in tricks to win the game points and to earn the maximum in multiplier points.

Card-Value Points: In Skat, cards are valued as follows: an Ace is worth 11 points, a 10 is worth 10 points, a King is four points, a Queen is three and a Jack is worth two. The other cards—7, 8, 9—have no value. At the end of the hand, players add up the value of the cards they collected in tricks. The person who was the highest bidder must have a total of 61 points or more in order to win his game. Only then can he earn game points.

Multiplier points: The amount that any individual game is worth (see Scoring System) is increased by multiplier points to arrive at the Player's final score. Multiplier points are based on card values, tricks and the trump cards held in the hand before play began.

If the total value of the cards taken in tricks is 61 points or more, the Player earns 1 multiplier point. A total of 91 or more is a *Schneider*, and earns 2 multiplier points. If the Player announced before play began that he would make a Schneider, and he does, he earns 3 multiplier points.

Taking all the tricks is called a *Schwarz* (German for black). If the Player scores a Schwarz without predicting it, he earns 3 multiplier points. If he predicts a Schneider and scores a Schwarz, he multiplies the game value by 4. If he predicts a Schwarz and makes it, he multiplies the game value by 5.

The Player also scores multiplier points for *Matadors* (Spanish for killers). Matadors are trumps that follow in sequence from the Jack of Clubs (the highest trump) down. For instance, in the game illustrated, the dealer has bid and become the Player, making Diamonds trump. He holds the J♣ and J♠, but lacks the next

Scoring System: Skat

Card-Value Points

Ace	11
10	10
King	4
Queen	3
Jack	2
Total point value of cards in deck	120

Game Points

Games with trump suits

	♦	♥	♠	♣
Frage (skat picked up)	1	2	3	4
Tournée (skat turned)	5	6	7	8
Solo (no skat)	9	10	11	12

Games with only Jacks as trump

Ramsch (no skat, take no tricks)	10
Grand Tournée	12
Guckser (skat picked up)	16
Grand Solo	20
Grand Ouvert (no skat, hand exposed)	24

Games with No-trump

Gucki Nullo	15
Nullo	20
Gucki Nullo Ouvert	30
Null Ouvert	40

Multiplier Points

Making game (61 to 90 points in counter cards)	1
Schneider (91 points or more in counter cards)	2
Schneider announced and made	3
Schwarz (taking every trick)	3
Schneider announced, Schwarz made	4
Schwarz announced and made	5
Each Matador (with or without)	1

Per hand minimum (2)
Maximum (16)

Penalties

Failure to make a bid	bid entered as negative
Failed Second Turn Tournée	bid doubled, entered as negative
Failed predicted Schneider or Schwarz	multiplier total times failed game point, entered as negative
Looking at tricks other than the last	loss of 10 points

trump in sequence, the J♥, and therefore he is said to be playing "with two Matadors." He actually has six trumps altogether—J♣, J♠, J♦, plus the Ace, 10 and Queen of Diamonds—but only the two in sequence from the highest trump down count as Matadors.

If he also had the J♥, he would be playing "with six Matadors," since he would have an unbroken sequence from J♣ to 10♦. If J♦ was the Player's highest, he would be "without three Matadors" because there are three higher trumps—J♥, J♠ and J♣.

The Player receives a multiplier point for each Matador—each trump in sequence from J♣ down—that he is "with" or "without" at the beginning of play. (In the game illustrated, V gets two multiplier points for being

"with two Matadors" before play begins.) The Player will always get at least one Matador point, since someone will have the J♣, which amounts to a sequence of one. The maximum is 11 multiplier points for Matadors, since every trump suit potentially has 11 cards: J♣, J♠, J♥, J♦, A, 10, K, Q, 9, 8, 7.

At the end of a hand, all the multiplier points are added up and the value of the game that was played is multiplied by the total multiplier points to arrive at the successful bidder's final score. In any hand, there is a minimum of two multiplier points (1 for making game and 1 for a Matador) and a maximum of 16 multiplier points (11 for Matadors and 5 for a Schwarz announced and made).

The Games: Each of the games that can be played in Skat is valued individually according to risk and difficulty. (See the Scoring System on page 271.) Tournée and Solo are played with full trump suits; Ramsch Guckser and the "Grand" games use only Jacks (the fifth, Grand suit) as trumps; and the Nullo games are played with no trump. The skat, the two-card widow on the table, is used in different ways in each game.

Frage is the simplest game. The Player simply picks up the skat cards, adds them to his hand, names trump as he wishes, and discards two cards to the table. (The discards count toward the total value of his cards at the end of the hand.) The value of a *Frage* game increases from 1 to 4 points

Skat

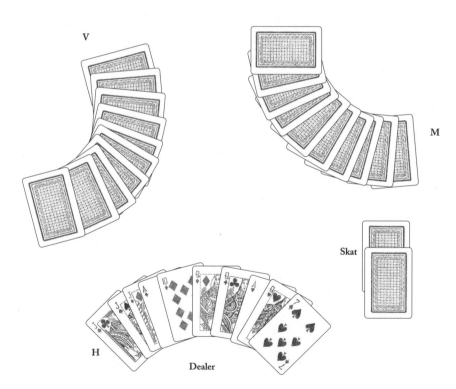

The New Games Treasury

depending on the rank of the suit named as trump.

In *Tournée*, the Player peeks at one of the skat cards, not letting the others see it. If he likes the suit, he displays it and this suit becomes trump. He then adds both skat cards to his hand and discards two to the table. (These are still considered the Player's cards and will be used to calculate the point total of his cards at the end of play.) The value of the Tournée game rises from 5 to 8 points according to the rank of the suit named as trump.

If the Player doesn't like the suit of the top card in the skat, he can add that card to his hand and turn over the remaining skat card for all to see, and that suit automatically becomes trump. This *second turn*, or *passt mir nicht tournée* as the traditionalists call it, is done at some risk: the downside of taking the second card is that the Player suffers double penalties if he fails to make his bid.

If the Tournée player turns up a

Jack on the first card, he can name a *Grand Tournée*, in which case only the four Jacks are trump and the game is worth 12 points. In all cases, both skat cards are added to the Player's hand and two are discarded to the table.

In the *Solo* game, the skat is ignored. The Player names trump and plays the hand without touching the skat. However, after the tricks are all taken, the value of the skat cards are counted toward the Player's point total. Solo is worth 9 to 12 points, according to the rank of the suit named trump.

The Player may, without looking at or adding the skat cards to his hand, name *Grand Solo*, playing with only Jacks as trump. Grand Solo is worth 20 points.

Guckser uses only Jacks as trump *and* allows the Player to add the skat cards to his hand, discarding two to the table before play. This is sometimes called *Gucki Grand* and is worth 16 points.

In *Nullo* or *Null*, the Player contracts

to lose every trick. It was introduced, apparently, as a consolation to players who are repeatedly dealt bad hands. No trump is called, the skat is not used and there are no multiplier points. (For that reason, a person who bids more than 20 cannot opt to play *Nullo*.) Usually, this game is played with the natural order of cards and no suit rank. Given the terrible hand one must have to win, Nullo games score very high: 20 for basic Nullo, 30 for *Gucki Nullo Ouvert* and 40 for *Null Ouvert*.

In *Ouvert*, as the name suggests, the Player exposes his entire hand before the first trick. In *Grand Ouvert*, he contracts to win all the tricks using only Jacks as trump. In *Null Ouvert*, the Player contracts to lose all the tricks using no trump. If a Player has bid more than 40, he cannot declare *Null Ouvert*.

Ramsch is played only when M and H (the dealer) have passed and V (the person on the dealer's left) must play the hand. The game is played with no

Skat

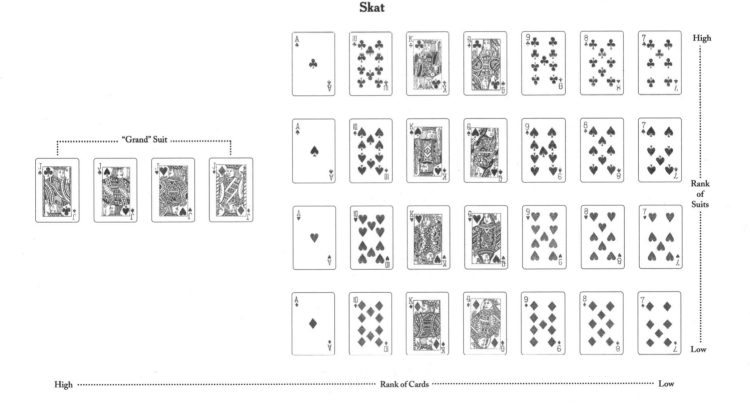

trump and the Player must not take any tricks. The skat cards are not used during play but go to the person who takes the last trick.

The scoring in *Ramsch* is somewhat different. The person with the fewest points is the winner and scores 10 points. If he takes no tricks, he scores 20. In the case of a tie among all three players, V gets 10. If two players tie for low points, the game and 10 points go to the one who did not take the most tricks taken by either. If someone loses all tricks at *Ramsch,* he loses 30 points.

Evaluation of the Hand:

Players evaluate their hands for a good potential trump suit, and on that basis decide which Skat game they are likely to win. Since the Player only earns game points if the value of his cards at the end of play adds up to 61 or more, hands must also be evaluated for high-value cards, both those held and those likely to be taken in tricks. Remember: the actual number of tricks doesn't matter, only the point value of the cards in them. In the illustrated hand on page 272, it is likely that H's Jacks, Diamonds and A♥ will all take tricks. These cards alone have a total point value of 41, so, together with the value of whatever cards he wins in tricks, he can be fairly sure of reaching the required point total of 61. Game points are increased by multiplier points, so hands are checked as well for Matadors and for Schneider and Schwarz potential.

Therefore, as each player looks at her hand, she must first decide which game she wants to play, what her chances are of winning it (i.e., can she take cards adding up to 61 points) and what her final score is likely to be when the game points are multiplied. This estimated final score is a player's top bid. When the hand is finally scored, the successful bidder must earn at least as many points as he bid; otherwise, the score is entered as negative and penalties may even be levied.

The Bidding:

Players bid for the right to name the type of game that will be played, and to name the trump suit, if necessary. They bid in turn and the highest bidder becomes the *Player*; the other two team up temporarily as the *Opponent.*

M (on the dealer's right) declares himself first. He can pass or name the number of points he expects to win. (Ten is the minimum bid; the highest practicable bid is usually around 100.) No game is named during the bidding.

V (on the dealer's left) says, "Yes," if she thinks she can match or exceed M's bid. M then has to increase his bid or pass. The bidding between M and V continues until one of them passes. Then H (the dealer) bids against the survivor, either naming a higher bid or saying, "Pass." If he names a higher bid, the survivor of the first bidding round either raises the bid or passes. The person who, in the end, makes the highest bid becomes the Player and names the game of Skat the three will play. (If everyone passes, the hand is thrown in and the deal passes to the left.)

The game can be any one of the Skat variations, so long as its point value is the same or higher than the Player's bid. Having deduced something of his opponents' hands from the bidding process, the Player may opt to name a different game than he originally had in mind.

The Play:

After the Player has named the game, picked up the skat, if appropriate, and discarded from his hand, play begins. Before the opening lead, however, the Player may attempt to increase his score by making a prediction (in effect, a contract): he can say he will Schneider (take at least 91 points) or he can say he will Schwarz (take all tricks).

V (on the dealer's left) leads to the first trick. The others play a card in turn, following suit if possible and, if not, discarding or playing trump. During a Grand game, if a Jack is led, players must follow suit with other Jacks since they are trump. Players are not obliged, however, to try to win a trick. The highest card of a suit takes the trick unless it is trumped, in which case, the highest trump takes the trick. (The rank of the suits has no bearing during play, except in establishing rank among the four Jacks.)

The winner of each trick leads to the next, until all cards are played. Tricks are kept separate and any player can look at the last trick taken only. Players who look at tricks other than the last one are penalized 10 points.

After the hand is scored, the deal moves to the left. Three hands (one deal per person) constitutes a round. Players agree amongst themselves how many rounds will be played before a winner is declared.

The Score:

In each hand, only the Player scores. To win the hand and score, the Player must take cards worth at least 61 points and the final value of his game (game points times multipliers) must be equal to or greater than his bid.

First, the Player adds up the point values of the cards in the tricks he took. To win his game, he must have a total of at least 61, which earns him 1 multiplier point for making game. If the total is 91 or more, he earns 2 multiplier points for a Schneider. If he predicted the Schneider and made it, he earns 3 multiplier points. If he took every trick (a Schwarz), he earns another 3 multiplier points. If he predicted the Schwarz and made it, he earns 5 multiplier points. He also figures out how many Matadors he held in his dealt hand.

The Player adds up all his multiplier points and multiplies the basic game-point value by the total (which is always at least two because of the game point and the Matador). If the result is more than the amount he bid, he scores the points. If he falls short, he loses the amount of his bid, which is entered on the scorepad as a negative number. If he fails to fulfill his predictions of Schneider or Schwarz, the multiplier total is used to calculate the penalty.

The exceptions to the above are *Nullo* and *Ramsch:* see the descriptions under "The Games" for scoring specifics.

Sometimes Skat is played for money. At the end of the final round, the scores are added up and the total divided in half to determine the median score. Players earn a penny a point for every point their score is above the median and have to pay a penny a point for every point their score is below the median.

Strategy: Skat is played on many levels as the game proceeds in stages through bidding and play. First to master is how to evaluate the hand, but equally important are how to bid successfully, how to play out the hand and, if you are not the Player, how to combine forces with the other opponent to defeat the Player.

In general, when bidding, go for a sure thing. Don't count on help from the skat: odds are against finding the card you need there. A doubtful Solo is generally safer than a risky Tournée. In bidding a Tournée, remember that the greater the strength of a suit in your hand, the less likely you are to turn up useful cards in the skat.

Typically, for a Tournée bid, the hand should contain at least one Jack with the other cards fairly evenly divided in three suits. With two Jacks, four suits of two cards each is acceptable, since you can discard two and make a void. Usually a Solo bid requires a five-card trump suit with at least two Aces or the Ace-King of a suit. Bidding Solo on four trump cards is not very safe, unless you have some side Aces. With six trumps and an outside Ace, however, H is safe making a Solo bid on the illustrated hand.

A Grand without trumps is relatively safe, provided you have the lead, two Jacks and two good suits, preferably two Aces. A Grand can also be bid without Jacks in hand if you have four Aces, or three Aces and four 10s.

There is risk, however, in all bids. A player who never bids unless absolutely safe is called a *Maurer*, one who only builds on a solid foundation. As the saying goes, you can't win if you don't play, and in Skat, that means taking the risk of making bids, because only bidders can score.

Good judgment in naming the game is almost as important as evaluating the hand correctly, since the point difference in naming a Frage in Hearts, for instance, when the hand could actually support a Tournée, means a huge difference in a Player's final score.

In play, don't consider the skat a trash pile: it is often better to discard valuable cards, since even as discards they still count toward your card point total. For instance, it would be better to discard an Ace or 10 if there is a danger that the opponents might take them. You might also discard the Ace and 10 if you have the King. When you play the King, an opponent might throw off a high-value card, thinking her partner will take the trick, when in fact you have already insured that the King is high. In general, discard unguarded 10s, which are unlikely to win tricks but which count well when the card point total is tallied. Try to make

voids wherever possible so you can trump into those suits.

If the Player has the lead, it is wise to lead trump to draw that suit out so that high cards in other suits will not be at risk later in the game. If you have a string of trumps, especially Jacks, it is common practice to start with the lowest and hope to lure your opponents into dumping valuable cards thinking their partner will take the trick. If you aren't the Player, beware of this strategic underplay. On the other hand, if the Player only has one Jack, the Ace, 10 and some smaller trumps, it is a good idea to play the small trumps to force out the high trumps and make your own cards valuable.

To defeat a Player, it is best if the Player is between his opponents, i.e., that the Player has the lead. In general, if you sit on the left of the Player and have the lead, lead a short suit up to him. If you sit on the right, lead long suits through him. Try to force him to play trump on your plain suit cards. If the Player is void in a suit, keep leading it, no matter what you hold. This will weaken his trump or, if your partner takes the trick, give your partner valuable discards.

Partners should try to protect one another's 10s by keeping Aces of plain suits. In other words, don't play an Ace as last hand to a trick that contains only small cards, if avoidable. ✄

Pitch

- OTHER NAMES: **Setback**
- NUMBER: **two to seven players; four or five is best; each plays for himself**
- EQUIPMENT: **one deck of 52, Ace high**
- DESCRIPTION: **a very old trick-taking game with trump; lots of fascinating variations**
- COMPLEXITY: **easy enough for conversation**

PITCH DEVELOPED from the old game of All Fours, whose name refers to the four principal points scored in the game: High Point (the highest trump), Low Point (the lowest trump), Jack Point (Jack of trump) and Game Point (taking the highest total in certain cards during play). The two-person variation of All Fours is known as Seven-Up; Pitch is the more popular multiplayer incarnation of the game.

The Deal: Cut the deck; high card deals. The dealer shuffles and deals six cards to each player three at a time, facedown, clockwise around the table. The rest of the deck is set aside. Players arrange their cards by suits.

Scoring System: Pitch

High Point: 1 point for *holding* the highest trump in that hand
Low Point: 1 point for *holding* the lowest trump in that hand
Jack Point: 1 point for *winning* the Jack of trump in that hand
Game Point: 1 point for *winning* the highest count in honor cards, any suit

Card Values	Points
10	10
Ace	4
King	3
Queen	2
Jack	1

Game is 7 points.

The Object of the Game: To score as many points as possible by capturing the Jack of trump and honor cards: A-K-Q-J-10 in any suit.

The Play: The player on the dealer's left establishes trump by *pitching* any card faceup onto the table. The other players must then follow suit, playing trump if they can. If they have no trump, they discard from a side suit. The highest trump takes the trick, and the winner of each trick leads to the next. Play continues with players following suit when they can and otherwise playing a trump card or discarding. The highest card of the suit led wins the trick unless it is trumped, in which case the highest trump card wins. Play continues until all the cards have been taken in tricks, then the points scored are added up, and the cards are shuffled and dealt for another hand. The game is over when one player reaches the target score.

The Score: At most, 4 points are scored at the end of each hand. The person who was dealt the highest trump card scores the High Point (1). The person who was dealt the lowest trump card scores the Low Point (1). The player who won the Jack of trump in a trick scores the Jack Point (1). At the end of the hand, the players add up the point value of the honor cards —A-K-Q-J-10 of all suits—in the tricks they took. The player with the highest honor-card total scores the Game Point (1).

If the honor-card count results in a tie, neither player scores the Game Point for that hand. The first person

to reach 7 wins, unless players agree in advance to play the game to 11 or 21.

Strategy: The Jack of trump may be buried, so don't count on a high trump garnering that extra point for you. Something worth remembering is that if the player making a pitch throws out a Jack and neither he nor anyone else has any other trump cards or honor cards, he can win 4 points with that single play: the Jack wins him the High Point, Low Point, Jack Point and Game Point—a rare but possible feat.

Variations: Auction Pitch is a little more demanding in that it includes bidding. Beginning at the dealer's left, players pass or bid depending on the number of points (1 to 4) they think they can make. The lowest bid allowed is usually two. The bidding moves clockwise around the table, each bid higher than the last. The final bidder (the dealer) does not have to top the third bid: he can take the same number and become the maker, provided the bid is less than four. If everyone passes, the deal is thrown in, shuffled and redealt. Otherwise, the highest bidder becomes the *maker* and names trump by pitching a card faceup onto the table. Play continues as above. In scoring, if the maker fails to make the number of points he bid, he is *set back* that many points, which may put him *in the hole* (a minus score).

In a variation called **Smudge,** a player who bids to win all 4 points says "Smudge." The dealer cannot take this bid away.

Pedro is a variation of Auction Pitch that replaces the Game Point for honor cards with a point for the 10 of trump. The 5 of trump, known as *Pedro,* also scores. Players bid for 9 possible points in each deal: High, Low, Jack and 10 of trump, each worth 1 point, and the Pedro, worth 5. All points are awarded to the person who wins that particular card in play. (In Pitch, players who are *dealt* the highest and the lowest trump cards score.) Pedro is bid and played like

Auction Pitch. A game goes to 21 points.

Originating in Denver, Colorado, around 1885, **Cinch** is like Pedro, except players are allowed to draw to improve their hands and there is yet another pay card added. The 5 of trump (*Right Pedro*) and the 5 of the same-color suit (*Left Pedro*) are each worth 5 points. Fourteen points are possible in each game: High, Low, Jack and 10 of trump for 1 point each and the Right and Left Pedros for 5 points each. Players are dealt nine cards, and they bid as in Auction Pitch, the bid going around only once. The successful bidder names trump, then players each throw three or more cards faceup onto the table. Three are discards; if he throws more, a player can draw from the stockpile to restore the hand to six cards. The player who names trump begins the play by leading any card. In play, the Right Pedro keeps its natural position and the Left Pedro is next highest in value, before the 4 of trump. Game is 51 points (or 61, if scored on a **Cribbage** board).   ∾

Euchre

- ◆ NUMBER: best with four players, as partners
- ◆ EQUIPMENT: a deck of 24, A-K-Q-J-10-9 of each suit; scored with 2s and 3s or with 5s
- ◆ DESCRIPTION: a game of tricks and trump, with limited strategy and no bidding
- ◆ TIP: fast and lighthearted; a good choice for after-dinner cards and conversation

THE ORIGINS of Euchre are less well defined than most card games, despite its relative youth. According to Mike Brandly, chairman of the National Euchre Players Association, research "strongly suggests Euchre originated in the United States . . . born of hearsay and piecemeal rules of Écarté and other various games played in Europe." One of these was almost certainly the Alsatian game of Jucker or Juckerspiel. The American version was first played in Pennsylvania in the 1850s and spread west with settlers. Within 20 years, over 65 percent of the American population—some 25 million people—knew how to play the game.

Euchre is characterized by a trump suit in which two cards supersede the Ace: the Jack of trump, called the Right Bower, and the Jack of the same-colored suit as trump, called the Left Bower. For instance, if Spades is trump, the highest card is J♠, the second highest is J♣, then A-K-Q-10-9♠. In some variations of the game, the highest trump of all is the Best Bower—the Joker. According to David Parlett in *A History of Card Games*, it was for Euchre that the Joker was invented, probably in the 1850s. The card was initially decorated with a tiger and called the Imperial trump. Only at the very end of the century was a Jester added to the court cards of a standard deck.

Cardplayers' manuals invariably specify a Euchre deck of 32 (Ace to 7), as in **Klobiosh** and **Piquet**, which mystifies those who already know how to play the game. "I have yet to meet or otherwise know of anyone who has ever played four-player partnership Euchre with anything but 24 cards," agrees Brandly, pointing out that books published in 1870 also dictate the larger deck. "It does force us to think 32 cards made the pack at some time in history." With 32 cards, 11 cards are buried in the stock; with 24, only three cards are out of play, making the game one of skill more than luck. Despite what other books say, this is the way Euchre is played today.

The Deal: Deal a card faceup to each player in turn until one person gets a black Jack: this is the dealer. The dealer shuffles the deck and deals five cards facedown to each player in groups of three, then two. The next card is turned up for trump. Players arrange their cards in sequence, high to low, within suits. In trump, cards rank Right Bower (Jack of trump), Left Bower (Jack of same-color suit), A-K-Q-10-9. In all suits except trump, cards rank A-K-Q-J-10-9 (unless the Jack is the Left Bower). For the sake of discussion, the player on the dealer's left is the First Hand, the next is the Second Hand, then the Third Hand (partner to the First) and the dealer, or Fourth Hand (partner to the Second).

The Object of the Game: With or without a partner, to win three of the five tricks in each hand; the first team to score 10 points wins.

The Trump: Starting with the First Hand, each player may pass or accept the turned-up card as trump. If a player accepts the trump, his team is obliged to win at least three of the five tricks. The First Hand and Third Hand accept the turned-up trump by saying, "I order it up." The Second Hand accepts it by saying, "I assist," and the dealer accepts it by saying, "I take it up." (Although the official Euchre laws do not mention it, many house rules specify that the dealer can make the turned-up suit trump only if she has a card of the same suit in her hand. For these purposes, the Left Bower is considered a same-suit card.) If the turned-up card becomes trump, the dealer picks it up and adds it to her hand, discarding another card facedown before play begins.

If no one accepts the turned-up card as trump, the dealer says, "I turn it down" and turns the card facedown.

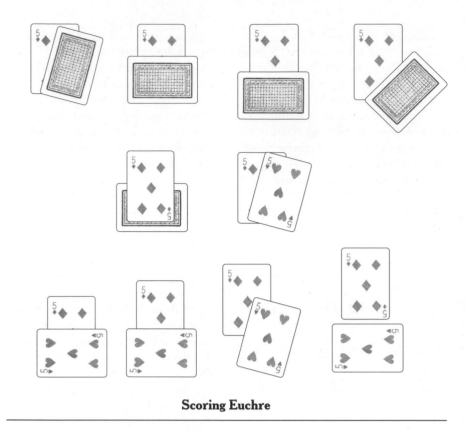

Scoring Euchre

Each player in turn then has the opportunity to pass or to make another suit trump, with the same obligation to take three out of five tricks. If everyone passes, the cards are thrown in for a redeal. The player who accepts or names trump is the *maker* and may offer to "go alone," in which case his partner lays her cards facedown, and the hand is played two against one. (Officially, only the maker can play alone, but according to some house rules, if one of the opponents has a particularly strong hand, he may say, "I defend alone," and the game is played one against one. Another common house rule specifies that once trump is established, if a player finds she has a hand with "no face, no Ace, no trump," she can ask for a new deal.)

The Play: The First Hand leads to the first trick. In a lone game, the player on the solo player's left leads. Players must follow suit if possible and either discard or trump if they cannot. Highest card of the suit led takes the trick unless it is trumped, in which case the highest trump takes the trick.

The winner of one trick leads to the next. The winner gathers the cards and lays each trick facedown in front of him overlapped so that players can readily count the tricks. Play continues until all five cards are taken in tricks.

Each team counts the tricks it won and scores its points, then the deal passes to the left, the cards are shuffled, and another hand is dealt. Several hands are played until one team reaches the target score.

The Score: Three tricks is the *point*. If the team that bid trump is successful in making its point, it scores 1; if it makes all five tricks—a *march*—it scores 2. (There is no extra score for making four tricks.) If a solo player makes her point, she scores 1; if she takes all five tricks, she scores 4. A lone defender wins 2 points for taking three tricks or 4 points for taking five. If the bidding team does not make its point, it is *euchred*, and the other team scores 2 points (see scoring system on the following page).

Euchre is traditionally scored with a 2 and a 3 of one suit or two 5s, laid across one another to expose pips that count 1 to 10, as illustrated.

Several hands are played in each game, which goes to 10 points. Euchre

is often played in rubbers, like **Whist** and **Bridge**. The team that wins the rubber (two out of three games) scores *rubber points*: 3 points if the losers scored 0 or 1; 2 points if the losers scored 2, 3, 4 or 5; and 1 point if the losers scored 6 or more.

Strategy: You can usually count on your partner to take one trick, so if you have two guaranteed tricks in your hand, it is appropriate to order up trump or to make trump in your best suit. Order up if you have any three trump cards or a duo of the Ace and any other card in that suit or the King and any other card. This varies somewhat according to which hand you are playing. The First Hand should hold three clear trump tricks, since if the trump is turned down, he has the first opportunity to make another trump. The dealer, however, should pick up the trump if at all possible.

If you have the lead and two or more cards in the trump suit, lead trump. Even if it doesn't take the trick, it will draw out four of the six possible trump cards on the first round, making your other trump cards the top cards in the game and certain trick-takers. Otherwise, lead a plain suit. Take a trick whenever you can: holding onto a high card in a suit that has already gone around once is a losing proposition. Most important, avoid doubling up your high trump— for instance, playing an Ace on the same trick on which your partner played a Bower. Early in the game, play a Bower if you have it so that your partner knows where it is.

Variations: Three-handed Euchre is often called **Cutthroat Euchre**. The maker always plays alone against the other two, who temporarily become partners. Scores are kept individually for each player. The maker scores 1 point for winning three tricks, 3 points for five tricks. If she is euchred, each of the other players scores 2 points. Two-handed Euchre can be played exactly like the game for four, but it is not a particularly engaging form of cards.

In **Railroad Euchre**, the Joker is

Best Bower, a higher trump than the Right Bower. If the Joker is the turn-up card, Hearts is automatically trump. If a player decides to go alone, she can discard one of her cards face-down and call for her partner's best card in exchange. When the Second Hand plays alone, the dealer may give him the turn-up card. In this version, a player who goes alone can lay his cards faceup on the table and allow his opponents to decide what he should lead or play. If he wins all five tricks, he scores 8 points—a *jambone*. If a player has a hand made up of the top five trump cards, he lays them down, declares a *jamboree* and scores 16 points. (The hand is not played out.) The jamboree inevitably puts the score over the 10 point game limit, so when a player scores a jamboree (or, in some cases, a jambone), the extra points over 10 are credited to the next game in the rubber.

In 1904, the United States Playing Card Company copyrighted **Five Hundred**, also known as Bid Euchre. An offshoot of Euchre in the direction of Bridge, Five Hundred includes Right, Left and Best Bowers. For three players, deal a 33-card deck (Ace to 7 in each suit plus the Joker), 10 cards to a player, in batches of three,

four and three. After the first round of the deal, lay three cards facedown in the center as the *widow*, then continue dealing until all the cards are used. There is no turned-up trump card.

Starting with the First Hand, players each have one turn to bid, naming a suit and a number of tricks: for instance, Six Spades or Seven Hearts. Each bid must overcall the last, which means it must have a higher scoring value, as illustrated in the scoring system below. The highest bid becomes the contract, and the other two players

become temporary partners against the maker. The maker adds the widow to his hand, then discards three cards. The hand is played in tricks, and the maker leads to the first trick. (If the maker bids no-trump, the Joker is the only trump card.)

If the maker takes the number of tricks he bid, he scores according to the table. If he takes all the tricks, he scores 250 or the value of the tricks he bid, whichever is more. If he fails to make his bid, the value of his bid is subtracted from his actual score in that hand. Whether the contract is made or not, each opponent scores 10 points for each trick he takes. The first player to reach 500 wins. In Five Hundred for four, a 43-card deck is used (a 52-card deck with the 2s, 3s and black 4s removed and the Joker added). For five-handed play, a full 52-card deck and a Joker are used. Odd numbers of players play for themselves; even numbers play as partners. ∽

<table>
<tr><td colspan="2">Scoring System: Euchre</td></tr>
<tr><td></td><td>Points</td></tr>
<tr><td>Point (bidding team takes 3 tricks) . . . .</td><td>1</td></tr>
<tr><td>March (bidding team takes 5 tricks) . . . .</td><td>2</td></tr>
<tr><td>Solo Point (lone player takes 3 tricks) . . . .</td><td>1</td></tr>
<tr><td>Solo March (lone player takes 5 tricks). . . . .</td><td>4</td></tr>
<tr><td>Euchre (defending team takes 3 or more tricks) . . . .</td><td>2</td></tr>
<tr><td>Solo Euchre:</td><td></td></tr>
<tr><td>   lone defender takes 3 tricks. . . . .</td><td>2</td></tr>
<tr><td>   lone defender takes 5 tricks . . . .</td><td>4</td></tr>
<tr><td>Rubber Points:</td><td></td></tr>
<tr><td>   losers score 0-1 . . . .</td><td>3</td></tr>
<tr><td>   losers score 2-5 . . . .</td><td>2</td></tr>
<tr><td>   losers score 6 or more . . . .</td><td>1</td></tr>
<tr><td>Game is 10 points.</td><td></td></tr>
</table>

Scoring System: Five Hundred

Number of Tricks	6	7	8	9	10
Spades	40	140	240	340	440
Clubs	60	160	260	360	460
Diamonds	80	180	280	380	480
Hearts	100	200	300	400	500
no-trump	120	220	320	420	520

Whist

- ◆ NUMBER: **four players as partners**
- ◆ EQUIPMENT: **one deck of 52, Ace high**
- ◆ DESCRIPTION: **the forerunner of Bridge, with trump but no bidding**
- ◆ COMPLEXITY: **easy to learn; skill improves with play**

WHIST IS THE grandparent of **Bridge**, and anyone who wants to become proficient at Bridge would do well to play a few hands of Whist first. In 1742, when Edmond Hoyle published his groundbreaking treatise on the game in London, England, he made his name famous among games players and started a British card craze that emigrated across the Atlantic. In 1767, Benjamin Franklin returned the favor: he took an American variation called Boston Whist to Paris, where it became a French fad.

The Deal: Cut the deck for partners: low cards play together and sit across from each other at the table; lowest card deals. (Ace is low for the cut.) The dealer shuffles and deals the entire deck one card at a time, facedown, until the last card, which he turns faceup. This is trump. When it is his turn to play to the first trick, the dealer adds the trump card to his hand, then plays a card to the trick.

The Object of the Game: To take more than six tricks in each hand; the first team to reach 7 points wins the game.

The Play: The person on the dealer's left leads to the first trick. The others must follow suit if they can. If a player cannot follow suit, she can play a trump card or discard from a side suit. The highest card of the suit led wins unless the trick is trumped, in which case the highest trump wins.

The winner of the trick gathers the cards together and turns them facedown in front of her; tricks won by both partners are kept together, overlapped so that everyone can easily count the tricks at a glance. No one may look at the tricks after they are turned facedown. The winner of each trick leads to the next.

Play continues until all cards have been taken in tricks. Partners then add up their tricks and record their scores. The deal passes to the left, the cards are shuffled, and a new hand is dealt. Several hands are played in each game.

The Score: There are 13 possible tricks in each hand. The first six tricks taken by a team are called a *book*. They count nothing, but each trick taken above a book—every *odd-trick*—scores 1 point. For instance, if a team takes six tricks, it scores zero; if it takes eight tricks, it scores 2 points. The first team to reach 7 points wins the game. Three games are usually played at a time: the winner of two out of three wins the *rubber*. After the rubber, players change partners.

There are several methods of scoring Whist. The British game is played to 5 points, a rubber is worth 2 points, and honor cards in the trump suit (in this case, A-K-Q-J, not the 10) contribute to the score of each game: 4 points for holding all four trump honors, 2 points for holding three.

Strategy: Because Whist requires a team effort to take tricks, the card you play serves two purposes: it takes the trick, and it gives your partner an idea of what you have in your hand so that she can more effectively play hers. Above all, you both want to avoid playing a high card on the same trick.

For the sake of discussion, the player who leads to the trick is the First Hand, the person on her left is the Second Hand, then the Third Hand (partner to the First) and the Fourth Hand (partner to the Second).

Although there are some basic rules of thumb for the game, there are also strategies particular to the position you are playing during each trick. Many of these have been adopted and elaborated in Bridge, but Whist is a good game in which to develop your team-tricks card sense. In general, keep the following in mind: return your partner's lead; Second Hand plays low; Third Hand, high.

Since the object of the game is to take tricks, the guiding principle is to make every card a trick-taking card. You can do this by getting higher cards out of the way or by making sure that players with high cards can't use them because you have the lead. Trump cards are useful not only in taking tricks but also as reentry cards— a way of regaining the lead at a strategic point in the game.

A fundamental strategy in both Whist and Bridge is the *finesse*, a play which might lose you the trick but which reveals information necessary to win future tricks. For instance, suppose your partner leads a 9. The player on your right follows suit with the 10. You hold the A-Q-J of the suit led. You don't know who holds the King. If you play by the Third-Hand-high rule, you will play the Ace, but if the Fourth Hand has the King and a low card to throw on the trick, you will never know whether your Queen and Jack are then safe. Instead, you finesse by playing the Queen: you will flush out the King if he has it, which means your Jack is good to take a trick later. If the player on your left doesn't play the King, you take the trick, and you've narrowed down the prospects for the owner of the King to your partner or the player on your right. Either way, you win, since they both play before you do, and you can save your Ace for the occasion.

When discarding from a side suit (neither following suit nor playing trump), try to create voids (no cards) in a particular suit so that you can trump if that suit is led. Never leave an Ace or a King unguarded as a singleton in a suit; always guard it with a lower card you can throw on the trick if your partner plays a high card. Keep reentry cards—trump cards and high cards in any suit—that will win you the lead and get you back in the game at strategic points. In general, discarding any small card tells your partner you are weak in that suit.

If you are the First Hand, lead a trump if you have five or more cards in the trump suit, regardless of what the rest of your hand is like. With three or fewer trump cards, never lead trump, unless your hand is very strong in all other suits. If it is, leading trump will draw out some of the powerful trump cards and make your other cards more playable. If you have four trump cards, lead them provided you have one other good suit and a reentry card.

Beginners should lead from their longest suit, unless they have a short four-card suit that includes very good high cards. By leading from a long suit, the high cards are siphoned off from the other players, making the lower cards valuable. A player can then use them to take tricks later in the game, provided he has high cards in his short suits to win him the lead. If you have a strong suit but neither trump cards nor reentry cards to support it, take your tricks while you can. Whenever a player holds two or more of the best cards in a suit, he should play one of them. If you hold the second and third best, playing one will force the best out of the way, leaving you with a trick-winning card.

If you have a long suit with sufficient high cards, you can lead from high to low, exhausting the other players' cards in the suit and continuing to take tricks with your lowest cards. This only works, of course, if the trump cards are gone: as soon as your opponents are void in the suit led, they will trump the trick. In general, then, it is safer to lead the fourth highest of your longest suit.

If you have the Ace and King of a suit, it doesn't matter, from a trick-taking point of view, which you lead. But the convention in Whist is to lead the King: this tells your partner that you have the Ace or the Queen or both. If you lead a Jack, you are telling your partner you have the Queen and King. There is only one time you lead a Queen: if you have the Queen, Jack and 10 but not the Ace and King. If you lead a 10, it means you have neither Ace nor Queen. If you lead an Ace, it means you have at least five cards in that suit or both the Queen and Jack.

Once you have led with a suit, stick with it. Scrambling from one suit to another is a sure sign of a beginner. Change suits only when you are forced to: because it is hopeless, and you have a better chance in another suit; because you want to lead a trump card to defend the rest of the cards in the suit; because you hold only high cards in that suit, and you want to avoid forcing your partner to play a high card on your lead.

If you are the Second Hand, the card you choose to play does not signal anything about your hand. If a 10 or higher is led, play low, unless you hold the Ace. If a Jack, 10 or 9 is led, try to take the trick if you have the King and Queen. If a low card is led, do your best to take the trick as cheaply as possible. If a low card is led and you have a short suit—for instance, Q-J-7— play the Jack or the Queen, since there is a chance the move might make your other high card good. If you only have cards below the Jack in the suit led, it is useless to try to win the trick, and it only complicates your partner's play if you play one of the higher cards. If you have cards immediately above and below the card led (a *fourchette*), play the higher card. If you have a void in the suit led, trump if the card led is the best of the suit or if you have a lot

of trump cards. If not, discard from a side suit, saving your trump to take a high card. Your partner may still take the trick, and you want to avoid wasting two good cards on one play.

If you are the Third Hand, when your partner leads high, follow suit as low as you can. When your partner leads low, try your best to take the trick as cheaply as possible. The Third Hand may finesse with a Queen if she holds the Ace and others in the suit. If you cannot follow your partner's lead, trump if he has played anything except a King or an Ace.

If you are the Fourth Hand, your duty as the person playing last is to take tricks whenever and as cheaply as you can. This position holds the least room for judgment. If you can't win the trick, play your lowest card.

Variation: In Auction Bid **Whist**, instead of turning up trump, each player announces the number of tricks he thinks his team can take during play. (Players do not declare trump, only tricks.) The bidding starts with the player on the dealer's left and goes clockwise around the table, each player raising the bid until three players pass in succession. The dealer may declare the same bid as the previous player, without raising it, and this then becomes the final bid. The person who makes the final bid—and takes the *contract*—declares the trump suit and leads to the first trick. (Trump need not be led.) If the bidder successfully makes his contract, his team's points are counted (1 point for each trick) and the other team's points are subtracted from the total, for the final score. If the bidder's team fails to take the number of tricks he declared, the bidding team scores zero, and whatever points the team earned for tricks taken are given to the opponents. ❧

Bridge

- ◆ OTHER NAMES: **formally known as Contract Bridge**
- ◆ NUMBER: **a game for four players, often called North, South, East and West; played in partners (N-S versus E-W)**
- ◆ EQUIPMENT: **a scorepad, a pencil and a deck of 52, Ace high; suits rank (high to low) Spades, Hearts, Diamonds, Clubs**
- ◆ COMPLEXITY: **easy to learn—the basics can be grasped in an hour—but complex to play**
- ◆ TIP: **the more you learn, the more fun it can be**

WHIST DEVELOPED into Bridge in 1896, then Auction Bridge in 1904 and Contract Bridge in 1925. By the end of World War II, it was the most-played card game in the United States. Although Bridge Clubs are no longer the mainstay of the middle class, the game persists not only because it is challenging but because it can be played and enjoyed at the most elementary level as well as the most advanced. Even adults who are unfamiliar with the basic rules of cards can be playing a passably good game of Bridge within an hour.

At its most professional, Bridge is extremely complex, with a language of communication that allows partners to tell each other what they hold while they bid. Not everyone aspires to that sort of game, but even for duffers, a few words of basic Bridge are worth learning in order to make the rules and conventions clear. A *rubber* is two games; the *book* is six tricks taken during one hand; an *odd-trick* is every trick over six taken in a hand; an *over-trick* is each trick a team takes over the number it has contracted to take.

Suits are *ranked* from high to low as Spades, Hearts, Diamonds and Clubs. The two lowest suits, Clubs and Diamonds, are the *minor suits*, and the two highest, Hearts and Spades, are the *major suits*. A *balanced hand* has the four suits in a pattern of 4-3-3-3 (four cards in one suit, three cards in each of the other three suits), 4-4-3-2 or 5-3-3-2. A *singleton* is a card that is the only one in a suit; a *doubleton* is only two cards in a suit. No cards at all

in a suit is a *void*, or a *blank suit*. An unbalanced hand contains a void or a singleton in one or more suits: for instance, 5-5-2-1 (which contains a singleton and a doubleton) and 5-4-4-0 (which contains a void) are both unbalanced.

The Deal: The shuffled deck is spread, and players draw for partners; the two people drawing the highest cards play together. Highest card deals. The dealer shuffles the deck and deals all the cards, one at a time, facedown. Each player receives 13 cards and arranges them in sequence (Ace high) within suits.

The Bidding: The hand is played out in tricks, and there are 13 tricks in each hand. Six tricks are a team's book, for which it earns nothing. Every odd-trick (every trick over six) scores. During the bidding stage of Bridge, each player specifies the number of tricks over six he undertakes to win with the help of his partner, at the same time naming one suit as trump or declaring no-trump. In making the bid, only odd-tricks are named. For instance, a bid of One Diamond is a bid to win one trick over book (seven tricks in total) with Diamonds as trump.

The players evaluate their hands for trick-taking potential (see Evaluating the Hand, page 284). Then the dealer begins: he either *passes* or *opens the bidding*. Moving clockwise around the table, each player in turn passes or makes a *sufficient bid*, naming either a greater number of tricks or the same

number of tricks in a higher suit than the previous bid. (No-trump is a higher bid than any suit.) For instance, when four players bid One Club, One Diamond, One no-trump and Two Diamonds in succession, each bid is higher than the last.

A player can *double* a bid made by the other team. As in **Poker**, this raises the stakes of the game: the team that made the original bid will score double the trick points plus a bonus if it makes its contract. However, if it fails, the team that doubled the bid scores a bonus. There are two kinds of double: a *penalty double*, which a player makes when he expects his team can defeat the opponents' contract, and a *take-out double*, which a player makes before his partner has bid. The latter is simply Bridge shorthand for asking his partner to name his best suit. A player doubles only an opponent's bid, never his partner's.

Doubling changes the scoring and increases the risk, but it does not change the actual bidding procedure. For instance, if the dealer bids Two Diamonds and the next person doubles, the third can make a sufficient bid with Three Diamonds and thus cancel the previous double. A team that has been doubled can, in its next turn, *redouble* its own bid. This doubles the trick points again and increases the bonus (and the penalty). Such a redoubling signifies that the player is confident his team can make its contract. A bid can be doubled and redoubled only once.

If all four players pass, the cards are thrown in for a new deal. Once the bidding opens, it doesn't end until three consecutive players pass. The last bid becomes the *contract*. The player who first named the suit on the successful bidding team becomes the *declarer*. The declarer's partner is the *dummy*.

The Object of the Game: To win the number of tricks bid or more.

The Play: The player on the declarer's left leads to the first trick,

Trick Points (scored by the declarer below the line)   Points

Each odd-trick bid and made in ♦ or ♣. 20

Each odd-trick bid and made in ♥ or ♠. 30

First odd-trick bid and made in no-trump 40

Subsequent odd-tricks bid and made in no-trump 30

If bid was doubled, multiply trick score by two.

If bid was redoubled, multiply trick score by four.

Game is 100 trick points.

Overtrick Points (scored by the declarer above the line)

Each trick over contract in ♦ or ♣:

undoubled . . . . 20 (20 if vulnerable)

Each trick over contract in no-trump or ♥ or ♠:

undoubled . . . . 30 (30 if vulnerable)

Each trick over contract in any suit:

doubled . . . . 100 (200 if vulnerable)

redoubled . . . . 200 (400 if vulnerable)

Undertrick Points (scored by the defender above the line)

Each undertrick, undoubled . . . . 50 (100 if vulnerable)

First undertrick, doubled . . . . 100 (200 if vulnerable)

Each subsequent undertrick, doubled . . . . 200 (300 if vulnerable)

First undertrick, redoubled. . . . . 200 (400 if vulnerable)

Each subsequent undertrick, redoubled. . . . . . . 400 (600 if vulnerable)

Bonus Points (scored by the declarer above the line)

Small Slam:

(6 odd-tricks bid and made). . . . . 500 (750 if vulnerable)

Grand Slam:

(7 odd-tricks bid and made). . . . . 1,000 (1,500 if vulnerable)

Rubber Bonus:

if the opponents won 1 game 500

if the opponents won no games 700

Honors Points (scored by either team above the line)

Four trump honors in one hand 100

Five trump honors in one hand. 150

Four Aces in one hand (no-trump bid). 150

playing any card he chooses. After the card is led, the dummy lays down her hand faceup on the table, the cards grouped in suits, with trump cards on the player's right. The declarer plays both his own hand and the dummy's, laying cards on the tricks in the proper order during each turn.

Moving clockwise around the table, each player plays a card to the one led. Players must follow suit if possible, but if they have a void, they may trump or discard from a side suit, as they choose. The highest card of the suit led wins unless trump cards were played, in which case the highest trump wins. The winner of the trick gathers the cards and turns them facedown in front of her, overlapping tricks so that they can be easily counted by all players. Partners keep their tricks together. The winner of one trick leads to the next, until all 13 cards are played.

A card, once played, cannot be withdrawn. The declarer plays a card from the dummy hand when he touches it or names it. For the other three hands, a card is played when it is shown or named.

The Score: In Bridge, tricks are scored according to the trump suit. If a minor suit (Clubs or Diamonds) is trump, each trick bid and won over six counts 20 points. If a major suit (Hearts or Spades) is trump, each trick bid and won over six counts 30 points. In no-trump, the seventh trick scores 40 points, and each additional trick bid and won scores 30. If the bid was doubled, the score is multiplied by two; if the bid was redoubled, it is multiplied by four. If the declarer fails to make his contract, each trick less than the number bid is called an *undertrick*. The opposing team—the defenders—scores 50 points for each undertrick, the stakes rising rapidly if the bid was doubled or redoubled.

Bridge uses a special scorepad with a separate column for each team and a horizontal line across the center, as illustrated opposite. The trick points just described are entered *below the line*, and the bonus points (awarded for overtricks) are entered *above the line*. For instance, in the score sheet illustrated, We bid Two Spades in the first hand and took three odd-tricks. Two odd-tricks were recorded below the line (30+30 = 60), and the overtrick (30) was recorded above the line. In the next hand, They bid and made Three no-trump, taking the required three odd-tricks for a score of 100 (40+30+30) below the line. They won the game, so a line is drawn below the score before another hand is dealt.

The first team to score 100 trick points wins the *game*, and a single line is drawn below the score. With the next hand, the teams start again at zero. A team that has won one game is considered *vulnerable*, which ups the ante for bonus points. Play continues until one team wins two games, thereby winning the rubber. After the rubber, a double line is drawn under the score. Each column, both above and below the line, is added up, and the lower total is subtracted from the other to determine the margin of victory.

As well as scoring for tricks, a team

that bids and wins six odd-tricks earns a bonus of 500 points (750 points if the team is vulnerable) for a *small slam*. If it bids and wins seven odd-tricks (which means taking all 13 tricks), it scores a 1,000-point bonus for a *grand slam* (1,500 points if the team is vulnerable). There are also *honors points*, a bonus for holding four or five honor cards (A-K-Q-J-10) of the trump suit in one hand or all four Aces if the final bid is no-trump.

Evaluating the Hand:
To make a reasonable bid, players must be able to evaluate their hands for trick-taking potential. Various systems have been developed to facilitate this evaluation, but the most common used in the United States is the *point-count system* created by Charles H. Goren. The following will get you started; for a thorough introduction to the complexities of evaluating a Bridge hand, read *Point Count Bidding* or *Contract Bridge for Beginners* by Charles H. Goren, published by Simon and Schuster, New York.

Goren's system awards points for certain valuable cards and combinations of cards: the point total guides your opening bid and your response to a partner's bid. (See Point-Count Bidding on the following page.)

First, count your *high-card points*, awarding 4 points for each Ace, 3 for each King, 2 for each Queen and 1 for each Jack. If the high-card points add up to a total that is borderline for an opening bid, give yourself points for *quick tricks*: the Ace-King of a suit is worth 2; the Ace-Queen is worth 1½ (because the Ace is a certainty, but your Queen will be good only if the King is played in the same trick as the Ace); the Ace alone or the King-Queen is worth 1; and the King with any small card is worth ½, since you may be able to make the King good by throwing off the other card on the Ace.

The *distribution points* (points for the number of cards in each suit) are counted differently depending on whether you are making an opening bid or responding to your partner's bid. For an opening bid, count 3

points for a void, 2 for a singleton and 1 for a doubleton. If you have all four Aces, give yourself an extra point; if you have no Aces, deduct a point. Deduct a point, too, for each un-guarded honor card (Ace to 10 without sufficient low cards to discard against higher face cards so that you can save the face card until it is the highest in the suit).

When you are responding to a bid, a void is worth 5 points, a singleton is worth 3 and a doubleton counts 1. If you have honor cards in your partner's bid suit, give yourself a point. Deduct a point if you have only three trump cards or if your hand is evenly split between suits. (A suit distribution of 4-3-3-3 is a liability, since you are not likely to create a void in which you can play a trump.)

For opening bids, use the following rules of thumb. You should have at least 12 or 13 points and two quick tricks to bid *One*. You can bid *Two* if you have 21 points with a good seven-card suit, 23 points with a good six-card suit, 24 points with two good five-card suits or 25 points with one good five-card suit. An opening bid of Two is a *forcing bid*: you are telling your partner not to pass until a game contract is made.

For no-trump opening bids, count only high cards. To bid One no-trump, you should have 16 to 18 points with a balanced distribution of suits and with a Queen or better in the doubleton. With a balanced hand of 22 to 24 points, you can bid Two no-trump, and with 25 to 27 points, bid Three no-trump, but in both cases, you should have *stoppers* in each suit. (A stopper is a trick-winning card that returns the lead to you: Aces are stoppers on their own, while Kings, Queens and Jacks are stoppers only if you have one, two or three other cards, respectively, to discard when higher cards are played so that the stopper becomes good.)

In general, when making an opening bid, bid your longest suit. If two suits are equal, bid the one with the highest points. Any five-card suit is biddable, but in order to make an opening bid for trump in a four-card

Bridge Scorepad

Goren's Point-Count Bidding System

High-Card Points   Points

Ace. 4

King 3

Queen 2

Jack. 1

Quick-Trick Points

A-K in one suit 2

A-Q in one suit. 1½

K-Q in one suit 1

Ace 1

K + any card in the suit . . . . ½

Distribution Points

Opening Bids:

void. 3

singleton 2

doubleton 1

4 Aces 1

no Aces . . . . -1

each unguarded honor card. . . . . -1

Responding Bids:

void. 5

singleton 3

doubleton. 1

honor card in partner's bid suit 1

3 cards or less in partner's bid suit . . . . -1

balanced hand . . . . -1

Point Totals

Minimum Hand 13-16

Good Hand 16-19

Very Good Hand 19-21

For an Opening Bid of:

One =	12-13 points + two quick tricks
Two =	21 points + seven-card suit
	23 points + six-card suit
	24 points + two five-card suits
	25 points + one five-card suit
One no-trump =	16-18 points + balanced hand
Two no-trump =	22-24 points + balanced hand
Three no-trump =	25-27 points + balanced hand

suit, you should have 4 high-card points.

Two players make opening bids; the other two players either pass or respond to their partners' bids by raising the bid in the same suit, making a higher bid in a new suit or making a bid in no-trump. For instance, if North bids One Diamond, South could respond with Two Diamonds or One Spade. To respond to your partner's bid, you should have at least a five-card suit or a four-card suit with an Ace, a King or a Q-J-10. Let your point-count total be your guide. If you have less than 10 points in your hand, raise from One to Two if the opening bid was in a major suit and you have adequate trump support. If the opening bid was in a minor suit, respond in a new suit at the One level. (This gives your partner the opportunity to raise the opening bid to Two himself.) If you have 11 or 12 points, raise to Two in the same suit. If you have 13 to 16 points and at least four trump cards, raise to Three. If you have 9 high-card points or less but at least five trump cards and a singleton or a void, raise to Four. If you have 13 points or more, keep the bidding going until your team reaches a game contract. If you have 19 points, try for a slam.

If you don't have good cards in your partner's suit but have four or more cards in another suit with a total of 6 to 10 points, switch to a new suit but keep at the One level. With 11 to 17 points, you can bid Two of a new suit, and with 18 or more, you can jump to Three in another suit.

With a balanced hand of 6 to 9 points, the usual response to an opening bid of One is One no-trump. Go to Two no-trump with 13 to 15 points and Three with 16 to 18 points, provided you have stoppers in all suits and a 4-3-3-3 distribution among the suits. If the opening bid was One no-trump, raise to Two if you have 8 or 9 points, Three with 10 to 14 points, Four with 15 or 16 points, Six with 17 or 18 points and Seven with 21 points, provided that in each case, your hand is balanced.

An opening bid of Two is a demand to keep the bidding open until a game contract is reached. If a partner has less than 7 points, he should respond Two no-trump no matter what he has: this indicates his hand is almost worthless. With 7 or more points and one quick trick, he should respond Three in the opening suit or Two in a high-ranking suit. With 8 or 9 high-card points, a balanced hand and more than one quick trick, he should respond Three no-trump, which means he has a good hand.

An opening bid of Three, Four or Five is a *preemptive bid*, usually based on a good suit of seven cards or more. This bid declares that you have less than 10 high-card points and are over-bidding by two or three tricks. To raise such a bid, a partner should have Aces and Kings and at least one or two trump cards. An opening bid of Three no-trump indicates 25 or more points, so the responder should bid higher only if he thinks the team can make a slam.

After a team's opening bid and the partner's first response, the opening bidder, or opener, *rebids*, often the most important bid of the bidding. Remember that 13 to 16 points is a minimum hand, 16 to 19 points is a good hand, and 19 to 21 points is a very good hand.

If the opener holds a *minimum hand* and the partner has made a limit re-sponse (a single raise or One no-trump), the opener should pass, since the team probably can't win a contract. If the partner bid a new suit at the One level, the opener can raise to Two if he has good support in the partner's trump, or he can rebid Two of his own suit, One no-trump or One of a new suit.

If the opener has a *good hand* and his partner has made a limit response (a single raise or One no-trump), he can rebid, jumping a raise in his own suit if he has six trump or in his partner's suit if he has four trump, or he can bid a new suit.

If the opener has a *very good hand* and his partner made a limit response of a single raise or One no-trump, the opener can jump to *game* (as many points as the team needs to reach 100) in either his suit or his partner's, depending on his distribution of suits.

Normally, between two partners, 26 points produces a game, 33 points produces a small slam and 37 points produces a grand slam. If you think you have the points, go for it. There are various conventions by which partners can figure out whether the other has a certain number of Aces or specific Aces, but this wades into the intricacies of advanced Bridge. The preceding instructions should be enough to get you started and keep you playing until you decide whether your interest in the game warrants a detailed Bridge manual.
❧

Poker

◆ NUMBER: **from 2 to 14 players; 5 or 6 makes a good table; 7 or 8 is considered ideal; each player plays for himself**

◆ EQUIPMENT: **standard deck of 52, usually Ace high (one or more Jokers sometimes added as wild cards), and counters**

◆ DESCRIPTION: **relaxing and challenging; can be played for serious stakes or just for fun**

MANY POKER players insist that they play for the cards, not the cash: the stakes are a means of measuring skill. Certainly, money adds pressure and piquancy to the play. Some families keep a jar of pennies for the purpose; others use candies or beans. It doesn't really matter. The games by themselves are fun, and if you like playing cards, don't bypass this large family of games. Poker variations abound, but the principles of them all are much the same. Once you know the values of the Poker hands and the betting procedures, the idiosyncrasies of individual games take only a few minutes to grasp.

The Deal: Because money is usually involved, the rules for shuffling and dealing Poker are strict, designed to foil would-be cheaters. At the start of a game, any player shuffles the deck and deals the cards faceup, one at a time, to each player around the table until a Jack is turned up, designating the dealer of the first hand. Thereafter, the deal passes to the left around the table.

Any player can ask to shuffle the deck before the deal. It should be shuffled three times altogether; the dealer shuffles at least once and always has the last shuffle. The player on the dealer's right cuts the shuffled deck. If he chooses not to, any other player may do so. If more than one want to cut the deck, the player nearest the dealer gets the chance. If any card is exposed during the cut, the deck is reshuffled and recut. The deck is cut only once after the shuffle.

The dealer distributes cards from the top of the deck, one at a time, beginning with the player on her left and moving clockwise around the table, ending with herself.

The Poker Hands: Each Poker hand has five cards. The value of each hand is as follows:

Straight flush is the highest hand; all five cards of the same suit and in sequence: for instance, Q-J-10-9-8♥. The highest straight flush is A-K-Q-J-10 of one suit, called a *royal flush*. For a straight flush beginning with 5, the Ace can be counted as 1, so the lowest straight flush is 5-4-3-2-A of one suit. (In games with wild cards, a straight flush loses to five of a kind, where the wild card makes the fifth card.)

Four of a kind ranks under a straight flush. The higher the denomination, the more valuable the four of a kind. (In games with wild cards, two players can hold the same four of a kind, in which case the highest fifth card in the hand determines the winner.)

Full house is three cards of one denomination, two of another: for instance, 5♦-5♥-5♣-J♦-J♠. The player with the higher-ranking three of a kind wins. (With wild cards, if two three of a kinds are the same, the higher pair wins.)

Flush is five cards in the same suit but not in sequence: for instance, A-K-J-8-3♣. Between two flushes, the one with the higher card wins; if the highest card in each hand is the same, the next highest card wins, and

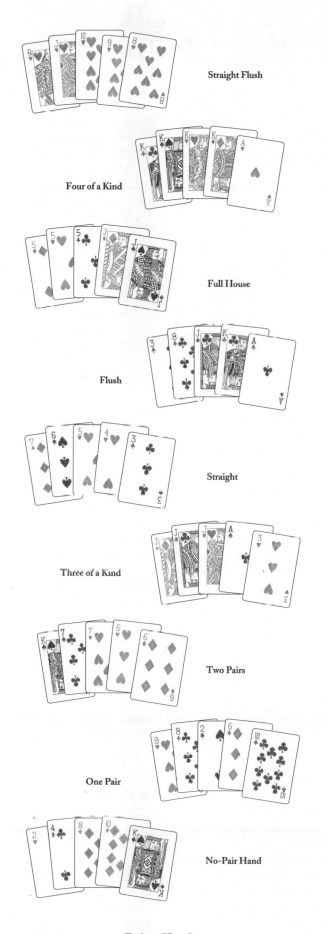

Straight Flush

Four of a Kind

Full House

Flush

Straight

Three of a Kind

Two Pairs

One Pair

No-Pair Hand

Poker Hands

so on. (Four cards of the same suit are called a *four flush* or, sometimes, a *bobtail*.)

Straight is five cards in sequence but not all from the same suit: for instance, 7♦-6♠-5♥-4♥-3♣. A straight loses to a flush but beats pairs and three of a kind. For a sequence beginning with 5, Ace may be used as low. The straight starting with the highest card wins. (An *inside straight* is four cards broken in the middle, so it needs a fifth card on the inside to make a straight. A *bobtail straight* is four cards in a sequence that can become a straight if a card at either end is drawn. For instance, 9-8-6-5 is an inside straight; 8-7-6-5 is a bobtail straight, but A-K-Q-J is not.)

Three of a kind is better than a pair but not as good as a straight. The highest denomination wins. (With wild cards, if the denominations are the same, the higher unmatched card wins.)

Two pairs are better than one but not as good as three of a kind. The highest pair wins. If both are the same, the higher unmatched card wins.

One pair beats a random hand. The higher pair wins, or if they are the same, the higher unmatched card wins.

No-pair hands are ranked by the highest card they contain. If two hands contain the same highest card, the second highest card determines the winner.

The Betting: Before starting a game, players set betting limits—the minimum and maximum bets allowed in the game. It can be anything from a penny to a dollar or more. If three figures are mentioned—5¢, 10¢ and 15¢ —the first is the ante and the opening bet, and the others are the minimum and maximum bets after the draw. Sometimes, players set a *pot limit*, which means a player may, at any time, bet an amount up to the total in the pot.

Often, the betting starts before a hand is dealt. Players have to *ante*, or make an initial contribution to the pot, before the game begins. The ante is usually the minimum bet allowed.

In the course of each hand of Poker, there are one or more *betting rounds* in which a player can bet on the cards in his hand. In each betting round, a player is designated as the first bettor (according to the rules of the particular game). Moving clockwise around the table, each player bets only in his turn.

Each betting round begins when the first bettor makes a bet or *checks*— a bet of nothing, which allows a player to remain in the game without risking any counters. After the first bettor has put her money in the pot, each subsequent player either *calls* the previous bet by putting in an equal number of counters or *raises* the bet by putting in more. (A player may check only if no one before him has bet in that betting round.) A player may also *drop*, which means she discards her hand or *folds*, dropping out of the game and automatically forfeiting any counters she has added to the pot up to that point. The principle is, if you want to stay in the game, you have to put into the pot at least as many counters as the last player put in.

Each player announces whether he is checking, calling or raising and, if so, by how much, then he puts his counters in the center of the table. The betting round ends when all the active players—players who have not folded—have put the same number of counters in the pot. Sometimes, everyone in a betting round checks: no money is put in the pot, and the next round of play begins.

For each Poker hand, there are usually two or three betting rounds, separated by rounds of play during which players improve their hands by exchanging or drawing cards. After the final betting round, each player who is still in the game shows her hand faceup on the table in a *showdown*. The best Poker hand takes the pot. If two or more hands tie for the pot, they divide it evenly, the odd counter going to the player who bet last.

If, at any time during the hand, a player makes a raise that no other player calls, he automatically wins the pot, without showing his hand.

The Object of the Game:
To win the poker pot (all bets made by the players in one deal).

Strategy: "Know when to hold 'em; know when to fold 'em," sang Kenny Rogers. It is good advice and is the key to success in Poker.

The value of each Poker hand is based on mathematical probability. There are 2,598,960 possible Poker combinations in a 52-card deck. The less likely you are to be dealt a particular hand, the higher it ranks and the more it is worth. For instance, the odds that a cardplayer will be dealt a straight flush are 1 in 65,000. But you are likely to get two pairs once in every 21 hands, and your hand will hold a pair about 50 percent of the time. Poker is a numbers game, and if you want to play it that way, you should study the probabilities in a book such as *Scarne on Cards* (Crown Publishers Inc., 1965).

But Poker can also be fun for those who are neither mathematical geniuses nor neophyte sharks. Although Poker has a high-risk reputation, it is a game where conservatism pays, especially for beginners. In general, *stay in* only if you think you have the best hand. You can, of course, *bluff*, betting on a hand which you know is not the highest, in the hopes that the other players will believe you are unbeatable and will drop out. Bluffing is a time-honored tradition in Poker and the origin of the expression poker-faced. If you have nothing in your hand, drop out. You may start with good cards, but if, on the next deal, your cards are clearly beaten by the exposed cards of the other players, drop out. Don't pray for a better card on a future deal. Count the cards that are exposed and the number that are buried, and if you calculate you have a 1 in 26 chance of getting what you need, drop out. On the other hand, as they say, if you get 'em, bet 'em. When you have a good hand, make the others pay to see it. Many serious Poker players rely as much on intuition as arithmetic: play a winning streak, but if the streak is a losing one, drop out.

There are two main types of Poker:

Draw Poker (closed Poker) and *Stud Poker* (open Poker). They require slightly different strategies. In Draw Poker, if you aren't dealt a pair, a four-card straight or a flush or better, drop out: the draw improves only a hand that has some potential. As a rule, if you have a pair above a 10 in the hand, stay in the game.

Serious players tend to prefer Stud Poker, since it has more betting rounds and demands more strategy. In general, if, on the first deal, the card *in the hole* (dealt facedown) is under 10, fold unless your faceup card makes a pair. If you have a face card or an Ace in the hole, make the minimum opening bet. In the next deal, if any player has an exposed pair and you don't, fold. Never play a hand that is lower than the exposed hands of the others. Remember that the chances of being dealt a pair in a hand of five cards is about one in two, so the winning hand at the table will inevitably have a pair or better. Don't play for a flush because you hold three cards of a suit: your chances are only 1 in 24. If your hand is uncertain, check, if possible, or fold. You won't lose much by folding early in the game, since the serious betting usually takes place in the last few rounds.

DRAW POKER: Players are dealt five cards each, facedown, one at a time. After the deal, there is a betting round. The player on the dealer's left is the first bettor. When the betting round is over, each player in turn, beginning with the active player to the dealer's left, discards one or more cards. From the top of the deck, the dealer deals her as many cards, facedown, as she discarded. This is the *draw*. A player may opt to *stand pat* and receive no new cards. There is another betting round after the draw, followed by the showdown.

In **Jackpots**, each player antes before the deal. After five cards are dealt facedown, each player, starting with the person to the dealer's left, has the right to *open* (make the first bet) or pass. A player may not open unless he has a pair of Jacks or a hand that would beat a pair of Jacks in a showdown. If no one opens, everyone antes, the deal passes to the next player, and a new hand is dealt. If a player opens, the first betting round has begun, and the rest of the players, in turn, drop, call or raise. The betting round ends. Before the first player discards, he must *show openers*, revealing only enough of his hand to prove that he had sufficient cards to open. After the draw, there is another betting round, followed by the showdown, when all the players reveal their hands.

Progressive Jackpots adds the rule that if no one opens on Jacks, on the next deal, Queens or better are needed to open; if no one opens on Queens, then Kings or better are needed, and so on, until someone opens.

High-Low is played exactly like Jackpots, except Jacks or better are not needed to open the pot and, in the showdown, the pot is divided equally between the two players with the highest and the lowest hands.

Deuces Wild is a regular game of Jackpots with the 2s wild, which means the player who holds a 2 can make it any card of any suit. As a result, Q♦-Q♥-2♦ count as three of a kind, and 10♦-9♦-8♦-7♦-2♣ count as a straight flush. The highest possible hand is five-of-a-kind Aces.

Jokers Wild is like Deuces Wild, except players decide how many wild cards to add to the pack: the more Jokers, the higher the winning hand.

Lowball, also called Lowboy or Burn and Squirm, is one of the most popular forms of Draw Poker. Instead of Jacks, the lowest hand showing opens, and low hand wins. Aces are low, so the lowest pair is two Aces. Straights and flushes don't count, so the lowest possible hand consists of the five lowest cards, with no pairs or three or four of a kinds: 5-4-3-2-A in random suits, known as *the bicycle*, after the popular brand of playing cards. The game can be speeded up by adding a Joker as a wild card, popularly known as *the bug*, the lowest card in the deck. Before the draw, players have to bet or drop; after the draw, they may check. Since the point of Lowball is to get the worst hand possible, don't draw too many cards: you

are liable to end up with at least a pair. A good pat hand should stand.

Shotgun deals three cards facedown to each player. After the betting round, a fourth card is dealt facedown to each player, then there is another betting round, and a fifth card is dealt facedown. After the third betting round, players draw to improve their hands. There is one final betting round, then the showdown.

Spit in the Ocean comes in many forms, but generally, four cards are dealt facedown instead of five. After everyone has four cards, the next card is turned faceup on the table—a fifth card common to all players, a kind of community wild card. In the betting round, the player to the dealer's left must open the pot, regardless of her hand. Players bet, then discard and draw one or two cards and bet again before the showdown, during which each player counts the upturned card as his own.

In **Pig in a Poke**, an extra card is turned faceup after everyone has been dealt four cards facedown, as in Spit in the Ocean. Cards of the same denomination as the upturned card are wild, but not the upturned card itself. For instance, if 3♦ was turned up, 3♥, 3♠ and 3♣ would be wild, but not 3♦.

STUD POKER: Because it has four or five betting rounds instead of two, as in most games of Draw Poker, Stud Poker allows more room for strategy and is preferred by serious players. According to the game, players ante, then starting with the player on the dealer's left and moving clockwise around the table, each player is dealt one card facedown, known as the *hole card*, followed by one card faceup. The dealer places the rest of the deck facedown on the table in front of her. Each player examines his hole card, being extremely careful not to expose it to any other players, since this is the only card that remains hidden throughout the hand.

The dealer assesses the exposed cards of all the players and designates as first bettor the player with the highest-ranking exposed card, saying, "Ace bets" or "Jack bets." (If two players

have the same faceup card, the one closest to the dealer starts.) The betting round begins, and when all players who want to stay in the game have an equal number of counters in the pot, the dealer deals each one a third card faceup. (The dealer does not lift the stockpile off the table but simply turns up the top card and places it in front of the player receiving the deal.) The dealer again names first bettor, and the second round of betting begins. When all bets are made, the dealer deals a fourth card faceup to each active player. A third round of betting begins, then a fifth card is dealt faceup to the active players, and a final round of betting begins. If there are still two or more players in the game, the one who called starts the showdown by *rolling*, or turning, his hole card faceup. Each player does the same, and the highest-ranking hand wins the pot. If, at any time during a betting round, only one player remains active, he automatically wins the pot without showing his hand.

Six-Card Stud is played exactly like Stud Poker, except a sixth card is dealt facedown like the hole card, and the best five out of six make the Poker hand.

Seven-Card Stud, also known as Seven-Toed Pete and Down the River, begins with the dealer distributing two hole cards to each player, one at a time. The third card is dealt faceup, then the first betting round begins. The fourth, fifth and sixth cards are dealt faceup, followed by betting rounds. The seventh card is dealt facedown, and the last betting round takes place. (In the end, players have three facedown cards and four faceup.) In the showdown, the best five out of seven cards make the Poker hand.

Seven-Card Stud High-Low is played exactly like Seven-Card Stud, except the highest- and the lowest-ranking hands split the pot.

In **Dealer's Choice**, you can choose the game you want to play when it is your turn to deal and explain the rules to those around the table. You may decide to make 2s or Jokers wild or to play **Dimestore** (5s and 10s wild).

In **Baseball**, 9s and 3s are wild (for the innings and strikes), and you draw a free card for every 4 (a walk).

In **Blind Baseball**, the game is still Seven-Card Stud, but instead of a conventional showdown, players place their five Poker-hand cards facedown in a pile and roll them faceup one at a time, with another betting round after each card is exposed. There are nine betting rounds in all, making for a huge pot of winnings in each hand.

Several games turn up a center wild card that everyone can use to make a Poker hand. In **333 Spit**, three cards are dealt facedown and three cards faceup (one at a time, with a betting round after each), and a card is turned faceup in the center, which is wild, as are the other three of the same denomination. There is a final round of betting, and as usual, the best five cards make the Poker hand.

A Canadian gambling brotherhood in eastern Ontario has another variation called **Flounder**, which is, the players say, a refinement of **Go Fish**. Basically, it is Seven-Card Stud with four cards facedown in the center. There is a betting round after each of the three cards is dealt facedown to the players and a round of betting as each center card is turned faceup.

Fiery Cross is the same as Flounder, except two cards are dealt facedown to each player, and five cards are laid in the center in the shape of a cross. ∾

11

Cards with a Future: Tarot Games

Tarot was the big card-game fad in the 18th century, just as **Piquet** was in the 16th, **Ombre** in the 17th, **Whist** in the 19th, and **Bridge** and **Poker** have been in the 20th. That might seem incredible to North Americans, who associate tarots almost exclusively with fortune-telling, but in fact, some of the earliest card games were played with tarots, games that have survived in one form or another for over half a millennium. This is especially true in Italy, where a 15th-century fresco in Milan's Palazzo Borromeo shows a table of three ladies and two knights playing Tarot, and where the game is still played in city cafés.

Dabblers in the occult believe that the spread of these beautiful pictorial cards reveals "the secret wisdom of the ages," and so it might, but the cards had been used to play games for at least 300 years before a Parisian wigmaker named Alliette had the brainstorm to use them to tell fortunes. In the late 18th century, Alliette reversed the letters of his name, becoming the Grand Etteilla, set himself up in a Paris hotel and, almost overnight, became the father of cartomancy, or fortune-telling. The real fortune in the telling was Alliette's: he grew rich in Robespierre's France foreseeing which nobles were headed for the guillotine.

A few years before the Grand Etteilla set up shop, a fellow Frenchman,

Antoine Court de Gebelin, published *Le Monde Primitif*, which proposed that the pictorial tarots were actually pages from *The Book of Thoth*, an ancient Egyptian book salvaged from a burning temple. According to Gebelin's theory, the symbols and figures on the tarots contained all the principles of Egyptian mystic philosophy. Two centuries later, Paul Foster Case suggested the fanciful but equally unsupported hypothesis that scholars from around the world met in the city of Fez, Morocco, around A.D. 1200 and devised the tarots as a means of communication, a picture book understandable only to the wisest of men.

Tarots are ripe for such speculation because their true origin is unknown. The first playing cards arrived in Europe, probably from Egypt, in the 12th or 13th century. The deck is based on one used by the Mamluks, the military caste that ruled Egypt from the 13th to 16th centuries. Their deck had 52 cards in four suits: Swords, Sticks (later, ceremonial Batons), Cups and Coins. There were 10 numerical cards and three court cards in each suit: King, Deputy King and Second Deputy. Within a hundred years or so, a fifth suit was added to serve as trump in trick-taking games. One of the oldest complete decks of playing cards in existence is a gold-embossed tarot deck painted in the mid-15th century for the Duke and Duchess of Milan by Bonifacio Bembo, one of Lombardy's most famous painters. The first rules for five-suited games appeared at about the same time, in *Capitoli del gioco dei Tarocchi*, by the poet Matteo Maria Boiardo.

The fifth suit was numbered and, although there were no court cards, all the cards were fancifully painted. The French call these cards *atouts*, the Italians, *trionfi*. This was the original name not only for the fifth suit but, by extension, for the entire deck and the games played with it—games in which one suit could override (triumph over, or trump) cards of any other suit. When the trump concept was adopted for games played with a standard deck, the picture cards were designated *tarocchi* to avoid confusion. The French *tarot* and German *Tarock* both derive from the Italian term. Exactly where *tarocchi* comes from remains a mystery, although its Arabic root helps confirm the Mamluk genesis of playing cards in general.

Tarots probably arrived in Italy first, but before long tarot games were played throughout Europe. One of the most famous lists of early card games appears in Rabelais's rollicking *Gargantua*, published in 1534. "Having sluggishly mumbled over some scraps of grace, Gargantua rinsed his hands in fresh wine, picked his teeth with a pig's trotter, and chatted gaily with his people. After which a green cloth was laid and a stock of cards, of dice and of games-boards were laid out." Gargantua proceeds to play some 195 games, the first 35 being cards, including *le Tarau*.

After their burst of popularity in the 1700s, Tarot games faded, partly because the standard deck of cards was simpler, smaller and easier to produce and use, and partly because fortune-telling with tarot cards superseded their use in games. However, Tarot games have persisted in Italy, particularly in the north Piedmont area, and remain favorites throughout central Europe, especially in Austria and France, although they have never made inroads in Britain or North America.

Tarot games are played with the same cards sold for fortune-telling purposes. The standard 78-card tarot deck consists of two parts. One will be familiar to card players: four suits of cards valued from Ace to 10 followed by a series of court cards. The difference in the tarot deck is that there are four, instead of three court cards—the King *(Roi* or *Re)*, the Queen *(Reine* or *Dama)*, the Knight or Horseman *(Cavalier* or *Cavallo)* and the Jack or Page *(Valet* or *Fanti)*—and the suits are usually the old Italian and Spanish suits of Swords, Cups, Coins and Batons. (In the Italian deck, the swords are curved and the ceremonial wands or batons are straight; in the Spanish deck the two suits are easier to differentiate because the batons are knobbly clubs.)

Four court cards and 10 numerical cards in each of four suits equals 56 cards, roughly equivalent to the standard playing-card deck. These 56 are referred to as the Lesser, or Minor, Arcana, a fortune-telling designation that is of little consequence for playing games. The other part of the tarot deck is a fifth suit of picture cards, 22 cards that are referred to as the Major Arcana. This is a permanent trump suit, now called *atutti* in Italian. Although the illustrations and names on the picture cards vary from deck to deck, they are generally numbered 1 to 21, in either Arabic or Roman numerals. There is also an unnumbered picture card—The Fool—which is not actually a trump but a wild card, something like the Joker in a standard deck. (The similarity is purely coincidental.)

It is the picture cards—the trumps—that truly distinguish the tarot deck. Traditionally, each picture card represents certain standard allegorical and ecclesiastic figures. These are often so intricately illustrated that the deck is a handheld gallery of miniature paintings. Indeed, certain famous decks are known by the name of the painter who illustrated them, the city where they were produced or, as is the case with the Visconti Tarot, the noble who commissioned them.

One of the most famous decks, the Tarot de Marseilles, became popular around the end of the 15th century and is still widely available. The Tarot Classic Deck, based on 18th-century woodcuts by Claude Burdel, has also been reissued and is available today. Most of the designs dating from the 18th century forward use the French suit system of Spades, Hearts, Diamonds and Clubs and designate the picture cards of the trump suit with Arabic numerals, illustrating them not with figures but with scenes of people at work or play.

One of the most famous 20th-century decks, and the one most often used by New Age devotees, is the Rider-Waite Tarot, issued by Rider & Co. in 1910. Drawn by Pamela Colman Smith, it was developed by Arthur Edward Waite, a scholar of occultism who wrote *The Key to the Tarot* and *The Holy Kabbalah*. Like many tarot designers, Waite changed some of the allegorical figures in the trump suit. The Fool comes first instead of last, the Female Pope becomes the High Priestess, the Pope becomes the Hierophant, Justice (8) becomes Fortitude and Strength (11) becomes Justice. Perhaps most disconcerting for game players (as opposed to fortune-tellers), the numerical cards also have symbolic pictures, so that the 4 of Swords, for instance, not only shows four swords but also a prayerful Knight lying on his tomb.

The World

The characters depicted in today's tarot designs are as likely to be unicorns as Zoroaster or Nostradamus. Design traditions are constantly evolving, which is why tarot decks are not only beautiful and collectible but also a pictorial history of cultural interests. In the past decade or so, designs have proliferated to such a degree that, just as you can buy standard playing cards with virtually any design on the back, you can find tarots illustrated with almost any theme: the feminist New Amazon Tarot, the Native American Tarot, the sci-fi Future Solleone Tarot, the Tarot of the Cat People, the Smokers' Tarot, even the Fantastic Shoe Tarot. In 1922, when T. S. Eliot wrote of those "wicked cards" in the hands of Madame Sosostris, famous clairvoyant of *The Waste Land*, tarots were little known and rarely seen far from a crystal ball. Now the vast array can be confusing to those choosing a pack for playing games.

Fortunately, as far as the games are concerned, it doesn't matter what pictures are on the cards. Only three are significant in play and these tend to retain their names and numbers regardless of the illustrations used: Number 1, the lowest trump, traditionally The Magician or The Juggler; Number 21, the highest trump, usually represented as The World; and the 22nd card, The Fool. For ease of play, make sure the tarots are numbered, preferably with Arabic rather than Roman numerals. The other suits often cause more difficulty. The Swords and Batons look alike and all the suits are brightly colored instead of two each of the familiar red or black. Novices will find it much easier to play with a French tarot deck, which uses traditional suits. If you have no choice but to buy tarots with the old suits, make certain they are easy to distinguish.

Tarot games appear in dozens of variations, but they all share certain characteristics. They are trick-taking games that involve trump, and the picture cards are the permanent trump suit. Play always proceeds counterclockwise as in Spanish card games. Players must play to tricks according to this strict rule: follow suit if possible, otherwise trump if possible, otherwise play any card. The Fool or, as it is known in some games, The Excuse, is like a suitless, wild Joker. It is not considered one of the trumps—it is definitely outside the pack—but it is involved in play, occasionally as the very highest trump (as in some forms of Euchre) but most often as a card that can be played instead of following suit or trumping a trick, in other words, as an "excuse."

Tarot games might include competitive bidding, a widow (usually called a scat, or sometimes a dog), and the melding of special scoring combinations of cards but essentially they are all point-trick games: the object is not to collect the most tricks but to use the tricks to capture certain valuable cards that score points. David Parlett, in *A History of Card Games*, suggests a practical reason for this. Tarot cards are so large and there are so many tricks involved in a three-person game (the usual) that the point-trick aspect may have developed as a matter of convenience: it is easier to throw the tricks in a pile and sort through them at the end for counter cards than to try to make the traditional overlapping trick "ladder" and score according to which player collects the most tricks.

Tarot is a family of games, all variations on the basic game but each distinctive to the part of Europe where it evolved. Classic Tarot, the most popular game during Tarot's heyday, developed in the east of France. It was played with the Tarot de Marseilles and, even after Classic Tarot died out in France, it persisted in 19th-century Germany as *Grosstarock* or Great Tarock. In the late 18th century, cardplayers in the Lombardy area of Italy incorporated bidding characteristics from **Hombre** to create Tarok L'Hombre and, though it didn't survive there, its rules are still distinctive of the game played in Austria and Slovenia. Modern **French Tarot** comes from a form played in Besançon and Dijon and also incorporates features from Tarok L'Hombre. Given Tarot's age, it isn't surprising that the deck has been refined for other games: Tarocchini, for instance, uses a 62-card deck with the 2s and 5s omitted, while Austro-Hungarian games use a 54-card deck with cards running 7 to 10 in black suits and Ace to 4 in red suits, four court cards per suit and 21 tarots plus The Fool.

After playing card games with standard 52-card decks, the tarots take some getting used to—they are big and most games use all the cards—but there is no doubt that the beauty and intricacy of these cards add considerable interest to the game.

Suzanne Jacob, the Québécoise chanteuse and writer, is a devotee. "When you play, it is on many levels: it is a game, but you are creating a story, too, with the cards. It is unlike anything else. You will see: this is not a game that allows chitchat at the table. You get inside it; and it gets inside you."

The allusions, allegories, double meanings and story potential of the picture cards has always been part of Tarot's charm at the games table. In 1969, Italo Calvino went so far as to write a book based on the Visconti Tarots. At first, he lined up the tarots at random, trying to read a story in the images, "but I felt that the game had a meaning only if governed by ironclad rules." After years of playing and writing, he wrote *The Castle of Crossed Destinies* with the note, "I publish this book to be free of it: it has obsessed me for years." And he ends with the line, "At every drawing of cards from this tarot pack, at every turning of a page in this maze of tales, all different, and all the same."

So perhaps Tarot players should be forewarned: at the very least, playing with tarots will make the standard deck seem terribly bland. But even more than the pleasure of handling the tarots, and the seduction of the stories revealed in images as each game unfolds, is the knowledge that, in playing the game of Tarot, you are participating in the oldest of card-playing traditions.

Basic Tarot

- ◆ NUMBER: three players
- ◆ EQUIPMENT: a 78-card tarot deck, including 56 suit cards, 21 trump cards and The Fool; Ace low
- ◆ DESCRIPTION: a trick-taking, trumping game in which players try to collect high-scoring cards
- ◆ COMPLEXITY: scoring is more complex than play
- ◆ DURATION: 15 minutes per hand, more at the beginning

THE SIMPLE GAME of Tarot is a good way to become acquainted with this family of card games. It will familiarize players with the deck and with the encumbrance of handling so many large cards. (The size and quantity of cards generally make Tarot games inappropriate for children.) At first, even organizing these strange cards into suits will be a challenge. Try taking the cards into your hand one at a time instead of picking up the lot and sorting them all at once. In general, Tarot play proceeds at a leisurely pace, affording time to enjoy the pictorial nuances of the cards.

The notion of a permanent trump suit may be familiar, since it has survived in games like **Skat**, where the four Jacks form a separate "Grand" trump suit that is superior to, or sometimes replaces, a named trump suit. Like Skat (and **Hombre** and **Solo**), most Tarot games are alliance games where one player goes solo against the combined forces of the other opponents. Basic Tarot, however, involves no partnerships; each person at the card table plays for himself.

The Deal: Shuffle the deck and deal to the right, three cards at a time, facedown, until the whole deck is used up (26 cards each). Players arrange their hands according to the five suits, high to low within each suit. The suit of picture cards is automatically trump.

The Object of the Game: To take high-scoring cards in tricks.

The Play: Before play begins, everyone agrees on how many cards will be counted off together at the end of play to calculate the score. (See the Scoring System.)

The player to the right of the dealer leads to the first trick. Moving counterclockwise around the table, each player must follow suit if possible; if he cannot follow suit, he must trump; and if he can neither follow suit nor lay down a trump, he can play any card he wishes.

If a player has a trump card or a card of the suit led but does not wish to play it, he can play The Fool instead, as an Excuse.

The highest card of the suit led wins the trick unless it is trumped, in which case the highest trump takes the trick. The winner of each trick leads to the next. Tricks are collected in a pile in front of each player.

Play continues until all cards are taken in tricks.

The Score: Each player calculates his score according to the value of the cards taken in tricks.

First, players separate their trick cards into scoring cards and nonscoring cards. Then they count the cards off in batches of two, three, four or five, as the players decided beforehand. Each batch must contain at least one scoring card, though it may contain up to four. If the batch contains one scoring card, it counts the value of that card. If it contains two scoring cards, it counts the value of the two cards combined minus 1 point. If it contains three scoring cards, it counts the combined value of the scoring cards minus two. If it contains four scoring cards, it counts their combined value minus three.

After counting off batches with scoring cards, there may be several nonscoring cards left over. These are also counted off in batches, scoring one point each.

Scoring System: Basic Tarot

Card Values

Trump XXI	.5 points
Trump I	.5 points
The Fool	.5 points
Each King	.5 points
Each Queen	.4 points
Each Cavalier/Knight	.3 points
Each Jack/Page	.2 points

Counting off the trick-cards

Players decide before play how many cards will be in each batch of trick-cards counted off at the end of the game. If a batch has:

No scoring cards	.1 point
1 scoring card	.score the card value
2 scoring cards	.combined value minus 1 point
3 scoring cards	.combined value minus 2 points
4 scoring cards	.combined value minus 3 points

The Tarot

	English	French	Italian
I	The Juggler or The Magician	Le Bateleur	Il Bagatto
II	The Popess or The High Priestess	La Papesse	La Papessa
III	The Empress	L'Empératrice	L'Imperatrice
IV	The Emperor	L'Empéreur	L'Imperatore
V	The Pope or The Hierophant	Le Pape	Il Papa
VI	The Lovers	L'Amoureux	Gli Amanti
VII	The Chariot	Le Chariot	Il Carro
VIII	Justice	La Justice	La Giustizia
IX	The Hermit	L'Ermite	L'Eremita
X	The Wheel of Fortune	La Roue de Fortune	Rota di Fortuna
XI	Fortitude	La Force	La Forza
XII	The Hanged Man	Le Pendu	Il Penduto
XIII	Death	La Mort	Il Morte
XIV	Temperance	La Tempérance	La Temperanza
XV	The Devil	Le Diable	Il Diavolo
XVI	The Tower	La Maison de Dieu	La Torre
XVII	The Star	L'Etoile	La Stelle
XVIII	The Moon	La Lune	La Luna
XIX	The Sun	Le Soleil	Il Sole
XX	The Last Judgment	Le Jugement	L'Angelo
XXI	The World	Le Monde	Il Mondo
	The Fool	Le Mat	Il Matto

The player with the most points wins.

Strategy: Unlike most trick-taking games, it is not always wise to take a trick, since the tricks themselves don't count, just certain cards captured in the tricks. However, with the exception of The Fool, the order of play is strictly controlled, so players might not always have the option of passing up a trick. Therefore, whenever possible, play low unless you can take the trick. Even a Page or a Knight can take a trick later in the game and score you two or three points. Remember, the Ace is low, so the King is the highest card in each suit.

Take your tricks early in the game. There is no point in holding back. In most cases, players will hold two or three cards in a suit, so you'll be able to take tricks with a King and Queen. (Remember: players *must* follow suit if possible, then must trump if possible.) If you hold the Knight as well, don't play it first: it would take the trick, but it would also draw suit cards, leaving your high-scoring court cards vulnerable to trumping.

If it is your lead and you have no King, lead low in a suit in which you hold another court card. This will draw out the court cards above yours and enable you to take a trick. Don't wait too long. Later in the game, as voids are opened in players' hands, suit cards are likely to be trumped.

In the trump suit, only #21 (The World) and #1 (The Magician) are worth points, so save these cards to trump court cards in the other suits, if possible. If played to a trump lead, The World will take the trick, but may take nothing but two other pointless trumps.

The Magician is a tricky card. It is the lowest trump and will never take a trump trick. However, it can take tricks containing scoring suit cards. For example, if the King of Cups is led and you have none, but you have been counting Cups and know that there are still four outstanding, it is probably safe to play The Magician. You will not only take the trick, but you will have a card worth five points in your trick pile. If you aren't sure what the other players hold and aren't keen to get the lead, take tricks with low trump other than #1.

Much strategy hinges upon The Fool. Although it is worth five points, it never takes a trick, so if you are dealt The Fool, you will be giving those points away. Use it wisely to buy yourself time and save your high trump or court cards for better tricks. Pay attention to whom you give The Fool: try to hand it off to the player with the lowest points to give yourself a better chance of scoring highest.

(In other Tarot games, The Fool stays with the player who receives it in the deal, and you can experiment with adding this rule to Basic Tarot. A player can play The Fool to a trick, but once the trick is taken, he replaces The Fool with a nonscoring captured card and puts The Fool in his trick pile. With this rule, The Fool functions solely as an Excuse and benefits only the player who holds it.)

As in most trick-taking games, observation and memory are reliable keys to success. At the very least, you must keep track of which court cards and trump cards have been played, in order to know which cards in your hand can still take tricks that contain scoring cards. ❦

Tarocco

- OTHER NAMES: **Tarok, Tarock, Taroky and Tarocchini**
- NUMBER: **three players**
- EQUIPMENT: **a 78-card tarot deck, including 56 suit cards, 21 trump cards and The Fool**
- DESCRIPTION: **a game with tricks, trumps and points for certain melds**
- COMPLEXITY: **simplified, less strategically demanding than French Tarot**
- DURATION: **a half hour or more**

Tarocco is the progenitor of the Bezique family of games, of which **Pinochle** is probably the most widely played in North America. Tarocco is rarely played on this side of the ocean, but it is still a popular pastime in the Piedmont region of northern Italy.

Given Tarocco's venerable age, it is not surprising that the game is marked by complex, elaborate rituals. It is not necessary to observe these to enjoy the game, but players who enjoy a game with a historical edge should read the Tarocco Players' Code (page 301) and incorporate these refinements into play. A rule that is quite common among Tarot players of all types is the rule of silence: this is not a game for chitchat, but is played quietly to fully appreciate the nuances of the cards.

Tarocco is similar to **French Tarot** in the rules of play and the use of The Fool, but there is no bidding and no partnerships or temporary alliances; everyone plays for himself. There is, however, a declaration of melds, which is typical of the Italian branch of the Tarot family. For these melds, the five highest picture cards (17 to 21) are called the Great Trumps, the five lowest (1 to 5) are called the Little Trumps. The Fool, The Magician (#1), The World (#21) and the four Kings are called, collectively, the *Tarots par Excellence*, or the Best Trumps.

The Deal: Read the Players' Code to determine how to select a dealer. The dealer shuffles the deck and deals 25 cards to each player, five cards at a time, facedown, to the right. The three cards left over are the widow, or the scat (from the Italian *scartare*, "to discard," or *scatala*, "a place of safe-keeping"). The scat automatically belongs to the dealer: he picks up the cards, adds them to his hand and discards three cards of inferior value.

The trumps rank from 21 to 1, high to low. The Fool is played as an Excuse. In Batons and Swords, cards rank from King high to Ace low. The court cards of Cups and Coins rank from King to Page, as usual, but the remaining cards are in reverse order, ranking from Ace high to ten low.

The Object of the Game: To win by melding high-scoring combinations of cards and capturing high-scoring cards in tricks.

The Melds: A meld in this game is an announcement that a player holds certain combinations of cards in hand: they are not laid down for all to see.

Starting with the player on the dealer's right, each player declares his melds by announcing the number of points earned from the cards he holds in his hand. (See **Meld Values** below.) For instance, if a player holds two Kings, The Fool and trump cards #16, #18 and #20, he would declare 20

Scoring System: Tarocco

Meld Values

Great Trumps (#17-21) . . . any 3 count . . . . .5 points
. . . any 4 count . . . . .10 points
. . . any 5 count . . . . .15 points
Little Trumps (#1-5) . . . . . any 3 count . . . . .5 points
. . . . . any 4 count . . . . .10 points
. . . . . any 5 count . . . . 15 points
Best Trumps	
(Kings, The Fool, #1, #21) . . any 3 count . . . . .15 points
Same-suit sequences	
(including trumps) . . . . any four-card sequence . . .5 points
any seven-card sequence . .10 points
any 10-card sequence . . .15 points
any 13-card sequence . . . 20 points

Card Values

Tarot #1 or #21 . . . . 5 points
King . . . . 5 points
Queen . . . . 4 points
Knight . . . . 3 points
Page . . . . 2 points
Any other card . . . . 1 point

points: 15 for the two Kings and The Fool and five for the three lesser trumps.

The Play: Once players declare their melds, the cards are played for tricks. The player to the right of the dealer leads to the first trick. Play proceeds in a counterclockwise direction. The highest trump takes the trick; if no trump is played, the highest card in the suit led takes the trick. The winner of one trick leads to the next.

Players must follow suit if possible, and trump if they cannot follow suit. The Fool is played as an Excuse: it can be laid down instead of following suit or playing trump, regardless of what cards are held in hand.

The Score: Tarocco is a point-trick game. In other words, it doesn't matter how many tricks each player takes: what counts is the value of the cards captured in the tricks.

After the last trick is taken, players add up the points of the cards they captured in tricks, using the card values listed in the Scoring System box.

Each player adds his meld score to his card-value score from the tricks. The player with the highest score subtracts the second highest score from his total: the result is the final winning score for the game. For instance, if one player scores 20 points in trick card values and 15 points in melds, his total is 35. If the next highest player scores 16 in trick cards and 15 in melds, his total is 31. The first player wins with a score of four points (35 minus 31).

Instead of tabulating totals on a scorepad, players can settle scores with poker chips or other counters, each loser paying the winner the value of the game. Or players can agree on a stake, which they each ante to the pot before the deal. The winner of the hand takes the pot. ∾

The Tarocco Players' Code

1. Before the deal, players decide on the stake for each hand. This also determines the penalty for certain misdemeanors, such as breaking the rule of silence, dealing out of turn or playing out of turn.

2. To determine who deals first, the cards are shuffled and dealt (or players may draw from the deck) until a player receives a major trump or a certain card (such as The Magician) agreed on beforehand.

3. The dealer shuffles the deck and announces how many cards he will deal at a time. This announcement must precede the cutting of the deck. If, during the deal, the dealer wants to change the number of cards dealt at a time, he must ask permission of the other players. If he doesn't do so, he must pay a penalty of a single game.

4. The dealer hands the shuffled deck to the player on her right to cut the deck. If the player refuses, the deck is handed to the right until someone agrees to cut it. If no one will cut the deck, the dealer distributes the cards from an uncut deck.

5. If a player looks at the bottom card while cutting the deck, she must pay the penalty of a single game.

6. If the dealer makes a mistake while dealing, giving a card too many or too few, he must pay for a single game.

7. If a card is accidentally turned faceup during the deal, the dealer must stop and ask the players if they want him to start again. If so, he must gather up the cards, reshuffle, and have the cards cut again before beginning a new deal. The same dealer hands out the cards: the deal does not move to a new player because of the mistake.

8. Once the cards are dealt, talk is forbidden, as are looking at one another's cards and making signs between players. Players who break this rule must pay a penalty decided on before the game begins.

9. If there are only two players and one plays out of turn, she may take the card back immediately with no penalty. If there are three players, the offender must pay the agreed-upon penalty.

10. A player may count the points in his own tricks but not the points in the tricks of others.

11. A player who doesn't follow suit, either inadvertently or on purpose, must pay for a single game, unless the cards are still on the table and have not been taken up. In this case, the first player leaves her card, but any of the others may exchange to follow suit.

12. Honor is all in this game, so if a player decides to abandon the game, for whatever reason, the others must allow it.

13. When the game is finished, the points earned by each player must be calculated precisely.

14. If, on a subsequent round, a player deals out of turn, either in error or on purpose or out of habit, he must stop as soon as someone notices, gather up the cards and hand them to the person whose proper turn it is to deal. The player can be assigned a penalty decided on beforehand. Should the mistake not be noticed until the scat has been picked up and the discards made, the game continues but the incorrect dealer must pay for a single game. After the hand is finished, the players resume the original dealing rotation as if the mistake had not occurred.

French Tarot

- ◆ OTHER NAMES: Le Jeu de Tarot
- ◆ NUMBER: three to five players, best with four
- ◆ EQUIPMENT: a 78-card tarot deck including 56 suit cards, 21 trump cards and The Fool, Ace low; suit values, high to low, are Spades, Hearts, Diamonds, Clubs (Swords, Cups, Coins, Batons/Wands)
- ◆ DESCRIPTION: a trick-taking game with trumps; players bid to make a contract
- ◆ COMPLEXITY: the strategic equivalent of Bridge, though it can be played simply too
- ◆ DURATION: a half hour per hand; an afternoon for a game

FRENCH TAROT combines elements of **Hombre** with elements of **Whist** and **Bridge** to produce a game that is played throughout France, both competitively and at home. The directions below come from Noël Chavey's, *Le Jeu de Tarot*, which lays out the rules recommended by the *Fédération Française de Tarot*, the body that governs tournament play. Recognizing that Tarot has been played in France for about 500 years, the Fédération not only runs adult and junior tournaments but has introduced the game to schools, claiming it cultivates memory, observation, logical thinking and independent, strategic action while preserving a pleasurable aspect of French culture.

The rules for French Tarot are similar to Basic Tarot, with the added intricacies of bidding, declarations and bonuses. The four court cards are referred to as honor cards (as in **Pitch** and Bridge). Honor cards are worth points, as are three of the trump cards—The Magician (#1), The World (#21) and The Fool—known collectively as *les Bouts*, or the Oudlers, a word that crosses languages but seems to defy translation. Much of the strategy of the game is organized around the Oudlers. They are worth maximum points, but even more important, having them among the captured trick cards reduces the number of points a player must have to win his

contract. The Magician (#1) is called *Le Petit* by the French, the Little Trump, and this card alone is often key to winning the game. The Fool, often referred to in French manuals as *L'Excuse*, is usually marked by a star, and is represented in the official tournament deck (produced by Carta Mundi in France) by a young man playing a mandolin.

In the two previous Tarot games, every player plays for himself. French Tarot, however, is an alliance game like Hombre and **Solo**. The player who is the last to bid makes the contract and becomes the Player; the others join forces against him as the Opponents. (This is a loose translation from the French, in which the lone player is *le Déclarant* and the others, *les Défenseurs.*) As with other alliance games, the partnership lasts for only one hand. New alliances are made with every deal.

Like Bridge, French Tarot can be learned in an afternoon, but it takes a lifetime to become skilled at play. The rules that follow give only the bare bones of the game. For a full description of the bidding conventions and strategies of play, contact the Fédération. (See Sources, page 407.) Better yet, find a table of Tarot players who will let you sit in on their games. Although official play is ruled by rigorous conventions, the ethics of the game are based on two simple words

that do not need translation: *honneteté et courtoisie.*

The following rules assume four players: if three or five are at the games table, see the Variations.

The Deal: Before the first deal, players cut the deck; low card deals. (Remember: Ace is low and the four suits are all lower than the trump suit.) In the case of a tie, the order of suits (Spades, Hearts, Diamonds, Clubs or Swords, Batons, Cups, Coins) determines the dealer. A player who exposes The Fool must cut again.

The player opposite the dealer shuffles the cards and hands them to the player on the dealer's left, who cuts the deck. Moving counterclockwise, the dealer deals three cards at a time, facedown, to each player. During the deal (but not on the first or last round) he deals a "widow" of six cards, one at a time. Although we sometimes call this the kitty or the scat, French Tarot players refer to it as *le chien* or "the dog," which is how it will be known throughout the game. These six cards eventually become the property of the winning bidder.

If there is a mistake during the deal, players throw in their cards without looking at them and the same player redeals a new hand.

Players organize the 18 cards in hand according to rank within each of the five suits. If a player is dealt a hand in which The Magician is his only trump, he must announce it before bidding begins. The hand—which is known as *Le Petit Sec*, or The Emaciated Magician—is thrown in, and the deal moves to the right.

The Object of the Game: To be the final bidder, then to take tricks that contain sufficient points to equal or better the contract.

The Bidding: The player on the dealer's right bids first. Moving counterclockwise, each player either passes or supersedes the bid of the previous player. Each player bids only once. In making a bid, a player undertakes to

The Oudlers

play alone against the others and win.

If a player has a poor hand, he passes. If all four players pass, they turn in their cards and the deal passes to the right. (This happens frequently in French Tarot.)

If a player has a good hand, he makes one of the four following bids, depending on how good he thinks his hand is. The bids are ranged low to high. In other words, each can be overbid by the one that follows. The last bid is the final one: no one can overbid it. Each bid is worth a certain number of multiplier points, which contributes to the player's final score: the riskier the bid, the more points it is worth.

The four possible bids in order are:

I take (Je prends): This is the bid of a player with a mediocre hand that promises a 50-50 chance of succeeding, a hand that relies heavily on the luck of the "dog" to win. If no one makes another bid, he becomes the Player: he picks up the six cards of the

dog, adds them to his hand and discards six facedown to the table. The discards are not used in play, but count toward the Player's final score. This bid, called *La Petite,* has virtually disappeared from competitive play, but is still useful in home play, especially among beginners. (One multiplier point.)

I keep (Je garde): This can also be used as a first bid when the player figures his chances of success are pretty good and he doesn't want to be overbid. Or it can be used by a second bidder to outrank the first. Basically, the contract is the same. The successful bidder becomes the Player, picks up the dog, adds the six cards to his hand and discards six cards facedown to the table. These cards are not used in play but count towards the Player's final score. (Two multiplier points.)

I keep without the dog: A player who has a very good hand may outrank the two previous bids by offering to play the hand *without* picking up the dog.

The Player doesn't use the dog cards in play, but they belong to him nonetheless, and count toward his final score when it is tallied at the end of the hand. With this bid, no one may look at the cards in the dog until after all the tricks have been taken. (Four multiplier points.)

I keep against the dog: With a very exceptional hand, a player might overbid the previous one by offering to play without picking up the dog and furthermore, giving the dog to his Opponents. No one looks at the dog cards or picks them up, but any points they contain belong to the Opponents and contribute toward their final scores. (Six multiplier points.)

Each hand is worth a base value of 25 points. Depending on how many Oudlers are in the Player's captured tricks, she must earn a certain number of points in order to win the hand. (With none, 56 points; with one, 51 points; with two, 41 points; with all three, 36 points.) Any points earned

Scoring System: French Tarot

Card Values:

Cards are always scored in pairs. Each of the following cards, when paired with a nonscoring suit card or trump card, is worth the following:

Each Oudler (Trump #1, #21, The Fool) . . . . 5 points
Each King . . . . 5 points
Each Queen . . . . 4 points
Each Knight . . . . 3 points
Each Page . . . . 2 points

Any two nonscoring cards . . . . 1 point
Total card points in the deck . . . . 91 points

Points Needed to Win a Contract

The points the Player needs to win depend on the number of Oudlers in the tricks he took during play:

With no Oudlers . . . . 56 points
With 1 Oudler . . . . 51 points
With 2 Oudlers . . . . 41 points
With 3 Oudlers . . . . 36 points

Multipliers:

Each hand is worth 25 points, plus the points that the Player is above or below the number of points needed to make the contract (above). This total is multiplied, depending on the original bid, as follows:

"I take" bid . . . . multiply by 1
"I keep" bid . . . . multiply by 2
"I keep without the dog" bid . . . . multiply by 4
"I keep against the dog" bid . . . . multiply by 6

Bonuses:

A single fist (10 trumps) . . . . .20 points
A double fist (13 trumps) . . . . .30 points
A triple fist (15 trumps) . . . . .40 points
Bonuses are not multiplied: they are added to the hand's total score.

The Last Magician (#1 Trump in the last trick taken) . . . . .10 points
Bonus is multiplied according to the contract regardless of who wins.

30 points for a *double fist* (13 trumps) and 40 points for a *triple fist* (15 trumps). No matter who holds the fist—the Player or one of the Opponents—the bonus goes to whichever side wins the hand.

If any player has 10 or more trumps but a number other than 10, 13 or 15, he may show only the fist and keep the others back, so long as he respects this rule: if he shows The Fool, this implies that he has *no other trump*. The absence of The Fool may mean he has more trumps, or it may mean he wasn't dealt The Fool.

Whoever wins the hand earns the fist bonus, regardless of who declared it. In other words, if the Player declares a fist and loses the hand, the Opponents earn the bonus points.

The Last Magician (Le Petit au Bout): If the #1 trump card (The Magician or *Le Petit*) is played to the last trick, whoever takes that trick earns a bonus of 10 points, regardless of which side wins the hand. This bonus *is* multiplied. For instance, if the Player bid "I keep without the dog," which is worth four multiplier points, and he takes the last trick, which contains The Magician, he earns a 40-point bonus even if he loses the hand.

A Slam (which comes from the French word *chelem*): A Slam occurs when the Player takes all 18 tricks. This is exceedingly rare. A person can play French Tarot all her life and never pull off a Slam. The value of a Slam depends on whether or not the Player declares it in advance. If the Player announces that she intends to try for a Slam and she takes all the tricks, she wins a bonus of 400 points, which is added after the rest of the hand is scored. If she announces a slam and fails, she incurs a penalty of 200 points. If the Player thinks she may win a Slam, but does not to declare it, she earns a bonus of 200 points if she succeeds. It is unusual, but if an Opponent wins a Slam, each of the Opponents wins a bonus of 200 points.

When the Player announces a Slam, the person to the right of the dealer leads to the first trick. The Player

above that number are added to the base value and this total is multiplied by the multiplier points to arrive at the final value of the game.

The last bidder becomes the Player. The other three at the table join forces to become the Opponents.

The Declarations: Before play begins, players are required to declare if they hold certain cards. These declarations earn bonuses, which are added at the end to each player's score. (Bonuses are not multiplied.)

The Fist (la Poignée): Players earn a bonus for holding a large number of trump cards. If any player's hand contains 10, 13 or 15 trump cards, he must show them before play begins. (The Fool is considered a trump for this count.) A player earns a bonus of 20 points for a *single fist* (10 trumps), must save The Fool until last and play it to the final trick. In this case, The Fool takes the trick.

When the Player announces a Slam and plays The Fool to the final trick, the Last Magician bonus applies to the second to last trick.

The Play: The Player, if appropriate, picks up the six cards from the dog, adds them to his hand and discards six others facedown to the table. These discards may not include Kings, Oudlers or trumps. If the Player's hand is so good that he must discard some of the above, he may discard trumps (other than Oudlers), provided he informs his Opponents. When he is finished discarding, he declares, "Play!"

The person to the right of the dealer leads to the first trick. (If a Slam has been announced, the person to the right of the Player leads to the first trick.) Play proceeds in a counter-clockwise direction. The highest trump takes a trick; if no trump is played, the highest card in the suit led takes the trick. The winner of each trick leads to the next.

If a trump card is led, each person must play the highest trump in his hand, even if it means overtrumping a partner (that is, one of the other Opponents). If a suit card is led, players must follow suit, although they are not required to play their highest card in that suit. If a player cannot follow suit, she must trump. If a previous player has already trumped, she must trump higher, if possible. If she doesn't have a higher trump, she can play any trump, although she would usually play her lowest. In the words of the French, a player who under-trumps "pisses." If a person cannot follow suit and cannot play trump, he can play any card he wishes.

The Fool is the exception to the order of play above. The Fool may be played as an Excuse at any time except during the last trick: it excuses the person who plays it from following suit or trumping (even if they have such cards in hand). Played as an Excuse, the Fool cannot take the trick, and neither is it collected in the trick. It remains the property of the person

who played it. Once the trick is decided, she takes back the Fool and replaces it with a nonscoring card from her pile of captured cards. (If a nonscoring card has not yet been captured, it can be handed over as soon as it is taken in a trick.) The Fool is added to her captured cards and contributes to her score at the end of the hand.

A player may lead The Fool as an Excuse, in which case the next card determines the suit for that trick. If The Fool is played as an Excuse in the last trick, whoever wins the trick keeps The Fool. However, if The Fool is played to the last trick in a Slam, it is not an Excuse: it takes the trick.

Tricks taken by any of the Opponents are picked up by the person who sits across from the Player. Only the most recent trick taken can be looked at. No one may play out of turn and no one may take a card from his hand before his turn arrives.

The Score: Scoring is complicated. Outside of tournament play, beginners often play for counters instead of points. Before play begins, the dealer adds an agreed upon stake to the pot. If the Player wins, he gets the pot. If he loses the hand, he adds an equal stake to the pot, which carries over to the next game.

Serious French Tarot players calculate scores. Only the Player tallies the points in his captured tricks, but once he determines whether he won or lost his contract, the value of the hand becomes each player's score—as a negative number for the losing side and as a positive number for the winning side.

The total for each hand must always equal zero. Think of it this way: if the Player wins, he takes his points from the three Opponents, so if the hand is worth 50 points, each Opponent scores -50 and the Player scores 150 (50x3). If the Player loses, he has to give points to the Opponents, so each of them scores 50 and he scores -150. Either way, the Player's score and the Opponents' scores add up to zero.

First, the Player adds the dog cards (if appropriate) to her captured trick cards. Then she counts off her cards in pairs, one scoring card and one non-

scoring card in each pair. When she runs out of scoring cards, she pairs off the remaining nonscoring cards, counting one point per pair.

The number of card points needed to win the hand is determined by the number of Oudlers in the Player's trick pile. If she has no Oudlers, she needs 56 points to make her contract; if one, 51 points; if two, 41 points; if she has all three, 36 points.

If the Player's card-point total is greater than the contract points needed, she wins the hand. If the card-point total is less than the required contract points, she loses the hand and must enter her final score as a negative.

Each hand is worth 25 base points. To calculate the value of the hand, the Player adds the base points to the number of points earned above or below what was needed to win the game. This total is then multiplied by the multiplier points of her bid.

For example, suppose the Player bid "I keep without the dog," which is worth four multiplier points. She took 10 tricks during play, capturing 11 scoring cards. She pairs the scoring cards with 11 nonscoring cards, counting off a total of 39 points: The Magician (5), The Fool (5), two Kings (5x2=10), a Queen (4), three Knights (3x3=9) and three Pages (2x3=6). The eight remaining nonscoring cards make four pairs at a point apiece, bringing her total to 43 points (39+4). Since she captured two Oudlers, she had to take 41 points to win the hand, and she did: she made her contract plus two. The hand, therefore, is worth 27 points (25 base points plus two points gained). Since she won a bid of "I keep without the dog," she now multiplies those 27 points by 4. The hand is worth a total of 108 points.

Therefore, each Opponent must give the Player 108 points. Each Opponent enters -108 on the scorepad, indicating the points he had to give to the Player. The Player earns 324 points (108x3). Note that the total of the four scores equals zero.

If the Player had lost—suppose she took only one Page and her card-point

The Fool

total was therefore 39, two points under the required number—she would lose 108 points (25+2)x4. She has to give each Opponent 108 points, so each enters a score of +108 and the Player enters a score of -324 (-108x3).

Bonuses are not affected by the multiplier and are added to players' scores after the value of the hand is tallied.

Strategy: French Tarot is one of those rare games that keeps skill and luck in almost perfect balance. The other factors that govern the game are memory and observation. It is vital to keep track of which cards have been played, and by whom, if a single Player is to outwit the combined force of three Opponents. One of the subtleties of the game is the shifting loyalties it requires. From hand to hand, French Tarot switches from a solo game to partnership play, depending on who is the final bidder.

The Oudlers are the key to the game, The Fool more so than the others. Whoever is dealt The Fool can count on it as part of her score, since even if it is taken in a trick, it has to be given back to its original owner, who substitutes a replacement card from her pile of captures. Similarly, The World (#21) stays with the player to whom it is dealt, since it is the highest trump and is guaranteed to take any trick. Of the three Oudlers, therefore, only the Magician, the #1 Trump, changes hands. For this reason, much of the strategy of the game revolves around this vulnerable card.

Much of the skill is in the bidding and learning to assess a hand, since the multipliers earned by making a game without or against the dog increase points dramatically.

As in Bridge, numerical values have been established to help novices determine whether to pass or to overbid a previous player. Assess your hand as follows. Count 10 points if you have The World, eight if you hold The Fool, zero if you have The Magician alone, but five if you have The Magician and five other trumps, seven if you have six other trumps and eight if you have The Magician plus seven other trumps. For the rest of the picture cards, give yourself two points for every trump other than the Oudlers, provided you have four or more. Give yourself another two points for every trump between 16 and 21. Honor cards are worth one point for the Page, two for the Knight, three for the Queen, six for a King without a Queen and 10 for a King-Queen marriage in the same suit. For a run of five cards in a suit, add five points, seven points for a run of six, nine points for a run of seven or more. Add up the points in your hand. If there are less than 40, pass. If you have between 40 and 55, bid "I take." If you have between 56 and 70, bid "I keep." If you have 71 to 80, you can bid "I keep without the dog" and over 80 should win you a game against the dog. This is only a general guide, but it will help beginners get a feel for certain bids.

Tarot players are traditionally poker-faced. When you pick up the dog, don't reveal disappointment or elation at what you find there. Similarly, when arranging your cards, don't always keep the tarots on the outside. Give your adversaries as few clues as possible about your hand.

When discarding, try to create voids or singletons so you can trump in early. A void is especially helpful if you have The Magician, because most players expect a suit to make it around all the players at least once. Also, try to go for long suits that will continue to take suits after trumps are gone. Although you cannot discard Kings, you can discard other Honor cards, and it is sometimes a good idea to discard Queens, Knights and Pages. In the discard they will still count toward your score, but in your hand they are likely to be taken in tricks. If you keep a Queen, make sure you have a low card in the same suit to play to the King so you can keep your Queen for a trick.

Observation is key to this game. Take careful note of which trumps are played and the order in which they are played: remember that if trump is led, a player must play his highest to the trick. This should give you a good idea of who holds the high trump. Keep a good mental count of how many trumps have been played; also how many Honor cards and in which suits.

Variations: Although this is not regulation play, some abide by the house rule that when the Player picks up the dog cards in a take or keep bid, she first turns them faceup for everyone to see.

With three players, cards are dealt

The Magician

four at a time. Each player gets 24 cards. The Fists are 13, 15 and 18 trumps. Because the tricks contain an odd number of cards, there may be a single card left over after the count, in which case it is worth half a point. This is usually rounded off in favor of the Player if she wins or in favor of the Opponents if the Player loses.

With five players, cards are dealt three at a time (each Player gets 15) and the dog only contains three cards. The Fists are 8, 10 and 13 trumps. In this game, there are partners. The per-son who is the successful bidder calls for a King of his choice. Whoever has that card becomes his partner for the hand. If the Player holds all the Kings, he calls for a Queen. The holder of the designated card does not identify herself immediately. The Player and the other Opponents do not know who she is until she plays the named King or Queen. Nevertheless, the partner helps the Player from the beginning of the game. If the card is in the dog or in the Player's own hand, he plays alone against four Opponents.

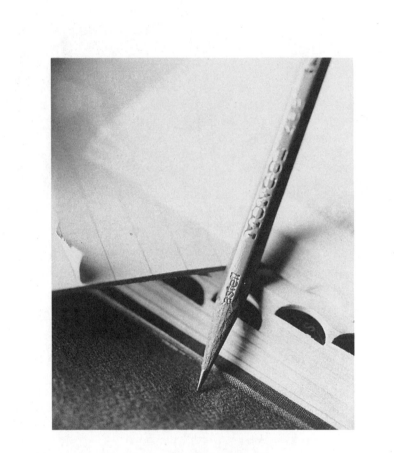

4

MIND OVER MATTER

*Games of Guessing
and Deduction*

———————

*Next, when you are describing
A shape, or sound, or tint;
Don't state the matter plainly,
But put it in a hint;
And learn to look at all things
With a sort of mental squint.*
—Lewis Carroll
Rhyme? and Reason?

12

Trivial Pursuits: Parlor Games

W ITH A FLOURISH, two of the children pull apart the sliding mahogany doors that separate the dining room from the parlor. Standing on a footstool, a woman strikes a noble pose, still as a marble statue. Before her, a man stands stooped, in a parody of age, and at his side, a young woman kneels to child size, both of them staring slack-jawed at the statue, as if they have just seen a ghost. Behind the statue, a woman with a scarf tied under her chin and an apron around her waist appears to be presenting the statue to the ersatz old man and his offspring. A woman at the piano begins to play softly, and the statue steps elegantly from the stool, extending her hand to the old man, who embraces her.

"A Winter's Tale!" shouts someone in the audience, assembled on chairs in the dining room. "Hermione and Leontes—of course! Brilliant. Bravo!"

It is hard to imagine a group of family and friends today playing a quick game of Tableaux Vivants as an after-dinner diversion. For one thing, our houses no longer have parlors, and if we are bored or craving entertainment, there is always the television, videotapes or video games. Yet in the 19th century, this particular form of **Charades** was the rage, one of dozens of guessing games that families played together, honing their wit and wisdom.

One might think that parlor games have gone the way of parlors, but many are still as popular as ever, though somewhat transformed. Balderdash and Scattergories have been dressed up in fancy boxes and given a board, cards and "men," but they are the same games our grandparents played as **Dictionary** and **Guggenheim**.

Although the new incarnations have inventors and trademarked names, the parlor games from which they are derived are so old that little is known of their provenance. **Blind Man's Bluff** appears in ancient Greek writings, the Romans certainly played word games, and Charades is at least 200 years old, but beyond that, the history of parlor entertainments is mostly surmise. They are handed down from generation to generation, the rules (the few there are) adapted to the mores of the day. Blind Man's Bluff, for instance, was originally Blind Man's Buff and had players beating or fondling the blindfolded one; only in the past 150 years has it developed from a sadistic pseudosexual game into one of guile and cunning.

Some games eventually disappear altogether. *The Phoenix Dictionary of Games*, revised as late as 1965, includes a parlor game called Slave Market, destined for the dustheap of games history. "The most attractive girls present are put up for auction—they may stand on the table if they promise not to giggle; otherwise, they stand at one end of the room. Each player is provided with 25 or 50 counters with which he bids for the ladies. The auctioneer tries to get as good a price as possible; the players egg one another on and yet retain as many counters as they can. The buyer who has the most slaves at the end wins. There should also be a prize for the slave who fetched the highest price and consolation prizes for the slaves who didn't."

Parlor games are mostly word games, which isn't surprising, given that parlors themselves were originally small sitting rooms set aside not so much for formal entertainment as for private conversation, an oasis from the chaos of children and household chores. As word contests, parlor games further subdivide into two types: guessing games and tests of general knowledge. In guessing games such as **Dumb Crambo, Conversations** and **Picture Charades,** one person tries to convey a word, a phrase or his or her own identity to the group using only gestures, pictures or synonyms, anything but straightforward speech. In most of these games, the person in the know wants the others to make a correct guess, so the game is a test of acting skill or vocabulary, but in some, such as Dictionary and Blind Man's Bluff, deception is the object of the game. The brain-buster parlor games are based on the premise of building or remembering words, as in **Anagrams** and Guggenheim, and find their apogee in **The Trivia Game**, wherein players try to outdo each other's recall of arcane information.

It isn't the educational value of parlor games that has made them last; parlor games have persisted because they are adaptable. They require no equipment, except perhaps paper and pencil, and are infinitely expandable, playable with a family of 4 or 14 or 40, if all the cousins and neighbors drop by. Everyone from the neophyte speller to old Uncle Sid can join in, and there are precious few rules to learn.

With most of these games, the only preparation is dividing the group into teams or deciding who is It. Teams can be entirely random. Put the people with birthdays in even-numbered months on one team and odd-numbered months on the other or people whose mother's first names are in the first half of the alphabet (A to M) on one side. Since some of these skills are impossible to predict—who would have thought that little Beth would know the capital of Angola or that Dick the physicist would be such a ham?—appointing captains and choosing teams are a waste of time and usually embarrassing to someone. To choose It, roll a die, and play in numerical order, highest number going first. Or in word games, have everyone pick a **Scrabble** tile, and play in alphabetical order, the letter closest to A going first.

Parlor games may have few rules, but they come with a peculiar means of enforcing those that do exist. Traditionally, an evening's entertainment would include several parlor games, perhaps Dictionary to break the ice, followed by an active game of Charades, a quiet round or two of **Crosswords**, then up again for Blind Man's Bluff and, finally, a bout of Guggenheim. Throughout the evening, whenever a player broke a rule—spoke during his turn at Charades, for instance, or failed to find all his neighbor's words in Crosswords—he would be penalized with a forfeit, a stunt or a puzzle designed to make a person look ridiculous and performed for the amusement of the others. The final event of the evening would be the redemption of the forfeits. Since everyone would have accumulated at least one forfeit during the course of play, all were made ridiculous together, which could be sublime. The forfeits were written on papers before the evening began, and players would draw them out of a basket, or one of the group would pronounce judgment, making up forfeits to suit the occasion. One of the standards was: "Bow to the prettiest, kneel to the wittiest, and kiss the one you love the best." For the uninitiated, a list of sample forfeits appears at the end of this chapter. If nothing else, the forfeits prove that these games are not to be taken too seriously. Parlor games are, for the most part, open-ended and scoreless—they are played just for fun.

Blind Man's Bluff

- OTHER NAMES: **Blind Man's Buff**
- NUMBER: **at least six or eight players; the more the merrier**
- EQUIPMENT: **needs only a scarf for a blindfold**
- DESCRIPTION: **an active guessing game—push the furniture to the walls**
- COMPLEXITY: **anyone over the age of 3 can play; traditionally a children's game but can be fun for adults too**

PLAYED CONTINUOUSLY for over 2,000 years, Blind Man's Bluff has evolved both in spirit and in name according to the sensibilities of the day. The ancient Greeks played it as Brazen Fly: players swatted a blindfolded boy with papyrus switches until the "fly" caught one of his tormentors.

The Elizabethans replaced the switches with knotted ropes and called the game Blind Man's Buff—a buff is a blow, short for "buffet." Later, courtiers turned it into a game of tag; instead of the blindfolded one being whipped, he chased the courtesans, and under the pretext of trying to identify the woman he caught, he fondled her.

The Victorians replaced fondling with the tag touch, accomplished with a long cane that avoided any prospect of human contact. The blindfolded player attempted to identify the tagged one by her answers to certain questions, while she, of course, tried to disguise her voice. In keeping with the shift in intent and the rules of the game, the name gradually changed to the more appropriate Blind Man's Bluff.

Preparation: Move furniture, especially breakables, out of the way.

The Object of the Game: For the blindfolded player, to guess the identity of one of the others; for the others, to avoid being identified.

The Play: Tie a blindfold on the person who is It. The blindfolded player stands in the middle of the room, and the others join hands and move in a circle around her. The circle keeps moving in one direction until the blindfolded person claps three times, the signal to stop.

The blindfolded player points, and the player she indicates has to slip inside the circle and try to elude her grasp. When he is finally tagged, he must stand still while the blindfolded person attempts to identify him by touching him, for example, on his hair, clothes and face. She is allowed one guess, and if correct, the tagged player is blindfolded, and the person who was It joins the circle.

Variations: Instead of the circle moving, everyone in the room stands still. The blindfolded person is turned around three times to disorient her, then she stumbles around the room, arms out, until she bumps into someone, whom she tries to identify by touch.

A less active version adds audio to the guessing game. The players circle around the blindfolded one singing. When she claps, they stop circling and fall silent. She points to someone and makes a sound that the other person must imitate—barking, meowing, crying, singing, clattering like a typewriter, roaring like the wind. The blindfolded person tries to identify the player by the sound he makes, and of course, the designated player does his best to fool her. If the blindfolded person is correct, she joins the circle, and the person she identified is blindfolded. If she guesses wrong, the players start singing and moving in a circle again until she claps and points to someone else.

Instead of identifying the designated player by touch or sound alone, the blindfolded person asks three questions, to which the person can reply in a feigned voice, although the answers must be correct.

In **Shadow Bluff**, It sits close to a blank wall. All the lights are out except one, placed well behind It and shining on the wall. The players walk between the lamp and It so that their shadows fall on the wall. It tries to identify the players by their shadows, which they attempt to disguise by adding cushion humpbacks and fingertip horns, smoothing frizzy hair, wearing hats, and so on. ∽

Charades

- NUMBER: **unlimited participants—invite the neighborhood**
- EQUIPMENT: **paper, pencils and a timer**
- DESCRIPTION: **a pantomime guessing game**
- COMPLEXITY: **any age can play; all ages can play together**

ACCORDING TO the Shorter Oxford English Dictionary, the word charade is exactly as old as the United States. It comes from the Provençal word for chatter and originally referred to a riddle that was composed to describe each syllable of a mystery word and then the word itself. For instance, a modern version of a classic charade might be:

My first is a story,
My second is not heavy,
If you see one before you,
It might be a Chevy.

The first syllable is "tale," the second is "light," and the whole word, as defined by the last two lines, is, of course, taillight.

In the 19th century, charades were often complex theatricals. As an illustration of how the game is played, *Cassell's Book of Sports and Pastimes* (1881) reproduces a two-scene play that was mounted to induce the audience to say **Go-Bang**. "Nothing is needed beyond a few old clothes, shawls, hats and a few good actors or, rather, a few clever, bright, intelligent young people, all willing to employ their best energies in contributing to the amusement of their friends."

Needless to say, this is not how the game is played today. Over 200 years, Charades has evolved from full theatricals into pantomime, the person or team that is It acting out each syllable of a word or each word of a phrase in an attempt to get the audience to guess it correctly. The object of the guessing game can be a word, a saying, a book title or the name of a famous person or of a television show.

During the Depression and again after World War II, Charades made a minor stir in the United States as "The Game," a variation that turned the parlor entertainment—actors in front of a guessing audience—into a competitive team sport. For a large group of mixed ages and stages, however, standard Charades is still best. Everyone is involved at the same time, and released from the pressure of competition, even the shiest wallflower may blossom. If there are some real hams in the crowd, consider giving them a handicap—for instance, play with one hand behind your back, with your back to the group or wearing mittens. Have everyone write a handicap on a piece of paper, and put the papers into a separate hat. When it is their turn, advanced players have to draw a handicap as well as a charade.

Preparation: If you decide to time the charades, get an egg timer or a clock with a second hand and designate one player as the timekeeper. Agree on a time limit for each charade: one or two minutes is sufficient.

Give the players several pieces of paper, and ask them to write a charade on each. The group should decide whether the game will be limited to words or book titles or whether it will be a free-for-all of familiar phrases from categories such as songs, movies, proverbs or sayings and television shows. If the group decides to do single words only, make the words at least three syllables long, and consider limiting yourselves to categories such as countries, food or the names of famous people. Old hands at the game might try advertising slogans ("A little dab'll do ya"), tabloid headlines ("Madonna Gives Birth to Mermaid") or actual news clips. If the game is a free-for-all, have players write on the paper the category into which the phrase falls. (If there is an age range in the group, some songs, books and movies may not cross the generation gap.)

Players should write their names at the bottom of their charades. When each player has thought up two or three charades, have everyone fold the papers and collect them in a hat or a bowl.

The Object of the Game: To act out a word or a phrase so that the audience guesses it as quickly as possible.

The Play: Players take turns being the actor. Everyone else is in the audience. The actor draws a paper from the bowl, reads it and puts it out of sight. He names the player who made up the charade; that person sits out the round. (She can act as the timekeeper.) The actor is allowed to take a few minutes to think about how to do the charade. When he is ready, the timekeeper gives the signal to begin. From this point on, he must not speak a word.

First, the actor must establish the category of the word or phrase. A book is indicated by the hands held together palms up; a song, by mouthing words and performing an operatic gesture; a film, by holding a movie camera to his eye and panning the crowd; a television show, by drawing a square box around his head and shoulders; a proverb or saying, by making quotation marks in the air. The other players call out the category, and if they are correct, he nods his head or puts his finger on his nose, a gesture that means "Correct!"

Next, the actor conveys how many words are in the phrase, holding up the appropriate number of fingers. Then he indicates which word he intends to act out first: for instance, he raises three fingers if he is starting with the third word. (Words do not have to be acted out in order.) If he decides to mime the whole phrase at once, instead of word by word, he puts his arm across his chest. At each stage, the audience verbalizes his gestures, and he puts his finger to his nose to indicate "Correct!" or shakes his head for "No!"

An actor cannot talk, he cannot mouth the words (although the temptation is powerful), and he cannot point to the actual object if it is in the room. Otherwise, he can do just about anything to get the audience to say the right word. He can use props if it advances his cause, and he can point to people or himself. As he pantomimes, the audience shouts out a barrage of guesses, which are often as hilarious as the actor's thespian attempts. When someone makes a correct guess, the actor points to her and nods. She repeats the word, he nods, everyone then knows that is the word, and he goes on to the next one, holding up fingers to indicate which word he intends to do.

The whole event transpires at breakneck speed, of course, because the goal is to get the audience to guess the phrase as quickly as possible.

Certain gestural shorthand is standard in Charades. If an actor holds out one arm and appears to chop it in three with his other hand, that means the word he is about to enact has three syllables. If he then points to the middle section of the arm, it means he is going to act out the second syllable.

Cupping the ear or pulling on the earlobe means "sounds like." For instance, if an actor had the misfortune of drawing the book title *Jude the Obscure*, he could pantomime taking off his clothes and hope that someone would guess "nude." He would then point to his nose to indicate that nude

get-out-of-town gesture (don't worry, it comes naturally).

If someone guesses a longer version of the right word, the actor makes shrinking motions with his hands; if he wants a longer version, he draws his hands apart. For instance, someone may guess "walking" when the word is

A-B-C-D-E. This is not a bad idea for kids who are just starting out in Charades, but for older or more experienced players, it is a cop-out.

The Score: If you time the charades, the actor whose audience guesses the charade in the shortest time wins. (This isn't entirely fair, of course, since the degree of difficulty varies dramatically.) Or you can set a time limit of two minutes per charade; each actor who gets the audience to guess the phrase correctly within that time scores a point, and the person with the most points at the end of the game wins. But there doesn't have to be a winner in Charades. The fun of acting out and guessing the phrases is an end in itself.

Variations: In **The Game**, the group is divided into two teams. Each team makes up a series of words or phrases and writes each one on a separate piece of paper. A representative of the opposing team draws one of the phrases from the hat and acts it out to her own team members. (Some house rules have the teams prepare specific phrases for certain individuals, which are handed out in turn.) The rules are the same as above: no talking, no sign language, no mouthing of words and no pointing except to people. If the team guesses correctly within the time limit (usually a minute or two), it scores a point. If it doesn't, the other team gets a point for thinking up the stumping phrase. The teams alternate acting out the charades of the other team until every player has had a turn. The team with the most points wins. (Instead of points, teams can add up the minutes used for each charade, and the team with the lowest total wins.)

The advantage of this variation is that teams are motivated to devise excruciatingly difficult words for the other team to pantomime. The downfall is that only half the group is actively engaged at any one time. Still, it can be entertaining, especially if everyone is of a similar age and skill. The pressure of scoring points for the team can be intimidating, however, for shy,

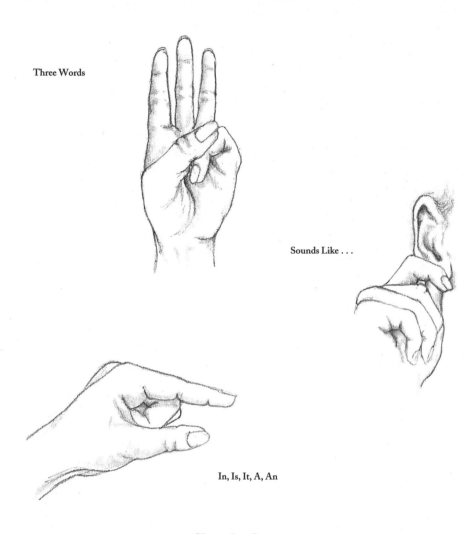

Three Words

Sounds Like . . .

In, Is, It, A, An

Charades Gestures

was correct and pull his ear, and the audience would call out "rude," "food," "mood," "sued" and "wooed," eventually coming up with "Jude."

To indicate that the audience's guesses are close, the actor makes a broad beckoning motion. If one particular person is close, he can point to her and beckon, meaning that she alone is on the right track. A finger on the nose means the guesser has hit the word right on.

If the audience is on the wrong track altogether, the actor makes a

"walk" or call out "play" when the word is "playful." If the verb is right but he wants a different tense, he motions forward for future, backward for past.

Little words, such as "in," "is," "it," "a" and "an," are indicated in the same way one would show that the pie was *this* thick. The traditional time-out signal in sports is Charades shorthand for "the."

Some house rules allow an elementary level of spelling, chopping the air with little horizontal jabs to indicate inexperienced or very young players.

Another way to play team Charades is to divide the players into two groups and have them go into separate rooms. Each group thinks up a charade and plans how to act it out as a group. For *A Midsummer Night's Dream*, for instance, one team might stage a re-enactment of Titania's wedding. The groups get 5 or 10 minutes to think up a phrase and to work out their strategy, then they return, and each group mimes its charade for the other. This is most fun (and comes closest to Tableaux Vivants) if everyone on the team helps act out the scene. This is pure entertainment: everyone wins.

Dumb Crambo

- ◆ NUMBER: **an absolute minimum of four players**
- ◆ EQUIPMENT: **none**
- ◆ DESCRIPTION: **a rhyming pantomime guessing game**
- ◆ TIP: **needs a fairly large space—push the furniture to the walls**

D UMB CRAMBO, aside from having a delightfully memorable name, is a forerunner of **Charades** that keeps all the players guessing. It is a large-group pantomime version of **Crambo**, played as if everyone in the room had suddenly been struck dumb.

The Object of the Game:
To guess the word of the team that is It; to guess the guesses of the guessing team.

The Play: Divide the group into two teams. One team leaves the room. When that team is out of earshot, the team left behind decides on a word which the others must guess. (Early versions of the game specified that the target words be verbs, which are easier to act out and to guess than other parts of speech.) The team also decides on a clue word that rhymes with the target word. For instance, the target word might be "speak" and the clue word "peek" or perhaps "tweak."

The team is called back to the room and given the clue word "tweak." After hearing the clue word, they retire for a moment to consult, then return and act out what they guess the target word to be. For instance, one player mimes carrying a bucket, while the others try to catch invisible drips seeping out the bottom. The first team understands that the guess is "leak" and hisses loudly to indicate it is wrong. The acting team then mimes its second guess, the players holding their noses and fanning the air. "Reek" is also incorrect, so that pantomime is met with more hissing. The team tries again, pantomiming deep conversation. Recognizing the right answer, the audience team begins to applaud.

The acting team is allowed three incorrect guesses. If the fourth one is wrong, the audience team reveals the word and scores a point for stumping the other side. In this case, the acting team correctly guessed "speak" and acted out the word on the third try, so it scores a point.

In the next round, the teams switch roles, the actors becoming the audience, well motivated to find a real brain buster of a word for the opposing team.

From the time the clue word is announced until the applause begins, not a single word can be spoken (except when the team retires to consult). If someone so much as utters a syllable, he must pay a forfeit (page 329) after the game ends.

The Score: The first team to reach 10 points (or whatever the group agrees on) wins. As in Charades, however, keeping score is not essential to the enjoyment of the game.

Conversations

- ◆ NUMBER: **a large group of players**
- ◆ EQUIPMENT: **none needed, just imagination**
- ◆ DESCRIPTION: **an acting guessing game; talking is allowed**
- ◆ COMPLEXITY: **better for adults than young children**

A LTHOUGH THE IDEA of this game might seem quite foreign at first, it makes for great family fun and gradually involves everyone in the action. The game has neither winners nor losers. It begins with two actors and an audience, but by the end, everyone is playing along.

The Object of the Game:
To guess who is having the conversation, then surreptitiously to join in.

The Play: Two players agree to go first. They leave the room, where they decide which characters they will be. They can choose any famous people, from the realms of fiction or real life. The two people can be a well-known duo like the Hardy Boys or Tristan and Isolde, but they do not necessarily have to be from the same country, the same time period or even the same fictional world. They must, however, have something in common—otherwise, how could they have a conversation? Imagine what Elizabeth Taylor and Cleopatra would

have to say to each other or Henry Ford and Lee Iacocca. Players are free to choose anyone at all, but they should choose characters they know a fair bit about.

When the players have made their choice, they return to the room and begin to converse in character, discussing a topic of mutual interest, us-ing the mannerisms and expressions of the people they have chosen to be but, at the same time, attempting to conceal their identities. The other players listen and try to figure out who the conversationalists are. They may not ask for clues, and they should not share their hunches.

When someone in the audience fig-ures out the characters' identities, she joins the conversation in such a way that the actors know she knows who they are. The three people continue the conversation until, gradually, everyone in the audience has joined in—or given up. ∾

Picture Charades

- ◆ OTHER NAMES: **Illustrated Proverbs; the basis for the commercial game Pictionary**
- ◆ NUMBER: **four or more players, divided into teams**
- ◆ EQUIPMENT: **paper and pencil for each team, a stash of words and a one-minute timer**
- ◆ DESCRIPTION: **a word-guessing game with illustrated clues, but artists don't necessarily have an advantage**
- ◆ COMPLEXITY: **provided the words are chosen carefully, anyone over the age of 3 can play**

I N THE POPULAR FORM of **Cha-rades,** players try to guess single words acted out by the other members of the team. In Picture Charades, instead of acting out a word or a phrase, a person draws it for his teammates, the sketches leading them to the correct answer. American playwright and games designer Stephen Sniderman admits that he played Picture Charades for years, never thinking to package it as a commercial game. But Rob Angel, a young Canadian working as a waiter in Seattle, deftly joined Picture Charades with the **Password** concept—teams of two in a word-guessing game—added a beat-the-clock timer and came up with Pictionary. The commercial game comes with a playing board, but it is superfluous to the fun.

Preparation: Divide the players into two teams. The people on each team take turns being the artist; the rest guess what the drawing represents. A timekeeper isn't necessary: one team keeps track of the time, while the other draws and guesses a word.

This game depends on having prepared mystery words: use cards from Pictionary or Password games, make up a list well in advance before the players arrive, or at the beginning of every turn, open a dictionary at random and have one team select a word for the other team to draw. (Because players are choosing for their opponents, the difficulty of the words usually balances out.) The choices are practically endless. Concrete nouns and active verbs are relatively easy; adverbs, adjectives and abstract nouns or concepts such as "far," "new" and "beauty" can be difficult.

The Object of the Game: To guess a word illustrated by your teammate's drawings; to draw pictures that clearly convey a given word to your team.

The Play: Players decide which team goes first. The artist from the first team is given a word (either on a card or whispered to her by someone from the other team) and takes a few seconds to think about it. No dawdling is allowed: five seconds, maximum. Someone from the other team takes the timer, yells "Go!" and the artist starts to draw, trying to represent the word in a picture. The rest of the team shouts out answers to which the artist shakes her head or nods if the word is correct.

Picture Charades

The artist cannot speak, nor can she use any kind of physical communication other than with the pencil. (No acting allowed; this is not standard Charades.) Drawings cannot include numbers, letters of the alphabet or symbols. For instance, to convey "car," you can draw a vehicle but not a Volkswagen logo.

The artist keeps drawing, and the team keeps guessing until it gives the right answer or the time is up. If it guesses within the one-minute time limit, the team gets a point.

The turn passes to the other team, the artist for that team is given a word, and the drawing begins. The teams play an even number of rounds, and the one with the most points wins.

Variation: In **Beat-the-Clock Picture Charades,** the artists from both teams take the same mystery word. (Or, together, they choose one word from a randomly selected page of the dictionary.) One of the guessers is designated timekeeper. When the timekeeper says "Go!" both artists start drawing, and the guessers call out answers. The first team to guess the mystery word wins. This is extremely loud and hectic, made particularly frantic because you are trying to watch your own artist while at the same time keeping an ear cocked for the wrong guesses of the other team. Separate the teams for this variation, but not too far: the gawking and eavesdropping are part of the fun. ∾

Password

- ◆ OTHER NAMES: based on the television game show, the inspiration for the board game Password
- ◆ NUMBER: four or five players; more in teams
- ◆ EQUIPMENT: requires a stack of prepared mystery words or a dictionary
- ◆ DESCRIPTION: a word-guessing game with word clues

PASSWORD ADAPTS the word-guessing concept of **Charades** and turns it into a vocal team game that involves everyone at once. The same word is given to one member of each team at the same time; they take turns giving clues to their teammates; the winner is the team that guesses the password first. Password works best as a game for four, with a fifth playing quiz master.

Preparation: You need a stock of words that none of the players has seen. You can use the words provided in a commercial Password or Pictionary game; you can spend an afternoon writing out words, storing them on the games shelf until some rainy day (when you have forgotten what you wrote); you can ask a nonplayer in the house to come up with a dozen or so; or you can appoint the fifth person in the group as quiz master and have her hand out the words to the teams. If the players are cooperative, the two clue givers can open the dictionary at random and find a mutually acceptable password at the beginning of each turn.

Whatever system you use, remember that nouns are the easiest for this game. The quiz master is also the timekeeper; otherwise, use a kitchen timer set to one minute.

The Object of the Game: To guess the password as quickly as possible based on your partner's synonym clues.

The Play: The four players are divided into two teams of two. One person on each team is the clue giver; the other is the guesser. The two members of each team should sit facing each other and at the opposite side of the table from the other team. The teams decide which one goes first, then they alternate in subsequent rounds.

The two clue givers are given the same password, either written on pieces of paper or whispered in their ears. The clue giver of the first team offers her partner a synonym or a word related to the mystery word. For instance, if the password is "game," the first clue might be "pastime." The clue giver can say only one word, and her teammate is allowed only one guess. If he can't think of anything, he says "Pass." If the guesser passes or guesses incorrectly, the other team takes a turn, one person giving the other the second clue, which might be "toy."

The two teams alternate; each hears the clues and guesses of the other team and uses this information to try to guess the password when its turn comes again. The round ends when one team guesses the word or if the players remain stumped after six clues.

Proper nouns cannot be passwords, but they can be clues. For instance, a player might say "Liberace" as a clue for the password "piano." Players are allowed to use inflection to convey part of the message. For instance, a player can say "flash . . . ," drawing out the word and raising her voice so that it is clear what is being asked for is the second part of the word: light. Or she might whisper "books" to elicit the password "library." A player can grimace, look mildly pleased or act peeved to indicate exactly how far off the mark the teammate is. Conversation and hand gestures, however, are not allowed.

In the next round, the other team begins. An even number of rounds are played, so each side has an equal advantage.

The Score: Players score 1 point each time they correctly identify a password; the first team to reach 10 points wins.

For a more competitive game, play to 25 points. Award 6 points if a team correctly identifies a password after the first clue, 5 points for naming it after the second clue, 4 points after the third clue, 3 points after the fourth clue, 2 points after the fifth clue and 1 point after the sixth clue. If neither team guesses the password after the sixth clue, the round ends, and the mystery word is revealed.

Variation: A relatively recent board game using the Password premise is **Taboo.** Each person tries to get his teammate to say a mystery word, but certain clue words are forbidden. For instance, if the mystery word is "tea," the taboo words might be "India," "drink" and "cup." If a taboo word is spoken by either the clue giver or the guesser, that team automatically loses. This is a useful variation for home play if you can find only easy words in the dictionary. Use the simple words as passwords and have the clue givers agree on a list of forbidden clues. ∽

Dictionary

- ◆ OTHER NAMES: **Definitions; the original inspiration for Balderdash and Slang Teasers**
- ◆ NUMBER: **the more the merrier; less than four is not much fun**
- ◆ EQUIPMENT: **a dictionary, a pencil for each player and a stack of notepaper**
- ◆ DESCRIPTION: **a hilarious bluffing-and-guessing game, especially for people who love words**
- ◆ COMPLEXITY: **not suitable for young children—players should be able to read a dictionary well**

"LAUGH, LEARN and Lie" promises the box of the Balderdash game: laugh and lie, certainly, but learn? Balderdash and its predecessor, Dictionary, both have educational underpinnings that appealed to Victorians as much as they do to denizens of the Information Age. But does anybody really remember that "fenks" is blubber fertilizer or that "zloty" is an old Polish coin? The appeal of this game is surely not knowledge but wit and guile, the satisfaction of successfully pulling the wool over everybody's eyes.

A parlor standard for generations, Dictionary was transformed into the board game Balderdash in 1984 by two Canadians, restaurateur Paul Toyne and actress Laura Robinson. As in the original game, Balderdash players make up definitions for bizarre but real words. Instead of finding the words in a dictionary, Balderdash provides them on printed cards (which somehow makes the words themselves seem like a put-on). Players who devise a definition that others believe and players who pick the correct definition from amongst the balderdash concocted by the others score points

that move markers along a board.

Dictionary, despite its prosaic name, is still a better game. There is no superfluous board, and players have the pleasure of paging through the dictionary for the perfect improbable word to stump the gathering. Don't despair of finding one: most English dictionaries contain about half a million words; the average player's vocabulary is only 50,000 words. For example, when was the last time you heard gnomon, dabster, palfrenier or tomium in polite conversation?

Preparation: Players sit so that they can't peek over each other's shoulders. Have at hand a large dictionary, preferably not a concise or abridged edition. Give each player a pencil and several small pieces of scrap paper. The papers should be similar or small enough to be concealed in the hand so that players can't identify the definition by the paper it is written on.

The Object of the Game: To write phony but probable-sounding definitions; to identify the true definition.

The Play: One player leafs through the dictionary to find a word with a peculiar, unexpected or arcane definition. (The impatience of the group sets a natural time limit on the search.) She announces the word and spells it. If anyone recognizes it, she has to find another. Everyone writes the chosen word and a definition on a piece of paper. The player who found the word transcribes the correct definition from the dictionary; the others try to concoct a definition which sounds plausible so that the rest of the players will believe it is, in fact, the true meaning of the word. Remember: Dictionary is essentially a bluffing game.

Players fold their papers and pass them to the person with the dictionary. She looks at them and arranges them in random order, setting aside any that are close to correct. (The writer still scores, but two similar definitions read aloud may tip off the crowd as to the real meaning of the word.) One by one, she reads the definitions aloud, being careful not to give away the correct answer with her intonation. Although kibitzing is part of the game, players must not identify the definition they wrote.

When all the definitions have been read aloud, each player votes for the one he thinks is correct. (This usually requires a second reading.) To avoid confusion or scoring disputes, the reader writes on the definition the initials of each person who votes for it. The person who found the word doesn't vote, of course. After the votes are in, the correct definition is revealed.

The Score: Imagination rates higher than erudition in this game.

Players who vote for the correct definition score 1 point. A player who writes a definition the same as or close to the real one scores 1 point. A player who makes up a definition that others believe scores 3 points for each person who votes for it. If no one votes for the right definition, the player who chose it scores 5 points. A player who votes for his own definition does not score.

Players can keep a running tally and play to 25; the first person to get that many points wins. The game, however, is not competitive; most people are in it for the laughs. Instead of keeping a running score, pass the dictionary to the person who wins the round, or simply hand it to the left, and play until everyone has had a turn picking a mystery word. ∾

Guggenheim

- ◆ OTHER NAMES: **the inspiration for the commercial game Scattergories**
- ◆ NUMBER: **two or more players; good for large groups**
- ◆ EQUIPMENT: **a pencil and paper for each player and an egg timer or watch with a second hand**
- ◆ DESCRIPTION: **a relatively quiet word game; fun and challenging, but not raucous**
- ◆ COMPLEXITY: **anyone who can read and write can play; about 8 years and up; kids can play with—and easily beat—adults**

NOT LISTED in the older compendiums of parlor games, Guggenheim appears to be a 20th-century game, probably a 1920s offshoot of Crosswords and part of the general word craze that has gripped North America since the invention of the crossword puzzle in 1913. It is undoubtedly American, although whether it is named for the museum, the Foundation or the seven sons of the powerful Philadelphia mining family is open to speculation.

Guggenheim, and its popular commercial incarnation, Scattergories, is a word game, but it is not a test of knowledge so much as a test of originality and the ability to second-guess other players. Players try to think of words that start with a certain letter and fit into a certain category, but they earn more points for words which do not appear on anyone else's list.

For instance, if the category is Birds and the letter is R, everyone's first thought is robin. All but one of the players discard robin as being too common: two list red-headed woodpecker; three write red-winged blackbird; and another lists red-eyed vireo. The vireo and the robin earn the highest score, because no one else wrote them down. Of course, if a player listed the rosy-breasted nitpicker, the others would have to decide democratically whether to allow it as an actual word. Without a well-stocked reference library at hand, the game, among adults at least, often becomes one of shameless bluffing.

When Milton Bradley reworked Guggenheim into Scattergories, it increased the number of categories to 12 and added a die that dictates the first letter of the words to be listed and a noisy timer that heightens the panic

	H	E	A	R	T
Food	Ham	Egg	Asparagus		
Tools	Hacksaw	Edger	Arc Welder		
Birds	Heron	Egret			
Composer	Handel	Elgar			
Books	Hamlet	East of Eden			

Guggenheim

of hitting the inevitable mental blocks which add tension to the game.

Preparation: Each round has a time limit. Games manuals from the 1930s and 1940s suggest 20 minutes a round. Newer books recommend 10 or 12. But the game is more fun if the head scratching is done under pressure: a minute or two is great for adults; three to five minutes is fine for kids (they think just as fast, but they take longer to write). Appoint one person as timekeeper, and give him a stopwatch or a kitchen timer, preferably one with a loud buzzer.

Give each player, including the timekeeper, several pieces of paper. Before the game begins, players put their heads together and come up with a list of categories, such as Vegetables, States, Occupations, Clothes, Tools, Trees, Presidents, Breakfast Cereals, Cartoon Figures, Provinces, Insects, Desserts, Jewels, Songs, Body Parts, Television Shows, Rivers, Artists, Countries, Cars, Birds, Girls' Names, and so on. Don't choose categories that give one player a special advantage, but for adults, the more arcane and specific the category, the better.

Players rule their papers into a grid, with seven horizontal and seven vertical lines at least an inch apart (6 squares each way, 36 in all). Leaving the top square blank, players write the names of five categories in the boxes down the left side of the paper. (Gear the type of categories to the age of the players.)

The Object of the Game: To list items in a series of categories within the allotted time.

The Play: One player chooses a five-letter word with no double letters: for instance, in the game illustrated on the previous page, the word is HEART. Players write the word across the top of the grid, one letter in each square. (The top left square remains blank.) When the timekeeper says "Go!" players write a word in each box that fits the category to the left and starts with the letter directly above. For instance, if the five categories are Food, Tools, Birds, Composers and Books, someone might write ham, hacksaw, heron, Handel and Hamlet in the boxes under the H; egg, edger, egret, Elgar and East of Eden under the E.

Use the time to jot as many words as you can in each box, but get at least one, the more unusual the better, since you earn more points if no one else lists the same word. When the time limit is up, the players compare the words they listed in each category, giv-ing themselves a check mark for each one that no one else has listed. Any questionable words are decided by a majority vote. Spellings do not have to be correct.

Players add up their scores for that round, then list categories on a fresh page (the same or new ones). The player to the left of the first player calls out a new five-letter word—for instance, TRAIN—the timekeeper says "Go!" and players list another round of words.

The Score: Players score 1 point for every word they list; 2 points if the word does not appear on anyone else's list. Players tally their scores at the end of each round. When everyone tires of the game, the highest score wins.

Variation: Categories is only slightly different. Players list more categories down the left side of the page. The commercial game of Scattergories has 12, but you can list as many as you want; 20 makes a good game for adults. Instead of playing the game with a five-letter word, Categories is played with one letter, which is chosen by the first player. The game is played exactly the same, but players do not score at all for words that other players list. Only unique words count, earning a player 1 point each. ⌒

Anagrams

- OTHER NAMES: Logomachy; the inspiration for Scrabble
- NUMBER: any number of players; excellent for two; more than six is too slow
- EQUIPMENT: one set of Scrabble tiles, or preferably two, and a dictionary
- DESCRIPTION: a brain-twisting word game; a grab-and-switch Scrabble that is best played on the floor
- COMPLEXITY: with patient adults, even kids just learning to spell can play; a great game for grown-ups
- DURATION: less of a commitment than Scrabble—takes only an hour or so to play

THE ART of making anagrams is probably as old as language itself. Where there are words, there are wordsmiths who take delight in scrambling the letters of one word to make another. Anagram as a word has been part of the language since the 16th century. It comes from the Greek, meaning to write anew, and refers to the transposition of the letters of one word to make a new word. For example, both SKATE and STAKE are anagrams of STEAK. There is a fascination in the exercise, particularly if the meanings are related: for instance, an anagram of HIBERNATES is THE BEAR'S IN; CONVERSATIONS is VOICES RANT ON; and, of course, BART (as in the

Simpsons) is an anagram of BRAT.

Classical anagrams involve a straightforward rearrangement of letters. This game, however, is based on adding a letter as well as transposing the existing ones, which is a little easier. Early games manuals promoted this game for its improvement value. "Like cross-word puzzles, it has educational advantages," wrote Milton Goldsmith in *The Book of Anagrams* (1930), "and is a great help in the proper formation and spelling of words." In fact, you have to be a pretty good speller to play it; but at the end of the game, your brain feels as lithe as your body does after a 20-minute workout.

Preparation: Make your own anagram letters, writing them on little squares of cardboard. The distribution of letters is as follows:

A-29	J-4	S-24
B-5	K-5	T-36
C-12	L-16	U-14
D-16	M-9	V-8
E-50	N-30	W-8
F-9	O-28	X-4
G-8	P-8	Y-9
H-20	Q-3	Z-3
I-28	R-30	

This adds up to 416. Although the letter distribution differs, you can also use **Scrabble** tiles. (Treat the blanks as "wild" letters: they can become anything.) With two players, a game to five words can comfortably be played with 100 tiles; a game to 7 or 10 words needs 200 tiles; the more players, the more tiles you need.

Players can agree, however, to play until all the letters are used up, making as many words as they can. Fewer tiles simply shortens the game. As in Scrabble, players should agree on a dictionary to arbitrate disputes.

The Object of the Game:
To be the first to build five words.

The Play:
Scatter the tiles facedown on a table or the floor. Players each draw a letter; the one closest to A goes first. The first player turns a tile faceup. The other players do the same in turn, moving clockwise around the table. As soon as any player sees a word that can be made with the faceup tiles, she calls out the word, takes the tiles and places the word in front of her. The word does not have to use all the turned-up tiles—the player just takes what she can use—but it must be at least four letters long, must not be a proper noun and must be good English, not slang.

A player can capture a word from another player by adding new letters to it *and* making an anagram. For instance, if one player has the word FLIRT and an E is turned up, another player can grab both the E and FLIRT to make TRIFLE.

Simple plurals do not count as four-letter words: for instance, CATS. Likewise, to grab another player's word, you must add a letter or letters that make a completely new word. Adding S or ES or even ING is not an anagram, because the meaning of a word is unchanged by the suffix. For instance, adding S to make a plural of STEAL is not allowed, but adding an S and changing the word to SLATES is acceptable and so is adding T to CLOSE to make CLOSET.

If two players call out a word at ex-

Anagrams

actly the same time or want to steal the same word, the person who calls out the longest word gets preference. For instance, in the game illustrated on the previous page, both players want the R. H calls out "answer," planning to steal WEANS and add the R. At the same time, M calls out "chagrin," adding the R to ACHING. M gets the R because hers is a seven-letter word. If both words are the same length, the other players vote on who should get it—usually the person with the cleverest anagram.

If a player calls out a word then finds he doesn't have the necessary letter or can't make the word he thought he could, he must return his last word to the stockpile, turning the tiles face-down and shuffling them in. This may seem harsh, but it eliminates a lot of precipitous calls.

As in Scrabble, players can challenge words that sound made-up. If the dictionary proves the challenger right, the player loses the word she just made as well as her previous word. If the challenger is wrong, he must put his last word back in the stockpile, turning the letters facedown and mixing them in with the others.

As the game progresses, there can be deadly lags after each new tile is turned over, while players strain mentally to scramble the existing words into anagrams. If the game slows down too much, set a time limit: a new tile is turned over every minute, ready or not.

The first player to get the target number of words (usually five) wins. Alternatively, the game ends when all the tiles are used up and no one can make another word. The player with the most words wins.

Variation: In the older, more refined version of Anagrams, the person who turns over the new tile has a minute to make a word. If he cannot, then the turn passes to the left; that player turns over a new tile, and she has a minute to make a word. A player can take another player's word only when it is her turn. This is not as rude or as lively as the grab-a-word version, but it works better with young children, especially if they are at different spelling levels. ❧

Crosswords

- OTHER NAMES: Word Squares, Word Exchange and Stock Exchange
- NUMBER: two or more players; especially fun with large groups
- EQUIPMENT: a pencil and paper for each player and a dictionary to settle disputes
- DESCRIPTION: a Lotto-style word game
- COMPLEXITY: anyone who can spell five-letter words can play

CROSSWORDS combines **Scrabble** with **Bingo**: players make words using letters that are called out and written at random on a grid. Although it seems simple, it is in fact highly strategic, especially if played between two people with an equal mastery of the English language.

Preparation: Each player draws a five-by-five-square grid (six horizontal and six vertical lines). The squares should be no smaller than an inch each way. If there are only a couple of players, each can make several grids for each round, just as Bingo players keep several cards going at once. Young children can use smaller four-by-four-square grids; for longer games or games with more than five people, draw larger grids: six-by-six for six people, seven-by-seven for seven people, and so on.

The Object of the Game: To make the most words in the grid.

The Play: Players decide who begins, then the first person calls out one letter of the alphabet. Each person writes the letter anywhere on the grid. Play moves clockwise around the table, each person calling out a letter of the alphabet, which everyone adds to the grid in such a way that words are created both vertically and horizontally. (Letters can be called more than once.)

The words must be at least three letters long; if a short word is completely contained within another, only the longer one counts. For instance, the player who makes TWINS scores for a five-letter word but not for TWIN, WIN, WINS or INS. Two words can overlap, however, and use some of the same letters. For instance, the letters S-A-R-I-G form the four-letter word SARI and the three-letter word RIG; both words count, since they share only the RI. Proper nouns such as people's names, place names or days of the week are not allowed.

When all the squares in the grid are filled with letters, players read out the words they have made, scoring for words of three letters or more. A player can challenge a word, checking in the dictionary to see whether it is acceptable English. If everyone agrees, a penalty can be imposed for false words and false challenges. The player who concocts a word subtracts those points from her score; the player who makes a challenge that proves incorrect subtracts the points of the challenged word from his score.

The person with the highest score after each game wins.

The Score: Although there are several ways to score this game, advanced players should allot 10 points for five-letter words, 5 points for four-letter words and 2 points for three-letter words, allowing nothing for shorter words. (Beginners can score 1 point for every letter in words of two letters or more: for instance, 5 points for five-letter words, 4 points for four-letter words, and so on.) In the game illustrated, M scores 25 and H scores 67.

Variations: If everyone agrees, diagonal words can be counted. In the illustrated example, scoring for diagonals adds 11 points to H's score and 17 points to M's score. Players can also spell words backwards on the horizontal, vertical and diagonal, but they should specify the house rules before the game begins.

Instead of players calculating their own scores, each player can make a list of the words on his or her grid, fold the paper so that the list doesn't show and pass it to the player on the left. Then, within a certain time limit—say, two minutes—the neighbor writes a list of all the words he finds in the grid. The person who made the grid scores full points for all her words. Any words the neighbor fails to locate are deducted from his score; any words the neighbor locates that the grid maker didn't know were there are added to his score.

In a two-person variation on the Crosswords theme, the players draw one nine-by-nine-square grid and set it between them. One person writes a word anywhere in the grid, scoring 1 point for each letter in the word. The next person adds a word, Scrabble-like, incorporating at least one letter from the other word on the board and scoring 1 point for each new word thus formed. The players alternate, making words anywhere on the grid until it is full or until no one can think of another word. (Any letters that touch vertically or horizontally must make actual words.) At the end, the player with the highest score wins.

Crosswords

Lotto

- ◆ OTHER NAMES: **Loto and, at gambling casinos, Keno; the inspiration for Bingo**
- ◆ NUMBER: **any number of players**
- ◆ EQUIPMENT: **numbered disks or squares and a pencil, paper and about 20 counters for each player**
- ◆ DESCRIPTION: **an addictive game of chance; fun for a large group**
- ◆ COMPLEXITY: **any age, from about 3 up**

A N AMERICAN variation of Lotto, Bingo was invented by Edwin S. Lowe, a former toy salesman who had started a games company just before the stock market—and the games market—crashed. According to legend, he found his inspiration one night on his way from Atlanta, Georgia, to Jacksonville, Florida, when he stopped at a roadside carny and watched a game of Beano— a homespun style of Lotto played with dried beans as counters. Players paid a nickel to play; the first to get five beans in a row won a Kewpie doll. One of the players, in her excitement at winning the doll, yelled "Bingo!" instead of "Beano!" and a new game was born. Lowe manufactured it, using 6,000 nonrepeating cards devised for him by a Columbia University mathematics professor. Although it began as a gambling game, Bingo has since become a fund-raising mainstay for Catholic congregations around the world.

Lotto is Bingo's forerunner by several hundred years. It was derived from an old Italian game, Tumbule, which in turn took as its model *Lo Giuoco del Lotto del Italia*, the Italian National Lottery, in operation almost continuously since 1530. Although the English name has its roots in the word lottery, Lotto does not have to be played as a gambling game.

Lotto cards contain a rectangular grid, nine squares long and three squares wide—27 in all. On each horizontal row, there are four blanks and five numbered squares, all randomly distributed, as illustrated. The playing pieces in the commercial game are little wooden (formerly ivory) disks with embossed red numbers, 90 in all. The numbered disks are drawn at random one at a time and called out, as in Bingo, and if a given number appears on their cards, the players mark it with a counter. The first person to get five counters in a row horizontally wins. At the turn of the century, there were dozens of variations on this theme— Picture Loto, Botanical Loto, Historical Loto, Geographical Loto—each substituting appropriate pictures for numbers on the squares. In this form of the game, instead of using prefabricated cards and numbered disks, players can make their own, which can be filled in as easily with magazine cutouts as with numbers.

Preparation: Cut 90 small cardboard squares, or buy a box of 90 poker counters; number the squares or counters 1 through 90. Put the numbers in a hat, a box or a bag from which they can be drawn without being seen. Give each player a paper and pencil and have each person draw a 27-square grid (4 lines across and 10 lines down). Color any four squares in each of the horizontal rows; these are the 12 blanks. Number the squares in the vertical rows as follows: put any

Lotto

numbers between 1 and 10 in the first vertical row, between 11 and 20 in the second row, between 21 and 30 in the third row, between 31 and 40 in the fourth row, between 41 and 50 in the fifth row, between 51 and 60 in the sixth row, between 61 and 70 in the seventh row, between 71 and 80 in the eighth row and between 81 and 90 in the last row. Players can make several cards if they want to and play them all at once. Each player gets a handful of counters of a size that fits the squares of the grid (M&Ms or pennies or beans). Alternatively, put a pile of counters in the middle of the table within everyone's reach.

The Object of the Game: To be the first player to fill in all five numbers in a horizontal row.

The Play: One player is the caller. (She also has a card.) She draws a number from the hat and calls it out. If a player has that number on his board, he puts a counter on it. The caller continues drawing numbers and calling them out. When a player has filled one horizontal row with counters, she calls "Lotto!" and wins.

Variation: Some house rules dictate that the whole card must be filled before a player calls "Lotto!"

Before the game begins, players can ante a coin or a gumdrop in the center, one for each card they have drawn. The player who wins gets the pot. In another twist, the player who first covers a row wins a quarter of the pot, the next to cover a row wins another quarter, and the person to cover the entire card wins the remaining half. A more democratic (and delicious) variation is to use candies as counters, and when someone calls "Lotto!" all players get to eat the counters on their cards. ❧

The Trivia Game

- ◆ OTHER NAMES: **an at-home version of Trivial Pursuit**
- ◆ NUMBER: **any number of players**
- ◆ EQUIPMENT: **questions and answers, a die and a timer**
- ◆ DESCRIPTION: **an information game; the more arcane the questions, the more fun the game**
- ◆ COMPLEXITY: **players of any age, as long as the questions are geared to the appropriate level**

IF MAH JONGG, **Monopoly** and **Scrabble** dominated the first half of the 20th century, Trivial Pursuit is the rags-to-riches games story of the latter half. Invented in Montreal in 1979 by two Canadian journalists, Chris Haney and Scott Abbott, the game hit the market in the middle of the video-game craze yet still sold 15 million copies in its first three years, shattering every board-game sales record.

While the pursuit of trivia may be new, games of knowledge are not. Victorian parlors often rang with question-and-answer games, although they sound heavy-handed and anything but entertaining to our ears. Take The Schoolmaster, for instance, described in *Cassell's Book of Sports and Pastimes* (1881) as: ". . . among stirring games, one that is always a success when played with energy." One person agreed to be the teacher, while the others sat in a row as the class. The teacher "examines his subjects in all different branches of education in succession," asking questions that the "student" must answer within the count of 10. Stripped of their pretty boards, the guiding principle of Go to the Head of the Class, Jeopardy! and Trivial Pursuit is exactly the same.

The actual Trivial Pursuit game is not reproducible at home, although the game can certainly be played without the board: players simply ask each other the questions and enjoy the thrill of getting the right answers. In 1984, Sarsaparilla Ltd. in Chicago published *In Further Pursuit of Trivial Pursuit*, a reference book in which Joseph DeBartolo embellishes on the bare-bones answers provided with the game. The book is divided into the same categories—Geography, Entertainment, History, Art & Literature, Science & Nature and Sports & Leisure—and could easily be used instead of the game's official cards to play the game at home.

Horn Abbot has produced several spin-offs from the original Trivial Pursuit, including Baby Boomer, All-Star Sports, RPM and Silver Screen editions. Likewise, many trivia aficionados have made up their own versions of the game, with questions and answers in subject areas of personal interest. One man produced a game for his community complete with questions of local history, gossip and lore, including "Whose wedding ring lies at the bottom of the lake?"

Preparation: Play as individuals, or divide the group of players into teams of equal size. The questions and answers can be taken from *In Further Pursuit of Trivial Pursuit*, from any question-and-answer reference book (kids' encyclopedias are great), from the official Trivial Pursuit question boxes or from a list of personal questions drawn up and kept on file in the family games drawer. It isn't difficult to make up a game for your friends. For instance, "What color was Lori and Andrew's last car?" "What is the name of Tom's dog?" or "What year did Wayne get contact lenses?" In making up your own game, write one question and answer to a card. If using question cards from a commercial trivia game (more than a hundred have come and gone since Trivial Pursuit), roll a die to decide which question on the card to answer, numbering them from top to bottom.

The Object of the Game: To score points by answering questions correctly.

The Play: Decide which team or player goes first. If playing as individuals, one of the group draws a question and asks it of the first player. If she answers correctly, she scores 1 point and gets the chance to answer another question. When a player gives the wrong answer, she draws a question and asks it of the person on her left. To keep the game moving, use a timer and give players only one minute to think of a reply.

If playing in teams, one player draws a question and asks it of the rest of his team. If they answer correctly, another question is drawn; if not, the turn passes to the other team. Each correct answer scores 1 point for the team. Team members take turns being the asker, and after everyone has had a turn, the team with the most points wins. ✎

Murder

- ◆ OTHER NAMES: **Assassin, Killer and, more innocently, Wink**
- ◆ EQUIPMENT: **a deck of playing cards or pencil and papers**
- ◆ NUMBER: **especially good with large groups**
- ◆ DESCRIPTION: **an elimination game of observation and deduction**
- ◆ TIP: **best played during another game**

MURDER CAN BE played by itself, while a group of people are sitting around in the evening, or it can be played concurrently with another game, such as **Hearts** or **Monopoly**. With kids, it usually isn't very subtle, but with wily adults, the game can persist for as long as an hour.

Preparation: From a deck of playing cards, separate out as many cards as there are players. One of the cards must be the Joker. Or get the same number of pieces of paper as there are players, and mark an X on one. Put the cards or papers into a hat.

The Object of the Game: To "murder" your victims by winking without being caught; to identify the killer before you are murdered.

The Play: The players each draw a card or a paper, being careful to keep it to themselves. The person with the Joker or the X is the killer. All the others are potential victims and, at the same time, detectives. The cards are returned to the hat, and the players continue doing whatever they like, playing another game or conversing.

During the evening, the killer murders someone by surreptitiously winking at her. Noticing that she has been winked at, she waits 10 seconds, then says, "I'm dead." This is usually accompanied by the appropriate theatrics. The rest of the players try to figure out who did it and keep a keen watch on everyone, hoping to catch the killer-winker. The dead person, of course, cannot reveal the identity of the murderer; she is simply out of the game.

The killer keeps winking, picking off his victims, trying to murder as many as possible before he is caught. The others may guess the killer's identity when they think they know who is winking, but if a player guesses wrong, he, too, is dead and drops out of the game. (The dead people can of course continue to converse or play whatever game is simultaneously under way; they are simply no longer trying to guess the identity of the wicked winker.)

When the killer is caught, the cards are reshuffled and drawn again for a new game. At the end of the evening, the killer who murdered the most victims wins; all the others pay forfeits. ✎

Forfeits

ALTHOUGH SOME OF them may sound quaint, these forfeits, adapted from *Cassell's Book of Sports and Pastimes* (1881), are still good fun today. When the moment of judgment comes, the person designated to pronounce on the others can either read a forfeit from the list below or make up something equally ridiculous. A forfeit can take any form: a riddle to solve, a dare to perform, a skill to master. (In the case of riddles, the answers are given here in parentheses.) The object of the exercise, of course, is to make the player appear absurd as he struggles to redeem his forfeit.

1. Put yourself through a keyhole. (Write the word "yourself" on a piece of paper, roll it up, and pass it through a keyhole.)

2. Take a friend upstairs, and bring him or her down on a feather. (Go upstairs with a friend, then find a feather, sprinkle down on it, and present it to the other person.)

3. Read a book inside and out without opening it. (Read the title in the room, then go outside the room, and read the title again.)

4. Put one hand where the other cannot touch it. (On the elbow.)

5. Leave the room with two legs, return with six. (Walk out of the room, and come back holding a chair.)

6. Put four chairs in a row, take off your shoes, and jump over them. (Jump over the shoes, not the chairs.)

7. Ask a question that cannot possibly be answered in the negative. (What does Y-E-S spell?)

8. The Statue. The person paying the forfeit must stand absolutely still and allow himself to be put in various positions by the rest of the group, staying frozen in one position until the next player moves his limbs.

9. The Sentence. Each player calls out a letter, and the person paying the forfeit must make up a sentence using words starting with those letters, in the order given.

10. Pay compliments to five people in the room, being careful to exclude all A's from the words you say to the first person, all E's from the second, all I's from the third, all O's from the next and all U's from the last.

11. The person paying the forfeit should hold his arms straight out on either side. A small object is placed in each hand. Without moving his arms, he must put both objects in one hand. (Put one object on a shelf, then turn around, and retrieve it with the other hand, keeping both arms still all the while.)

12. Make a five-minute laudatory speech about yourself.

13. Have two people stand on the same newspaper so that they cannot touch each other. (Put it over a doorsill, and close the door between them.)

14. Say the alphabet backwards.

15. Cut a caper.

16. Put a candle in a position so that everyone can see it except yourself. (Put it on your head.)

17. Give an animated three-minute speech on the subject of prunes (or any subject).

18. Ask a person for a dollar, offering six good reasons why he should give it to you. A bigger forfeit: Go outside and ask the first passerby.

19. Make one of the gathering laugh.

13

Family Pastimes: Travel Games

It was a Game called Yes and No, where Scrooge's nephew had to think of something, and the rest must find out what; he only answering to their questions yes or no, as the case was. The brisk fire of questioning to which he was exposed, elicited from him that he was thinking of an animal, a live animal, rather a disagreeable animal, a savage animal, an animal that growled and grunted sometimes, and talked sometimes, and lived in London, and walked about the streets, and wasn't made a show of, and wasn't led by anybody, and didn't live in a menagerie, and was never killed in a market, and was not a horse, or an ass, or a cow, or a bull, or a tiger, or a dog, or a pig, or a cat, or a bear. At every fresh question that was put to him, this nephew burst into a fresh roar of laughter; and was so inexpressibly tickled, that he was obliged to get up off the sofa and stamp. At last the plump sister, falling into a similar state, cried out:

"I have found it out! I know what it is, Fred! I know what it is!"

"What is it?" cried Fred.

"It's your Uncle Scro-o-o-o-oge!"

Which it certainly was.

I N THE DECADES since Dickens included this variation of **Twenty Questions** in *A Christmas Carol,* humans have taken to the road in droves; the pastimes that once entertained in the parlor are now more often reserved for the backseat. Although Fred could not jump up and stamp his feet with glee and his plump sister could not roll out of her chair, playing Twenty Questions in the car tickles the funny bone as effectively as it ever did at home.

The games in this chapter are more properly called pastimes than games. A game is a contest of sorts, guided by rules of play, with a winner at the end who can claim some mastery that eludes the losers. A pastime, on the other hand, is an unassuming form of play, designed merely to pass the time in an agreeable way. A generation ago, pastimes filled the moments between dinner and bedtime, but television has taken over that role. Today, pastimes are more likely played on the road, in cars, trains and planes, at bus stops and in movie lineups, where people are thrown together with nothing but their wits to entertain them.

For all their apparent gentleness, pastimes are the wild things of the games world. Spontaneous, often short-lived, they are confined by few rules, and what rules exist can be bent to fit the circumstance. Perhaps because they have escaped the close scrutiny of the rule makers and archivists, these games have hardly evolved at all: they are handed from generation to generation virtually intact. When families launch into a game of Twenty Questions and **Hangman** today, they are passing the time exactly as their parents, grandparents and great-grandparents did. And when they play **Scissors, Paper, Stone,** they are enjoying themselves as people have since the pharaohs reigned.

Pastimes have at least three characteristics guaranteed to ensure their survival: they can be played anywhere; they require no equipment (except occasionally a borrowed pencil and the back of a paper napkin); and they work best with a small group of people, as few as two or three. And no one needs to move a muscle, except in their heads.

Family pastimes can be categorized as guessing games such as **Jotto** and **Coffeepot,** memory games such as **Roll Call** and word-play puzzles such as **Ghost** and **No! No!** Most of them are brainteasers, often with a ridiculous bent. To figure them out, it helps to have what Lewis Carroll called "a mental squint." Carroll, or Charles Lutwidge Dodgson, as he was christened, was a master at them and invented a few, including **Doublets**, which is still played today. In 1879, several months after submitting the first Doublets to *Vanity Fair*, Dodgson wrote to a friend, describing the pastime as "what doctors call 'an alterative,' i.e., if you happen to have a headache, it will charm it away: but if you haven't one, it will probably give you one."

Doublets today is played under at least half a dozen names, as are most of the other games in this chapter. The rules are as difficult to pin down as the names; they are usually made up on the spot to suit the players and the day. There is nothing formal or formalized about these games, nor should there be, so consider the directions on the following pages to be little more than starting points for creating your own. For instance, the staff at a Canadian restaurant in Kingston, Ontario, evolved **Questions of Character** from **Who Am I?** a parlor standard of a century ago. The game goes on all day: the bartender is It, and the others offer guesses every time they return to place an order.

Choosing It is about the only formal part of these games. Often, someone in the group simply offers to start, and players take turns from there, moving clockwise around the car or at random down the movie lineup. More than once, my son and I have turned heads at the grocery store when we have suddenly launched into a game of No! No! while waiting in line at the cash register. For a more ritual start to the game, roll a die or draw cards from a deck (the highest number begins), flip a coin, or play a round of Scissors, Paper, Stone. In guessing games, the winner of one round can start the next, or in games such as **Taboo**, the person who loses one round begins anew.

Most of these games include some means of declaring a winner, although in practice, players rarely keep score. The games just go on and on, which in fact is part of their charm. The first time we played **Botticelli**, we became so engrossed in identifying the mystery woman whose name started with B that we drove 50 miles past our turnoff.

Mora

- ◆ OTHER NAMES: **more widely known by its variations Buck, Buck and Scissors, Paper, Stone**
- ◆ NUMBER: **two players**
- ◆ EQUIPMENT: **just your hands**
- ◆ DESCRIPTION: **extremely old guessing game**
- ◆ TIP: **use the game to choose It or to pass a few minutes, hardly more**

MORA AND ITS companion game, Scissors, Paper, Stone, have their roots on the Mediterranean coast and in the Orient. In Japan, the game is called Jan-Ken-Pon. Mora is Italian, the name of the game borrowed from the word for a very short beat in poetry. Mora has been played in Italy since at least 1706, but it has a much longer history than that. Egyptian hieroglyphic paintings from 2000 B.C. show a finger-guessing game much like Mora in progress, and Roman children in Nero's day played Bucca, Bucca, Quot Sunt Hic? which sounds for all the world like "Buck, Buck, how many fingers do I hold up?" a Mora variation that is still played by American children today.

Mora is often played to decide who is It for another game. If there are more than two or three players, run elimination rounds. Pairs play Mora, and the winners of each pair play each other until a single winner, or It, is declared.

The Object of the Game:
To predict the number of fingers the other player will expose.

The Play:
Two players sit facing each other with their hands in fists. Each has a pile of counters (beans, gumdrops, baseball cards). At exactly the same time, each person puts out one or two fingers and calls "One!" or "Two!"—the number of fingers each predicts the other person will expose.

If both players are right or if both are wrong, the game is a draw, and no one wins. If one player guesses right, the other gives him as many counters as the number of fingers he showed. Each round takes a matter of seconds. The game is played until one person runs out of counters or until both find something else to do.

Scissors, Paper, Stone

Variations: In a more complex version of Mora, three and four fingers can also be exposed. When the players put out their fingers, they try to predict the exact number of fingers the other player will expose: anything from one to four—or five, if the thumb is in the game. In another variation, they call "Evens!" (two or four fingers) or "Odds!" (one or three fingers).

Buck, Buck is a game for three that combines leapfrog with finger guessing. One person is the Master and stands as the judge for that round; one is the Buck, who bends over and blinds himself by burying his head in the Master's stomach; and one player is the Frog, who leaps on the Buck's back and sits there for the round. The Frog holds out her right hand with some of her fingers exposed and says, "Buck, Buck, how many fingers do I hold up?" If the Buck guesses correctly, he becomes the Master, the Master becomes the Frog, and the Frog becomes the Buck. If he guesses wrong, the Frog keeps asking, exposing a new set of fingers each time, until the Buck gets it right.

In **Scissors, Paper, Stone**, two or three players hide one fist behind their backs. On the count of three, each shows his or her hand, holding it either in a fist (stone), flat (paper) or with the first two fingers pointing in a sideways V (scissors). The winner is decided on the principle that scissors cut paper, paper wraps stone, and stone blunts the cutting edge of scissors. If each person shows something different, the round is a draw, because the three cancel each other out. If two people show paper and one shows scissors, scissors wins; if two show stone and one shows paper, paper wins. The winner gets a counter from each of the losing players (or becomes It for another game); if there are two winners (two papers and a stone, for instance), each scores 1 point or gets a counter from the loser. ∾

Twenty Questions

- OTHER NAMES: Yes and No; familiar to many as the variation Animal, Vegetable, Mineral; the basis for television quiz shows such as *What's My Line?* and *Front Page Challenge*
- NUMBER: any number of players
- EQUIPMENT: none
- DESCRIPTION: a classic question-and-answer game

MADE FAMOUS by a radio quiz-show broadcast shortly after World War II, Twenty Questions has been popular under a variety of names for centuries. It is just as much fun now as it was in Dickens' day. Traditionally, one person, designated It, asked questions of the other players, all of whom knew the mystery word. For traveling, however, the game works better if the person who is It thinks of the mystery word, and all the others do the asking and guessing.

The mystery word in this game is always an object, a noun such as Asparagus or Submarine. Twenty clues—the answers to 20 questions—may not seem like much help, but in fact, the identity of just about anything, even abstract nouns such as Beauty and Evil, can be deduced within that time, provided sufficient forethought is given to the questions. According to convention, the first question is: "Is it animal, vegetable or mineral?" (This is the only question that is not answered either Yes or No.) The next question is usually: "Is it bigger than a breadbox?" The general strategy is to find out the composition of the object, then the size, its location and whether it is useful or ornamental.

There are dozens of variations which limit the category of the objects to be guessed or the kind of questions that can be asked, but basically, the method is always the same. Remember: These are guessing games, not bluffing games. You can try to throw your questioners off the track, but your answers must be technically true.

Preparation: If there are more than six players, divide them into teams; one team is It, and the others take turns asking questions—one question per team, which is decided by consulting among themselves.

The Object of the Game: To guess the mystery word by asking 20 questions or less.

The Play: The person who is It thinks of an object that fits easily into one of the categories of animal, vegetable or mineral. The others take turns asking questions that can be answered with either Yes or No. (Some house rules accept replies of Partly or Sometimes.) The players are allowed 20 questions altogether, within which they have to guess the correct answer.

The person (or team) who is It keeps track of the number of questions he has been asked. If he stumps the others, he gets to think of another word; otherwise, the person (or team) who guesses correctly is It.

Variations: Strictly speaking, in **Animal, Vegetable, Mineral,** there is no limit to the number of questions that can be asked, but there is a time limit for guessing the right answer, say, three minutes. (Otherwise, it is exactly like Twenty Questions.) For young kids, you may have to clarify what objects fit into the categories: Animal is anything that moves and breathes (including, in this game, fish and insects); Vegetable includes anything that grows (trees, plants); and just about everything else is Mineral. The name of the game belies its age. Contemporary players might add another category: Synthetic, which would include objects made of plastic and other manufactured materials. For instance, in 1890, a ball would be Vegetable, since it was made of rubber tapped from trees; nowadays, it would be Synthetic.

In **Who Am I?** players choose a well-known person, instead of an object, for the others to guess. The person can be alive or dead, fictional, famous or the next-door neighbor, as long as it is someone with whom everyone in the game is familiar. In the original version of this game, the questions must be answered Yes or No. For instance: Is it a woman? Yes. Is she American? No. French? Yes. A singer? Yes. Is she Edith Piaf? Yes.

Questions of Character is a variation on Who Am I? that taxes the observational and deductive powers of both the questioners and the person giving the answers. The person who is It decides on a character for the others to guess and tells them up front whether it is a man or a woman. The person's name must be deduced from her answers to their questions, which always ask that the character be described in terms of another object. For instance: If he were a car, what kind would he be? A big black limousine. If he were a drink, what kind would he be? Bourbon, straight up. If he were a tie, what kind would he be? A black string tie with a silver-rope clasp. Is he Johnny Cash? Yes. Obviously, the person who is It should choose someone they know, or think they know, quite well. ∽

Botticelli

- NUMBER: **any number of players**
- EQUIPMENT: **a keen brain**
- DESCRIPTION: **a two-level name-guessing game; the most refined variation of Twenty Questions**
- COMPLEXITY: **an absorbing game for older kids and adults**
- DURATION: **each round takes 15 to 20 minutes, sometimes longer**

LIKE **Who Am I?** Botticelli is an impersonation game, one that keeps both the questioners and the impersonator guessing. The person who is It decides on a character, living or dead, fictional or real, famous or simply well known to everyone in the game; a male must choose a man, and a female a woman. You don't have to know a lot about the person you choose to be, but you do have to know a lot of other people whose last names start with the same letter. Be wary of people such as Joyce Carol Oates and Ivan the Terrible: dictionaries of biography have the shortest listings under I, O, U, X, Y and, of course, Q and Z.

The Object of the Game:
To guess the name of It.

The Play: The person who is It decides on a character to impersonate, then identifies herself by the first initial of the mystery person's last name, announcing, for instance, "I am M." The other players in turn try to guess who she is. Each questioner thinks of a person whose last name starts with the same letter, then asks whether It is the person they describe; It has to figure out who the questioner has in mind and answer with that name—or any name which starts with the same letter and fits the description. For instance: "Are you a singer who made a movie?"

"No, I am not Madonna."

The next person might ask, "Are you an actress who committed suicide?"

"No, I am not Marilyn Monroe."

The questioners have to give enough of a description that It has a fair chance of figuring out who they have in mind, but the real purpose is to try to stump It. If she cannot think of anyone who fits the description and whose last name starts with the required letter, she says, "I pass," and the questioner wins a chance to ask one yes-or-no question, the kind typical of **Twenty Questions**. While the first questions in Botticelli eliminate some possible identities, it is the bonus questions that narrow down who the person might be. For instance, It is asked, "Are you an educational theorist?"

She does not remember Maria Montessori, so she says, "I pass."

The other player then asks, "Are you dead?"

"Yes," she replies. Every yes earns the questioner another yes-or-no question.

"Are you a writer?"

"Yes."

"Are you American?"

"No."

The turn now passes to the next player, who goes back to asking a question with a specific person in mind. For instance: "Are you a short-story writer from New Zealand?"

"Yes, I am Katherine Mansfield."

There is no maximum number of questions that can be asked, which is why the game can sometimes last all the way from New York to Boston. The person whose question reveals It's identity is It in the next round. ❧

Coffeepot

- OTHER NAMES: **Mousetrap, Teakettle and Teapot**
- NUMBER: **any number of players; perfect for two**
- EQUIPMENT: **none**
- DESCRIPTION: **a wonderfully silly word-guessing game; a new twist on Twenty Questions**
- COMPLEXITY: **good group game for all ages; young kids especially love it**

MORE OPEN-ENDED than **Twenty Questions**, Coffeepot (the American version of the British game Teapot) allows It to choose any word at all for the others to guess—an object, an action, an event, anything. It replies to the other players' questions with a sentence that contains clues, in each case substituting the mystery word with "coffeepot." The game taxes everyone's brain, but best of all, it keeps players in stitches as coffeepots crop up in the most unexpected places. To confuse the questioners, choose a mystery word that has several homonyms—words that sound the same but have different meanings, such as pare, pear, pair or sea, see, C (the alphabet letter, the vitamin and the musical note).

The Object of the Game:
To guess the mystery word by asking questions.

The Play: One player thinks of a word (an object or an action verb). He composes a sentence around the mystery word but replaces the actual word with "coffeepot." The other players take turns asking questions that It answers in a sentence which gives one of the meanings of the mystery word but again uses "coffeepot" instead of the word. He can make the coffeepot sound as ridiculous as he likes, but the answer must use the mystery word correctly according to one of its meanings.

For instance, the player who is It begins, "When I go to the zoo, I coffeepot animals."

The first questioner, thinking the word might be "watch," asks, "Do you wear the coffeepot on your wrist?"

"No, when I am in the coffeepot, I take off my watch."

"Is the coffeepot wet?"

"No, but vitamin coffeepots can dissolve in water." (The answer is see/sea/C.)

The game continues until a player guesses the word. Some people include a house rule that anyone who laughs is out of the game, but this seems unnecessarily cruel: laughter is not only inevitable, it is the point of the game. ❧

Do you wear a coffeepot on your wrist?

Crambo

- ◆ OTHER NAMES: **I'm Thinking of a Word . . .**
- ◆ NUMBER: **any number of players; best with more than four**
- ◆ EQUIPMENT: **none; can be played anywhere**
- ◆ DESCRIPTION: **a rhyming word-guessing game**
- ◆ COMPLEXITY: **anyone who can rhyme can play**

CRAMBO, A forerunner of **Charades**, is based on riddles and rhymes. In the Victorian parlor-game version, a player drew papers from two hats, one containing a single noun, the other a phrase. The player would have to compose a rhyme containing both the noun and the phrase. But the game is much older than that, first appearing in print around 1600 and mentioned as a welcome traveling companion from time to time ever since: the famous British diarist Samuel Pepys played it on his way to The Hague, and Jonathan Swift describes it in *Gulliver's Travels*. The root of the game's name is apparently the Greek word for cabbage, although the relationship between the thick-headed vegetable and repeating rhymes is tenuous. Nevertheless, both the name and the rules have survived virtually unchanged for four centuries, and players today love it as much as ever, especially kids, who are often better than adults at the free association the game demands.

The Object of the Game:
To guess the mystery rhyming word.

The Play:
One player thinks of a mystery word and a word that rhymes with it, then announces, "I am thinking of a word that rhymes with _____." The others take turns asking a question that defines a word which also rhymes. The player who is It has to figure out the rhyming word each questioner has in mind, then answer, using the new rhyme.

For instance, It says, "I am thinking of a word that rhymes with jar."

The first player says, "Is it a long way away?"

"No, it isn't far."

The next player asks, "Is it where you go to have a drink?"

"No, it isn't a bar."

"Does it shine in the sky?"

"No, it's not a star."

"Do you drive it to work?"

"Yes, it's a car."

If It cannot figure out the rhyming word a questioner has in mind—for instance, if she asks, "Does it burn?" and he can't think of "char"— the questioner reveals her word and takes another turn. The person who guesses the mystery word correctly becomes It for the next round. ❧

No! No!

- ◆ NUMBER: **two or more players**
- ◆ EQUIPMENT: **none**
- ◆ DESCRIPTION: **a somewhat complicated but hilarious rhyming-word game**
- ◆ COMPLEXITY: **best for older kids and adults**

ANYONE EAVESDROPPING on this game will think that the players have gone completely, collectively bonkers. It takes some mental agility, but even young kids can play once they get the hang of it.

The Object of the Game:
To answer the previous definition with the proper rhyme; to add a definition for your own rhyming word.

The Play: One player thinks of a word, then adds a definition for a word that rhymes with it. The next player identifies the word for the previous definition, then adds a definition for another word that rhymes. Players who cannot figure out the word for the previous definition or who cannot add one of their own drop out. The last person to add a rhyme to the chain wins.

For example, the first person starts with, "Top, what happens when you let something go."

The next person says, "No! No! You mean Drop, what you use to clean the floor."

"No! No! You mean Mop, jumping on one foot."

"No! No! You mean Hop, to hit someone."

"No! No! You mean Bop, a soft drink."

"No! No! You mean Pop, to trade for something else." And so on.

I Spy

- ◆ NUMBER: **two or more; with more than five players, it is too long between turns**
- ◆ EQUIPMENT: **none**
- ◆ DESCRIPTION: **a guessing game for anyone who can identify colors**
- ◆ DURATION: **easily absorbs 20 minutes or more**
- ◆ TIP: **good for slow-speed daytime trips**

I SPY WAS, UNTIL as recently as 1883, the common name for **Hide and Seek,** but it is as an object guessing game that most of us have played it. It is an ideal travel game, although it can be played only in daylight and players must agree to choose mystery objects either inside the vehicle or in the distant landscape; otherwise, the objects disappear before the others have a chance to guess. If you think you know all about I Spy, read on: there are a couple of twists that can make it more interesting.

The Object of the Game:
To guess the object spied.

The Play: The person who is It decides on a mystery object that is in clear view of all the players and says, "I spy, with my little eye, something that is _____," identifying the object by its

I spy, with my little eye, something that is orange . . .

color alone. The other players take turns guessing what it could be, naming objects of that color. Choosing an object of a common color such as green or blue extends the game; if the player names chartreuse and there is nothing but a yellow-green scarf in sight, the game is quickly over.

Variations: Some claim that the original game involved identifying the object by its first letter, rather than its color: for instance, "I spy, with my little eye, something that begins with W." A slightly more challenging game, it is just as much fun to play.

Guessing objects of a specific color or those whose names begin with a certain letter can get tedious if it goes on too long. For a faster game, allow each player only one guess based on the color or letter clue. The Spy then gives another adjective clue, for instance: "I spy, with my little eye, something that is red and soft." The players each take a turn guessing, and if no one comes up with the answer, the Spy gives another clue: "I spy, with my little eye, something that is red and soft and fits me." This version of the game keeps everybody happier. The Spy is more involved, and the other players are less frustrated by their own dim-wittedness.

An 8-year-old named Claire invented **Alphabet I Spy**, in which a player can select an object of any color, but the first player must choose one that begins with the letter A, the second must have one that begins with B, and so on. For instance, the third player says, "I spy, with my little eye, something that is orange." Since her letter is C, the others guess car, child's hat, cantaloupe, Chiclets package and crayon before finally getting the right answer—the hands of the car clock. This makes for a more challenging travel game: there are lots of F words —field, farm, fence, factory—but how many K words are there in the landscape or in the car? This game easily keeps the passengers occupied for the better part of an hour. ∾

Fortunately/Unfortunately

- ◆ NUMBER: **any number of players; especially good with just two**
- ◆ EQUIPMENT: **none**
- ◆ DESCRIPTION: **a short-lived storytelling game; lots of laughs while it lasts**

THIS GAME STRETCHES the imagination and is good exercise for those who are always inclined to see the glass as half empty—or half full. The routine has been used to good effect for decades by vaudevillians and comedians.

The Object of the Game: To take the opposite view of what was just said.

The Play: The player who goes first starts the story by saying just about anything at all that could begin with the word Fortunately. For instance, "Fortunately, it is a beautiful day today."

The next player continues the story, starting his sentence with Unfortunately. He cannot hesitate, and he must turn the story completely around, but what he says must also make perfect sense. "Unfortunately, I don't have any sunscreen."

The next person sees the brighter side: "Fortunately, I can borrow some from Aunt Ginny, who just came back from Mexico."

The pessimist continues, "Unfortunately, her trip was cut short when she got malaria."

"Fortunately, she left just before the earthquake." And so on.

Eventually, a player will find it impossible to find any redeeming feature in a particularly bleak situation—or the dark side of an event that is unremittingly bright—and will have to drop out of the game. ∾

Fortunately/Unfortunately

Taboo

- ◆ OTHER NAMES: **Poison Letter**
- ◆ NUMBER: **any number of players**
- ◆ EQUIPMENT: **none; can be played anywhere**
- ◆ DESCRIPTION: **a question-and-answer avoidance game that strains the brain**
- ◆ COMPLEXITY: **players must be able to spell quite well**

IF PLAYED WITH people of various ages and abilities, gauge the questions to the level of the player who must respond. Played competitively, a slight hesitation is enough to bump a player out of the game, but some degree of tolerance is usually applied among friends. Even adults can sometimes take a while to figure out a taboo-free reply.

The Object of the Game: To answer the question without using the taboo, or poison, letter.

The Play: Players take turns asking the questions. The person who is It decides which letter of the alphabet is forbidden, or taboo. He then poses a question to each player in turn, asking anything at all that comes to mind but trying to formulate the question so that the player will find it difficult to avoid the taboo letter. The players, for their part, must answer the question honestly, without using the forbidden letter in any word. They cannot answer with a simple Yes or No. If an answer borders on the ridiculous, the rest of the players decide whether it is admissible.

For instance, the person who is It decides that for this round, R will be taboo. He asks the first player, "Have you ever been in a race?"

"No, I don't like to be that active."

He asks the next, "How is your mother?"

"She is fine now that I am going to school."

"Who was it that the big bad wolf ate?"

"He ate a little female child who had a hooded cloak dyed the hue of poppies."

Finally, he asks, "What do trains travel on?"

The player hesitates, trying to think of a reply that does not use railroad, rail or track. She waits too long and has to drop out of the game. The last person in the game is It in the next round.

Variation: Another game based on random questions and qualified answers is **Initials**. The questioner asks questions of the other players in turn, naming each according to how the person prefers to be addressed. Each player must respond with answers that begin with his or her own initials. The players can use two initials or three (or four if they have that many names), but the initials must be used in order, and the answers must be plausible, if not actually correct. For instance, "What do you like to read, Ross Rogers?"

"Robust Romances."

"What are your favorite animals, Janice McLean?"

"Jumping Monkeys."

"What did you do at school today, Erik Robert Franz?"

"Etched Ridiculous Fables."

Karl and Zach are in big trouble in this game. ❧

Questions

- ◆ NUMBER: **more can play, but best for two**
- ◆ EQUIPMENT: **none; can be played anywhere**
- ◆ DESCRIPTION: **an avoidance game**
- ◆ COMPLEXITY: **can be played by anyone who can ask a question (kids are experts)**

A GAME DESIGNED for 4-year-olds, this is usually only a few minutes' entertainment, but it is good for a few laughs too.

The Object of the Game: To reply to every question with a question.

The Play: One person begins by asking a question. Players take turns in order, each replying to the previous question with a question. Anyone who delays too long or who goofs and makes a statement is out of the game. When only one player remains, she is the winner.

For instance, one person starts by asking, "Where is your mother?"

The next replies, "Don't you remember that she said she was going to work?"

"Where does she work?"

"Why don't you ask your father?"

"Where is my father?"

"Isn't he at home?"

"Is his house the one with the red shutters?" And so on.

The last person in one round starts the next. ❧

Ghost

- OTHER NAMES: also known as Add-A-Letter and by the name of its variation, Donkey
- NUMBER: two to four players; three is best
- DESCRIPTION: a word game that requires spelling and, occasionally, bluffing
- COMPLEXITY: kids at grade-three level can play comfortably with adults; also fun for adults with a love of language
- TIP: an absorbing nighttime traveling game

SOME PLAY THIS as Donkey, but it is properly called Ghost. Its name is derived from the century-old tradition of calling anyone eliminated from the game a "ghost." The game is a good one, since it keeps players involved even after they have dropped out of one round. It can last 10 to 15 minutes and, if played as Donkey, even longer.

The Object of the Game:
To add a letter without spelling a word.

The Play: The first person thinks of a word and says the first letter. For instance, if she thinks of "peanut," she says P. (She does *not* say the word peanut.) The next player thinks of a word that starts with P—for instance, "pot"—and says the first two letters, P-O. The next person thinks of a word starting with PO and says the first three letters. For instance, he thinks of "possible" and says P-O-S. If the next person can only think of "post," he says P-O-S-T, ending the game, because he has made a word. He loses one of his three lives and becomes a third of a ghost.

If, instead of a T, the player had said S, the game would continue, since POSS is not a word but is the beginning of the word "possum." The next player says P-O-S-S-U, and finally, the next one must add M, completing the word in the only way possible.

Several rounds are played in each game. When one word is spelled, the next player in turn starts another word. Each time a person adds a letter that spells a word, she loses a life and becomes another third of a ghost. When a player loses three lives and is a full-fledged ghost, he drops out of the game. As a ghost, he can no longer call out letters, but he can talk to the other players, giving them advice and hints. A player, however, cannot talk to a ghost: if he forgets himself and converses with the ghost for any reason whatsoever, he, too, becomes a full-fledged ghost (even if he still has all his lives) and leaves the game.

Every time a player adds a letter, she must have a real word in mind. If another player thinks the person who added the last letter is bluffing, he can challenge her, but only if he is the next player. If she can produce an actual word, spelled correctly, the challenger is penalized: he loses a life, as well as his turn. If he is right, the bluffer loses

a life, and the challenger continues playing, adding a letter to the word as it was before the bluffer played.

Bluffing is a good strategy, but don't get caught. A dictionary is the final arbiter, and failing that, the consensus of the players holds sway. (Proper names and foreign words are usually not allowed.)

Sometimes, players lose a life accidentally. A player may be thinking of a longer word, but if his contribution actually makes a word, he is out of the game. For instance, if the player before him says T-H-A, he might add N, thinking of the word "thank." But since THAN is a word, he loses a life.

As a courtesy, players should call out all the letters accumulated to that point, then add one of their own so that all the players can keep in mind what is being spelled.

Variations: A trickier version for advanced spellers is **Super Ghost.** Players can add letters to either the front or the back of the letters already stated, so long as they have an actual word in mind. For instance, after POSSU, a player could add O to the front, making OPOSSU (for "opossum"), leaving it to the next player to complete the word.

Ghost is sometimes scored without lost lives. Instead, a player who completes a word earns the first letter of the word ghost. When he has lost fives times, he becomes a ghost (one life for each letter). **Donkey** is exactly the same game, except when a player completes a word, she earns a letter of the word donkey. The game is over when someone loses six times and becomes a full-fledged donkey. ∾

Word Chains

- NUMBER: two or more players; with more than five, it is too long between turns
- EQUIPMENT: none
- DESCRIPTION: a progressive word game
- COMPLEXITY: can be played by anyone who knows the alphabet; variations require some special knowledge of geography, animals, and so on
- DURATION: a classic travel pastime that can go on practically forever

THERE ARE DOZENS of twists on this theme, but the basic method of play is the same: building word chains by making a word that begins with the last letter of the previous word. Players usually limit themselves to words in specific categories—Cities, Countries, Food, Animals. The more expert the players, the narrower the field. For instance, real pros may play Word Chains with the names of Living Female American Authors or Retired Baseball Players.

The Object of the Game:
To think of a word in the selected category that begins with the last letter of the previous word.

The Play: The first player names the category and says a word—any word—that fits. The next player must make a word which starts with the last letter of the first word and which fits the category. For instance, the first player announces the category, Birds, then says Thrush, the next player says Hummingbird, and the following players add Dove, Egret, Tern, Nuthatch, Heron, Nightingale, and so on.

Players continue in turn. If a player cannot think of a word, she either passes and is allowed to play again on the next turn or drops out of the game, depending on what everyone agrees before the game begins.

Technically, the last person still in the game wins, but in practice, the game usually stops when everyone is ready for something new.

Variations: For a more competitive game, players try to make a word from the last *two* letters of the previous word. This is quite difficult, so dispense with categories: any old word will do, as long as it is four letters or more. For instance, Table, Lemon, Only, Lyme, Melon, Onset, Etymology, Gymnast, Stamina, and so on. Advanced players can set a minimum of five or six letters per word. If you play the game so that the point is to stump fellow players, it can quickly be brought to a halt with a word like Stack or Stagnant. It is much more absorbing for players to work together to keep the chain growing as long as possible.

A related game is **Alphabet Geography** (or Alphabet Animals, Alphabet Vegetables, and so on). Instead of using the last letter of the previous word, the word chains are created by making words in alphabetical order, beginning with A. For instance, if Geography is the category, the first player might say Australia, the next would add Brazil, then Canada, Denmark, England, France, Germany, Holland, Iceland, and so on. The first time through the alphabet isn't so hard, but progressive passes become excruciating as players try to think of an animal besides Zebra that starts with Z. After a decent interval, most players just agree to pass, skipping the tough letters and continuing to move through the alphabet until every option is exhausted—many miles down the road.

One of the oldest forms of the word-chain family of games is **I Love My Love**. Players take turns declaring their love for a person whose name begins with the next letter of the alphabet, who lives in a city beginning with that letter and who has an appealing quality which also begins with that letter. For instance, the first player starts, "I love my love with an A, because her name is Abigail, she lives in Albuquerque and she is agile."

The next player continues, "I love my love with a B, because his name is Biff, he lives in Boise and he is brusque."

This game is not particularly taxing intellectually, but it can certainly be hilarious.

Another spin on the same theme is **The Parson's Cat** (the cat, historically, has also belonged to the minister and the preacher). The first player says, "The parson's cat is an active cat, and his name is Andrew."

The next player continues with A, "The parson's cat is an adorable cat, and her name is Alexandra," and so do all the other players.

When the turn comes around to the first player again, he switches to B: "The parson's cat is a brave cat, and his name is Bob." All the players take a turn with each letter of the alphabet. The game is best with large groups, but even with a handful of players, some letters of the alphabet can be tricky. "The parson's cat is a querulous cat, and her name is Queenie." ∾

Slogans

- ◆ OTHER NAMES: **Headlines and Telegrams**
- ◆ NUMBER: **two or more players**
- ◆ EQUIPMENT: **pencil and paper (optional)**
- ◆ DESCRIPTION: **a fast, funny game; good for only a few rounds; can be played anywhere**
- ◆ COMPLEXITY: **a creative word game for those who can spell**

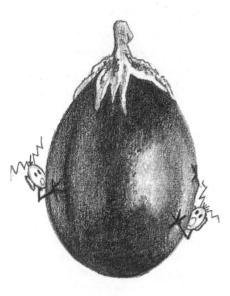

**Timid Aliens Barter
Leviathan Eggplant**

THIS GAME IS fun for adults, kids or a mixed group, anyone who is good at free association. As a travel pastime, limit the letters to half a dozen so that players can work out the sayings in their heads. At home, you can hand out papers and pencils, and the players can come up with more convoluted slogans.

The Object of the Game:
Using certain letters, to create the funniest saying.

The Play: Players take turns calling out random letters of the alphabet, the number of letters geared to the age and skill of the players: five is good for young children, up to a dozen or more for keen adults. Within a time limit of five minutes (or three or one), players make up a saying, an advertising slogan, a tabloid headline or a telegram to a distant friend (or enemy) using each of the letters to begin a word. The letters must be used in the order they were given.

At the end of the time limit, players call out their slogans. The winner is the one whose slogan elicits the most laughs.

Variation: Instead of using letters of the alphabet, the player who is It calls out a four-, five- or six-letter word, and everyone uses this to provide the first letters for the words in the slogan. For instance, the illustration shows one player's slogan for the word TABLE. ∿

Demonic Mnemonics

- ◆ NUMBER: **any number of players**
- ◆ EQUIPMENT: **none, other than good recall and a bent for the ridiculous**
- ◆ DESCRIPTION: **the gaming equivalent of the song *The Twelve Days of Christmas***
- ◆ COMPLEXITY: **even young children can play**

MEMORY GAMES are great for the road, because they take no preparation and no equipment and generally last quite a long time, creating more than a few laughs along the way. This collection offers several variations on the theme, but the principle is always the same: to keep in your head an ever-growing list of absurd and usually completely unrelated things.

The Object of the Game:
To remember everything the players before you have said and to add an appropriate item of your own.

In **Roll Call**, the first player begins with the number One and adds a noun and an adjective, both starting with the letter O. For instance, One Ornery Ostrich. The next player begins his count by repeating One Ornery Ostrich, then adds a similar alliterative phrase for the number Two: Two Tantalizing Tattletales. Players continue in turn, each time counting from One, remembering all the phrases that have gone before and adding the next one in sequence: Three Throbbing Thrushes; Four Flighty Flibbertigibbets; Five Furry Felines. Players can insist that the adjectives make some kind of sense when attached to those particular nouns. And for a more challenging game, increase the adjectives so that after the number Three, each phrase contains a corresponding number of words. For instance, Four Flighty, Flustered Flibbertigibbets; Five Furry, Fussy, Fat Felines.

In another variation called **In the Attic**, players add a phrase starting with the next letter of the alphabet, repeating all those that came before. For instance, "In the attic, there's an aardvark acting, a bison bouncing, a cartoon character caterwauling, a dogfish dithering, an electric eel entertaining," and so on.

Instead of building by numbers or letters, **I Packed My Trunk** creates a random list, threading the objects together in a story, of sorts. For instance, the first player begins by saying, "I packed my trunk for Grandmother's house, and in it, I put a red bandanna." (The player, of course, can say any object she likes.) The next player continues the story, repeating what the player said before and adding another item to the trunk: "I packed my trunk for Grandmother's house, and in it, I put a red bandanna and my pet pony." The items quickly become ridiculous, and the task of remembering them all, in exact order, becomes Sisyphean. A player who makes a mistake becomes a half-ghost and can try again in his next turn. Two mistakes, and the player becomes a spectator to the antics of the others. The last player remaining in the game wins. There are dozens of ways to start the story. Among the traditional prologues are: When I go to California, I'll take my _____; When my ship comes in (or, When I win the lottery), I'll _____; or, if you play this on a trip, When I get to _____, I'll _____. (The last two require full sentences instead of phrases, which become quite complex to remember.) ❧

Car Capers

- ◆ NUMBER: **two or more players**
- ◆ EQUIPMENT: **paper and a pencil for each player**
- ◆ DESCRIPTION: **classic car games using the landscape, passing cars and their license plate numbers and letters**
- ◆ COMPLEXITY: **requires keen observation and some spelling or counting skills**
- ◆ DURATION: **keeps kids occupied for hours, but drivers can't always play**

LICENSE PLATE GAMES may soon become a glitch in games history. They have existed only as long as widespread car travel—a mere 70 years or so—and are becoming harder and harder to play as high speeds and divided highways make the license plates (let alone the numbers and letters) increasingly difficult to see. Nevertheless, on a leisurely drive along the nation's "blue highways," they still make for good family fun, and even on superhighways, the passing cars and the landscape can become material for road play.

For **License Plate Lotto**, each player makes a Lotto card, as described on page 326. Every time a player sees a number on a license plate that matches a number on his card, he crosses it off. The first player to cross off a horizontal row wins. (If that is too easy, make the goal the crossing out of all the numbers on the card.)

You can simplify this by having all the players put their heads together to come up with a list of objects that might be seen along the way. Everyone copies out the list for herself; the first person to see an object on the list calls it out and crosses it off her list. Each individual object can be claimed by only one player. For instance, if a white horse is on the list and one appears, only the player who calls out first crosses it off. If a white horse appears later in the trip, however, another player can claim it.

In **License Plate Slogans**, players watch oncoming or passing cars carefully. One player calls out the letters of a license plate, and everyone tries to think of a slogan that uses each letter, in order, as the first letter of the words in the slogan. A player earns 10 points for the slogan and a bonus of another 10 points if the slogan befits the car or the driver. For instance, if a car passes with the license 475-BOE and a player calls out, "Blue Orient Express," she would earn 10 points for the slogan and a bonus, since the car was a speeding navy Toyota.

In **License Plate Language**, players take the passing plates in turn and, by filling in letters, make a single word using the license plate letters in the order they appear. For instance, HCN is "halcyon," VNL is "venal." You can establish a maximum time limit or a minimum word length. Have one of the players keep a list of the words, and when there are 5 (or 10), the first person who can make a sentence using them all in order wins the round.

In **Alpha Travel**, players collect letters from the license plates of passing cars, completing the alphabet in order. Players can agree to take the license plates in turn, or if they are well matched in age and skill, they can play competitively, claiming a letter by calling it out as soon as they see it. A variation on this theme is to collect the alphabet from objects in the passing landscape, players calling out their choices. For instance, Ash Tree, Boy, Car, Doghouse, Electric Wires, and so on. Only one person can claim a given object, although the same object can be claimed again if it appears later in the trip (such as electric wires).

Car Snap uses the color of the passing vehicles, rather than their license plates. Each player chooses a car as his or her own, such as a red Jaguar or a white Cadillac, but preferably something more conventional, like a blue Ford. When a matching car passes, the player yells Snap and earns 1 point. Players choose new cars and start again. After five rounds, the player with the most points wins.

In another variation, **Color Collection**, players choose a primary color—red, blue or yellow. (This game, obviously, is limited to three players.) Every time a car of the right primary color passes, the player earns 1 point. But players also earn a point if the color of the car contains their primary color. For instance, green is made by mixing blue and yellow, so a green car earns 1 point for the Blue player and 1 point for the Yellow player. Orange is red and yellow; purple is red and blue; and brown, gray and black are made by mixing the three primary colors together, so all the players earn 1 point. White cars don't earn any points, because they have no pigment at all. Two-tone cars are like blanks: the first player to call out either color gets the point. This game can last for hours on a deserted highway or become a hectic race in a traffic jam. After a specified time, the player with the most points wins. ❧

Jotto

- ◆ OTHER NAMES: **the basis for MasterMind**
- ◆ NUMBER: **two players only**
- ◆ EQUIPMENT: **a piece of paper and pencils**
- ◆ DESCRIPTION: **a word-guessing game that tests deductive logic to the extreme**
- ◆ COMPLEXITY: **best for older kids and adults**

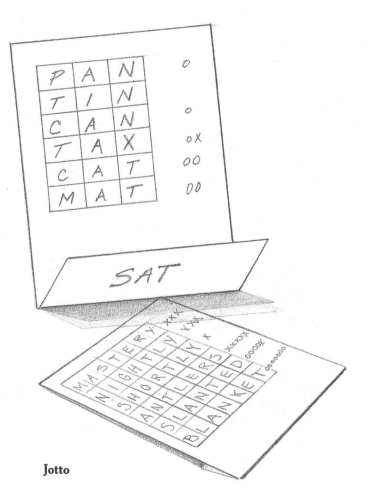

Jotto

ALTHOUGH TRADEMARKED for several decades, Jotto has been played as a game of logic for hundreds of years. With a matched set of crayons, you can even play the non-verbal spin-off, MasterMind. Both are brainteasers that, like **Chess**, bear playing over and over again. Five-letter words are a challenge, but three-letter combinations teach the basics to beginners with less frustration.

The Object of the Game: To guess the word in as few guesses as possible.

The Play: Privately, so that the other person cannot see, one player writes a word at the top or bottom of the piece of paper and folds the paper to cover what he wrote. (The word cannot contain duplicate letters and cannot be a proper noun; length is optional, but five or six letters make a good game.) Then he draws a guessing grid with the same number of squares across the top as there are letters in the word and six squares down, representing the number of guesses allowed.

The grid is passed to the other player, and she writes her first guess in the top row, one letter per square. (Her word should also have no duplicate letters.) He then compares her guess with the mystery word and marks an O for every letter in the word that is correct and in the right position and an X for every letter that is correct but in the wrong position. If the guess has no correct letters at all, she gets no marks.

She studies her score, decides which letters to keep and in which position, then writes a word in the second row of the grid. The other player scores her second guess with X's and O's, then she guesses again, each time using the information from all her previous guesses to deduce which letters to use and where to put them. Guesses can be limited to six, or the grid can be extended for difficult words. For instance, in the bottom game illustrated on the previous page, the player can deduce by the third guess that only the T is common to all three, so there are two other correct letters in the first and another two in the second guess. She decides to try the most commonly used letters of the alphabet: A, E, L and N. Together with the T, she can make TALENTS and LANTERN, but both have duplicate letters. She tries ANTLERS and, from this, correctly determines positions for T, L and A, and on the last attempt, she gets the answer right.

When the player correctly identifies the mystery word, she can then make up a word for the other person to try to guess. The player who determines the word in the fewest guesses wins.

Variations: Instead of scoring an X for a correct letter in a wrong position, a player scores only an O for a correct letter, regardless of whether it is in the right place or not. It is possible, therefore, to have five O's and still not have guessed the right word. For instance, BRAKE has all the right letters, but the mystery word is BREAK. Once a player has all the correct letters, she has to guess anagrams.

For those with advanced deductive skills, some house rules allow the player who is scoring the guesses one lie, which can be perpetrated at any time during the game.

Jotto can be played while traveling, without pencil and paper by those with very good memories. And it can also be played by a group. One person thinks of a mystery word, and the others take turns calling out their word guesses. The person tells them each time how many letters they have correct (and how many are in the right position, if you like). A player who thinks he has the answer must wait his turn to reveal it.

MasterMind is a commercial variation that distills Jotto from a word game to one of pure deductive logic. The marketed game uses colored pegs, but you can do the same thing at home with a set of crayons in six colors. One person marks four dots (or three) on the paper, in any order, using any of the given colors. Duplicates are allowed. Cover up the mystery code. The other player then makes a row of four colored dots; his guess is awarded an O for each correct color in the right place and an X for each correct color in the wrong place. (The O's and X's correspond to the black and white pegs in the game, respectively.) The player continues to guess until his color code correctly matches the mystery code. ∽

Doublets

- ◆ OTHER NAMES: **Word Golf, There and Back, Transformation and Changelings**
- ◆ NUMBER: **one or more players**
- ◆ EQUIPMENT: **paper and pencil (although some can do this in their heads)**
- ◆ DESCRIPTION: **a delightful word-manipulation game**
- ◆ TIP: **a good solo travel pastime**

DOUBLETS WAS invented by Charles Lutwidge Dodgson, a logician, mathematician and avid games player better known to the world by his pen name, Lewis Carroll. Two of his young friends once asked for some riddles, and since no new ones sprang to mind, he set himself to devise "some other form of verbal torture which should serve the same purpose." The result of his meditations was what he called Doublets. He submitted the game to *Vanity Fair* in March 1879, and it was a hit, revitalizing a magazine that had owed much of its appeal to competitive Acrostics.

A fitting game from the author of *Alice's Adventures in Wonderland*, Doublets is a topsy-turvy kind of word play in which one word is gradually transformed into another, one letter at a time, with each change of letter creating a new and legitimate word.

Although you can try changing any word to another with the same number of letters, Dodgson's own examples show his characteristic wit: Drive PIG into STY (4); raise ONE to TWO (7) and FOUR to FIVE (6); make WHEAT into BREAD (6) and BREAD into TOAST (6); dip PEN into INK (5); change TEARS into SMILE (5); make HARE into SOUP (6); turn RICH into POOR (5); get WOOD from TREE (7); prove GRASS to be GREEN (7); change CAIN into ABEL (8); get COAL from a MINE (5); change BEER into WINE (5); derive MAN from APE (4) and LOVE from HATE (2); make BLUE into PINK (8) and change BLACK to WHITE (6).

The first and last words Dodgson called doublets; the intermediary words he called links. The numbers in brackets show the minimum number of links required to make each transition. Dodgson scored his game by giving a point for each letter in the two doublet words and subtracting a point for each link used to make the transformation.

The Object of the Game:

Transforming one word to another by changing one letter at a time, creating a new word at every step.

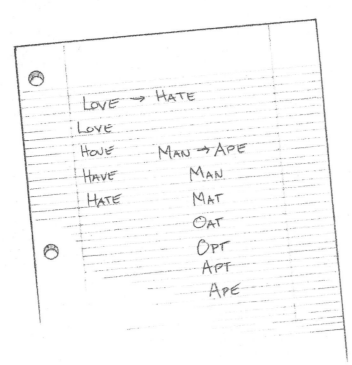

Doublets

The Play: Write a four- or five-letter word at the top of a page and another the same length at the bottom. At each turn, make a new word, changing only one letter of the word before. Players take turns shifting and replacing letters until the first word is changed to the second. For instance, LEAD-LOAD-GOAD-GOLD. The point is to accomplish the transformation in as few turns as possible.

In 1892, Dodgson ruled that instead of substituting a new letter each time, the existing letters can be rearranged to make an anagram. For example, in going from BREAD to TOAST, you could substitute a K and change BREAD to BREAK and, in the next step, change BREAK to BRAKE, rearranging the letters without adding a new one.

You can also change a three-letter word to a four-letter word—for instance, RED to BLUE—using one turn to add a new letter altogether; or turn five-letter words to four-letter words by taking one turn to drop a letter. Some words, however, cannot make the transition, no matter how hard you try: for instance, only in baseball can a player get from FIRST to THIRD. If, after 20 tries, you fail to turn DROSS to GOLD, start again.

Hangman

- ◆ OTHER NAMES: **the basis for the popular television game** *Wheel of Fortune* **and the board game Probe**
- ◆ NUMBER: **two or more players**
- ◆ EQUIPMENT: **paper and pencil**
- ◆ DESCRIPTION: **a classic word-guessing game**
- ◆ COMPLEXITY: **an elementary game that can be played by beginning spellers, but also fun for adults**

GALLOWS HUMOR has outlived the scaffold. This game is as popular with kids as ever, and it has been around a long, long time. But it isn't a bad game for adults either, provided the contestants choose little-known words made up of odd combinations of unusual letters, such as RUBIGINOUS or ERLKING. Long words are not necessarily more difficult than short ones, however: a three-letter series with an O in the middle can be dozens of different words.

Avoid words with common multiple letters; a word such as AARDVARK will be recognizable as soon as the player guesses A, although SYZYGY will likely defeat your opponent, who is unlikely to ask for a Y.

And instead of single words, try phrases (as in *Wheel of Fortune*). This turns Hangman into a sort of written **Charades.** To give the victim a fighting chance, the hangman usually reveals the category of the phrase and indicates the spaces between words.

The Object of the Game: To guess the mystery word before your entire body is hanged.

The Play: The person who is the hangman chooses a mystery word and draws a series of dashes on the paper, one dash for each letter in the word. Above or beside the dashes, she draws the gallows.

The other player (or each of the other players in turn) guesses a letter that might be in the word. If it is, the hangman prints the letter on the appropriate dash (or dashes, if the letter appears more than once). If the letter is not part of the mystery word, the hangman draws a head hanging from the gallows.

The players continue guessing, and every time they guess incorrectly, another part is added to the body on the gallows. The usual order is head, body, two arms, two legs, allowing six guesses for a four-letter word. If the word is very long, say, seven or eight letters, the hangman might also add eyes, nose and mouth, allowing nine guesses before the other player is hanged. (Players can also start with an empty paper and include the drawing of the gallows in the guessing, taking three or four turns to build the gallows.) Players can decide in advance how many guesses to allow, but most house rules leave it up to the hangman in his or her infinite mercy.

The person who guesses the mystery word becomes the hangman. If no one guesses the word, the next person in turn becomes the hangman. If two are playing, each tries to guess the other's word in fewer guesses. ~

Hangman

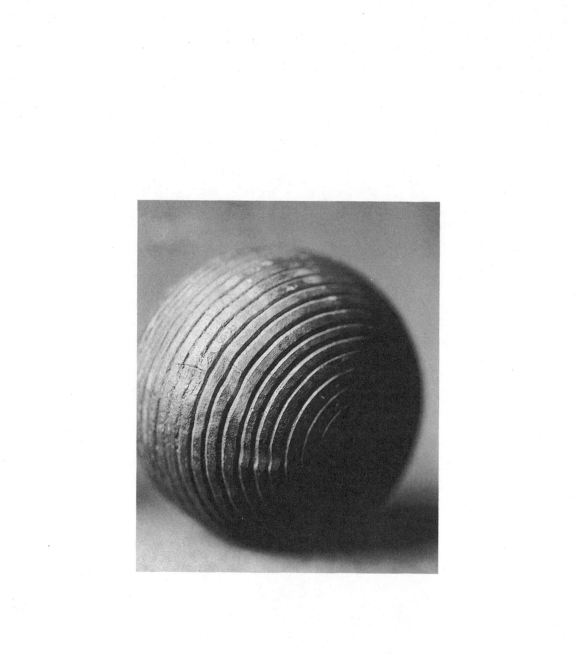

5

TIME OUT!

Outdoor Games

For when the One Great Scorer comes
To write against your name,
He marks—not that you won or lost—
But how you played the game.
—Grantland Rice
Alumnus Football

14

Good Sports:
Organized Outdoor Games

EVERY SUMMER, near the first of August, on a sunny Sunday afternoon, friends begin to arrive at our house around 3 p.m. We don't have the ball diamond until 4:00, but no one really relaxes; we palm our bats and toss balls back and forth across the yard, recalling last year's goofs and gaffes and vowing to make a few good plays today. The kids pull at our shirttails until, finally, at 3:45, we head down the street to the ballpark.

The spectators climb the wooden bleachers, and the players range onto the field. "Go by birthdays," someone suggests, and the group parts like the Red Sea into even- and odd-numbered months. There is a bit of shuffling—Tom and Steve move to different teams, the kids under 10 are spread out between the sides—then someone tosses Steve the bat wrong side down, and he catches it midshaft. Tom grips it above Steve's hand, and they grip their way alternately to the knob at the end: Steve's team is in the field. There is a frantic exchange of gloves, the batters sort themselves into a lineup, and the pitcher throws a few warm-ups. "Everybody ready?" she yells. "Batter up!"

Merrily pitches, lobbing the ball easily to the kids at the plate, making

Wayne and Tracy work for their hits. When Nick connects, 25 fielders head for the ball like gulls to a tossed French fry. The score is 3 to 2 when 5-year-old Madeleine steps to the plate. She holds the bat like the leash of an errant puppy and swings, eyes closed. The catcher is calling the strikes; he jams at two, two, two. Finally, wood nicks leather, and Madeleine toddles up the baseline, lugging the bat. Zalman and the gaggle of 8-year-olds covering first all fumble the ball, and Madeleine is safe, her grin as shy and wide as Dave Winfield's. The crowd goes wild. We play for an hour or two, then straggle back up the street for cold drinks, burgers and not-so-instant replays. Before the summer night falls, the kids disappear, returning to the ball diamond to squeeze another inning or two out of the day.

The outdoor sports we see on television—the groomed, squared-off playing fields; the numbered, padded players; the semaphore men in striped shirts—is the end result of an evolution that began in the backyard with a gang of people getting together for some fun and exercise on one of those exhilarating gotta-be-outside days. Most books would have you believe otherwise. They cite the rules for Football or Hockey, adding in a patronizing postscript that of course, you can also play in an organized home league. A pale imitation for aging athletes and wanna-be's. Not quite the real thing.

Nothing could be further from the truth. The professional associations may have codified the rules, but they didn't invent the game; ordinary folks did. When you play a round of **Shinny** or pitch an end or two of **Horseshoes**, you are part of a vital tradition of homely outdoor games that is as old as the human race. This is where organized sport was born; this is where it is still kept alive today.

Most of the games in this chapter can accommodate large or small groups of people, but they need a fair amount of space, more than a typical urban backyard offers. If you don't have a sprawling country lawn, look for a park nearby or a beach or a schoolyard where you can play. The professionals notwithstanding, you don't need a "green" to pitch a few ends of **Lawn Bowls**, and you don't need a white-lined court to play **Badminton**. All these games can be adapted for ungroomed open spaces and odd numbers of players without compromising the basic moves that make them so much fun to play.

The principles that govern these games are elementary: getting the ball over the other team's goal line or around the course first. The few rules that exist are applied only to keep things fair. In **Croquet**, for instance, you can't hammer the same player's ball twice in a row, and in Horseshoes, the winner of one round starts the next; after all, the second player has the advantage. Umpires and referees are unnecessary; the fouls and misdemeanors they are hired to catch go unremarked. Players often don't even keep score; one team is content to be "one up" or "two up" on the other. Yet the games don't suffer for it. Left to their own devices, kids and adults alike exhibit an impressive sense of fair play and self-preservation. The games are often physically aggressive, yet players rarely indulge in fights. On home turf, you make up rules as you go along, the honor system prevails, and the end result is a game that is good sport and players who are good sports.

The best of the professionals know all this. When Bobby Hull played for the Winnipeg Jets, he would often drive to an outdoor rink after a game and park his car so that the headlights lit the ice. He'd lace on his skates, haul out a puck and zigzag up and down the ice, practicing his famous slap shot. Within minutes, the neighborhood kids would be there with their sticks, and a couple of decades later, they would boast to their own offspring, "I played Shinny with the Golden Jet." Hull loved a good backyard game too.

Horseshoes

- OTHER NAMES: derived from Quoits; also called Barnyard Golf
- NUMBER: for two players, or four playing as partners
- EQUIPMENT: two horseshoes for each player, two stakes and a clear patch of ground at least 44 feet long and 6 feet wide
- DESCRIPTION: an easygoing game that requires minimal physical fitness or strategy but a strong arm and good eye-hand coordination; not unlike bowling
- COMPLEXITY: best for kids over 10; the pitch is long and the shoes are heavy for younger sports

HORSESHOES is a North American twist on the British game of Quoits, a pitching game that probably evolved from the Greek game of throwing a discus. Quoits players toss flat metal rings toward a stake in the ground, earning points by lobbing a ringer over the stake. Quoits undoubtedly came to North America with the first settlers. Exactly how it became Horseshoes is unknown, but games historians speculate that in this case, necessity really was the mother of the invention: instead of using manufactured metal rings, sodbusters in the Midwest substituted what they had on hand—Old Nellie's cast-off footwear. The game was called Barnyard Golf, until President Warren Harding made it respectable in the 1920s, moving it out of the shadow of the manure pile and onto country-club lawns. In 1921, the National Horseshoe Pitchers Association was formed, and the Minnesota State Fair hosted a world championship for what was fast becoming the most popular game on the Great Plains.

Horseshoes faded after the Depression, but the game enjoyed a brief resurrection in the 1980s, when President George Bush admitted to an affection for the homely sport. Bush's endorsement, unlike that of Harding, did not launch a national craze, but with or without a presidential stamp of approval, pitching horseshoes is still a pretty good game.

As well as adding a bit of magic to the game, the switch from metal rings to horseshoes also proved to be a strategic boon, since it requires considerable skill to pitch the broken-ring shape over the stake. All in all, Horseshoes is more rigorous than it looks. Political pundits may call it an old man's game, but in the course of one Florida tournament, master horseshoe pitcher Blair Nunamaker tossed the equivalent of more than seven tons of steel and walked an estimated 26 miles back and forth across the pitch.

inch in diameter and about three feet long) firmly into the ground so that about 14 inches extends above the surface. The stakes are not perpendicular: they lean toward each other, three inches off the vertical. The ground between the stakes can be uneven and riddled with tree roots, but dig out the area immediately around the stakes, and fill it with clean dirt, sand or clay—a cushion for the horseshoes. Make the *pit* around each stake about four feet long and three feet across, confining the dirt with two-by-sixes driven into the ground on edge. For tournament play, the soil in the pit is kept at a puttylike consistency, but at home, the pits can double as sandboxes when not being pummeled with horseshoes.

The pitching court is six feet wide, creating a 1½-foot alley on either side of the pit. This is where players stand to pitch to the opposite box. One foot in front of the pit is the pitching foul line: players must not cross this line when pitching a shoe.

Horseshoe Pitch

The Playing Field: The *pitching court*, or *pitch*, measures 40 feet from stake to stake (30 feet for women; 20 for children). If possible, lay out the court on a north-south axis so that the sun won't be in anybody's eyes when it sinks low in the sky. Drive metal or wooden stakes (one

Equipment: Two horseshoes for each player marked so that each set is easily identified. Actual horseshoes—a size-8 draft shoe—can be used or regulation pitching shoes: 7¼ inches wide and 7⅝ inches long, with an opening at least 3½ inches wide. Each shoe weighs about 2½ pounds, has no holes

A Ringer for White; a Leaner for Black

but has three ridges, or *calks*, on one face of the shoe (one on each prong of the open heel and one at the rounded toe), which anchor the shoe in the dirt. Claws at the inside of each prong encourage the shoe to *ring* the stake.

The Object of the Game:
To earn points by throwing ringers; the first to reach the target score wins.

The Play: Players decide who goes first. The first player stands beside or behind the pit, being careful not to step over the foul line when making his throw. He pitches both of his horseshoes, one after the other, then stands aside while the other player tosses both of her shoes.

After all four horseshoes are thrown —the first *inning*—players walk to the opposite stake, count their scores, pick up their shoes and smooth the sand in the pit. Then they toss their shoes back to the first stake. Players can alternate first pitch, or the winner of one round can pitch first in the next (the second player has the advantage).

A player cannot cross to the other stake during an inning to check the position of the opponent's horseshoes. Shoes are scored as they lie at the end of the inning. For instance, if the first

player's ringer is knocked out by the second player, it doesn't count. Any shoes that fall outside the pit are disqualified, as are shoes that land outside and roll back in. To count as a ringer, a horseshoe must completely encircle the stake: a straight stick laid across the heel of the shoe must not touch the stake. A *leaner*, or *hobber*, does not count as a ringer, but it does count as a shoe close to the stake.

The Score: A ringer counts 3 points. Each horseshoe closer to the stake than an opponent's shoe counts 1 point. If a player has two shoes closer to the stake than either of her opponent's shoes, she scores 2 points. In tournament play, "close" means within six inches of the stake: a shoe scores the single point only if it is closer than the opponent's and within six inches of the stake. In backyard play, however, distance is measured with horseshoes, not rulers: a shoe scores if it is closer than the opponent's and within a horseshoe width of the stake. Beginners can waive the width rule: any shoe closer than the opponent's shoe scores, as long as it is inside the pit.

In tournament play, ringers cancel each other out, but in backyard games,

players usually count all their earned points. (The maximum score for an inning is 6 points—two ringers.) For instance, in the game illustrated, White scores 3 points for her ringer, and Black scores 1 point for the leaner, which is closer than the other White shoe. You can agree to play 25 innings or to play to a target score of 21, 40 or 50 points. (Singles usually play to 50, doubles to 21.)

For a faster game, players can agree to score 1 point for all shoes within six inches of the stake, regardless of the position of the opponent's shoes.

Technique: World-famous American pitcher Ted Allen holds the record for throwing 72 consecutive ringers. But getting the horseshoe around the stake is not as easy as players like Allen make it look. There are two basic grips that, when the horseshoe is released with a gentle underhand lift, give the shoe either 1¼ or 1¾ clockwise turns from the time it leaves your hand to when it lands in the opposite pit, headed toward the stake. Experiment to determine which is most comfortable for you.

Hold the horseshoe with the calks facing down, all four fingers underneath and your thumb resting on the smooth top side. If you hold the shoe open to the left, it will make 1¼ clockwise turns. In this case, rest your little finger on the heel calk to balance the shoe. If you hold the shoe open to the right, it will make 1¾ turns. Stretch your little finger to the toe calk for balance.

To make your pitch, stand to the left of the stake if you are right-handed (lefties do the opposite). Using either grip, hold the horseshoe in front of you. Lead with the foot opposite your throwing arm, being careful not to step out of the pitching court. (Some players actually take a step while pitching; others plant their feet and move only their upper bodies.) Keep your arm in line with the center of the opposite pit, and lift so that the shoe arcs up and forward, spinning horizontally like a plate toward the stake at the other end.

Distance, direction and arc all depend on delivery: that easy, graceful pendulum swing which releases the horseshoe at exactly the right moment. Only practice makes perfect. The sole downfall of Horseshoes is that you won't be able to practice in private. The first characteristic twang of metal on metal is guaranteed to bring neighbors to the pitch, and before you know it, another game is under way.

Variation: For doubles, partners stand at opposite ends of the pitch. There is no walking back and forth. The rules and scoring are identical: each partner of the set simply returns his teammate's horseshoes, taking alternate turns to play.

1¼ Turn

1¾ Turn

Horseshoe Grips

Lawn Bowls

- ◆ OTHER NAMES: played by the British as Bowls and Flat Green Bowls, by the French as Boules and by the Italians as Bocce
- ◆ NUMBER: for two players or two teams of up to four each
- ◆ EQUIPMENT: four bowls for each player, one target bowl, a throwing mat (optional) and a rink 33 to 44 yards long and 14 to 19 feet wide
- ◆ DESCRIPTION: the skill and technique of indoor bowling played outdoors at the pace of Horseshoes
- ◆ COMPLEXITY: anyone who can hoist the ball can play

BOWLING A BALL down a runway, aiming to hit other balls at the end, is a game as old as Western civilization. Middle Eastern cultures have played it for 4,000 years, the Greeks considered it to be excellent exercise, and the Romans spread it north: a bowling green in Southampton, England, has been bowled upon continuously for more than 700 years. Before the American Revolution, lawn bowling was the leading leisure activity in the United States. There was a green laid out at Mount Vernon, George Washington's family

home, as early as 1732. The game died out almost completely after the War of Independence, but in 1879, the Dunellen Bowling Club was formed in New Jersey, part of a worldwide bowling revival. It may no longer be as ubiquitous a pastime in rural America as it is in Britain, France and Italy, but Lawn Bowls is still a worthwhile addition to the roster of backyard games.

Some incarnations, such as the Italian Bocce and the French Boules, are played on sand or gravel pitches; the traditional British version is played on a flat stretch of grass. The size of

the field and of the balls varies, but the point is much the same: to get the bowls, bocce or boules closer to the target ball—called variously the *jack*, *pallino* or *cochonnet*—than the opposition. Bowls in all its forms is a little like Horseshoes, played with balls and a stake that can roll away. Although the official games have been taken over by fanatics who insist on manicured surfaces and straight lines, all three can be played as they have been for centuries, on any level yard or driveway, substituting softballs or croquet balls for the precision tournament equipment. People of all ages enjoy the game, although players of a certain age can take heart in the French opinion that a *bouliste* does not reach his prime until middle age, when strength and cunning converge and peak.

The Playing Field: Individual *rinks* of a bowling green are large: 132 feet long and anywhere from 14 to 19 feet wide. Formal greens have ditches around the outside, but a flat rectangle of lawn marked with string or a toed line is fine. Drive a small peg into the ground at the midpoint of each end of the rectangle: a line sighted between these two pegs divides the rink in half lengthwise. (The jack and the throwing mat are always positioned on this invisible centerline.) On the long sides of the rectangle, mark a point 27 yards from each end: this is as close as a bowler can stand when delivering his bowls to the opposite end.

On formal rinks, bowlers pitch with one foot on a black rubber throwing mat. The mat is a movable start line. At the beginning of the game, the mat is laid on the centerline with its back edge four feet from the end of the rink. During the game, the back edge of the mat cannot be less than four feet from the end, and the front edge cannot be closer than 27 yards to the opposite end. At the beginning of each round of play, the mat is laid down and is not moved until the bowlers start the next. (There are several rounds of play, or *ends*, to a game.)

In the backyard, players can dispense with the mat and simply make sure that bowlers pitch from the center of the rink, never crossing the 27-yard line.

Equipment: If two players are in the game, each has four bowls, black balls made of wood, rubber or a composite material, 5¾ inches in diameter

Lawn Bowls Rink

and weighing about 3½ pounds, a little heavier than a horseshoe. A bowl looks somewhat like a cross between a mandarin orange and an egg, flattened on both ends but also somewhat elongated on one side so that it swerves on the bias, curling in slowly just before it comes to rest. The smaller jack, or target bowl, is white and perfectly round; it is about 2½ inches in diameter and weighs just under 10 ounces. Begin-

ners can substitute softballs or croquet balls for bowls and a tennis ball for the jack. Although it isn't essential, a black rubber mat or a piece of carpet, about 24 inches long and 14 inches wide, can serve as a movable start line, as described above.

The Object of the Game: To place the bowls nearer to the target than the opposition.

The Play: Players decide who goes first. The person or the leader of the team that plays first throws, or *delivers*, the jack, then repositions it on the centerline, parallel to where it landed. If it travels within two yards of the opposite end of the rink, it is centered on the two-yard line; if it travels less than 25 yards, it passes to the other player, who delivers it again.

The first player then throws a bowl, trying to place it as close to the jack as possible. It doesn't matter whether the bowl hits the jack as long as the jack stays within the rink.

The turn passes to the other player, who tries to get her bowl closer to the jack, dislodging her opponent's bowl, if necessary. Players take turns, deliv-

Live Balls and Dead (X)

ering their bowls alternately until all eight have been played.

If a bowl hits the jack out-of-bounds, the jack is dead. The end is void and must be replayed, the same person delivering the jack. If the jack is hit out-of-bounds but rebounds onto the rink, it is still live provided it is more than 22 yards from the mat. A jack on a boundary is also live. It must be completely outside the rink to be dead.

Any bowl that fails to travel 15 yards, stops outside the boundaries, is driven off the rink by another bowl, stops in the ditch at the end of the rink without having touched the jack or rebounds from the opposite end without having touched the jack is *dead*. All other bowls, including those on the boundaries or those which rebound onto the rink, are *live*. A bowl that touches the jack when it is first bowled is called a *toucher* and is marked with chalk; if the toucher is later driven into the ditch, it remains live. The chalk marks are erased after each end. In the game illustrated at the bottom of the facing page, five bowls are live and three (indicated by an X) are dead.

After the eight bowls are delivered, players walk to the other end of the rink, tally their scores, retrieve their bowls and the jack, reposition the mat, deliver the jack and throw the bowls again. The winner of one end pitches first in the next. (The second player has the advantage.)

The Score: Only one person scores after each end: she scores 1 point for each bowl nearer to the jack than her opponent's best bowl. Game is usually 21 points.

Technique: Although some players throw the bowl from a stooped or crouched position, the usual delivery in Lawn Bowls is not unlike that in indoor bowling. The player stands upright on the mat, the bowl palmed so that it faces the opposite end, with fingers just below the disk on the inside of the bowl (or the little finger stretched around the other side). The biased side of the bowl is always kept to the inside of the rink. The player

takes aim, bends, swings the bowl back, steps forward with his opposite foot and delivers the ball in a single smooth movement down the center-line toward the jack. At the moment of delivery, the rear foot must be on or above the mat.

Players aim to get a *draw*, a bowl close to the jack; a *guard*, a bowl that blocks the opponent's path to the jack or protects a draw; or a *tap*, a bowl that knocks away an opposing bowl which touches or is close to the jack. If two bowls are positioned away from the jack, try for the *trail*, knocking the jack toward your bowls so that they will score. The *yard-on* is a heavy shot that breaks up a *head*, a formation of opponent's bowls around the jack. As in **Crokinole** or Billiards, much of the skill of the game rests in sophisticated shots that use the opponent's bowls to get your own closer to the jack. In the *rest*, a bowl pushes the opponent's bowl out of the way and takes its place; if the hit is hard and knocks the opposing bowl off the rink, it is a *drive*. A *cannon-off* is a ricochet shot, or carom, that bounces off an opponent's bowl toward the jack. The *follow-on* knocks the opponent's bowl out of the way in one direction

and continues on toward the jack.

Variations: If playing Lawn Bowls in teams of two, one member of each team stands at either end of the rink. The players at one end bowl four bowls each, delivering the bowls alternately. They score, then their teammates at the other end bowl the eight balls back, also scoring. After 18 or 21 ends, the team with the highest score wins.

The tournament form of Lawn Bowls involves a team of four and is much like a fair-weather version of Curling. Each of the four team members has a role: the lead delivers the jack, the second scores, the third measures disputed shots, and the fourth, the skip, is captain. Each of the four players places two bowls, one at a

Boules Rink

time and in turn. A game is 21 ends.

The French **Jeu de Boules** (also called Pétanque) and the Italian **Bocce** are played almost exactly like Lawn Bowls, but in many ways, they make better backyard games. (Boules and Bocce are essentially the same.) The balls are made of metal and are smaller and lighter—at least 3½ inches in diameter and 1½ pounds. The rink can be any kind of surface but is usually a

Lawn Bowl and Jack

hard, level strip of gravel or sand. It is a little smaller than a Lawn Bowls rink: 80 to 90 feet long and 10 feet wide. At each end, there is a line at 6½ feet, beyond which the boule is out of play, and a line at 16 feet 3 inches, which the *bouliste* cannot cross when throwing the boule. When the jack—a wooden ball about 1½ inches in diameter—is thrown at the beginning of the game, it must land between these two lines at the other end and be at least 20 inches inside the side boundary lines.

The players draw lots to determine who will throw the jack in the first end; in subsequent ends, the player or team that last scored throws the jack and delivers the first boule. The boules themselves are either rolled along the ground (*boule pointée*), thrown through the air (*portée*) or aimed at a specific target (*tirée*). The player crouches, keeping his feet together with the boule in the crook of his hand, held away from the target so that it is flicked up and forward. He may not step over the throwing line until the boule lands. The closest boule to the target is the *best boule*. As soon as a player (or team) has best boule, he stops. (The first to play always throws only one boule; it is automatically the best.) The other player then throws

boules until she gets one closer to the target. She now has best boule, so she stops, and the other player throws until he has best boule. The game is over when all the boules have been thrown (three or four each for two players; three each for teams of two.) Players count the score as in Lawn Bowls—each boule that lies closer to the target than the opponent's best boule earns a point. If two opposing boules are equidistant from the jack, the end is void and must be replayed. A *baguette*, an iron rod 20 inches long with a two-inch angle at one end, is used to measure distances precisely. After the score, players change ends, and the winner of the previous end throws the jack and the first boule. Games are usually played to 13 or 15 points.

Duck on a Rock is a rambunctious kids' version of Lawn Bowls, or perhaps it is just the same instinct manifest in a game that blends sedate Lawn Bowls with a vicious game of tag. Any number can play, but they should be of similar age and size to avoid mishaps.

Players each find a rock, called a *duck*, about the size of their fists. They agree on a target—a stump or a large rock with a generous clearing in front of it. About 20 or 30 feet in front of the rock, players mark a line in the dirt to denote home base and, standing there, take turns throwing their ducks at the target. The one whose duck lands farthest from the target is It. All the players pick up their ducks: It sets hers on the rock; the others go back to home base and throw their ducks, trying to knock It's duck off the rock. At this stage of the game, no one bothers to take turns. Once a player has thrown his duck, he moves up near it, and when there is a break in the barrage, he grabs his duck and races

back to home base to throw again. It, for her part, tries to tag a player racing home. She can make a tag only as long as her duck is on the rock, so during the chase, all the other players try madly to unseat her duck.

When It manages to tag another player, they both race to the target rock, the other player clutching his duck. (Everyone else stops throwing, since the tag has been made.) If It can tap her duck three times on the rock before the other player puts his duck on the rock and tags her, she can go back to home base. The other player then becomes It, puts his duck on the rock and tries to tag another player.

There is yet another phase of the game: if, during the attempt to dislodge It's duck, a player lands his duck within a hand span of the rock, It can challenge that player, calling, "Span." The others stop throwing and running while It goes back to home base and

Boule and Cochonnet

throws her duck. If It's duck lands closer to the rock than the challenged duck, the other player becomes It. American children have been playing Duck on a Rock for more than a hundred years: as William Newell notes in *Games and Songs of American Children* (1883), "The game is not without a spice of danger." ∽

Croquet

- **NUMBER:** usually up to six players at a time; more if you have the equipment
- **EQUIPMENT:** a colored ball with a matching mallet for each player, nine wire hoops, or wickets, two pegs and a relatively smooth stretch of lawn (rough patches are acceptable, but not an incline) at least 50 feet long by 20 feet wide
- **DESCRIPTION:** a leisurely game that lends itself well to conversation; the outdoor summer equivalent of a friendly game of Pool

CROQUET is the hot new backyard game. Not as energetic as Badminton nor as bucolic as Horseshoes, Croquet is the perfect pastime for the lawns of our mock-Victorian houses, a game as elegantly nostalgic as contemporary taste in domestic architecture. Stores can't keep Croquet sets in stock, even the $1,000 variety; advertisers such as Rolex use Croquet pros to promote their products; entertainers such as Anne Murray and Larry Hagman have been snapped wielding mallets; Dennis the Menace makes quips about Croquet in his cartoon strip; and, a sure sign of success, Revlon has named a line of cosmetics after the homely sport.

Croquet may enjoy a reputation now as a refined game of crisp-pleated slacks and polite conversation, but it was banned in Boston a century ago by a Reverend Skinner, who called upon his brethren to suppress "the immoral practice of Croquet." He didn't have to worry. Croquet, a fad in the mid-1800s in both England and North America, quickly fell into disfavor when Tennis took over the lawn.

Although its precise evolution is unclear, Croquet likely derives from Paille Maille, a French game in which players used clubs to knock balls through bent willow branches. The game migrated to England, where it was called Pele Mele, then Pall Mall; the hoops were made of wire, often decorated with flowers, and the mallet was a long, curved club, not unlike a thick hockey stick. The Shorter Oxford English Dictionary, in fact, suggests that "croquet" comes from *croche*, an Old French word meaning a shepherd's crook.

Pall Mall faded away (although the London park where it was played has kept the name). In the mid-1800s, an almost identical game traveled from Ireland under the name of Crooky. It struck a chord with the British and, by 1865, was widely played throughout the Empire, immigrating eventually to Canada and the United States. Manuals were published; tournaments were arranged; the equipment and rules were refined; the game was even played in Alice's Wonderland. The more popular it became, the more it was frowned upon for the cavorting that accompanied it on the field: Croquet, after all, was one of the few outdoor sports genteel enough for women to play. When Lawn Tennis hit the United States in the 1890s, Croquet went into a quick decline, much to the relief of its detractors.

"The ingenuity of man has never conceived anything better calculated to bring out all the evil passions of humanity than the so-called game of Croquet," wrote an anonymous critic in 1898 in the American magazine *Living Age*. "It is not long before every honorable feeling, every dictate of morality has been obliterated. The hoop is the gaping jaws of hades."

As Croquet evolved, the hoops shrank in both size and number. The standard court setting of the 1860s consisted of two pegs set about 50

Nine-Wicket Croquet

yards apart with two hoops in front of each stake and three ranged on both sides in the space between. In 1872, the hoops were reduced to six, and in 1922, the British settled on the so-called Willis setting of six hoops and one peg, which is how they still play it. In the United States, the game retained the 10 (sometimes 9) hoops set in a figure eight, an arrangement that the United States Croquet Association (USCA), formed in 1977, refers to as Garden Croquet. The USCA promotes the six-wicket game, the basis of international competition and USCA tournaments.

The Playing Field: The USCA recommends a smooth stretch of lawn 100 by 50 feet for the nine-wicket layout. As long as the layout of the hoops and the relative spacing between them remains the same, however, the game can be shrunk to fit any yard. Knock the stakes into the ground at the midpoint of either end of the playing surface. About 18 inches should show above the ground. Set the wickets in the ground as illustrated on the previous page, two in front of each stake and the remaining five arranged in the space between like the five spots on a die. If there are 10 wickets with the set, you can put the tenth one crosswise over the center wicket, creating a cage that is more difficult to shoot through. (Victorians used to suspend a bell inside the cage to herald each player's passing through the midpoint.) The wickets should rise about 10 inches out of the ground and be firmly and vertically in place, their legs about 4 inches apart so that there is minimum clearance for the balls.

Equipment: Each player has one ball and a mallet marked with a matching color. The mallets can be any length, although the shafts are usually about 36 inches long. The mallet end is a cylinder, typically round but sometimes squared. The overall size and weight of the mallets are variable, although they usually weigh about three pounds. The balls are wooden, just under 3¾ inches in diameter, and weigh about a pound

each. The wickets for regulation play are made of rounded iron and are 12 inches tall and 3¾ inches wide, just barely enough for a ball to squeeze through. In backyard sets, the wickets are often lightweight wire hoops with legs that can be spread as much as six inches apart, although they should be set in place with a maximum four-inch spread. The stakes are wooden dowels about 24 inches long. They are painted at the top with colored rings to match the balls and mallets: top to bottom, blue, red, black and yellow. This determines the usual order of play in a game of Croquet.

The Object of the Game: To hit the ball from the first stake through the hoops, in order, to the far stake and back again.

The Play: To determine the order of play, players can follow the colored stripes on the stake, blue going first, then red, and so on. Or the players can take turns hitting one ball toward the stake from 20 paces: the person who comes closest goes first, second closest plays second, and so on.

The first player sets his ball one mallet length in front of the stake and takes his shot. Players then take turns in rotation, each taking one shot. Players move through the course

counterclockwise. Each time a player runs a ball through a wicket, she earns another stroke, called a *continuation shot*. To determine whether a ball is completely through a wicket, the mallet head is laid against the legs of the hoop on the side opposite the ball: if the mallet is flush with the wicket and doesn't touch the ball, it is through. Halfway through the course, each player must hit the opposite stake with his ball, which also earns him another turn.

If a player makes a *roquet* (hits another player's ball), she earns two extra strokes, which can be taken either as two continuation shots or as two separate shots: one can be used to *croquet* the other player's ball, and the other can be used to advance her own ball. For the croquet shot, she places her ball next to his so that the two balls are touching, puts her foot on her own ball to hold it firmly in position and whacks the side of it, sending the other player's ball away. The opponent must play his ball from where it stops. If it rolls outside the playing field, however, the player can bring the ball back to the point where it crossed the boundary. (Some play that the ball is set one mallet length outside the line.) A good house rule, borrowed from six-wicket play, forbids a player to roquet the same ball twice unless his

Golf or Irish Grip

Reverse Palm Grip, Center Stance

Reverse Palm Grip, Side Style

Croquet Grips and Stances

ball has passed through a wicket in between the two hits.

If a player runs a wicket while making a roquet shot, he does not earn an extra stroke. Similarly, if a player runs two wickets in a single stroke, he earns only one continuation shot. In this game, the bonuses are not cumulative. The first person to go through the course and come back to hit the starting stake wins. Most games continue until everyone is home.

Technique: A novice will not have as much difficulty learning to manipulate the mallet and ball as Alice had trying to bat the hedgehog with her flamingo. There are basically two mallet grips: in the British or reverse palm grip, hold the palm of the upper hand toward your body and the palm of the lower hand away from you. In the golf or Irish grip, both palms face away from the body. The hands can be together at the top of the shaft, but the American style is to slide the lower hand down the shaft a bit, which provides more leverage in rough terrain.

The ball is always hit with the round face, not the side, of the mallet. There are several stances to choose from. You can swing sideways, hitting the ball like a golf ball: this offers good control but poor aim. You can use the side-style stance, swinging the mallet to the right or left of your legs. This gives more power and freedom of movement, but your aim might be off, since you aren't hitting from exactly behind the ball. Or you can use the center stance, swinging the mallet like a pendulum between your legs, hitting the ball dead on. This requires some awkward bending and more wrist control but generally produces more power and better aim.

A good shot depends on your swing. Walk up to the ball from behind, facing the direction you intend it to go (called *stalking the ball*). Find a comfortable stance, bring the mallet back slowly; the arms and the mallet move as one, but the rest of the body remains still. Keep your eyes on the back of the ball, at the spot where you want to hit it. You should make contact with the ball about an inch from

Six-Wicket Croquet

the bottom of the mallet face. The arms control the mallet, but the swing comes from the shoulders. Keep the wrists flexible. Too much wrist, and the hit will go awry. Remember to follow through with your mallet after the hit. If the mallet bounces on contact, you are standing too close to the ball; if the ball wobbles, you are probably too far from it. The idea is to sweep the ball forward, not to thwack it.

Learning the basic techniques will get you started. There are a dozen or more different kinds of shots, but one of the most useful is the *split shot*, in which a player aims his ball at the side of an opponent's ball, hitting it out of the way but, at the same time, ricocheting his own ball off the side so that it goes through a wicket. (This advances the ball but doesn't earn an extra stroke.) You can also hit your ball slightly underneath, rather than square on the side, making it jump over a ball that is in your way. Once you've mastered the basics, get a copy of the USCA's *Croquet: Its History, Strategy, Rules and Records* and learn the more sophisticated shots and strategies. As *Cassell's Book of Sports and Pastimes* (1881) grudgingly admitted: "A vast amount of head-work as well as nerve and manual neatness is essential to all who wish to excel in what is really, in many respects, a

most interesting and difficult game."

Variations: If playing partners, one member of a team starts, an opponent follows, then the other teammate plays. Otherwise, the rules are the same.

According to the USCA, the layout for **Six-Wicket Croquet** requires a somewhat larger field—84 by 105 feet—but you can shrink the size as long as you keep the same proportions of roughly 4:5. The lone stake is in the center of the court, with wickets on the four corners and one on either side of the center stake, called the penultimate wicket and the rover (in the illustration, shown below the stake).

The equipment is heftier than in the garden-variety game: the balls are 3⅝ inches in diameter and weigh one pound each, the mallets have 36-inch handles, and the wickets are ⅝-inch cast iron with an opening only ⅛ inch wider than the diameter of the balls. Given the tolerances, you'll probably take to rolling your lawn.

Six-Wicket Croquet can be played as singles (two players each having two balls) or as doubles (four players, blue and black as teammates; red and yellow playing together). The balls are always played in sequence: blue, red, black, yellow. The players move through the course as indicated. Every time your ball roquets another ball, either your own or an opponent's, you earn two strokes. You *must* take a croquet shot first; however, you may not put your foot on your ball (this eliminates the mile-long drives into the woods). The second shot can be either a croquet shot or a continuation shot. As far as the ball you just hit is concerned, you are *dead*: you can't hit it again until you pass through a wicket. As in the nine-wicket version, if a player goes through a wicket and makes a roquet in a single shot, he earns only two bonus strokes, the maximum for any one play.

There is more strategy to this form of the game. Experts plan their shots several strokes in advance. For instance, in a singles game, in which each player has two balls, it is possible to get around much of the field in one turn. As soon as he can, a player roquets his own ball, earning two bonus shots. He uses one to croquet one of his balls, the *pioneer ball*, ahead, at the same time sending his other ball through the wicket. With the second bonus shot from the roquet, he hits the pioneer ball forward again, past the next wicket. With the bonus shot earned by going through the first wicket, he hits that ball through the next wicket, roqueting the pioneer ball again. With skill, he can continue leapfrogging around the field, roqueting his own ball and using the bonus shots to advance both.

After a ball goes through all the wickets twice, it can peg out or become a *rover*. A rover can move around the court at will, hitting any ball, but not more than once per turn unless it passes through a wicket in between hits. (It can go through wickets in either direction.)

Instead of a formal course, you can also set up the wickets at random around the yard for a game of **Croquet Golf**, a homemade version of Miniature Golf. Make the course as long, meandering and difficult as you like, complete with sand traps and water jumps. The point of this form of Croquet is still to get the ball from the starting stake around the course and back again.

Finally, Lewis Carroll devised two variations: Arithmetical Croquet, a mental game played entirely without wickets, mallets, balls or field, and Castle Croquet, which combines some elements of **Chess** with the traditional game. Both are described in *The Magic of Lewis Carroll*, edited by John Fisher and published by Thomas Nelson and Sons Ltd. (London; 1973). 　⌒

Shinny

- ◆ OTHER NAMES: **Field Hockey, Street Hockey, Ball Hockey, Boot Hockey, Bandy, Hurley, Shinty and, when played on skates, Ice Hockey or Pond Hockey**
- ◆ NUMBER: **any number of players, divided into two teams**
- ◆ EQUIPMENT: **a stick for each player, a ball or a puck, something with which to mark the two goals and a 100-by-40-foot field or a 60-by-25-foot patch of ice**
- ◆ DESCRIPTION: **a freewheeling stickball game; extremely active and often rough**

ACCORDING TO LEGEND, Shinny was the first game of the first people on this continent. Among the Wichita native Americans, the first man, called Darkness, was guided to the Light along the flight path of a shinny ball. The native game, played with wooden, bone or buckskin balls and long-handled clubs, figures in the legends of many tribes: mythic animals often joined the fray and played with their tails, and the outcome could be deadly. In one account: "Each side tried to force the ball through the other's goal. When one side was beaten, it immediately began to kill those of the other side."

Shinny's roots, however, are practically universal. It was played by Greeks in 500 B.C., 12th-century Anglo-Saxons, 15th-century Dutch and 20th-century Russians. The word we use comes from Scottish dialect, via the Gaelic Shinty, a corruption of "Shin ye!" The British codified the field version of the sport in 1875, first as Bandy, then as Hockey, taking the name, as they did **Croquet**, from the Old Norman word for shepherd's crook. The first organized Ice Hockey games were played in Canada, and a Canadian student at Johns Hopkins University, in Baltimore, introduced the formal game to the United States in the late 19th century. But Shinny—two teams batting a small object toward a goal with sticks on whatever surface they can find—is so universal that no one can claim credit for its invention.

Shinny is a rough-and-tumble game, but it is great fun and exercise for adults, families and kids with lofty ambitions. "How much can you teach a 10-year-old?" asks Wayne Gretzky, one of professional Ice Hockey's greatest stars. "There's only so much he's going to take in. Do the basics—that's all they do in Russia. The Soviets get all their 10-year-olds on the ice and say, 'Play Shinny.'"

Even after you know you'll never be another Gretzky, Shinny is still fun to play. A community center in Toronto, Ontario, has four regulation hockey rinks, one of which has a continuous game of Shinny, 24 hours a day, all

Shinny on Ice

winter. Anyone with a yen to play just takes a stick, laces on her skates and waits on the sidelines until someone drops out. There are no teams and no scores, and there's never a time, night or day, when *everybody* goes home.

Shinny is one of the few all-weather games. Although there's no reason why **Softball** and **Volleyball** can't be played in the snow, Shinny is the only outdoor family game that is played as often on ice with skates and a puck as it is on the street with sneakers and a tennis ball. The basic rules are the same no matter where it's played, although there are plenty of regional variations. Most outdoor sports are played within the boundaries of a diamond, a pitch or a rink, but one of the attractions of Shinny is the wide-open space and the freewheeling comradeship of the game. As Doug Bearsley writes in *Country On Ice*, Shinny is "a game that dishes out fun and friendship in equal doses."

The Playing Field: A regulation Ice Hockey rink is 200 feet long by 85 feet wide, and a regulation Field Hockey field is 300 feet long by 165 to 180 feet wide, but a place to play Shinny is as big as what you've got. Most city yards aren't quite big enough, but a playground, an alley or a dead-end street is. Country backyards

can usually accommodate a round of Field Hockey, and it is worth scraping a pond or making a backyard rink (see Sources) for a winter's worth of Shinny. A playing field 100 feet long and 40 feet wide is luxurious: Wayne Gretzky grew up playing Shinny on a backyard rink about 60 by 25 feet. Whatever the dimensions, keep the proportions close to 2:1. For Field Hockey, dirt or close-cropped grass is best—pavement is hard on the knees —and, of course, ice or hard-packed snow serves in winter. Toe a line across the center of the field, dividing it in half. Each team takes one half of the field. The goals are set at either end—hockey goal nets, two posts or orange crates about six feet apart or a railroad tie lying crosswise in the grass.

Equipment: Although hockey sticks are ideal for either field or ice Shinny, players often substitute anything from a broomstick to a hickory cudgel with a natural crook. Or use a full-fledged broom to play the gentler sport of Broom Hockey. You can use a hockey puck, a tennis ball, a rubber ball, a tuna can, a knot of elm wood or even frozen "road apples" donated by local horses. In summer, keeping a tennis ball in the freezer gives it good heft. On ice, players usually wear skates or boots; in the yard or street,

good running shoes. If the game gets too fast and furious, wear protective equipment.

The Object of the Game: For one team to get the ball or puck into the goal of the other team.

The Play: Divide the players into two teams. Field Hockey has 11 players to a side, and professional Ice Hockey has 6; Shinny is best with 5 to 8 per team. If lots of people want to play, allow a maximum of 12 or 14 players on the field at a time; even that may reduce the game to long periods of standing around interspersed with short passes. Instead, play substitutions: when a player gets tired, he switches places with someone waiting on the sidelines.

To choose teams, all the players throw their sticks into the center of the field, and one person, without really looking at them, tosses an equal number of sticks to the left and to the right. Those who retrieve their sticks on one side form one team. If, after the group has divvied up, one team has all the good players, rearrange the teams to balance skills: it isn't unusual for one team to have fewer (but better) players than the other.

The ball or puck is put in the middle of the field or the ice, and a player

Broomball

from each team is chosen to start the game with a *face-off*, or *bull-off*. The rest of the team is spread out in its half of the playing field. The two players at center field stand on either side of the puck with their left hands toward their own goals. Simultaneously, they tap the ground with their sticks, tap their sticks together three times, then both try to get control of the puck and start the drive toward the opposing goal.

The puck is passed between teammates as they advance toward the goal, trying to hit the puck in. A few stay back to guard their goal in case the other team gets the puck; one person usually acts as goalie. (With six per side, there are typically three forwards, two on defense and a goalie.) The other team tries to defend its goal and

to prevent the puck from going in, while at the same time attempting to steal the puck away and advance toward the goal at the opposite end.

Although players can go by the traditional Field Hockey or Ice Hockey rules, observing professional niceties such as icing and offside, there are usually not a lot of rules. In general, players must *shinny on their own sides* —face the other team when defending their goal. The sticks must be kept low when hitting the puck. The puck cannot be pushed or kicked into the goal or touched with the hands except by the goalie. A puck that leaves the playing field (or rolls under a car or into the woods) is out-of-bounds; it is brought back to the edge of the field and played from that spot by whoever went to fetch it. Body checking isn't allowed. There are no referees: players are on their honor, and the unwritten codes of conduct prevail.

When one team scores a goal, the puck or ball is returned to center field, and two other players are chosen to face-off.

The Score: "You are taking the game too seriously," writes Bearsley, "if you keep score." Scores are counted not by how far you are from some specified target but by how one team stands in relation to the other. If it isn't a tie game, one side is always one up or more on the other.

Technique: The wide-open, free-flowing nature of Shinny depends on being able to control the puck, to do some fancy stickhandling and to pass the puck precisely and quickly. The game is more like Russian-style hockey than the body-checking North American game. Professional hockey on this continent may be bloody, but Shinny is actually a game of cooperation and dexterity; played in winter, it develops superb skaters adept at backtracking, crisscrossing and fast stops and starts.

Variation: In Broom Hockey, only five or six people from each team are on the field at a given time. The field is the same, but the goal is a little bigger, and brooms are used instead of sticks, a volleyball instead of a puck. To start the game, the volleyball is set at the center point in the field with the brooms laid in a row on either side, as illustrated. At a signal, the players run onto the field, grab their brooms and start swatting the ball, trying to get it through the opposite goal. Each team has a goalie, who is the only player allowed to touch the ball with his hands. He can catch it and throw it back onto the playing field. As in Shinny, the team that gets a goal scores 1 point, then a new round starts with the volleyball in the middle.　　∽

Softball

- ◆ OTHER NAMES: **Scrub Baseball, Kitten Ball, Mush Ball and Diamond Ball**
- ◆ NUMBER: **at least 10 players, preferably 18**
- ◆ EQUIPMENT: **bats, softballs, three bases and a home plate (optional), gloves for half the players at a time and a field at least 50 feet square**
- ◆ DESCRIPTION: **a leisurely afternoon ball game that involves throwing, catching, batting and running as well as considerable strategy**
- ◆ COMPLEXITY: **thrilling when played well, but equally a delight for duffers**

IN AMERICA's Colonial days, the only ball game besides Field Hockey was Base-ball. The way it is played today became known as the "New York game," but a cruder form had been played at least since the late 1700s. As William Newell describes it in his 1883 book, *Games and Songs of American Children*: "There were three 'bases' besides the 'home' base, at about the same distance as at present; but the number of players was indeterminate. The pitcher threw the ball, and the catcher stood close behind the striker. When the batsman struck the ball, a run must be made; and the ball

Sandlot Softball

was not, as at present, thrown *to* the base, but *at* the runner, usually with all the force possible. If he was hit, he was out." There's more. "As there was never any umpire in these games, the field for controversy was unlimited. One way, as we recollect, of settling disputes was as follows: All proceeding to the spot of the doubtful catch, the best player on one side hurled the ball with all his force upwards; if it was caught by the designated player of the other party, the point was given in the latter's favor, and *vice versa*."

This is a form of Rounders, a British children's game, and gives the lie to A.G. Spalding's heartfelt hope that Baseball is as true-blue American as the Stars and Stripes. Unfortunately, the nation's national sport was not born at Cooperstown, New York, in 1839; it was a variation (as most games are) of a venerable ball game that had been played since America was first settled, with as many people as showed up on the village green. The old game continued to be played under the name Boston Baseball even

after the Knickerbocker Club of New York drew up the first official rules for the New York game in 1845.

The New York game, played with a tag instead of a knockout and with a smaller, harder ball, quickly became the purview of adults and professionals. In 1887, a milder form with a bigger, softer ball, a shorter, lighter bat and a smaller field was introduced at the Farragut Boat Club of Chicago. It was played indoors in North America until the 1920s, when Canadians moved it outside to small playgrounds. Americans picked up the practice, and in 1933, after a national tournament at Chicago's world's fair, the ball game played on a scaled-down outdoor diamond was dubbed Softball. Together with its hard-hitting cousin, Baseball, it has become the national American game—"the very symbol," wrote Mark Twain, "the outward, and visible expression of the drive and push and rush and struggle of the raging, tearing, booming nineteenth century."

In its fundamental principles and strategies, sandlot Softball is the same

game played in the major leagues, except the bat is smaller, the ball is bigger, the diamond is reduced, there is no pitcher's mound and the pitching is underhand (as it was in the beginning). In the absence of umpires, the rules, of course, are more flexible. Traditionally, there are nine players per side, but seven will suffice, and you can play with as few as five. The method of divvying up a gang of friends into teams is the same today as it was in Newell's day: "The two best players, or any two selected, toss the bat from one to another; the tosser places his right hand above the hand of the catcher, who in turn follows with his own left, and so on. He who can get the last hold has first choice; but the hold must be proved by ability to whirl the bat three times round the head and throw it."

The Playing Field: A regulation Softball diamond has 60-foot baselines, with 46 feet between pitcher and batter, 40 feet for women. (A regulation Baseball diamond has 90-foot baselines and 60 feet 6 inches between pitcher and batter.) The diamond can be shrunk even further, provided the relationship between the length of the baselines and the distance between the pitcher's mound and home plate is maintained. If the baseline is 45 feet, for instance, the pitching distance is 37 feet; if the baseline is 35 feet, the pitching distance is 30 feet. Make the diamond to suit the age and skill of the players, or use the diamond at a park or a schoolyard.

Equipment: Among the players, there should be at least one bat, smaller around and shorter than a baseball bat. Any type of hittable ball can be used. (The younger the players, the shorter the pitching distance and the larger the ball.) A softball is typically 12 inches around its circumference; a baseball is only 9¼ inches in circumference, too small and hard for home play. Even with a softball, the fielders should wear baseball gloves to protect their hands. Toe the bases in the dirt, or use cushions or squares of cardboard.

The Object of the Game: When your team is at bat, to hit the ball and score runs; when your team is in the field, to catch the ball and to prevent the other team from scoring runs.

The Play: Divide the players into evenly matched teams; players decide which positions they will play. One team takes the field, while the other is at bat.

The team in the field should have a pitcher and a catcher, a first-base player, one player on second and one on third, a shortstop between second and third and, standing farther back, a left fielder, a center fielder and a right fielder, as illustrated on the previous page. If more people play, spread them around the outfield. If fewer than nine play, just cover the bases. With fewer than five players, try Box Softball or Triangle Softball (see Variations).

The batting team decides on a lineup, and the first batter "up" goes to the plate. The pitcher pitches the ball underhand. The batter swings at any good pitch. There is usually no umpire to call balls and strikes, so players decide for themselves what is within the strike zone.

Pitches that are too high or too low are balls; if the pitcher throws four balls, the batter can walk to first base. No bunting is allowed. If the batter misses the ball, it is a strike. If he hits the ball outside the *foul lines* (the lines connecting home plate with first base and third base), it counts as a strike the first two times; after that, it is a foul and does not count against the batter. When the batter has three strikes, he is out. If he hits the ball fair, he runs to first base.

The members of the other team try to catch the ball. If someone catches the ball before it hits the ground, the batter is out. If the ball hits the ground before a player touches it, the hit is good, and it becomes a race between the batter and the ball: the player picks up the ball and throws it to the first-base player. If the batter gets to first base before the ball does, he is safe. If the first-base player catches the ball and touches the base before the batter gets there, the batter is out. If the ball is hit hard enough, the batter can touch first base and continue on to second or third or, if it's a home run, all the way to home plate, which he must touch without being tagged by an opponent with the ball.

After the first batter is safe or out, the next person comes up to bat, and play continues in the same way. If the second batter gets a hit, she runs to first base. If there is a player on first base, he runs to second. The players on the other team try to get one or both out by touching first base before the runner gets there and/or by tagging the other player before he reaches second base. In Softball, base stealing is allowed, but the runner must stay on base until the ball has left the pitcher's hand and is on its way to the batter.

Each team gets three outs and tries to score as many runs (once around the diamond) as possible while at bat. An out is made when a batter gets three strikes; when a hit is caught by anyone on the other team, including the catcher; when the first-base player tags the base before the batter gets

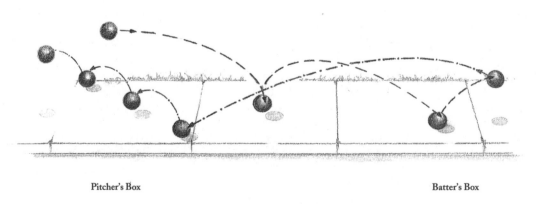

Pitcher's Box   Batter's Box

Box Softball

there; or when a fielder tags a runner between bases.

After one team gets three outs, the teams change positions, the batters going into the field and the fielders coming up to bat. An inning is complete when each team has three outs. Softball is usually played to seven innings, but five is a good workout among friends. The team with the highest score after the agreed-upon innings wins.

Variations: In Stickball, the street version of Softball, a tennis ball replaces the softball, and a broom or mop handle (one end taped for a better grip) is substituted for the bat. The diamond is as big a space as you can find, and the bases are marked with chalk or found objects. The players form two teams. There should be at least three per side—a pitcher, someone to cover first base and someone to cover second and third—but it is better if there are also a couple of people in the outfield. A member of the batting team serves as catcher, returning balls to the pitcher. The pitcher stands closer than usual, about 30 feet away. The pitcher throws the ball, letting it bounce once before it reaches the batter. (If the teams are really stretched thin, the batter can toss the ball herself and hit it in the air or on the bounce. This is called *hitting fungo*.) The batter tries to hit the ball and run the bases. The strike zone is wide, and there are no walks. Some play that there are no balls, either: three pitches, and you are out. Period.

Otherwise, the rules are the same, except for one important feature. In Softball, if a ball is hit out of the park —beyond the boundaries of the playing field—it is an automatic home run; in Stickball, if a ball is hit out-of-bounds, it is an automatic out, and the batter must retrieve the ball, no matter how unfriendly the dog on the other side of the fence. The main reason for this rule is to define responsibility for broken windows. If there are only three players per side, and all three get on base, the person on third is allowed to bat, creating a ghost runner who is automatically propelled home if the other runners advance. Played in the street, Stickball lacks none of the excitement of the more sophisticated game.

Kickball does away with the bat altogether and substitutes a large rubber ball for the tennis ball. The diamond is the same (though perhaps smaller: 20 feet or so between bases). The rules of basic Softball apply, except the ball is rolled to the person at home plate, who kicks it into the field instead of batting it.

The same holds true for **Punchball** or **Slapball**, except the ball is bounced to the "batter," arriving at about waist height; the batter punches the ball with her closed fist or smacks it with her open palm. (Players can also pitch to themselves, bouncing the ball in front of them.) Bases are run as in regular Softball.

Triangle Softball is Punchball played with as few as four players. Instead of a diamond, mark out a triangle with each side about 30 feet long: home plate, first base and second base. Two players bat, while on the other team, one pitches and one fields from near the center of the triangle, as illustrated above.

The pitcher bounces the ball to the batter from behind the baseline connecting first and second bases. The batter slaps or punches the ball. It must bounce once inside the triangle and not go beyond the foul lines connecting home plate with the bases. If it does or if the batter swings and

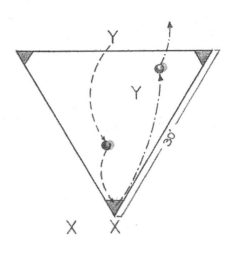

Triangle Softball

misses, he is out. If the batter makes a hit, he runs the bases and can be tagged out or thrown out as in regular Softball. There is a lot of running and second-guessing to this game, but all the regular rules apply.

Box Softball is another form of Punchball played by two to four people, but in an even more limited space. Use a rubber ball or a tennis ball, and mark out three five-foot squares in a row, as illustrated on the facing page (a sidewalk is perfect) The pitcher stands outside one box, and the batter stands outside the box at the opposite end. The pitcher tosses the ball so that it bounces once in the center box and once in the batter's box. If he fails, it is a ball. If he succeeds, the batter must try to slap or punch it back into the pitcher's box. If he swings and misses, it is a strike; if he hits it but it doesn't bounce in the right box, it is an out. If it enters the box and the pitcher catches it on the first bounce, it is an out. Otherwise, the batter scores a base for every extra bounce before the pitcher catches it.

Badminton

- ◆ NUMBER: two or four players
- ◆ EQUIPMENT: a racket for each player, a net and poles, several shuttlecocks and a 44-by-20-foot field
- ◆ DESCRIPTION: a vigorous backyard racket game; played like Tennis, but with a shuttlecock instead of a ball and no bouncing allowed

BADMINTON derives from Shuttlecock, which has been played in the Far East for more than 2,000 years. Young Oriental cadets kicked a small feathered ball to hone their agility; shopkeepers kicked the ball in the streets to keep warm on slow winter days. In another version of the game, the feathered ball was batted from player to player with small rackets called battledores, which were probably originally used as rug beaters. Eventually, the rackets were made of parchment or rows of gut stretched across a frame. The game of Battledores was depicted in Greek drawings; it was also played in Tudor England by British girls who relied on the shuttlecock to foretell their futures. As they batted it back and forth, trying to keep it off the ground, they would sing, "Shuttlecock, Shuttlecock, tell me true, How many years have I to go through? One, two, three . . ." Experts can often keep the shuttlecock in the air for a count of 100.

British military officers in India in the 1870s added a net to the traditional Battledores and Shuttlecock, naming the new game Poona, after the village where they were stationed. While on leave in England in the summer of 1873, some of the officers played Poona at Badminton Hall, the Cotswold country estate of the Duke of Beaufort. The game began to be known by the name of the Duke's country seat—Badminton.

Badminton arrived on the scene a few years before Lawn Tennis, and a good thing, too, according to Tennis aficionados, who claim that the milder game would never have stood a chance had the two competed head to head. Away from India's balmy weather, the game quickly moved indoors, where it was played in huge Victorian salons, often bisected by sliding doors—which meant that the net was at least four feet narrower than the back lines. In 1901, the court straightened out its hourglass shape, and although competitive Badminton stayed inside, the layperson's game returned to the backyard for play.

The Playing Field: A regulation Badminton court is 44 feet long and 20 feet wide for doubles (four players), 17 feet wide for singles (two players). Outdoors, the court can be enlarged or shrunk, depending on the size of the yard and on the agility of the players. Stretch the net across the middle, at the 22-foot point, and draw a *short service line* 6½ feet from the net on either side. (This line can be set anywhere from 9 to 5 feet away.) For doubles games, draw a *long service line* 2½ feet from the back boundary. A serve must clear the short service line near the net, and in doubles games, it must not go past the long service line. Draw a centerline from the short ser-

Doubles Badminton

vice line to the back boundary, dividing the court into equal halves.

Equipment: The net is 30 inches wide and at least 20 feet long, held up by poles on either side of the court. The distance from the top of the net to the ground should be exactly five feet in the center, a little higher at the poles in case the net sags. Although inexpensive Badminton sets can be had, it is worth spending a little more to get rackets, shuttlecocks and a net that will survive beyond the first game.

Shuttlecocks (also called shuttles, birdies and birds) were originally large and solid, made of leather-covered cork weighted with lead and stuck with feathers that were interlaced with thread so that the fan could be spread or drawn tightly together to change the shuttlecock's speed according to wind conditions. The same models are still widely available, at extremely low cost, yet most players settle for the lightweight plastic varieties that come with backyard sets. An official shuttlecock weighs 2½ to 3 ounces and has 14 to 16 feathers with a 2½-inch spread on top.

There is no specified size for a badminton racket, but it generally ranks between a tennis racket and a squash racket. It weighs about 5 ounces and is strung with 20-gauge gut or high-test nylon.

The Object of the Game:

To return the shuttlecock to the other side of the net, always keeping it in the air and never committing a fault.

The Play: Players decide who goes first by flipping a coin or spinning a racket (when the racket falls, the player closest to the handle has her choice of ends and can opt to serve first or not).

In singles, the server stands on the right side of the court and serves diagonally across the net to the other player's right court. She serves by dropping the birdie and hitting it underhand when it is at or below her waist. Both feet must be within the serving half-court, and the birdie must cross the short service line on the other side and

be returned from the other player's right court. (The long service line near the back boundary is not used in singles.) After the serve, players can hit the birdie from anywhere on their side of the net.

Players bat the birdie back and forth across the net. The server scores 1 point if the other player fails to return the birdie, and she serves again. If the

Shuttlecock

server fails to hit it back across the net, however, she loses the serve, and no one scores a point. In any volley, only the serving side scores. With each new serve, players move to the other half-court, serving and receiving first from one side, then the other.

If the server commits an error—a *fault*—she loses the serve. A server is at fault if she serves overhand, serves with one or both feet outside the boundary lines or serves either from or into the wrong court. She is also at fault if the birdie falls short of the service line, goes outside the court boundaries, goes through the net or fails to clear the net altogether. (A birdie that touches the net is still in play as long as it falls on the opponent's side.) A receiver is at fault if he is not standing with both feet in the half-court diagonally opposite the server: in this case, the server scores 1 point.

During play, if the server commits a fault, she loses the serve; if the other player commits a fault, the server scores 1 point and serves again. Any player is at fault if his body or his racket touches the net, if the birdie touches the ground before he returns it, if he sends the birdie into the net or

out of the court, if he hits the birdie twice or if he hits it before it actually clears the net. If a birdie hits a line, it is considered in. It must fall completely outside the line to be dead.

Letting is a tradition in informal Badminton games: if a player makes a minor fault inadvertently (a toe edging beyond her half-court, for instance, or a birdie stuck in the net), the other player may let her take the play again.

After each game, players change sides, and the winner of the last game serves first in the next. If playing a third game in a match (best two out of three), players switch after one side has earned half the points necessary to win the game.

The Score: The usual game for singles is 11 or 15 points; doubles play to 21 points. A player or team must win by 2 points, so if the score is 9-9, 13-13 or 19-19, respectively, the person who first reached the tie score has the choice of playing on until someone wins by 2 points or *setting the game*, in which case the side that first scores 3 points wins. A match of two out of three games is generally played.

Technique: One of the unusual characteristics of the birdie is its tremendous speed on impact—up to 110 miles per hour—which brakes to a meandering glide within seconds. A hard hit may propel the birdie quite high, but it descends so slowly that players can get into position to whack it back before it hits the court. Controlling the birdie's peculiarities of flight so that your opponent cannot return the volley is the secret to Badminton success.

There are four basic Badminton strokes: the high *clear shot*, also known as a *lob shot*; the *smash*, a hard downward angle; the *drop shot*, which plummets as soon as it crosses the net; and the *drive*, which is a fast, flat shot that zooms horizontally over the net, barely clearing it. The best strategy is to perfect a variety of shots and mix them up. Deception is a big part of the game: never let an opponent know what is coming.

One of the downfalls of Badminton, in the opinion of serious players, is the birdie's vulnerability to wind. This adds a certain element of luck to the game that is not always unwelcomed by amateurs, but skilled players prefer to rely on their own devices and not on the vagaries of the weather. To ensure that neither player has an advantage, arrange the net so that it is in line with the direction of the wind. If your yard enjoys a rather constant breeze, buy a heavier birdie (the weight is coded by the color around the neck of the ball) or move indoors for a game of **Ping-pong**.

Variations: When playing partners, a full 20-foot court is used. The person in the right-hand court serves first. The serve in doubles must land between the short and the long service lines of the receiver's court diagonally opposite. If the server scores a point, she continues to serve, switching sides with her partner. When she loses the serve, it passes to her teammate, who serves from the left-hand court. Then the serve moves to the opponent's right-hand court and, finally, to the opponent's left-hand court. No matter who is serving, service always alter-

nates between right and left courts.

Indoors, use a badminton birdie and a pair of ping-pong rackets to play **Shuttlecock**. Play by yourself or with a friend, and bat the birdie, seeing how long you can keep it in the air. Or the birdie can be kicked between two players until one lets it fall. If playing by yourself, keep score by counting every hit until it falls, then play for your personal best high score.

Basketball

- ◆ NUMBER: **two or more players**
- ◆ EQUIPMENT: **a basketball, a backboard, a hoop and a playing area as small as 20 feet square**
- ◆ DESCRIPTION: **a fast-moving game that hones control and stamina**
- ◆ COMPLEXITY: **kids and adults are well matched; the agility of one balances the strength and judgment of the other**
- ◆ TIP: **needs little space and equipment and few players; ideal for city lots**

BASKETBALL HOOPS are probably the most underused pieces of outdoor games equipment in the country. Every garage in suburbia seems to have one jutting off its side, but if you had a nickel for every person you ever saw playing, you'd still be short the price of a cup of coffee. Yet as anyone who has seen *Father of the Bride* knows, not only is Basketball good exercise, it is an effective bonding agent for parents and kids.

Basketball was invented during the exercise craze of the late 19th century by James Naismith, a Canadian who was working as a physical-education instructor at the International YMCA Training School in Springfield, Massachusetts. Naismith set out to devise a game for his students that would be as good a workout as calisthenics and as much fun as Football or Soccer, that could be played indoors like **Badminton** but that would involve a

large group of people. He used a soccer ball, incorporated lots of running, but without tackling, and extended the

Basketball

---

space vertically by nailing half-bushel peach baskets on either end of the gym as elevated "goals." Basketball was born.

The rules were published in the campus paper in 1892; the metal hoop with its bottomless, netted basket was invented in 1893; the next year, a distinctive ball was manufactured; in 1895, the backboard appeared; and in 1896, the first official rules committee was struck. The first national tournament was played in 1897, and the first professional league was formed in 1898. A hundred years later, it is, with Baseball and Football, one of the three top sports in the United States.

Of all the organized sports that are also played as home games, Basketball requires the least space and needs the fewest players. It is a good workout and hones ball-handling and shooting skills; besides, it is fun. For backyard play, you don't need a full 94-by-50-foot court with hardwood floors—just a hoop and a backboard attached to the garage or house wall, with a hard-pack driveway to dribble on. There are lots of games that can be played with a couple of people and a single hoop: among them, they combine all the elements of team play.

The Playing Field: Ideally, you should have a clear area about 20 feet square in front of the basket. If you want to mark lines for a half-court on the driveway, consider the midpoint of the basket, where it attaches to the wall, as the center of the end line. Six feet on either side of the midpoint, draw parallel lines extending forward from the backboard 15 feet.

Join the ends with a 12-foot line that is parallel to the backboard: this is the free-throw, or foul, line. (In the gym, the backboard is four feet in from the end line, and the end line is 19 feet from the free-throw line.) Using the midpoint of the free-throw line to define the six-foot radius, draw a half-circle beyond the free-throw line. If you have room, 28 feet beyond the free-throw line and parallel to it, draw the centerline, the division that defines the half-court. At the midpoint of the division line, draw two half-circles, one with a two-foot radius, the other with a six-foot radius.

Equipment: A regulation basketball has shrunk over the years from 32 inches in circumference to the standard now of about 30 inches and weighs 20 ounces. The ball is laceless and is inflated so that when it is dropped from a height of six feet, it rebounds at least four feet. The "basket" is a ⅝-inch metal ring, or hoop, with an inside diameter of 18 inches; the net that hangs from the hoop is not essential, except for making the satisfying "swish" when a ball passes through the basket without touching the rim. The basket is mounted firmly in the middle of a backboard that is either a 4-by-6-foot rectangle or a 54-inch-wide fan shape. The backboard should be mounted so that the ring is perfectly horizontal and 10 feet above the ground.

The Object of the Game: To sink a basket; to prevent the opponents from doing the same.

The Play: General Basketball rules apply to most hoop games. The ball is passed, batted, tapped, rolled or dribbled (but never kicked or carried) between players until one can get into a position to sink a basket. In the absence of referees, players are on the honor system when it comes to fouls and violations. Basketball is a noncontact sport: when a player who does not have the ball makes contact with the player who does, that is a defensive *foul*: the offended player gets to take a free throw. If the offended player was

Driveway Basketball

in the act of shooting when he was touched, he gets two free throws if he missed his shot, one if he made it. If the player with the ball contacts another player, it's an offensive foul, and the offended player gets one free throw. If neither player has the ball and there is contact, it is still a foul, but there are no free throws: the ball is given to the offended player's team. In organized Basketball, a player who commits five fouls is out of the game.

If a player commits a *violation,* he loses the ball. A violation occurs when a player travels (takes two steps without dribbling); double dribbles (dribbles the ball, stops, holds the ball with two hands, then starts dribbling again); sends the ball out-of-bounds; steps over the line when taking a free throw; fails to pass the ball within five seconds; runs with the ball or hits it with his feet or fist; stays in the free-throw lane for more than three seconds when he or a teammate has the

ball; or jumps up to make a shot and comes down without having released the ball. After a violation, the ball goes to the other team and is brought back into play from out-of-bounds.

The ball is usually put into play with a jump shot at center court. One person tosses the ball into the air between two opposing players. After it has reached its highest point, each player tries to tap it to a teammate or to take control of the ball. If there are only two players, they decide who gets the ball first and play an even number of games to balance the advantage.

After each successful basket and after a successful free throw, the ball is brought back into play by the opposing player or team from the end line behind the basket. If the free throw does not make a basket, all players vie for the rebound, and play continues.

The Score: In regulation Basketball, a successful basket from the floor scores 2 points; a successful basket from the free-throw line scores 1 point. For adults, a game consists of two 20-minute halves; for teenage players, four 8-minute quarters; and for younger players, four 6-minute quarters. The team or player with the most points at the end of the game wins.

Technique: *Dribbling*, or bouncing the ball on the floor, is the main means of moving around the court with the ball. (A player must start dribbling before he takes a second step.) When a player touches the ball with both hands, the dribble is done, and he must then either pass the ball to another player or shoot at the hoop. A double dribble is not allowed. The ball must touch the backboard, the basket or another player before the same person can dribble again.

Players move the ball between them by passing. In the *chest pass*, a player holds the ball with both hands at chest level and pushes it straight at a teammate. With a *bounce pass*, a player bounces the ball to a teammate. The *roll pass* rolls the ball along the floor to a teammate. The *hook pass* is lobbed sideways or overhead around another player. And the *baseball pass* pitches the ball to a teammate a long distance away, as if it were a very large baseball.

In the *lay-up shot*, the shooter dribbles in and throws the ball against the backboard so that it rebounds into the basket; in the *over-the-rim shot*, better known as the *dunk shot* or the *slam dunk*, the player jumps and drops the ball over the rim of the hoop directly into the basket; from a distance, a player might use a *one-hand shot*, thrown from a jump (and called a *jump shot*), a stride or a standing position; the longer-range shots are called *set shots*, usually two-handed throws from the chest.

The player in possession of the ball tries to move with it, pass it or make a shot. The opponent tries to get the ball, intercepting a bounce pass, stealing a dribble. At the same time, he also tries to prevent the person with the ball from getting near the hoop—

this is called *screening*—without making direct contact, delaying or preventing the other player from making his move.

Variations: A favorite two-player game is **One-on-One**, played on a half-court. The ball is put into play by a jump ball at center court. If there is no one else around to toss the ball, the players can decide who gets the ball first. Baskets are worth 1 point each, and a game is played to 21 points.

There are two major variations on the game: if the rule is "make it and take it," the player who makes a basket keeps the ball; some play that after a basket, the person who scored gives up the ball to the other player. The latter makes for a fairer game. Players should also agree whether to play the rebounds or to follow the rule that if you recover a rebound, you must dribble it behind the free-throw line before trying to make another basket.

Next to One-on-One, **Horse** is the most common two-player hoop game. The object of the game is to spell HORSE. Players decide who gets the ball first, then that player takes a shot —any kind of shot—from anywhere on the court. If he doesn't make it, the other player gets the ball. However, if the first player sinks the basket, the other person must match it, making the same shot from the same place. If he misses, the first player scores an H. If the second player succeeds, he gets the ball. To keep the game interesting, agree that a shooter cannot take the same shot twice in a row. There are dozens of variations on this theme— in some games, the loser earns the letters—but it doesn't matter. The real object of the game is practicing baskets.

In **Twenty-One**, one player stands at the free-throw line and takes a free throw. The other waits under the backboard. If the shooter sinks the basket, he earns 2 points, and the other player returns the ball to him. He continues to shoot until he misses. When the shooter misses, the person under the basket grabs the rebound and tries a lay-up. If she sinks the

basket, she earns 1 point and switches positions with the other player so that she now shoots from the free-throw line. If she misses the lay-up, the ball goes back to the shooter for another free throw. The first player to reach 21 points wins. If a player goes over 21, her score is wiped out, and she starts again at zero.

To play Twenty-One with more than two players, everyone takes turns at the free-throw line. Each player takes shots until he misses, running up to grab his own rebounds. If he makes a free throw, he earns 2 points; if he makes a basket from where he catches the rebound, he earns 2 points; if he catches the rebound and dribbles in closer for a lay-up shot, he earns only 1 point. If he misses the rebound, the next person in line gets a chance. This game is also played to 21.

Greedy is a game for two players each with her own ball. Tape or chalk an X on one ball. Both players shoot baskets at the same time, retrieving their own rebounds and trying again. Each can shoot only with her own ball. If a player shoots with her opponent's ball, she automatically loses. The first to score 10 baskets wins.

Around the World is a little more controlled than Horse but is good practice for sinking baskets and can include as many players as you like. Players mark seven spots in a semicircle around the hoop. The player who goes first shoots from the first spot; if she makes the basket, she moves to the second spot and shoots, continuing her trip around the world until she misses. The ball then passes to the second player, who gets as far as he can before missing; he passes the ball to the third player, and so on, until everyone has had a turn. Then the first player gets the ball again, picks up where she left off and continues around the world. The first player to go from the first spot to seven and back again wins. Some players choose nine spots and call this **Basketball Golf**, recording the number of shots per hole and keeping a running tally. The player with the lowest total at the end of 18 "holes"—there and back—

wins. In either game, it is wise to set a 10-shot limit for each spot, especially with novice players.

Most games depend on sinking baskets, but **Steal the Dribble** is good practice in ball handling and defending. There is no shooting at all. Players decide who gets the ball first, then the first player starts at the free-throw line and dribbles to a point under the basket, screened all the way by the other player, who tries to hit the ball away, steal it or force a violation. Every time a player makes it from the free-throw line to the basket, she earns 1 point, and the dribbler and defender switch roles. When a defender steals the ball or forces an error, he earns 1 point, and the players switch roles. ∾

Volleyball

- ◆ NUMBER: **12 players is standard, but a minimum of 6 can play (3 per side)**
- ◆ EQUIPMENT: **a volleyball, a net and a field 60 feet by 30 feet or less**
- ◆ DESCRIPTION: **a volley game like Badminton, with a ball instead of a birdie and no rackets**
- ◆ COMPLEXITY: **various ages play well together, from age 8 or so and up**
- ◆ TIP: **active and fast-paced without demanding great physical fitness; almost no body contact**

A GENUINE AMERICAN sport, Volleyball was invented in 1895 by William G. Morgan, the physical director of the YMCA in Holyoke, Massachusetts, as a less demanding alternative indoor sport to the brand-new game of **Basketball**, which many members found too rigorous. It became a bit of a fad during the 1930s: more than five million Americans played regularly, seduced by its easygoing nature. The rules are few and simple, the court is adaptable, the skills elementary. As *The New York Times* noted at the time: "It can be played during the noonhour outside the factory; it can be played on a roof, and in the backyard or in rural surroundings, where a fence takes the place of a net. If a fence is not available, a piece of rope will serve."

Volleyball was included in the Olympics for the first time in 1964, but it wasn't until the 1980s that it became really popular. **Croquet** may be enjoying a heyday among the trendier elements of society, but Volleyball is also an up-and-comer among younger, brawnier, less affluent folk, especially the ones who hang out at the beach. There is now a 28-event professional tour for the two-man beach version of the game, with hundreds of thousands of dollars in prizes. The seaside professionals have a point. The poles are relatively easy to drive into the ground, and the landings are soft if a player dives for a ball and misses. The sand makes it a little harder to move, but with the water close by, players who work up a sweat can take a quick cooling dip.

The Playing Field: Regulation Volleyball is played on a court 60 feet long by 30 feet wide, but for

Volleyball

Forearm Pass

home play, the court can adapt to the number of people playing, as long as it is roughly twice as long as it is wide. For instance, with three to a side, a court 36 by 18 feet is adequate. Lay out the boundaries of the court with ropes, pegged at the corners, or toe a line in the sand. The net divides the court across the center into two square half-courts, one for each team. Official courts have a *spiking line* marked parallel to the centerline 10 feet from the net on either side—back-line players can't go beyond this line to spike—but for home play, this is unnecessary. The outside boundaries parallel to the net are the baselines. Facing the net, start at the right-hand corner of each baseline and mark off a third of the baseline as the serving line: players must stand behind this line to serve.

Equipment: The regulation volleyball is lightweight and is 25 to 27 inches in circumference, and really, nothing else will do. The official net is 3 feet wide and 32 feet long, but just about anything can serve as a net for a spontaneous game: a fence, a piece of rope with a blanket draped over top or two pieces of rope interlaced closely enough with string that the ball will bounce back. For regular use, however, it is worth buying a regulation net.

String the net tightly, top and bottom, between stable uprights that won't sag after a few vigorous rebounds. If there aren't trees about 35 feet apart, sink two heavy wooden poles into the ground and guy them back with ropes. If the net droops,

simply tighten the guys. John Thorndike, who organizes an annual Volleyball tournament at his Ohio farm, recommends using a posthole digger to dig two 24-inch-deep holes, 36 feet apart. He cuts small trees (about 6 inches in diameter at the base and 15 feet tall), trims the branches and sets them in the holes so that they lean away from each other at a 15-degree angle. He firms them in place, then ties a rope between the trees and tightens it to draw the trees back to the vertical. After he attaches the net, he removes the top rope. The poles want to spring apart, and thus the net stays tight game after game after game.

The net should extend about a foot on either side of the court. The official

Volleyball

net height is 8 feet for men, 7 feet 6 inches for women and teenagers and 7 feet for youngsters, but adjust it to suit the players, especially children. In general, the top of the net should be just a little higher than the players' upstretched fingertips.

The Object of the Game: To hit the ball over the net so that it can't be returned; to return balls hit over the net by the other team.

The Play: Official teams have six players to a side, three forwards positioned close to the net, three players in the backcourt. With four to a side, play two people up and two back. Three players on a team cover a third of the court each as best they can, usually playing two net and one back.

More than six to a side makes for a frustrating game, with players more likely to hit each other than the ball. Instead of letting everyone on the court at once, have one person leave and another come on the court with each rotation.

Players decide which team begins. The person at the back right serves the ball from behind the serving line, hitting it over the net into the opposing team's court. It doesn't matter where it goes as long as it clears the net without touching it and falls within the sidelines and the baseline of the opposite court. Players on the other team hit the ball, returning it to the serving team. The volley continues, the ball going back and forth across the net, until one team makes a fault.

Each team is allowed three hits on one side before returning the ball to the opposing court, although no player is allowed to touch the ball twice in a row. Technically, a ball can be hit by any part of the body above the waist. Once the ball is in play, it can touch the net as long as it makes it over; it must not, however, touch the ground.

The volley ends when a team fails to return the ball, when the ball touches the ground or goes out-of-bounds or when a player makes an error. If the serving team wins the volley, it earns 1 point and serves again. The same person serves until the team loses a volley. When the other team wins the volley, it is a *side out*: no one

The Set

earns a point, but the serve passes to the other team. Only the serving team can score a point.

Every time a team gets the serve, that team's players rotate clockwise one position. This way, everyone has a chance to play each position. At the beginning of each volley, the players in the back and front rows must stay in position (a back-row person cannot be farther forward than a front-row person), but after the serve, players can move anywhere on the court.

The rules are simple. Players can step on the centerline but not over it. And they can reach over the net to block a shot but not to attack. If a ball hits a boundary, it is in; to be out of play, it must be completely beyond the line. The ball can bounce into the net and out again and remain in play as long as it doesn't hit the ground, but if a player touches the net, it is a side out. According to regulation play, if a player uses two hands, they must touch the ball at exactly the same time; otherwise, it counts as a *double hit*. If the ball comes to rest in the palm of the hand for even a split second, it is an illegal *lift*.

The Score: The first team to score 15 (or 21) points wins; a game must be won by a margin of 2 points. Matches are usually two out of three games, with players switching courts between games and again in the middle of the third game, if a third game is necessary. The team that loses one game serves first in the next.

Technique: To serve, hit the ball with the open palm or the fist, tossing it up in the air and pummeling it overhand or holding it with one hand and swinging the other arm like a pendulum to hit it underhand.

Once the ball is in play, there are three main types of hits: the forearm pass, the set and the spike, and they are often used in this order, batting the ball between three players before returning it to the other side of the net.

The *forearm pass* is a relatively painless way to handle a spike and avoids any hint of a lift with the palms of the hands. To make a forearm pass, cradle the four fingers of one hand palm up in the other, make your thumbs parallel and point your hands toward the ground, creating a tight V with your forearms. Bend your knees to get under the ball, hitting it from below with the flat surface between the wrists and elbows. Use this to return a serve, *bumping* the ball to the setter.

The *setter* is a player in either the front or the back row with good control and strong fingers. He receives the ball from the first player and sets it up so that a third teammate can spike it over the net. For good control in setting, hold your hands palm out and make a triangle with your thumbs and forefingers, then move your forefingers about three inches apart. The ball is hit with all 10 fingertips, hands held high above your face, the strength coming from your wrists, not your whole arms. The setter propels the ball high in the air toward the person who will put it over the net.

The *spike* is the most difficult volley to return and is therefore most often used to put the ball into the other court. It is a hard slam with an open palm or a fist, delivered from above so that the ball takes a fast nose dive into an empty spot on the opposite court. A player's hand cannot be in the other team's air space when delivering a spike: the ball must be on the spiker's side of the net when it is hit, although in the follow-through, the spiker's hand may enter the opponents' air space. ∽

Touch Football

- ◆ OTHER NAMES: Tag Football
- ◆ NUMBER: 6 to 11 players per side
- ◆ EQUIPMENT: a football and a very big yard
- ◆ DESCRIPTION: a safe, scaled-down version of the professional game that is just about as fast and exciting and uses the same skills and strategies

THROW-AND-KICK ball games have been around since the Greeks, and probably earlier. In ancient and medieval Britain, they were played under the general rubric of mêlées, or mellays, in which a group of children punched, kicked, shoved and, in any possible way, maneuvered some round or oval object—usually a filled animal bladder—toward a goal.

The games were played mostly on feast days, much as Touch Football is traditionally played at Thanksgiving family gatherings. The mellays were barred by a succession of monarchs, from Edward III to Elizabeth I, but the games were as irrepressible as they were rowdy. In the 18th century, a French spectator commented that if this was what the British called play-ing, what on earth would they call fighting.

At Britain's public (in other words, private) schools, the mellays were harnessed into more structured games, but each school seemed to have its own version. The only thing the mellays had in common was that the games were primarily for kicking and booting, with occasional batting: the ball was never actually carried. In 1823, William Webb Ellis broke this hallowed rule at Rugby School: He picked up the ball and ran. From this point on, the mellays divided into foot games (Soccer) and foot-and-hand games (Rugby).

On the other side of the Atlantic, students at American universities were also playing ball-kicking games; all were slightly different, but all except

Flag Football

one forbade running with the ball. Only Harvard demurred, allowing a player to pick up the ball and, if chased, to run with it. In 1874, Harvard played a series of games against McGill University of Montreal, alternating between Harvard rules (a kicking game with a round ball and limited hand contact) and the Canadian rules (essentially Rugby), which used an elongated ball and included running with the ball as well as touchdowns. The contact with the Canadian team galvanized Harvard's commitment to its unconventional game; it adopted the Rugby rules and the elongated ball and eventually convinced Yale, Princeton and Columbia to do the same.

The American game, although called Football, was based on Rugby. Over the next 50 years, it continued to evolve into the game it is today, shrinking the field by 100 feet and the teams from 20 players each to 11, adding the quarterback, the huddle, downs and numerical scoring. In 1906, at the insistence of no less a fan than President Theodore Roosevelt, the American Inter-Collegiate Football rules committee was formed to make the game safer. It did so by introducing the forward pass, a ploy that successfully opened up the play and, coincidentally, made College Football a distinctive American game. And a wildly popular one. More than 133 million Americans

—almost half the population of the United States—watched the 1993 Superbowl.

Touch Football comes full circle, moving off the public school grounds and college campuses and back to the streets. To reduce the body contact, tagging replaces tackling as the means of halting the opposing team's advance. Exactly what constitutes a "tag" or a "touch" varies across the country. In two-hand Touch Football, it takes a tag with both hands to "down" an opponent; sometimes, the tag must be between knees and shoulders; others allow only a one-hand tag.

Altogether, Touch Football involves more running and passing than tagging. Instead of taking four downs to move the ball 10 yards, backyard players can agree to take four downs to score a touchdown, which isn't that difficult given the shrunken field. Otherwise, the rules of College Football and Touch Football are much the same. Above all, this is a team effort: players can decide among themselves how strict or how free-form a game they want to play. Whatever the veneer of rules that are applied, Football, like the mellays it evolved from, is still a robust, aggressive and enduring game.

The Playing Field: A regulation Football field in the United States is 360 feet long and 160 feet wide, marked in 5-yard lines from 50

at the midpoint of the field to 0 at the goal line. (The Canadian field is 300 feet long.) Beyond the goal line lies the 30-foot end zone and, at the back of it, the end line where two goalposts are centered 18 feet 6 inches apart. The crossbar is 10 feet above the ground, and the posts extend up another 20 feet beyond that.

The game can be scaled down, however, for play in a park, a backyard or a stretch of vacant beach. A 100-foot playing area is big enough for a workout but compact enough so that there will actually be a score. (If the field is smaller, change the number of downs from four to three.)

Divide the field in half with a centerline that represents the 50-yard line, and mark goal lines at either end. Goalposts are optional, and end zones disappear.

Equipment: An oval leather football inflated to a pressure of 12½ to 13½ pounds; in home games, helmets and pads aren't necessary, and cleats aren't allowed.

The Object of the Game: To carry the ball over the opponents' goal line or to kick the ball between their goalposts; to prevent the other team from doing the same.

The Play: Divide the players into two teams. On a College Football team, there are 11 players: four backs (quarterback, left halfback, right halfback and fullback) and seven linemen (left end, left tackle, left guard, center, right guard, right tackle and right end). Many high school teams play with six to a side. Touch Football teams generally have nine players, but backyard teams can have as few as four to a side: choose a quarterback, but otherwise, leave the positions undefined.

Touch Football has as many house rules as **Shinny**: it is played by whatever rules the teams agree on. In its loosest, most elementary form, each team has four downs in which to get the ball over the other team's goal line. On a larger field, in more organized play, a team has four downs to move the ball the traditional 10 yards (or one-tenth of the field). If the team is successful, it keeps the ball and tries for another 10 yards, inching down the field toward the opposition's goal line.

To start the game and after a score, the ball is put into play by a place kick from the kicking team's 40-yard line. The kicker's team is behind him, and the receiving team must be behind the restraining line (a line 10 yards in front of the ball). Kickoffs are recovered by the receiving team. (The ball must go beyond the restraining line.) The player who catches the ball charges toward the opponents' goal line, flanked by his protective teammates. The other team tries to block their advance. The player carrying the ball gets as far as possible before being tagged. (If none of the players is a good kicker, start the game at the centerline in the same way as a first down, giving the ball to the team that wins the coin toss.)

When the ball carrier is tagged, the action stops, and the ball is put down in the middle of the field parallel to where the player was tagged. This is the *first down*. The receiving team has four downs, or four tries, in which to get the ball to the opponents' goal line (or to travel 10 yards). For each down, the team that has the ball goes into a *huddle* to figure out its next move: one person is appointed to receive the pass and carry the ball forward toward the goal line.

After the huddle, the players line up behind the ball along their *scrimmage line*, facing their opponents but separated from them by a neutral zone as wide as the ball is long. One player snaps the ball back to the quarterback, who advances with it or passes it to the player chosen to advance the ball. The ball carrier can run forward with the ball, pass it forward or pass it directly to the side in a *lateral pass*. The other team tries to tag the ball carrier; his own teammates try to keep the other players away. If the ball carrier is tagged, it is the *second down*. (If the field has goalposts, a team may decide, on any down, to try for a *field goal*: the

quarterback receives the ball and holds it vertically on the ground, and another player tries to kick it between the opposing team's goalposts, above the crossbar.)

On the fourth down, if a team is sure it cannot score, it may kick, or *punt*, the ball down the field so that the opponents will have as far to move the ball as possible. The team must announce its intention to punt before the down begins, and no one can cross the scrimmage line until after the kick.

If, after four downs, the team with the ball has not scored a touchdown or advanced 10 yards, the other team gets the ball, starting the play from the last scrimmage line or where the team was tagged after catching the punt. The direction of movement on the field reverses as the new ball carriers try to move the ball toward the other goal.

The rules during the game are basically the same as for College Football, except there is no tackling, the ball is *dead* whenever it touches the ground, and if there are no goalposts, there is no try for an extra point after a touchdown.

A ball is dead and a player is "downed" if a player on the other team tags him. A fumbled ball goes to whichever team pounces on it first. It is put back into play at the point of the fumble. If, during a play, a pass is intercepted by someone on the other team, that team gets the ball, and the action on the field reverses as those players run to the opposite goal line to score.

Any number of passes can be thrown in a series of downs, and any player on the field can catch them. Forward passes can be thrown from any point back of the scrimmage line, and lateral passes can be thrown from anywhere. Passing back to a player behind you is not allowed.

Blocking is allowed, although a player's feet cannot leave the ground, and he cannot use his arms or hands to impede another player's progress. This means, effectively, no jumping and no grabbing.

A player who crosses the other team's goal line carrying the ball scores

a touchdown for his team. If a team gets close to a goal line but doesn't think it can carry the ball over, it can choose, instead, to have the kicker propel the ball over the goal line (or between the goalposts), earning a field goal, which scores only half as much as a touchdown. After a touchdown, there is no try for an extra point, as in professional Football. The other team gets the ball, and play starts at center field, as at the beginning of the game.

Although there are no referees, players can decide on penalties for obvious infractions, such as using hands and feet in blocking, roughing, pushing, holding, tackling or tripping. The usual penalty is 15 yards (or a proportional distance on a smaller field). If a player goes into the other team's territory before the ball leaves the center, there is a 5-yard penalty.

College games are one hour of play, divided into 15-minute quarters, with rest periods in between. In the backyard, friends usually play until it is time for dinner.

The Score: A field goal scores 3 points. A touchdown scores 6 points. The team with the most points at the end of the game wins.

Variations: The game can be played entirely without kicking. The game begins with a pass instead of a kick, and field goals are omitted.

In **Razzle Dazzle**, the rules are relaxed a little further. All the rules above apply, except the ball can be passed backward, laterally and forward as many times as the team wants during a single down. If someone drops the ball, it is dead, and the line of scrimmage is where the ball was thrown from (not where it landed).

Flag Football, or **Tail Football**, reduces the contact a little more and makes for tighter defensive play. Each player stuffs a rag, a bandanna or a shirt into the waistband of his pants. Instead of tagging a player, the flag must be pulled out to stop the play. ❧

15

Home Free: Games of Search, Chase and Capture

S UDDENLY, IT'S SPRING. It's not that the snow is gone—it's been
gone for days, maybe weeks—and it's not that the sky is clear. It's
something in the air, as warm and soft as a mother's good-night
kiss. And it's something in the earth, a certain firmness that
tells you winter has, at last, drained away. The signs are unmistakable:
it's marble time.

Outdoor games have a seasonal rhythm that has remained unchanged
for centuries. William Newell noted it in his 1883 collection, *Games and Songs
of American Children*: "These 'times' succeeded each other almost as regularly
as the flowers of summer, the children dropping one and taking up another
every year at the same season. This succession, which the children themselves
could hardly explain beforehand, but remembered when the occasion came,
has impressed itself on observers as almost a matter of instinct."

As surely as **Marbles** is followed by **Jump Rope** and Jump Rope by
Dodge Ball and **Tag,** so do the games themselves seem to arise from some
collective memory shared by all of us who play. Generation after generation
plays **Red Rover, Squat Tag** and **World,** yet few can remember where or how

they learned these games. No one takes a rule book into the playground, yet everyone knows, as if by genetic code, how to draw a **Hopscotch** grid or how to stamp the **Fox and Geese** maze in the snow.

The persistence of these games over centuries and through countries is nothing short of astounding. Many of them appear in Rabelais' list of games that Gargantua played; Shakespeare mentions them in his plays. It isn't so surprising that simple chase and search games like Tag and **Hide and Seek** should endure, but more complex pursuits such as **Prisoner's Base** and **Red Lion** have had hardly a rule change in hundreds of years.

Without putting an unseemly academic burden on such innocent amusements, many of these games have inadvertently become an unwritten and often only vaguely understood historical record. Red Lion, for instance, has nothing to do with safaris: it is more likely an anticonscription game that dates from pre-American Revolution days. When children chant, "Red Lion, Red Lion, come out of your den; Whoever you catch will be one of your men," they are taunting their old British masters, the redcoats.

Ring-Around-the-Rosy goes back even further to London's Great Plague of 1665. The first line—originally "ring-a-rosy"—describes the rash that encircled the body; "a pocketful of posies" was how some attempted to forestall the dread disease; "ashes, ashes" was originally "achoo, achoo," the violent sneezing that marked the last stage of the illness; and "we all fall down" was the unhappy result for thousands of people.

While the story behind Ring-Around-the-Rosy is well known, even the writers of most games books seem mystified by the word "chivy" that American children yell when they play Prisoner's Base. "Chivy" or "chivvy" is an old word meaning to harass persistently; it is a variant of "chevy," from the term "Chevy Chase," which most Americans associate with a very funny actor but which in fact is the name of a ballad about the territorial rivalries between two prominent families on the Scottish border. In Britain, the expression came to mean any border skirmish or running battle, which perfectly describes the game.

If kids go to school, they probably already know how to play the games in this chapter. The rules (such as they are) are written down not for kids so much as for adults who, remembering their own childhoods, may want to bring the old pastimes home to play. Although traditionally called street games or playground games, they are fun for the whole family. Most of them adapt easily to a wide range of ages—the usual state of affairs on school playgrounds—and most can be played within the relatively narrow confines of a backyard. None require equipment more complex or costly than a piece of chalk or a big rubber ball.

One of the most interesting aspects of these games is that there is almost never a mechanism for scoring. Many are based on elimination: the last one in the game is the loser, and the penalty is that the loser is It in the next round. Other games are simply played until they are over, until everyone is found or tagged or gets to home base or is taken prisoner by the other side. Even in more formal games such as Marbles, there is rarely a score: only marbles change hands, not numbers, making this a game of capture as surely as Tag.

These games may not have hard-and-fast rules, but they do have conventions and a language that is part of the distinct culture of play. If a player calls "Times!" and crosses her fingers during a game, she is safe—she can go into the house for a drink of water without fear of being tagged. "Times!" is a respite from the game, not an act of all-out surrender like "I give!" "Dibbs" means "it's mine" or "finders keepers" but is a lot faster out of the mouth. It can be heard in Marbles games or when several kids come upon a Hopscotch grid or a skipping rope lying in the grass. "Butts" is the correct way to ask to join a game like Red Rover and butt into line. "I call my place" reserves a player's spot in a game should he call "Times!" Universally understood but rarely documented, these are laws based not on recognized authority; they are the laws of custom, observed and broken by common consent.

The games in this chapter each have dozens of names and as many faces. In the end, it doesn't really matter what you call them or how you play them, as long as you have fun. They are free-form, made up on the spur of the moment, the outdoor equivalent of parlor games—and the kind of games that adults too rarely relax enough to play. They spring from the underworld of children's culture, where they have, for the most part, remained immune from the commercialization and codification of play.

Statues

- ♦ NUMBER: **fun with as few as four players; more fun with a crowd**
- ♦ EQUIPMENT: **none; can be played in a small yard or even indoors**
- ♦ DESCRIPTION: **not particularly exerting, but good for a laugh**

A GAME WITHOUT a history and with more variations than a fugue, Statues is, nevertheless, a fixture from most American childhoods.

The Object of the Game: To hold the position you find yourself in.

The Play: The person who is It grabs each player in turn and swings him or her by the arm. As she swings, she asks, "Coffee, tea or milk?" If the player answers "Milk," he is swung gently; if he answers "Tea," he gets a slightly harder turn; and if he answers "Coffee," he is spun with all of It's might. When It releases her grip, the person spins around and stops in some grotesque posture, his limbs and even his face as still as that of Lot's wife after one glance at Gomorrah. Her statuary garden complete, It (the sculptor) wanders between the motionless forms. Anyone who moves, laughs or otherwise breaks the pose is out of the game and joins It in taunting and even tickling the stony-faced players who remain. The last one to hold the pose wins and becomes It in the next turn.

Variations: Instead of spinning the other players, It moves from person to person and arranges their bodies in hard-to-hold poses. Or everyone runs around the yard until It yells "Freeze!" transforming the players into flash-frozen athletes. In yet another variation, the players are swung, but instead of becoming statues, they fall to the ground in death throes. The most convincing corpse or the one that returns to life last wins. ∾

Tag

- ♦ NUMBER: **at least five or six players, but the more the merrier**
- ♦ EQUIPMENT: **none, but needs a large yard or park**
- ♦ DESCRIPTION: **an active running and chasing game**
- ♦ TIP: **fun for a group of mixed ages provided the older ones give the little kids a break**

TAG IS SUCH A simple game that at first, it may be difficult to understand why it has persevered. It was one of the most popular games at the court of Queen Elizabeth I, and according to Greek myth, it was also the favored amusement of Diana and the nymphs. Hundreds of years later, kids raised on Nintendo continue to play Tag as enthusiastically as if they had just invented it, which in fact, many children believe they did.

The answer lies perhaps in the magic and mystery of Tag. In early forms of the game, It was conceived as an aged but powerfully malignant dwarf who could stop a player in her tracks with the touch of a finger. Writhing and racing would elude the evil finger for the moment, but the only true safety lay in touching iron, an ancient protection against evil (remember, witches rode brooms because horses wore iron shoes). Deep down, maybe we really believe this is how it is: the swift and lithe can outfox life's evils, and with a touchstone, the rest of us can too.

According to William Newell's 1883 survey, *Games and Songs of American Children*, Iron Tag was the usual British version. He quotes a writer who describes the game in the February 1738 issue of *Gentleman's Magazine*: "The lad saves himself by the touching of cold iron," although "in later times, this play has been altered amongst children of quality, by touching of gold instead of iron." Newell adds, "Owing to the occasional scarcity of iron objects, wood-tag and stone-tag have been varieties of the sport in America." Among the Tag games he lists are Squat Tag and Cross Tag, still favorites in North America today.

The crux of every Tag game is It, a person who, in 19th-century manuals, was invariably referred to as "He." Choosing It can be a simple matter among kids: one person says, "Let's play Tag," and immediately, there is a chorus of "Not It! Not It!" The last voice to be raised is It. As a testament to the fair-mindedness of children, It is often chosen by counting out. Everyone stands in a circle and thrusts a fist toward the person in the center, who counts on the fists in turn, chanting: "Eeny, meeny, miny, mo, Catch a tiger by the toe, If he hollers let him go, Eeny, meeny, miny, mo." "Mo" is It. If "mo" has been It too recently, the rhyme is extended with, "O-U-T spells out, So out you must go." The person who is "go" may be It, or after several rounds, the person left is It.

Tag is best played on a grassy area: it can sometimes get physical, the evil touch evolving into a full body check. And it is best played at dusk, when darting bodies become shadows, and the fall of night adds an ancient touch of mystery to the game.

The Object of the Game: For It, to touch someone else; for the others, to avoid being tagged by It.

The Play: The most elementary of these games of chase is **Touch Tag.** Players decide who is It. The person who is It closes her eyes, counts to 10 to allow the others time to scatter, then gives chase. She pursues the rest of the group until she tags one, who then becomes It and tries to tag someone else. It can tag someone by running him down, or It can use strategy, luring players close enough to touch by pretending to be tired or hurt.

Variations: In **Touch One, Touch All,** It gives chase until she tags someone, who then joins her in the chase. Everyone tagged joins It until no more fugitives remain. The first person tagged is It in the next game.

Duck, Duck, Goose is a simple form of Tag that young children especially like. Everyone sits in a circle while It walks around the outside, tapping each person on the head and saying, "Duck, duck, duck . . ." When It taps someone on the head and says "Goose," the goose jumps up and chases It around the circle. (Doubling back is not allowed.) It tries to get to the goose's spot in the circle before being tagged. If It is tagged by the goose, she must start over in her search for another goose. If It gets to the goose's spot in the circle with-out being tagged, the goose is It.

In **Squat Tag,** It calls out the number of "squats" each player is allowed. Players who squat while being chased are immediately safe from being tagged, but once a player uses up all her squats, she is fair game.

In **Touch Wood Tag,** players agree that either wood, iron or stone is safe. Anyone who touches the designated material cannot be captured.

In **Floating Tag** or **Hang Tag,** players are safe as long as both feet are off the ground: they climb a tree, a fence or a chair or hang from a branch with both hands to avoid being tagged.

In **Cross Tag,** It is obliged to run after anyone who comes between him and the person he is pursuing. The fleet of foot can save the slower runners, and all can gang up against It, prolonging the game indefinitely.

In **Poison Tag,** also called **Hospital Tag** or **Doctor Tag,** It tags someone who then becomes It. The new It must give chase while holding one hand on the spot where he was tagged, or poisoned. Not only does this add humor to the game, but It can be so hobbled that tagging someone else is almost impossible. The strategy is for each It to tag the next person in a hard-to-hold place—the ankle, the big toe, the knee.

Shadow Touch is best played in the lengthening shadows of the late afternoon. To make a tag, It steps on a player's shadow. There is no physical contact at all.

Spotlight Tag is played at dusk or in the dark. It has a flashlight and tags players by catching them in the beam of light.

In **Freeze Tag,** a player who is tagged must immediately freeze his position. While It is chasing someone else, a person can sneak up and touch a frozen player, bringing him back into the game. In some versions, a player must crawl between the frozen person's legs in order to unthaw him. A player frozen three times is It.

Bronco Tag, Chain Tag or **Hook-On Tag** is most fun with 10 or more people. Decide who is It, then divide the others into at least three teams of three players each. (The more teams, the better.) The members of each team line up, each player holding onto the person in front of him around the waist. The first person in line is the head of the "bronco"; the person at the back is the tail; the body may be several players long. The broncos start running. It tries to join a bronco by grabbing the "tail" person around the waist. If It is successful, the head breaks off and becomes the new It.

Shadow Touch

There are no winners or losers. The game just continues with the broncos bucking around the yard trying to elude capture until everyone is exhausted.

Dragon Tag also needs a lot of people. Four people are It. They link arms to make the dragon, then chase the others, always staying linked. They catch another player by forming a circle around her. The captive then becomes part of the dragon, chasing after the others. Some people call this, more appropriately but less poetically, Fish and Net: the Its form the net, and the others are the fish.

The Blob is a Tag game with definite boundaries. Players mark off a square and put spotters on the four corners to alert the Blob when someone steps out-of-bounds. The person who is It is the Blob. She chases the other players, and if she tags a player or forces him to step out-of-bounds, that person becomes part of the Blob. They join hands and continue the chase. Each person tagged or forced out-of-bounds joins the Blob (which actually looks like a snake). Only the person on each end can make a tag.

Horseyback Tag or **Piggyback Tag** is one of the wildest incarnations of Tag, perfect for 10-year-old boys or a mixed party of teenagers. The group pairs off into two-person teams: one is a horse, the other a rider. Each rider has a strip of masking tape stuck on his back or a bandanna tucked into the back of his pants. At the signal, the riders mount their "horses," jumping on their backs with their arms around their necks. The teams chase each other, each rider trying to grab the tape or bandanna from the others' backs. (The horses do not grab; they are merely two-legged beasts of burden.) The team with the last rider with a bandanna or tape on his back wins. ❧

Hide and Seek

- ◆ NUMBER: **good for large groups of mixed ages**
- ◆ EQUIPMENT: **none**
- ◆ DESCRIPTION: **an active running and tagging game that can go on for a long time**
- ◆ TIP: **best in a big yard with lots of trees, bushes and other hiding spots**

IN THE LAST CENTURY, this game was known as **I Spy**, which today is played as a quiet visual-clue guessing game, not a rambunctious game of Tag. Whatever it is called, the game is as old as the Roman Empire. Does this description, from a thesaurus of terms written by the Greek scholar Julius Pollux in the second century, sound familiar: "One of the party places himself in the middle of his comrades and closes his eyes, unless some other covers them for him. The players run away and scatter. Then the pursuer opens his eyes and proceeds to look for them. It is each player's object to reach that one's ground before him."

Hide and Seek games can be played anywhere, indoors or out, but the place should have lots of interesting "cover." Be sure to establish the limits of the hiding area before the game begins: someone concealed in the rain barrel next door might not be found for days. Also, warn kids about unsafe hiding places, such as abandoned refrigerators and parked cars.

The Object of the Game: For It, to find the other players; for the others, to avoid being found or to touch home base before being tagged.

The Play: A place is designated as "home." The person who is It stands at home, closes her eyes and counts to some number, 50 or 100, for instance. The rest of the players hide while she counts. When she finishes, she calls, "Ready or not, here I come!" and starts to look for the others. When she spots someone, she says, "One-two-three on _____," naming the player, then both It and the discovered player race for home. If It reaches home first, the other person is caught. If the player reaches home before It, he yells, "Home free!" or "Allie, Allie, oxen free!" and is safe. It continues to look for the rest of the players, but a player doesn't have to wait to be found: he can race for home at any time. If It sees him, she tries to outrun him and tag him before he gets home. The game continues until everyone is caught or home free. The first person who was caught is It in the next round.

Variations: A reversal of the usual order of the game, **Sheep and Wolf** has one person, the wolf, hide while all the other players stay at "home" and close their eyes. When the wolf is ready, he howls. The others, who are the sheep, begin wandering around the yard (in truth, looking for the wolf), and when someone sees him, she yells, "I spy a wolf!" The sheep scatter, and the wolf immediately gives chase. Whoever is caught by the wolf before reaching home is the wolf in the next round.

Sardines is also a reverse Hide and Seek, made infamous by the film *Pretty Baby*. Instead of counting, It hides while all the others close their eyes and count. When they are done, they shout in unison, "Ready or not, here we come!" and fan out to find It. If someone finds It, he doesn't reveal the hiding place but instead crawls in beside her. This continues, each person who discovers the fugitives joining them, until the players are packed in like sardines. The last one to find the hiding spot is It in the next game.

Kick the Can is undoubtedly the

Home Free

noisiest version of Hide and Seek. If all the cans have gone to the recycling plant, substitute a block of wood, a puck or a stone. The person who is It decides on home base—a square of sidewalk, a patio block, a flat stone— or draws home base on the ground. It places the can on home base and tries to protect it, while all the other players mill about trying to distract It and knock the can off its base. When a player succeeds in kicking the can, sending it as far as she is able, she shouts for everyone to run and hide. Before he can pursue the other players, It must chase after the can and kick it back home. (No handling is allowed.) When the can is back at home base, It begins his search, and when he spots someone, he runs back home, puts his foot on the can and yells, "One-two-three on _____." The person named

must return to home base a prisoner. (There is no chase or tag.) Prisoners are confined to base, but while It is out searching for the others, a rescuer can sneak up and kick the can, yelling, "All free! All free!" liberating the captives. Once again, It must kick the can back to home base before he can continue his search. The game is over when everyone is captured—not an easy task. The first person caught is It next time round.

Ring-o-lievio or **Relievio** is a team version of Hide and Seek. Players divide themselves into two teams and define part of the yard, about 10 feet square, as the jail. The hiding boundaries are clearly established. One team is It. The players on that team close their eyes and count while the other team hides. When the counting is done, some members of the It team

stay back to guard the jail, and the rest begin the search. When a fugitive is found, he is taken back to the jail and put under guard. (In some versions, the catcher has to hang onto her victim and yell, "Caught, caught, caught!" to complete the capture. If the victim can wriggle away before the chant is done, he is free.) A prisoner can escape from jail only if a teammate can sneak within the boundaries and yell, "Ring-o-lievio!" or "Relievio!" before the guards catch him. (The more prisoners there are, the easier it is to sneak up unnoticed and spring them from jail.) This usually sets all the prisoners free, although some play that only one prisoner can be released at a time. The game ends when all the members of the fugitive team are in jail. ❧

Prisoner's Base

- ◆ NUMBER: **best with 20 players or more**
- ◆ EQUIPMENT: **none, but needs a large, square playing area**
- ◆ DESCRIPTION: **a fast-paced, chaotic taunt-and-tag game that can go on for hours**
- ◆ COMPLEXITY: **requires great agility and endurance as well as alertness; best for older children and adults**

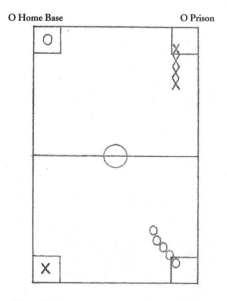

O Home Base   O Prison

X Home Base   X Prison

Prisoner's Base

PRISONER'S BASE has been around for a long time. Shakespeare mentions it in *Cymbeline*; 300 years before that, Edward III banned it from the grounds of Westminster Palace because it interfered with parliamentary affairs. It is the basis of dozens of **Tag** games played in teams, which some games historians interpret as mock war, rather than play.

The Object of the Game: To tag the members of the opposing team, putting them in prison; to avoid being tagged and to release your own teammates who are in jail.

The Play: Divide the group into two teams, each with a leader. Differentiate the teams: players on one side wear a bandanna or take off their

shoes (if the field is grassy) or put their shirts on backwards (if everyone is the same gender).

Divide the playing field in half, and draw a circle about two feet in diameter in the center of the dividing line. In one corner, draw a home base for one team, and in the other corner of that side of the field, mark that team's prison. Of the remaining two corners, one is the home base for the other team; the other is its prison.

The players decide which team goes first. The captain of the first team sends a good runner toward the circle. When he gets there, he yells "Chivy!" taunting the opposite team to come and get him. A player from the other side runs out toward the center to tag the challenger; the first team sends another player out to intercept him. The captains keep sending a pursuer to pursue the previous pursuer. Each player tries to capture a member of the opposite team by tagging.

Although there may be dozens of players on the field, each one is chasing only those who came onto the field before her and is being chased only by those who came after. Whenever a player returns to home base, she is safe and, upon reentering the field, can chase anyone who is on the field at the time but can be pursued only by those who come after.

A tagged player is put in prison in enemy territory. The first captive must keep one foot inside the prison. When another prisoner joins him, the second prisoner must have one foot in the prison, but the first one can stand outside as long as they are holding hands. Each new prisoner keeps one foot in the prison, and the others form an unbroken chain that stretches into the field in the order they were captured. If a teammate tags the prisoner at the end of the line, he is free, and the two

can go back to home base, immune from being tagged on the way. A player cannot free a teammate on his way back from delivering an opponent to prison: he must deliver his captive, go back to home base, then venture out to free his friends. However, if a player can run around the field, touching each base and prison (in other words, each corner) without being tagged, all his teammates in prison go free. The game is over when one team captures everyone on the other team.

Variation: In the more modern and less complex **Capture the Flag,**

the playing area is marked out the same, but near its prison, each team puts a flag—a bandanna tied to a stick and stuck in the ground. Instead of simply taunting each other, the members of each team try to get to the opposing team's prison and capture its flag without being tagged. Anyone caught in enemy territory can be tagged, captured and put in prison, where he must stay until a teammate frees him with a tag, as in Prisoner's Base. The game is over when one team has both flags.   ∾

Red Lion

- ◆ NUMBER: **most fun with 10 or more players**
- ◆ EQUIPMENT: **none, but needs a small yard or driveway**
- ◆ DESCRIPTION: **chase, tag and capture game that can be quite physical**

RED LION is one of several games that combine elements of Tag and Hide and Seek: one person is It and tries to tag the other players, but instead of hiding from the evil one, the others boldly taunt It. William Newell lists Red Lion in his 1883 survey, *Games and Songs of American Children*, played exactly as it is today, but he also lists an older form of the game called Red Line. Red Line refers to the uniforms of the British soldiers and originally meant running the gauntlet. Since the game does not occur in Britain under the name Red Line (and the position of keeper seems to be a later addition), Red Lion may refer not to a zoo of mutants but to Colonial conscription.

The Object of the Game: To tag the others so that they become lions.

The Play: One person is the lion, another is the lion's keeper. The lion chooses a place for his den and stays inside or beside it, with the keeper nearby. The rest of the players sneak

up to the den and chant: "Red Lion, Red Lion, come out of your den; Whoever you catch will be one of your men." Suddenly, when the others least expect it, the keeper yells "Loose!" and the lion roars out of his den, racing

Fox and Geese

after the scattering horde, trying to catch someone. If the lion can repeat "Red Lion" three times while holding onto the tagged player, the tagged one also becomes a lion, and the two return to the den. The game continues until all the players are lions. The first two players caught become the keeper and the lion in the next round.

If the keeper yells "Cowcatcher!" after "Loose!" any two lions can tag a player by joining both their hands and trapping the player inside (in the same way that a player is trapped when London Bridge falls down). If the keeper yells "Tight!" all the lions must join hands and surround the captive. If the keeper yells "Doubles!" the lions must hunt in pairs, linking arms to pursue their prey two by two.

Variations: There are many other games that dress up the tag concept in a predator-prey guise. **Fox and Geese** can be played on a sidewalk with chalk, but it is usually played in winter, after a fresh snowfall has covered all previous tracks. The players stamp a huge wheel in the snow, adding six or eight spokes. (For obvious reasons, the game is also called Wheel Tag, Cut the Pie and, 100 years ago, Picadill, after the famous traffic circle in London, England.) The player who is It is the fox; the rest are geese. The geese start in the center, which is a safe area where no one can be tagged. The geese run down the spokes and around the outside circle, jeering at the fox, who tries to catch them as they race back to the safety of the center. The first goose caught is transformed into a fox, who also chases the geese. In another version, a goose is eliminated from the game when she is tagged. The play ends when all the geese are caught or become foxes.

In a more complicated variation, a roughly circular trail is stamped in the snow or the sand around the boundary of the play area with a maze of paths in the middle, some leading to dead ends, many crisscrossing. Somewhere in the tangle is a den for the fox and a coop for the geese. The fox imprisons tagged geese in the den; the coop is a safe haven for the geese. Both predator and prey must stick to the trails: no jumping across the snow to a nearby path, and watch out for the dead ends!

Pom Pom Pullaway is similar to Red Lion. One player is It and stands in the middle of a rectangle about 25 feet long; the others line up at one end. It shouts, "Pom Pom Pullaway; If you don't come, I'll pull you away!" which is the signal for all the players to run to the opposite end of the play area; as they pass, It tries to tag one or more. Players may not run outside the boundaries. If they do or if It tags them, they must stay in the center. When It again shouts, "Pom Pom Pullaway; If you don't come, I'll pull you away!" the tagged players help It catch the others. Each time the chant is called, the remaining free players race from one end to the other, dodging the growing band of Its in the center, until everyone is caught. The last

person caught is It in the next game.

Crows and Cranes is another chasing game, this one with teams instead of one It against the crowd. The players choose a "caller" and divide themselves into roughly equal teams called Crows and Cranes. The teams draw goal lines quite a distance apart, 30 feet or more, and stand in front of them, facing each other. When the caller yells "Start!" the two teams begin advancing toward each other. At some point before they meet in the middle, the caller yells either "Crows!" or "Cranes!" The team that is named races back to its goal line, and the other team gives chase. Any players who are tagged join the team in pursuit. When all the remaining players of the named team are behind their goal line, the other team also returns to its goal line, and the caller again yells "Start!" The game is over when either the Crows or the Cranes are extinct. The game is quite dramatic, with the teams creeping cautiously away from their goal lines and the caller prolonging the suspense by yelling "Crrrr . . ." so that the players don't know until the last second whether they are the hunters or the hunted. ❧

Red Rover

- ◆ NUMBER: **a team game that is best with a large group of players**
- ◆ EQUIPMENT: **none, but needs an open space about 15 feet square**
- ◆ DESCRIPTION: **a very physical game requiring strength, stamina and courage**

ONE OF THE most popular children's games, Red Rover is played by virtually every North American at some time during the formative years.

The Object of the Game: To break through the barrier of the other team.

The Play: Players divide the group into two equal teams. Each

team designates a leader, and the two teams decide which goes first. Then the members of each team join hands and form two parallel lines about 15 feet apart, the players facing each other. (If everyone agrees, players clasp each other by the wrist instead of the hand to make a stronger chain.) The leader of the first team yells, "Red Rover, Red Rover, let _____ come over," naming one of the players on the other side. The person named

charges at the other team's chain and tries to break through. If she does, she takes the two people whose link she broke back to her own team, and they join the line. (In some versions, breaking through earns only one captive.) If she can't break the chain, she joins it. Then the second team calls out to the first, "Red Rover, Red Rover, let _____ come over," and the person named charges at the second team, trying to break through. The teams call on the weakest members of the other side first, hoping they won't be able to break through.

Technically, the game is played until one team is reduced to a single player, but most often, players agree to end the game when one team obviously has more players than the other team does.

Variations: In **Bull in the Ring**, all the players but one join hands to form a ring; the lone player is the bull inside the ring, who charges at the ring trying to break out. When he does, everyone gives chase, and the person who tags the bull becomes the bull in the next round.

The Wolf and the Lamb or **Cat and Mouse** are variations on the Bull in the Ring. Players form a circle with one player inside as the prey and another outside as the predator. The predator tries to break into the circle to catch the prey, and the prey tries to break out so that she can avoid being trapped inside with the hunter. If the predator breaks into the circle and tags the prey, he continues as predator. If the prey successfully breaks out of the circle without being tagged as she makes her exit, she becomes the predator. In both cases, one of the players who formed the weak link in the chain becomes the new prey. ∾

Simon Says

- ◆ NUMBER: **three or more players**
- ◆ EQUIPMENT: **none; a driveway or a porch is room enough**
- ◆ DESCRIPTION: **a game of alert observation, compliance and elimination**
- ◆ TIP: **just as much fun—perhaps more—with adults as with kids**

MIMICRY GAMES were popular in England in the 1850s, especially one known as Wiggle-Waggle, in which It would turn thumbs up or thumbs down, and the rest would follow suit. The person who was inattentive or slow would then become It.

The original American name was more doctrinaire—Do This, Do That—but according to Alan Milberg in *Street Games*, a man named Simon, who worked as a social director at a resort in the Catskill Mountains of New York, renamed the game, and it was as Simon Says that the game swept the East Coast of the United States and back to Europe.

The Object of the Game: To obey commands quickly and correctly.

The Play: One person is designated the leader. The rest of the players stand in front of her as she shouts rapid-fire commands. When the command is prefaced with "Simon Says," the players must do as they are told. When that key phrase is omitted, the directions must be ignored. Anyone who follows instructions not authorized by Simon is out of the game. The last one left to obey the commands earns the right to be leader in the next round.

Variations: In **Contrary Children**, the leader must be alert too. Whatever It says, the rest of the players must do the opposite, and the leader sends out of the game anyone who actually follows her orders.

Another copycat game is **Follow the Leader**, which is really an active free-form version of Simon Says. All the players follow It single file, repeating every motion, jumping across ditches, climbing trees, jumping off rocks. The players are challenged to match It's prowess. Whoever cannot drops out, and the last person to drop out becomes It next. In one variation, the leader can, at any time, shout "Freeze!" The followers immediately hold their postures, and the leader turns to stare. Anyone who moves is out of the game. The last one to follow the leader is It—in these games, a reward rather than a punishment. ∾

Mother May I?

- ◆ OTHER NAMES: **played in Israel as Father May I? in Italy as Queen, Little Queen and, in earlier times, as Giant Steps**
- ◆ NUMBER: **most fun with a large group**
- ◆ TIP: **needs a fairly long playing area; a driveway is perfect**

THIS OLD BRITISH game is a combination of **Simon Says** and a racing game. It is a little more complex than the variation Red Light, Green Light, but unlike other race games, it is controlled enough to play indoors. It can also be played by as few as two. Recently, a mother and her 5-year-old amused themselves playing Mother May I? all the way home from the store. The child, noticing his parent's flagging enthusiasm, finally said, "Mother, may I take 555 running steps?" She gratefully nodded, and he ran all the way to the front door of their house.

The Object of the Game: To get to "mother" by asking her permission before obeying her commands.

The Play: One person is chosen to be the mother and stands at the far end of the driveway or the room. The rest of the players are at the opposite end. The mother addresses one of the players by name, giving her a command: for instance, "Sarah, take two giant steps." Before making a move, the player must beg permission to follow the order, saying, "Mother, may I?" Those who forget to be polite are sent back to the starting line. If a player asks properly, the mother may give her permission, deny it or change the command, in which case the player must ask again, "Mother, may I?"

The mother gives commands to the players in turn and is required by unwritten law not to play favorites. The usual commands are for baby steps and giant steps, a holdover from the earlier name of the game. Some of the other steps are: banana split (sliding one foot forward along the ground as far as you can stretch), umbrella step (twisting around while moving forward, a kind of pirouette), choo-choo train (shuffling forward until told to stop), crab walk (lying on the ground, stretching out your arms and pulling yourself forward as far as you can), frog jump (taking one big lunge from a crouching position), bunny hop (taking a little hop from a semicrouch position), camel step (walking on both hands and feet with bottom in the air), duck waddle (walking forward while in a crouch) and blind step (walking forward with eyes closed). According to Primo Levi, the traditional Italian lexicon includes the shrimp step, which obliges the Queen's subject to move backwards.

The players, for their part, try to inch forward without the mother's permission and without getting caught. (Kids are more adept at this kind of subterfuge than adults.) If the mother notices, she sends them back to the starting line. The first player to reach the mother wins.

Variation: In Red Light, Green Light, the person who is It stands at one end of the course, and the rest of the players line up at the other, at least 30 feet away. It has his back turned to the group. When he calls "Green light!" everyone runs forward, and when he calls "Red light!" they must stop in their tracks. Immediately after he utters "Red light!" he whips around, and if he catches anyone moving, that player must go back to the starting line. The first person to tap It on the shoulder is It in the next round.   ∾

Hopscotch

- NUMBER: **a solo game that can also be played with any number of friends**
- EQUIPMENT: **a piece of chalk, a stone or a stick, a clear patch of earth or sidewalk about 12 feet long and 4 feet wide and a stone, a chain or a shoe heel for a marker**
- DESCRIPTION: **a game of personal challenge, requiring good aim, physical balance and agility**

A SCOTCH IS A line drawn or scored on the ground, and Hopscotch is a game of hopping across those lines, which children have been doing around the world for centuries. It is played in Russia, India and China, as well as Europe and North America: one of the oldest Hopscotch diagrams is incised into the floor of the Forum in Rome. In the early years of Christianity, the Hopscotch grid represented the journey of the soul from earth to heaven: reaching the end meant everlasting glory. Although its religious symbolism has long since ebbed away, Hopscotch remains a rite of spring, a formalized version of that walking-home-from-school game "Step on a crack, break your mother's back." The grid itself has as many variations as there are players: one researcher found 20 different Hopscotch grids on the streets of San Francisco alone.

A piece of chalk or a stick for drawing in the dirt is all you need for these games. Make each block of the grid fairly large, about 16 by 24 inches. For a marker, or *potsie*, use a flat stone, a chain, a hockey puck, the heel of a cast-off shoe or an old shoe-polish can filled with dirt.

The Object of the Game: To complete the course, hopping on one foot.

The Play: Each player, in turn, stands at the beginning of the course and throws a marker into the first block. The player hops on one foot from the starting block to the end of the grid, hopping over the square that contains the marker, then turns (staying inside the last block) and hops back again, stopping at the second block to pick up the marker from the first and, still on one foot, hopping back to the starting block. Wherever there are two blocks side by side, a player can land with one foot in each block; single blocks are hopped on one foot. Both coming and going, a player must avoid the block with the marker, and he must use the same hopping foot throughout the course.

After successfully completing the course once, the player tosses the marker into the second block and hops from the start to the end of the grid, avoiding the block with the marker, and on her way back, she picks up the marker and hops to the starting block. In another version, the player throws the marker to each block in turn, then hops to that block, picks up the marker and returns to the start: instead of maneuvering the whole course, each trip is only one block farther than the last. In an older form of Hopscotch, the player hops to the block, but rather than picking up the marker, she kicks it back over the start line with her hopping foot.

Each player continues until he makes a mistake: throwing the marker into the wrong block or landing it on a line; stepping on a block that contains a marker; losing his balance and putting the other foot down while hopping; or stepping on a line. The turn then passes to the next player. At the end of each player's turn, the marker stays where it landed, and subsequent players must avoid those squares as well as the square with their own markers. When it is the first player's turn again, she can pick up where she left off: for instance, throwing the marker on #7 if her last successful hop was with the marker on #6. Play continues until each person has completed the entire course, retrieving the marker from the first to the last block and, sometimes, back to the first again.

Variations: Heaven and Earth is a ladder grid with 11 steps from the planet to the celestial reward, the tenth being Hell, which must be avoided at all costs. A player must hop on one foot, one square at a time, from Earth to one and back, Earth to two and back, and so on, until she hops from Earth to nine.

On the next throw, she tosses the marker into Heaven and hops there, jumping over Hell; in Heaven, she can rest on both feet, then she hops back to Earth.

On the next turn, she tosses the marker to Heaven again, hops there and, instead of tossing the marker back to Earth, kicks it back from block to block.

On the following turns, she brings it back balanced on her elevated foot, then on her head, her finger, her forearm, her right knee and her left knee.

On the next turn, with her eyes closed and head held high, she hops from Heaven to Earth, her friends guiding her with "Hot" if she lands correctly, "Cold" if she hops outside the line.

Finally, standing on Earth with her back to the diagram, she tosses the marker over her shoulder. If it lands in a block and not on a line, she chalks her initials in that block. In subse-

Heaven and Earth

quent games, she can rest there with both feet, and the others must skip over the block completely.

If, at any time during the game, the marker lands on a line or in the wrong block, a player loses her turn. If it lands in Hell, she must start the whole sequence again, from the beginning.

In **Japanese Hopscotch**, 19 blocks are drawn on the ground in the arrangement of a sideways M. There is no marker. Each player begins at one end and hops through all 19 blocks and back again. If successful, a player writes his initials in any block he chooses. In subsequent turns, a player can land with both feet in his own initialed block; everyone else must hop over that square. If a player doesn't make it through the course, she starts the next turn from the beginning. The

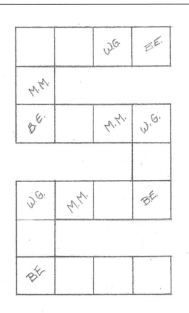

Japanese Hopscotch

page 322 for suggestions). The players take turns moving through the blocks in order, kicking a marker or bouncing a ball from block to block and naming an object that fits each category.

For instance, if the categories were Countries, Birds, Presidents, Fruits, Athletes, the player would hop from block to block, kicking the marker or bouncing the ball, and, without hesitation, would say, Brazil, Parrot, Kennedy, Orange, Gretzky. To make it more difficult, insist that all the categories be filled by words starting with the same letter: for instance, Brazil, Bluebird, Bush, Banana, Beliveau. Dropping the ball, hitting or hopping on a line or hesitating with an answer makes a player lose his turn, but he can pick up where he left off next time. The first player to get through the course wins. ◞

Window Hopscotch

person who "owns" the most blocks at the end of the game wins.

Window Hopscotch is similar to Japanese Hopscotch, but with a grid of 21 squares in three columns of seven squares each, instead of a snake-like shape. Each player throws a stone into a square, hops there, picks up the stone and goes back to the start, writing her initials in the square if she was successful. An initialed space is a rest spot for the owner but must be avoided by everyone else. The person who owns the most squares at the end of the game wins.

French Hop or **Snail** is exactly the same as Window Hopscotch except the grid is a spiral of 16 blocks, with "home" in the center.

In **English Hopscotch**, players draw a grid of six foot-square blocks. Instead of hopping on one foot, each player holds the marker between his feet and hops like a kangaroo from square to square. A player who drops the marker or lands on a line loses his turn.

Potsie is an outdoor game of **Guggenheim** played on a Hopscotch grid. Mark off a diagram with as many blocks as you want (8 or 10), and write a category in chalk in each box (see

Snail

Jump Rope

- NUMBER: **for one, two or several players**
- EQUIPMENT: **a skipping rope of the appropriate length and a space big enough to swing it in**
- DESCRIPTION: **requires balance, rhythm and endurance as well as the hand-foot coordination necessary for most other sports games**
- TIP: **good for the heart and the circulation and for general physical fitness**

LIKE HOPSCOTCH, jumping rope is, for reasons unknown, largely a female activity, despite the fact that it is also an accepted fitness routine for such "manly" pursuits as boxing. Even in the 1850s, it was a girls' game, although manuals warned against being too enthusiastic: "It is a healthy exercise and tends to make the form graceful; but it should be used with moderation. I have known instances of blood vessels burst by young ladies, who, in a silly attempt to jump a certain number of hundred times, have persevered in jumping after their strength was exhausted."

Jumping rope is good physical exercise, but the rhythmic slap of the rope on pavement has inspired songs and poems too. This is the stuff of kids' culture—enduring chants, often rooted in history, repeated generation after generation, a kind of audio graffiti. Every country has them, sometimes the same ones. "Teddy Bear," for instance, has been heard in Japan, Ecuador and South Africa. Altogether, more than 3,000 different skipping songs have been noted.

Although once made of wild grapevines, hop stems or plaited straw, ropes today are usually plastic or woven cotton. For a single skipper, the rope should be long enough to reach up under the arms when the skipper holds one end in each hand and stands on it. If two people are holding the rope, a 15- or 20-foot length is about right. Handles aren't essential: just knot the ends of a piece of clothesline, ¾-inch rope or #10 sash cord.

The Object of the Game:
To skip rope for as long as you can.

The Play: If skipping by yourself, hold the rope, one end in each hand, so that it drapes behind you. Keep your upper arms fairly close to your sides, your forearms out about a foot and your wrists loose. Bend your knees slightly, and keep your hips loose. Swing the rope in an arc over your head, and as it swings down to your feet, jump over it. You only have to jump about an inch, just high enough to clear the rope. Jump on the balls of your feet, raising both at the same time and landing on both at the same time, in the same spot. Practice jumping at a rate of about a bounce a second. Once you have the basic bounce down pat, try some fancier footwork. With your feet together, bounce twice, once to clear the rope and a second little bounce in between. With the running bounce, you basically run in place as you jump, jumping first with one foot then the other.

With two people, stand side by side, each holding one end of a slightly longer rope, or stand facing each other and close together, one person holding both ends of the rope. As the rope completes its arc, both jump in unison.

With three players, two *enders* hold the rope and swing it round and round while the other runs into the center, skips and runs out, never making the rope miss a beat. When the third person misses or causes the rope to stop, she changes places with one of the enders. To determine who is going to be an ender in a three-person game, coil the rope in loops, have everyone grab a loop, then unwind the rope: the two people closest to the ends are the enders.

When skipping with enders, you have to accommodate yourself to their rhythm. A good way to start is to have the enders sway the rope from side to side, making only half an arc under your feet. When you are comfortable jumping over the half arc, ask them to turn a full arc. Don't jump too high, and stay in the middle of the rope: closer to the ends, the rope takes less time to complete the circle.

The next step is to learn how to *run in* while the rope is turning. *Running in the front door* is easiest, because the rope is falling toward you. Stand just outside the arc of the rope, and watch its rhythm, swaying in sync. As soon as the rope passes you, run to the spot where it hits the ground. Stay relaxed: you have almost a full arc to prepare for that first jump, and once you get it, the rest are easy. If you *run in the back door*, the rope is rising toward you. Run in as soon as it passes and be prepared to jump right away: by the time you are in position, the rope is almost under your feet again.

Experienced skippers can *duck skip* in a crouched position and do *hopsies*, jumping on one foot, with the other one raised and bent at the knee like a flamingo. They can also skip on alternate feet, first one, then the other, or skip *up and down the ladder*, moving from the center of the rope to one end, then the other, never missing a beat.

Skipping style also changes with the speed of the rope. *Hot peas*, *hot pepper*, *hot tamales* or *red-hot bricks* is a fast-turning rope. In many places, *salt* is slow, *mustard* is intermediate, *pepper* is fast, and *vinegar* is the speediest of all. (Sometimes, mustard and vinegar are intermediate, pepper is fast, and red-hot pepper is superfast.) *High water*, or *licking*, usually means high, slow turning (although in some parts of the country, licking also means a fast rope). *Low water* is a low-turning rope, so low that the player must crouch when she jumps. Some jump-rope games have to be played *on time*:

the enders must turn the rope at a steady rhythm, and the jumpers must keep to that rhythm, jumping in and out, never leaving the rope empty.

Variations: The following are just a few of the most common among thousands of skipping games.

Crossie is a favorite solo skipping game. The skipper crosses her arms tightly at the elbows as the rope descends, creating a wide loop to skip through.

In **Double-Skip**, another solo skipping game, the skipper turns the rope fast enough that the rope goes under his feet twice between each jump. For best form, he bends at the waist a little, keeps his legs straight and points his toes.

This rhyme has been a solo endurance test for at least 100 years: "Down in the valley where the green grass grows, There stands _____ pretty as a rose, Along comes _____ and kisses her on the cheek. How many kisses did she get this week? One, two, three . . ."

Crossie

Or skippers can try to get through the alphabet with this chant: "A, my name is Angela, and my husband's name is Archibald. We live in Alaska, where we sell Asparagus. B, my name is Bethany, and my husband's name is Billy. We live in Bangladesh, and we sell Bicycles. C, my name is Candy, and my husband's name is Cecil. We live in Canada, and we sell Candelabra. D, my name is . . ."

Visiting is a century-old game played with one rope and several friends. One skipper turns the rope, and another player runs in, facing the skipper to visit. Then the visitor jumps out so that another visitor can enter. This usually goes with a skipping rhyme such as "I call in my very best friend, And that is _____. One, two, three." On the count of three, the person named jumps in. Try inviting two friends to visit at once, one in front and one in back.

A simple game with one long rope, two enders and several skippers is **Follow the Leader**. One person runs in, skips a certain way and runs out, then each of the others must follow

suit. If one misses, that person takes an end, releasing the ender to skip. Among the motions copied are *the ladder*, skipping first on one foot, then the other, as if climbing a high flight of stairs; *winding the clock*, counting to 12 and turning around with each jump; and *cut the moon*, running in at one end, touching the ender's hand, skipping once in the middle and running out the same side she ran in, but at the other end. In each round, the number of skips grows until the skipper runs in one end, touches the ender's hand, skips 12 times toward the other end, touches the other ender's hand and runs out.

Instead of a full arc, the rope can be swayed from side to side by the enders. In **Rocking the Cradle**, the rope sways three times, then does three full turns, then sways three times, and so on, until the skipper misses.

More than one skipper can jump a single rope turned by two enders. In **Coffee Grinder**, one skipper jumps in place while another circles tightly around her, like a coffee grinder.

Begging keeps several people moving in and out of the turning rope. Two players start skipping. While jumping, they switch places, and as they pass, the beggar says, "Give me some bread and butter." The other skipper replies, "Try my neighbor" and runs out. Another jumps in, the two switch places, and as they pass, the same beggar says, "Give me some bread and butter." This continues until the beggar misses and the other skipper becomes the beggar.

The most chaotic of the multiskipper games is **All in Together**, jumped to the rhyme: "All in together, This is fine weather; Trips stay out, And the last is pepper. January, February, March . . ." All the skippers run in together and leave on the months of their birthdays. Anyone who trips is eliminated, and the last one in jumps hot pepper for as long as she can or for a predetermined number of jumps. If she misses, she becomes an ender.

A favorite calling-in rhyme for multiskipper games is: "Mother, Mother, I am ill, Send for the doctor to give me a pill. In comes the doctor (second skipper runs in), In comes the nurse (third skipper runs in), And in comes the lady with the alligator purse (fourth skipper runs in). I don't want the doctor (second runs out), I don't want the nurse (third runs out), And I don't want the lady with the alligator purse (fourth runs out)."

Double Dutch is the standard two-person, two-rope game. (Some call it Double French, Dutch Ropes or French Ropes.) The enders hold one rope in each hand, their arms outstretched. They turn the ropes inward, toward each other, first one, then the other, using an overhand action, somewhat like a horizontal eggbeater. When one rope is at the top of its arc, the other is slapping the ground. The jumping motion for the skipper is like running in place, one foot up for each rope. To start, however, it is easier to keep your feet together and jump side to side with little two-foot jumps rather than alternating feet.

In a variation on Double Dutch, sometimes called **Double Irish, Double Orange** or **Dutch Irish**, the ropes are turned in an outward, underhand motion. This is much more difficult to jump, since the ropes are crossing under you instead of overhead. You have to jump higher, kicking out your legs. In double-rope games, if the two ropes kiss and lose their momentum, the skipper can start again, since the kiss is likely the enders' fault.

When you run in for a two-rope game, watch only one rope, not both. In Double Irish, always run in the front door; in Double Dutch, always run in the back door.

The favorite Double Dutch rhyme, worldwide, is: "Teddy Bear, Teddy Bear, turn around; Teddy Bear, Teddy Bear, touch the ground; Teddy Bear, Teddy Bear, shine your shoes; Teddy Bear, Teddy Bear, read the news; Teddy Bear, Teddy Bear, go upstairs; Teddy Bear, Teddy Bear, say your prayers; Teddy Bear, Teddy Bear, blow out the light; Teddy Bear, Teddy Bear, spell good night; G-O-O-D-N-I-G-H-T." The chant is accompanied by appropriate actions and finished off with top-speed spelling and a red-hot-pepper rope.　　　～

Marbles

- ◆ NUMBER: **any number of players, but usually two to six**
- ◆ EQUIPMENT: **at least half a dozen marbles and one shooter for each player; any clear patch of bare earth, big enough for a large circle or a raceway; indoors, a carpeted or cement basement floor offers enough resistance to keep marbles from skittering across the room**
- ◆ COMPLEXITY: **prime marble years are 8 to 11, but if you can crouch, you can shoot, and the fun never dulls**

IT IS DIFFICULT to say when children started playing Marbles. Pieter Brueghel, the Elder, includes marble players in his 1560 omnibus painting *Children's Games*, and before that, there are plenty of pictures of kids shooting polished nuts and stones and bones into holes. But Marbles is not only a children's game. England once celebrated Good Friday as Marbles Day, an attempt to divert holidaymakers from less innocent pursuits, and taverns often had built-in marble "alleys" for their patrons' amusement. (Specific laws prohibited the playing of Marbles in either the library at Oxford University or the Great Hall at Westminster.)

The game probably came to America on the *Mayflower*. Thomas Jefferson, John Quincy Adams and Abraham Lincoln were all prodigious shooters, and the game continues to be popular with politicians. According to Fred Ferretti in *The Great American Marble Book*, the late Senator Estes Kefauver once shot marbles on the floor of the Senate; Bella Abzug, he says, was "great at immies." Not only is Marbles virtually universal, but the game has been credited with spawning the respectable adult pursuits of Bowling, Billiards and Golf. Furthermore, it is one of the few children's pastimes that has become an organized sport, complete with a world championship.

Most marbles sold in department stores today are made of glass (glassies), but they can also be made of marble, limestone, agate (aggies), alabaster (alleys), clay (migs or mibs), glazed or fired clay (commies or immies), porcelain (crockies or potteys), steel (steelies), brass, iron and, at the two extremes, gemstones and plastic. By tradition, the aggie is the heart of any marble player's collection: it is never bought, only acquired. Players may have as many marbles as they like, but for some games, they also need at least one shooter, a larger marble that is used to hit the smaller target marbles. Playing marbles are roughly half an inch in diameter, while shooters are about three-quarters of an inch.

Individual Marbles games are classed as one of three types: *chase games* and *circle games*, wherein opponents shoot at each other along a course or within the confines of a specific area, like **Crokinole**, and *hole games*, in which marbles are shot or bowled into a series of holes, like Golf. Chase and hole games are competitive but friendly; circle games are cutthroat: the marbles you hit are yours to keep, and the object of more ruthless players is to send opponents packing without an aggie to their name.

Marbles is generally an outdoor sport, played in spring and summer on expanses of dry dirt—lanes, vacant lots, playgrounds, anywhere there is a swath of packed earth about 10 feet in diameter. Rainy seasons make for poor Marbles, as do droughts that pack the

Marble-Shooting Technique

earth too hard to dig holes. However, marble players are persistent and resourceful: there is even a New Hampshire variation, called Last Clams, played in the snow.

The Object of the Game:
During play, to capture as many marbles as you can.

The Play: Each player has a shooter and several marbles. If all players are using crystal or kitty-eye boulders, do not use steelies, which can crack the glass varieties. If you are playing "for keeps"—whoever hits a marble gets to keep it—make sure everyone understands the ground rules before you start. These are high stakes. If, instead, you are playing "for fair" and are returning the marbles after the game, be sure that the marbles are identifiable. At the end of a game played for fair, the player with the most marbles wins, but she gives back the marbles to their rightful owners.

Deciding who goes first in a Marbles game can be done several ways. In circle or chase games, players each shoot, or *bowl*, their shooters toward a *lag line*, or target line, while standing at a *pitching line* about 10 feet away. The person who gets his shooter closest to the lag line goes first, the next

closest goes second, and so on. In hole games, players determine the shooting order according to who shoots closest to the hole on the first turn.

To shoot a marble, a player lays his writing hand, knuckles down, on the ground so that the first joint of his first finger (Peter Pointer) is flat against the surface. The shooter is held in position with the ball of the first finger; the thumb is tucked behind the shooter, ready to propel it straight forward. The key to success is a steady hand and good aim, and that takes practice. It doesn't matter whether a player squats, crouches, kneels or sits on the ground to shoot, but the movement must be a flick: he cannot thrust his whole hand forward. (Experts refer to shooting as firing, flicking, pinching, dribbling, pinking, dribbying, drizzying and bowling.)

Players usually invoke a rule of "no hunchies"—leaning closer than necessary to the opponent's marble when shooting. If players see another player hunching forward or moving a hand forward, they yell "No hunchies," and the player must correct his posture. On the other hand, if the leaner yells "Hunchies" first, he is allowed to lean. A player is also not allowed to raise his hand when shooting, a move often called "histing." Players sometimes

agree to invoke the *pops rule*: on rough ground, a player can throw overhand rather than roll the marble along the ground.

If a shooter slips out of a player's hand and travels less than a foot, the player can yell "Slips!" and take the shot again, provided everyone agrees it was a legitimate slip. It is considered bad form to switch shooters during a game: the one a player starts with is the one she finishes with, unless it breaks during the game. If a player walks through the marble ring or the hole course, he must give up a marble to each of the other players. No one can stop a marble in motion, and anyone who touches a marble in action loses his or her turn.

Where the marbles are shot from, what they are aimed at and how the game is scored depend on the specific kind of Marbles being played. Following are just a few of the hundreds of Marbles games played on American playgrounds on any given spring day.

The standard chase game is **Boss-Out**, also called Chasies, Trailing, Bomber, Hits and Spans, Curb and Plumpers. Kids play it today in almost exactly the same way Ovid described the Emperor of Rome at play. Like all chase games, it is best played on the way to school (or work), although players are advised to get an early start: it can add hours to the trip.

When two people play, the first person starts by throwing a marble several feet ahead on the ground. The other person bowls his marble, trying to hit the first or lay it within a *span*—the distance between the tip of the thumb and the tip of the little finger with the shooter's hand outstretched. If the bowler doesn't hit the target marble or span to it, the first person shoots his marble at his opponent's marble, also trying to hit it or span to it. If he is successful, he wins the marble. His own marble stays where it lands, and the other player has another chance to hit it. If more than two people play, after the first two miss, the third aims for either player, and so on.

In a variation called **Bomber**, marbles more than a span apart but less than a footstep away can be bombed: the player picks up her marble and drops it from eye level at the other's aggie. If she hits it, it is hers.

Ringer is the oldest and most common circle game. In its simplest form, a circle about six feet in diameter is drawn in the sand or on the ground with chalk (for younger kids, three to four feet in diameter). Each player antes the same number of marbles into the center of the circle, then everyone takes a turn trying to hit the others' marbles outside the circle and thereby claim them. Players shoot from any point on the ring; the marbles must be knocked outside, but the shooter must remain inside for the hit to count. If a person hits a marble or another player's shooter, he shoots again from the point where his shooter stopped inside the circle. If a player knocks two marbles at once, he is usually entitled to the rewards of both shots. If a marble is resting on the "ring line" of a circle game, it is out of the ring if its center is outside or exactly on the line; it is inside if its center is inside the line.

A player continues to shoot as long as she makes a hit. If a shooter goes outside the circle or no marble is hit, the turn is over. After a miss, the shooter must remain inside the circle, a target for other players. On the next turn, it is shot from where it lies. If

Schoolyard Ringer

the shooter rolls outside the circle, it can be moved to any point on the ring and shot from there on the next turn. (If a shooter hits a marble and also rolls out of the circle, the player claims the marble, but his turn is over.) *Roundsters*, the privilege of taking a different position on the ring, is allowed only at the beginning of the game or after a shooter leaves the ring.

In a high-stakes variation called **Potsies** or **Dubs** (which loosely translates as double or nothing), the first player to knock a majority of the mar-

bles out of the circle claims the rest.

The official game of Ringer played in the annual National Marbles Tournament has 13 marbles arranged in a cross in the middle of a 10-foot-diameter ring, a marble in the center and three in each arm of the cross, each marble three inches from the next. Players sit at the edge of the ring and, with their shooters, try to knock marbles out of the ring; the first player to score seven hits wins.

In **Knuckle Box**, players draw a square with 18-inch sides, then ante a specified number of marbles inside. Players decide who goes first. The first player chooses his shooting spot outside the square by spanning from any side of the square (one hand's width, thumb to outstretched pinkie). He shoots from here and keeps any marbles he hits out of the square, but his shooter must leave the square too. If he misses or if his shooter stays in the square, the turn passes to the next player, and his shooter becomes a target marble, the property of whoever hits it out of the square. This is a fearsome game, played for keeps. Of course, if the next player misses, the first player retrieves his shooter and takes his next turn from his old shooting spot. If several are playing, the shooter stays in until everyone has had a shot at it.

Tournament Ringer

Persian

An indoor variation of Knuckle Box is **Persian**, played on a patterned rug, using one of the rug designs to define the "knuckle box" for the marbles. Everyone antes a certain number of marbles into the designated area and takes turns shooting from a spot one span outside the enclosure. Any marbles shot out of the design are the property of the player who shot them.

Holy Bang is a simple hole game. A shallow hole, a little deeper than the marble is wide, is dug in the ground (a saucer shape is better than a cone shape; make sure the lip of the hole is flush with the ground). Players shoot marbles from a shooting line 8 to 15 feet away (4 to 6 feet for young children; more than 15 feet for older players with well-muscled thumbs). The first person to land a marble in the hole gets all the other marbles that missed.

Potty is a variation on the one-hole game that adds considerable strategy. The hole is about seven feet from the shooting line. Players throw their marbles toward the hole; the closest gets first shot. This is an all-or-nothing kind of game. When they shoot their marbles, players try to get into the hole, but if they miss, they don't want to be too close, because the rule is: whoever gets in the hole wins all the marbles that come within a span of the

lip of the hole, as illustrated below. Once a player's marble is in the hole, she wins the marbles that come close to it, but she is also vulnerable to the next marble that lands inside the hole. That player gets three chances to knock her marble out, and if he does, he wins it. If he fails, she gets three chances to win his marble by knocking it out. If she misses too, he gets another three chances, and so on.

Spanning is a hole game for experienced shooters. Hollow out three holes in a line with about 10 feet between them. Start at a shooting line roughly 20 feet from the first hole. Players try to hit the holes in sequence. As long as he makes a hole,

a player keeps bowling his marble. When he misses, the next player takes a turn and has the choice of aiming for the hole or "kissing" her opponent—shooting him off the track. If she does, she earns an extra shot. The first person to make all three holes can then shoot at his opponent's marbles, but instead of just shooting them out of the way, the player can either claim the hit marble or return it to the owner in exchange for a stake, usually five or six marbles.

Poison has three holes in a row about seven feet apart and a fourth—the "poison" hole—about five feet to the side of the third. Players go from first to second to third, back to first, then through second and third again to the poison hole. After he makes the poison hole, a player can shoot at any other marble and, if he hits it, claim the marble or some agreed-upon stake.

Black Snake is a seven-hole version of Poison, a game of personal skill with no captures. Dig seven holes at irregular intervals to produce a snake-like twisting track. A player must go through all the holes to the end and back again to become a Black Snake, at which point he can shoot at other players' marbles, eliminating them from the game. If a player shoots into a hole after becoming a Black Snake, he is out of the game.

Arches is a target game, a variation on the basic hole game that is often played indoors. Cut arches in a shoe box or a cigar box—a small one-inch-wide arch in the center worth 10

Measuring a Span

points, two slightly larger arches on either side worth 5 points each and a large arch at either end worth 2 points each (or cut five holes of decreasing size from a large 2-point hole on one end to a very small 10-point hole on the other). Set up the box about 30 inches from the shooting line. Each player in turn knuckles down and shoots the same number of marbles toward the arches. The highest score wins, or players can play several rounds until someone reaches the target score of 50 or 100 points. ∾

Arches

Dodge Ball

- ◆ NUMBER: **10 or more players**
- ◆ EQUIPMENT: **a bouncy rubber playground ball (about 10 inches in diameter) and a fairly large yard, about 40 feet square**
- ◆ DESCRIPTION: **an elimination game; a large-format organized form of ball Tag**

BALL GAMES are as ancient as civilization itself, although they were originally played as part of religious rituals and to solve political quarrels. The first bouncing balls were made from distended bullocks' bladders covered with leather. The ball was so hard that players had to protect their hands and forearms with leather gauntlets. By the 19th century, British imperialists had brought a softer, bouncier ball to the playground and even indoors. "Balloon balls" were hollow, airtight, brightly painted balls made of gutta-percha, an elastic material extracted from Malaysian trees. Synthetics such as polyethylene and vinyl have since replaced gutta-percha, but whatever the equipment is made of, games with big bouncy balls continue to be a fixture of outdoor play.

The Object of the Game:
To tag the others out by hitting them with the ball; to avoid being hit by the ball yourself.

The Play: Make a square about 30 feet on each side, and draw a line down the middle to divide it into two courts. Divide the players into two teams, and decide which team has the ball first. Each team takes a half court. One of the players from the team with the ball throws it at a player in the other court. If the ball hits the player and he doesn't catch it, he is out of the game. The first person to catch the rebounding ball throws it at someone on the opposing team and tries to get her out. If the target player catches the ball, the person who threw it is out of the game. The person who caught it throws it back across the line trying to hit an opponent and eliminate him from the game. Anyone who steps over the centerline or out-of-bounds while trying to dodge the ball is out. The first team to eliminate all opponents wins.

Variations: Prison Dodge Ball is more fun, because it keeps everyone involved in the game. When a player is sent out of the game, she doesn't retire permanently. She waits on the sidelines of her team's court, and as soon as a teammate catches a ball intended to hit him, she can return to the game. This variation is best with 20 or more players. It can last a long time. The game usually ends when one team has more players still on the court than the other.

Circle Dodge Ball can be played with fewer players in a smaller space. Divide the players into two groups. One group forms a loose circle, and the other spreads out inside the circle. The players who form the circle have the ball. They try to hit the players in the center, who try to dodge the ball. In this game, however, a player may not catch a ball that was intended to hit him: no one in the center ever catches the ball. If the ball falls to the ground, someone kicks it back out to one of the players in the circle. Players who are hit join the circle. (In a double hit, only the first player hit joins the circle.) The last player remaining in the center wins the game. For the next round, players switch places, the circle players going to the center, and vice versa.

Wall Dodge Ball is a small-space city adaptation of the field game. Divide the players into two teams. The team with the ball lines up about

15 to 25 feet away from a wall. The dodging team lines up along the wall, facing the opposition. Each person on the wall team can move only within a two- or three-foot space chalked on the ground (or defined by partitions in the wall). The rules are the same: the team with the ball tries to hit the players standing against the wall, who try to dodge the ball. If a player is hit, she is out of the game. If a target player catches the ball, the thrower is out, and the catcher can try to hit an opponent. The team with the last remaining player wins. On the next round, the teams switch places. ∾

Wall Dodge Ball

Spud

- ◆ NUMBER: **six or more players**
- ◆ EQUIPMENT: **a large bouncy ball (not a tennis ball) and a spacious yard free of breakables**
- ◆ DESCRIPTION: **a formal sort of ball Tag with punishments for the loser**
- ◆ COMPLEXITY: **requires quick catching and accurate throwing**
- ◆ TIP: **it sounds a little rough, but the ball is soft, the throws are not missiles, and the targets always turn their backs**

WHETHER IT REFERS to a potato or to a short, stumpy person, Spud is only the latest in a long line of names by which this ball game has been known. William Newell lists a variation in *Games and Songs of American Children* (1883) as Call-Ball, Callie-ball or Ballie-callie. *Cassell's Book of Sports and Pastimes* (1881) has a variation called Days of the Week. A 19th-century report from Austria describes exactly the same game, with a penalty for every single miss: "If he misses his aim, he must place himself in a bent position with his hands against a wall, until every player has taken a shot at him." With a ball, of course. The ritual humiliation of the loser is as much a part of the game as calling on the catcher by number or name.

The Object of the Game: If your name or number is called, to catch the ball and tag another player with it.

The Play: The person who is It counts out the fists of the other players and, after the last "Eeny, meeny, miny, mo," begins to count, "One, two, three . . . ," assigning numbers to each of the players in turn and ending with herself as the last number.

All the players gather around It, but not too close. She throws the ball up in the air (or bounces it hard on the ground) and yells a number. (In some variations, It calls out a name.) The player called runs to catch the ball, while the others, including It, take off in all directions at top speed. As soon as the player catches the ball, he yells

"Spud!" and everyone must stop running immediately. They cannot move their feet, although they can twist away from the ball—or toward it to catch it. The person with the ball is also frozen in the spot where he caught it. He throws the ball from there toward one of the other players. (Some variations allow him to take four giant steps, spelling out S-P-U-D, before he throws.) If the ball makes contact, the tagged person gets one letter of the word SPUD and becomes It. If the ball misses or if a player catches it, the person who threw it gets one letter of the word SPUD and becomes It.

The player who spells the word SPUD first is the loser and usually has to endure some kind of humiliation. It may be the windmill: all the other players line up, legs spread, and the SPUD has to crawl through the tunnel of legs, being paddywhacked by everyone along the way.

Variations: In Baby, the numbers are dispensed with. Players crowd around a wall. The person who is It bounces the ball against the wall and calls out someone's name. Everyone runs, while the person named tries to catch the ball. When she picks it up, she calls "Baby!" and everyone halts. The person with the ball is allowed to take three giant steps toward the others, then she tries to tag one of them by throwing the ball. If her throw misses, she earns a B; if it is a hit, the person tagged gets a B. The first to spell BABY must go through the ordeal of the "hot oven": being spanked by everyone else (usually delivered with more merriment than malice).

World, also known as Territories and Around the World, is a longer, complex version of Spud that can be played with as few as three people. A circle about 15 feet in diameter is drawn in the dirt with a stick or on cement with chalk, then the circle is divided into as many equal parts as there are players. Each person claims a section and writes the name of a country in it—a real domain, a fantasy land or one bearing the player's own initials.

One player is chosen as It, usually by counting out. It stands at the center and bounces the ball on the ground, yelling, "I declare war on _____," and names one of the countries. Everyone runs except the person whose country was named. He retrieves the ball, runs back to his own country and, when he gets there, yells "Freeze!" Everyone stops, and the person with the ball tries to tag someone, either by rolling the ball on the ground or by throwing it. If he is successful, he can claim one foot of land from the person he hit: he steps onto the territory and marks out the land around his foot with the stick or chalk. In later rounds, a player can throw the ball from his own country or from claimed bits of land in other countries. The first player to claim all the land in the whole circle wins (or the first to claim more than half).

Often a stick takes the place of a ball. Each person may only stand in his or her own country or walk on the borders between countries. (If, during the game, a player touches another person's land, that person can claim some of the player's territory.) The game starts with It running around the world (around the outside of the circle), everyone watching intently. It throws the stick into someone's country, and everyone takes off except the owner of that country, who quickly steps on the stick and yells "Stop!"

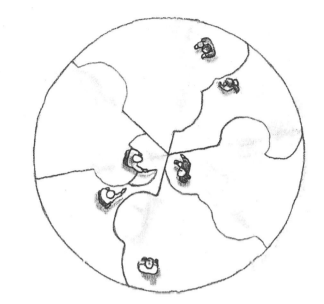

World

Then she moves around the boundaries of the world to get in a good position and lobs the stick underhand at one of the others. (No hard or overhand throws are allowed.)

If she hits someone, she gets as much of that person's country as she can reach. Stepping carefully only on the boundaries, she draws an arc of claimed land with the stick. (If, in drawing the arc, she touches the other person's land with any part of her body, that person can claim some of her territory.) The new owner writes her initials in the claimed land and erases any boundaries between it and her own. Then the rest of the players return to their countries, and the person who was tagged with the stick is It, running around the world.

The game can go on for hours: a player may be reduced to standing on tiptoes in a few square inches of his country, then suddenly he gets a run of good hits and gradually extends his boundaries. In World, the imperialist is not the winner: the game ends simply when one player's land is completely overtaken. "It's no fun if someone is out," my sons patiently explain, "so we just start another game." ∽

Further Reading

The History of Games

The History of Board Games by Robert McConville (Creative Publications, Inc.; Oak Lawn, Illinois; 1974).

Not really the history of all board games so much as the rules and strategies for some of humankind's oldest games, most of them variations on Tit-Tat-Toe. Somewhat academic in tone, the book was intended as a teacher's guide for math classes.

The World of Games: Their Origins and History, How to Play Them, and How to Make Them by Jack Botermans, Tony Burrett, Pieter van Delft and Carla Splunteren (Facts on File; New York; 1989).

An excellent full-color book with interesting historical anecdotes, clear instructions and directions for making beautiful, unique game boards.

Panati's Parade of Fads, Follies, and Manias: The Origins of Our Most Cherished Obsessions by Charles Panati (HarperPerennial, a division of HarperCollins Publishers; New York; 1991).

Puts the games of our youth and our grandparents' youth in the context of the fads, dances, books and popular songs of the time.

Games of the Gods: The Origin of Board Games in Magic and Divination by Nigel Pennick (Century Hutchinson Ltd.; London; 1988).

An academic paperback that investigates the roots of board games. For anyone seriously interested in the subject.

Games and Songs of American Children by William Wells Newell (Dover Publications; New York; 1963).

This republication of Newell's 1883 survey of children's games in the United States makes for fascinating reading. It is reassuring to learn that not much has changed in more than a century.

Games of the North American Indians by Stewart Culin (Dover Publications; New York; 1975).

This is a reprint of Culin's landmark 1907 survey of Native American games, originally published by the Government Printing Office in Washington, which also published Culin's *Chess and Playing Cards* (1898).

One Potato, Two Potato . . . The Secret Education of American Children by Mary and Herbert Knapp (W.W. Norton & Company Inc.; New York; 1976).

A sympathetic, wide-ranging and sensitive exploration of children at play.

PART I: Board Games

The Boardgame Book by R.C. Bell (Cavendish House; London; 1979).

The best book devoted exclusively to board games, over 80 of them, written by one of the world's foremost authorities on the subject. Beautifully illustrated with antique game boards big enough to play on; paper playing pieces are included too. Bell also wrote the landmark two-volume set *Board and Table Games From Many Civilizations* (Oxford University Press; London; 1969).

Wonders and Curiosities of Chess by Irving Chernev (Dover Publications, Inc.; New York; 1974).

A grab bag of delightful information about Chess as well as bits from famous games. Chernev has written more than a dozen books on Chess, any of which will improve your game.

Backgammon by Paul Magriel (Optimum Publishing; Montreal; 1976).

A complete book of rules and strategies, written in a style understandable to newcomers to the game.

Go and Go-Moku by Edward Lasker (Dover Publications Inc.; New York; 1960).

Originally published in 1934, this manual is still among the best, written by a Chess player who remains "convinced that Go will gradually share with Chess the leading position among intellectual games in the Occident just as it has reigned supreme in the Orient for the last three or four thousand years."

The Monopoly Book: Strategy and Tactics of the World's Most Popular Game by Maxine Brady (David McKay Company, Inc.; New York; 1974).

Although it perpetuates the myth of Darrow's unilateral invention of the game, the book is thorough and entertaining, with detailed strategic tips, including an appendix of Property Development Tables.

The Scrabble Book: Winning Strategies for the World's Most Popular Word Game by Derryn Hinch (Mason/Charter; New York; 1976).

An excellent book on Scrabble with just enough lore and lots of strategy, including lists of two-letter words, three-letter words and letters to keep that almost ensure a bingo within a few draws.

The Official Scrabble Players Dictionary is a hardcover book including more than 100,000 words, all of them acceptable in Scrabble tournaments, official or otherwise; in fact, only words permissible in Scrabble are found here. If you can't find it at a bookstore, write to the publisher c/o Consumer Sales, Merriam-Webster Inc., 47 Federal Street, P.O. Box 281, Springfield, MA 01102.

Mancala Games by Larry Russ (Self-published, 1984).

The most complete collection of Mancala games available in English. The book is out of print, but paperbound photocopies are available from Larry Russ at 613 Hudson Street, Hoboken, NJ 07030. E-mail address: lruss@vaxc.stevens-tech.edu.

PART 2: **Games With Playing Pieces**

Scarne on Dice by John Scarne (Stackpole Books; New York; 1974).

A fairly complete guide to dice games with a strong emphasis on gambling and casino games as well as crooked dice, hustlers and cheats. As a former shark, Scarne is knowledgeable and loquacious on the darker side of dice.

Dominoes: Five-Up and Other Games by Dominic C. Armanino (David McKay Company, Inc.; New York; 1959).

Almost 200 pages of explanations, rules and strategies not only for Five-Up but for all the basic games. The best—and perhaps only—source for those who take the game seriously.

Mah-Jongg: The Fascinating Chinese Game by J.P. Babcock (Mah-Jongg Sales Company of America; San Francisco; 1923).

This is by far the best introduction to Mah Jongg, and copies still turn up in used-book stores. Most of the other books use Japanese terminology; Babcock's version is faithful to the Chinese.

A Mah Jong Handbook: How to Play, Score, and Win the Modern Game by Eleanor Noss Whitney (Charles E. Tuttle Company; Rutland, Vermont; 1964).

A complete guide that covers Japanese, Chinese and American play, which emphasizes high scores over skillful play by including a large number of "limit hands." Good sections on strategy and scoring.

The Crokinole Book by Wayne Kelly (The Boston Mills Press; Erin, Ontario; 1988).

The only book on the subject of Crokinole, this is a brief history as well as an introduction to play.

Darts: The Complete Book of the Game by Keith Turner (David & Charles; London; 1980).

An excellent overview of the game from a layperson's point of view; infused with the spirit of Darts night at the pub.

Table Tennis Illustrated by Douglas Cartland (A.S. Barnes and Company; New York; 1953).

Clear instructions on various strokes with understandable photographs. Takes a more relaxed approach to the game than most British manuals.

PART 3: **Card Games**

Playing Cards: The History and Secrets of the Pack by W. Gurney Benham (Spring Books; San Francisco).

A wonderfully wry British look at the evolution of card making, not card playing.

A History of Card Games by David Parlett (Oxford University Press; New York; 1991).

A thorough and readable history of what Dr. Samuel Johnson called playing "at cards."

Illustrated Games of Patience by Lady Adelaide Cadogan (Leslie Frewin; London; 1968).

This is a facsimile of the Sampson, Low et al. edition published in 1875. Lovely, if you can find it.

An Expert's Guide to Winning at Gin by Chester Wander, with Cy Rice (Wilshire Book Company; Hollywood, California; 1965).

Written by international Gin Rummy champion Chester Wander, with an introduction by none other than Desi Arnaz, this is a highly personal account of how to win at Gin Rummy.

All About Cribbage by Douglas Anderson (Winchester Press; New York; 1971).

Somewhat dour, this is, nevertheless, a thorough and helpful guide to the intricacies of Cribbage.

Goren's Bridge Complete by Charles Goren (Doubleday & Co.; New York; 1971).

One of a veritable library of books that Charles Goren has written on Bridge. They are all good, but this is, as the title suggests, the most complete.

The Rules of Neighborhood Poker According to Hoyle by Stewart Wolpin (New Chapter Press; New York; 1990).

One of the few Poker books written for rec-room, rather than back-room, gamblers. As Wolpin says, "It isn't about winning. It's about having a good time." He even tells you the right food to serve at a Poker party.

PART 4: Games of Guessing and Deduction

The Oxford Guide to Word Games by Tony Augarde (Oxford University Press; New York; 1984).

A good source of word games and puzzles.

In Further Pursuit of Trivial Pursuit by Joseph A. DeBartolo (Sarsaparilla Ltd.; Chicago; 1984).

Organized in the same categories as the game, this book expounds on the short answers included on the Trivial Pursuit cards. It is also a handy source of questions and answers for a boardless version of the game.

PART 5: Outdoor Games

Croquet: Its History, Strategy, Rules and Records by James Charlton and William Thompson, with Roger, Katherine and Andrew Adler (The Stephen Greene Press; Lexington, Massachusetts; 1988). Available from the United States Croquet Association (page 408).

The definitive source for six-wicket rules and some fascinating bits of trivia about the early game.

"Home Ice" by Paul Quarrington, *Harrowsmith* (Nov./Dec. 1990, No. 94, page 47; Camden East, Ontario).

All you need to know to make a backyard rink big enough for family-sized Shinny.

Rules of the Game: The Complete Illustrated Encyclopedia of all the Sports of the World by the Diagram Group (Paddington Press Ltd.; New York; 1974).

A brief outline of all the outdoor sports, including specifics on the field, equipment, techniques, plays, strategies and scoring. Compiled from a professional, not a backyard, perspective, but useful in sorting through the details of outdoor-sport games.

Street Games by Alan Milberg (McGraw-Hill Book Company; New York; 1976).

An irreverent and entertaining look at the games most of us used to play, complete with great photographs and anecdotes from famous people about the games they once played.

New Games for the Whole Family by Dale LeFevre (Putnam Publishing Group; New York; 1988).

Part of a long list of books written about noncompetitive and mostly outdoor games.

Red Rover, Red Rover by Edith Fowler (Doubleday; Toronto; 1989).

A survey of Canadian children's games in their own words. When it comes to games, national borders aren't observed: these are commonly played in the United States too.

Jump Rope! by Peter L. Skolnik (Workman Publishing; New York; 1974).

Jumping rope for fun and fitness, complete with all the favorite rhymes and lots of new ones.

The Great American Marble Book by Fred Ferretti (Workman Publishing; New York; 1973).

Everything you ever wanted to know about marbles—the toys and the games.

Museums and Archives

The Museum and Archive of Games University of Waterloo, Waterloo Ontario, Canada.

A unique institution dedicated to the collection, exhibition, preservation and research of games and game playing. Founded in 1971, the collection includes 1,500 games and an equal number of documents.

Games Manufacturers and Distributors

ABBA Wood Products Ltd.
RR1
Neustadt, Ontario, Canada
N0G 2M0
The only major Canadian manufacturer of Crokinole boards.

Canada Games Company Ltd.
75-'T' West Drive
Bramalea, Ontario, Canada
L6T 2J6
Sells a wide variety of games, including Tiddley Winks, Snakes and Ladders and Backgammon.

Carta Mundi
72, rue Regnault
75013 Paris, France
01-44-24-58-58 (tel.)
01-44-24-58-59 (fax)
Supplies French tarot cards for tournament play.

Dufferin Game Room Store
52 Titan Road
Toronto, Ontario, Canada
M8Z 2J8

A mail-order outlet for all kinds of games equipment: playing cards, Ping-pong paddles, tables and nets, Backgammon, Cribbage, Chess, Mah Jongg, Darts, Crokinole, dice and a few board games as well as billiard and general-games tables.

Les Editions Section B (Canada) Inc.
4570 rue Chambord
Montreal, Quebec, Canada
H2J 3M7
Manufactures classic board games designed by modern artists, beautiful enough to hang on the wall.

Farkle Games, Inc.
3884-T S. Shiloh Road
Garland, TX 75041
Manufactures Farkle.

Game Gang Ltd.
21 E. 4th Street
New York, NY 10003
Distributes Balderdash and Pictionary.

Hasbro Inc.
1027 Newport Avenue
Pawtucket, RI 02861
Manufactures a variety of educational, action and card games.

Inca Perudo
2 Brydges Place
London, England WC2
Manufactures Perudo and sells dicing cups.

A.F. Kopp Company
30930 Camas Swale Road
Creswell, OR 97426
Manufactures elegant Croquet equipment. Ask for a catalog.

Marble King, Inc.
Dept. 10, P.O. Box 195
Paden City, WV 26159
Sells a large variety of glass marbles.

Merdel Game Manufacturing Co.
218 E. Dowland Street
Ludington, MI 49431
Manufactures Caroms boards.

Milton Bradley Company
443 Shaker Road
East Longmeadow, MA 01028
   Manufactures board games, such as Scrabble, Scattergories, Chutes and Ladders, Battleship and more, as well as Chess, Checkers, Yahtzee and Bingo in its Lowe Division. Milton Bradley himself was a prolific games inventor and America's first games magnate; his company is still a leader in the field—and generous too. If your Scrabble tiles have gone missing or are defective, write to Milton Bradley's Consumer Service Department for free replacements.

Parker Brothers
P.O. Box 900
Salem, MA 01970
   Manufactures Monopoly, Risk, Clue, Sorry and, in the United States, Trivial Pursuit.

Pressman Toy Corp.
200-T 5th Avenue
New York, NY 10010
   Manufactures Backgammon, Chess, Bingo and Checkers.

Queen City Forging Co.
223 Tennyson Street
Cincinnati, OH 45226
   Sells official pitching horseshoes direct to consumers.

Rose Art Industries Inc.
555 Main Street
Orange, NJ 07050
   Manufactures Pick-Up-Sticks.

Schindel & England
854 Palmerston Avenue
Winnipeg, Manitoba, Canada
R3G 1J5
   Sells beautiful reproductions of classic 18th- and 19th-century paper games and pastimes as well as hand-made glass marbles, exotic wood tops, hoops and hand-held glass-topped puzzles.

Western Publishing Co.
1220 Mound Avenue
Racine, WI 53404
   Manufactures Pictionary.

Games Organizations

Amateur Softball Association of America
2801 N.E. 50th Street
Oklahoma City, OK 73111-7293

Founded in 1933, this is the governing body for amateur Softball in the United States. It maintains a Hall of Fame and publishes an official guide and rule book as well as a newsletter called "Balls and Sticks."

American Checker Federation
220 Lynn Ray Road
P.O. Drawer 365
Petal, MO 39465

Founded in 1949 by master and expert Checkers players, the federation promotes the game as "a dignified intellectual pastime." It sponsors a world-title match in odd-numbered years and a U.S. open tournament in even-numbered years. It also publishes a newsletter, maintains a Hall of Fame and sells books and videos on Checkers as well as handmade inlaid-wood game boards and pieces.

American Darts Organization
7603 E. Firestone Boulevard
Suite E6
Downey, CA 90241

Affiliated with the World Darts Federation, this organization has 100,000 members, sponsors 250 tournaments a year and holds a biennial meeting in Las Vegas.

American Lawn Bowls Association
17 Buckthorn
Irvine, CA 92714

Founded in 1915, the organization sponsors national, divisional and sectional play-offs and is the ruling body for Lawn Bowls in the United States.

Chicago Bar Point Backgammon Club
2726 West Lunt Avenue
Chicago, IL 60645-3039

Although there is no national Backgammon association, the president of this club, Bill Davis, brought together 15 tournaments to form the American Backgammon Tour. The Chicago Bar Point Backgammon Club is the largest in the country; it publishes an international newsletter, "Chicago Point," and distributes the *United States Backgammon Tournament Rules & Procedures.*

Fédération Francaise de Tarot
1 bis, rue des Cornillons
71100 Chalon-sur-Saône, France

Organizes tournaments and school programs and supplies a free brochure (in French), "Creating a Tarot Club."

International Bocce Association
187 Proctor Boulevard
Utica, NY 13501

Founded in 1977, this association serves as the international governing body for Bocce. It publishes rules and regulations for competitive Bocce and organizes tournaments.

International Table Tennis League
1319 Dexter Avenue North
Suite 103
Seattle, WA 98109

Founded in 1971, the group sponsors tournaments and maintains a

Professional Table Tennis Hall of Fame.

National Amateur Basketball Association
6832 W. North Avenue, Suite 4A
Chicago, IL 60635

This organization promotes amateur Basketball and hosts an annual tournament.

National Euchre Players Association
P.O. Box 09732
Columbus, OH 43209

The organization promotes the game by sponsoring competitions and compiling statistics and historical information. It publishes a newsletter as well as *The Official Laws of Euchre* and several pamphlets that will improve your game.

National Horseshoe Pitchers Association
Box 7927
Columbus, OH 43207

Founded in 1909, the association has 17,000 members and promotes Horseshoes as both a recreational pastime and a competitive sport. It publishes a bimonthly newsletter and a manual of rules and sponsors an annual world tournament.

National Mah Jongg League
250 W. 57th Street
New York, NY 10107

Founded in 1937, the league still boasts 150,000 members. It sponsors a yearly tournament and publishes the annual *Official Standard Rules* and *Mah Jongg Made Easy With Tiles and Kards*.

The National Scrabble Association
P.O. Box 700
Greenport, NY 11944

For $15 ($20 U.S. outside the United States), you can join the club, which entitles you to a one-year subscription to the *Scrabble News*, special word lists and hints to improve your play, strategy tips, calendars of tournaments and more.

National Touch Football Leagues
1039 Coffey Court
Crestwood, MO 63126

This group sponsors competitions, gives awards, maintains a Hall of Fame and publishes the quarterly "NTFL Newsletter."

North American Tiddlywinks Association
10416 Haywood Drive
Silver Spring, MD 20902

Founded in 1966 and affiliated with the International Federation of Tiddlywinks Associations in England, it publishes the official *Rules of Tournament Tiddlywinks* and maintains an archives and a "Closet of Fame."

United States Badminton Association
1750 E. Boulder Street
Bldg. 10, Rm. 127
Colorado Springs, CO 80909

This is the governing body for the Olympic Sport of Badminton in the United States. Publishes the bimonthly *Badminton USA Magazine*.

United States Croquet Association
500 Avenue of the Champions
Palm Beach Gardens, FL 33418

Founded in 1976, the USCA has 5,000 members and, with the Croquet Foundation (same address), maintains a Hall of Fame. The USCA publishes a quarterly, runs tournaments and selects the U.S. National Croquet Team. It also sells a book of Croquet rules and is a source for mallets, balls and complete sets of equipment from the first British firm to manufacture Croquet hardware, John Jaques.

United States Flag Football League
5834 Pine Tree Drive
Sanibel, FL 33957

Devoted to promoting and developing men's Flag Football, the league conducts a national tournament and publishes the *USFFL Rule Book*.

United States Othello Association
920 Northgate Avenue
Waynesboro, VA 22980

This small group of Othello supporters conducts tournaments and maintains a national rating system for active players. It publishes *Othello Quarterly* and instructional materials, including *Othello: Brief and Basic*.

United States Stickball League
P.O. 363
East Rockaway, NY 11518

Founded in 1984, the league is devoted to organizing Stickball competitions and championships. It also publishes a bimonthly newsletter.

The United States Volleyball Association
3595 E. Fountain Boulevard
Colorado Springs, CO 80910-1740

Formed in 1928, the association has 64,000 members. It is the national governing body for the sport and publishes a quarterly newsletter called "Inside" as well as the *Official United States Volleyball Rule Book*.

Games on the Net

Following is a sampling of game sites on the Internet. They are offered in the knowledge that, especially in these early years of Web-crawling, sites will come and go and URLs will change frequently. The best advice is to use a search engine to find out what's new. Each engine is a little different: for games, Yahoo seems to be the best organized, cutting through the small personal home pages to the sites with the fullest information and the most links. This engine allows you to start with a broad request on board games and still find out fine points, like what a "squop" means in a game of Tiddlywinks.

General Games Sites

Directories
http://www.yahoo.com/Entertainment/Games
  This is an excellent general games directory for the Web and will lead you to many board and card game sites.

http://www.inrete.it/games/telnete.html
http://www.io.com/games/servers.html
  Both of these are lists of game servers.

http://www.dos.qmw.ac.uk/~steed/Games/bygame.html
  Games and puzzles.

On-line Games Magazines
http://www.gamecabinet.com/
  A monthly games magazine that includes reviews of commercial games and books as well as rules to traditional games and new, original games. The focus is on family games: those who like this book will become regular visitors to this site.

http://www.wolfenet.com/~peter/tgr/
  This is the Web site for *The Game Report*, a Web quarterly on board, party, dice, card, family and strategy games. It includes game and book reviews, with a full index of back issues. It also includes a useful link to games manufacturers.

Museums/History
http://www.ahs.uwaterloo.ca/~museum/index.html#exhibits
  The Museum and Archive of Games at the University of Waterloo in Ontario, Canada, is dedicated to the research of games and game-related behavior and to the collection, preservation and exhibition of games. Their site offers a virtual visit to their games collection, complete with detailed color photographs. (Of particular interest is their Mancala board exhibit.) The site includes links to other museums specializing in games.

http://www.inmet.com/~justin/game-hist.html

This is the Medieval and Renaissance Games Home Page, where you can find rules for ancient games, including hnetafl, senet and very old card games like Bone-Ace, Gleek and Primero. It includes links to manufacturers of historical board games and shareware games and also to the records of the Carolingian Low Company, a group of game players and researchers.

http:www.usa.net/~rfinn/agca.html

This is the Web site for the American Game Collectors Association, a nonprofit group interested in collecting and preserving old games and researching the history of American games, including cards, tops, marbles and puzzles. It includes a calendar of events, a sample issue, a five-year index for *Game Times* magazine and instructions for more than 1,800 commercial games. Although they cannot be downloaded, photocopies can be ordered for a small fee.

Specific Games Sites

Backgammon

http://www.cybercom.net/~damish/backgammon/bg-faq.html

This site by Mark Damish is a Backgammon Baedeker. In addition to basic rules and strategies, there is a good bibliography of Backgammon books, with reviews, links to private Backgammon pages, lists of clubs around the world and tournaments across the United States, reviews of Backgammon software, addresses for snail-mail and e-mail games, as well as lists of sites where you can play on-line.

Card Games

http://www.netlink.co.uk/users/pagat/

This site, developed and maintained by John McLeod, is a bonanza for card lovers. It features an alphabetical index of card games that leads you to the rules of play for hundreds of games, as well as links to rules at other sites. There is in-depth information on national and regional games, special playing-card decks, basic procedures and strategies common to most games, lists of newsgroups, on-line games, books and museums and a great FAQ (Frequently Asked Questions) section. Bookmark this site for sure.

Checkers

http://web.cs.ualberta.ca:80/~chinook/

At this site you can test your skill against a computer program designed by Dr. Jonathan Schaeffer at the University of Alberta, Canada. You'd better practice: this computer beat the human world champion!

http://www.Gamercafe.com/checkers/

Accounts are free (unlike a lot of sites for on-line game-playing) but the site was still in development at press time, and the address changes. If you cannot reach it at that URL, e-mail the café at checkers@gamercafe.com.

Chess

http://www.princeton.edu/~jedwards/cif/intro.html

There are dozens of Chess sites, but this one is particularly good for beginners. Maintained by Jon Edwards, the United States Correspondence Chess Champion, the site gives thorough strategies for each Chess piece and clear instructions. It also includes links to huge databases of Chess games, such as ChessBase and SmartChess, to the free weekly the *Week in Chess* and to the Internet Chess Club where players can sign up for games any time of the night or day, for a fee.

Crokinole

http://www.vivanet.com/~crokinol/

As well as a useful primer of rules, this site includes upcoming events, Frequently Asked Questions and Crokijokes, as well as links to the *Crokinole Quarterly* and good sources for Crokinole boards.

Darts

http://www.mnw.net/crow/darts.html

This is a private but well-designed Web site with a good range of links to suppliers, tournaments and dart games on the Web as well as useful rules of play for lots of games.

Dominoes

http://neon.ingenia.com/dominet/

Jack Mitchell's site should come with a warning. This is a gonzo site, and the language is a little crude, but it is a fascinating repository of Domino arcana including the history of the game, strategies, a bit about the patron saint, links to shareware games and Usenet groups and even footage from a Fellini film showing a robot playing Dominoes!

http://www.xs4all.nl/~spaanszt/Domino_Plaza.html

This Dutch site, created by Z. Teun Spaanz, lays out all the basic games and has great links to sites where you can play Dominoes or download shareware.

Scrabble

http://www.teleport.com/~stevena/scrabble/faq.html

This is a listing of Frequently Asked Questions, but it also lists clubs, tournaments, championship bouts, books and, best of all, a host of new admissible words.

Tiddlywinks

http://www.cpcug.org/user/rwtucker/tiddlywinks.html

This wonderful site by Richard Tucker is worth a visit. In addition to rules, techniques and answers to FAQs, he includes a Tiddlywink lexicon, history, patents and trademarks, scientific reports and links to *Newswink* from the North American Tiddlywink Association, *Winking World* from the English Tiddlywink Association and *The Squopsman* from the Scottish Tiddlywink Association.

Games Index

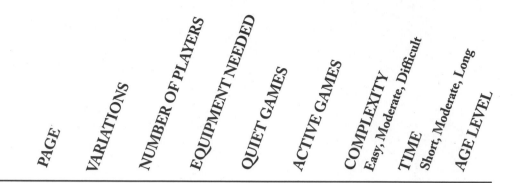

	PAGE	VARIATIONS	NUMBER OF PLAYERS	EQUIPMENT NEEDED	QUIET GAMES	ACTIVE GAMES	COMPLEXITY Easy, Moderate, Difficult	TIME Short, Moderate, Long	AGE LEVEL
◆ BOARD GAMES ◆									
1. Games on Homemade Boards									
Boxes	25	3	2+	◆	◆		E	S	7+
Sprouts	26		2+	◆	◆		E	S	5+
Tit-Tat-Toe	27	3	2	◆	◆		E	S	7+
Picaria	28		2	◆	◆		M	S	10+
Go-Bang	29	1	2	◆	◆		M	M	10+
Nine Men's Morris	30	3	2	◆	◆		M	S	10+
Alquerque	32	4	2	◆	◆		M-D	M	10+
Fanorona	34		2	◆	◆		D	L	10+
Seega	35	1	2	◆	◆		M	M	10+
Four Field Kono	36	1	2	◆	◆		M	M	7+
Cows and Leopards	37	2	2	◆	◆		M	M	7+
Solitaire	38	4	1	◆	◆		M	M	7+
Salvo	39	1	2	◆	◆		M	L	10+
2. Games on Checkerboards									
Checkers	46	9	2	◆	◆		M	M	7+
Giveaway Checkers	50		2	◆	◆		E	M	7+
Box the Fox	51	2	2	◆	◆		E	S	7+
Reversi	51	2	2	◆	◆		M	M	10+
Halma	53	2	2, 4	◆	◆		E	M	7+
Chess	54		2	◆	◆		D	L	12+
3. Games With Special Pieces									
Steeplechase	66	1	2+	◆	◆		E	S	5+
Snakes and Ladders	67	1	2+	◆	◆		E	S	5+
Pachisi	68	5	2+	◆	◆		M	M	7+
Backgammon	71		2	◆	◆		M-D	M-L	10+
Chinese Checkers	75	2	2+	◆	◆		E	M	7+
Go	76		2	◆	◆		D	L	10+
Monopoly	80	4	3-7	◆	◆		M	L	10+
Scrabble	85	6	2-4	◆	◆		M	L	10+
4. Mancala Games									
Wari	96	7	2	◆	◆		E	S	7+
The Cow Game	99	1	2	◆	◆		E	S	7+
Bechi	100		2	◆	◆		M	M	10+

	PAGE	VARIATIONS	NUMBER OF PLAYERS	EQUIPMENT NEEDED	QUIET GAMES	ACTIVE GAMES	COMPLEXITY Easy, Moderate, Difficult	TIME Short, Moderate, Long	AGE LEVEL
Qelat	101		2	◆	◆		D	M	12+
Ayoayo	102	5	2	◆	◆		E	M	7+
Gamacha	104	3	2	◆	◆		M	M	10+
Giuthi	106	1	2	◆	◆		M	M	10+
Bao	107		2	◆	◆		D	L	12+
The Game of Daughters	109		2	◆	◆		M	L	10+
Deka	110	3	2	◆	◆		E	M	7+
Abalala'e	111		2	◆	◆		E	M	7+
Gabata	112	1	2	◆	◆		M	L	10+
Njombwa	113	3	2	◆	◆		M	L	10+
Nsumbi	114	1	2	◆	◆		D	L	12+

◆ **GAMES WITH PLAYING PIECES** ◆

5. Dice Games

	PAGE	VARIATIONS	NUMBER OF PLAYERS	EQUIPMENT NEEDED	QUIET GAMES	ACTIVE GAMES	COMPLEXITY	TIME	AGE LEVEL
Bugs	123	1	2-6	◆	◆		E	S	5+
Dreidels	123		2+	◆	◆		E	S	5+
Going to Boston	124	1	2+	◆	◆		E	S	5+
Dice Golf	124		2+	◆	◆		E	M	7+
Ohio	125		2+	◆	◆		E	S	7+
Sevens	126		2+	◆	◆		E	S	7+
Drop Dead	126		2+	◆	◆		E	S	7+
Straight Shooter	127		1+	◆	◆		E	M	7+
Farkle	127		1-3	◆	◆		M	M	10+
Help Your Neighbor	128		2-6	◆	◆		E	S	5+
Aces in the Pot	129		2+	◆	◆		E	M	7+
Yacht	129	5	1+	◆	◆		M	M	7+
Craps	131		2+	◆	◆		M	M	12+
Barbudi	132		2+	◆	◆		M	M	12+
Poker Dice	133	4	2+	◆	◆		E	S	10+
Liar's Dice	134		2	◆	◆		E	S	7+
Dudo	134		2+	◆	◆		M	L	12+

6. Dominoes Games

	PAGE	VARIATIONS	NUMBER OF PLAYERS	EQUIPMENT NEEDED	QUIET GAMES	ACTIVE GAMES	COMPLEXITY	TIME	AGE LEVEL
Block and Draw Dominoes	142	7	2-5	◆		◆	E	M	7+
Blind Hughie	144		2-5	◆		◆	E	M	5+
Bergen	145		2-4	◆		◆	M	M	7+
Matador	146	4	2-4	◆		◆	M	M	7+

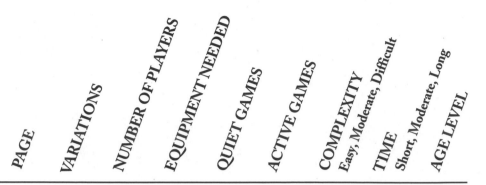

	PAGE	VARIATIONS	NUMBER OF PLAYERS	EQUIPMENT NEEDED	QUIET GAMES	ACTIVE GAMES	COMPLEXITY Easy, Moderate, Difficult	TIME Short, Moderate, Long	AGE LEVEL
All Fives	147	3	2-4	◆		◆	M	M	7+
Five-Up	149	2	2-4	◆		◆	D	L	10+
Mah Jongg	151	4	4	◆		◆	D	L	12+
7. Games With Special Equipment									
Jacks	163	6	1+	◆		◆	M	M	5+
Pick-Up-Sticks	164		2-4	◆	◆		E	S	5+
Tiddlywinks	166	4	2-6	◆		◆	E	M	5+
Crokinole	167	1	2-4	◆		◆	M	L	7+
Caroms	170	1	2, 4	◆		◆	M	L	7+
Darts	171	6	2	◆		◆	M	L	10+
Ping-pong	175	1	2, 4	◆		◆	M	L	10+

◆ **CARD GAMES** ◆

	PAGE	VARIATIONS	NUMBER OF PLAYERS	EQUIPMENT NEEDED	QUIET GAMES	ACTIVE GAMES	COMPLEXITY	TIME	AGE LEVEL
8. Card Games for One									
Idiot's Delight	184	1	1	◆	◆		E	S	5+
Monte Carlo	184	5	1	◆	◆		E	S	5+
Clock Solitaire	186		1	◆	◆		E	M	7+
Trusty Twelves	187	1	1	◆	◆		E	M	7+
Kitty in the Corner	187		1	◆	◆		E	M	7+
Four Winds	188	1	1	◆	◆		M	M	10+
Klondike	189	6	1	◆	◆		E	M	10+
Fascination	192	6	1	◆	◆		M	M	10+
Trefoil	193	6	1	◆	◆		M	M	10+
St. Helena	196	4	1	◆	◆		M	M	10+
Beleaguered Castle	197	2	1	◆	◆		M	M	10+
King Albert	198		1	◆	◆		D	M	10+
Spider	199		1	◆	◆		D	M	12+
9. Card Games for Two									
Memory	208		2+	◆	◆		E	M	5+
Beggar My Neighbor	208	5	2+	◆	◆		E	M	5+
Spit	209		2	◆	◆		E	M	7+
Go Fish	211	4	2+	◆	◆		E	M	5+
Cassino	212	7	2+	◆	◆		E	M	7+
Conquian	215		2	◆	◆		E	M	7+
Gin Rummy	217	1	2	◆	◆		M	M	10+
Canasta	220	5	2	◆	◆		M	L	10+

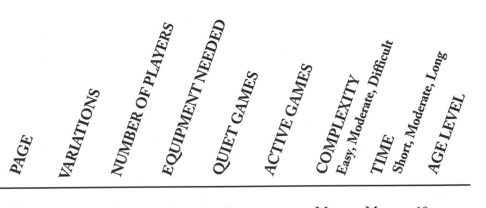

	PAGE	VARIATIONS	NUMBER OF PLAYERS	EQUIPMENT NEEDED	QUIET GAMES	ACTIVE GAMES	COMPLEXITY Easy, Moderate, Difficult	TIME Short, Moderate, Long	AGE LEVEL
Cribbage	223	2	2	◆	◆		M	M	10+
Russian Bank	226		2	◆	◆		M	M	10+
Crapette	228	1	2	◆	◆		M	M	10+
Stung	231		2+	◆	◆		M	S	10+
Spite and Malice	233	1	2	◆	◆		D	L	12+
Piquet	235	1	2	◆	◆		D	L	12+
Pinochle	238		2+	◆	◆		D	L	12+
Klobiosh	241	2	2+	◆	◆		D	L	12+
10. Card Games for Three or More									
I Doubt It	248		3+	◆	◆		E	S	5+
Pig	248	4	3+	◆	◆		E	S	5+
Michigan	249	1	3-8	◆	◆		E	M	7+
Play-or-Pay	251	2	3+	◆	◆		E	S	7+
Rummy	253	9	2-6	◆	◆		M	S	10+
Go Boom	258		2+	◆	◆		E	M	7+
Hearts	259	6	3-6	◆	◆		E	M	7+
Oh Hell	260	1	3-7	◆	◆		M	M	10+
Nine-Five-Two	262		3	◆	◆		M	M	10+
Napoleon	263	4	3-6	◆	◆		M	S	10+
Hombre	264		3	◆	◆		M	S	10+
Solo	267	3	4	◆	◆		D	M	12+
Skat	270		3	◆	◆		D	L	12+
Pitch	276	4	2-7	◆	◆		M	M	10+
Euchre	277	3	4	◆	◆		M	M	10+
Whist	280	1	4	◆	◆		M	L	10+
Bridge	282		4	◆	◆		D	L	12+
Poker	286	19	2-14	◆	◆		M	S	10+
11. Tarot Games									
Basic Tarot	298		3	◆	◆		M	S	10+
Tarocco	300		3	◆	◆		D	M	12+
French Tarot	302		3-5	◆	◆		D	L	12+

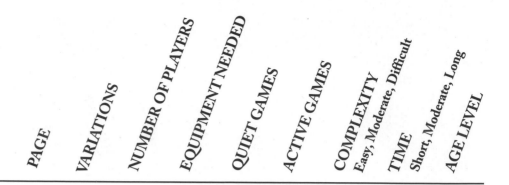

◆ Games of Guessing and Deduction ◆

	PAGE	VARIATIONS	NUMBER OF PLAYERS	EQUIPMENT NEEDED	QUIET GAMES	ACTIVE GAMES	COMPLEXITY Easy, Moderate, Difficult	TIME Short, Moderate, Long	AGE LEVEL
12. Parlor Games									
Blind Man's Bluff	314		6+	◆		◆	E	S	5+
Charades	314	2	3+	◆		◆	E	S	5+
Dumb Crambo	317		4+	◆		◆	E	S	5+
Conversations	317		5+		◆		M	M	7+
Picture Charades	318	1	4+	◆		◆	E	M	5+
Password	319	1	4+	◆	◆		M	M	7+
Dictionary	320		4+	◆	◆		M	M	10+
Guggenheim	321	1	2+	◆	◆		E	M	7+
Anagrams	322	1	2-6	◆	◆		M	M	7+
Crosswords	324	3	2+	◆	◆		M	M	7+
Lotto	326	2	3+	◆	◆		E	M	5+
The Trivia Game	327		3+	◆	◆		M	M	7+
Murder	328		5+	◆		◆	E	L	7+
13. Travel Games									
Mora	333	3	2		◆		E	S	5+
Twenty Questions	334	3	2+		◆		E	M	5+
Botticelli	335		2+		◆		E	M	10+
Coffepot	335		2+		◆		E	S	5+
Crambo	336		2+		◆		E	S	5+
No! No!	337		2+		◆		E	S	7+
I Spy	337	3	2-5		◆		E	S	5+
Fortunately/Unfortunately	338		2+		◆		E	S	7+
Taboo	339	1	2+		◆		E	S	7+
Questions	339		2+		◆		E	S	7+
Ghost	340	2	2-4		◆		M	M	7+
Word Chains	341	4	2-5		◆		M	M	7+
Slogans	342	1	2+		◆		M	M	7+
Demonic Mnemonics	342	2	2+		◆		M	M	7+
Car Capers	343	6	2+		◆		M	S	7+
Jotto	344	3	2	◆	◆		D	L	10+
Doublets	345		1+	◆	◆		D	S	10+
Hangman	346		2+	◆	◆		M	M	7+

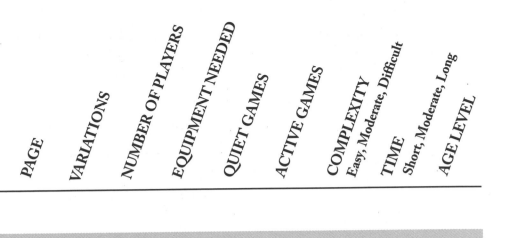

	PAGE	VARIATIONS	NUMBER OF PLAYERS	EQUIPMENT NEEDED	QUIET GAMES	ACTIVE GAMES	COMPLEXITY (Easy, Moderate, Difficult)	TIME (Short, Moderate, Long)	AGE LEVEL

◆ Outdoor Games ◆

14. Organized Outdoor Games

	PAGE	VARIATIONS	NUMBER OF PLAYERS	EQUIPMENT NEEDED	QUIET GAMES	ACTIVE GAMES	COMPLEXITY	TIME	AGE LEVEL
Horseshoes	353	1	2, 4	◆		◆	M	M	10+
Lawn Bowls	355	4	2, 8	◆		◆	M	M	10+
Croquet	359	2	2-6	◆		◆	M	M	7+
Shinny	362	1	10-16	◆		◆	M	L	7+
Softball	364	5	10-18	◆		◆	M	L	7+
Badminton	368	2	2, 4	◆		◆	M	L	7+
Basketball	370	7	2+	◆		◆	M	M	7+
Volleyball	373		6-12	◆		◆	M	L	10+
Touch Football	375	2	12-22	◆		◆	M	L	10+

15. Games of Search, Chase and Capture

	PAGE	VARIATIONS	NUMBER OF PLAYERS	EQUIPMENT NEEDED	QUIET GAMES	ACTIVE GAMES	COMPLEXITY	TIME	AGE LEVEL
Statues	381	1	4+			◆	E	S	5+
Tag	381	11	5+			◆	E	S	5+
Hide and Seek	383	4	5+			◆	E	M	5+
Prisoner's Base	384	1	8+			◆	E	M	5+
Red Lion	385	3	10+			◆	E	L	7+
Red Rover	386	2	10+			◆	E	L	7+
Simon Says	387	2	3+			◆	E	M	5+
Mother May I ?	387	1	5+			◆	E	M	5+
Hopscotch	388	6	1+	◆		◆	E	M	5+
Jump Rope	391	10	1+	◆		◆	E	M	5+
Marbles	393	12	2-6	◆		◆	M	M	5+
Dodge Ball	397	3	10+	◆		◆	M	M	7+
Spud	398	2	6+	◆		◆	M	L	7+

General Index